What Will Dr. N...

John Henry Newman
and
Papal Infallibility,
1865–1875

John R. Page

A Michael Glazier Book
THE LITURGICAL PRESS
Collegeville, Minnesota

A Michael Glazier Book published by The Liturgical Press

Cover design by David Manahan, O.S.B. Portrait of Cardinal Newman, by Willium Roden, 1874, Manchester Art Gallery.

1   2   3   4   5   6   7   8   9

Library of Congress Cataloging-in-Publication Data

Page, John R., 1940–
    What will Dr. Newman do? : John Henry Newman and papal
infallibility, 1865–1875 / John R. Page.
        p.   cm.
    "A Michael Glazier book."
    Includes bibliographical references and index.
    ISBN 0-8146-5027-9
    1. Popes—Infallibility—History of doctrines—19th century.
2. Newman, John Henry, 1801-1890—Contributions in doctrine of papal
infallibility.   3. Vatican Council (1st : 1869-1870)   I. Title.
BX1806.P34   1994
262'.131—dc20   94-5538
                                                                CIP

Contents

Acknowledgments

It will be clear how much this study, based primarily on Newman's letters, owes to *The Letters and Diaries of John Henry Newman* and to the principal editor of that multi-volume collection, the late Father Charles Stephen Dessain of the Birmingham Oratory. The many annotations throughout each volume and the "Index of Persons and Places" at the end of each volume are themselves invaluable sources of information on Newman and his times.

I am especially indebted to Father John C. Ford, C.S.C., professor of theology in the School of Religious Studies at The Catholic University of America, who read the manuscript and offered numerous helpful suggestions and improvements along the way. I have greatly profited from his vast knowledge of Newman's life and thought and from his equally sure knowledge of the First Vatican Council.

I am deeply grateful to many people associated with the International Commission on English in the Liturgy, especially to the former chairman of its Episcopal Board, the Most Reverend Denis E. Hurley, O.M.I., Archbishop Emeritus of Durban, South Africa. At a critical point in this study, the Episcopal Board voted me a sabbatical leave. That I came most days to the office instead, taking very little advantage of this gracious gesture, is my fault entirely. I owe thanks to the members of ICEL's committees and my colleagues on the staff of the ICEL secretariat. They gave encouragement all along the way and cheered me on. I am particularly grateful to Monsignor Frederick R. McManus and to Mr. Peter C. Finn and Mr. James M. Schellman. James Schellman read parts of the manuscript and commented on it.

The work would never have been finished but for the dedication and skill of Mrs. Mary L. Fowler. Early and late, Mrs. Fowler kept at the task of preparing the manuscript from the note-taking stage, through many drafts, and through the several stages of "final" corrections. She frequently worked from my handwritten notes and drafts, my once clear Catholic school penmanship growing more and more ragged as the work proceeded. And in the process Mrs. Fowler became a devoted Newmanite. At a stage when highly sophisticated word-processing techniques became essential, I was guided and helped by the knowledge, experience, and thoroughness of Mr. Edmund O. Yates. Mary Fowler and Edmund Yates put up with my relentless perfectionism; I derived many benefits from theirs.

A sincere word of thanks to Father Joseph F. Wimmer, O.S.A., professor of biblical studies at the Washington Theological Union, who provided me with English translations of excerpts from the Döllinger correspondence.

Now that I am at last finished, I must thank all of those—family, friends, acquaintances, passers-by—who asked how the work was going and, even worse, when or whether it would ever be finished. I realize now that they had an important role in the process.

Finally, I wish to acknowledge the encouragement given to me as a graduate student in history at Georgetown University by Dr. Michael F. Foley. His sudden death in June, 1984, at age forty-four, was a terrible loss to his wife and their children. It was a loss too for many others, particularly the undergraduate students of Georgetown, then and since. *Justus ut palma florebit . . . plantatus in domo Domini.*

26 April 1994
Our Mother of Good Counsel

Introduction

In the third week of July 1870, the Catholic world waited to hear news from Rome where the Vatican Council was expected to promulgate its dogmatic definition of papal infallibility. Among those who waited, and indeed with far more interest and concern than most, was the superior of the Birmingham Oratory, John Henry Newman. The formal decision was made in Rome on Monday, 18 July, in the midst of a violent and dramatic thunderstorm. It would be five days before Newman saw the text of the definition. Whether he set down any reactions on that first sultry summer day in Birmingham[1] is now impossible to tell. It would have been characteristic of him to wait and consider.

On the next day, Sunday, 24 July, Newman wrote a long letter to his friend of twenty years, the enthusiastic and at times eccentric lay convert, Ambrose Phillipps De Lisle. The second paragraph of that letter is easily one of the most remembered and scrutinized passages of Newman's nearly twenty thousand extant letters. It has received almost as much notice and attention as any of his vast output of books, essays, reviews, and poems. Newman had held a face to face conversation with De Lisle earlier in the week. The subject had undoubtedly been the definition of papal infallibility, the news of which decision they certainly had received, though they had not seen its exact wording. In the letter of 24 July to De Lisle, Newman proposed to take up again and "finish his thoughts" on this "anxious and large subject." He got down to business straightaway: "I saw the new Definition yesterday, and am pleased at its moderation, that is, if the doctrine in question is to be defined at all. The terms used are vague and comprehensive; and, personally, I have no difficulty in admitting it. The question is, does it come to me with the authority of an Ecumenical Council?"[2] Newman wrote on for several more pages. He took the trouble to write a first draft and then a final copy, but in the end he did not send the letter. It remained unused and filed away until four and a half years later when he would give it a far wider audience than he had at first intended by including it in an appendix to his *Letter to the Duke of Norfolk*.

A long and complex story had led up to that warm, close day when Newman first saw the text from Rome. A long and complex story would

---

1. See *The Letters and Diaries of John Henry Newman,* eds. Charles Stephen Dessain and Thomas Gornall, S.J. (Oxford: The Clarendon Press, 1973) 25:163.
2. *The Letters and Diaries,* 25:164.

follow after. The whole of the story was played out over a decade, the events of July 1870 coming nearly in the middle.

There is a generally received picture of Newman and papal infallibility that can be briefly summarized. Newman accepted the doctrine of papal infallibility when he decided to enter the Roman Catholic Church in 1845, though it was not for him a major reason for his decision. Prior to the definition at the Vatican Council in July 1870, he was against the definition of papal infallibility since he held that there was no call, no necessity for it in the Church at that time and that it would needlessly unsettle Catholic consciences and deter converts to Catholicism. The matter needed further time and study. It was too important to be hurried and agitated. When the definition came in 1870, Newman accepted it after, at most, only a brief struggle. From that time he went on largely at peace with what had taken place. He decided in 1874 to speak out publicly on papal infallibility because he believed that Gladstone had unfairly attacked the civil loyalties of English Roman Catholics by insinuating that the definition of papal infallibility had exalted the pope over every temporal ruler. In the *Letter to the Duke of Norfolk,* published in 1875, Newman gave a moderate but unquestionably orthodox exposition of the definition that succeeded in routing Gladstone and ending any lingering controversy or uneasiness over the definition within the English Roman Catholic community.

The subject of Newman and papal infallibility has been treated in some detail by Newman's principal biographers, Ward, Trevor, Dessain, Ker, and Gilley. Necessarily they had to limit their discussion of the topic. Newman's is a crowded life, full of drama and detail, spanning nearly the whole of the nineteenth century. The surviving sources are manifold. The need to keep the story moving forward meant that every color and tone could not be filled in. More perhaps than in any other area of his life, Newman's approach to the question of papal infallibility is one of nuance and shading. It defies swift, bold strokes, calling instead for sifting and winnowing, for pausing to consider some small detail, some secondary passage or letter, some casual or hurried aside.

For each of the principal biographers, Newman is definitely a heroic figure, and possibly a saint. In some sense this view has influenced their presentations, perhaps most notably in such a complex and sensitive area as Newman and papal infallibility. This is not to suggest that their accounts and estimates of this aspect of Newman's life distort or depart from the evidence, but that these writers may not in the end have been fully sensitive to the evolution of Newman's position on this difficult and controversial topic. This is especially true of Ward and Trevor, but even to some degree of Dessain, Ker, and Gilley. It is probably fair to say that the biographers have for the most part written for an audience and in an atmosphere strongly influenced by the definition of 1870 and by the part that definition has played in the life of the Roman Catholic Church in the century since.

Most students of Newman, while acknowledging some inconsistencies in his approach to the subject of papal infallibility, have chosen to highlight the positive aspects of his dealings with the subject and the central, undeniable fact that he did in faith and obedience accept the definition of 1870, making it a part of his life as a Catholic in the twenty years of his life that followed. For various reasons, chiefly the constraints imposed in treating such a long and full life, writers on Newman have given little attention to the depth of Newman's struggle with the question of papal infallibility, particularly in the crucial years of 1865 to 1875.

The earliest of the major biographies of Newman was Wilfrid Ward's *The Life of John Henry Cardinal Newman,* published in two volumes in 1912. In some ways it will never be surpassed. Though Ward did not have the advantage later biographers had of having access to all of the primary material (and in an organized form),[3] he had the unique advantage of having known Newman and of having had firsthand conversations and correspondence with many who had known Newman longer and more intimately than he. Not least of these was his own father, William George Ward, a figure large in Newman's life and perhaps never more so than in the controversies of the 1860s and 1870s over papal infallibility. Wilfrid Ward treats the subject of Newman and infallibility in four chapters. He makes use of a number of Newman's letters, from which in some instances he quotes at length. In each of the four chapters there is a fairly direct, chronological account, with only occasional side topics introduced. It is important to recall that Ward finished his study at the height of the Roman antimodernist campaign. To some of those who directed or sympathized with that campaign, Newman was indeed a figure of suspicion.[4] Ward does acknowledge some of the difficulty surrounding the subject of Newman and papal infallibility: "It is sometimes suggested that Newman's

---

3. For a description of the difficulties Ward had with Newman's literary executors, particularly Father William Neville, in obtaining access to Newman's papers and correspondence, see Nadia M. Lahutsky, "Ward's Newman: The Struggle to be Fair and Faithful," *Newman and the Modernists,* ed. Mary Jo Weaver (Lanham, Md.: The College Theology Society and University Press of America, Inc., 1985) 47–67.

4. Mary Jo Weaver says of Ward that "on a strategic level he had to vindicate Newman from any suspicion of Modernism at a time when some Church officials, Newman scholars, and Modernists themselves were saying that *Pascendi* [1907] condemned Newman along with Modernism," and that Ward himself definitely believed that *Pascendi* was at least in some sense aimed at Newman. See Mary Jo Weaver, "Wilfrid Ward's Interpretation and Application of Newman," *Newman and the Modernists,* 29–30. See also John Coulson, "Was Newman A Modernist?" *John Henry Newman and Modernism,* Newman-Studien, 14, ed. Arthur Hilary Jenkins (Sigmaringendorf: regio Verlag Glock und Lutz, 1990) 74–84. And in the same collection see the important essay by Edward E. Kelly "Newman, Ward, and

line of action in 1869 and 1870 in connection with the Vatican Council was an episode which showed a certain deficiency in whole-hearted loyalty to the Holy See and is best forgotten by his admirers."[5] But when treating the actual event of the definition, Ward tells the reader that Newman, "though accepting the definition at once himself, . . . did not at first feel justified in speaking of it publicly as *de fide* until the Council should be terminated,"[6] and that Newman "very soon treated the dogma as of obligation, and urged on all his friends the duty of submission."[7]

Meriol Trevor, who completed her work just before the opening of the Second Vatican Council, tells the story of Newman and papal infallibility in six chapters in her second volume, *Newman: Light in Winter*. While her approach is also chronological, unlike Ward she often spends considerable time on other events in Newman's life in the period covered rather than focusing sharply on Newman and papal infallibility. Though she frequently refers to Newman's correspondence on the subject, she quotes fairly sparingly from the letters. Rather, she prefers to go on with swift, colorful strokes—almost breathlessly at times—making sure to cover Newman's long life in countless small and large details. But her selection of details more often serves the vigor of her account than its depth. Her biography is the most readable of the major studies. She tells the story vividly and carries the reader along. Her narrative, however, is at times too partial to Newman, to the point that she does him some injustice by a partisan presentation of his views while opponents' views are often depreciated. Of the major biographies, Trevor's fascinating account comes closest to being hagiography. Not surprisingly, then, Trevor speaks succinctly and with sureness of Newman and the 1870 definition: "To accept the dogma presented no difficulty to Newman, but he did not change his mind about the behaviour of the dogmatists [proponents of the definition]."[8]

Father Charles Stephen Dessain's brief, spare account, *John Henry Newman,* first published in 1966, can be read almost as a companion to Trevor. One wonders if Father Dessain in fact intended it to be so. It deals far more with Newman's thought, and the voice of the narrator is always

---

Modernism: Problems with Infallible Dogmatic Truth," 168–79. Kelly writes: "Ward submitted to *Pascendi* after much internal distraction, but he was not really at peace after it. His irritation with the objectionable encyclical persisted through the period of his writing Newman's life. He prepared several drafts of an introduction which was intended to relate Newman to Modernism, but he abandoned this plan after opposition from the Birmingham Oratorians and warning from Cardinal Mercier," 177.

5. Wilfrid Ward, *The Life of John Henry Cardinal Newman* (London: Longmans, Green, and Co., 1912) 2:279.

6. Ibid., 308.

7. Ibid., 373.

8. Meriol Trevor, *Newman: Light in Winter* (London: Macmillan & Co., Ltd., 1962) 492.

careful, judicious, and measured. Surely no one has had a deeper knowledge of Newman than Dessain. He was the principal editor of all twenty-one of the volumes of *The Letters and Diaries* that cover Newman's Catholic years. That he did not live to finish the ten volumes planned for Newman's Anglican years was a great loss to Newman scholarship; and this is in no sense meant to detract from the quality of the six volumes that have so far appeared. Father Dessain chose to deal with the definition of papal infallibility and its aftermath in a chapter that also treats Newman's attempts to found an Oratory at Oxford, efforts that were frustrated in the end by Archbishop Henry Edward Manning and Rome. Dessain, in keeping with his plan to present a concise overview of Newman's life and thought, quotes from only a small number of the Newman letters dealing with papal infallibility. He covers the subject of Newman and the definition almost by indirection and with a certain reserve: "The final form of the definition was moderate enough. . . . In fact the form of the definition was in reality something of a defeat for the extremists. It was nonetheless an over-emphasis in one direction, always a dangerous thing when revealed truth is at stake. Newman spent much time in the years after 1870 reassuring and explaining matters to the many Catholics who were disturbed in their faith by what had happened."[9]

A very recent biography of Newman is Ian Ker's masterful *John Henry Newman: A Biography,* published in 1988. To call a biography definitive is always risky, but Ker's study certainly deserves to be considered such. Ker's work is based almost entirely on Newman's writings and correspondence, and he quotes generously from both. His organization of and selection from such a vast amount of material is astonishing. His approach is far more centered on Newman the thinker and writer than is Trevor's, though he succeeds in handling the biographical aspects of his task with passages that at times rival hers in verve and color. His account is in some ways a vast filling out of Dessain's. It should be recalled that Ker was a close collaborator of Dessain and took up the work of editing *The Letters and Diaries* after Dessain's sudden death in 1976. Ker, who deals with Newman and papal infallibility in a chapter of forty-two pages, gives emphasis to one of the peculiarities of Newman's reaction to the definition in the uncertain days just after it was passed: "Personally, Newman accepted the somewhat circular argument that if the Pope himself enforced the definition as a dogma of faith, then 'I should consider that the fact of the Pope being able by his power of jurisdiction practically to enforce his claim of infallibility . . . was a providential intimation that the claim was well founded and I should receive the dogma as a dogma.' "[10]

9. Charles Stephen Dessain, *John Henry Newman,* 2nd ed. (Stanford, Calif.: Stanford University Press, 1971) 139.

10. Ian Ker, *John Henry Newman: A Biography* (Oxford: The Clarendon Press, 1988) 656.

Of the major biographers, Ker comes closest to presenting something of the dilemma that the definition occasioned for Newman in his seventieth year and a quarter century after his reception into the Roman Catholic Church. He shows how Newman found a way forward by looking toward "a new Pope, and a reassembled Council [that] may trim the boat."[11] And in addition, Ker writes of Newman's stance: "The implication is clear enough: while not to be dismissed as an unmitigated disaster, the definition was at best a necessary evil."[12]

Sheridan Gilley's biography *Newman and His Age,* issued in 1990 to coincide with the centenary of Newman's death, deserves to be ranked with the other great studies of Newman's life. It is at once an intellectual biography and a colorful chronicle of Newman's life and times. Considerable attention is given to contemporaries of Newman, both Anglican and Roman Catholic, who played major and minor roles in Newman's long life. Gilley's overall achievement is much to be admired. His portrait of Newman is in some sense sharper than that of any of the other major biographers, and while in general highly sympathetic to Newman, Gilley is not averse to exposing Newman's personal lacks and weaknesses. Gilley relies fairly often on Newman's letters, diaries, and other writings. However, he makes less use of Newman's letters than does Ker and prefers to add more narrative and analysis.

Gilley deals with Newman and papal infallibility in a chapter of nineteen pages. While giving the standard account of Newman's reactions to the Vatican Council, before, during, and immediately after, Gilley also indicates aspects of Newman's struggle over the definition. He quotes from Newman's letter of 21 August 1870 to Mrs. William Beckwith, "I doubt whether it is yet an article of faith."[13] Gilley goes on to say, "Newman also felt that the definition had brought its own punishment. It was immediately followed by the Franco-Prussian War. . . . The Pope had been declared infallible but had lost the temporal power that had been his for a thousand years."[14] In his last allusion to any hesitation or negative feelings on Newman's part, Gilley states: "Any lingering doubt was resolved in Newman's mind by the submission of the *orbis terrarum* to the infallibility decree, as even the gallant Gallicans of France and the proud prelates of Austria and Hungary surrendered one by one. . . ."[15]

Two of the lesser biographies should also be added to this survey of how the topic of Newman and papal infallibility has been handled. John

11. Ibid., 660.

12. Ibid., 683.

13. Sheridan Gilley, *Newman and His Age* (London: Darton, Longman, and Todd, 1990) 369.

14. Ibid.

15. Ibid., 370.

Moody's fairly brief account, *John Henry Newman,* appeared in 1945 and had a certain popularity, especially in the United States, in the long interval between Ward and Trevor. It was not in any sense intended to be an original study. Moody felt, as did Ward, the necessity of dealing with persistent reports that Newman's acceptance of the definition had been less than complete: "But what of his attitude to the third declaration during the Pontificate of Pius IX—Papal Infallibility, . . .? This is the instance in which, his critics have said, he failed to conform to the mind of the Church—at least in which he did not interiorly conform. But let us see."[16] Moody then goes on after a brief analysis to present the following confident conclusion: "Though he had felt the pronouncement of any definition at this time was hardly necessary and that, in any event, the matter should be approached more deliberately, . . . he was now to rejoice that the Council had simply defined a doctrine of the Faith in the form which had been held explicitly from ancient times and in which he had believed ever since he became a Catholic."[17]

A more recent popular study is Brian Martin's *John Henry Newman: His Life and Work,* which appeared in 1982. Martin's account is careful and readable. He deals tersely and somewhat indirectly with Newman and papal infallibility, almost backing into the subject when he writes: "It was not that Newman failed to believe this doctrine: he simply found that its prosecution at the Council disturbed the faith of so many."[18]

To add to this overview of how the subject of Newman and papal infallibility has been handled in the years since his death, it is also useful to look at several of the works of commentators on Newman's theology or other aspects of his religious thought. These writers too reveal by their somewhat different approaches and emphases that this is an aspect of Newman's life deserving of greater attention and a fuller probing. An important treatment along this line is Paul Misner's *Papacy and Development: Newman and the Primacy of the Pope,* which appeared in 1976. Though papal infallibility is a secondary consideration in his study, Misner does not overlook the problematic aspects of Newman's approach to papal infallibility. Misner appears to contrast Newman's views on papal infallibility with his far more consistent approach to the question of papal primacy when he writes that "even when he had his difficulties with the notion of the pope's infallibility, there was never any doubt in his mind about his primacy."[19] Another important voice on Newman and papal

16. John Moody, *John Henry Newman* (New York: Sheed and Ward, 1945) 283.
17. Ibid., 287.
18. Brian Martin, *John Henry Newman: His Life and Work* (New York: Oxford University Press, 1982) 123.
19. Paul Misner, *Papacy and Development: Newman and the Primacy of the Pope* (Leiden: E. J. Brill, 1976) 147.

infallibility is that of Edward Jeremy Miller, whose *John Henry Newman on the Idea of Church* was published in 1987. Miller characterizes Newman's reaction to the definition: "The restrictive language of the definition actually pleased Newman. It said far less than the ultramontane party had wished. The pope's infallibility was limited to the deposit of revelation; it did not apply to the political arena, such as the pope's temporal powers. Furthermore, the doctrine was to be understood negatively; it was a protection from error in the statement alone that was explicitly being taught. . . . Finally, Newman sensed that the wording looked to future modifications—he called it 'trimming'—from another council or pope."[20] Miller is here actually summarizing the position that Newman came to in time and he appears to acknowledge that Newman's first reaction and his acceptance of the definition are two very distinct moments when he writes:

> The issue of corporate dissent, following Vatican I, never fully materialized. The bishops of the minority either individually or in regional synods, came to accept the decree and to promulgate it in their dioceses. As this opposition was melting, the decree was gaining conciliar authority in Newman's mind. The doctrine of papal infallibility, in which he had long believed, was receiving *de fide* corroboration.
>
> The second phase of *securus iudicat* [the universal acceptance of the definition] then began.[21]

Writing in the *Ampleforth Journal* in 1975, Roderick Strange clearly does not see Newman's acceptance of the definition as simple and untroubled. Rather, he seems to highlight the individuality of Newman's approach to the definition by implying that it was distinctive then and has in fact not fully gained favor since. At the conclusion of his article, "Newman on Infallibility: 1870 and 1970," Strange writes: "The suggestion here is that Newman's interpretation of infallibility, if adopted, might have been, and could still be, of vital importance for the health and well-being of the Church."[22]

The most concentrated study of Newman and papal infallibility is Wolfgang Klausnitzer's *Päpstliche Unfehlbarkeit bei Newman und Döllinger: ein historisch-systematischer Vergleich,*[23] published in 1980. Klausnitzer is concerned primarily to compare the positions of Newman and Döllinger. In order to show Newman's position in its strengths as well as its lacks,

---

20. Edward Jeremy Miller, *John Henry Newman On the Idea of Church* (Shepherdstown, W.Va.: The Patmos Press, 1987) 112.

21. Ibid., 118.

22. Roderick Strange, "Newman on Infallibility: 1870 and 1970," *Ampleforth Journal* 80 (Spring 1975) 70.

23. Wolfgang Klausnitzer, *Päpstliche Unfehlbarkeit bei Newman und Döllinger: ein historisch-systematischer Vergleich* (Innsbruck: Tyroliaverlag, 1980). See esp. 89–117.

he relies chiefly on Newman's notes on infallibility from the 1860s, the *Letter to the Duke of Norfolk,* and the preface to the third edition of the *Via Media* (1877). Klausnitzer's aim is more theological than historical, more analytical than chronological. Consequently, he relies on only a small number of Newman's letters.

Further important witnesses on Newman and papal infallibility are Joseph Fenton, writing in 1945, Josef Altholz, writing in 1962, Owen Chadwick, writing in 1983, and Avery Dulles and Francis Sullivan, both writing in 1990. Altholz, the preeminent historian of the nineteenth century liberal Catholic movement in England, agrees with several of the biographers in characterizing Newman's acceptance of the definition as fairly straightforward: "Newman had no difficulty in submitting and advising others to submit; he devised a 'minimalistic' interpretation of the dogma which satisfied nearly all the Liberal Catholics."[24] Chadwick also appears at first to see Newman's acceptance of the definition as immediate, even easy, though he concludes his estimate on a less certain note: "When at the Vatican Council of 1870 they [the Fathers of the Council] insisted on defining that the Pope is infallible whenever he makes decisions on faith and morals, and even though the Church at large has not formally expressed its agreement, he cheerfully accepted what was decided though he still was not sure what was meant. He was quite serene. The Church will mediate further, and one day will give further light."[25]

In "Newman on Infallibility," Avery Dulles, S.J., takes the position that while the council was sitting, Newman "nervously expressed his opposition to the proposed definition of papal infallibility. When the dogma was defined in 1870 he initially hesitated as to whether it was binding on Catholics. Soon, however, he overcame his doubts and became a leading apologist for the definition. At that stage he confined the dogma within narrow limits, glorying in his own minimalism."[26] Dulles's view appears to foreshorten the several stages of struggle that Newman went through in the months and even years following the definition.

Francis Sullivan, S.J., in his contribution on Newman and infallibility in *Newman after a Hundred Years,* acknowledges somewhat more of Newman's struggle than the other writers by saying that "even as an Anglican, as we shall see, he believed that the Church enjoyed something akin to infallibility; but it was only some months after the definition by Vatican I that he could give his full assent to papal infallibility as a dogma of his faith."[27] Fenton, on the other hand, brooks no uncertainty on New-

24. Josef L. Altholz, *The Liberal Catholic Movement in England: the "Rambler" and Its Contributors 1848–1864* (London: Burns and Oates, 1962) 241.

25. Owen Chadwick, *Newman* (Oxford and New York: Oxford University Press, 1983) 66.

26. Avery Dulles, S.J., "Newman on Infallibility," *Theological Studies* 51 (1990) 434.

27. Francis A. Sullivan, S.J., "Newman on Infallibility," *Newman after a Hundred Years,* ed. Ian Ker and Alan G. Hill (Oxford: The Clarendon Press, 1990) 419.

man's position. More than any other commentator, he believes that Newman's acceptance of the definition was less than wholehearted. A determined antimodernist, Fenton characteristically expresses his views on Newman and papal infallibility strongly and bluntly: "As a whole Newman's stand on the doctrine of papal infallibility was doctrinally inexact and unfortunate in its influence."[28] Fenton chides biographers of Newman for giving a misleading, if not false, impression of Newman's views on papal infallibility: "Some popular accounts of Newman's life seem calculated to make us believe that his position on the Vatican Council's definition was basically satisfactory. Such a belief would be inaccurate . . . his capacity for good is too powerful to allow us to dally with the notion that his stand on the infallibility controversies is as valuable as his other contributions to Catholic thought."[29]

The treatments of Newman and papal infallibility by the principal biographers and other commentators have necessarily been governed by their own special aims—full-length biographies or close concentrations on specific aspects of his theological writings, for example, on papal primacy. The purpose of the present study is to look closely and searchingly at Newman and papal infallibility from the year 1865, when the topic became the subject of controversy in England, largely owing to the writings of W. G. Ward, editor of the *Dublin Review,* to the year 1875, when Newman's *Letter to the Duke of Norfolk* appeared and by most accounts succeeded in quieting the long contention. It is in the main a biographical rather than a theological exposition, though in the end no such absolute separation can be made.

What is the proper characterization of Newman's views on papal infallibility, and particularly his attitude toward the definition of 1870? Is there any way to gauge the depth of Newman's difficulties with the question? Is there any way to look into the matter more deeply, to study it in a new light? Are there any openings for further exploration? Newman's letters would appear to offer the way forward. Few figures in history have left such a massive record of their lives as John Henry Newman has in his extant letters, collected to date in twenty-seven full volumes, with at least another four still to come. In many ways these letters provide an almost daily record of his life and thought, his concerns and preoccupations, fears and prejudices. In the letters he breathes and takes on flesh more than in the somewhat artificial and limited exposition of his *Apologia pro Vita Sua* and far more fully and concretely than in the scattered jottings that have been collected together as his *Autobiographical Writ-*

---

28. Joseph Fenton, "John Henry Newman and the Vatican Definition of Papal Infallibility," *American Ecclesiastical Review* 113 (October 1945) 318.
29. Ibid., 320.

ings. In the "Introduction" to his study of Newman, Sheridan Gilley calls Newman "one of the greatest letter writers in the English language. . . ."[30]

That twenty thousand letters survive is for the most part no accident. Newman carefully collected his letters from friends and acquaintances. Especially from the early 1860s, he spent long hours cataloguing and, in some cases, annotating his correspondence. He did not want a biography, but he knew that there were likely to be accounts of his life despite his wishes and he feared that his life might be misrepresented by people who did not know him. Better to leave something for his friends to set the record straight. "Had I my will," he wrote in 1874, "no Memoir should be written of me, except such a thin running notice as would suffice to hold together a series of my letters. Letters I don't mind, for they are facts, and belong, for good or bad, to the personality of the writer of them; but a Memoir, or at least a life, is more or less the product of the imagination, a conclusion from facts, more or less theoretical and unauthoritative."[31] In a letter to his niece, Jemima Mozley, written in 1863, Newman had dealt in a similar vein with the part that letters can play in telling the story of a person's life. In his view they have a truth that no biographer, however objective, can achieve, for "biographers varnish, they assign motives; they conjecture feelings. . . ." In asking for the loan of some of his letters that he had sent to his niece, Newman said, "It has ever been a hobby of mine (unless it be a truism, not a hobby) that a man's life lies in his letters."[32]

As has been pointed out, some of the Newman letters dealing with papal infallibility between 1865 and 1875 have been used by the biographers and commentators—perhaps about a dozen letters have in some way been relied upon by all the major writers that have treated the topic directly or indirectly. But a large number of the letters involving papal infallibility have received only small or passing mention or no mention at all. Many of these could perhaps be called "lesser" letters on the topic, but often they have as much or more to say than the famous handful on which the majority of writers have based their expositions and analyses. At times these letters are brief or mention the subject of papal infallibility among several other subjects. At times they are addressed to some of the "minor"

30. Gilley, *Newman and His Age,* 3.
31. Henry Tristram, ed. *John Henry Newman: Autobiographical Writings* (New York: Sheed and Ward, 1957) 23. See also Newman, "Memorandum on Future Biography", 15 November 1872, *The Letters and Diaries,* ed. Charles Stephen Dessain and Thomas Gornall, S.J. (Oxford: The Clarendon Press, 1975) 27:200, in which he states: "I don't wish my life written—because there is so little to say. . . . Moreover in the Apologia I have virtually written my life up to 1845—and there is little or nothing to say since."
32. Newman to Mrs. John Mozley, 18 May 1863, *The Letters and Diaries,* ed. Charles Stephen Dessain (London: Thomas Nelson and Sons, Ltd., 1970) 20:443.

characters in the crowded *dramatis personae* of Newman's life. There has been no close examination of all that the letters offer toward a fuller understanding of Newman and the definition of papal infallibility. The letters get inside the topic in a unique way. The letters afford a vivid and penetrating look at Newman grappling, largely in private, with the possibility of the definition and then with its consequences, both personal and public.[33]

An analysis of Newman's letters in this period casts light on his views on papal infallibility in ways that his published writings do not, even those writings that Newman appealed to in the late 1860s and early 1870s as giving clear evidence of what he termed his longheld views on the matter. The letters reveal the intensity of Newman's struggle against the nearly daily background of his many duties and distractions, some of them major, such as the completion of the *Grammar of Assent,* others of small moment, such as his reassuring report to the parent of a prospective pupil of the Oratory School after an outbreak of scarlet fever among the students. The story told in the letters casts new light not only on Newman but on the Roman Catholic Church in England in the opening decade of Cardinal Manning's long sway over it, a dominance that in many ways persisted after his death in 1892 right down to the present. The Newman letters dealing with papal infallibility reveal him as a vital and believable human person who did not so overestimate the virtue of faith as to make meaningless the equally great virtue of hope. In the end, they offer new support, but in a more real and appealing way, for the portrait of Newman as a hero, and possibly a saint.

As Nicholas Lash has written of Newman's influence upon theology—both before, but more important—after the Second Vatican Council, " . . . I would hazard the remark that Newman's influence is extraordinarily difficult to chart because that very *closeness* of speech to speaker, of text to thinker ('it was the man who was in all these things') means that it is *Newman* who makes a difference to those touched by his spell, far more deeply than his arguments or ideas considered in abstraction from the man."[34]

The method of this study is chronological rather than topical. A chronological approach seemed better suited to capturing the human drama, the vividness of the struggle, the depth of the dilemma. A chronological approach allows the reader to see Newman going back and forth on the question, now confident and secure, now hesitant and given to

---

33. Father Avery Dulles writes in "Newman on Infallibility": "Many of Newman's most interesting observations on infallibility are found in personal diaries or in private correspondence," 434.

34. Nicholas Lash, "Tides and Twilight: Newman and Vatican II," *Newman after a Hundred Years,* ed. Ian Ker and Alan G. Hill (Oxford: The Clarendon Press, 1990) 451–52.

painstaking second thoughts. One week he is sure that no definition will come from the Vatican Council, the next he consoles himself with the belief that the definition is simply what he and others fearful of its passage have always held.

The first chapter of this work takes Newman up to the year before the council opened. It sets the stage by introducing many of the key players, especially in England, and showing Newman's reluctance to become actively involved in the English debate over the pope's infallibility. The second chapter treats the heightening tension that was building up in England and on the Continent in 1869, the year the council opened, and Newman's response (or lack of response) to it. This chapter also looks at Newman in the months the council was sitting. It is not meant to be a history of the council, but rather a history of Newman's reaction to the council as events in Rome unfolded and became known. The third chapter looks at Newman from the time of the definition and in the year after. Here Newman is at first caught up in a tense and uncertain situation, which over the course of the year gives way to an atmosphere of acquiescence and acceptance. From mid-1871 to mid-1874, the public controversy over the definition largely subsided, but Newman still had to deal with its consequences, both publicly and in private. The story of the lingering consequences for Newman is detailed in the fourth chapter. Chapters five and six show Newman struggling with a way to answer Gladstone's *Expostulation,* his success after several trying weeks in finding a way forward, and the generally positive response that his answer to Gladstone achieved in England, from both Catholics and Anglicans.

Newman and the topic of papal infallibility continue to be of great interest to Christians at the close of the twentieth century. Interest in Newman has grown steadily since the end of the Second World War. The Newman centenary year, 1990, appears to have intensified and deepened the continuing fascination with Newman and his thought. That two major biographies, each a unique and valuable contribution to Newman studies, should appear within a two-year period is a testimony to this continuing interest. Since the close of the Second Vatican Council a quarter century ago, there has also been a reawakened interest in the subject of papal infallibility.[35] This interest has focused on both theological and historical aspects of the topic, and especially the definition of 1870. In 1971, Hans Küng's *Infallible? An Inquiry*[36] was published. Later in the 1970s, Peter Chirico's *Infallibility: The Crossroads of Doctrine*[37] appeared. A decade

35. For a comprehensive overview of books and articles on papal infallibility, especially since the close of the Second Vatican Council, see John T. Ford, C.S.C., "Infallibility: A Review of Recent Studies," *Theological Studies* 40 (June 1979) 273–305.

36. Hans Küng, *Infallible? An Inquiry* (New York: Doubleday, 1971).

37. Peter Chirico, *Infallibility: The Crossroads of Doctrine* (Kansas City: Sheed, Andrews, and McMeel, 1977).

after Küng's provocative book appeared in English, August Bernhard Hasler published in English his equally provocative *How the Pope Became Infallible: Pius IX and the Politics of Persuasion*[38] with an introduction by Küng. Very recently a more scholarly approach has been taken by Margaret O'Gara in *Triumph in Defeat: Infallibility, Vatican I, and the French Minority Bishops*[39] and by Luis Bermejo in *Infallibility on Trial: Church, Conciliarity and Communion.*[40]

As historical and theological inquiry into topics dealing with the definition of papal infallibility continues, Newman's part in the debate that preceded and followed the definition of 1870 cannot be ignored. Newman's struggle is, to be sure, only one aspect of his involvement with the issue, but it is an extremely important one. An examination of the human struggle of this great figure of the modern Church has value in providing not only a fresh and deeper understanding of the man but also of the 1870 definition itself in the life of the Church in the century since Newman's death.

---

38. August Bernhard Hasler, *How the Pope Became Infallible: Pius IX and the Politics of Persuasion* (Garden City, N.Y.: Doubleday & Co., Inc., 1981).

39. Margaret O'Gara, *Triumph in Defeat: Infallibility, Vatican I, and the French Minority Bishops* (Washington: The Catholic University of America Press, 1988).

40. Luis Bermejo, *Infallibility on Trial: Church, Conciliarity and Communion* (Westminster, Md.: Christian Classics, 1992).

Chapter 1

"I Put All This on Paper with Great Diffidence"
1865–1868

By the late 1850s, Newman, wearied by his experience as rector of the Catholic University of Ireland and by a series of disappointments in his life as a Catholic, saw his permanent return to Birmingham as a time of quiet preparation for his life's end. He already considered himself an old man. Though he had some projects in mind, he thought that on the whole his accomplishments were behind him. He had lived largely in obscurity since his reception into the Catholic Church in 1845. His life had been narrowed to the confines of ecclesiastical duties. Beyond a rather small circle of Catholics he was all but forgotten. The honors that had been foreseen by both Catholics and Anglicans when he entered the Roman communion had been kept from him. Though Newman would in 1864 acerbically decline Monsignor George Talbot's[1] invitation to preach in Rome with the famous remark, "Birmingham people have souls,"[2] Birmingham was thought in the great world to be a backwater. Newman's admirers as well as his detractors could not comprehend why a man of his gifts had chosen to make himself an exile there.

In fact, from 1858 when Newman officially gave up his duties in Dublin, he would live another thirty-two years, and in that time would write *On Consulting the Faithful in Matters of Doctrine* (1859), the *Apologia Pro Vita Sua* (1864), the *Dream of Gerontius* (1865), the *Grammar of Assent* (1870), the *Letter to the Duke of Norfolk* (1875), the Preface to the third edition of the *Via Media* (1877), and prepare new editions of his sermons and other writings, both from his Anglican and Catholic years.

1. George Talbot, after several years as an Anglican clergyman, became a Catholic in 1840. Ordained a priest in 1846, four years later he was named a canon of St. Peter's and a papal chamberlain. Trusted by Pius IX, he had a great influence in English Catholic affairs and was a close confidant of Manning's. He had a serious mental breakdown in 1868 and spent the last eighteen years of his life in an asylum outside Paris. There was little sympathy between Newman and Talbot, a fervent ultramontanist.

2. See Newman to George Talbot, 25 July 1864, *The Letters and Diaries of John Henry Newman,* ed. Charles Stephen Dessain and Edward E. Kelly, S.J. (London: Thomas Nelson and Sons, Ltd., 1971) 21:167.

Newman's biographers have noted that it was Charles Kingsley's attack in 1863 on the veracity of the Catholic priesthood that brought Newman back into the public eye—both Catholic and Anglican. He was like a man returned from the dead. From 1864 Newman would again take a place in the public arena and far from ending his life in obscurity, there would come recognition by his dear Oxford in 1878 and in the following year the lifting of the cloud that had come over his Catholic years, when he was named a cardinal by the new pope, Leo XIII. Between the mid-1860s and the honors of the late 1870s, Newman would know several triumphs, but he would also continue to experience bitter disappointments, both at the hands of the leaders of the English Catholic Church and the Roman authorities. In 1867 the suspicions that Rome had harbored against him since the *Rambler*[3] affair were allayed, but they had had too long a life not to linger on. Newman would remain suspect. Even in the nearly universal triumph of the *Letter to the Duke of Norfolk* in 1875, voices of dissent—though more muted than in the past—would be heard in England and in Rome. There is no doubt that Newman was elated by the success of the *Apologia,* but from the first he saw his restored renown as a mixed blessing. It gave him his chance to have his say, to speak calmly and moderately in an atmosphere of suspicion, accusation, and heightened rhetoric that he deplored. But it also put before him the prospect of having to deal with certain controversies that he would have preferred to avoid. In 1864 Newman could not, for example, ignore the controversies and debates surrounding the papacy, and perhaps more precisely, the papacy of Pius IX. Debates over the pope's temporal power had intensified in the face of a determined Italian nationalism, and allied to this issue, but going well beyond it, was the great question of papal infallibility.

There were many reasons for the increasing debates over the exercise and authority of the papal office. In 1854 Pius IX, after consultation with the worldwide episcopate, had proclaimed the dogma of the Immaculate Conception. This exercise of the papal office had helped to bring the centuries-long debate between conciliarists and infallibilists to the fore again. Further, as a consequence of the threat to the Papal States, great sympathy was aroused for the pope and expressions of support and affection were addressed to Pius IX from Catholics all over the world. In addition, there was in the 1860s a belief that revealed religion was under attack from scientific discoveries and a pervasive rationalist philosophy.

---

3. Newman's article, "On Consulting the Faithful in Matters of Doctrine," in the July 1859 issue of the *Rambler* was delated to Rome by Bishop Thomas Brown of Newport. In 1860 Newman was made aware of this by Bishop Ullathorne of Birmingham. Newman then wrote to Cardinal Wiseman to ask in what way his article had failed to convey the Church's teachings. Wiseman obtained a list of the parts of the article that Rome found questionable, but he never sent it on to Newman. Newman learned this only in 1867. In the meantime, the Roman authorities decided that Newman had refused to reply.

The Church began to take on the appearance of a beleaguered bastion, and the role of the pope as the universal champion against irreligion and indifferentism (often seen as synonymous with social and political liberalism) was promoted by a number of Catholics who were convinced that the authority of the papal office must be clear and unassailable in the coming night battle if the Church was to emerge triumphant. A leading English proponent of papal infallibility wrote at this time,

> It is in these days a very trite remark—yet not on that account the less true—that an internecine conflict is at hand, between the army of dogma and the united hosts of indifferentism and unbelief. Looking at the matter practically, the one solid and inexpugnable fortress for the army of dogma, is the Rock of Peter. But we cannot submit to the Pope's authority by *halves;* we cannot accept what we please and reject what we please; we must humbly embrace that whole body of Christian doctrine, which he infallibly inculcates. By denying to him then that measure of infallibility which he so undeniably and peremptorily claims, you would lay open our one position of security, and leave us an easy prey to our enemies.[4]

In the practical order, the authority of the pope over local bishops had considerably increased from the time of the French Revolution and the Napoleonic Wars. For example, in the appointment of diocesan bishops, Rome had begun a centralizing policy that took the right of naming bishops away from diocesan chapters. This was especially true during the pontificate of Pius IX, 1846–1878.[5] There were other evidences of Roman centralization, particularly in the government of religious orders, in the imposition of the approach of the Roman schools upon the teaching of philosophy and theology in Catholic seminaries, and in the liturgical life and discipline of the Church.

In the midst of Newman's controversy with Charles Kingsley, Pius IX issued his Munich Brief, *Tuas Libenter* (21 December 1863), in which he said that "the Catholic scholar was bound not only by the solemn definitions of the Church, but also by the 'ordinary magisterium,' the decisions of the Roman curial congregations, and by the common teaching of theologians."[6] In the apostolic brief, the pope rejected "the freedom claimed for Catholic thinkers at a recent conference of theologians in Munich."[7]

4. William George Ward, "A Second Letter to the Rev. Father Ryder," *Dublin Review,* n.s. 10 (January–April 1868), appendix to April issue, 65.

5. See Garrett Sweeney, "The 'wound in the right foot' unhealed?," *Bishops and Writers: Aspects of the Evolution of Modern English Catholicism,* ed. Adrian Hastings (Wheathamstead-Hertfordshire: Anthony Clarke, 1977) 207–34.

6. Charles Stephen Dessain, *John Henry Newman,* 2nd ed. (Stanford, Calif.: Stanford University Press, 1971) 124.

7. Ian Ker, *John Henry Newman: A Biography* (Oxford: The Clarendon Press, 1988) 541.

At the end of 1864, Pius IX issued the Encyclical *Quanta cura* and the attached *Syllabus of Errors*. These two documents, along with the Munich Brief, gave the clear impression that the Church viewed the social, political, and intellectual ideas of nineteenth-century Europe with great suspicion and even disdain. These Roman documents created deeper divisions between the two opposing views in the Church on papal teaching authority.

In March 1865, several months after the publication of the *Apologia,* Pius IX convened in secret a commission of cardinals to study whether an ecumenical council (which would be the first in three hundred years) should be called and what topics it should consider. The question of papal infallibility was not given a prominent place in these discussions. With the notable exception of the discussions of the preparatory doctrinal commission in 1869, this would remain true—so far as the Roman authorities were concerned—right up through the opening of the council five years later.[8] Although the subject of the revision of the Code of Canon Law, questions concerning the authority of diocesan bishops over exempt religious orders, and more theoretical issues such as the Church's response to secularism and rationalism were given as the reasons for a council, individuals in the Church began to look toward the council as an opportunity for clarifying once and for all the pope's authority as the supreme teacher in the Church.

The debate over papal infallibility intensifies

The debate in England over papal infallibility suddenly intensified in 1865. In May of that year Henry Edward Manning[9] was nominated to the see of Westminster. Manning was already a determined and publicly vocal defender of the papal temporal power, according it the status of Catholic doctrine. His views on papal infallibility were equally fervent. One of those who was encouraged by Manning's ascendancy was William George Ward, editor of the *Dublin Review* since 1863 and an equally en-

---

8. See *Collectio Conciliorum Recentiorum Ecclesiae Universae* (hereafter cited as Mansi), ed. Ludovicus Petit and Joannes Baptista Martin, 49 (1865-1869) Tomus Decimus Tertius, Sacrosancti Oecumenici Concilii Vaticani: Pars Prima, Acta Praesynodalia (Arnhem & Leipzig: Société Nouvelle d'Edition de la Collection Mansi [H. Welter], 1923) 668-73, 695-96, 711-12.

9. Henry Edward Manning, born in 1808, became an adherent of the Tractarian party in the 1830s. In 1833 he married Caroline Sargent, who died in 1837. Manning entered the Roman Catholic Church in 1851 as a result of the Gorham Judgment. Ordained a Roman Catholic priest two months later, he afterwards studied in Rome where he was befriended by Pius IX. Returned to England, he became a close associate of Cardinal Nicholas Wiseman, archbishop of Westminster since 1850, and succeeded to that see in 1865 after Wiseman's death. Manning died in 1892.

thusiastic advocate of papal infallibility.[10] In the pages of the *Dublin Review,* in effect the leading Roman Catholic journal in England, Ward expressed strong views on papal infallibility and the necessity for all true and loyal Catholics to accept wholeheartedly the position on infallibility that he espoused. Early in 1866, the new Archbishop of Westminster in his first pastoral letter, *The Reunion of Christendom,* took the same line. Manning and Ward were both Oxford converts but there their similarities with Newman diverged. Though Manning and Ward were divided from Newman on a number of issues facing the life of the Church in England and the universal Church, none would divide them more than the question of papal infallibility.[11]

Aside from his own personal struggles with the question, Newman had many reasons for wanting to avoid confrontations with officials in the Church, both in Rome and in London. Perhaps more than any other reason during the mid-1860s was Newman's bitter disagreement with Manning and his allies over Catholics attending Oxford (and Cambridge). Twice between 1864 and 1867 Newman seemed to have the approval needed for founding an Oratory for Catholic students at Oxford, where he himself would live at least for a time. Twice he was thwarted in this hope by Manning and, through Manning, by Rome. The starts and stops of the Oxford Oratory issue, a project so important to Newman that he could imagine in anticipation the faces of the undergraduates who would hear his sermons, cannot be discounted as a reason for Newman's appearing to hold back in this period from publicly dealing with the issue of papal infallibility.[12]

Newman and infallibility in the Apologia

It is of course true that Newman dealt with the subject of infallibility in the *Apologia,* but in the *Apologia* he took a careful path and dealt more with the Church's infallibility than with the pope's. "I am not," he wrote,

10. Born in 1812, William George Ward, after studies at Oxford, became one of the leaders of the Tractarian party in the 1830s. His views were condemned by the Oxford Convocation in 1845. After becoming a Roman Catholic that same year, Ward, as a layman, taught philosophy and theology at the major seminary of the Westminster diocese. He was editor of the *Dublin Review* from 1863 to 1878, and died in 1882.

11. In an autobiographical note written in 1887, Manning stated: "During these years three subjects were uppermost: (1) The Temporal Power; (2) The Oxford Question; and (3) The Infallibility. On all these Newman was not in accordance with the Holy See." Manning continued: "I am nobody, but I spoke as the Holy See spoke." Edmund Sheridan Purcell, *Life of Cardinal Manning: Archbishop of Westminster* (New York and London: The Macmillan Company, 1896) 2:350–51.

12. Newman and the Oxford Oratory question are treated in Ker, *John Henry Newman: A Biography,* 560–617.

"here determining any thing about the essential seat of that power, because that is a question doctrinal, not historical and practical. . . ."[13] Newman could not altogether avoid dealing with the question of infallibility in replying to Charles Kingsley. Kingsley had implied that Catholics would accept unthinkingly anything that the Church asked them to believe. Newman saw Kingsley's charge as this: "That I, as a Catholic, not only make profession to hold doctrines which I cannot possibly believe in my heart, but that I also believe in the existence of a power on earth, which at its own will imposes upon men any new set of *credenda,* when it pleases, by a claim to infallibility; in consequence, that my own thoughts are not my own property; that I cannot tell that to-morrow I may not have to give up what I hold to-day, and that the necessary effect of such a condition of mind must be a degrading bondage. . . ."[14] The principal thrust of Newman's reply to this charge was to take a middle course, to keep away as far as possible from the question of the pope's role in the definition of truth. The Church of its very nature as a teacher of truth founded by God was ensured of a divine guarantee that it would not fail in its mission. Newman wrote:

> Supposing then it to be the Will of the Creator to interfere in human affairs, and to make provisions for retaining in the world a knowledge of Himself, so definite and distinct as to be proof against the energy of human scepticism, in such a case—I am far from saying that there was no other way—but there is nothing to surprise the mind, if He should think fit to introduce a power into the world, invested with the prerogative of infallibility in religious matters. Such a provision would be a direct, immediate, active, and prompt means of withstanding the difficulty; it would be an instrument suited to the need; and, when I find that this is the very claim of the Catholic Church, not only do I feel no difficulty in admitting the idea, but there is a fitness in it, which recommends it to my mind. And thus I am brought to speak of the Church's infallibility, as a provision, adapted by the mercy of the Creator, to preserve religion in the world, and to restrain that freedom of thought, which of course in itself is one of the greatest of our natural gifts, and to rescue it from its own suicidal excesses.[15]

In two instances in his reply to Kingsley, Newman made remarks that would have particular bearing on his attitude toward the definition of papal infallibility six years later. In both he was dealing with the doctrine of the Immaculate Conception, proclaimed in 1854. Newman was attempting to show that definitions of dogma neither introduced new beliefs out of the blue nor asked unprepared and uncomprehending Catholics to ac-

13. John Henry Newman, *Apologia Pro Vita Sua,* standard ed. (Garden City, N.Y.: Doubleday & Co., Image Books Edition, 1956) 326.
14. Ibid., 323.
15. Ibid., 322–23.

cept them. When a definition came about, it came only after centuries of preparation and acceptance by the Catholic faithful. It simply made clear and in a solemn way what the whole Church had come to accept as a truth of the faith: "The new truth, which is promulgated, if it is to be called new, must be at least homogeneous, cognate, implicit, viewed relatively to the old truth. It must be what I may even have guessed, or wished, to be included in the Apostolic revelation; and at least it will be of such a character, that my thoughts readily concur in it or coalesce with it, as soon as I hear it. Perhaps I and others actually have always believed it, and the only question which is now decided in my behalf, is that I am henceforth to believe that I have only been holding what the Apostles held before me."[16] Then Newman went even further, removing the qualifications and subjunctives: " . . . there is no burden at all in holding that the Blessed Virgin was conceived without original sin; indeed, it is a simple fact to say, that Catholics have not come to believe it because it is defined, but it was defined because they believed it."[17]

Though Newman tried to set aside the question of the seat of infallibility, he could not help touching on it. "This [the Immaculate Conception] of course is an extraordinary case; but it is difficult to say what is ordinary, considering how few are the formal occasions on which the voice of Infallibility has been solemnly lifted up. It is to the Pope in Ecumenical Council that we look, as to the normal seat of Infallibility. . . ."[18] Dr. Charles Russell, the president of Maynooth,[19] who had been a friend to Newman since his Anglican years, found this and other passages in the *Apologia* questionable and he wrote to Newman in May 1865 suggesting various corrections and clarifications. In his first response to Russell on 5 May, Newman said, " . . . I have availed myself of your suggestions to leave out one passage and to modify another. But I do not see my way to withdraw the statement that the Pope in Ecumenical Council is the normal seat of Infallibility. . . ."[20] When Russell persisted in making his criticisms, Newman responded again but without changing his position on this point:

> I will only say, that still, with my best lights, I do not see that the Pope's judgments out of Council are other than extraordinary utterances, and therefore, if they are extraordinary, they are not normal.

16. Ibid., 329–30.
17. Ibid., 330.
18. Ibid., 331.
19. Charles Russell, born in Ireland in 1812, was ordained a priest in 1835 following studies at Maynooth where he soon after joined the faculty. In 1857 he became president of Maynooth. Russell's friendship with Newman began in 1841 when Newman was still an Anglican. Newman valued Russell's advice, especially on theological issues.
20. Newman to Charles Russell, 5 May 1865, *The Letters and Diaries,* 21:460.

> If a Council were held now, I conceive one of its first acts, would be formally to receive and repeat the condemnation of Jansenism and the definition of the Immaculate Conception. It would be natural indeed for it to do so any how; but I think it would consider it a duty.[21]

Newman would take the same position when writing to E. B. Pusey[22] in 1867 after the council had been formally announced by Pius IX. Indeed he found it quite plausible that one of the purposes of the council was a kind of ratification by the bishops gathered in council with the pope of the definition of 1854.[23]

While the *Apologia* was hailed by many English Catholics, including Newman's bishop, and Newman received a number of congratulatory letters from the Catholic community, Manning and Ward took an opposite view, especially because Newman had taken what to them was a "minimizing" stance on the question of papal infallibility.[24] They could not help feeling that Newman in at least one passage was taking an oblique aim at the position they were championing: "And all those who take the part of that ruling authority [the papacy], will be considered as time-servers, or indifferent to the cause of uprightness and truth; while, on the other hand, the said authority may be supported by a violent ultra party which exalts opinions into dogmas, and has it principally at heart to destroy every school of thought but its own."[25] The hard attitude that Newman here reveals toward those he would later call, following St. Francis de Sales, "the Pope's lackies," continued to be evident in his private correspondence as the debate over papal infallibility intensified, and even after its definition. His reference to those who took the part of Manning and Ward as the "violent" party and other such vivid phrases would be characteristic in the difficult years ahead.

Newman hesitates over a public reply to Pusey on papal infallibility

Since the late 1850's some Roman Catholics and some Anglicans, chiefly of Anglo-Catholic views, had had discussions about eventual unity between the Roman Catholic and Anglican Churches. In 1857 the Roman

21. Newman to Charles Russell, 17 May 1865, *The Letters and Diaries,* 21:470.

22. Edward Bouverie Pusey, born in 1800, was a leader in the Tractarian Movement at Oxford in the 1830s and became its chief influence after Newman became a Catholic. In time, Newman and Pusey resumed their earlier friendship, principally through correspondence. Pusey died in 1882.

23. See Newman to E. B. Pusey, 21 July 1867, *The Letters and Diaries,* ed. Charles Stephen Dessain and Thomas Gornall, S.J. (Oxford: The Clarendon Press, 1973) 23:272.

24. See Purcell, *Life of Cardinal Manning,* 2:326, and Meriol Trevor, *Newman: Light in Winter* (London: Macmillan & Co., Ltd., 1962) 342–43.

25. Newman, *Apologia,* 334.

Catholic convert Ambrose Phillipps de Lisle had founded the Association for the Promotion of the Unity of Christendom for the purpose of fostering discussion between Roman Catholics and Anglicans. In 1864 Rome, chiefly at the instigation of Manning, forbade Catholic participation in the association. At the same time Manning produced a pamphlet, *The Workings of the Holy Spirit in the Church of England: A Letter to the Rev. E. B. Pusey,* which was meant to refute Pusey's position that the Anglican Church was a true and valid branch of the one Catholic communion just as much as the Roman Catholic Church was another branch of the great ecumenical Church. E. B. Pusey, Newman's former colleague, was the principal spokesman of the Anglo-Catholic party and in 1865 he published his reply to Manning in a pamphlet entitled *The Church of England a Portion of Christ's One Holy Catholic Church, and a Means of Restoring Visible Unity. An Eirenicon, in a Letter to the Author of 'The Christian Year.'* While this pamphlet dealt with the topic of unity, its author acknowledged that there were still great obstacles in the way of any rapprochement between Rome and Canterbury. In particular, Pusey decried the Roman Church's promotion of various practices of piety, particularly devotions in honor of our Lady, and the Church's teaching on the authority of the pope. Newman thought that Pusey had gone too far and had taken the position of some Catholics, particularly some leading Catholics in England, as synonymous with the teaching of the Church. Newman felt compelled to answer Pusey and early in 1866 he published his *A Letter to the Rev. E. B. Pusey, D.D. on his recent Eirenicon,*[26] which was an answer to Pusey on the subject of our Lady and the Church's devotional practices. In answering Pusey, Newman demonstrated that though there were excesses evident in the devotional practices of some Catholics, the Church's true teaching, and in fact the traditional practices of English Catholics, did not countenance such excesses. It was evident that Newman in replying to Pusey was at the same time criticizing what he considered to be the encouragement given by Manning, Ward, and Faber[27] (who had died in 1863) to practices that were not in fact to be identified with the stated teachings of the Church.

26. *A Letter to the Rev. E. B. Pusey, D.D. on his recent Eirenicon* is published in John Henry Newman, *Certain Difficulties Felt By Anglicans In Catholic Teaching* (London, New York, and Bombay: Longmans, Green, and Co., 1907) 2:1-170.

27. An Anglican clergyman from 1839 until his reception into the Catholic Church in 1845, Frederick William Faber founded a religious community soon after. In 1848 he and his followers joined the newly-established English Oratory under Newman. Newman placed Faber in charge of the London Oratory community when it was founded in 1849. When it became an independent house in 1856, Faber was chosen superior. A poet and devotional writer of a highly romantic temperament, Faber was frequently in disagreement with Newman from the early 1850s until Faber's death in 1863.

Having dealt with the question of Catholic devotional life, Newman began to consider a response to Pusey's second charge against the Catholic Church, the position and authority of the pope. From 1865 Newman started to make various notes and jottings on the question of papal authority. He continued these in 1866 after the publication of *A Letter to the Rev. E. B. Pusey,* but increasingly he began to retreat from the idea of a public answer to Pusey on the question of the exercise of the papal office. It was one thing to deal with questions of devotion and piety, it was quite another to grapple with the difficult topic of infallibility, especially in the midst of an evident campaign by Manning and Ward to promote the dogma of papal infallibility. Newman had treated the subject of infallibility cautiously in the *Apologia,* and now Pusey, his one-time ally, had brought the question of infallibility forward in such a way that Newman, if he did respond, could not help but become embroiled in a public controversy. He shrank from this task. There is evidence to suggest that Newman's struggles with the question of whether he should make a public reply to Pusey resulted in part from a realization that the more he studied the subject of infallibility, the more he understood that his own position was not consistent and that he could not afford in such a frame of mind to get into conflict with Manning and Ward, whose own position was rigorously straightforward. He could deal with Pusey on the question of our Lady and the Church's devotions, though even here he could not avoid a critical, if indirect, comment on the position of Manning, Ward, and Faber, but the question of the papal office was a quagmire in which he did not wish to become trapped.

On 26 February 1866, Newman wrote in the notes that he was making with a view to replying to Pusey on papal infallibility his reasons for hesitating to tackle the subject. "My doubts about a second Pamphlet," Newman recorded,

> in continuation of my letter to Pusey are such as these—arising from my feeling more and more the *extent, difficulty,* and *variety of views* taken, of the Treatise de Ecclesiâ and de Summo Pontifice.
>
> I have not enough to say, nor would it be tanti, to write simply against *him,* unless I did something to establish a moderate view about the Pope and the Church, as against Ward, as in my first Pamphlet I had established a moderate view about the Blessed Virgin as against other extreme writers.
>
> Now the case is very different of the former undertaking, from that of this new one.
>
> The doctrine of Catholics about the Blessed Virgin is plain and simple; there are no varieties of opinion. I could lay it down broadly, and defend it. . . . All I had to animadvert on, was a certain extravagance of devotion in detail, and I could throw this off, as being foreign.
>
> But on the other hand, there is no one received doctrine on the Church, but several—several on the power of the Church, on the extent of the sub-

ject matter of its infallibility, and the seat of that infallibility. Whatever view I took, I could not, from the nature of the case, carry all Catholics with me. I should divide them into parties—some would be with me, and more would be against me; more,—for I could only take one view out of several or many views. There is no received English view—no books to appeal to.

Instead of taking all Catholics with me in a point of doctrine, to criticize points of devotion, I should be taking only some Catholics with me in a doctrine to attack another, and an authoritative view of the same doctrine. If I noticed that other view, Anglicans would say "*This* is your unity of creed"—If I did not, Catholics would say, I was ignoring what had at the time greater authority and popular acceptance than my own.

Moreover, I could truly and safely call certain devotions to our Lady, foreign, Italian;—but it will not do so to speak of a doctrinal view of the Pope and the Church, which is so highly sanctioned at Rome, and just now by the Episcopate.

I should not be writing against Pusey, but making a case against Ward, and every one would say so.[28]

Two days later Newman, writing to the Jesuit Henry James Coleridge, the son of the judge who had imposed sentence against Newman in the Achilli case,[29] said, "I have *almost* entirely given up the thought of finishing my subject in a second Letter." He used as his primary reason for hesitating the time it would take him to do the work and he felt that "by the time . . . I get a second Letter published, the state of the controversy would have changed perhaps." Newman again underscored the differences in writing about the doctrine of the Immaculate Conception and devotion to our Lady, and in writing on questions of the Church and the Holy See: " . . . even though I were ever so successful in keeping within allowable limits, (and that is not very easy to compass), yet I could not carry with me the sympathy of *all* Catholics, *whichever* line of theological opinion I took, and, even though, I should *only* attempt (which would be the case,) to keep 'libertas in dubiis,' yet, in doing that very thing I should

28. *The Theological Papers of Newman on Biblical Inspiration and On Infallibility*, selected, edited, and introduced by J. Derek Holmes (Oxford: The Clarendon Press, 1979) 111–12.

29. In a public lecture, given in 1850, Newman denounced the anti-Catholic lecturer, Giacinto Achilli, for scandalous behavior during his years as a Catholic priest in Italy. Newman made these charges on the basis of documentary evidence gathered by Cardinal Wiseman. Wiseman, however, was unable to marshal the evidence in time. Newman was indicted for libel and the matter went to trial in 1852. The jury found for Achilli. In 1853 Newman was sentenced to pay a fine of £100, a virtual acquittal. The judge who handed down the sentence was Sir John Taylor Coleridge. His son, Henry James Coleridge, became a Catholic and a Jesuit priest. From 1865 to 1880 he was editor of the Jesuit publication, the *Month*. Father Coleridge and his brother, John Duke Coleridge, an Anglican who became Lord Chief Justice in 1873, were both staunch friends of Newman.

be doing the most offensive thing of all to some influential people. Yet I may be challenged to write, till I am obliged to write."[30]

In the same month Newman wrote to W. G. Ward. In this instance Newman, no doubt annoyed by Ward's assertion, "All the world says you are writing on the infallibility of the Pope,"[31] downplayed the necessity of treating papal infallibility in a second response to Pusey. "As to writing a volume on the Pope's infallibility," Newman said,

> it never so much as entered into my thoughts. I am a controversialist,[32] not a theologian. And I should have nothing to say about it. I have ever thought it likely to be true, never thought it certain. I think too, its definition inexpedient and unlikely; but I should have no difficulty in accepting it, were it made. And I don't think my reason will ever go forward or backward in the matter.
>
> If I wrote another pamphlet about Pusey, I should be obliged to have a few sentences to the effect that the Pope's infallibility was not a point of faith—that would be all.[33]

Several weeks later Newman, writing to Emily Bowles,[34] gave further insights into his hesitancy over writing a second pamphlet in answer to Pusey. The first letter he said had tired him out. Miss Bowles must recall that he was "an old man and must husband [his] strength." But more deeply still, Newman revealed his fear of getting into yet another scrape with those in authority. "Recollect," he asked Miss Bowles, "to write theology is like dancing on the tight rope some hundred feet above ground. It is hard to keep from falling, and the fall is great."[35] What Newman meant by that "fall" and the kind of harm that could result from it, he revealed in the same letter of 16 April: "The questions are so subtle, the

30. Newman to Father Henry James Coleridge, S.J., 28 February 1866, *The Letters and Diaries,* ed. Charles Stephen Dessain (London: Thomas Nelson and Sons, Ltd., 1972) 22:166–67.

31. William George Ward to Newman, 17 February 1866, *The Letters and Diaries,* 22:157, n. 1.

32. Newman, both as an Anglican and as a Catholic, consistently referred to himself as a "controversialist." He considered his greatest strength his ability to argue against the writings or statements of those who publicly attacked the teachings of the Church. With some notable exceptions, for example, the *Grammar of Assent,* he did his best work in answer to specific challenges.

33. Newman to William George Ward, 18 February 1866, *The Letters and Diaries,* 22:157.

34. Emily Bowles had met Newman before she became a Catholic in 1843. She was for a time a member of Cornelia Connelly's religious community but left the community after a disagreement with Mother Connelly. She lived afterwards in London where she wrote religious works and carried on various charitable activities. She was a frequent correspondent of Newman.

35. It is interesting to note that after Newman had finished writing the *Letter to the Duke of Norfolk* in 1875, he likened the task to a man going up in a balloon, uncertain of his landing.

distinctions so fine, and critical jealous eyes so many. Such critics would be worth nothing, if they had not the power of writing to Rome, now that communication is made so easy—and you may get into hot water, before you know where you are. The necessity of defending myself at Rome would almost kill me with the fidget. You don't know me, when you suppose I "take heed of the motley flock of fools." No—it is *authority* that I fear. Di me terrent, et Jupiter hostis."[36]

Just at the time that Newman was struggling with the question of writing a second letter to Pusey, Manning issued his pastoral on *The Reunion of Christendom*.[37] It was disturbing to Newman and a further evidence that a public reply to Pusey would bring him into an equally public dispute with the new Archbishop of Westminster. On 21 February, Newman wrote:

> Here I come across the judgment of an old friend now occupying a post of great authority, and who has felt it his duty to combine authority and controversy in one publication. I have asked myself whether in that necessary collision which must take place I should speak without an express allusion to him or not—and I felt that, since, do what I will, I shall be considered to allude to him, I had better speak of him freely. The Archbishop's pastoral will to them who are his subjects necessarily be taken on its aspect of authority; to others it comes as a controversial paper.[38]

Newman was gratified by the response to his first answer to Pusey. Many Catholics had shown their approval, including his bishop, William Ullathorne.[39] But Newman was also very conscious that there had been some dissent.[40] "There are," he acknowledged, "just two or three cliques

36. Newman to Emily Bowles, 16 April 1866, *The Letters and Diaries,* 22:215–16.

37. Manning's first pastoral letter was published in February 1866. It took a strong position in upholding the claims of the Roman Church to be the only Church which had the right to use the name "Catholic." The letter greatly disappointed the hopes for unity of various Roman Catholics and Anglicans in England. See Purcell, *Life of Cardinal Manning,* 2:284–88.

38. *Theological Papers of Newman,* 109.

39. See William Bernard Ullathorne to Newman, 12 February 1866, *The Letters and Diaries,* 22:154, n. 1. William Ullathorne, born into an old Yorkshire Catholic family, entered the Benedictines at Downside in 1823. After ordination as a priest in 1831, he served for ten years in Australia. In 1846, several years after his return to England, he was named Vicar Apostolic of the Western District and in 1848 Vicar Apostolic of the Central District. When the hierarchy was reconstituted in 1850, he was named first bishop of Birmingham and remained in that post until his retirement in 1888. He died the following year. Ullathorne's sympathy and appreciation for Newman grew over the years.

40. See Newman "Memorandum I—W. G. Ward And A Letter to Pusey," 26 March 1866, *The Letters and Diaries,* 22:189–91. See also Wilfrid Ward, *The Life of John Henry Cardinal Newman* (New York: Longmans, Green, and Co., 1912) 2:112, and Cuthbert Butler, O.S.B., *The Life and Times of Bishop Ullathorne 1806–1889* (New York: Benziger Brothers, 1926) 2:356–64. Newman's *Letter to Pusey* occasioned a famous exchange between Talbot and Manning in which Talbot said: "Dr. Newman is more English than the English

in London who are the other way"; but this was enough to give him pause. "The less I do myself," he averred,

> the more others will do. It is not well to put oneself too forward. Englishmen don't like to be driven. I am sure it is good policy to be quiet just now.
>   I have long said "the night cometh etc," but that does not make it right to act in a hurry. Better not do a thing than do it badly. I must be patient and wait on God. If it is His will I should do more, He will give me time. I am not serving Him, by blundering.[41]

The notes that Newman made on the infallibility question in the period 1865 to 1868 and the letters that he wrote show that he approached the topic with great diffidence. In May 1866, Newman wrote in his notes, "I never have been against the doctrine of the Pope's Infallibility— certainly strong acts from the beginning but I don't see that the munus pascendi requires infallibility."[42]

Newman grapples in private with the subject of papal infallibility

The one constant of Newman's position was that he evidently thought the position of Manning and Ward to be exaggerated, if not intolerant. While he repeatedly recorded his own belief in infallibility, his notes evidence a lack of clarity in taking a consistent approach. Newman professed to have accepted papal infallibility before his entrance into the Roman Catholic Church, though he made clear throughout the controversy that this teaching had not been for him, as it had for some of his contemporaries among the converts, a reason for entering the Church. But he was troubled over what he saw as the newness of the doctrine and the haste of those who would see it proclaimed a dogma as soon as possible. Newman's notes and letters from this period are important for an understanding of his position on infallibility through all the events of the late 1860s and the first half of the 1870s. The position sketched out in the notes and letters of 1865 to 1868 continued in great measure to be the position that Newman would maintain in his private correspondence in the time leading up to the definition of Vatican I and immediately following, and in many ways it is the same position he would finally declare publicly in the *Letter to the Duke of Norfolk,* ten years after he had made his first private notes on the topic of papal infallibility.

[as opposed to being a Roman]. His spirit must be crushed," and Manning said of Newman and his views: "In one word, it is worldly Catholicism, and it will have the worldly on its side, and will deceive many." See Butler, *Ullathorne,* 1:358 and 359.
    41. Newman to Emily Bowles, 16 April 1866, *The Letters and Diaries,* 22:216.
    42. *Theological Papers of Newman,* 102.

Newman could not understand why there was such agitation for an immediate proclamation of the definition of papal infallibility. In his earliest notes he alludes to the discussions between various leading Irish bishops and the British government in the negotiations that led up to the declaration of Catholic Emancipation in 1829. An issue in those discussions had been the matter of papal infallibility, a question that the government saw as having more than an incidental bearing on giving Catholics full rights as citizens of the nation. The Irish bishops were able to give assurances, presumably with the approbation of Rome, that Catholics were not obliged to hold the infallibility of the pope. "Common sense," Newman wrote in his notes in 1865, "tells us that what was an open question 30 years ago is an open question now."[43]

Two years later, in July 1867, he would take up the same theme in his notes, but more extensively:

> . . . it is most important to bear in mind that this doctrine is unheard of till late centuries. This is not any proof that it is not true, because it may be a development of the Depositum. But such developments, even though in the objectum fidei, do not become generally obligatoria till they have some public recognition. In saying this, I am not denying that a consent of modern divines, clear, perfect, and lasting through centuries, might not almost obliterate a contrary consent in former times—but it must be recollected, that even in the case of the Immaculate Conception, no one asserted that the doctrine was binding on our internal assent *till* the Definition in 1854.[44]

Continuing in the same vein, Newman wrote: "First they have to get over the modernness of their doctrine. It is hardly mentioned till the time of the Jansenist controversy. We can trace the authors in whose writings it arose, etc. etc. It is not generally received now."[45]

Newman knew that any treatment of the topic would need an investigation into the history of the teaching authority of the pope and how it had been exercised in the Church. "And it is difficult," he wrote in 1866, "to read history without seeing that they [the popes] have a wonderful instinct of what is true, and what is good for the Church. That it has never failed, or is infallible, is another question."[46] But Newman's historical researches left him with the conviction that the *pascendi actio* of the pope consisted more in enforcing old and known truths than in making declarations of what could at least for the sake of argument be called new truths. The enforcing of old and known truths did not demand, according to New-

43. Ibid., 103.
44. Ibid., 149.
45. Ibid., 150.
46. Ibid., 117.

man, infallibility, "any more than a Bishop's enforcing them." Rather, Newman saw the pope's *pascendi munus* as consisting "very much more in directing conduct than in any dogmatic determination of points of faith and morals—and by aiming at the latter he may miss the former."[47]

Newman, taking up another theme that would be evident in all his dealings with the subject of papal infallibility in the period from 1865 to 1875, thought that the supreme governing power of the pope in the Church made it "*unlikely* that he would have the infallible legislative or dogmatic authority; for, the ordinary constitution and working of the ecclesiastical system being carried on solely by human laws, and the result only being overruled, we have a right to judge of what is likely or not by our political experience, and to say that such a union of legislative and executive powers in one person is not like[ly], as being, as human politics teach us, too great for man to sustain, and a temptation to abuse."[48]

But above all, after a year and a half of intermittent study on the question, Newman continued to maintain the position that he had highlighted in the *Apologia*, that the primary question to be decided, if in fact anything needed just then to be decided, was the infallibility of the Church.[49] Weighing the issues on both sides, Newman took the position in July 1866 that the definition of papal infallibility was simply not a practical necessity, a position which he would maintain with various changes and qualifications right up until the definition. Yet even as he showed in 1866 that he could not see the need for a definition, he was careful to say that he himself believed that the infallibility of the pope admitted of definition.[50] The full statement of his position at this time runs as follows:

> There is very little *theoretical* difference between the *opinions* of the maintainers of the infallibility of the Pope and its deniers. They both hold that he is the centre of unity, teacher of the faithful, possessed of universal jurisdiction. They both hold that, when his decision is generally accepted, it binds. The question merely turns on this, *whether* that acceptance is necessary as a *condition* of his decision being accepted as infallible. Where then does lie the difference between the parties? it is *ethical and practical*. How then would the definition of the Pope's infallibility, if made, change the state of things in these respects? It would leave things ethically just as they are, it would be injurious practically.[51]

As Newman wrote this opinion in the calm of his study at Birmingham, he was evidently seeing himself as putting forth a moderate, reasonable

47. Ibid.
48. Ibid., 144.
49. Ibid., 143.
50. Ibid.
51. Ibid.

position, but it is difficult to believe that the proponents of the definition, the "violent party," would have recognized themselves as believing that the difference between themselves and their opponents was simply "ethical and practical."

Ignatius Ryder stands in for Newman in the debate with Ward

Despite his hesitations Newman continued through 1866 to make notes on the topic of papal infallibility. At times they are brief jottings, at other times long passages, marshalling various theological opinions from the Fathers through current theologians of the Roman school. In addition to the goad provided by Pusey, there was also the strong voice of the *Dublin Review,* taking up a determined ultramontane position on infallibility, especially from April 1865.[52] In fact, Newman's notes began in time to be more a preparation for a response to Ward than to Pusey. At this same time one of Newman's fellow Oratorians at Birmingham, Henry Ignatius Dudley Ryder, a nephew of Archbishop Manning, was annoyed by the sweeping doctrine of papal infallibility that Ward was proclaiming in the *Dublin.* Ryder was never an intimate of Newman's, but Newman respected him as a theologian and he would succeed Newman as superior in 1890.[53] He urged Newman in 1865 to make a public response to Ward.

As he continued his study of infallibility, Newman, who was at the community's country house at Rednal,[54] wrote an important letter to Ryder on 16 July 1866 showing why he was having difficulty in finding a method for dealing with the topic:

> I send you another paper. I wish I could bring out clearly what I am at.
> Primarily, I am attempting to put on some intelligible ground, of reason, of philosophy, what has to be said about the Church's (Pope's) infallibility. To say that it is a gift, to guarantee to the end of time the integrity of the original revelation, made once for all through the Apostles, is *perfectly* intelligible—and, I suppose, till the utterances of these modern schools, sufficient as well as intelligible. Now if we are to believe more, it ought to be placed on an equally intelligible basis.

52. In the April 1865 issue of the *Dublin Review,* William George Ward in his essay, "The Encyclical and the *Syllabus,"* 441–99, strongly stated his convictions concerning the infallible status of *Quanta cura* and the *Syllabus.* See, for example, *Dublin Review,* n.s. 4 (January–April 1865) 443–44.

53. In his journal Newman made the following note on 30 October 1870: "He [Ignatius Ryder] is not quite of my sort, and one does not make new friends, when one is old." See John Henry Newman, *Autobiographical Writings,* ed. Henry Tristram (New York: Sheed and Ward, 1957) 266. An appreciative essay on Ryder can be found in Wilfrid Ward, *Ten Personal Studies* (London: Longmans, Green, and Co., 1908) 117–38.

54. Newman used the spelling *Rednall.* The present day spelling is *Rednal.* This usage is followed by Ker. See pages 503 and 745 of *John Henry Newman: A Biography.*

ter section of this letter Newman expressed more directly his exasperation with "these modern schools":

> I want then some better ground than the ipse dixit of Cardenas, Fénelon, and Muzzarelli, before I receive the doctrine that what the Pope says, (that is, what the Church says, for no one says that the Pope is infallible except as being in himself the Church) is certain, when he is not professing to explain or declare the Apostolic depositum which has [come] down to him by tradition. The Church (or Pope) can determine the sense of the depositum—she can declare its implicit meanings—she can declare what contradicts it—she can declare what in its nature subserves it (i.e. pious opinion) or is prejudicial to it, (i.e. what is erroneous, false, near heresy, savouring of heresy, etc.)—she can declare its concrete manifestations . . . but all these enunciations are to be received by Catholics BECAUSE they *directly* relate to the depositum, *not* as being mere utterances of the Church or Pope. Next, I have said, "they are to be received;—" but *how* received? as *infallible*? I have no difficulty in so receiving them myself, but I have yet to discover that it is de fide, or that there is a consensus scholae, that they *are* infallible.[55]

Newman, it would appear, had agreed to reply to Ward, but when he continued to delay, Ryder eventually took it on himself to prepare his own draft response to Ward.[56] He presented this to Newman, who gave Ryder his support as well as his notes to go on with the project. Indeed, Newman continued to make notes expressly for Ryder after giving the work over to him.[57]

In April 1867 Ryder's *Idealism in Theology: A Review of Dr. Ward's Scheme of Dogmatic Authority* appeared. It was the work of Ryder, but outside the Birmingham Oratory it was taken to be the response of Newman to the positions of Ward and Manning on infallibility. Certainly Newman recognized this in a note made on 29 January 1868. "It was natural," Newman wrote, "that, though every part of both pamphlets was the work of his [Ryder] own mind, that at first they, or at least the first pamphlet was attributed to me. . . . Gradually this opinion has been set right; still he has had the advantage of my name, and his Pamphlets have come from this Oratory, and must have had my sanction."[58] Newman throws fur-

---

55. Newman to Henry Ignatius Ryder, 16 July 1866, *The Letters and Diaries,* 22:261–62.

56. See Newman, 29 January 1868, *Autobiographical Writings,* 265. It is not clear why Newman, having decided that he could not risk a public reply to Pusey, apparently decided to answer Ward's views on the pope's infallibility. It can only be speculated that Newman believed Ward's views posed a far more immediate threat to the faith of Catholics than did the writings of the Anglican Pusey.

57. See *Theological Papers of Newman,* 151.

58. Newman, *Autobiographical Writings,* 265. See also Newman to W. G. Ward, 30 April 1867, *The Letters and Diaries,* 23:197. The Ryder-Ward exchange is treated in Damian McElrath, *The Syllabus of Pius IX: Some Reactions in England* (Louvain: Publications Universitaires de Louvain, 1964) 153–84.

ther light on the extent to which Ryder's pamphlet could be said to have his support in a letter to Canon John Walker of Scarborough.[59] In this letter of 11 May 1867, Newman also takes careful aim at Ward and the tyranny of the *Dublin:*

> You are mistaken—not indeed in thinking that I do not substantially approve of and agree with Fr. Ryder's Pamphlet, but in treating it as mine. The idea of writing is solely his—"facit indignatio versus." So were the topics, the line of thought, the illustrations, and the tone and temper. I agree with your criticism on it—indeed, I had made the same when I saw it in manuscript. He is ever in deep Devonshire lanes—you never know the lie of the country from him—he never takes his reader up to an eminence, whence he could make a map of it. This is partly my fault—partly his, if it *is* a fault. A fault it certainly is in the *composition*—but it is not strictly a fault in *determining* on committing such a fault of composition. My own share in it is this—that I thought it was good generalship for various reasons directly to attack Ward, not in the first place his opinions—I wanted him to show from Ward's character of mind how untrustworthy he was—also I thought he would enlist the feelings of oppressed and groaning Catholics, if he presented himself in the character of a young, chivalrous rebel—Then, on his side, since he was proposing, not primarily to teach his betters theology but to answer Ward, he felt himself obliged to follow Ward's lead and to take the very points for consideration which Ward's publication suggested.
>
> As to his professing himself, not in any *true* sense, but in the sense people sometimes *injuriously* use the word a Gallican, he *wished* to say what he has said—and *I* confess I have a great impatience at being obliged to trim my language by any conventional rule, to purse up my mouth, and mince my words, because it's the fashion.[60]

The Ryder-Ward Exchange

The Ryder-Ward exchange continued into 1868. In all, Ryder produced two letters and a postscript. Ward answered each of these publications with a reply of his own. Ward had the advantage of the *Dublin Review.* Not only were his replies printed in full in the *Dublin,* while only extracts of Ryder's position appeared, but tendentious critiques of Ryder's letters also appeared in the "Review of Books" section.

The sharpest dispute between Ryder and Ward came over the extent of infallibility. Ward took the position that the pope's teaching authority

59. Canon John Walker of Scarborough in the diocese of Beverley was a priest of the old Catholic school. A friend of Lingard, he also had great sympathy for Newman and wrote to him frequently. He is not to be confused with Canon John Walker, an Oxford convert and priest of Westminster, who was also a correspondent of Newman.

60. Newman to Canon John Walker of Scarborough, 11 May 1867, *The Letters and Diaries,* 23:227.

needed to be viewed as extending to every facet of human life because as he expressed it:

> Those perils then to which the Faith is now exposed, lie far more in the sphere of history, politics, and philosophy, than of theology proper. And hence the peculiar importance of vindicating and clearly exhibiting the Church's infallibility in Allocutions, Encyclicals, and the like, which are the very instruments she now adopts for condemning religious error in things secular. Those who deny the infallibility of such pronouncements, in fact deny that the Church is infallibly guarding the Deposit against particular dangers [indifference], which at this moment are far more formidable than any others.[61]

Ryder maintained that the Church's infallibility was confined within the limits of the Deposit. He protested that Ward was going far beyond the Church's teaching and tradition in maintaining that every doctrinal exposition of the pope as long as it was intended for the instruction of the whole Church was infallible.[62] Thus Ward would extend the infallible teachings of Pius IX beyond the declaration of the dogma of the Immaculate Conception to include encyclicals, letters, and allocutions that could be construed as having been addressed to all Catholics. Ward maintained strongly that the pope's infallible pronouncements extended well beyond the case of *ex cathedra* definitions: "My thesis then may be thus summed up: (1) The Pontiff may speak infallibly no less in expositions than in propositions. (2) His expositions are infallible always and only, when they are intended for the purpose of inculcating doctrine on the Universal Church. Yet (3) they need not be addressed *formally* to the Universal Church, but may be otherwise authenticated as obliging the absolute assent of Catholics."[63]

Ward saw the differences between himself and Father Ryder in the end as unmistakably clear. He wrote, referring to Ryder's first pamphlet, " . . . you remark (pp. 62–63), on the evil of mixing up what is certain with what is merely probable. Such remarks can have no bearing on my own conduct; for my contention has been throughout, that the doctrine on infallibility which I advocate is in substance absolutely certain. In fact this is precisely the point at issue. I maintain, and you deny, that the

---

61. "F. Ryder and Dr. Ward," *Dublin Review,* n.s. 9 (July–October 1867) 155. This review of Ryder's and Ward's pamphlets, as was customary, is unsigned but is surely the work of Ward.

62. See William George Ward, "A Second Letter to the Rev. Father Ryder," *Dublin Review,* n.s. 10 (January–April 1868), appendix to April issue, 52–53.

63. William George Ward, "A Brief Summary of the Recent Controversy on Infallibility; Being a Reply to Rev. Father Ryder on His Postscript," *Dublin Review,* n.s. 11 (July–October 1868), appendix to July issue, 19.

Church teaches this doctrine as vital and essential."[64] In defending his position, Ward could at times take his argument to such intricate lengths that he ended up making preposterous claims. In his second reply to Ryder, he said: "I quite admit (as I have stated in January, 1868, p. 90) that the Pope may inculcate some doctrine, not as certain, but only as the more probable; only I would add that in such case the faithful are bound to accept it, as infallibly the more probable at the time of such inculcation."[65]

Ward was especially concerned to make clear that he believed *Quanta Cura* and the *Syllabus* infallible and that all Catholics were bound under pain of sin to hold the same:

> You think (p. 54) "that there are very considerable grounds for supposing that the Syllabus is nothing more than an index" to Pius IX's briefs, and has in itself no infallible authority. Now a very large number of bishops, from the Cardinal Vicar of Rome downwards, have officially and most emphatically pronounced it infallible; and moreover—the former being a manifest and overt fact—no one bishop has so much as publicly hinted any different view. If therefore this deplorable notion of yours could be maintained, it would follow that the Ecclesia Docens—our divinely appointed guide to Catholic Truth—has been banded in one vast conspiracy for the corruption of that Truth.[66]

Ward wrote further of the *Syllabus*:

> My third argument was that "our one model as to the suitable manner of accepting the Syllabus, is most assuredly the way in which it was accepted at Rome under the eye of the very Pontiff who issued it" (p. 69). But the Cardinal Vicar of Rome declared it was to be received "as the very word of God" Ergo & etc. You reply that I do not myself *maintain* it should be so received. But I do. If God has conferred on Pius IX the gift of infallibility, then we are bound to accept all his infallible utterances, "as the very Word of God," Who guarantees them from error.[67]

Ward professed throughout the controversy to have a high respect for Father Ryder and for his theological learning, but he considered him dangerously wrong in his position on infallibility. Ward allowed that Ryder might not be entirely culpable for his erroneous position, but nonetheless

64. William George Ward, "A Letter to the Rev. Father Ryder on His Recent Pamphlet by William George Ward, D.Ph.," *Dublin Review,* n.s. 9 (July–October 1867), appendix to July issue, 30.

65. Ward, "A Second Letter," Dublin Review, n.s. 10 (January–April 1868), appendix to April issue, 56.

66. Ward, "A Letter to the Rev. Father Ryder," *Dublin Review,* n.s. 9 (July–October 1867), appendix to July issue, 27.

67. Ward, "A Brief Summary," *Dublin Review,* n.s. 11 (July–October 1868), appendix to July issue, 17.

his narrowing of the extent of infallibility was objectively sinful and was a source of scandal to lay people: "But speaking (as becomes me) under correction, I must maintain that your attitude towards such Constitutions as the 'Unigenitus' and the 'Auctorem Fidei,'[68] is gravely censurable and in itself mortally sinful. You will not, I am sure, misunderstand me as saying this in personal disrespect and disparagement of yourself; for it is one of your very complaints against me that I extend so widely the doctrine of invincible ignorance."[69] Writing in the same vein, Ward said: "We have undoubtedly alleged that F. Ryder—however confessedly excellent his motives and intentions—does in fact materially violate a grave obligation imposed by the Holy Father on all Catholics; and, moreover, threatens the Faith with grievous injury."[70] With a note of condescension Ward announced to Ryder: "It is not against *you* that I consider myself really contending; but against those who would make a stepping-stone of you, and of others also, for the purpose of their intolerable misbelief."[71] Undoubtedly one of the "others" was Newman. Later in the exchange Ward spoke very bluntly of the dire consequences of Ryder's position: "I consider that your principles lead, by necessary and very speedy consequence, to a denial of the Church's infallibility altogether; or, in other words, to apostasy from her communion."[72]

The controversial exchange between Ryder and Ward revealed again the long-standing acrimony between the Oratories of London and Birmingham.[73] The superior of the London Oratory, Father Thomas Francis Knox, wrote in 1868 to the editor of the *Revue des Sciences Ecclesiastiques* to make very clear that Father Ryder was not a member of the London house, nor were his positions supported by the Fathers there:

> Sir,—I request that you will have the kindness to correct an inadvertency which has crept into your last number, page 221.
>   F. Ryder is not a member of the London Oratory, but of that of Birmingham.

68. The Bull *Unigenitus Filii Dei,* condemning 101 propositions attributed to the Jansenists, was issued by Clement XI in 1713; the Bull *Auctorem fidei,* issued by Pius VI in 1794, condemned eighty-five of the articles enacted by the Synod of Pistoia in 1786.

69. Ward, "A Brief Summary," *Dublin Review,* n.s. 11 (July–October 1868), appendix to July issue, 9–10.

70. "Notice of Books," *Dublin Review,* n.s. 10 (January–April 1868) 566–67.

71. Ward, "A Second Letter," *Dublin Review,* n.s. 10 (January–April 1868), appendix to April issue, 20.

72. Ward, "A Brief Summary," *Dublin Review,* n.s. 11 (July–October 1868), appendix to July issue, 27.

73. The disputes between the London and Birmingham Oratories, especially those of the 1850s, are treated at length by Trevor, *Light in Winter.* See 73–84; 112–49. See also Placid Murray, "Newman's Oratory Papers," no. 27, 31 August 1856, *Newman the Oratorian* (Leominster, Hertfordshire: Fowler Wright Books Ltd., 1980) 349–59.

The congregations of the Oratory, according to the law of our institution, have a totally separate existence and direction. They have no mutual relations of subordination, not even as regards the Oratory at Rome.

Consequently, each Congregation is responsible only for the acts and the writings of its own members.

I think it right to add that F. Ryder's sentiments with regard to the infallibility of the Church, are very different to those which have always been professed by the Fathers of the London Oratory. As for myself, I considered it my duty to testify, without naming Father Ryder, to what an extent I disapprove of his doctrine on this subject, by publishing a pamphlet, entitled, *"When does the Church speak infallibly?"*[74]

Newman gives his views in private letters; he will go no further

Just as important as Newman's notes in this period for determining his attitude on infallibility, are a number of his letters in the years 1865 to 1868. Among the most important letters on this topic are those to Pusey. After the *Apologia*, Newman and Pusey began a fairly full correspondence. While Newman hesitated to respond to Pusey publicly, he took great pains to describe his position on a number of points, including papal infallibility, in his letters. Soon after the appearance of Pusey's *Eirenicon*, Newman wrote to his former colleague: "As to the Infallibility of the Pope, I see nothing against it, or to dread in it—for I am confident that it *must* be so limited practically that it will leave things as they are. As to Ward's notions they are preposterous. . . ." "But I don't think," Newman wrote in the same letter, "there will be any such decree, or about the temporal power."[75]

A year and a half later Newman again dealt with infallibility in letters to Pusey on 22 and 23 March 1867. Many of Newman's Catholic opponents on the infallibility question saw him as a dangerous minimizer. Pusey and the Anglo-Catholic bishop of Brechin (Scotland), Alexander Forbes, accepted this view of Newman and attempted to gain his support for their own view that a minimalist approach was precisely what was needed to bring the Roman Catholic and Anglican communions into unity. In these two long letters, in which the place of the pope in the Church has a large

---

74. An English translation of Father Knox's letter is given in the *Dublin Review,* n.s. 11 (July–October 1868) 315–16. In his essay Knox wrote: "Nothing is clearer, from the whole history of the Church, than that the Sovereign Pontiffs have never tolerated any practical doubt of their infallibility on the part of the faithful, but have exacted from all the most unreserved submission to whatever they might decree." *"When Does the Church Speak Infallibly?"* or *The Nature and Scope of the Church's Teaching Office,* 2nd ed. enlarged (London: Burns, Oates, and Co., 1870) 31. Ward lavishly praised Knox's pamphlet in a review in the April 1870 issue of the *Dublin Review.* See n.s. 14 (January–April 1870) 523–27.

75. Newman to E. B. Pusey, 17 November 1865, *The Letters and Diaries,* 22:103–04.

part, Newman made it clear to Pusey that he could not accept Pusey's view of him as a minimizer. In the course of the first of the two letters Newman felt it necessary to give what he characterized as "a sort of Sermon against Minimism and Minimists":

> The words then of Councils etc on the subject of the Pope's powers are (to a certain degree) vague, as you say, and indefinite; even for this reason, viz. from the strong reluctance, which has been ever felt, to restrict the liberty of thinking and judging more than was absolutely necessary, as a matter of sacred duty, in order to the maintenance of the revealed depositum. It has always been trusted that the received belief of the faithful and the obligations of piety would cover a larger circuit of doctrinal matters than was formally claimed, and secure a more generous faith than was imperative on the conscience. Hence there has never been a wish on the part of the Church to cut clean between doctrine revealed and doctrine not revealed; first indeed, because she actually *cannot* do so at any given moment, but is illuminated from time to time as to what was revealed in the beginning on this or that portion of the whole mass of teaching which is now received; but secondly, because for that very reason she would be misrepresenting the real character of the dispensation, as God has given it, and would be abdicating her function, and misleading her children into the notion that she was something obsolete and passé, considered as a divine oracle, and would be transferring their faith from resting on herself as the organ of revelation . . . simply to a code of certain definite articles or a written creed (or material object) if she authoritatively said that so much, and no more, is de fide Catholicâ and binding on our inward assent. Accordingly, the act of faith as we consider, must ever be partly explicit, partly implicit; viz "I believe *whatever* God has revealed, whether I know it or not;" or "I believe whatever has been and whatever shall be defined as revelation by the Church who is the organ of the revelation;" . . . . and "I absolutely submit my mind with an inward assent to the Church, as the teacher of the whole faith."[76]

But in the second part of this letter, written the next day, Newman dealt directly with the question of papal infallibility and showed a willingness to retreat somewhat from this rather defensive stance by giving his own candid views on the subject. "For myself . . ." Newman wrote, "I think the Church *may* define it (i.e. it possibly may turn out to belong to the original depositum), but that she *will* not *ever* define it; and again, I do not see that she can be said to hold it." Newman then gave a further glimpse into the less than fixed attitude that he maintained on the topic of papal infallibility: " . . . I think there is a good deal of evidence, on the very surface of history and the Fathers in its favour. On the whole then I hold it; but I should account it no sin if, on grounds of reason,

76. Newman to E. B. Pusey, 22 March 1867, *The Letters and Diaries*, 23:99–100.

I doubted it."[77] But, as if remembering again the general object of his letter he took a firmer stance on the question of the pope's jurisdiction. "Nor is the point, which is the direct subject of your question much, or at all, less an elementary difference of principle between us; viz. the Pope's jurisdiction;—it is a difference of principle even more than of doctrine. That that jurisdiction is universal is involved in the very idea of a Pope at all."[78]

Some weeks later Newman sent Pusey a copy of Ignatius Ryder's first reply to Ward. He said that he did not expect Pusey to agree with Ryder's views, but he felt it important that Pusey should know, "what men of moderate opinion among us at this day hold."[79]

In the summer of 1867, soon after the first public announcement of the council at Rome, Newman continued his exchanges with Pusey. Speaking of the coming council, Newman showed that he was heartened by the news, especially since a council was the "normal way of doing things." "I don't like," he wrote, "that half and half way which sets people by the ears—I am not denying the Pope's Infallibility—but questions arise, as to what are the conditions of his exercising the gift—no such difficulties (*to me*) arise as to a General Council."[80]

It was in this period that Newman wrote his impassioned letter to Ward, decrying the position that Ward was proclaiming in the pages of the *Dublin*. Newman had written to Ward just a few days before when he sent him a copy of Ignatius Ryder's first pamphlet. In that letter Newman had made very clear his disagreement with Ward and his views. Speaking of Ignatius Ryder, Newman wrote:

> I think he is but a specimen of a number of young Catholics, who have a right to an opinion on the momentous subject in question, and who feel keenly that you are desirous to rule views of doctrine to be vital, which the Church does not call or consider vital. And certainly, without any unkindness towards you, or any thought whatever that you have been at all wanting in kindness to me personally, I rejoice in believing, that, now that my own time is drawing to an end, the new generation will not forget the spirit of the old maxim, in which I have ever wished to speak and act myself. "In necessariis unitas, in dubiis, libertas, in omnibus charitas."[81]

Ward must have answered a few days later, and Newman gives a summary of what he said in a letter written on 3 May to Ambrose St. John,[82]

77. Newman to E. B. Pusey, 23 March 1867, *The Letters and Diaries,* 23:105.
78. Ibid., 105–06.
79. Newman to E. B. Pusey, 1 May 1867, *The Letters and Diaries,* 23:198.
80. Newman to E. B. Pusey, 10 July 1867, *The Letters and Diaries,* 23:265.
81. Newman to William George Ward, 30 April 1867, *The Letters and Diaries,* 23:197.
82. Ambrose St. John was born in 1815 and was graduated from Oxford in 1836. Ordained an Anglican priest, he joined Newman at Littlemore in 1843 and was received into

who was in Rome. "In spite of his personal liking for me," Newman reported, "we must regard each other in a public point of view with the 'greatest aversion'; and that we belong to 'different religions!' "[83] It was undoubtedly this reference to "different religions" that caused Newman to state in his reply to Ward of 9 May: "Pardon me if I say that you are making a Church within a Church, as the Novatians of old did. . . ."[84] Newman went on to say,

> . . . you are doing your best to make a party in the Catholic Church, and in St. Paul's words are *"dividing Christ"* by exalting your opinions into dogmas, and shocking to say, by declaring to me, as you do, that those Catholics who do not accept them are of a different religion from yours.
>
> I protest then again, not against your tenets, but against what I must call your schismatical spirit. I disown your intended praise of me viz that I hold your theological opinions "in the greatest aversion," and I pray God that I may never denounce, as you do, what the Church has not denounced.[85]

But Ward would persist in not seeing himself as part of the "violent ultra party" referred to in the *Apologia*. Rather, in 1869 he pretended not to see Newman's meaning in using that phrase. Ward in his piece, "Catholic Controversies," in the April number of the *Dublin Review* wrote that

> F. Newman considers ("Apologia," p. 401) that there is "a violent ultra party" in the Church, "which exalts opinions into dogmas, and has it principally at heart to destroy every school of thought but its own": in other words, a party which claims untruly the Church's authority for its own private opinions. We are not ourselves aware of any persons who seem to us guilty of this intolerable presumption; but if such dull tyranny do exist, surely it should be steadily discountenanced and opposed by loyal Catholics. This was undoubtedly F. Newman's purpose.[86]

Another important correspondence on infallibility in this period took place between Newman and John Stanislas Flanagan in 1868. Flanagan, then the parish priest of Adare in Ireland, had for a time been a member of the Birmingham Oratory. Newman had a high regard for Flanagan's theological ability. Flanagan wrote to Ryder after his second response to Ward

---

the Roman Catholic Church in 1845, a few days before Newman's reception. He accompanied Newman to Rome in 1846. Their close association in the Birmingham Oratory lasted until St. John's death in 1875. Trained in Hebrew and classics and at home in modern languages, which Newman was not, he took on many tasks within the Oratory at Newman's bidding, particularly the direction of the Oratory School from 1862. The tribute Newman paid to him at the end of the *Apologia* is evidence of their close friendship.

83. Newman to St. John, 3 May 1867, *The Letters and Diaries,* 23:203.
84. Newman to William George Ward, 9 May 1867, *The Letters and Diaries,* 23:217.
85. Ibid.
86. "Catholic Controversies," *Dublin Review,* n.s. 12 (January–April 1869) 365.

to express his concern about what seemed to him Ryder's widening of the scope of infallibility, so that it not only involved the Depositum but also "the whole *logical outcome* of these Divine Truths, whether elicited by comparison with one another, or with truths absolutely certain naturally."[87] Flanagan, assuming that Ryder's work had Newman's "imprimatur," was surprised by Ryder's view since he thought it completely at variance with Newman's writings and with conversations Flanagan had had with Newman.[88] Newman, to whom Ryder had shown Flanagan's letter, wrote a letter and an accompanying essay to Flanagan on 15 February. In many ways Newman's response to Flanagan was the most carefully expressed statement of his views on infallibility since the *Apologia*. It was not at the time made public but is of great importance since it addresses the topic in a systematic presentation and is a pulling together of various points that are disjointedly treated in Newman's notes on infallibility.

Newman began his essay to Flanagan by stating: "I dare say I have not been consistent or logically exact in what from time to time I have said about the extent & subject matter of the Church's Infallibility, for it is a very large question and I have never set myself formally to answer it." Early in the essay Newman was once more careful to state his own acceptance of papal infallibility "as a theological opinion." "But," he went on,

> I carefully abstain from asserting it in the general view which I give of Catholic doctrine. I felt I should be as obviously wrong in setting down theological opinions, when I was declaring the Church's doctrine as such, as I have thought Archb^p Manning obviously wrong in introducing into his Pastorals the Pope's Infallibility; and I think I bore in mind, as I wrote, because I have ever remembered, our Bishop's [William Bernard Ullathorne] remark that what made F^r Faber's book on the Holy Eucharist[89] so unsettling to Nuns was that he mixed up dogma with theological opinion, and that in a popular work theological opinions ought to be kept under."[90]

At the end of this essay Newman, taking up Flanagan's chief criticism of Ryder's views, wrote:

> I conceive then that the Depositum is in such sense committed to the Church or to the Pope, that when the Pope sits in St. Peter's chair, or when a Council of Fathers & doctors is collected round him, it is capable of being presented to their minds with that fullness and exactness, under the operation of supernatural grace, (so far forth and in such portion of it as the occasion re-

---

87. *Theological Papers of Newman*, 154.
88. Ibid., 153.
89. *The Blessed Sacrament; or the Works and Ways of God*, published in 1855.
90. *Theological Papers of Newman*, 154-55.

quires,) with which it habitually, not occasionally, resided in the minds of
the Apostles;—a vision of it, not logical, and therefore consistent with errors of reasoning & of fact in the enunciation, after the manner of an intui-
tion or an instinct. Nor do those enunciations become logical, because
theologians afterwards can reduce them to their relations to other doctrines,
or give them a position in the general system of theology. To such theologians
they appear as deductions from the creed or formularized deposit, but in
truth they are original parts of it, communicated per modum unius to the
Apostles' minds, & brought to light to the minds of the Fathers of the Council, under the temporary illumination of Divine Grace.[91]

It is perhaps noteworthy that Newman who began this passage by speaking directly of papal infallibility ends by speaking only of "the Fathers
of the Council." In the concluding sentence of this essay for Flanagan,
Newman sounded a note characteristic of his writings on this topic. "I
put all this on paper," he wrote, "with great diffidence, though it is the
view I have entertained for so many years."[92]

In this essay Newman spoke of his treatment of infallibility in his past
writings: "So much on what I have said in my Essay on Development &
in the Apologia; I don't recollect having said any thing on the subject
elsewhere"[93] But as the debate grew more intense in the months leading up
to the definition of 1870 and in the time just after it when acceptance of
the definition became a test of orthodoxy, Newman would appeal to other
of his earlier writings in defense of his longheld views on papal infallibility and he would place particular stress on *Loss and Gain (1848),* and lectures he had given in the early 1850s in Birmingham and in Dublin.[94]

Apart from the letters to Pusey, Ward, and Flanagan, Newman found
many other occasions in his correspondence during this period to deal with
the subject of papal infallibility. As the council grew nearer, his correspondence on infallibility increased and took in a wider circle of friends
and inquirers. In July 1867 in a letter to Henry Wilberforce,[95] Newman

91. Ibid., 159–60.
92. Ibid., 160.
93. Ibid., 156.
94. See, for example, Newman to Emilie Perceval, 15 August 1870, *The Letters and
Diaries,* ed. Charles Stephen Dessain and Thomas Gornall, S.J. (Oxford: The Clarendon
Press, 1973) 25:185; Newman to Alfred Plummer, 19 July 1872, *The Letters and Diaries,*
ed. Charles Stephen Dessain and Thomas Gornall, S.J. (Oxford: The Clarendon Press, 1974)
26:139.
95. Born into a renowned Anglican family in 1807, Henry William Wilberforce was
graduated from Oxford in 1830 where he came under the influence of Newman. After becoming an Anglican clergyman in 1834, he served in various parishes until his entrance into
the Roman Catholic Church in 1850. He then supported himself as a journalist. He remained
a close friend of Newman, who preached a moving eulogy at Wilberforce's funeral in 1873.
Wilberforce's wife Mary, whom he married in 1834, was the sister of Manning's wife Caroline.

began by decrying the campaign being waged by Ward and Louis Veuillot, the editor of *L' Univers,* in favor of the definition of papal infallibility: " . . . what is extraordinary is that the battle should pass from the Schools[96] (which, alas, are not) to Newspapers and Reviews, and to *lay* combatants, with an appeal to the private judgment of all readers. This is a deplorable evil—and from all I have heard Ward has hindered various people from becoming Catholics by his extreme views, and I believe is unsettling the minds of I can't tell how many Catholics." He continued:

> For myself I have never taken any great interest in the question of the limits and seat of infallibility.[97] I was converted simply because the Church was to last to the end, and that no communion answered to the Church of the first ages but the Roman communion, both in substantial likeness and in actual descent. And as to faith, my great principle was "Securus judicat orbis terrarum."[98] So I say now—and in all these questions of detail I say to myself, "I believe whatever the Church teaches as the voice of God— and this or that particular inclusively, *if* she teaches this"—it is this *fides implicita* which is our comfort in these irritating times. And I cannot go beyond this—I see arguments here, arguments there. I incline one way to-day, another tomorrow—on the whole I more than incline in one direction— but I do not dogmatise—and I detest any dogmatism when the Church has not clearly spoken . . . for I have only an opinion at best (not faith) that the Pope *is* infallible, and a string of arguments can only end in an opinion, and I comfort myself with the principle "Lex dubia non obligat—" What is not taught universally, what is not believed universally, has no claim on

96. In the years leading up to the definition but even more insistently after it, Newman would speak of the critical importance of the theological schools, the *Schola Theologorum,* in the life of the Church. Already in a letter of 9 November 1865 to Henry Nutcombe Oxenham, Newman had given a very forceful exposition of the place that he believed the *Schola Theologorum* had in the working out and enunciation of the Church's teaching. He said in part: "It is a *recognised* institution with privileges. Without it, the dogma of the Church would be the raw flesh without skin—nay a tree without leaves—for, as devotional feelings clothe the dogma on the one hand, so does the teaching of the Schola on the other. Moreover, it is the immediate authority for the practical working and course of the Church . . . , *The Letters and Diaries,* 22:99.

97. This statement is at odds with the position that Newman maintained at times after the Vatican Council, namely, that he had, since becoming a Catholic, maintained a clear view of papal infallibility. See for example his letter to the Editor of the *Guardian,* 12 September 1872, in which he says: "I will, . . . quote one out of various passages, in which long before the Vatican Council was dreamed of, at least by me, I enunciated absolutely the doctrine of the Pope's Infallibility. It is my Discourse on University Education, delivered in Dublin in 1852," *The Letters and Diaries,* 26:167.

98. St. Augustine's rule for deciding where the true Catholic position lay, a rule he had used in the Donatist controversy, played a major part in Newman's deciding in 1839 that the Church of Rome, not the Anglican Church, had remained true to the Church of the Fathers. Newman was to refer to St. Augustine's maxim again and again during the debate over papal infallibility.

me—and, if it be true after all and divine [[though not universally held]] my faith in it is included in the implicita fides which I have in the Church."

In November 1867, Newman wrote to Canon John Walker of Scarborough in an effort to encourage him to write an essay on papal infallibility. Newman thought that Walker as a born Catholic could show that the extreme ultramontanism of the late 1860s was not in keeping with the history and tradition of the English Catholic community, which had survived since the sixteenth century. Referring to letters that Walker had written to him, Newman said:

> I will tell you what they brought home to my mind, what indeed I have not once or twice thought of before—that you should really write a pamphlet, *bearing witness* to the views taught to Catholics when you were young. No one can do it but one who can speak as an authoritative witness, and such you would be. There are very few who could do it but you—and it is really most necessary. Here is the Archbishop in a Pastoral or Pamphlet putting out extreme views—getting it read to the Pope, and circulating that the Pope approved of it—all with a view of anticipating and practising upon the judgments of the Bishops, when they meet for a General Council. Of course what the General Council speaks is the word of God—but still we may feel indignant at the intrigue, trickery, and imperiousness which is the human side of its history—and it seems a dereliction of duty not to do one's part to meet them. You are one of the few persons who can give an effective testimony, and I hope you will.[100]

It is interesting to see the reluctant Newman advising someone else to put views opposed to Manning's forward for public consideration. There is no evidence that Canon Walker ever did so.

Some months later Newman wrote to Richard Clarke, a Fellow at St. John's College, Oxford, who was soon to be received into the Roman Catholic Church, in terms that would anticipate the *Letter to the Duke of Norfolk*. Newman stated: "We give to the Pope and to the Church an authority above the law of the land in spiritual matters. If the State told us to teach our children out of the Christian Knowledge Society's books, and the Pope told us not to do so, we must disobey the State and obey the Pope."[101] In the summer of the same year Newman was in cor-

---

99. Newman to Henry Wilberforce, 21 July 1867, Georgetown University, Special Collections, Newman Collection, Box 3, A283. This letter is published in *The Letters and Diaries*, 23:274–76. Double square brackets indicate later additions that Newman made in the original.

100. Newman to Canon John Walker of Scarborough, 10 November 1867, *The Letters and Diaries*, 23:367. The pastoral letter referred to is Manning's *The Centenary of St. Peter and the General Council.*

101. Newman to Richard Clarke, 21 April 1868, *The Letters and Diaries*, 23:64.

respondence with Peter le Page Renouf,[102] whose pamphlet on Pope
Honorius Newman had encouraged.[103] Renouf in his *The Condemnation
of Pope Honorius* attempted to demonstrate that the teaching of Pope
Honorius in the seventh century on Christ as God and man having a single will was not only erroneous but also an *ex cathedra* statement, and
thus irrefutable evidence against the position of the ultramontanists. Newman thought that Renouf had gone too far in his argument, but he saw
Renouf's research as necessary for any full discussion of the history of
the exercise of papal infallibility in the Church. Newman's letter to Renouf
is another evidence of his painstaking efforts to try to look at the controversy from all sides and to attempt to rein someone in when be thought
he was taking a risky path:

> I am glad you have had the boldness to publish on the subject, because I
> think it is intolerable that one side of a question should be ostentatiously
> obtruded on us in the *Dublin Review* and elsewhere, as the one Catholic
> Faith, and that authoritative writers should hold a pistol to our ear after
> the fashion of "Your money or your life," when there is another side with
> as real a right to be heard and to make converts, if it can, and with, in times
> past, as great a following of theologians; and because I consider this in-
> tolerable state of things is occasioning the loss of souls. Though I myself
> consider the Pope's formal definitions of faith to be infallible, I rejoice to
> see a pamphlet which has the effect of reminding the world that his infalli-
> bility is not a dogma, but a theological opinion.[104]

In the same letter Newman wrote: "I hold the Pope's Infallibility, not
as a dogma, but as a theological opinion; that is, not as a certainty, but
as a probability. You have brought out a grave difficulty in the way of
doctrine; that is, you have diminished its probability, but you have only
diminished it. To my mind the balance of probabilities is still in favour
of it."[105] Though Newman disagreed with Renouf's conclusions, it was
generally known that he had encouraged Renouf to write his pamphlet.
This would come back to haunt him as the controversy over the pamphlet
unfolded.

102. Peter le Page Renouf as a student at Oxford in the early 1840s was much influenced
by Newman. Renouf was received into the Catholic Church by Wiseman in 1842. Newman
brought him to Dublin in 1854 to teach on the faculty of the Catholic University. After
Newman left Dublin, Renouf returned to England and became an inspector for Catholic
schools. His pamphlet on Pope Honorius involved him in a bitter dispute with Manning,
and was placed on the Index. Renouf's wife, Ludovica Brentano, was, through her family,
a close friend of Döllinger.

103. See Frederick J. Cwiekowski, S.S., *The English Bishops and the First Vatican Council*
(Louvain: Publications Universitaires de Louvain, 1971) 98–99.

104. Newman to Peter le Page Renouf, 21 June 1868, *The Letters and Diaries,* ed. Charles
Stephen Dessain and Thomas Gornall, S.J. (Oxford: The Clarendon Press, 1973) 24:90–91.

105. Ibid., 24:92.

In another letter from this time Newman's anger at the position of the infallibilist party is evident. Writing to Monsignor James Patterson,[106] he said:

> *This* is where I differ from some other persons, viz in refusing to make my own views of doctrine necessary for a man being considered a good Catholic—I cannot endure narrowing the terms of Catholicity, as some would narrow them—I cannot abide those who would make belief in the Pope's Temporal Power (which I uphold myself) the "Articulus stantis vel cadentis Ecclesiae"—I will ever in heart and soul, and in my prayers, if I cannot in act, fight against a clique, who, though anonymous or at least without authority, give themselves out as exponents of the Holy Father's sentiments, . . . nor will I think myself disobedient to the Church because I utterly ignore them—[107]

As Newman grappled with the issues surrounding papal infallibility, he could not avoid dealing also with the question of the pope's temporal power, especially since the supporters of papal infallibility saw the pope's temporal rule as practically synonymous with his office in the Church. In his notes of 1866 Newman had written: "While I have never been anxious about his losing his temporal power (his temporals), being sure that, if Providence dispensed with one way, He would find another."[108]

Newman, already suspect in ecclesiastical circles in England and Rome on the subject of the pope's temporal power, greatly intensified these suspicions when on 7 October 1866, the feast of the Holy Rosary, he preached his sermon, "The Pope and the Revolution." The occasion was a special service to pray for the pope, mandated by the bishops of England. The particular focus of these commemorations was the growing challenge to the pope's control over his temporal domain. While Newman spoke with great sympathy and force about the pope's troubles and sufferings, he made it clear that he did not see the pope's temporal rule as essential to the carrying out of his office in the Church. Rather the papal states were a human invention only. God's divine protection of the pope in the carrying out of his office would continue until the end of time quite apart from the history or fate of the papal states. Newman's language was clear:

---

106. James Laird Patterson, an Oxford convert, succeeded Frederick Rymer as president of St. Edmund's College, Ware, in 1870, a post which he held for ten years. He was afterwards auxiliary bishop of Westminster. Given Patterson's close connection with Manning, it is not surprising that his dealings with Newman were not warm. Though Patterson lived until 1902, there is no surviving correspondence between him and Newman after this letter of 25 April 1867.

107. Newman to James Laird Patterson, 25 April 1867, *The Letters and Diaries,* 23:189–90.

108. *Theological Papers of Newman,* 107. This note written in 1866 seems to contradict what Newman said in his letter the following year to Patterson when he wrote, "the Pope's Temporal Power (which I uphold myself). . . ."

To say that the Church cannot live except in a particular way is to make it "subject to elements of the earth." The Church is not the creature of times and places, of secular politics or popular caprice. Our Lord maintains her by means of this world, but these means are necessary to her only while He gives them; when he takes them away, they are no longer necessary. He works by means, but He is not bound to means. He has a thousand ways of maintaining her; He can support her life, not by bread only, but by every word that proceedeth out of His mouth. If He takes away one defence, He will give another instead. We know nothing of the future: our duty is to direct our course according to our day; not to give up of our own act the means which God has given us to maintain His Church withal, but not to lament over their loss, when He has taken them away.[109]

This sermon would cause Newman many difficulties in the disputes and controversies of the late 1860s and the first half of the 1870s. Support for the pope's temporal power was often seen as a test of the depth of one's Catholic convictions. Newman's position on the temporal power was one of the chief reasons why some Catholics in London and Rome considered him only half a Catholic and a badly tinkered convert. Newman's views on the temporal power gave currency in some quarters to rumors that he had in fact pledged money for the support of Garibaldi. It was in this highly charged atmosphere that plans for the council went ahead and Newman's apprehensions over its outcome grew.

The opening of the council is announced; Newman refuses invitations to go to Rome

While Newman kept his counsel on the topic of infallibility and the Ryder-Ward exchange gave evidence of increasing divisions on the topic among English Catholics, plans for the council moved forward. In June 1867, on the occasion of the centenary observances in honor of the martyrdom of Saints Peter and Paul, Pope Pius IX announced to the many bishops from around the world present in Rome for the solemnities that the council would open, but again the date was not specified. It was only in June 1868 that the date was finally set for 8 December 1869. The observances in honor of Saints Peter and Paul as well as the certainty that the council would at last be held were the occasion for important pastoral letters from Archbishop Manning, letters which again made clear his own belief in the dogma of papal infallibility.[110] In fact, Manning had taken

109. John Henry Newman, *Sermons Preached on Various Occasions,* new ed. (London: Longmans, Green, and Co., 1898) 312–13. On this sermon, see also Paul Misner, *Papacy and Development: Newman and the Primacy of the Pope* (Leiden: E. J. Brill, 1976) 141–45.

110. *The Centenary of St. Peter and the General Council* (1867); *The Oecumenical Council and the Infallibility of the Roman Pontiff* (1869).

a vow during the centenary observances in Rome in 1867 to do all that he could to promote the definition of the dogma of papal infallibility.[111]

As the council drew closer, Newman was approached by Rome, by certain English bishops, and by Bishop Félix Dupanloup of Orléans about his taking part in the preparatory commission for the council or in the council itself.[112] Newman turned aside these requests, pleading his age, his inability to speak other languages, his awkwardness when serving on committees, his shyness in the presence of ecclesiastical authorities, and his desire to finish one of the great projects of his life, the *Grammar of Assent*.[113]

At the end of 1867, Newman told William Monsell, who was acting as an intermediary for Dupanloup by way of Montalembert, that his going to the council was simply out of the question: " . . . there are men, and some of them have been Saints, whose vocation does not lie in such ecclesiastical gatherings. St. Gregory Nazianzen, and St. Chrysostom, not to say St. Basil, are instances. And I suspect, also St. Jerome. I am their disciple. I am too old to learn the ways of other great Saints, as St. Athanasius, St. Augustine, and St. Ambrose, whom I admire, but cannot run with. They are race-horses—I am a broken-kneed poney."[114]

But there is evidence to suggest that Newman's disinclination to participate in the council was at least partially motivated by his lack of sympathy for the definition of papal infallibility. He told Pusey a year before the council formally opened: "I am not going to Rome. The Bishop of Orleans ⟨(this is not known)⟩ at the beginning of the year asked me to be his theologian. And lately the Pope sent a message offering me to be a Consultor—I have begged off—and, as far as I can see, rightly. I am not a theologian, and should only have been wasting my time in matters which I did not understand. I have ever more than inclined to hold the Pope's Infallibility—but as a matter of expedience, I wish nothing done at the Council about it."[115]

OVERVIEW

The success of the *Apologia* gave Newman a prominence and renown that he had not had since his Anglican days. But this success was not universal. Some prominent Catholics in England refused to join in the

111. See Purcell, *Life of Cardinal Manning,* 2:420.

112. See Cwiekowski, *The English Bishops,* 73-78.

113. See Newman, "Memorandum, Consultor Previous to the Council?," 14 October 1868, *The Letters and Diaries,* 24:161-62.

114. Newman to William Monsell, 31 December 1867, *The Letters and Diaries,* 23:396.

115. Newman to E. B. Pusey, 14 November 1868, *The Letters and Diaries,* 24:171. Angled brackets indicate Newman's own later interlinear explanations in copies or in the originals which eventually he asked his correspondents to send back to him.

encomiums addressed to Newman or limited their remarks to words of polite but decidedly muted praise. Within the Catholic community the heightened rhetoric over the pope's infallibility and his temporal power became even more soaring and intense just at the time of Newman's great success. Many people for totally opposite reasons wanted to see Newman come forward on the subject of the pope's authority and power.

Newman sensed a trap. His own views on papal infallibility, he acknowledged privately, had never been consistent. He held that the pope's infallibility was a theological opinion but not a matter of faith. This was as far as he was willing to go, and he refused to change this view simply because Manning and Ward were taking such a determined position in the opposite direction.

As the controversy grew apace in the late 1860s, Newman refused to be drawn out. He feared getting into new trouble with ecclesiastical authority, as he told Emily Bowles in 1866. For Newman the doctrine of papal infallibility was not a necessity, "it would be injurious practically." He had never dealt with the subject in an orderly or logical way and he had never, as he told Henry Wilberforce in July 1867, "taken any great interest in the question of the limits and seat of infallibility." "I see arguments here, arguments there," Newman said in the same letter to Wilberforce, and "I incline one way today, another tomorrow. . . ."[116]

Newman did actively encourage and assist Ignatius Ryder in replying to Ward. It was the task for a younger man, Newman somewhat conveniently decided. His time was past.

When the council was formally announced in June 1867, Newman was encouraged. An ecumenical council was the normal way of doing things. Newman did not expect the council to take up the question of papal infallibility, but he thought one beneficial result of the council would be to show that the body of bishops had a role along with the pope as the supreme teachers of the faith. In fact, he expected, as he told E. B. Pusey, that there would be a retrospective affirmation of the doctrine of the Immaculate Conception just to make this point clear.

Newman refused all invitations to take part in the preparations for the council or in the council itself. He did his best work, he maintained, in quiet and at home. He was a controversialist, not a theologian. One can speculate endlessly on what would have happened had Newman decided to go to Rome in 1869.

Though Newman excused himself from joining publicly in the debate over papal infallibility, he had an uneasy sense that this could not last. He told Father Coleridge in February 1866: "Yet I may be challenged to

---

116. Newman to Henry Wilberforce, 21 July 1867, Georgetown University, Special Collections, Newman Collection, Box 3, A283. See also *The Letters and Diaries*, 23:274–76.

write, till I am obliged to write.''[117] He could hardly have foreseen then that it would be nearly nine years before that challenge came.

117. Newman to Father Henry James Coleridge, S.J., 28 February 1866, *The Letters and Diaries,* 22:167.

Chapter 2

"Can Any Thing I Say Move a Single Bishop?"

January 1869–July 1870

The year 1869 began routinely for Newman. He was absorbed in various details of overseeing the smooth running of the Oratory, its church and school as well as the community of priests and brothers. On 5 January he sent to Ambrose St. John, his close friend and confrere, who was away for a brief holiday in the interval between school terms, a detailed diagram in his own hand of a proposed rearrangement of the Oratory Church that would allow our Lady's image to be seen from various parts of the church and would then be better "for *devotion.*" And the rearrangement would also have the effect of allowing part of the church to be separated off, which, as Newman told St. John, "would make a famous place for me to lecture in. . . ."[1] Newman's interest in practical affairs—financial arrangements, the care and design of buildings and property—is a surprising side to a man who is remembered chiefly as a scholar and writer.

In the first days of 1869, Newman had also to assure his friend, William Monsell, whose son was to become a pupil and boarder at the school in the new term, that a few recent cases of scarlet fever among the boys at the school should give Monsell no reason for alarm.[2] There is in addition a brief glimpse into the life of the Oratory community when Newman in a letter of 3 January tells Catherine Bathurst,[3] "we have two new Deacons, who soon will be Priests—and who are two new Preachers already—

---

1. Newman to Ambrose St. John, 5 January 1869, *The Letters and Diaries of John Henry Newman,* ed. Charles Stephen Dessain and Thomas Gornall, S.J. (Oxford: The Clarendon Press, 1973) 24:201–02. Perhaps Newman had in mind the Adam de Brome chapel at St. Mary's, Oxford, where he delivered his *Lectures on Justification* in 1837. See Charles Dessain, *John Henry Newman,* 2nd ed. (Stanford, Calif.: Stanford University Press, 1971) 45.

2. Newman to William Monsell, 11 January 1869, *The Letters and Diaries,* 24:205.

3. Born in 1825, Catherine Bathurst was received into the Roman Catholic Church in 1850. She tried her vocation with several religious communities, and was for a time in charge of an orphanage associated with the Birmingham Oratory. A frequent correspondent of Newman, she eventually founded a convent and school at Harrow.

which is a great relief to us. You know several of us are getting old now.''[4]
Despite all of these ordinary obligations and details of daily living, Newman was also very much looking forward at the beginning of 1869 to continuing his work on the *Grammar of Assent*. And indeed the greater part
of what has come to be recognized as one of Newman's most enduring
contributions to the history of religious thought was finished before the
year was out.

Newman in October 1868 had declined an invitation from Rome to
take part in the preparatory work of the council. A number of his friends
were dismayed by his refusal, and Newman throughout 1869 had to deal
with letters chiding him for his refusal to go to Rome and urging him to
reconsider. But Newman remained adamant. He would not go back on
the reasons he had privately set down for himself on 14 October 1868.
He preferred to remain in Birmingham and thought it his obligation. But
even in the quiet of the Oratory with its ordinary routines and the time
spent on the *Grammar of Assent,* Newman could not escape the coming
council. It was frequently on his mind both because of his own fears and
uncertainties about its course and because friends and strangers asked his
opinion of what he thought was likely to happen in Rome. In many instances they looked to him as someone who could calm their fears and
steady them for what seemed likely to be bleak days ahead. Newman would
have this role through the next several years, during the council and after
it, until the publication of his *Letter to the Duke of Norfolk* in 1875.

In one of the first letters of the new year, Newman defended his not
going to Rome as a consultor to one of the preparatory commissions for
the council. On 3 January 1869 he told his longtime friend Henry Wilberforce: "I was not invited to the Council—but to be one of a few foreigners
who were to be placed amid Cardinalitian commissions or committees,
to prepare matters to be treated of in the Council. Such a work requires
a strong memory for theological passages and a quick eye in turning over
pages—and I have neither. Ignatius [Ryder] would be just the man for
it." In fact, Newman confessed to Wilberforce that he was having a hard
enough time just then getting down to work on the *Grammar of Assent*.
"As to my own essay," he lamented, "I have neither the patience nor
the vigour to think; and how can I do any thing without thinking and
reading.''[5]

The coming council very likely intruded in another way on Newman's
routine at this time. On 12 January he noted in his diary: "Dr. Errington
calls." Archbishop George Errington, forced by Pius IX in 1860 to give
up his right to succeed to the see of Westminster after a bitter dispute

---

4. Newman to Catherine Bathurst, 3 January 1869, *The Letters and Diaries,* 24:197.
5. Newman to Henry Wilberforce, 3 January 1869, *The Letters and Diaries,* 24:200.

with Cardinal Wiseman, would show himself at the Vatican Council a determined "inopportunist." He would be the last of the English bishops
to give his adherence to the definition of papal infallibility. This would
come in April 1872 after strong urgings from Rome. Newman did not record the discussions he and Dr. Errington had on January 12, but continuing references to Errington in Newman's letters during and immediately
after the council give reason to believe that they had discussed the council
and their fears about the possibility of a definition of papal infallibility.

The subject of Newman's having some role at the council came up
once more in the early part of 1869 in a letter from his friend of many
years, Sister Maria Pia Giberne, a nun at the Visitation Convent in Autun,
France. A convert from Anglicanism, she was one of the people in Newman's life who was accustomed to speak to him frankly and she had made
it evident that she did not think he should excuse himself from attendance
at the council. Newman replied to her chiding on 10 February. "Don't
be annoyed. I am," he wrote,

> more happy as I am, than in any other way. I can't bear the trouble which
> I should have, if I were brought forward in any public way. Recollect, I
> *could* not be in the Council, unless I were a Bishop—and really and truly
> I am *not* a theologian. A theologian is one who has mastered theology—
> who can say how many opinions there are on every point, what authors
> have taken which, and which is the best—who can discriminate exactly be-
> tween proposition and proposition, argument and argument, who can pro-
> nounce which are safe, which allowable, which dangerous—who can trace
> the history of doctrines in successive centuries, and apply the principles of
> former times to the conditions of the present. This is it [sic] to be a
> theologian—this and a hundred things besides. And this I am not, and never
> shall be. Like St. Gregory Nazianzen I like going on my own way, and hav-
> ing my time my own, living without pomp or state, or pressing engagements.
> Put me into official garb, and I am worth nothing; leave me to myself, and
> every now and then I shall do something. Dress me up and you will soon
> have to make my shroud—leave me alone, and I shall live the appointed time.
> Now do take this in, as a sensible nun. . . .[6]

The public debate over the definition of papal infallibility intensifies

In the same month a storm was caused by the publication in the *Civiltà
Cattolica* of a report from the nuncio to France submitted to the papal
secretary of state, which purported to give the view of the French Church
on various issues that should engage the attention of the Vatican Council. The report suggested that the *Syllabus of Errors* should be clarified
and then solemnly proclaimed by the council. It also espoused the procla-

---

6. Newman to Sister Maria Pia Giberne, 10 February 1869, *The Letters and Diaries,*
24:212–13.

mation by the assembled bishops of the dogma of papal infallibility by acclamation.[7] The *Civiltà* was known to have a kind of semiofficial status as a vehicle for expressing the mind of the Roman curia and even of the pope. Though the Bull convoking the council had not even remotely referred to the possibility that the topic of papal infallibility would be discussed, it was of course an open secret that leading figures in Rome and in the worldwide episcopate were determined to broach the subject once the council convened. But the *Civiltà* piece had the effect of thrusting the subject forward into the public arena and of putting an end to the relatively quiet discussion that both proponents and antagonists had thus far been carrying on. From that moment the public debate in newspapers, journals, pamphlets, and books began. Those who had hoped that the topic would not be addressed by the council or that some consensus could be easily achieved found themselves frequently swept aside in the rush of words that came forth from extremists on both sides. The immediate and most far-reaching answer to the *Civiltà* piece came in a series of articles that appeared in March and April in the Augsburg *Allgemeine Zeitung.* The articles were signed "Janus" but all Europe knew that their principal author was Ignaz von Döllinger.[8] Newman made no direct comment on these dramatic events until the end of April in a letter to the Jesuit Henry Coleridge, editor of the *Month,* and even then he was somewhat oblique.

While Newman maintained close and cordial contacts with a number of English Jesuits, he considered some members of the Society, especially the editors of the *Civiltà Cattolica,* to be in the forefront of those who were determined at any cost to secure the passage of the definition of papal infallibility at the coming council. Speaking of the Jesuits, Newman in a letter of 29 April intended for Father Coleridge said: "I cannot regard unmoved their present position. They are said to have the Pope in their hands—and the *Civiltà* seems to me, as far as I hear about it, to be hurrying on measures which I cannot contemplate without pain. Of course God will, as I have said, provide. Men cannot, not even the Pope, go further than he wills."[9]

7. See the *Civiltà* piece in Roger Aubert, *Vatican I* (Paris: Editions de l'Orante, 1964) 261–70.

8. Ignaz von Döllinger was for many years professor of church history at Munich. His reputation for scholarship was recognized all over Europe. Although an almost exact contemporary of Newman (Döllinger was born in 1799 and died in 1890), his relationship with Newman through letters and intermediaries was cordial but not close. During the Vatican Council the relationship between Newman and Döllinger became strained. As a consequence of his refusal to accept the definition, Döllinger was excommunicated in April 1871. His relationship with Newman continued but became very distant. Döllinger could not understand Newman's acceptance of the council.

9. Newman to Father Henry James Coleridge, S.J., 29 April 1869, *The Letters and Diaries,* 24:247. A year later, after the unexpected publication of his 28 January 1870 letter

Early in May, Sir John Simeon[10] sent Newman the record of a conversation that had taken place in Rome on 23 April between the agent of the British Government in Rome, Odo Russell, and Cardinal Antonelli, the papal secretary of state. Simeon had been sent a copy of Odo Russell's minute by Russell's brother, Arthur. In the course of his conversation with Cardinal Antonelli, Odo Russell asked, "May I say that the Press is wrong and that the so-called new Dogma of the personal infallibility will not be submitted to the Council?" Antonelli replied, "Certainly and it stands to reason—I ask you yourself—How could a Divine truth be submitted for discussion to men. The Pope need not ask the Council whether he is infallible since God has made him so."[11] Simeon was eager to have Newman's reaction to what seemed to Simeon a startling and unexpected piece of news. Newman began by standing back from the issue, putting it at some remove. By the same time a year later he was far more disturbed by the news out of Rome: "Persons like myself, shut out from the world, are apt to make great mistakes, when they attempt to interpret the words and deeds of those who live in it, and I have too much experience of my own failures, when I have attempted to do so, not to feel that it is rash in me to play the interpreter of so great a diplomatist as the Cardinal, especially as I never saw him." But as he went on his reserve receded somewhat and he became almost caustic:

> My notion is that he thinks the Council a great blunder—that things go on very well when a Pope and Secretary of State and a few others settle matters—but who can say what trouble a host of Yankees, French, Spanish, German, bishops well may give—We may have put our foot into it, and be unable to get it out. Therefore our great consolation is, that they are really worth nothing at all, and are an anachronism. All is settled already, and, if we want any thing new, all can be settled without them—nor do we wish them to pass this as a principle or dogma. It is already the fact and the truth, without a Council to settle it. . . .

---

to Bishop Ullathorne, Newman would go to great lengths to make clear that his statement in that letter about "others . . . angry with the Holy See for listening to the flattery of a clique of Jesuits, Redemptorists, and converts" was not meant to apply to the Society as a whole but only to a small number of its members.

10. Sir John Simeon was born in 1815 and was graduated from Oxford in 1834. He became a Catholic in 1850 and soon after a close friend and supporter of Newman. Simeon, elected to Parliament in 1865 when W. G. Ward refused to vote for him because he was a "liberal" Catholic, had a wide circle of friends, including Manning and the poet Tennyson. Simeon died while the Vatican Council was sitting.

11. *The Letters and Diaries,* 24:250–51, n. 2. On 1 May 1869, Russell told Lord Clarendon, the foreign minister: "From the conversation [with Antonelli] I infer that the dogma of the Pope's personal infallibility will never be submitted to a debate, but will be presented in such form to the Council as to enable the bishops to confirm it *'nem. con.'*

"To judge from the pastorals and pamphlets published by the leading bishops of the

Despite his cynical appraisal of Antonelli's remarks, Newman still felt obliged as he had in the past to make clear that should there be a definition of papal infallibility at the council, it would not trouble his own faith. "In the same way that I hold the See of Rome to be the centre of unity on the word of the Church, so I should believe that See infallible, if the Church so determined, and I believe a General Council to be her voice in determining—and I don't believe at all that a General Council can decree any thing which the Divine Head of the Church does not will to be decreed."[12] But, as in other letters from this period, Newman appears to place more emphasis on the role of the council than on the role of the pope as the seat of infallibility.

Later in the same month Newman's friend, William Monsell,[13] writing from the Atheneum, passed on a piece of news to Newman which in an atmosphere of conflicting rumors could be seen to be a kind of corroboration of the truth of Cardinal Antonelli's curious conversation with Odo Russell. Monsell told Newman: "The Bishop of Orleans who is at Rome wrote to Montalembert to say that the idea of any definition of the limits or extent of the Pope's authority has been abandoned."[14] If Cuthbert Butler's surmise that the *Civiltà* article was in fact a " 'ballon d'essai', to test how such ideas would be received," it is possible that in the late spring of 1869, the authorities at Rome had decided as a consequence of the raging debate unleashed by the *Civiltà* piece and indications of negative reactions from various European governments that the subject of papal infallibility should not be part of the council's agenda.[15]

Roman Catholic world, this measure [papal infallibility] is ardently desired by them. Some few who think otherwise have published their pamphlets anonymously and they will find it difficult to hold an independent opinion once they are in Rome and under the dome of St. Peter. . . .

"When therefore the bishops meet on 8 December they will find the subjects they are called upon to consider already studied and sifted by the Roman committees and all further discussion almost superfluous, and the Pope's infallibility will be established *de facto*. Some opposition, however, is expected on the part of the French bishops. . . ." Noel Blakiston, ed., *The Roman Question: Extracts from the despatches of Odo Russell from Rome, 1858–1870* (London: Chapman and Hall, 1962) 362–63.

The record of the conversation that Simeon sent to Newman was addressed by Odo Russell to his brother, Arthur, and is a fuller and livelier account of the conversation with Antonelli than the one sent to Lord Clarendon.

12. Newman to Sir John Simeon, 8 May 1869, *The Letters and Diaries,* 24:250–52.

13. William Monsell, born in 1812, was a member of Parliament for Limerick from 1847 to 1874. He was associated with Gladstone and other leading members of the Liberal Party. He became a Roman Catholic in 1850, and was a devoted friend of Newman for almost forty years.

14. William Monsell to Newman, 27 May 1869, Archives of the Birmingham Oratory, Vatican Council file I, no. 15.

15. Cuthbert Butler, *The Vatican Council: The Story Told From Inside In Bishop Ullathorne's Letters* (London: Longmans, Green, and Co., 1930) 1:109.

Newman maintains his private counsels but is willing to aid others in their efforts to speak out against the definition

Through the summer of 1869 Newman was busy with the *Grammar of Assent*. He carried on a very full correspondence with Father Charles Meynell, professor of philosophy at Oscott College, who assisted Newman with the *Grammar of Assent* by reading the draft manuscript and making detailed comments on it. As he carried forward the work on his book, Newman went back and forth to Rednal, the Oratorians' country retreat. Speculation about the council and what was likely to happen there played no great part in his life. This interlude was broken at the end of August by a correspondence with Magdalene Helbert, an Anglican who was very much drawn to the Roman Catholic Church and, as many others had done and would do after, was seeking the help of Newman as she prepared to take this significant step. She was undoubtedly troubled by rumors about the council, particularly about the possible proclamation of papal infallibility. In the end, she did not enter the Catholic Church until 1872, but her correspondence with Newman in the late summer and autumn of 1869 is among the most important records of his views on papal infallibility before the council. Newman began the correspondence by trying to encourage Mrs. Helbert not to let the agitation over papal infallibility stand in the way of her entrance into the Catholic Church:

> When a man is perplexed by a difference between different teachers, if he cannot solve the difficulty at once, it is his duty to say "I believe what the Church holds and teaches." He cannot be wrong in that—the differences cannot be about any thing important *because* they *are* differences. Catholics do not differ about any thing important. If any one says to you "this is of authority or that—" "the Pope, for instance, is certainly infallible," you have to ask "do you hold it as an article of faith?" and again, "Do *all Catholics* hold it as a matter of faith?" and the answer will be sure to be in the negative. Therefore, *supposing* the Archbishop [Manning] says that the Pope is infallible in formal teaching, he has quite a right to say so, as I have myself, but he never will say that it is part of THE FAITH, for the Church has never so pronounced.[16]

Newman then reiterated his point but in more personal terms:

> If the Pope's infallibility were to be determined now, I should say after the event, that doubtless there were good reasons for its being done at this time and not sooner. And I can *see* such reasons; for instance, in the present state of the world, the Catholic body may require to be like an army in the field, under strict and immediate discipline. I tell you frankly, that, in *my*

16. Newman to Mrs. Magdalene Helbert, 30 August 1869, *The Letters and Diaries,* 24:324.

own mind, I see *more* reasons for wishing it may *not* be laid down, by the Council, than for wishing it should be; but I know that I am fallible, and I shall have no difficulty in accepting it, if the Council so determine—and then there will be a point of private judgment less—but till then it *is* a point of private judgment.[17]

Although Newman, who was not at home in other languages, did not himself have much correspondence with leading figures of the continental Church, a number of his English friends had close links to leading churchmen and laymen in Europe, particularly in France and Germany. One of those who brought Newman more directly in touch with European theological and ecclesiastical opinion was William Monsell, perhaps Newman's most trusted confidant among his lay friends.[18] In the late spring and early summer several statements from prominent German lay people, including some of those who were to have a leading role in the German Center Party, were addressed to individual bishops in Germany or to the whole German hierarchy. These statements took an inopportunist (the question was not ready for definition) stance with regard to the definition of papal infallibility. One of them, thought to be the work of Döllinger, began to circulate among leading inopportunists in various European countries in August.[19] Monsell, who was in France at the time, came by a French translation of the document, possibly through Dupanloup with whom Monsell had stayed toward the end of August.[20] Monsell was undoubtedly asked by Dupanloup or others in France to arrange for an English translation of the document that could be privately given to the English-speaking bishops before the council. The document would have to be secretly printed, and Monsell thought of Newman as the one who would best know how to arrange this. Accordingly, he wrote to Newman from France on 31 August: "It is possible that I may have a French confidential document addressed to the Bishops given me to translate. Would you mind looking over my translation for me, and letting me know how I can have *secretly* printed a sufficient number of copies to send to the English, Irish and American bishops."[21] Newman replied on 3 Septem-

---

17. Ibid., 325. Newman says in this letter, "but I know that I am fallible," whereas in a letter six months later, when his concern over the possibility of a definition was intense, he wrote: "My rule is to act according to my best light as if I was infallible, before the Church decides. . . ." See *The Letters and Diaries,* ed. Charles Stephen Dessain and Thomas Gornall, S.J. (Oxford: The Clarendon Press, 1973) 25:100 and also 93.

18. See Hugh A. MacDougall, *The Acton-Newman Relations: The Dilemma of Christian Liberalism* (New York: Fordham University Press, 1962) x.

19. See Butler, *The Vatican Council,* 1:112–13; also Aubert, *Vatican I,* 78, though Aubert does not mention Döllinger's role in any of these addresses.

20. *The Letters and Diaries,* 24:325–26, n. 2.

21. William Monsell to Newman, 31 August 1869, *The Letters and Diaries,* 24:326, n. 2.

ber, agreeing to look over the English version and suggesting a course for the private printing of the text. "The best way, I think, of getting it printed secretly," Newman wrote, "would be for me to write in confidence to Longman, and to get him to put one of his printers upon it. . . . A Protestant Printer would look at such a pamphlet as a matter of course. Or *you* might write to Longman."[22]

Newman did go ahead and make the arrangements with Longman. The original plan, it would appear, was to send the pamphlet to the English-speaking bishops confidentially. Monsell, however, was looking to a wider audience. Newman was not. When the pastoral letter of the German bishops, drawn up during a meeting of the bishops at Fulda in early September, was printed in *The Times*, Monsell saw an opening for his plan.[23] In a letter of 21 September, Monsell, writing from the Colonial Office, of which he was undersecretary, asked Newman: "Does the publication of the address of the German Bishops alter your view as to the inexpedience of letting the Times *get hold* of our memorandum? . . . If we were to decide on letting the Times get hold of it I could probably manage that they should write a judicious article on it."[24] Newman would not take a stand but in reality gave in by having the word "confidential" removed by the printer from the title page. Newman insisted, however, that the pamphlet must go to the "Bishops of England, Scotland, and Ireland" before it went to *The Times*. "When this is done," he told Monsell, "it will come upon you to decide." He added, "I have not seen the Fulda manifesto in the Times—only an allusion to it."[25] A week later Newman wrote again to Monsell, who was concerned that the printing of the pamphlet was taking so long. Newman shared his annoyance. "Of course it is very provoking," he said. "I wrote last night [to the printer] to say that, if delayed a few days, the use of the Pamphlet would be gone." Newman was anxious to have copies of the pamphlet because opportunities to make them available to the American bishops were being lost. Two bishops from the United States had already stopped at the Oratory on their way to the council. But there was still a chance. Newman told Monsell: "There was a report that the American, Father Hecker[26] certainly comes round by BM

22. Newman to William Monsell, 3 September 1869, *The Letters and Diaries,* 24:326.
23. The German bishops' pastoral was moderate in tone and refuted the positions of Janus, especially that the council would not be free. Fourteen of the twenty German bishops also wrote a confidential letter to Pius IX in which they spoke strongly of the inopportuneness of the definition. The letter became public through an indiscretion of the bishop of Passau. See Aubert, *Vatican I,* 80; Butler, *The Vatican Council,* 1:113–14.
24. William Monsell to Newman, 21 September 1869, Archives of the Birmingham Oratory, Vatican Council file I, no. 20.
25. Newman to William Monsell, 22 September 1869, *The Letters and Diaries,* 24:335.
26. Isaac Hecker, founder of the American Congregation of St. Paul (The Paulists).

[Birmingham]. In case this be so, you had better send me a dozen or more copies of the Pamphlet at once."[27]

In his letter of 31 August, Monsell, in addition to asking Newman's help in getting the pamphlet printed, had also asked his help in recommending to Dupanloup "which of the English Bishops he may speak to in confidence and rely upon to aid him in his efforts to defeat the project—would you kindly let me know," Monsell went on, "the names of those

27. Newman to William Monsell, 29 September 1869, *The Letters and Diaries,* 24:341–42. Hecker arrived in England in the first week of November. According to William Portier, Hecker stopped in London for a few days before going on to the Continent and that he arrived in Rome on 26 November. Portier does not mention Hecker's being in Birmingham. See William L. Portier, *Isaac Hecker and the First Vatican Council* (Lewiston/Queenston: The Edwin Mellen Press, 1985) 26–27.

In his recent comprehensive biography of Isaac Hecker, David J. O'Brien makes it clear that Hecker did in fact see Newman. O'Brien writes: "In England Hecker called on John Henry Newman, who gave him a copy of an address to the German bishops of a number of French bishops opposed to infallibility; Hecker thought their argument 'very logical,' Newman reported. Newman also wrote a friend that the American bishops were 'likely to play an independent part' and that the best way to reach them was through Hecker and the Paulists." David J. O'Brien, *Isaac Hecker: An American Catholic* (New York and Mahwah, N.J.: Paulist Press, 1992) 228. The "friend" of Newman that David O'Brien mentions was E. B. Pusey. Newman had written to Pusey on 4 July 1869. Among other issues treated by Newman was the following: "I am *told* that our American bishops were likely to play an independent part [at the Vatican Council]. The best way at getting at them is through the community of St. Paul in New York—Father Hecker is their head. . . . As far as I know, he would do more for you than any one in America." *The Letters and Diaries,* 24:283. Pusey had written a pamphlet in which he expressed opposition to the definition of papal infallibility and its harmful effect upon any efforts at reunion between Anglicans and Roman Catholics.

There are several comments that must be made on Newman's dealings with Isaac Hecker just prior to the council. As noted above, Portier has Hecker in London early in November, but he makes no mention of Hecker's going to Birmingham to see Newman. O'Brien on the other hand makes specific reference to Hecker's seeing Newman in Birmingham but he gives no date for the meeting. He does mention Hecker's stopping in London but again with no date given. O'Brien reports that on 22 November, Döllinger told Acton that " 'Father Hecker from New York' had spent a couple of hours with him the day before. . . ." O'Brien then goes on to say "a short time later Hecker arrived in Rome" and he quotes from two letters from Rome, dated 4 and 6 December, that Hecker sent to his Paulist confreres in New York. *Isaac Hecker,* 228–29.

Strangely in a letter of 3 December to William Monsell, Newman writes, "Fr. Hecker is just here." *The Letters and Diaries,* 24:382. Perhaps by "is just here" Newman meant that Hecker had recently been at the Oratory, recently being early November.

There is yet another problem and this is David O'Brien's reference to "a copy of an address to the German bishops of a number of French bishops opposed to infallibility." The document is surely the one that Monsell on 31 August asked Newman's help with in having an English translation of the document secretly printed. The document was German in origin. Monsell had secured a French translation of the German text. Referring to the document the editors of the *Letters and Diaries* say: "This, it is clear from the correspondence, was the memorandum drawn up in the name of persons alarmed at the talk of a defi-

that answer this description. Dr. Clifford[28] of course would be one. What do you say of the Bishop of Birmingham?"[29] Newman responded frankly:

> Except Dr. Clifford there is no one you could depend upon. Most of them would be echoes of the Archbishop. The two who *fret,* are the Bishops of Liverpool and Newport[30], but I do not know enough of them to say they could not be talked over. As to the person you mention [Ullathorne], I can only account for his unreliableness by considering that, being a monk, he has the instinct of obedience so strong that he never would go against the Pope's private wishes. I think him in his own heart opposed to any doctrinal definition—he has clear and good views—very angry with Ward—not at all partial to Manning—but I expect nothing from him.[31]

---

nition of the personal infallibility of the Pope, and addressed to the Bishops of Germany." The authors made it clear that they were submitting it "to the episcopate [German] alone." The footnote in the *Letters and Diaries* goes on to state: "The original was in German, and Döllinger acknowledged the authorship." *The Letters and Diaries,* 24:326, n. 2.

From Newman's letter of 3 December to William Monsell, it is clear that Newman gave copies of the English translation of the address to the German bishops to Hecker. It would appear then that O'Brien has not clearly stated the origin of the document when he calls it "an address to the German bishops of a number of French bishops. . . ."

28. William Joseph Hugh Clifford was Newman's closest friend in the English hierarchy. A member of an aristocratic English Catholic family, he was ordained in Rome in 1850 and named bishop of Clifton (Bristol) seven years later. He was one of the leading candidates for the archbishopric of Westminster in 1865. At the Vatican Council he was a decided inopportunist. He preached the eulogy at Newman's funeral Mass.

29. William Monsell to Newman, 31 August 1869, Archives of the Birmingham Oratory, Vatican Council file I, no. 16.

30. Alexander Goss and Thomas Brown.

31. Newman to William Monsell, 3 September 1869, *The Letters and Diaries,* 24:326. It is especially curious that Newman did not mention Archbishop Errington. Nor did he mention the Bishop of Plymouth, William Vaughan, who voted *placet iuxta modum* on 16 July 1870 on the final determining vote on the schema *de infallibilitate Romani Pontificis,* though he assented to the definition at the solemn session two days later. See also Ullathorne to Brown, in Cuthbert Butler, *The Life and Times of Bishop Ullathorne, 1806–1889* (New York: Benziger Brothers, 1926) 2:50–51, in which Ullathorne shows in no uncertain terms his fears about the harm that an exaggerated definition would cause in the Church, especially in the episcopate. For a brief analysis of positions of the English bishops at the council, see Edward Norman, *The English Catholic Church in the Nineteenth Century* (Oxford: The Clarendon Press, 1984) 307. But surely Norman is wrong in saying that Ullathorne supported Manning. See also the definitive study on this topic, Frederick J. Cwiekowski, S.S., *The English Bishops and the First Vatican Council* (Louvain: Publications Universitaires de Louvain, 1971), esp. ch. 1, "The English Bishops in 1869-1870," 25-60. Cwiekowski says of Errington, "As we may expect, Errington sided with the minority at the Council," 38; of William Vaughan he writes: "Vaughan of Plymouth, . . . thought a definition of papal infallibility would be unnecessary and harmful," 236; and of Ullathorne, he says: "The Bishop of Birmingham and some of the others at the council, while disposed toward a definition, deliberately refrained from openly aligning themselves with either side, and in this sense they may be said to belong to the moderates of the council," 141.

Newman took the occasion of the letter to Monsell to speak fully of his own views on the definition. He recommended to Monsell the recent pamphlet of the Archbishop of Malines, Victor Dechamps,[32] as putting forth a moderate view on papal infallibility. He saw Dechamps's view as similar to that of Ignatius Ryder, "and the view I should take myself, though I don't want it defined." If there was to be any definition Newman thought that it could only come to pass if expressed in the limited, moderate terms favored by Dechamps.[33] Newman showed Monsell why he had found the position of Dechamps congenial:

> I don't know whether I am right, and write under correction of the Bishop of O.[rléans] viz those theologians, as the French, who deny the Pope's Infallibility and lodge the gift in the Church, *enlarge the subject matter.* Ultramontanes, who uphold the Pope's Infallibility *contract* the subject matter. Ward burns the candle at both ends—upholding the Pope's Infallibility *and* enlarging the subject matter. *This* it is that I dread—and, though there will be sharper and deeper wits than mine to see prospective dangers, yet I should be sorry if, while striving (perhaps in vain) to hinder the definition of the Pope's infallibility, men like the Bishop of O. allowed the *extended* subject matter to be defined. What made the Archbishop of Malines plausible, was the safeguards he made as to what Papal definitions were—I don't know what he said about the subject matter. One of the most important points is this—whether the Church is infallible *when not* evolving the depositum of faith.[34]

Newman remains steadfast in avoiding a public role

Exactly a week after his letter to Monsell, Newman was again deeply involved in the subject of papal infallibility. Mrs. Helbert, following on Newman's letter of 30 August, wrote immediately to take up again the various hesitations that troubled her in her thoughts about becoming a Catholic. She had lately read Peter Le Page Renouf's controversial pamphlet, "The Condemnation of Pope Honorius," which raised objections to the doctrine of papal infallibility on the basis of the sad history of Honorius I and his apparent espousal of the Monothelite heresy in the seventh century.[35] Newman told Mrs. Helbert that he could not agree with Mr. Renouf's definition of "ex cathedra." "You may be quite sure," he

32. "L'Infaillibilité et le concile général, étude de science religieuse à l'usage des gens du monde," June 1869.
33. Later, in a letter to Lady Henrietta Chatterton on 11 March 1870, Newman would speak less admiringly of Dechamps. See *The Letters and Diaries,* 5:47.
34. Newman to William Monsell, 3 September 1869, *The Letters and Diaries,* 24:326–27.
35. For a brief, readable discussion of the papacy of Honorius I and the Monothelite controversy, see J.N.D. Kelly, *The Oxford Dictionary of Popes* (Oxford, New York: Oxford University Press, 1986) 70–71.

told Mrs. Helbert, "that if the Infallibility of the Pope was ever defined, this point also, what is ex Cathedrâ, would be cleared up. At present it is unsettled, because the Pope's Infallibility is unsettled."[36]

In this second series of letters to Mrs. Helbert, Newman made an effort to persuade her of the reasonableness of papal infallibility. "When it is said," he told her, "that 'no Father favors the infallibility of the Pope,' I should ask what do you mean by Father? are the Popes themselves Fathers? and what do you mean by infallibility? it is a word;—define it." In his attempt to help this prospective convert overcome her doubts, Newman pointed to the consistent history of the Roman See's having the authoritative voice in Church disputes: " . . . in matter of fact there were continual collisions between Rome and nearly every Church and that Rome was always in the right. . . . *Why* did the Pope always interfere and (if you will) dictate, except that he had a tradition of his infallibility? and why was he always right, except that he *was* infallible?"[37]

Mrs. Helbert's anxieties persisted nonetheless and she became more uncertain and full of self-doubt, even to the point of wondering whether her enquiries were not in fact leading her to give up religious belief altogether.[38] In his reply Newman seemed to back away somewhat from his earlier concentration on the pope's infallible office:

> As to the history of Vigilius[39] and Honorius, it requires going into at length before it can be proved that the Pope's infallibility was compromised—for myself, taking the history by itself I should say that it told very strongly against the Pope's infallibility though I don't think it actually disproves it. I have no hesitation in saying this, because I have never urged you to believe the Pope's Infallibility. I think that infallibility a point which *can* be defined by an Ecumenical Council—but till it *is* so defined, I only hold it as an opinion. . . .
>
> All this, my dear Madam, let me say is away from the point. What you are called on to believe is the infallibility of the *Church*. If the Church, in the ensuing Council, said any thing about Papal Infallibility, it will be so strictly worded, with such safeguards, conditions, limitations, etc. as will

36. 10 September 1869, *The Letters and Diaries,* 24:329. See Ullathorne to Brown, late October 1869, in which Ullathorne says: "What I am anxious most about is to get a balance on the side of the episcopate, by defining its divine origin as a counter-balance, and by putting landmarks about the ex cathedra." Butler, *Ullathorne,* 2:50–51.

37. Newman to Mrs. Magdalene Helbert, 10 September 1869, *The Letters and Diaries,* 24:329.

38. See letter of 15 September 1869, Mrs. Magdalene Helbert to Newman, *The Letters and Diaries,* 24:338, n. 1.

39. Sixth-century pope who under intense pressure from the Emperor Justinian repudiated leading theologians who had supported the Cyrillian understanding of the Chalcedonian teaching on the two natures of Christ, namely that the union was hypostatic. See J.N.D. Kelly, *Oxford Dictionary of Popes,* 60–62.

add as little as is conceivable to what is *now* held—it will be so explained
and hedged round as not to apply to the case of Honorius etc. It will not
be, what Protestants fancy it will be, a declaration that "whatever the Pope
says is infallible."

"See how tightly," Newman tried to assure his correspondent, "the *cases*
of an ex cathedrâ decision will be restricted."[40]

While Newman was carrying on with great sensitivity and attention
this correspondence with someone whom he had never met, dramatic
events were occurring elsewhere with regard to the coming council. On
20 September, the celebrated French Carmelite preacher, Hyacinth Loyson, who had visited Newman in 1868, wrote a letter to the General of
his Order denouncing the General's efforts to silence him from speaking
out against the definition of papal infallibility. In perfervid language Loyson declared his withdrawal from the Carmelites rather than accept an
imposition of silence. And he raised "before the Holy Father and the
Council, my protest, as a Christian and a priest, against those doctrines
and those practices which are called Roman, but which are not Christian,
and which by their encroachments, always more audacious and more bane-
ful, tend to change the constitution of the Church. . . ."[41]

Loyson's passionate letter was regarded with a certain dismay among
those who were opposed to the definition. They felt that such a strong
public utterance disseminated through *Le Temps,* with its Protestant as-
sociations, would certainly play into the hands of their opponents. Monsell wrote to Newman on 24 September with concern over Loyson's letter.
He was especially distressed about its possible repercussions for Dupanloup and he saw it as a gain for Louis Veuillot, the editor of *L' Univers,*
who in France took an even more determined stance in favor of the definition than Ward did in England.[42] Newman was moved to write an impassioned letter to Loyson, decrying his action and urging him to avoid
dealings with Protestants. It was unlike Newman to write such an emo-
tional letter to someone he barely knew. While assuring Loyson of his
affection, he urged him to be obedient to his superiors and in his warnings against Protestants he took a strong stance: "Even good Protestants
are not trustworthy in matters of religion. They open the door to errors
which perhaps they do not hold themselves. I am not accusing them individually and personally, but warning you. You see them in couleur de
rose. There are Protestants who are nothing else than infidels—They will

40. Newman to Mrs. Magdalene Helbert, 28 September 1869, *The Letters and Diaries,*
24:339.
41. *The Letters and Diaries,* 24:342–43, n. 3, quoting the *Guardian,* 22 September 1869,
1050.
42. See William Monsell to Newman, 24 September 1869, Archives of the Birmingham
Oratory, Vatican Council file I, no. 22.

use you, and secretly smile at you; or if not they, then the Author of Evil, who uses them too."[43]

The Loyson affair had other consequences for Newman. All unexpectedly it had the effect of putting him forward in the public discussion in England of the council. On 28 September, the *Daily Telegraph* stated:

> Père Hyacinth's letter to the Father General of the Barefooted Carmelites has fallen among the Ultramontane party with the suddenness and force of a bombshell. From one end of Europe to the other the eloquent preacher is the subject for eulogy, remonstrance, denunciation, and curses both loud and deep. . . .
>
> Neither by Protestants nor by Catholics is the name of Dr. Newman ever mentioned without honour; and to both there must be something strangely significant in the report that, when invited to attend the Council, he excused himself on the plea that "the air of Rome did not agree with him." Possibly the story may be incorrect; or, possibly, Father Newman may have intended to convey no more than the literal meaning of the words; but the very circumstance that attention is drawn to the double signification of the message, when coupled with the notorious fact that the well-known convert from Anglicanism has more than once excited the open hostility of Ultramontane leaders like Dr. Cullen unmistakably marks the attitude which he is supposed to have assumed. Some such position as Dr. Newman occupies in England is held by Dr. Döllinger in Germany.[44]

Newman could not have been happy with the report in the *Telegraph*. He had carefully worked to keep himself out of the public controversy over infallibility in England and he could not have been cheered by a statement asserting he had had difficulties with Archbishop Cullen of Dublin over matters dealing with infallibility. Nor could he have been happy to see his own carefully quiet stance on infallibility compared to the position of Döllinger, whose polemics over the coming council had electrified Europe during the past several months.

William Monsell thought the *Telegraph* article gave Newman an opportunity to express his views publicly on the great question, but Newman, as he would again and again in the years ahead, refused his friend's urgings. Newman showed what it would take to get him to engage in public discussion. "As to the *Telegraph*," he wrote on 29 September, "it has sometimes struck me, that the way in which I naturally might be led to write, would be some strong published statement charging me, for praise or blame, with Gallicanism or quasi-Protestantism. But an anonymous leading article is not enough."[45] Whether Newman had in mind the pos-

43. Newman to Hyacinth Loyson, 1 October 1869, *The Letters and Diaries,* 24:343–44.
44. Archives of the Birmingham Oratory, Vatican Council file I, no. 29.
45. Newman to William Monsell, 29 September 1869, *The Letters and Diaries,* 24:341.

sibility that in time he would have to write on the subject of papal infallibility when he set down some notes on the subject earlier in September
is not clear. These notes are the first set in a series of three. This first
set of notes, written on 20 September 1869, was followed by those of 27
December 1869 and those of 28 June 1870. On 20 September, Newman
jotted down the following:

1. On Honorius's acts being compatible with infallibility, even if past.
2. Infallibility a fact—our *knowledge* of doctrine may develop, but facts
are facts from the first.
3. if defined, it needs be circumscribed. It must be so defined that it is
not possible to say his addresses to the soldiers are infallible.
4. against negative propositions, e.g. "Si quis dixerit nullam habere potesta-
tem directe vel indirecte" etc.
5. What is its field?
6. What its tests?
7. Why is it, if I believe the Pope's Infallibility I do not wish it defined?
is not *truth* a gain? I answer, because it can't be so defined as not to raise
more questions than it solves.
8. analyze how it is that the converts are all one way.
9. On expediency. We must not say that Pope or Council may do any inexpedient thing *after* it is done—but such a thing is possible—and we may
say so *before* it.
10. "Woe unto those thro' whom scandals come"[46]

Newman gave further evidence of his reaction to Père Loyson's public statement on his renunciation of his vows as a Carmelite in a letter
to his friend, Mary Holmes, one of several women for whom Newman
acted as a spiritual guide and to whom he often revealed his deepest feelings both of delight and disappointment. Newman's 7 October letter to
Mary Holmes was written just at the time when his friend, Emily Bowles,
was visiting Birmingham where she came to confide in Newman her strong
distress over a possible definition of infallibility.[47] In his letter to Mary
Holmes, Newman said: "I don't think Fr. Hyacinth has any right to do
what he has done. He is a monk and under obedience. . . . Then again
why should he *prejudge* the Council? What an insult to all the bishops
who compose it! and to appeal from the Church to our Lord in a matter
of faith is sheer Protestantism. The Church is the *voice* of our Lord. . . .

46. Newman "Notes," 20 September 1869, *The Letters and Diaries,* 24:334, n. 2.
47. See Newman to Emily Bowles, 29 September 1869, *The Letters and Diaries,* 24:341
and 341, n. 1, which gives an account of Miss Bowles's meeting with Newman during which,
in answer to her fear that the definition might force her to leave the Church, Newman said,
"You will not. We all must go through that gate of obedience, simply as obedience. And
mind if the dogma is declared, you will find that it will not make the slightest difference
to you."

That there are real grievances at Rome, which he has suffered from, I don't doubt—but he has managed to spoil a good cause."[48]

In a further exchange with Mrs. Helbert in late October, Newman continued his attempts to persuade her that she must try for a middle ground and go on to take her momentous step with confidence. Though Mrs. Helbert had been newly alarmed by Archbishop Manning's sermon on the *Syllabus of Errors* on 3 October,[49] Newman tried his best to put Manning's rather strong statements about the pope's power in a mild light. Nor did he, as he had not in his previous letters to Mrs. Helbert, show an unreserved acceptance of the doctrine of papal infallibility.

> As to the Archbishop's Sermon, it speaks to Catholics not to Protestants— Protestants are sure to take it in the sense which to a Catholic is not conveyed in its words. e.g. He makes the Pope say "I am the sole *last* Supreme Judge of right and wrong—" now look at that little word "last." Any Protestant would think it meant that man had no *natural conscience*—but that the Pope *made* right and wrong—which every Catholic knows to be a wicked heresy—but the Archbishop knew what he was saying, and he says no such thing, and any theologian, the high authorities at Rome, will quite understand the theological force of his words. He says "the sole *last* judge;" that is, to him is the *appeal* when men differ IN DETAIL."[50]

Newman did make an effort to take the Archbishop's side, but in the process he came near to standing Manning's words on end. It is doubtful that Manning would have been altogether happy with Newman's efforts at exegesis. And Newman in this passage to Mrs. Helbert already shows his views on the place of individual conscience in relation to papal authority. He was to spell these views out clearly in the *Letter to the Duke of Norfolk* five years later.

---

48. Newman to Mary Holmes, 7 October 1869, *The Letters and Diaries,* 24:346–47. Mary Holmes became a Catholic in 1844. She wrote frequently to Newman, who had been her spiritual director when she was an Anglican. Miss Holmes also corresponded with William Makepeace Thackeray and Anthony Trollope.

49. Manning's sermon was printed in the 4 October edition of *The Times*. Among other things he said, "The Syllabus contains 80 errors with their condemnation, and a reference to those formal acts and documents in which their condemnation has already made. Now those 80 errors were partly in matters of faith, partly in matters of morals, in both of which, as they [his hearers] knew, the Catholic Church, and the head of the Catholic Church, also by divine assistance, were infallible—that is, they were the ultimate interpreters of the faith, and the ultimate expositors of the law of God and that not by the light of human learning only, but by the light of Divine assistance which secured from error. Under morals were also included a number of errors relating to the political state of the world." *The Times,* 4 October 1869, 6.

50. Newman to Mrs. Magdalene Helbert, 20 October 1869, *The Letters and Diaries,* 24:355–56.

In another section of the 20 October letter, Newman tried to assure Mrs. Helbert that her assent need not be looked upon as an isolated, solitary event but must be viewed in the face of the whole life of the Church, past, present, and future. "How do we know," Newman asked, "that Pius IX is true Pope? Securus judicat orbis terrarum. How shall we know that the coming Council is a true Council—but by the after assent and acceptance of it on the part of that Catholic organization which is lineally descended, as one whole, from the first ages?—How can we interpret the decisions of that Council, how the Pope's decisions in any age, except by the Schola Theologorum, the great Catholic school of divines dispersed all over the earth?"[51] Newman's insistence on the place of the theological schools in the enunciation of the Church's teaching was to have a large part in his dealings with the subject of papal infallibility, both before and after the Vatican Council.

On the eve of the council Newman shows great interest in the historic event but declines invitations to go to Rome

The approaching council entered in further ways into Newman's life in October 1869. On 9 October, Bishop Henri Maret, dean since 1850 of the theological faculty of the Sorbonne and the leading French theologian of the Gallican school, sent to Newman his newly-published two-volume work, *Du Concile général et de la paix religieuse.*[52] Newman thanked Maret in a letter of 6 November. He wrote in English:

> I beg to acknowledge the honour you have done me in giving me a copy of your most learned work on the General Council.
>
> I hope to gain much instruction from it, and am sure I shall—but it has a far higher destiny than that of profiting an individual such as I am.
>
> It is an important contribution to our ecclesiastical literature and, in placing it in our Congregational Library, I look forward to its instructing and edifying Catholic students after my time.[53]

In the same month Peter Le Page Renouf came to visit Newman. Though there is no record of their discussion, it can be safely concluded that the

---

51. Ibid., 355.

52. Before the council there was uncertainty over whether Rome would invite titular bishops, at least those without jurisdiction such as Maret. It was said that Pius IX was not in favor of doing so precisely to keep Maret out of the council. In the end, titular bishops were invited to participate.

53. Newman to Bishop Henri Maret, 6 November 1869, *The Letters and Diaries,* ed. Charles Stephen Dessain and Thomas Gornall, S.J. (Oxford: Clarendon Press, 1977) 31:88*. It is interesting to note that Newman, while assuring Maret that his book would find a place in the library of the Oratory, gives no indication that he has himself read it.

prospect of the definition was not overlooked. And in October Manning issued his pastoral letter, "The Oecumenical Council and the Infallibility of the Roman Pontiff," in which he maintained that the pope's power to define was not in any sense dependent upon or allied to the consent of the college of bishops. It was this position which provoked Dupanloup, who responded with his *Observations sur la controverse soulevée relativement à la définition de infaillibilité au prochain concile.* It was also Manning's reduction of the place of the bishops in the life of the universal Church that made the moderate Ullathorne determined to keep clear of any of Manning's maneuvers at the coming council.[54]

Almost on the eve of the council, Newman would receive his last invitation to be present at it. The invitation was made by Montalembert on behalf of Dupanloup, who wanted Newman to accompany him to Rome as a personal theologian.[55] On 10 November, Newman declined the invitation without specifying his reasons: "It is an extreme honour to me that the Bishop of Orleans should wish to have me with him, and should speak to me through you. He is so great a man, that it is a serious trouble to me and a real distress, to feel that I cannot take advantage of so special and condescending a kindness—but there are reasons quite special which make it impossible."[56] Late in September one of the English bishops, Thomas Brown of Newport, who had delated Newman to Rome in 1859 over the *Rambler* article, "On Consulting the Faithful In Matters of Doctrine," had also asked Newman to go to Rome as his theologian. Newman replied: "There is nothing I could do there that others could not do. . . ."[57] Brown sent a further request to Newman on 2 November,[58] and this time Newman, as though annoyed by Brown's persistence, answered sharply:

> There was an English Bishop, just ten years ago, who, without a word to me, (which would have settled everything,) and in spite of the sacred direction, Matt. xviii, 15, denounced a writing of mine to the Authorities at Rome.

---

54. See Ullathorne's Advent Pastoral, 1869, in which he said: "It is for the bishops, then, in Council to bear witness, to deliberate, and to deliver their judgements by their votes on the matter in hand; and it is for the Pope to confirm or withhold consent from their decisions. The Church does not consist of body alone, or of head alone, but of head and body moving in joint action; but the head is the crowning authority alike in the Church's capacity of teacher, of lawgiver, and of ruler." Butler, *Ullathorne,* 2:49.

55. See Montalembert to Newman, 8 November 1869, Archives of the Birmingham Oratory, Vatican Council file I, no. 37.

56. Newman to Montalembert, 10 November 1869, *The Letters and Diaries,* 24:368.

57. Newman to Bishop Thomas Brown, 28 September 1869, *The Letters and Diaries,* 24:337.

58. See Cwiekowski, *The English Bishops,* 107.

He it is, who has created a prejudice against me there, such, as to be my sufficient justification in acting upon those positive inducements, which lead me at this time to remain quietly in my own place at home.[59]

On 9 November 1869, Richard Simpson in a letter to Lord Acton said that "Brown of Newport is, or has been teazing Newman to go with him as his theologian. N. is rather sorry now not to go. But having first refused the Pope, & then Ullathorne on the ground of that first refusal, he does not think it expedient to yield to the 2d thought."[60] There is certainly no evidence that Newman at any point regretted declining the several invitations he had had to be present at the council.

Tensions grow as opening of the council draws near; Newman critical of Manning's public stance

In the month before the council Newman wrote once more to Mrs. Helbert, who was now disturbed after reading the letters of Janus that had just been published in English under the title of *The Pope and the Council*. Newman gave the following somewhat contradictory opinion of the book in a letter to Mrs. Helbert on 5 November:

As to that book Janus, a man must be a strange Catholic to have written it, if what I hear of it is true. A friend of mine here, observing that he quoted in one place a rare book, which he happened to see in one of our bookseller's shops, bought the book, and found it said nearly the *reverse* of what Janus said. For myself, though I have the book, I have not at this time an hour at my disposal to give to it—but, as far [as] I have looked at it or heard of it, it seems a very able book written with a great exaggeration and colouring of facts.[61]

Another indication of Newman's reaction to Janus is found in a letter written in late October by Bishop Ullathorne to Bishop Brown of Newport. Ullathorne wrote: "Since I have read 'Janus' I can scarcely think it to be Döllinger's, it is so outrageous and extreme. Dr. Newman, who

59. Newman to Bishop Thomas Brown, 3 November 1869, *The Letters and Diaries,* 24:361–62.

60. Josef L. Altholz, Damian McElrath, and James C. Holland, eds., *The Correspondence of Lord Acton and Richard Simpson* (Cambridge: At the University Press, 1975) 3:282. Edmund Sheridan Purcell also implies that Newman did in fact want to go to the council but declined the invitations of various bishops because Pius IX had not named him a consultor to the council. See Purcell, *Life of Cardinal Manning, Archbishop of Westminster* (New York and London: The Macmillan Company, 1896) 2:448.

61. Newman to Mrs. Magdalene Helbert, 5 November 1869, *The Letters and Diaries,* 24:364. Evidently Newman's work on the *Grammar of Assent* kept him from reading many of the publications that were coming out in view of the approaching council.

thinks it will do immense mischief, thinks also that it cannot be Döllinger."[62]

Two weeks later Newman wrote another important letter on infallibility to someone who was concerned about the possibility of a definition in Rome during the months ahead. The correspondent was Mrs. William Froude, a convert who was married to the brother of Newman's close friend, Richard Hurrell Froude, who had died in 1836. Newman, writing to Mrs. Froude on 21 November, again made clear his opposition to the definition, while being careful to say that its passage would not greatly dismay him or trouble his faith: "I have ever held the Pope's Infallibility as an opinion, and am not therefore likely to feel any personal anxiety as to the result of this Council. Still I am strongly opposed to its definition—and for this reason. Hitherto nothing has been ever done at Councils but what is *necessary*; what is the necessity of this? There is no heresy to be put down. It is a dangerous thing to go beyond the rule of tradition in such a matter. . . . We must not play with edged tools." "I am against the definition," Newman went on, "because it opens a long controversy. You cannot settle the matter by a word—whatever is passed, must be a half, a quarter measure."

Newman ranged back over the history of the early Church, which he knew so well, as he explained to Mrs. Froude his uneasiness over the prospect of the soon-to-be convened council's defining papal infallibility. *"Now,"* he stressed,

> the Bishops of the Church are called upon to take the first step in opening a question as difficult, and not as justifiable, as the question which those early Councils [Nicea, Ephesus] were obliged to discuss. This question will lead to an alteration of the *elementary constitution* of the Church. Our *one* doctrine, in which all doctrines are concluded, is, "the Church's word is to be believed—" Hitherto "the Church's decision" means that of the Pope and the Bishops; now it is proposed to alter this for the Pope's word." It is an alteration in the fundamental dogma. Hitherto, *I personally* may be of *opinion* that the Pope is infallible by himself—*but I have never been called to act* upon it—no one has—and what is the consequence? that the Pope cannot act upon it. Hitherto the Pope has always acted, (for greater caution,) with the Bishops—he has not gone to the extent of what he might do, supposing him infallible. But, define his infallibility, and he will act alone. Well—God will direct him—but what is this but throwing away one of the human means *by* which God directs him? It is making the system more miraculous—and it is like seeking a bodily cure by miracle, when human means are at hand.[63]

62. Butler, *Ullathorne*, 2:50–51.
63. Newman in this passage twice makes reference to the role of bishops in infallible pronouncements. Misner would see Newman as giving little recognition to the role of the

Newman believed the council was taking on an almost impossible task if it thought that it could deal easily and in a relatively short space of time with such a complex question:

> Councils are formal things—and there is no need of drawing the line between their acts, or not much need, but a Pope is a living man, ever living, and it will be a great work to go through this question well. You have to treat it doctrinally—and then again historically, reconciling what you teach with the verdict of history.
>
> Then again recollect that this doctrine is a retrospective doctrine—it brings up a great variety of questions about *past* acts of Popes—whether their decrees in past ages are infallible, or whether they were not, and which of them, and therefore whether they are binding on *us*."

At the end of the letter, Newman added a telling postscript: "Keep this; I may want it. I have never before put my thoughts on paper."[64] Mrs. Froude thanked Newman for his letter which she and her daughter, Eliza (Isy),[65] had been "comforted" by. "I can understand and appreciate," she wrote, "your having kept so quiet—holding so strong a view as you do."[66]

---

episcopate. He speaks primarily of the *Letter to the Duke of Norfolk,* but in light of the letter to Mrs. Froude of 21 November 1869, the letter to J. R. Bloxam of 22 February 1870, the letter to Bishop Alexander Goss of 1 April 1870, and the letter to Isy Froude of 28 July 1875 as well as Newman's concern about the lack of a moral unanimity among the bishops after the solemn proclamation on 18 July 1879, *The Letters and Diaries,* 25:75–76, the following comments of Misner should perhaps be tempered: "It must be confessed that, when Newman came to interpret the Vatican Council, he overlooked or ignored the whole dialectic of papal and episcopal rule, preferring to take an idiosyncratic line. (I refer especially to the *Letter to the Duke of Norfolk* of 1875.) Unlike such moderates as his own bishop, Ullathorne, and Ketteler, bishop of Mainz, whose aversion to absolutism in all its manifestations was perhaps more natural and deeply-rooted than Newman's, he did not look upon episcopal authority as an important safeguard against abuse of papal authority. This despite the fact that the question was a natural and familiar one to the Anglican, one which he had discussed on a very few occasions also as a Catholic. His lack of interest in bishops' rights is one of those traits which make him an ultramontane *sui generis,* though he certainly did not favor the centralization of authority in Roman offices which was going on during this period, as attested by a remarkable letter of 1863 [Letter to Monsell, 13 January 1863, *The Letters and Diaries,* ed. Charles Stephen Dessain (London: Thomas Nelson and Sons, Ltd., 1970) 20:390–93] and an eloquent passage in the *Apologia*" [John Henry Newman, *Apologia Pro Vita Sua* (1864; 2nd ed., 1865), ed. Martin J. Svaglic (Oxford: The Clarendon Press, 1967) 238–40]. Paul Misner, *Papacy and Development: Newman and the Primacy of the Pope* (Leiden: E. J. Brill, 1976) 150.

64. Newman to Mrs. William Froude, 21 November 1869, *The Letters and Diaries,* 24:377–78.

65. Mrs. Froude and her children all became Catholics, though her husband William, brother of R. H. Froude, did not.

66. Mrs. William Froude to Newman, 30 November 1869, *The Letters and Diaries,* 24:378, n. 1.

In this time just before the opening of the council, when the name of Manning and his position on infallibility came up frequently in Newman's correspondence, Newman and Manning had another of their unhappy, albeit this time brief, exchanges. They had last corresponded in the summer of 1867 when the Archbishop had initiated the correspondence in the hope of assuring Newman that he had not been responsible for the fact that Newman's letter in 1860 (explaining his position to Rome on the *Rambler* article in 1859 and offering to retract any statements that were not correct) had never reached the Roman authorities. That exchange had simply intensified their mutual distrust, and they succeeded only in pledging prayers for one another. This new exchange in November 1869 was again begun by Manning, who wrote to ask Newman where he could obtain a copy of a pamphlet[67] which told how Newman had been shamefully treated in the *Rambler* affair and implicated Manning as a participant. It had been brought to Manning's attention by Edward Ffoulkes, who had been excommunicated by Manning in September 1869 for his pamphlet, *The Church's Creed or the Crown's Creed? A Letter to Archbishop Manning.* In his letter of 2 November to Newman, Manning said:

> It is my intention to obtain a copy of the Pamphlet referred to by Mr. Ffoulkes at p. 63 of his Letter[68] and to take any steps it may make necessary. I feel that I have no right to ask you to assist me in obtaining the Pamphlet: and Mr. Ffoulkes may be in error in supposing that you know the Author, and may know how to obtain a copy for me.
>
> If you are not unwilling to do so, you would confer on me a real and kind service.

Manning was soon to begin his journey to Rome for the council. In concluding his letter to Newman, he said: "On Friday I hope to leave England; and as return is always uncertain, and may, at best, be distant, I leave with you the assurance that the friendship of so many years, though of late unhappily clouded, is still dear to me."[69] Newman, who had already told Manning through Ullathorne that he harbored no suspicions

67. William Palmer's appendix to the French translation of Newman's 7 October 1866 sermon, "The Pope and the Revolution." See Palmer's Preface and Appendix, *The Letters and Diaries,* 23:397–406, appendix. Palmer wrote with the assistance of Newman's friends, especially Frederick Neve, rector of the English College in Rome, in the hope of dispelling various calumnious reports about Newman and his sermon then circulating in Rome among curial officials. The text of "The Pope and the Revolution" was included by Newman in the third edition (1870) of *Sermons Preached on Various Occasions.*

68. *The Roman Index and its late Proceedings, a Second Letter to the Most Rev. Archbishop Manning,* October 1869.

69. Archbishop Henry Manning to Newman, 2 November 1869, *The Letters and Diaries,* 24:362.

against Manning in the *Rambler* episode,[70] was, it would appear, annoyed by the stiff tone of Manning's letter and by Manning's implication that Newman was in touch with the author of the pamphlet. While the immediate subject of their correspondence was a series of incidents that had happened nearly a decade before, it is perhaps not at all an exaggeration to think that Newman's and Manning's positions on the coming council played a part in intensifying rather than lessening their estrangement. In any case, Newman closed this particular correspondence with his famous reply to Manning: "I can only repeat what I said when you last heard from me [2 September 1867]. I do not know whether I am on my head or my heels, when I have active relations with you. In spite of my friendly feelings, this is the judgment of my intellect."[71]

On 21 November, Newman thanked Robert Charles Jenkins, an Anglican clergyman and author, for his *A Letter respectfully addressed to His Holiness Pope Pius IX in reply to his appeal to the Members of the Reformed Churches* and for his pamphlet, *What do Popes say on their alleged Infallibility? A Letter respectfully addressed to the most reverend Archbishop Manning.* Newman professed to be happier with Jenkins's letter than with his pamphlet, but he took the occasion nonetheless to show his lack of sympathy for Manning's position. "I don't think Dr. Manning has put on any 'spectacles'," Newman wrote. "He says what he thinks, and knows what he is about. I cannot help thinking he holds that the world is soon coming to an end—and that he is in consequence careless about the souls of future generations which will never be brought into being. I can fancy a person thinking it a grand termination (I don't mean that he so thinks) to destroy every ecclesiastical power but the Pope, and let Protestants shift for themselves."[72] Newman was even more caustic about Manning's position just prior to the council in a letter he wrote to another Anglican clergyman. "I heard," he wrote to Malcolm MacColl on 29 November, "that Archbishop Manning considers the day of judgment certain to come in a few years. Whether this is better than the above gossip about myself [that Newman was writing a book on Rationalism] I know not, but it is an answer anyhow to your astonishment about his Pastoral.[73]

---

70. See Newman to Bishop William Ullathorne, 1 November 1869, *The Letters and Diaries,* 24:359.

71. Newman to Archbishop Henry Manning, 3 November 1869, *The Letters and Diaries,* 24:362–63.

72. Newman to Robert Charles Jenkins, 21 November 1869, *The Letters and Diaries,* 24:379.

73. Newman to Malcolm MacColl, 29 November 1869, *The Letters and Diaries,* 24:382. The pastoral was Manning's *The Oecumenical Council and the Infallibility of the Roman Pontiff: A Pastoral to the Clergy,* October 1869.

While Newman was corresponding with Manning and with clergymen from other Churches who approached him in the hope that he would comment on Manning's public viewpoint on the council, a new storm had broken on the Continent because of two pamphlets from the Bishop of Orléans, one of them in part a direct response to Manning's October pastoral, "The Oecumenical Council and the Infallibility of the Roman Pontiff." On 11 November, Dupanloup, against the advice of some of his friends, published *Observations sur la controverse soulevée relativement à la definition d'infaillibilité au prochaim concile.* In this pamphlet Dupanloup took a clearly inopportunist position, but he was also concerned by what he viewed as the risk of diminishing the role of the episcopate in the Church. On this point he was certainly taking issue with the statement in Manning's pastoral that "judgments *ex cathedra* are in their essence judgments of the Pontiff, apart from the episcopal body, whether congregated or dispersed."[74]

Just five days before the council Newman was again in touch with William Monsell. Somewhat surprisingly he makes a reference to Manning's pastoral that seems to indicate that he had not read it. At the end of a series of swift, short sentences dealing with various topics related to the council, Newman wrote, "I am told Archbishop Manning's Pastoral gives up the notion of any decree or acclamation in favour of Infallibility, and wishes it negatively ruled by condemning the Gallican propositions." In the same letter Newman told Monsell that Father Isaac Hecker was just then at the Oratory and that he had given Hecker copies of the pamphlet, *Is It Opportune to Define the Infallibility of the Pope?,* that Newman had had printed for Monsell in September.[75]

Hecker attended the council as the theologian of Archbishop Peter Richard Kenrick of St. Louis, a determined inopportunist (if not anti-infallibilist). Monsell and Newman were not alone in thinking that Hecker could play a role in Rome among the opponents of a definition. Acton and Richard Simpson thought that Hecker would be willing to encourage the English and Irish bishops to oppose the definition. On 9 November, Simpson wrote to Acton:

> I think that the English & Irish Bishops should be acted on through the Americans who are perfectly misunderstood at Rome—they have the art of hiding an uncompromising resistance under the show of the most hearty loyalty, & so they are more listened to than we are, who if we resist, generally resist without show. Hecker as a missionary, with a vocation to convert the semiliterary class in the U.S. puts this truth into the first place—that

74. *The Letters and Diaries,* 24:382, n. 1; on Dupanloup's pamphlet, see Aubert, *Vatican I,* 91–92 and Butler, *The Vatican Council,* 1:124–25.

75. Newman to William Monsell, 3 December 1869, *The Letters and Diaries,* 24:383. It is in this letter that Newman says "Fr. Hecker is just here." See above n. 27.

it is impossible to believe against evidence, & not only impossible but wicked to attempt it—So he is toto caelo opposed to the Jesuit school, whose triumph he thinks would be the greatest of calamities.[76]

And a month later, on the day the council opened, Simpson wrote to Acton, who was in Rome: "I hope things are going well at the Council—and that you have been able to concert with Hecker some plans for having the American Bishops represent in a body that the infallibility has never been taught on their continent."[77]

There were evidently various hopes and plans that a large number of the English-speaking bishops would meet together to take a common line. The *Tablet* had reported on 10 July that

> the Bulletin of the Apostolic Vicariate of Gibraltar insists upon the great advantage which would result from preliminary assemblies of the Bishops of England, Ireland, and the British colonies and possessions. The great distance that separates them would render such a meeting impossible previously to their arrival in Rome, but the writer is of opinion that, when once there, they might advantageously consult, with a view to community of action, on points which peculiarly interest them. "What incalculable benefits," he continues, "would not be the result, if the 66 Bishops of the British colonies united their action to that of the 44 Bishops of the mother country? The Bishops of English Sees form at least one-tenth of the Bishops of the world, and are more numerous than those of any other nation."[78]

But while Newman, Monsell, Acton, and Simpson thought that the coming together of the English-speaking bishops would work to the advantage of opponents of the definition, the *Tablet* was sure of the opposite result. In its issue of 25 December 1869, the *Tablet* announced: "We have received from Rome a report, for the truth of which we can in no wise vouch, to the effect that the Bishops of England, Ireland, America, and the Colonies are, as a body, likely to take one line in respect to the definition of the infallibility of the Pope. The truth of the report would in no way astonish us. The English speaking Bishops represent a singular independence of character, which raises them above the timidity of a hesitating or doubtful policy."[79]

76. Simpson to Acton, 9 November 1869, *The Correspondence of Lord Acton and Richard Simpson,* 3:282.

77. Simpson to Acton, 8 December 1869, *The Correspondence of Lord Acton and Richard Simpson,* 3:286.

78. *Tablet,* n.s. 2 (10 July 1869) 34:169.

79. *Tablet,* n.s. 2 (25 December 1869) 34:938. The *Tablet's* reference to "the timidity of a hesitating or doubtful policy" is meant as a slur against the inopportunist party.

The council solemnly convenes; Newman, absorbed in work on the Grammar of Assent, *shows concern about the council's outcome*

In early December, Newman was at Rednal hard at work on the *Grammar of Assent,*[80] and there are no indications from his diaries and letters that his thoughts were on the great council, which solemnly began in Rome on 8 December 1869. There are no extant letters dated 8 December, and the only entry in his diary, "Ambrose sang High Mass," is obviously a reference to the observance of the feast of the Immaculate Conception. But Newman returned to thoughts of the council the next day. He was in a somewhat confident mood. Again the recipient of his observations was Monsell. Newman wrote: "What a splendid letter to his Clergy is the Bishop of O's[Orléans]! I hope he has *thrown back* the movement. We hear from Rome that there is no talk of bringing forward the Infallibility except perhaps at *last.* What I fear is that Manning will attempt, by *delay,* to gain over Bishops whom he cannot carry with him at once. But the Bishop of O. will have his eyes about him."[81]

The approach of winter was signaled by a snowfall on Sunday, 12 December. Newman was in a reflective mood about the council and its likely outcome. He jotted down under nine headings some highly important notes on the question of the definition of papal infallibility. He kept them strictly for his private reference. They were set down in the way one would set down points for meditation or for an examen during a retreat. Though they were never published, one or other of them showed up in some form in the dozens of letters in which Newman treated or touched upon the subject of papal infallibility between 1870 and 1875.

The notes are as follows:

1. I have ever held the doctrine of the Pope's infallibility, but vaguely. *Why then not wish it defined*[?]
2. and more effectively, because vaguely[.] I doubt whether you do not lessen it by defining it.
3. Because you put it in *limits.* As it is there is nothing, when he *has done* it which does not stand.
4. What riles so many Catholics, is to have to believe as a *whole* dogma, what they would grant in each separate act.
5. I doubt whether the Immaculate Conception and the Assumption, being *defined,* will ultimately increase *devotion,* or not rather limit it.

80. See 5 December 1869, *The Letters and Diaries,* 24:383.
81. Newman to William Monsell, 9 December 1869, *The Letters and Diaries,* 24:383. An indication of the extent to which Newman lived from day to day far from the great world is evident in the Newman–Monsell correspondence through late 1869–early 1870. The council usually took second place in Newman's letters to reports of various small illnesses and other difficulties that Monsell's son, Gaston, was having as a boarding pupil of the Oratory school.

6. "Quieta non movenda." In the early Church they were *obliged* to define because of Arius etc.

7. But see what a large controversy they opened—2 or 3 centuries. There is another reason for not defining now, because you cannot do it at once. *This* is what I say in answer to "If you believe why not wish it defined?"

8. The increase of scoffers—the throwing back of inquirers.

9. "Save the church, O my Fathers, from a danger as great as any that has happened to it."[82]

After the council Newman would appeal to various of his works as evidence of his consistent belief in papal infallibility, but the works cited show, in most instances as he says here, that he held it "vaguely." It is difficult to know whether Newman's last point in the notes above was a rhetorical flourish or a deeply-felt conviction. If the latter, it is hard to see how some commentators can so surely place him in the camp of those who believed placidly in the dogma. Newman knew well the story of the tumultuous controversies that had characterized doctrinal disputes in the early Church. He had also a good knowledge of the subsequent history of the Church. Yet on 12 December 1869, he would fear the agitation for the definition as a great danger, as great as any of the major dangers that the Church had faced in its long history.

In mid-December, Newman was drawn into yet another inquiry involving papal infallibility from someone who was considering entrance into the Catholic Church. Writing his twentieth letter that day, Newman was frank. "I have long held," he wrote to J. F. Seccombe,

> the Infallibility of the Pope as a private or theological opinion—but I never have attempted to bring anyone into the Church by means of it, for I hold it principally because others whom I know hold it, as I may hold many doctrines which are not defined by the Church, as being pious to hold or agreeable to general sentiment.
>
> But if I am asked to defend it logically and prove it—I don't profess to be able—and I don't expect it will ever be made an article of faith. It did not bring me into the Church. . . . My own reasons for becoming a Catholic I have given in my Essay on Development of doctrine [sic]. Should I be able to find a copy, I will gladly offer it for your acceptance, if you think it may be of use to you—but, though I hold the Pope's Infallibility as most likely, and as having the suffrages of most people in this day, I cannot defend it in a set argument, and never would use it as the instrument of bringing inquirers into the Church.[83]

The year closed with Newman still hard at work on the *Grammar of Assent* and with his annual thanks to his close friend, W. J. Copeland,

---

82. Newman "Notes," 12 December 1869, *The Letters and Diaries,* 24:378, n. 1.
83. Newman to J. F. Seccombe, 14 December 1869, *The Letters and Diaries,* 24:390.

who had been his curate at Littlemore, for his yearly present of a Christmas turkey.

Newman follows news of the proceedings at Rome with interest and heightened concern

The new year had hardly begun when Newman was brought once more to the topic of papal infallibility. Again the correspondent was J. F. Seccombe, and Newman patiently responded to him a further time, taking in general the same line he had followed in his letter three weeks previously:

> As to the Pope's infallibility I have no difficulty about it myself, and have no objections to others (if they can) making it *the* argument by which they enter the Church, for there must be a liberty to such things, but for myself, though it were defined de fide by the present Ecumenical Council, that would only change it in my mind from an opinion to a dogma, and not tend to make it a reason before being a Catholic for being a Catholic.[84]

By mid-January the bishops assembled in Rome were just getting down to the actual business of the council. The various elections for representation on the deputations had been completed. Manning was elected to the deputation *de fide,* though the English bishops had favored Thomas Grant of Southwark. Ullathorne was elected to the deputation on discipline.[85] With the work of the council beginning to take shape, first reports of happenings at Rome began to reach England. Newman, who would remain fairly well informed throughout the council of what was taking place in Rome both from direct and indirect sources, had his first opportunity to comment on 14 January in a letter to his devoted friend Ambrose St. John. St. John was visiting Arundel where he had spoken with David Lewis, a friend of Manning. St. John told Newman that Manning felt that a definition would come "but the terms of it would be 'that the Pope is infallible whenever he defines a truth to be in the Depositum Fidei.'" St. John could not resist adding, "Ignatius [Ryder] may well crow a little."[86] Newman was skeptical. He replied to St. John: "Thanks for your news. If that *was* passed (which L. says) the effect *apparently* would

84. Newman to J. F. Seccombe, 2 January 1870, *The Letters and Diaries,* 25:5. Seccombe did not enter the Catholic Church. He had a varied religious career, including ordination as a bishop in 1867 by the "Bishop of Iona," a fact that Seccombe's second wife was unaware of until after his death in 1895.

85. See Butler, *The Vatican Council,* letter of Ullathorne, 18 December 1869, 1:169, in which he says: "All the world knows that most of the nations have got the man they wish except ourselves." See also Hugh Parry Liddon, *Life of Edward Bouverie Pusey* (London and New York: Longmans, Green, and Co., 1897), Pusey to Newman, 28 January 1870, 4:189, in which Pusey shows his discouragement over the election to the *Deputatio de Fide* of Manning, while Darboy, archbishop of Paris, and Dupanloup were passed over.

86. Ambrose St. John to Newman, January 1870, *The Letters and Diaries,* 25:8, n. 1.

be to cut off from the subject matter of *Church* Infallibility all but the depositum—for the Pope cannot have less than the Church has, if he has infallibility at all. This makes me think it impossible that the decree can take that shape, but, if it did, it would be the very view which I have from the first insisted on, and which Ignatius has with much learning advocated. But how will they deal with Honorius! for *his* letters were on the de fide."[87]

Two days later Newman was dealing with the council again. On the same day he announced to W. J. Copeland that, though some corrections remained to be made, he had essentially finished the *Grammar of Assent.*[88] In a letter to another of his longtime friends, James Hope-Scott, Newman gave an account of the proceedings at Rome. It was not accurate in every respect, but it indicates that Newman's sources were fairly sure. "As to the Council," Newman said,

> as far as I can make out, it stands thus:—Two hundred Bishops, many of them distinguished men, stand out; 400 or 500 have taken the popular view—but in this way. Manning found himself with perhaps a smaller number than Mgr. Dupanloup. A middle party arose, eclipsing the 2 extremes, as it was sure to do. This middle party was for a compromise. Mgr. Manning has thrown himself upon or into this middle party, joining them and raising the terms of the compromise—and in this way, I suspect, the full 400 or 500 are made up. The terms he is trying for are that "the Pope is inerrable in matters *de fide*"—this is *very far* short of Ward's wishes or Manning's self, but further than Mgr Dupanloup would grant. It has another difficulty. Since you cannot make a division in the Pope's divine gift, and say he is infallible *only in part* of the things in which the *Church* is infallible, to pass a decree that the Pope is infallible in matters *de fide* is to say that in all matters *not* de fide, there is *no where* any gift of infallibility—but this is contrary to the Gallican notion, which, lodging the gift in the Church, *not* the Pope, *enlarges* the subject matter of the gift, taking in, for instance, infallible condemnation of *books*. Therefore, tho' I know Manning's proposition is what I have said, still *it* can't pass. Time is everything—but the Ultras are hurrying on.[89]

In a letter to William Monsell several days later, Newman was showing cautious optimism. "From what I hear," he said, "the proceedings of the Bishop of O[rléans] etc. are very successful. They have encouraged the formation of a middle party. And I am told that Manning is in the way to lose influence. The Council is to be postponed in the summer—and that again is a great thing—for *time* is everything."[90]

87. Newman to Ambrose St. John, 14 January 1870, *The Letters and Diaries,* 25:8.
88. Newman to W. J. Copeland, 16 January 1870, *The Letters and Diaries,* 25:9.
89. Newman to James Hope-Scott, 16 January 1870, *The Letters and Diaries,* 25:9–10.
90. Newman to William Monsell, 26 January 1870, *The Letters and Diaries,* 25:15.

From the time that first reports of the council began to circulate in the mid-1860s, E. B. Pusey had carried on a regular correspondence with Newman about what was likely to take place when the council met. He had some hope that the council might signal a way to reunion between the Churches and he thought that the Ritualist party of the Anglican Church was in an especially favorable position to act as an agent for getting the Roman Church to consider some steps toward unity. Early in 1870, Pusey published his essay *Is Healthful Reunion Impossible? A Second Letter to the Very Rev. J. H. Newman.* Pusey looked to Newman for information on the proceedings at Rome and he relied on Newman to suggest to him which bishops might appreciate having a copy of Pusey's book. Newman told Pusey on 26 January: "It will be a great point to have the Council extended over another year. I hear that Manning is over shooting his mark, and losing influence. He has a wonderful gift of ingratiating himself with people—but still it is a difficult thing to retain that kind of influence. On the other hand I hear that leading men on the other side cannot foresee how the event will be. If it is true that Döllinger does not acknowledge the Council of Florence, that will be in favour of those who think with Manning. It seems a revolutionary doctrine." In a postscript to this letter, Newman showed that he was relying for information on sources other than the newspapers. "I hear," he said, "on the first authority that the notion of 500 being ready to sign the petition [in favor of the definition] which was in the papers, is a great exaggeration. I knew the exact number who had signed it but forget it; it was much under 200 perhaps not more than 140. As many as 110 had in writing protested against their act."[91]

In a reply to Newman two days later, Pusey followed up on Newman's unflattering references to Manning. "Manning's is a strange lot," Pusey

91. Newman to E. B. Pusey, 26 January 1870, *The Letters and Diaries*, 25:15–16. But see Butler, *The Vatican Council*, 1:204, who says that 380 signed the main petition in favor of the definition and that about 100 others signed various separate petitions which also in essence called for the definition. Butler says also that a petition asking that the subject not be introduced gained 140 signatures. Odo Russell had a slightly different report: "The Infallibilists or Definitionists . . . drew up their petition in favour of the dogmatic definition of Papal infallibility . . . which, it is said, has been signed by more than 400 bishops. This demonstration was met by the international committee in their turn by a counter petition against the definition of the dogma, to which they say they have obtained nearly 200 signatures . . . ." Blakiston, *The Roman Question*, 304. See also *Collectio Conciliorum Recentiorum Ecclesiae Universae* (hereafter cited as Mansi), ed. Ludovicus Petit and Joannes Baptista Martin, Tomus Decimus Quintus, Sacrosancti Oecumenici Concilii Vaticani, Pars Secunda, Acta Synodalia (Congregatio XXX-L, pars prima), (Arnhem and Leipzig: Société Nouvelle d'Edition de la Collection Mansi [H. Welter]: 1926) 51:639–77, where petitions in favor of the definition are given. Manning and Bishop Grant of Southwark signed petitions in favor of the definition. See Mansi, 51:651 and 658. Petitions against the definition are found in Mansi, 51:677–87. Among those signing petitions against the definition were Newman's friends, Errington, Clifford, and Moriarty of Kerry. See Mansi, 51:682.

believed. "With, I should have thought but a very moderate share of learning, by throwing himself into the tide, to seem to be at the head of a movement, which should revolutionise the Church. It is a mysterious lot, one which one should not like for oneself."[92]

Newman's letter of 28 January to Bishop Ullathorne

The day of Pusey's reply, 28 January, was a significant date in Newman's involvement with the Vatican Council. Indeed it would turn out to be one of the most important dates of his later life. It was the day of his celebrated letter, decrying to his bishop, William Ullathorne, the plans afoot at Rome to define papal infallibility. Despite the many letters Newman wrote dealing with the council and the definition, it is the letter of 28 January that will forever be attached to his name as showing his position on whether the council should take up the great question. All of the major biographers and commentators quote from it in full or at length, and its dramatic, ringing language, its vivid, soaring phrases have been cited repeatedly by Newman scholars and others interested in the history of the Vatican Council. Many interpreters have looked for ways to minimize his fears and the words he used to express them, not always satisfactorily. It was, as was often the case with Newman, one of several letters he wrote that day and one of several that dealt with the council.

Of the extant letters for 28 January the briefest is to Father Herbert Vaughan. We do not know which letter Newman wrote first on 28 January, the letter to Vaughan or the letter to Ullathorne. It is at least interesting to speculate that the Vaughan letter came first and put Newman "in the mood" for the impassioned rhetoric of the letter to Ullathorne. Vaughan, who was to be Manning's successor at Westminster, was a determined infallibilist and an ally of Manning. From November 1868 he controlled the *Tablet* and made of that journal (and its 1870 supplement *The Vatican*) an undisguised promoter of the views of the Ultramontane party.[93] Vaughan had written to Newman on 22 January. Newman could not have been glad to hear from Vaughan, whose views he abhorred, but Vaughan's request of Newman made it even less likely that Newman's response would be gracious. Vaughan wrote:

---

92. E. B. Pusey to Newman, 28 January 1870, in Liddon, *Life of Pusey,* 4:189.

93. Vaughan's biographer speaks as follows of the *Tablet* under Vaughan: "The peculiar policy of the *Tablet* at this period made many enemies. Its dogmatism, its intolerance of all opposition, its impatience of the attitude of those who dreaded the consequences of a Definition, and above all its readiness to cry down and discredit its opponents by suggestions of disloyalty or by open accusations of Gallicanism, alienated the sympathy of a multitude of moderate men." J. G. Snead-Cox, *The Life of Cardinal Vaughan* (London: Burns and Oates, 1910) 1:231.

We are endeavouring to get the enclosed Petition [in favor of the defini-
tion] as widely signed as possible and the Heads of Religious Orders and
Congregations are being asked—and so far their answers have been most
favourable—to lend the influence of their encouragement to the movement.
In bringing the matter under your notice and soliciting your signature and
a word of approval, I feel how efficiently we should be promoting the cause
we have at heart; and this will be, should you approve the movement, my
sufficient apology for troubling you with these few lines.[94]

Newman's reply was distant and caustic. "I am," he said, "not partial
to what you call 'movements—' In the Catholic Church I consider rest
to be the better thing. And, when I do 'move,' it is for the most part and
ordinarily at the suggestion of my own ecclesiastical Superiors—certainly
not on the interposition of strangers. I think it best to be frank.'"[95] It is
interesting to note that Newman opposes his belief in the need for "rest"
to Vaughan's being in favor of "movement" concerning the definition
of papal infallibility. In the months ahead Newman would frequently in-
voke the need for rest and quiet in terms of the controversies over the
definition. The notion of rest was for him another way of saying that the
definition was inopportune at best, that the Church must take its time
in making such a decision, that it must not be hurried on by agitation,
campaigns, and lobbying. The long view was needed. "Quieta non
movenda," as Newman had written in his notes several weeks earlier.

In addition to the well-known letter to Ullathorne, Newman on 28
January wrote also to another bishop who would figure very prominently
in his correspondence on the infallibility issue. Despite his years as rector
of the Catholic University of Dublin, Newman had never been at ease with
members of the Irish episcopate. He had no real friends among them with
the exception of David Moriarty, bishop of Kerry. Moriarty was also notable among the Irish bishops for his opposition to the definition. Only three
other bishops, including the redoubtable John MacHale of Tuam, joined
him in this opposition.[96] Moriarty's views on the definition were in many
ways similar to Newman's own. He decried the tactics of its promoters
and he thought it would be catastrophic to the Church, especially outside
of what he saw as the narrow Latin world.[97] But at the same time he wanted

94. Father Herbert Vaughan to Newman, 22 January 1870, *The Letters and Diaries,*
25:20, n. 5.
    95. Newman to Father Herbert Vaughan, 28 January 1870, *The Letters and Diaries,*
25:20.
    96. For an account of the Irish bishops' participation in the First Vatican Council, see
Emmet Larkin, *The Roman Catholic Church and the Home Rule Movement in Ireland,
1870–1874* (Chapel Hill and London: The University of North Carolina Press, 1990) 3–26.
    97. See Bishop David Moriarty to Newman, 3 February 1870, *The Letters and Diaries,*
25:17, n. 3.

to remain loyal and respectful toward the Holy See. At base he was against
the definition; in practice he settled for being an inopportunist. Moriarty
was one of Newman's principal sources of information as to what was
happening in Rome. Newman's letter of 28 January to Moriarty repeats
in many ways the sentiments of his more celebrated letter to Ullathorne
of the same day:

> The fears of some unknown definition, when everything is *at rest* is secretly
> distressing numbers. What heresy calls for a decision? What have we done
> that we can't be let alone? Hitherto definitions de fide were grave necessi-
> ties, not devotional outpourings. Can there be a clearer reductio ad absur-
> dum of the animus of the talked of definition, than the proposition to pass
> it by acclamation. Have the men who entertain such a project any regard
> at all for the souls of their brethren? . . . Where is the Arius or Nestorius,
> whose heresy makes it imperative for the Holy Church to speak. What has
> M. Veuillot, or the Civiltà not to answer for, if a secret unbelief is creeping
> over the hearts of our brethren, at the rumour of an event which I trust
> will never be realized!
>
> From what you say to Father St. John,[98] I know that in substance these
> are your feelings, and I earnestly pray that all will end well according to
> them. What a load of scandal is being exhumed against the Holy See on
> account of these precious editors, who think themselves so devout to it.[99]

Newman on 28 January undoubtedly thought of Herbert Vaughan among
the "precious editors."

Bishop Ullathorne had written to Newman on 20 January. He provided
Newman with a general description of what had happened since the council
opened, though he was very circumspect, careful about observing the oath
each bishop had sworn to observe the secrecy of the council's proceedings. It is not clear if something in Ullathorne's letter immediately inspired
Newman's passionate response. On the whole Ullathorne kept to the
moderate, balanced language that characterized his many letters to friends
written from Rome during the council. He did make the following statement which refers to movements, a word that, as has already been shown,
tended to elicit Newman's ire toward the infallibilists. Ullathorne wrote:
"You will hear a good deal of movements outside of the Council, and
indeed, I wish there was less of them; but they certainly began on what
may be called the "ultra" side, which naturally led to efforts at counter-
organization. But everything will find its level, though this may require
a little time. Many reputations will be marred and made in this Council,

---

98. Moriarty had stopped at Birmingham on his way to Rome and had spoken with
St. John, Newman being away.

99. Emphasis supplied. Newman to Bishop David Moriarty, 28 January 1870, *The Letters
and Diaries,* 25:17.

and the true metal, tried in the fire of patience, will come out at last."[100]

Newman's reply of 28 January may have been less a response to what Ullathorne had written than an occasion for Newman to express a whole host of thoughts on the council and the definition that had been building up within him over the past several months, indeed over the past several years. Not only did Newman respect Ullathorne, but he deferred to him as his immediate superior in the Church. A letter to Ullathorne gave him not just an excuse to have his say but an opportunity to do this on the high and unassailable ground of a privileged communication with his bishop. Students of Newman will ever puzzle over whether Newman thought about the possibility of the sentiments of his letter to Ullathorne becoming in some way public. Newman was careful to keep records of his correspondence and perhaps foresaw that what he said to Ullathorne would some day be known to the wide world. He apparently thought that Ullathorne would be sympathetic to his views and might share them, at least indirectly, with other bishops. All of this to say that Newman, while sincere in his belief that he was taking a most responsible course, a confidential letter to his bishop, may have written with some sense of others listening in, whether in his own day or at a later time.

In the famous 28 January letter to Ullathorne, Newman took up again the theme of "rest" that had run like a thread through the day's correspondence: "When we are all at rest, and have no doubts, and at least practically, not to say doctrinally, hold the Holy Father to be infallible, suddenly there is thunder in the clear sky, and we are told to prepare for something we know not what to try our faith we know not how. No impending danger is to be averted, but a great difficulty is to be created. Is this the proper work for an Ecumenical Council?" As he would do over and over in the months ahead, Newman was careful to separate out his own private position from a strong opposition to the definition on the basis of its dire effects on others: "As to myself personally, please God, I do not expect any trial at all; but I cannot help suffering with the various souls which are suffering, and I look with anxiety at the prospect of having to defend decisions, which may not be difficult to my private judgment, but may be most difficult to maintain logically in the face of historical facts." This last statement is especially significant in view of the many letters that Newman was called upon to write in the years ahead to explain the definition.

As Newman continued, his language became even more heightened, and in fact some of the more vivid phrases that follow would come back to haunt him. "What," he all but cried out,

---

100. Butler, *The Vatican Council,* 1:211; the full text of Ullathorne's letter is given on 209–12.

have we done to be treated, as the faithful never were treated before? When
has definition of doctrine de fide been a luxury of devotion, and not a stern
painful necessity? Why should an aggressive insolent faction[101] be allowed
to "make the heart of the just to mourn, whom the Lord hath not made
sorrowful?" Why can't we be let alone, when we have pursued peace, and
thought no evil? I assure you, my dear Lord, some of the truest minds are
driven one way and another . . . ; one day determining to give up all theology as a bad job, and recklessly to believe henceforth almost that the Pope
is impeccable; at another tempted to believe all the worst which a book like
Janus says; others doubting about the capacity possessed by Bishops, drawn
from all corners of the earth, to judge what is fitting for European society,
and then again angry with the Holy See for listening to the flattery of a
clique of Jesuits, Redemptorists, and converts.

Nor did Newman forget the interest of Pusey and other Anglicans of
Tractarian views in the outcome of the council. "And then again," he
wrote, "the blight which is falling upon the multitude of Anglican ritualists etc who themselves perhaps, at least their leaders, may never become Catholics, but who are leavening the various English denominations
and parties (far beyond their own range) with principles and sentiments
tending towards their ultimate absorption in the Catholic Church."
Newman's bleak attitude toward the council carried over into another
topic at the conclusion of his letter. He spoke of the *Grammar of Assent,*
a book he had attempted "three or four times in the last 20 years." "I
have had no confidence," he confessed, "that I should be able to complete it. I have done so—but now that it is done, I think it will disappoint
most people."[102]
The twenty-eighth of January, as were most of Newman's days, was
given over partly to his vast correspondence, but he would long live with
the consequences of this day, and new doubts and suspicions would come
his way because of his strong letter to his bishop.

Newman is in receipt of firsthand information from Rome and shares it with his friends

Both Bishop Moriarty and Bishop Ullathorne responded to Newman
within several days, an evidence of the efficient postal service between
England and what seemed to many in England the deeper reaches of the
Continent. Moriarty's letter of 3 February was not meant to reassure New-

101. Newman, who did not keep a good copy of the letter to Ullathorne, appears to have
written "an aggressive insolent faction." In the controversy that followed this phrase was
variously quoted, and Newman himself was not consistent.
102. Newman to Bishop William Ullathorne, 28 January 1870, *The Letters and Diaries,*
25:18–20.

man or to chide him for groundless fears. Rather Moriarty wrote: "Never before did I feel anxiety for the Church. Now it is all but a torment . . . the loss of souls who are near and dear to me—the fear of schism and of secret heresy make me miserable night and day." "The majority," Moriarty reported, "represents the curia Romana—Spain—Belgium—Ireland—South America etc. etc. It is composed of men who have not come into conflict with the unbelieving mind or in contact with the intellectual mind of the time." Moriarty concluded his letter to Newman with a report of a recent audience he had had with Pius IX, who, with some evidence of his well-known playfulness but more with indications of annoyance, had blessed the bishop of Kerry with the words, "Dominus benedicat te et *dirigat*."[103]

Ullathorne replied to Newman's letter on 4 February. He explained his own position on the definition and tried to assure Newman that such a moderate, carefully balanced approach was the only one that could in the end succeed with the bishops. Ullathorne began:

> Your letter received today, and written with true tact, and deep feeling of the position created by the zealots, but repeats with force what many here are feeling, as well as yourself. But I think I may venture to say that the zealots are doomed to future confusion. Some are in fact beginning to find it already.
>
> As the question of which you speak has not yet been even breathed within the Council Chamber, I may venture to give you some information as to its actual position outside of it.
>
> Cardinal Bilio (President of the special deputation *de Fide*) informed an American Archbishop, who informed me, only two days since, that although a Schema *de Summo Pontifice* had been prepared, it had been decided to put it aside, and not to present it, in so far as that important question of the infallibility was concerned. But when Maret and Dupanloup came out strongly in antagonism, then it was thought desirable to do something. . . .
>
> I, of course, do not forget that one of these prelates was roused up by excesses, nor do I forget who roused him.

After this reference to his colleague, the Archbishop of Westminster, Bishop Ullathorne continued in a personal vein: "For my part, I have quietly, and in private maintained that I should not oppose a calm and moderate definition, *provided* it was duly balanced by strengthening the authority of the Episcopate, provided also it was duly limited so as to save us from enthusiastic and fantastic interpretations. And I have insisted on the importance of reviving the old canon in the Sexto, against laymen lead-

---

103. Bishop David Moriarty to Newman, 3 February 1870, *The Letters and Diaries,* 25:17, n. 3.

ing in theological writing and publishing.''[104] Having made his own position clear, Ullathorne then attempted to give a wider view, but circumspectly: "One Cardinal assured me that, though in consequence of court intrigues and anti-papal writings, something must now come in, yet it would be proposed in such very moderate terms, that it will not fail to meet the wishes of all parties. . . . My general knowledge enables me to say that this, amongst other things, implies the omission of the word infallible, and I apprehend also the limitation to some such terms as the obedience due Pontifical decisions and their irreversibility. Ullathorne made one further attempt to calm Newman's fears. "Be assured, my dear friend," he wrote, "that, whatever mischief is doing outside by our own Newspapers, to which so many of us are alive, moderation will be the upshot in the Council.''[105] Newman was not entirely persuaded by Ullathorne's assurances. He replied almost immediately, saying:

> I feel the extreme kindness of your long letter, which is a very tranquillizing one. The only anxiety I have is about a thing, which, before you left us, you said was impossible;—lest a definition should not have *full time* given it. You speak of the matter soon coming before the Fathers of the Council— now you said last year that a subject, after *passing,* came up again, something like the three readings in Parliament. But there will be a great effort to get through the matter, and, though the Fathers have torn to shreds, as you say, certain schemata, yet all parties will wish to remove out of the way so terrible a contention, and to proceed to other matters. The only hope of those you call zealots lies in expedition. They first wished to acclaim, now they wish a swift definition.
>
> Since I last wrote, a document in Latin has been inserted in the Times— purporting to be a *compromise,* and speaking of the "judicia" of the Holy See as *universally* demanding an interior assent.[106] This is just what Ward wishes. There was another in the Pall Mall Gazette of yesterday giving the *Church* infallibility, not only in matters of the Depositum, and in all matters *necessary for the integrity* of the Depositum. This would be intelligible

104. Ullathorne's views on W. G. Ward were, of course, well known to Newman.

105. Bishop William Ullathorne to Newman, 4 February 1870, *The Letters and Diaries,* 25:25-27.

106. *The Times,* 2 February 1870, 10. In addition to the Latin document, "Schema Pro Infallibilitate Romani Pontificis Ex Principiis Jam Ab Ecclesia Universa Receptis Logice Clareque Definienda," *The Times* of 2 February also carried on p. 10 a long report from its Rome correspondent which took the position that the "compromise" was in fact a ploy by the dominant infallibilist party to take in those who were espousing a middle course. The writer said: "To one who has any acquaintance with the different shades and hues in the feelings of various sections, with the divergences existing in various quarters, it cannot but be manifest that this clandestinely concocted and privately circulated document is not the emanation of a frank impulse towards compromise, but the inspiration of an insidious spirit at sowing discord by means of, indeed, utterly inconsistent professions, but for each of which there is some particular ear in view."

when given to the Church, but, when given to the Pope, it would enable him without taking advice or other condition to say that a condemnation of the Copernican System was necessary for the depositum.

However, you have said to me all that need be said. And we must have a little more faith than we have—*and rest in quiet confidence* that all must turn out well.[107]

Newman must surely have thought that this would bring to a close the correspondence that Ullathorne had initiated on 20 January.

Early in February, Newman's help was again sought by a woman who was distressed at the thought of a definition of papal infallibility. Lady Henrietta Chatterton was a convert who had been received into the Church by Newman in 1865. Newman wrote to her on 3 February. He tried to assure her that her fears were groundless, that no definition would come from the council.

I have ever held the infallibility of the Pope myself, since I have been a Catholic—but I have ever felt also that others had a right, if they pleased, to deny it—and I will not believe, till the event takes place, that a Council will make the belief obligatory. If it takes place, I shall say that Providence has ways and purposes for His Church, which at present are hid from our eyes—but that [it] is His Blessed Will for a time to check the success of His Church upon the external world.

He often moves in a mysterious way—Before hand, we can often pronounce what seems *likely*—and I say it is most unlikely that the Infallibility of the Pope will be determined at the Council. —We cannot say *more.*

Newman also tried to discredit the popular notion that the *Syllabus* was to be declared a matter of faith at the council and in doing so he gave a revealing glimpse into his own youthful attitude toward nineteenth-century political liberalism. "As to the Syllabus," Newman wrote, "I think it will not be passed by the Council—but really if you ask me, there is little in it which when I was young, the Tory party did not hold, and which I did not hold myself."[108]

In addition to Pusey, others of Newman's Anglican friends looked to him for information, or perhaps for an informed interpretation, of what was happening in Rome. On 22 February, in a letter to J. R. Bloxam who had been a curate at Littlemore from 1837 to 1840, Newman was careful to avoid expressing his own feelings on the possibility of a definition at

107. Newman to Bishop William Ullathorne, 9 February 1870, *The Letters and Diaries,* 25:27-28. Emphasis in the final sentence supplied.

108. Newman to Lady Henrietta Chatterton, 3 February 1870, *The Letters and Diaries,* 25:23. Newman makes a similar reference to the Tory principles of his youth in the *Letter to the Duke of Norfolk.* See *A Letter Addressed to His Grace The Duke of Norfolk On Occasion of Mr. Gladstone's Recent* Expostulation (London: B. M. Pickering, 1875) as reprinted in *Newman and Gladstone: The Vatican Decrees* (Notre Dame, Ind.: University of Notre Dame Press, 1962) 140.

the council. Bloxam in a letter of 19 February, congratulating Newman on his sixty-ninth birthday (21 February), had said "in common Clerical Society, if the Roman Council is mentioned, some one unknown to you, starts up and says, 'I wonder what Dr. Newman thinks of it.' "[109] Perhaps in consequence of this picture of Anglicans eager to have his views, Newman began his reply to Bloxam by giving a somewhat remote appreciation of how he thought the bishops in Rome would be affected in their future ministry by the experience of coming to know other bishops from all over the world and the problems of their particular Churches firsthand. "As to this Council," Newman wrote to Bloxam,

> about *facts* I know little more than you do; but as to my expectations, I think untold good will come of it—first, as is obvious, in bringing into personal acquaintance men from the most distant parts. The moral power of the Church will be almost squared by this fact alone. Next, each part will know the state of things in other parts of Christendom, and the minds of all the Prelates will be enlarged, as well as their hearts. They will learn sympathy and reliance in each other. Further, the authorities at Rome will learn a great deal which they did not know of, and since the Italian apprehension is most imaginative and vivid, this will be a wonderful gain. It must have a great influence on the election of the next Pope. . . .
>
> They have come to Rome with antagonistic feelings, they will depart in the peace of God. I don't think much will come of this movement for Papal Infallibility—though something very mild may be passed.

At the close of his letter Newman thought better of leaving Bloxam with the idea that his own views on the possibility of a definition were so olympian and detached. He added in a postscript: "You must not suppose from any thing I have said that I do not sympathise with the Bishop of Orleans etc—for I do."[110]

From the close of January through the month of February a good deal of Newman's time had been taken up with letters on the council. And there were also visitors with whom Newman surely spent time discussing what was taking place in Rome. On 5 February, Dr. Russell of Maynooth was at the Oratory and exactly a week later William Monsell came from London to stay with Newman during the weekend.

Newman's fears about the council intensified in the late winter of 1870. On 2 March he wrote to Edward Bellasis: "We are all in great anxiety about the definitions of the Council. Of course in [sic] it cannot go beyond the will of God, but the spirit of many of the prime leaders is to me simply intolerable, and is *not* according to God's will surely."[111] But

109. J. R. Bloxam to Newman, 19 February 1870, *The Letters and Diaries,* 25:37, n. 1.
110. Newman to J. R. Bloxam, 22 February 1870, *The Letters and Diaries,* 25:37.
111. Newman to Edward Bellasis, 2 March 1870, *The Letters and Diaries,* 25:43.

as happened not infrequently in this period, Newman tempered his remarks when again, on 11 March, he tried to say calming things to Lady Chatterton: "The Archbishop of Malines [Victor Dechamps] is no historical reader—and cannot answer historical objections. Fr. Gratry takes a rather one sided view, but he brings out great truths. I think it impossible that the violent party, the zealots as I believe they call them, can have their way—whatever is passed dogmatically in the Council will come very short indeed of their hopes. I could desire nothing to be done, but whatever is done will be very neutral in character."[112]

An important letter from this period giving a different view on Newman's attitude toward the possibility of the pope's infallibility being defined was written on 16 February to Richard Holt Hutton, the editor of the *Spectator*, who was corresponding with Newman at this time with a view toward possibly becoming a Roman Catholic. Toward the close of a long letter Newman wrote very revealingly: "What the genius of the Church cannot bear is, changes in thought being hurried, abrupt, violent— out of tenderness to souls. . . . The great thing is to move all together and then the change, as geological changes, must be very slow. Hence we come to be accused of duplicity—I mean, the cleverer men see what is coming, yet from charity to others (and diffidence in themselves) don't speak out." After this oblique reference to the great excitement over the council and his own determination not to be drawn out publicly on the council's proceedings, Newman spoke directly of the definition. "But, while I think the Church might define doctrines to be true," he wrote, "which it has not yet defined, I hold strongly the distinction between dogma and theological opinion—and I am strongly opposed to the present attempt to make the Pope's infallibility a dogma, because I see no cause, that is, no sufficient motive, for doing so—and because I think we have difficulties enough on our hands, without burdening ourselves with a whole load of historical objections."

Again, Newman had spoken more strongly and openly about his opposition to the definition to someone who was not a member of the Church than he was willing to do in a number of letters to fellow Catholics, including his friends. Newman closed his letter on a note characteristic of so many of his letters on the theological issues surrounding the definition of papal infallibility. He wrote: "I am going to ask you to let this letter be 'private'. I think that all I have said will *stand*—and you may use it as you please—and find what other Catholics say—but I am no theologian—my memory is bad."[113]

112. Newman to Lady Henrietta Chatterton, 11 March 1870, *The Letters and Diaries,* 25:47.
113. Newman to Richard Holt Hutton, 16 February 1870, *The Letters and Diaries,* 25:31–32.

As the letter to Ullathorne gradually becomes known, Newman is under pressure to give a full and public exposition of his views

The council entered dramatically and unavoidably into Newman's life in mid-March, and the calm remove of his life at the Oratory was at least for several weeks upset when he was put on the defensive about various expressions and opinions in his confidential letter of 28 January to Ullathorne. The story of how Newman's letter became public will probably never be known. Ullathorne lent it with all kinds of cautions to several other bishops at Rome, including Newman's friends, Errington and Clifford. In many ways Clifford, the most determined anti-infallibilist of the English bishops, appears to have had the most reasons for breaking the strict confidence imposed by the always cautious Ullathorne. But there is some surprising evidence that Ullathorne himself was at least indirectly responsible. Certainly in lending it to bishops, such as Archbishop Connolly of Halifax, beyond Newman's small circle of friends, Ullathorne had taken a chance.[114]

Newman had no advance warning that his letter was to become public. Along with many other people in England he found references to it in the 14 March issue of the *Standard*. The *Standard's* report said: " . . . it will interest many people to know that Dr. Newman has written to his Bishop at Rome, Dr. Ullathorne, stigmatising the promoters of Papal In-

114. See *The Letters and Diaries,* 25:54, n. 1. Alfred Plummer, writing in July 1870 of a conversation he had had with Döllinger, seems to place the blame for the betrayal of Newman's letter on Clifford: "We talked of Dr. Newman's celebrated letter about the 'insolent aggressive faction' which was driving all things to extremes in the Roman Church. This letter written to Bishop Ullathorne of Birmingham, was (it was said) shown by him to Bishop Clifford of Clifton, and by him sent to England where it appeared in the *Standard.*" Alfred Plummer, *Conversations With Dr. Döllinger 1870-1890,* intro. and notes by Robrecht Boudens, with the collaboration of Leo Kenis (Leuven: University Press, 1985) 4.
Manning obtained a copy of the letter through Odo Russell, but there is no evidence to suggest that Manning had anything to do with the letter's becoming public. See Purcell, *Life of Cardinal Manning,* 2:454; see also Blakiston, *The Roman Question,* 392, quoting a letter of Odo Russell to the Earl of Clarendon of 15 February 1870, in which Russell, transmitting a copy of Newman's 28 January letter writes: "I have repeatedly asserted that many opportunists [Russell uses the term 'Opportunists' where most commentators use 'Inopportunists'] who oppose the definition of Papal Infallibility would submit their judgement once the Dogma has been decreed by the Council. As a proof of my opinion I enclose confidentially a copy of a private Letter from Dr. Newman to Bishop Ullathorne, which curiously illustrates the power Rome can exercise over the minds of the faithful." See also G. Swisshelm, "Newman and the Vatican Definition of Papal Infallibility," *St. Meinrad Essays* 12 (1960) 70-88. In a letter of 23 March 1873, Newman said with reference to the 28 January 1870 letter, "and in my letter to my Bishop which was stolen from his custody. . . ." There is no evidence to indicate why Newman three years later called the letter "stolen." See *The Letters and Diaries,* ed. Charles Stephen Dessain and Thomas Gornall, S.J. (Oxford: The Clarendon Press, 1974) 26:281.

fallibility as an insolent, aggressive faction, praying that God may avert this threatened peril from the Church, and affirming his conviction that, if He does not see fit to do so, it is because he has chosen to delay the Church's ultimate triumph for centuries."[115] Newman quickly informed Ullathorne that he was not responsible for giving the *Standard* any knowledge of his 28 January letter. On the day the report appeared in the newspaper, Newman wrote to Ullathorne: "I lose no time in sending you a line, in order to assure you that the following passage in to day's Standard has neither directly nor indirectly come from this House. No one saw my letter to Your Lordship but Father St. John—and neither he nor I have opened our mouths to any one about its contents."[116]

Newman also lost no time in writing to the Editor of the *Standard*. In the event it would have been better had he waited to consider calmly the *Standard's* report and to check its accuracy against the records he kept of his correspondence. In his letter of 15 March, Newman said:

> . . . I am bound to disavow what you have imputed to me, viz.—that I have "written to my bishop at Rome, Dr. Ullathorne, stigmatising the promoters of Papal Infallibility, as an insolent, aggressive faction."
>
> That I deeply deplore the policy, the spirit, the measures of various persons, lay and ecclesiastical, who are urging the definition of that theological opinion, I have neither intention nor wish to deny; just the contrary. But, on the other hand, I have a firm belief, and have had all along, that a Greater Power than that of any man or set of men will over-rule the deliberations of the Council to the determination of Catholic and Apostolic truth, and that what its Fathers eventually proclaim with one voice will be the Word of God.[117]

The letter to Ullathorne had brought Newman, however unwillingly, into the public controversy over the definition. With his letter to the *Standard* he had revealed beyond the circle of his friends and a few interested inquirers his deep-seated misgivings. The writer of the piece in the *Standard* readily accepted Newman's correction that he had not used the words "an insolent, aggressive faction," but he went on with considerable satisfaction to say: "Be this however, as it may, the public declaration by him for the first time, that he deprecates the affirmation of Papal Infallibility, will afford infinite encouragement to those who are struggling to avert its establishment."[118]

115. *The Letters and Diaries*, 25:54–55, n. 2.

116. Newman to Bishop William Ullathorne, 14 March 1870, *The Letters and Diaries*, 25:53.

117. Newman to the *Standard*, 15 March 1870, *The Letters and Diaries*, 25:55.

118. *The Letters and Diaries*, 18 March 1870, 25:61, n. 1. The *Tablet* for all its difficulties with Newman was sure that not even he could have used the phrase "an aggressive insolent faction." In the issue of 19 March 1870, n.s. 3, 35:350, the following appeared: "The

Within a few days there was trouble on every side. The consequences of the letter to Ullathorne and the reference to it in the *Standard* were growing rapidly. In the main these consequences were unfortunate for Newman. On 21 March, Sir John Simeon wrote from the House of Commons saying that several copies of what was purported to be Newman's letter to Ullathorne were circulating around London and that all of them did in fact contain the phrase "an aggressive, insolent faction." Newman was forced to go back and check the copies he had kept. With considerable dismay he realized that the *Standard* piece on 14 March had been correct. He knew that the only course for him was to admit his error and he did so immediately. On 22 March he wrote to the Editor of the *Standard*: "In answer to the letter of 'The Writer of the Progress of the Council,' I am obliged to say that he is right and I am wrong as to my using the words 'insolent and aggressive faction' in a letter which I wrote to Bishop Ullathorne. I write to make my apologies to him for contradicting him." Having rechecked his drafts and having learned that copies of his letter were circulating in England, Newman took the occasion of writing to the *Standard* to explain various references in his letter which he rightly judged would cause him difficulties, even with his friends. "I will only add," he told the editor, "that when I spoke of a faction I neither meant that great body of bishops who are said to be in favour of the definition of the doctrine nor any ecclesiastical order or society external to the Council. As to the Jesuits, I wish distinctly to state that I have all along separated them in my mind as a body from the movement which I so much deplore. What I meant by a faction, as the letter itself shows, was a collection of persons drawn from various ranks and conditions in the Church."[119]

Newman, who had had good relations with the Jesuits since going out to Rome in 1846 and who counted a number of English Jesuits among his friends, wrote to Father Henry Coleridge on the same day that he wrote acknowledging his mistake to the *Standard*. "I am sorry to say," he said, "I find I *did*, in my private letter to the Bishop, use the words, 'an insolent aggressive faction!' But I am sure you will believe that I had no in-

---

Standard, always too much inclined to indulge in personalities, wished to persuade its readers that a priest and a gentleman, as conspicuous for refinement of taste as for genius and learning, had bluntly described the advocates of the doctrine of infallibility as an 'insolent and aggressive faction.' Yet it might have occurred to the *Standard*, if it had taken time to reflect, that no man in his senses could speak in such terms of the great majority of the Bishops, priests, and faithful in communion with the Church. Our contemporary may be assured that grave men, especially men whose words have so much importance as those of Dr. Newman, do not indulge in outrages of this kind." In the same issue, the *Tablet* printed Newman's letter of 15 March to the *Standard,* 396

119. Newman to the *Standard,* 22 March 1870, *The Letters and Diaries*, 25:61.

tention whatever of aiming at the Society, or its general action, by those words. I was thinking of the Univers, the Civiltà, and the Tablet."[120]

Newman and his friends realized that now that Newman's views had become public, there would be a demand for him to write a more extended exposition of his position, if only to save his reputation from being damaged by promoters of the definition. There had, even before the *Standard* piece, been discussion among Newman's friends on whether he should make his views more public. This discussion had been especially intensified by his letters to Ullathorne and Moriarty on 28 January. Moriarty wrote from Rome on 20 February. He was not, as were several of Newman's lay friends, persuaded that Newman should express his views. Moriarty told Newman, "If it seems good to the Holy Ghost and to the Council that the definition should be made, it would be dangerous to have the public mind prejudiced against it."[121] But Moriarty continued,

> I fear that Maret and Dollinger have done us harm. Moderate men have said to me that they would never have harboured the idea of definition of Papal Infallibility only for those attacks on the Holy See. I know you would write in quite a different tone and sense. . . .
>
> Another reason induces me to dissuade you from publishing. The odium theologicum is fermenting. Men's motives, orthodoxy, character will be assailed. We can not allow *you* to become an object of this angry vituperation.

Moriarty was careful to point out that his reasons for dissuading Newman were shared by others in Rome. "I asked," he said, "Dr. Ullathorne and Dr. Clifford what they would advise you to do. They agree with me that it is better for you not to publish." Before closing Moriarty recounted a conversation that he had had recently with another participant in the council. "Strange to say," he told Newman, "if ever this definition comes you will have contributed much towards it. Your treatise on development has given the key. A Cardinal said the other day—'We must give up the first ten centuries, but the infallibility is an obvious development of the supremacy'."[122] Newman wrote to offer words of encouragement to Moriarty, but he also made it clear that he did not find the cardinal's position congenial with his own. He wrote to Moriarty on 20 March just as the *Standard* incident was showing signs of becoming a most unpleasant crisis:

> I am continually thinking of you and your cause. I look upon you as the special band of confessors, who are doing God's work at this time in a grave crisis; who, I trust, will succeed in your effort, but who cannot really fail—

120. Newman to Father Henry James Coleridge, S.J., 22 March 1870, *The Letters and Diaries,* 25:60.

121. Butler, *The Vatican Council,* 2:30.

122. Bishop David Moriarty to Newman, 20 February 1870, *The Letters and Diaries,* 25:57–58, n. 3, and 25:58, n. 2.

both because you are at the very least diminishing the nature and weight of the blow which is intended by those whom you oppose, and also because your resistance must bear fruit afterwards, even though it fails at the moment. If it be God's will that some definition in favour of the Pope's infallibility is passed, I then shall at once submit—but up to that very moment I shall pray most heartily and earnestly against it. Any how, I cannot bear to think of the tyrannousness and cruelty of its advocates, for tyrannousness and cruelty it will be, though it is successful.

Newman then turned to Moriarty's remarks on development. "As to development," he wrote equably enough, "I am quite aware of what you say." He went on in a more aggrieved voice: "It has been my fate to have my book [*Essay on the Development of Christian Doctrine*] attacked by various persons, praised by none—till at last it is used against me. However, I cannot be sorry for it, for without it I should never have been a Catholic. Of course I do not allow, as your Eminent friend seemed to think, that *anything* is a development; there are right developments and wrong ones. . . . nor do I think with your friend that infallibility follows on Supremacy—yet I hold the principle of development." Newman concluded his letter with an indication of how much the events at Rome were wearing on him: "I don't give up hope, till the very end, the bitter end; and am always praying about it to the great doctors of the Church. Any how we shall owe you and others a great debt."[123]

Despite the dissuasion of Moriarty and other bishops, several of Newman's lay friends thought that the *Standard* episode gave Newman an opportunity to speak out more fully on the definition. In many ways they had for a long time been hoping for such a chance. Sir John Simeon made his plea to Newman on 23 March: "Do, dear Dr. Newman openly speak out, and let us downtrodden liberal Catholics thank you as our best and truest friend."[124] On the same day Newman was seeking the advice of William Monsell on what he should do now that the likelihood of the full text of his letter to Ullathorne's becoming public was growing:

I suppose it would do less harm to get it into the Papers *now*, than *after* any definition. Its force, if published now would be blunted by three weeks hence—whereas if it came out after the definition, it might unsettle minds, from its strong language. And now it has some faint chance of doing good. As Dr. U. tells me to do what I will about it, the idea has occurred to me whether I had not better at once publish it myself—but I shall get into very hot water, if I do—however the water will not be hotter than it will be three weeks hence. On the other hand, it may be argued that, the matter ceasing

123. Newman to Bishop David Moriarty, 20 March 1870, *The Letters and Diaries,* 25:57–58.

124. Sir John Simeon to Newman, 23 March 1870, *The Letters and Diaries,* 25:66, n. 2.

with the definition, the Papers are not likely to insert it at a later date, if they do not now."[125]

Newman was obviously torn over the course he should follow concerning the Ullathorne letter. But he continued to be adamant against any suggestion that he take the present opportunity to write more fully of his views. On 24 March he responded to Sir John Simeon's plea in the following terms:

> Now, holding, as I do, the absolute divinity of any formal dogma, which an Ecumenical Council, as a Council, declares, should I be acting according to my conscience, if, under the above circumstances, I put forth any view which I might entertain about the matters which the Council was determining?
>
> Next, what exceedingly weighs with me is,—what call is there upon me to speak? If there is no call, I am simply putting my foot into what does not concern me, and gratuitously bringing responsibility and penalty upon myself. I am neither Bishop, nor theologian. I am but a convert, a controversialist, a private priest.

"Should I," Newman asked himself no doubt more than he asked Simeon, "persuade one single member of the Council at Rome, by any words I might use?"[126]

Simeon must have found Newman's reply unsatisfactory. Newman wrote again on 27 March, making clear that in the letter to Ullathorne he had had his say and there was no further need for him to speak out:

> . . . I am bound to act in my own place as a priest under authority and there was no call, nor excuse for my going out of it.
>
> One thing I could do without impropriety,—liberare animam meam to my Bishop, and that I did. I did so with great deliberation in one of the most passionate and confidential letters that I ever wrote in my life.
>
> I am glad I have done it; and moreover, I am not sorry that, without any responsibility of my own, which I could not lawfully bring on me, the general drift of what I wrote has been published.

But Newman stuck to his position. He had no "call" to go beyond what he had already said. He argued:

> There were two reasons which might be urged upon me for making my views known, viz in order that they might act as a means of influencing some of the Bishops of the Council, and as a protest against the action of a certain

125. Newman to William Monsell, 23 March 1870, *The Letters and Diaries,* 25:64. In a response to Newman from the House of Commons on 24 March, Monsell advised Newman against publishing the letter. See Archives of the Birmingham Oratory, Vatican Council file I, no. 70.

126. Newman to Sir John Simeon, 24 March 1870, *The Letters and Diaries,* 25:66.

party. What I have already done, is all that I can, all that I need, do. Would any thing more on my part move a single Bishop? Would any thing more make my mind on the matter more intelligible to the world? I think not.

I will add one thing. I do not at all anticipate any ultimate dissention. Like a jury, they will sit till they agree. I have full confidence in the French and German Bishops."[127]

Newman's great reluctance to be involved in any further public discussion over the definition is revealed in a postscript to this letter to Simeon. Simeon had told Newman that a number of Catholics were preparing a petition against the definition to be presented to Bishop Clifford as a counter to the several petitions that had been circulated among English Catholics in favor of the definition. Newman expressed satisfaction over the proposal but he would not be part of it. "Certainly I rejoice to hear from you," he told Simeon, "that an Address protesting against the definition of Infallibility would, if started, be largely signed; but what have I to do with such measures, beyond giving my opinion, which I have done?"[128] Newman's rather optimistic assessment of what was likely to happen at Rome seems inconsistent with more pessimistic assessments expressed in this same period and one wonders whether this tack was taken in an effort to fend off Simeon's importunings. Nor do Newman's indications that he would have no influence with any of the bishops ring altogether true. He knew that several bishops at Rome valued his opinion and he had evidence that even some bishops whom he did not know, particularly bishops from English-speaking countries, had spoken favorably of him to their colleagues at Rome.[129]

While the furor over Newman's letter to Ullathorne continues, the prospect of a definition by the council increases

March was drawing to a close but there were no signs of spring. In his diary for 26 March, Newman wrote, "snow lying."[130] It had been a difficult time for Newman. His anxieties about the council continued to

---

127. Newman to Sir John Simeon, 27 March 1870, *The Letters and Diaries,* 25:70. This is Newman's last letter to Sir John Simeon, who died several weeks later.

128. Ibid., 69–70.

129. In his letter of 20 January, Ullathorne had told Newman: "I see a good deal of the leading American Prelates, who all have a great affection and respect for you." Bishop William Ullathorne to Newman, 20 January 1870, *The Letters and Diaries,* 25:20, n. 2. At least one American bishop, James Roosevelt Bayley of Newark, had visited Newman on his way to the council. See Newman "Diary," 6 September 1869, *The Letters and Diaries,* 24:327.

130. Newman "Diary," 26 March 1870, *The Letters and Diaries,* 25:67.

affect him deeply. On 26 March he told Canon Walker of Scarborough: "And it is very pleasant to me to find you have hopes of the Council abstaining in a matter on which, I fear, the Pope has set his heart. What I dread is *haste*—if full time is given for the Synodal Fathers to learn and reflect on the state of the case, I have little doubt they will keep clear of the dangerous points."[131] And in a letter of 30 March to Robert Froude, Newman attempted again, as though preparing for the inevitable, to explain to an inquirer what he thought would be the likely outcome for Catholics should the definition come about: "But any declaration of the Pope's, if he were ruled infallible, would require explanation in the concrete in *another way* also—not only as to its application, but its interpretation. As lawyers explain acts of Parliament, so theologians have ever explained the dicta of Popes and Councils—and that explanation, when received generally, is the true Catholic doctrine. Hence I have never been able to see myself that the ultimate decision rests with any but the general Catholic intelligence. And so I understand it to be implied in the 'Securus iudicat orbis terrarum.' "[132]

Whether dealing with the actual proceedings of the council or offering theoretical explanations of how its possible decisions could be accepted in the life of the Church, Newman was troubled. On 26 March he told his confidante Mary Holmes: "What a misery this controversy about the Council is becoming—of course I cannot wish it over, for the longer it lasts, the more will the right principles gain, but it is most painful while we are in it."[133] In this very month when Newman found himself unwittingly but publicly involved in the debate over infallibility, it was announced to the council Fathers that the question of papal infallibility had been moved on to the agenda. Newman undoubtedly hoped to learn firsthand of what was going on in Rome from Sir Rowland Blennerhassett, who wrote on 23 March: "I have just come back from Rome where I went and got engaged to be married. . . . I have much to tell you of the state of affairs in Rome."[134]

The council continued to preoccupy Newman in the first half of April. In many ways he was even more caught up in correspondence over it than he had been in preceding months. Eventually a respite would come just after Easter, which was observed on 17 April. Late in March, Newman had begged off writing publicly on the council partly out of the belief that

131. Newman to Canon John Walker of Scarborough, 26 March 1870, *The Letters and Diaries,* 25:69.

132. Newman to Robert Froude, 30 March 1870, *The Letters and Diaries,* 25:71.

133. Newman to Mary Holmes, 26 March 1870, *The Letters and Diaries,* 25:68.

134. Sir Rowland Blennerhassett to Newman, 23 March 1870, Archives of the Birmingham Oratory, Vatican Council file I, no. 69. In June 1870, Blennerhassett married Charlotte von Leyden, a friend and correspondent of Döllinger.

anything he had to say would have no influence on the bishops. Ironically, on 1 April, Newman received a long letter from Bishop Alexander Goss of Liverpool, asking Newman's help in writing a pastoral on the infallibility question for his diocese. Goss showed in no uncertain terms his opposition to the definition and he evidently believed that Newman shared his sentiments. Goss entirely concurred in Newman's use of the notorious phrase, "an aggressive insolent faction." Among other things he said in his long letter of 29 March:

> The Pope is amiable & hence has won a sort of hysterical affection from ladies and young priests & he has unfortunately believed that he would be able to exercise the same fascination on the Bps. He began life as a liberal but was at heart an autocrat & he soon made known to the Cardinals that the white Zuchetto covered all the red ones. With him the Infallibility is a personal affair, & he works upon all who do not go in for it as enemies, personal enemies.
>   It has pained me much to write what I have written, but I have written it in the interest of truth.[135]

Goss was not at Rome. He had set out for Rome late in 1869, but ill health had forced him to stop his journey at Cannes. He never reached Rome but eventually returned to England where he died in 1872. Goss had little respect for the Roman Curia, nor did he have great respect for Pius IX. He was a Cisalpinist to the core. Newman replied to Goss on 1 April. He had not changed his determined position over the preceding days. He would not write even under the anonymity promised by reason of Bishop Goss's necessarily being the author of any pastoral letter to the people of the Liverpool diocese. Newman began on a practical note: "I doubt whether you have time to publish any thing. . . . Next I will say—it is quite possible that, if I wrote any thing for Your Lordship, as you are [so] kind and flattering as to wish, I should be sure to be found out—and I don't think this would be consistent with your dignity, because[?] I do not belong to your diocese, and have no official connexion with your person." But Newman, despite his refusal, showed that he was in many respects in sympathy with Bishop Goss's position. "You yourself suggest," Newman wrote, "excellent topics for an address to your people, such as the *tradition of the English Catholics*—for the Bishops at the Council are 'testes' as well as 'iudices.' Also that, considering the point in debate admits of being treated[?] not only as a point of doctrine but of discipline, coming home personally to every Bishop, if there is a question on which perfect una-

135, Bishop Alexander Goss to Newman, Archives of the Birmingham Oratory, Vatican Council file I, no. 75. Ordained at Rome in 1841, Goss became coadjutor bishop of Liverpool in 1853 and Ordinary of that diocese in 1856.

nimity is to be desired, it is this: a majority has no right to vote away the right of their fellow-Bishops.''[136]

Journalistic comment on Newman's letter to Ullathorne continued to appear both in England and on the Continent, though as yet the complete text had not appeared. On 4 April, *The Daily Post* of Liverpool reported the following:

> The Allgemeine Zeitung publishes a fuller account than has yet appeared of Dr. Newman's now famous letter on infallibility. In it Dr. Newman says that the party of the Civilta Cattolico [sic]—the Pope's party—have brought matters to such a pass that the report of the Council, instead of sounding a message of peace, excites only terror and alarm in the minds of the faithful; and that matters look as if the Council had been held to create a great difficulty, not to avert a great danger from the Church, as in times past. Dr. Newman asks how he is to defend and recommend decisions at variance with notorious facts of history? Of course, if it be God's will that Papal infallibility should be defined, nothing remains to him but to bow his head under so inscrutable a dispensation. The newspaper which publishes the letter says "it is well known to Dr. Newman that two of his Oxford friends and disciples are at the bottom of the whole agitation. Well for him he is not in Manning's diocese, if all that is said about that prelate's high-handed proceedings is true.''[137]

No doubt the appearance of this item in the *Daily Post* had a role in making Newman decide that it was best to go ahead and make his letter to Ullathorne public. On 5 April, Newman wrote a letter marked "private" to the Editor of the *Standard*. It read: "Dr. Newman presents his Compliments to the Editor of the Standard and begs the favour of his insertion of the inclosed in his paper.''[138] The *Standard* printed the full text of the letter to Ullathorne in its issue on the following day, 6 April. And on 7 April the text appeared in *The Times*.

By this time Newman was showing more and more concern that his worst fears over the council would be realized. He told J. R. Bloxam on 5 April, "No one, not I only, has any means of knowing what is going on in the Council since that time,[139] as regards the definition of the Pope's infallibility. However, I fear that the faction, which I have so strongly characterized in my published letters has great chance of success.''[140] And on 7 April, Newman told Ambrose De Lisle: "Anxious, as I am, I will

---

136. Newman to Bishop Alexander Goss, 1 April 1870, *The Letters and Diaries*, 25:75–76. Newman wrote on the copy of the letter that he kept, "sent in substance."

137. Archives of the Birmingham Oratory, Vatican Council file II, no. 6. The other Oxford friend referred to is surely Ward.

138. Newman to the Editor of the *Standard*, 5 April 1870, *The Letters and Diaries*, 25:80.

139. 28 January letter to Ullathorne.

140. Newman to J. R. Bloxam, 5 April 1870, *The Letters and Diaries*, 25:79.

not believe that the Pope's Infallibility can be defined at the Council till I see it actually done. . . . When it is actually done, I will accept it as His act; but, till then, I will believe it impossible. One can but act according to one's best light. Certainly, we at least have no claim to call ourselves infallible; still it is our duty to act as if we were, to act as strongly and vigorously in the matter, as if it were impossible we could be wrong, to be full of hope and peace, and to leave the event to God. This is right, isn't it?"[141] And on the following day Newman wrote to Bishop Thomas Brown of Newport, who had not gone to Rome because of illness, "I will not believe that the Pope's infallibility will be defined by the Council till it is actually done and over—when this is so, then of course, with every Catholic, I will accept it."[142]

On 19 March, Döllinger, having seen a copy of Newman's letter to Ullathorne, joined those who were begging Newman to add his voice to those who had shown public opposition to the definition of papal infallibility.[143] There is ample evidence to suggest that Döllinger and his protégé Lord Acton were annoyed at what they believed was Newman's timidity and his reputation for seeing the merits on both sides of every question. Döllinger was almost blunt: "In my opinion, and probably in yours too, the situation of the catholic Church has not been more dangerous in the last four centuries than it is at present. At such a time the true sons and friends of the church ought to be communing together. . . . Neutrality in such a case is too near akin to lukewarmness, but if you speak out, then let 'the trumpet give a clear and certain sound' and believe such a splendid opportunity to do signal service to the cause of the church will not be offered again."[144]

141. Newman to Ambrose De Lisle, 7 April 1870, *The Letters and Diaries*, 25:82. Ambrose Phillipps De Lisle became a Catholic in 1824 at the age of fifteen. A man of considerable wealth he used his energies and monies in promoting union between the Anglican and Roman Catholic Churches. In 1857 he was one of the founders of the Association for the Promotion of the Unity of Christendom. Ecclesiastical authority in 1864 forbade Catholic participation in the Association.

142. Newman to Bishop Thomas Brown, 8 April 1870, *The Letters and Diaries*, 25:83.

143. Döllinger had received a copy of Newman's letter from Acton, who said in the 10 March letter to Döllinger with which it was enclosed: "It would be perhaps good to translate the greatest part, as the letter circulating in many copies, of a well-known non-German theologian, to one of our bishops. But every sign that it is from Newman or from England ought to disappear. . . . We decided that we would have the right to make the letter known only if we give no clue as to its author. He would immediately write a rejoinder, equally ambiguous, but probably strong in the other direction." Acton to Döllinger, 10 March 1870, *Ignaz von Döllinger: Briefwechsel 1820–1890* (hereafter cited as *Breifwechsel*), ed. Victor Conzemius (Munich: C. H. Beck'sche Verlagsbuchhandlung, 1965) 2:209. The original is in German. English translation of this and other letters of Döllinger provided for the author by the Reverend Joseph F. Wimmer, O.S.A.

144. Ignaz von Döllinger to Newman, 19 March 1870, *The Letters and Diaries*, 25:84. Döllinger is perhaps alluding to Tract 1, "Thoughts on the Ministerial Commission," in

Newman, expecting a visit that never came from Döllinger's friend, Sir Rowland Blennerhassett, delayed his response to Döllinger until 9 April. Then he struck a characteristic note: "My feeling has been this on the question before the Council—can any thing I should say move a single Bishop? and if not, what is the good of writing?" Newman then used the unexpected publication of his letter to Ullathorne as releasing him from the need to say anything further. "It speaks," Newman declared, "in far more forcible, vehement terms, than I should have ventured to use in a letter which I had intended for publication. I suppose in all Councils there has been intrigue, violence, management, because the truth is held in earthen vessels. But God over rules."[145]

Newman receives some letters critical of his letter to Ullathorne but the overall reaction is positive

The public repercussions of Newman's letter to Ullathorne caused Newman much distress in the spring of 1870. Not only did he have to justify his opinions in print and in letters to close friends but also to strangers. Some of the letters from strangers had about them a tone of sorrow, a feeling that Newman by expressing such strong sentiments against the proponents of the definition had let the writers down. One of these let-

---

which Newman wrote: "But, if you will not adopt my view of the subject, which I offer to you, not doubtingly, yet (I hope) respectfully, at all events CHOOSE YOUR SIDE. . . . *Choose your side;* since side you shortly must, with one or other party, even though you do nothing." *Tracts for the Times* by Members of the University of Oxford, vol. 1 (London: J.G.F. and J. Rivington. Reprinted in 1969 by AMS Press, New York, from the bound editions of 1840–1842, London, which were collections of pamphlets published from 1833–1841).

Gladstone in letters to Acton and to Döllinger in March also touched on the theme of what he saw to be Newman's lack of boldness in action. To Acton on 1 March he said: "I have never read a more extraordinary letter than that of Newman to Bishop Ullathorne which doubtless you have seen: admirable in its strength, strange in its weakness, incomparable in speculation, tame and emasculated in action." Gladstone to Lord Acton, 1 March 1870. *The Gladstone Diaries,* ed. H.C.G. Matthew (Oxford: The Clarendon Press, 1982) 7:245. And on 25 March, Gladstone wrote to Döllinger: "No more singular phenomenon is exhibited I think in these strange critical times than the mind of Dr. Newman. Such an abundance of power, such an excess of beauty, hardly ever I suppose, have appeared in conjunction with some latent defect or peculiarity which seems to penetrate the effect of all his gifts, & to exhibit him in a position of impotence before the world at the cardinal moment which others have been showing him how to use." Gladstone to Ignaz von Döllinger, 25 March 1870, *The Gladstone Diaries,* 7:264.

145. Newman to Ignaz von Döllinger, 9 April 1870, *The Letters and Diaries,* 25:85. Döllinger commented on this letter to Acton as follows: "I received a short letter from Newman, who very clearly betrays his inclination and intention to salvage for himself a reversal and to leave open a capitulation to the fait accompli." Döllinger to Acton, April 1870, *Briefwechsel,* 2:323.

ters came from Father Samuel Walshaw, parish priest of St. Mary's, Sheffield. He wrote to Newman on 8 April: "I have just left my confessional from which, I saw, among the Choristers practising Holy Week music, four or five who were lately Anglicans; I was then led to think of several who may follow their example, but who are now kept back, and who from their veneration of your name may receive *irreparable* injury from the false statements, wh[ich], if uncontradicted will be only too willingly believed.''[146] Walshaw was sure that the reports in the press of what Newman was supposed to have written to his bishop could not be true. Newman replied on 11 April:

> Men are illogical, when they conclude, as the newspaper which you send me, that because I disapprove of the actions of certain Catholics, therefore my faith is unsettled as regards the Catholic Church. . . .
> I hold, and ever have held, that her Sovereign Pontiff is the centre of unity, and the vicar of Christ.[147]

In a letter to Newman of 12 April, W. R. Brownlow, a priest of the diocese of Plymouth who had been received into the Church by Newman in 1863,[148] complained that since "the whole Protestant and infidel press" were taking the side of the opponents of the definition, "I could not resist the impression that this was the devil's side.''[149] Brownlow, who had evidently seen the text of the letter to Ullathorne in *The Times,* thought that Newman's letter was a great mistake and that it had the effect of calling into question the definition of the Immaculate Conception in 1854. He carried his criticism further by saying, "As long as the Infallibility question remains undefined the [Anglican] Ritualists are able to say to enquiring souls: 'You will never find that infallible authority which you want in Rome, for they have never been able to settle where it is.' Besides the triumphs of the Church are generally brought about in a way that human prudence would never dream of, and so I cannot share your sad foreboding: 'If it is God's will etc.' "[150] Newman was gracious but unyielding in his reply. He conceded none of Brownlow's points:

> As to my confidential letter, where are we if we may not in the freest way discuss matters with *each other*? Whom am I to write to except my own

146. Father Samuel Walshaw to Newman, 8 April 1870, Archives of the Birmingham Oratory, Vatican Council file II, no. 22.

147. Newman to Father Samuel Walshaw, 11 April 1870, *The Letters and Diaries,* 25:90.

148. William Brownlow succeeded William Clifford as bishop of Clifton in 1894.

149. Father W. R. Brownlow to Newman, 12 April 1870, *The Letters and Diaries,* 25:97, n. 3. The editors of the *Letters and Diaries* add a note to Brownlow's comments: "It was argued in the press that the extremists illustrated the real nature of Catholicism."

150. Father W. R. Brownlow to Newman, 12 April 1870, Archives of the Birmingham Oratory, Vatican Council file II, no. 32.

Bishop? to who [sic] else have I spoken as I have to him? how can I communicate to him except by letter, when he is 2,000 miles off? how am I answerable if, to my utter surprise, someone reads my confidential letter over his shoulder?[151]

As to the Immaculate Conception, *by contrast* there was nothing sudden, or secret, in the proposal of definition in that case. It had been talked about years out of mind—and was approached, everyone knowing it, by step after step. This has taken us all by surprise.

The Protestant and Infidel Press, so far from taking part with Mgr. Dupanloup, have backed up all along the extreme party—and now all through the country are taking an *argumentative* position against me. . . .

The *existing* Ritualists may or may not be put back—but the *leavening of the country* will be checked.[152]

A number of priests of the Birmingham diocese were also upset by Newman's letter to their bishop. When the provost of the Chapter brought this to the bishop's attention, Ullathorne replied:

I think it well to remark that Dr. Newman's letter to me was private and intended to be private, and that neither Dr. Newman nor myself had the slightest intention of making it public. In that letter he communicates to me his personal conviction of the infallibility, whilst he is driven, through the difficulties of other persons, to put his ideas on the policy of the question of opportuneness before me. This in the private way in which it was done was a legitimate proceeding. But I think, and very prudent bishops, on what I may call both sides of the question, unite with me in thinking, that it would be unfair and ungenerous to treat that private letter addressed by a priest to his bishop, as if it had been a formal one and intended for publication.[153]

But Newman received far more evidences of support for what he had written to Bishop Ullathorne and the subsequent letters he had written to the *Standard*. These came largely from friends but also from strangers. Ambrose De Lisle wrote on 6 April:

I have been intending for some time to write a line to thank you for the 2 Letters, which I have read in the Papers, and which bear[?] your signature, in connexion with this ill-omened Question of the Separate Personal Infallibility of the Pope.

I heartily concur with the qualification you put upon those, who have forced it on, and I feel that it has thrown, as the Bishop of Orleans says in his Letter to the Archbishop of Malines of the 1rst March, not only the Catholic world into a state of perplexity and alarm, but that it is rekindling

151. Does this indicate that Newman thought Ullathorne could have been more careful?
152. Newman to Father W. R. Brownlow, 13 April 1870, *The Letters and Diaries,* 25:97–98.
153. Butler, *Ullathorne,* 2:63–64.

extinct animosities between Catholics and our separated Brethren of other
Xtian Communions.
    It is indeed a most critical moment.[154]

De Lisle wrote again on 12 April with words of encouragement for Newman that leave no doubt that he saw Newman as opposed to the definition: "I quite understand the annoyance you must feel at your Letter,
so private and confidential, getting into the public Papers, still I think
it will do a great deal of good and tend to give some check to the reckless
haste with which the Dominant Party are striving to force upon the Church
their own peculiar views, as a Dogma of Faith. With you I can hardly
believe that they will succeed, but it is certainly a duty to oppose them,
as much as we can, for God makes use of human means to effect His
purposes."[155] Evidently Newman's friends had more faith than he that
his words could indeed "move a single Bishop."
    Newman also received a letter marked "private," from Bishop Thomas
Brown, who said: "I cannot resist[?] my desire of thanking you for the
admirable letter you wrote to Dr. Ullathorne and am rejoiced at finding
it in print. With every word of it my feelings and judgment coincide—
though it would not be prudent in me to give them publicity."[156] Anglicans hoping for Church unity also wrote to thank Newman as is evidenced
in a letter of 13 April from W. F. Taylor, who said: "Will you be pleased
to accept from an Anglican and a member of APUC[157] an expression of
humble thanks for your recent letter to the Bishop of Birmingham in thus
using your influence to obtain postponement of the defining of the dogma
of Infallibility, as being inopportune."[158]
    On 13 April, the Irish Sulpician, John Baptist Hogan, who taught the-
ology for thirty-two years at St. Sulpice and would become one of the
first faculty members at the Catholic University in Washington, wrote to
Newman from Paris:

> Your last letters have already appeared in the french papers and will be a
> relief to a large number of enlightened Catholics whose feelings have been
> utterly disregarded, not to say violently trampled upon, during these last
> four or five months. I fear very much that the great bulk of these bishops

154. Ambrose De Lisle to Newman, 6 April 1870, Archives of the Birmingham Oratory,
Vatican Council file II, no. 11.
    155. Ambrose De Lisle to Newman, 12 April 1870, Archives of the Birmingham Ora-
tory, Vatican Council file II, no. 33.
    156. Bishop Thomas Brown to Newman, 7 April 1870, Archives of the Birmingham Ora-
tory, Vatican Council file II, no. 15.
    157. The Association for the Promotion of the Unity of Christendom. See page 102,
n. 141.
    158. W. F. Taylor to Newman, 13 April 1870, Archives of the Birmingham Oratory,
Vatican Council file II, no. 38.

in Rome have only a very inadequate knowledge of the real state of public feeling in France and through the Continent generally. Their information is chiefly derived from the popular Catholic organs, and those are only calculated to mislead them. The "Univers" in particular runs right counter to public opinion almost in everything. It is only too successful in generating and developing in the minds of a half educated clergy a general distrust and dislike for whatever the present generation cares for most, and is thus daily widening the Chasm that separates the Church from the world. The impending definition will act identically in the same way. . . .[159]

For all his troubles Newman must have been particularly gratified by a letter of 3 May from Emily Bowles. Miss Bowles quoted Mrs. Augustus Craven, a French writer married to a convert British diplomat: "As to Father Newman's Letter I think he ought never to have expressed the least regret at its publication, although it was not written with that intention. It gave comfort and edification to a great many—and a copy of it having reached Montalembert Fr. Newman may like to know that it gave him *his last sensation of joy upon earth*. He mentioned this to me in his *last* letter."[160]

Ullathorne himself saw Newman's letter as having on the whole a positive effect. On 19 April he wrote to a friend: "Everybody asks me how Dr. Newman's letter got out. Of course the infallibilists regret it, the oppositionists admire it, and it has a certain influence in combination with other demonstrations in urging in the direction of prudence."[161]

Newman continues in private to press strongly the case against the definition

On 11 April William Monsell, writing from the Colonial Office, sent Newman the following dramatic piece of news: "The international committee of liberal Bishops are going to draw up a last protest against definitions not unanimously or nearly so. If this be ineffectual they think of withdrawing from the Council."[162] It was probably the same day or the previous day that Newman received a letter from Father Robert Whitty, who was in Rome as the theologian to Newman's friend, Bishop Moriarty of Kerry. Whitty was to return to England in May, having been named

159. Father John Baptist Hogan to Newman, 13 April 1870, *The Letters and Diaries,* 25:123, n. 2.

160. Emily Bowles to Newman, 3 May 1870, Archives of the Birmingham Oratory, Vatican Council file II, no. 55. Montalembert died in the spring of 1870.

161. Butler, *The Vatican Council,* 2:36.

162. William Monsell to Newman, 11 April 1870, Archives of the Birmingham Oratory, Vatican Council file II, no. 29. See also Odo Russell to the Earl of Clarendon, 10 April 1870, in Blakiston, *The Roman Question,* 418.

provincial of the Jesuits in England. His long letter to Newman gave a
running account of the proceedings at Rome from 23 February to 3 April.
Among other items of news, Whitty attempted to give Newman some idea
of the position of the bishops from English-speaking countries on the definition. He tried to show that these bishops, apart from the Irish, were
largely against the definition.

Whitty began his long letter to Newman by defending his Jesuit brethren and by seeing a link between the response to the *Syllabus* of 1864 and
the agitation for the definition of papal infallibility at the council:

> There are some extra conciliar points on which I suppose I may speak, as
> the papers speak of them. For the sake of truth then I think you should
> know that the paper in the Civilta in which the flourish about defining the
> infallibility by acclamation occurred was not only not written by a Jesuit
> but was inserted (as I am told) contrary to the advice of the Fathers who
> have charge of the Periodical. I have heard also one fact since coming to
> Rome and it is a striking one. The Syllabus was prepared and published
> without asking the advice of a single Father of the Society upon it. This
> was done on purpose to save the Society from the odium of the measure,
> as Fr. General was afterwards assured.[163] There are disputes as to who be-
> gan the controversy on the infallibility. But I believe all agree that the pub-
> lication of the Syllabus gave occasion to it.

Concerning papal infallibility, Whitty maintained that

> in any General Council of the 19th or 20th century (if the world lasts so
> long) it *must have* come on. Against the Broad or No-Church systems so
> widely prevalent now, the Constitution of the Church has to be defined and
> in doing this we come to the Rock. I have never felt any difficulty in ac-
> cepting the doctrine of the Pope's infallibility as revealed. But how far the
> world is prepared for its definition now or will be the better for it, is an-
> other question. If defined, it will be so no doubt for higher reasons than
> those alleged now for the opportuneness. It has bearings on some future
> unknown to us.[164]

Newman's impassioned reply to Whitty, written on 12 April, the Tues-
day in Holy Week, may well have been inspired not only by Whitty's

163. Certainly it was assumed at the time that the Jesuits had had a major role in the
preparation of *Quanta Cura* and the *Syllabus*. See, for example, Odo Russell to Earl Russell, 17 January 1865, and a further communication from Odo Russell to Earl Russell the
same day in which Odo Russell wrote: " . . . I am assured that he [Cardinal Antonelli,
papal secretary of state] opposed its publication, but was overruled by the Pope, Mérode
[archbishop and one time minister of war in the government of the Papal States], and the
Jesuits, who are now all powerful in Rome," Blakiston, *The Roman Question,* 304–05. See
also McElrath, *The Syllabus of Pius IX,* 79–81, who deals with the prevalent belief in the
English press that the Jesuits were responsible for the encyclical and the *Syllabus.*

164. Father Robert Whitty to Newman, 23 February and 3 April 1870, *The Letters and
Diaries,* 25:92–93, n. 2.

detailed account of proceedings at Rome but also by the dramatic news Newman had just received from Monsell concerning the plans of the minority bishops. In beginning his response to Whitty, Newman sounded a theme that was characteristic of his thoughts on the definition in this period. In a letter to Ambrose De Lisle five days earlier Newman said, "Certainly we at least have no claim to call ourselves infallible; still it is our duty to act as if we were. . . ."[165] In the letter to Father Robert Whitty, Newman wrote: "One can but go by one's best light. Whoever is infallible, I am not; but I am bound to argue out the matter and to act, as if I were, till the Council decides; and then, if God's Infallibility is against me, to submit at once, still not repenting for having taken the part which I felt to be right. . . . We can but do our best." Newman went on to state his case in language that borrowed an important metaphor from the technical developments of the nineteenth century:

Well then, my thesis is this: you are going too fast at Rome;—on this I shall insist.

It is enough for one Pope to have passed one doctrine. . . . We do not move at railroad pace in theological matters even in the 19th century. We must be patient, and that for two reasons:—first, in order to get at truth ourselves, and next in order to carry others with us.

The Church moves as a whole; it is not a mere philosophy; it is a communion; it not only discovers, but it teaches; it is bound to consult for charity, as well as for faith. You must prepare men's minds for the doctrine, and you must not flout and insult the existing tradition of countries. The tradition of Ireland, the tradition of England, is not on the side of the Papal infallibility. You know how recent ultramontane views are in both countries; so too of France; so of Germany. The time may come, when it will be seen how those traditions are compatible with additions, that is, with true developments, which those traditions indeed in themselves do not explicitly teach; but you have no right rudely to wipe out the history of centuries, and to substitute a bran new version of the doctrine imported from Rome and the South. Think how slowly and cautiously you proceeded in the definition of the Immaculate Conception how many steps were made, how many centuries passed, before the dogma was ripe; —we are not ripe yet for the Pope's Infallibility. Hardly any one even murmured at the act of 1854, half the Catholic world is in a fright at the proposed act of 1870.

As Newman continued he became more insistent that the time was not ripe for the definition: "I say then you must take your time about a definition *de fide,* for the sake of charity; —and now I say so again for the sake of truth; —for the very same caution, which is necessary for the souls of others, is surely the divinely appointed human means of an infallible decision." "We need," Newman continued, "to try the doctrine by facts,

165. Newman to Ambrose De Lisle, 7 April 1870, *The Letters and Diaries,* 25:82.

to see what it may mean, what it cannot mean, what it must mean. We must try its future working by the past. And we need that this should be done in the face of day, in course, in quiet, in various schools and centres of thought, in controversy. This is a work of years.'' ''To outsiders like me,'' Newman told Father Whitty, ''it would seem as if a grave dogmatic question was being treated merely as a move in ecclesiastical politics.''

This searing letter, which ranks in intensity with the letter to Ullathorne, is notable in two other respects. It gives in two other passages Newman's impressions of why he thought the council had been convoked, impressions no doubt shared by others—even, Newman would appear to say, by bishops. The letter also evidenced Newman's fear that the definition would lead to an intensification in England of prejudice toward Catholics after the quiet, hard-won victories that had come over the past seventy-five years.

First, Newman's views on the reasons for the council:

> When indeed I think of the contrast presented to us by what is done now and what was done then [the definition of 1854], and what, as I have said, ought always to be done, I declare, unless I were too old to be angry, I should be very angry. The Bull convening the Council was issued with its definite objects stated, dogma being only slightly mentioned as among those objects, but not a word about the Pope's Infallibility. Through the interval, up to the meeting of the Council, not a word was said to enlighten the Bishops as to what they were to meet about. The Irish Bishops, as I heard at the time, felt surprised at this; so did all I doubt not. Many or most had thought they were to meet to set right the Canon Law.[166] Then suddenly, just as they are meeting it is let out that the Pope's Infallibility is the great subject of definition, and the Civiltà and other well informed prints say that it is to be carried by acclamation! Then Archbishop Manning tells (I believe) Mr. Odo Russell, that, unless the opposition can cut the throat of 500 Bishops, the definition certainly will be carried; and moreover, that *it has long been intended*! Long intended, and yet kept secret! Is this the way the faithful ever were treated before? is this in any sort of sense going by Tradition? On hearing this, my memory went back to an old saying, imputed to Monsignore Talbot, that, what made the definition of the Immaculate Conception so desirable and important was that it opened the way to the definition of the Pope's Infallibility. Is it wonderful that we should all be shocked? For myself, after meditating on such crooked ways, I cannot help turning to our Lord's terrible warning ''Vae mundo à scandalis! Quisquis scandalizaverit unum ex his pusillis credentibus in me, bonum est ei magis si circumdaretur mola asinaria collo ejus, et in mare mitteretur.[167]

166. In a letter of 18 June 1867, Bishop Ullathorne showed that he too thought that the chief work of the council would be the reform of the Code of Canon Law. See Butler, *Ullathorne*, 2:45.

167. Matthew 18:6; Mark 9:42.

Newman was also disturbed by evidences of new anti-Catholicism in England, especially the passage by the House of Commons on 29 March, with a majority of two, of a bill by Charles Newdegate to form a committee to investigate convents and monasteries.[168] "Am I bound," Newman asked,

> to take my view of expedience from what is thought expedient at Rome? May I not judge about expedience for Catholics in England by what we see in England? Now the effect upon the English people of the very attempt at definition hitherto does but confirm one's worst apprehension about it, for 1st The ministry is decidedly Pro-Catholic. Gladstone would help the Irish Catholic University, if he could, but he has been obliged to declare in the House, that what is going on in Rome ties his hands. And 2ndly Mr. Newdegate has gained his Committee to inquire into conventual establishments and their property. These are the first fruits in England of even the very agitation of this great anticipated expedient for strengthening the Church. That agitation falls upon an existing Anti-catholic agitation spreading through the English mind. Murphy[169] is still lecturing against priests and convents, and gaining over the classes who are now the ultimate depositary of political power, the constituency for Parliamentary elections.[170] And we,

168. For a discussion of Charles Newdegate and his bill for the inspection of convents and monasteries, see Walter L. Arnstein, *Protestant versus Catholic in Mid-Victorian England: Mr. Newdegate and the Nuns* (Columbia, Missouri, and London: University of Missouri Press, 1982) 123–35. Arnstein, 132, sees a direct link between the passage of Newdegate's bill and the council. He writes: "The factor that had contributed most to what the *Spectator* called 'the thrill of anti-Catholic panic' was no new revelation of convent life or any well-publicized conversion but 'what was, in every sense, the crisis of the nineteenth century, the Vatican Council.' " For the debate on the Newdegate Conventual and Monastic Institutions Motion for A Select Committee, see *Hansard's Parliamentary Debates*, Third Series, 200:872–908, 29 March 1870. The vote was very close: ayes 131; noes 129. Gladstone, who voted against the motion, directly related it to the proceedings at Rome in a letter to Odo Russell on 3 April: "The sage advisers of Pope Pius the Great, if they care about the condition of their co-religionists here, may find some material of instruction, as to the effect of their present proceedings, in the Parliamentary 'situation'. We maturely considered in Cabinet yesterday whether we should try to reverse or alter the vote on Conventual Institutions. We decided that we could not attempt it." Gladstone to Odo Russell, 3 April 1870, *The Gladstone Diaries*, 7:269–70. And in a letter to Archbishop Manning on 16 April, Gladstone wrote: "From the announcement of the Council, I have feared the consequences of (what we consider) extreme proceedings [the Vatican Council] upon the progress of just legislation here. My anticipations have been, I regret to say, much more than realised." *The Gladstone Diaries*, 7:277–78.

In the "Chronicle of the Week" in its issue of 11 December 1869, the *Tablet* noted: "Anti-Catholic Meetings. The Feast of the Immaculate Conception [the opening date of the Council] was duly honored this week by Protestants in London after their own peculiar fashion. They held three meetings against the Catholic Church." *Tablet*, n.s. 2, vol. 34, 11 December 1869, 873.

169. A former priest and notorious anti-Catholic lecturer.

170. The number of voters in parliamentary elections was doubled by the Reform Act of 1867.

when we are bound, if we can, to sooth the deep prejudices and feverish suspicions of the nation, we on the contrary are to be forced, by measures determined on at Rome, to blow upon this troubled sea, with all the winds of Aeolus, when Neptune ought to raise his "placidum caput" above the waves.[171] This is what we need at least in England. And for England of course I speak.[172]

In concluding Newman asked Whitty to "excuse my freedom."

Whitty replied to Newman on 15 May, just after his return to England:

> Before leaving Rome Dr. Moriarty and I had made a collection of pamphlets on the Infallibility for you. I hope you have received them by post.
> So far as I could see or hear both in Rome and on my way here, our F.F. [Fathers] Italian, French, and German don't criticise your expressions or words as seems to be the case in England.[173] But they feel deeply the weight of your authority on the question itself. It was very hard in the beginning of the Council to persuade some of them that the dislike of the definition was both sincere and widespread.
> I left your letter in Dr. Moriarty's hands. It expressed his own thoughts and I considered it might be useful to him in case he had to speak in the Council.[174]

Moriarty himself mentioned the letter to Newman in a letter of 28 April from the Irish Dominican house, San Clemente, where he was staying in Rome. "I saw your letter to Dr. Whitty," Moriarty said. "I wish we could get the Pope to take in your view."[175]

On the day following his impassioned letter to Whitty, Newman wrote to another of his Jesuit friends, Henry Coleridge, the editor of the *Month,* who had just informed Newman that he was writing an article on infallibility. "It is meant," Father Coleridge wrote, "to be a simple common sense view of the matter—taking the line—the only one I *can* take—that *hactenus* the movement for the definition of infallibility seems to be a genuine impulse of the assembled Bishops. . . . Somehow, I can't distrust the Church."[176] Coleridge also brought up the 28 January letter to

171. Aeneid I, 27.

172. Newman to Father Robert Whitty, 12 April 1870, *The Letters and Diaries,* 25:92–96.

173. This must refer especially to Father Paul Bottalla, a professor at St. Beuno's College, Wales, who was an ardent polemicist in favor of the definition.

174. Father Robert Whitty to Newman, 15 May 1870, Archives of the Birmingham Oratory, Vatican Council file II, no. 61. At the council Bishop Moriarty spoke in opposition to the definition on 27 June. Cardinal Cullen, a strong proponent of the definition, thought Moriarty's speech a "great failure." See Larkin, *The Roman Catholic Church and the Home Rule Movement,* 20.

175. Bishop David Moriarty to Newman, 28 April 1870, Archives of the Birmingham Oratory, Vatican Council file II, no. 49.

176. Father Henry James Coleridge, S.J., to Newman, 12 April 1870, *The Letters and Diaries,* 25:98, n. 2.

Ullathorne and said that some people thought that Newman should have written a pamphlet on the definition rather than the private communication meant for Ullathorne alone. Newman felt that Coleridge was gently taking him to task, especially by the description of the position he would take on the definition in the article he was planning. Newman sent Coleridge a copy of the letter he had just written to Whitty, perhaps to persuade him of another view. Newman defended his not having written a piece on the definition for publication: "Of course a pamphlet would have been far better than such a letter; but I was distinctly dissuaded from publishing; and then I asked myself this question, 'Can any thing I say move a single Bishop? and if not, what is the good of writing?' And this is the great charge which I bring against the immediate authors of this movement, that THEY HAVE NOT GIVEN US TIME. Why must we be hurried all of a sudden, to write or not to write? Why is a coup de main to settle the matter before we know where we are?" Newman reverted again to a railway image to deplore what he thought was the haste of the council: "What could such as I do, *but* cry out, bawl, make violent gestures, as you would do, if you saw a railway engine running over some unhappy workmen on the line? What time was there for being scientific? what could you do but collar a bishop, if you could get up to one? The beginning and end of my thoughts about the Council is, 'You are going too fast. You are going too fast.' "[177]

With the solemn days of Holy Week upon him, Newman was obviously greatly upset by the council. He celebrated the Mass of Holy Thursday, but on the same day he took time to tell Charlotte Wood:

> The Times has, I believe, published the whole of my letter to Dr. Ullathorne. It was one of the most confidential letters that I ever wrote in my life. I felt it a sacred duty to write it—I feel every word I have said in it—and, while I was bound to let my Bishop know what I thought, to him alone did I tell it. One friend in this House saw the letter before it went—and both of us kept a dead silence about its contents. But within a week of its getting to Rome, a copy of it was circulated through the place. Thence it got to London and Germany, I knowing nothing about its betrayal. Parts got into the Standard and Saturday Review, and of course incorrectly given. So by degrees it has oozed out. Whether there is more to give, they must say who have got the letter—I think not. The definition of the Immaculate Conception was not the work of a Council—and was the consequence of the spontaneous growth of belief through centuries in the Church.[178]

Because the copy Newman had kept of his 28 January letter to Ullathorne was in parts almost illegible, he was still not sure even after making a new

177. Newman to Father Henry James Coleridge, S.J., 13 April 1870, *The Letters and Diaries,* 25:98.
178. Newman to Charlotte Wood, 14 April 1870, *The Letters and Diaries,* 25:99–100.

copy to send to the *Standard* that he had in fact included everything he had said in the actual letter to Ullathorne. In a letter on the previous day to Emily Bowles, Newman had also interestingly spoken of the publication of his 28 January letter as a betrayal: "I believe it is quite a mystery who is the traitor."[179]

Even on Good Friday, Newman still spoke of his letter and of the proceedings at Rome. "It was one of the most confidential letters that I ever wrote in my life," he told the Dominican Reginald Buckler. "And I wrote it as an absolute duty."

> I have no claim as a theologian—but I have a claim to speak as one who is now near 70 years old, and has experience of various kinds in ecclesiastical matters. My rule is to act according to my best light as if I was infallible, before the Church decides; but to accept and submit to God's Infallibility when the Church has spoken. The Church has not yet spoken, and till she has, not only is my freedom of thought in possession, and I may fairly consider myself right in what I think, and I have a very strong view on the present question. I think the movement party is going too fast.

Then Newman turned again to the Immaculate Conception, another dominant theme in the various strong letters that he wrote in late March and in April 1870. "How differently things went in the case of the Immaculate Conception," he told Buckler. "Step after step was taken *towards* it. The Church patiently waited till all was ripe—No Council was necessary—the theological opinion grew into a dogma, as it were, spontaneously. But now it is as if certain parties wish to steal a march upon Catholics. Nothing is above board—nothing is told to bishops generally before hand—the gravest innovation possible, (for it is a change in the hitherto recognized basis of the Church,) is to be carried by acclamation.—Deliberation is to have no part in the work." Newman closed the letter to Buckler by using again the image of shouting a warning to a railway workman unaware that a train was fast closing on him. And he used a phrase so characteristic of his life and thought, "Slowness in decision, tenderness for weaker brethren, are first principles in the exercise of Ecclesiastical authority."[180]

Even on Easter Day, 17 April, Newman spent some time at his writing desk, but he wrote more calmly, the calm he knew when writing to the closest of his friends. The principal topic of his letter to Mary Holmes was the publication of his letter to Bishop Ullathorne: "No—it is one of those wonderful things, which cannot distress one, because simply it is

179. Newman to Emily Bowles, 13 April 1870, *The Letters and Diaries,* 25:96.
180. Newman to Father Reginald Buckler, O.P., 15 April 1870, *The Letters and Diaries,* 25:100–01.

in no sense one's own doing. I only wish, since the letter *was* to get out, I had introduced into it the awful text, which is much forgotten, 'Who shall scandalize one of these little ones who believe in Me, it were better than [sic] a millstone should be tied around his neck, and he cast into the sea.' What call have we to shock and frighten away 'the weak brothers for whom Christ died'?'' Newman ended by saying, ''Thank you for your prayers. Don't suppose I am cast down—not a bit of it, and, thank God, I am very well.''[181]

From the time of this brief reflective letter on Easter Day until the second week in May, a kind of quiet entered Newman's life so far as the council was concerned, at least from the evidence that his extant correspondence gives. Things were otherwise at Rome. On 29 April it was announced to the fathers of the council that the topic of infallibility would be moved forward in the order of debate. This announcement was a source of consternation to the bishops opposed to the definition and caused them to make new plans in the face of what they knew to be the great likelihood that the definition would be passed.

Newman begins to prepare for what he now sees as almost inevitable

This peaceful interlude for Newman was shattered when on 6 May, *Le Monde* printed a letter from Father Bernard Dalgairns of the London Oratory. The letter, written on 2 May, had the ostensible purpose of defending Newman against charges made by Louis Veuillot in *L'Univers* that Newman had never thanked Veuillot for the money he had raised through *L'Univers* to help Newman with the expenses of the Achilli trial in 1852. These charges Dalgairns refuted. But his letter had another, and more far-reaching, purpose. Calculated to keep up the old antipathies between the two English houses of the Oratory, it read in part:

> Before the Council of the Vatican was even convoked, Father Knox, at that time our Superior, wrote a pamphlet to prove the infallibility of the Holy See and to set forth the sphere of its action according to the opinion of the great majority of theologians; together with all my brethren of the London Oratory, I adhere entirely to this excellent treatise. . . . I deplore the unfortunate publicity given to a letter[182] in which the writer poured forth to his Bishop his wounded feelings. I deplore it, because it gives rise to suppositions of a complicity between Father Newman and a party with whom, practically, I am convinced, he has nothing in common. I am indignant that the few liberal Catholics who are to be found in England should dare to

---

181. Newman to Mary Holmes, 17 April 1870, *The Letters and Diaries,* 25:101–02; Matthew 18:6; Romans 14:15.
182. Newman to Bishop William Ullathorne, 28 January 1870.

use his name as their shield. With sorrow I admit that he has done wrong in affording a pretext for this accusation.[183]

When he learned of the Dalgairns letter Newman had just heard from Bishop David Moriarty, who had written an unusually candid letter from Rome. Moriarty told Newman that he had been one of a group of bishops who had asked Pius IX to postpone for a year any action on the infallibility question. In addition he told Newman:

> Speaking secundum hominem I would say that neither time nor place are suited for a general Council. The Pope, the Bishops of Italy, of Spain, of Mexico are smarting under a sense of recent wrong done under cover or pretext of those great principles of liberty of which we in England and America are enjoying the blessed fruit. The truth has gained half France— half the French Bishops say their position is better than before the Revolution.
>
> Nor does the place suit. The presence and presidence of the Summus Pontifex necessarily takes from the council the pouvoir constitutif. . . .[184]

Newman gave only passing notice to Moriarty's remarkable letter. He was greatly disturbed at the moment by the Dalgairns letter and he made this the principal subject of his reply of 8 May to Moriarty. "Why I write is this," Newman explained to the bishop of Kerry,

> —Fr. Dalgairns of the London Oratory has written a letter against me in the Monde—with the *object*, (as it seems to me,) of its preventing any possible [influence] my divulged letter may ex[ert on any] one at Rome; for instance on the French Bishops.
>
> The *point* of his letter seems to be this—that he is an old friend of mine of 30 years standing, and that he and other friends view with grief my having left them. . . .
>
> I could tell a very different tale, [but it] would not become me.

Newman concluded his letter by saying, "At first I thought to have written to the Monde briefly to say 'He is not a friend of mine of 30 years standing—' but I think I shall answer every purpose by thus writing to you.'"[185] Aside from expressing his anger to a friend, Newman must have thought that Moriarty could set the record straight in Rome, particularly with the French bishops. Moriarty responded on 14 May. He told New-

183. *The Letters and Diaries,* 2 May 1870, 25:121–22, n. 2: English translation from the *Tablet,* 7 May 1870, n.s. 3, 35:580–81.

184. Bishop David Moriarty to Newman, 28 April 1870, *The Letters and Diaries,* 25:120, n. 1.

185. Newman to Bishop David Moriarty, 8 May 1870, *The Letters and Diaries,* 25:120–22. The editors of *The Letters and Diaries* explain that the sections in brackets are attempts at reconstructing the letter, since the extant copy is in places torn.

man that the letter of Dalgairns "caused me to have a feeling of disgust."
Moriarty protested:

> What do these men mean by designating liberalism as a heresy, and liberal Catholics as heretics to be avoided? Is it not liberalism that gives them the right and protection by which they live and preach and practice? Restore the principle of intolerance and what will become of the London Oratory? I am glad you have not answered the letter. Let no abuse tempt you to break silence. Should the Papal infallibility be defined, you will render a signal service to the Church by writing in support of the truth, for the opportunity will then have ceased to be a question.[186]

Moriarty continued in a tone heavy with resignation:

> As far as human calculations can guide us, the Council will proceed to the definition, but the Providence of God may prevent it by means we cannot foresee. If God does not interfere, we must acknowledge that the result will be His Holy Will.
>
> The authorities will carefully avoid interference with the liberty of speaking or voting. If we are overwhelmed it must be by a majority of our own brethren in the episcopacy. On the other hand, if the Pope's cause has been damaged by the intemperate advocacy of the *Civiltà, Univers,* and *Tablet,* we have been damaged also by some of the pamphlets on our side. Some of our friends have not written "cum moderamine inculpatae tutelae." They furnish our adversaries with arguments for the necessity of an immediate definition. Let us all pray, "Dominus dirigat corda nostra et intelligentias nostras".[187]

Through the rest of May, Newman's life appears to have been largely uninterrupted by the council. He gave his attention to preparations for the feast of St. Philip Neri in late May, preparations complicated in 1870 by the coincidence of the feast of the Ascension on 26 May and thus the need to transfer the observances in honor of St. Philip, including the traditional festivities involving the Oratory School. There was a brief interruption in these domestic concerns when Newman wrote on 20 May to E. B. Pusey. Pusey had sent copies of his "Is Healthful Reunion Impossible?" to Bishop Clifford and Bishop Dupanloup in Rome but had never received an acknowledgement from them. Through Moriarty, Newman had finally ascertained that the copies had never reached the two bishops, owing it seemed to the vigilant Roman censors, though a copy intended for Moriarty had reached him and he had shared it with Dupanloup. New-

---

186. Bishop David Moriarty to Newman, 14 May 1870, *The Letters and Diaries,* 25:122–23, n. 2; *The Letters and Diaries* says "the opportunity will then have ceased." Butler, quoting the same letter, says "the opportuneness will have ceased." Butler, *The Vatican Council,* 2:62.
    187. Butler, *The Vatican Council,* 2:62. This section of Moriarty's letter is not quoted in *The Letters and Diaries.*

man concluded his recital of this explanation to Pusey by stating briefly but significantly, "I fear from Dr. Moriarty's letter, there is no chance of the Definition being avoided."[188] On 26 May, Newman's diary entry reads, "Ascension. I preached as for St. Philip's day," but the actual observance of the Founder's feast seems to have been celebrated on 31 May and 1 June.

On the day before Ascension Thursday, Manning spoke at the council for nearly two hours.[189] It was by all accounts one of the great speeches of the council. Whereas Newman in his letter to Whitty of 12 April had said that the definition would have adverse effects in England both on Catholics and non-Catholics, Manning in his speech of 25 May said "Nothing is so injurious to the spread of Catholicism in England as the doubts and controversies among Catholics on this matter of the infallibility." In the same speech he took other positions with which Newman could not have agreed, perhaps none so surely as his declaration: "The Pope's infallibility is Catholic doctrine of divine faith, and all are obliged to hold it; to question it is at least material heresy, for it is not an open theological opinion, but a doctrine contained in the divine revelation."[190] Bishop William Clifford spoke on the same day, against the definition. He urged that any consideration of the pope's infallibility not be separated from the Church's infallibility.[191]

On 1 June, Newman received another report from Rome from Bishop Ullathorne, who wrote: "We are in the thick of the discussion on the great question. . . . Some efforts have been made by conferences of members

188. Newman to E. B. Pusey, 20 May 1870, *The Letters and Diaries,* 25:130.

189. See Butler, *Vatican Council,* 2:50.

190. Butler, *The Vatican Council,* 2:49–50. See full text of Manning's speech in Mansi, 52:249–61.

191. See Butler, *The Vatican Council,* 2:52. See full text of Clifford's speech in Mansi, 52:274–84. Concerning Manning's and Clifford's speeches, Acton reported to Döllinger: "In the Council he [Manning] asserted that English Catholics are in favor of the teaching, that Protestants also bear witness to it, that they would strengthen his hand. He did not say that the most important English theologian, Newman, expressed himself so sharply against the definition. For it was in conformity with the bitter enmity that exists between these two men to ignore him. Nor did he say that the English bishops are now separated into two equal halves, but he read excerpts from Protestant papers which said that infallibility is, to be sure, the legitimate result of Catholicism. He had to descend to such miserable weapons in order to defend his case. Clifford, who spoke immediately afterwards, had an easy time exposing this nonsense. But one point of his speech escaped the listeners. Clifford said that the extent of damage to the Church by this definition—and to religion in England—can be seen from letters of outstanding statesmen, the existence of which can be witnessed to by one of the archbishops present. (It is the letter of Gladstone, April 25, which you sent me, and I showed Clifford.) The archbishop was Manning himself, and the allusion is to a letter from an English minister to him. . . ." Acton to Döllinger, June 1870, *Briefwechsel,* 2:389. The original, with the exception of the sentence in parentheses, is in German.

to bring things to an understanding but hitherto without success."[192] Ullathorne's letter drew Newman back into the discussion of the definition.
He had not changed the position that he had so strongly taken in April
in his letter to Whitty. Nor did he in writing to Ullathorne change his tone:

> I trust the account in the Papers is true, that the Pope intends to have mercy
> on the assembled Fathers from St Peter and St Paul [29 June] to the middle
> of October. However, such a respite involves a longer sitting when you meet
> again—and the sitting any how, I suppose, will be of formidable length,
> if the Fathers are to show a moral unanimity. Luckily they are not shut up
> without meat and drink like an English jury. But a moral unanimity is
> indispensable—for how could we take as the voice of the Council, which
> is infallible, a definition which a body of Bishops, of high character in them-
> selves, and representing large masses of the faithful, protested against? Per-
> haps Garibaldi will anticipate the unanimous decision.[193]

Is there hopefulness in Newman's closing remark?

Newman took up the theme of moral unanimity again in a letter he
wrote in late June to Francis Diederich Wackerbarth, an English as-
tronomer working in Sweden. Newman had met Wackerbarth just before
the latter became a Catholic in 1841. In his letter of 28 June, Newman said:

> I will not believe that this definition about Papal Infallibility is passed, till
> it actually is passed. It seems to me a duty, out of devotion to the Pope
> and charity to the souls of men, to resist it, while resistance is possible.
> It is very unlike the Immaculate Conception, in this, that no country
> raised its voice against that definition, and that Germany and good part
> of France, to name no other countries, are opposed to the present move-
> ment. I don't think any definition can be passed under a protest from French,
> German etc. Bishops. There must be a moral unanimity.
> We can but leave the matter to God, and rest confidently in His protec-
> tion of *His Infallible Church* and the guidance of the Holy Ghost."[194]

In late June and early July, Newman's other comments on the council
are almost exclusively confined to responding to people, such as Wackerbarth, troubled by the impending definition. On 27 June, Newman wrote
to an Irish member of Parliament, W. J. O'Neill Daunt, who had approached Newman with some questions from a friend. It is interesting
to note that whereas on 20 May in his letter to Pusey, Newman appeared

---

192. Bishop William Ullathorne to Newman, 1 June 1870, *The Letters and Diaries,*
25:138–39, n. 2.

193. Newman to Bishop William Ullathorne, 6 June 1870, *The Letters and Diaries,*
25:138–39.

194. Newman to Francis Diederich Wackerbarth, 28 June 1870, *The Letters and Diaries,*
25:153–54. Emphasis supplied.

sure that the definition was unavoidable, in this letter to Daunt he took a different position:

> As to the subject of your letter, I certainly think the agitation of the Pope's Infallibility most unfortunate and ill-advised—and I shall think so even if the Council decrees it, unless I am obliged to believe that the Holy Ghost protects the Fathers from all inexpedient acts, (which I do not see is any where promised) as well as guides them into all the truth, as He certainly does. There are truths which are inexpedient.
> . . . Your friend should not take it for granted that the Infallibility of the Pope will be carried. I am not at all sure it will—For myself, I refuse to believe that it can be carried, till it actually is. I think the great Doctors of the Church will save us from a dogma which they did not hold themselves.
> Next, if any thing is past [sic], it will be in so mild a form as, practically to mean little or nothing. There is a report, . . . that Cardinal Cullen said, when he was in Dublin at Easter, that he thought "the Pope would *never be able to use* the dogma, in the shape it was to be passed." In concluding Newman asked: "Lastly, is your friend sure she *understands* the dogma, even as Ultramontanes hold it. I very much doubt if she does. She should look carefully to this—The Pope did *not* force on us the Immaculate Conception. The whole of Christendom wished it."[195] Strangely Newman appears to be implying here that the whole of Christendom also wished for the definition of papal infallibility. This is yet another evidence of Newman's continuing inconsistency on the topic.

In the letter to Daunt, Newman made reference to a poem by Cowper, entitled "Needless Alarm." The next day he made the following note for himself, quoting the lines he alluded to but did not give in the letter to Daunt:

> Beware of desperate steps; the darkest day,
> Live till tomorrow, will have passed away.
> Vigil of SS. Peter & Paul [28 June] 1870. John H. Newman[196]

In the months ahead Newman would frequently use these lines to counsel caution for those who would write to him to say that their faith had been shaken by the definition. In some sense they should be seen as a watchword for himself. The day before, Newman had written, again for his own personal use, a "Memorandum on the Definition of Infallibility." This memorandum has interesting parallels with the notes that Newman wrote on 20 September 1869 and on 12 December 1869, just as the council was opening. The memorandum reads:

195. Newman to W. J. O'Neill Daunt, 27 June 1870, *The Letters and Diaries,* 25:150–51.
196. Newman "Notes," 28 June 1870, *The Letters and Diaries,* 25:150, n. 3.

If three Fathers, such as Justin, Tertullian, and Irenaeus, could be produced saying "the Pope is the Vicar of Xt" as they say, that "Mary is the second Eve."

Two subjects
    1. Councils have been scenes of violence etc.
    2. they have been followed by long disputes and schisms
    inopportune
To Him who sees the end from the beginning, whatever he does is *expedient* i.e. on the long run—but it may be inexpedient for *the time*

inopportune means   1. uncharitable
                     2. unecclesiastical—a false step[197]

    It is not clear what Newman intended this memorandum for. It might indicate that he was planning to write something either for his own use or for publication. Aside from the opening remark "if three Fathers," it might also have been a memorandum on which he expected to base letters in response to those who would write to him now that, according to most reports, the definition appeared imminent.

    In two letters on 3 July, Newman dealt with the council. In the one to Canon Walker of Scarborough there was still a touch of optimism: "As to the Council, it is wonderful that a definition has not yet passed, and gives one hope."[198] In the other to Mrs. Margaret Wilson, a convert disturbed by the possibility of a definition, Newman was more sober and spoke in terms close to those of his 27 June memorandum:

> I feel with you what a time of trial this is, the opinions of Catholics being so divided. All I can say is, that an Ecumenical Council has not unfrequently created such divisions, and that truth is ultimately promoted by what at the time is very painful.
>
>   To myself, with many others, it is the Presence of our Lord in the Blessed Sacrament which is the relief and consolation for all the troubles of ecclesiastical affairs. I wish you could make that your own consolation. What can I do better than call on you to go to Him who is your Life and your Strength?"[199]

    Six days later Newman resumed an earlier correspondence on the council with Mrs. F. R. Ward. The prospect of the definition was now, as Newman's letter shows, all but sure:

---

197. Newman "Memorandum on the Definition of Infallibility," 27 June 1870, *The Letters and Diaries,* 25:151.

198. Newman to Canon John Walker of Scarborough, 3 July 1870, *The Letters and Diaries,* 25:156.

199. Newman to Mrs. Margaret Wilson, 3 July 1870, *The Letters and Diaries,* 25:156.

This is certainly a most anxious time of suspense—though they say now it is to be at an end on the 16th or 17th. Councils have ever been times of great *trial*—and this seems likely to be no exception. It was always held that the conduct of individuals who composed them was no measure of the authority of their result. We are sure, as in the case of the administration of the sacraments, that the holiness of actors in them is not a necessary condition of God's working by means of them. Nothing can be worse than the conduct of many in and out of the Council who are taking the side which is likely to prevail.[200]

In mid-July, Newman received a letter that brought from him one of the great moments of his vast correspondence. The letter, written by Edward Husband, who had been received into the Church at the Birmingham Oratory in 1869 but had recently returned to the Anglican Church, was partly occasioned by the council. Husband told Newman that he intended to publish his letter to Newman, which he did later in 1870. Husband wrote:

I have a great hope . . . that . . . if the Infallibility of the Pope is declared an Article of Faith, you will retrace your steps. . . . You, under God, were really the originator of the "Oxford Movement." . . . You taught us how to love our Lord; His Mother; His Sacraments; and His Saints by setting before us the mind, and authoritative teaching of the Early Church. . . . You have sacrificed *every thing* for Christ's sake, and broken ties, which caused you agony. . . .[201]

And after this poignant recital, the question—"Have you found what you hoped and longed for?"—elicited from Newman his masterful and deeply revealing reply. Newman responded to Husband on 17 July, the eve of the definition:

"Have I found," you ask of me, "in the Catholic Church, what I hoped and longed for?" That depends on what I "hoped and longed for?" I did not hope or long for any "peace or satisfaction," as you express it, for any illumination or success. I did not hope or long for any thing except to do God's will, which I feared not to do. . . .

You add that my very look is one of disappointment;[202]—those who think me disappointed, will easily discern it in my face; but he cannot have much disappointment, who never had much hope. . . .

Then again, whether I have, since a Catholic, been treated well or ill, by high personages or confidential friends, does not touch the question of truth and error, the Church and schism.

200. Newman to Mrs. F. R. Ward, 9 July 1870, *The Letters and Diaries,* 25:158.
201. Edward Husband to Newman, 13 July 1870, *The Letters and Diaries,* 25:160, n. 2.
202. Husband had met Newman the previous year at the time of his reception into the Catholic Church.

Be sure, if I can answer for myself in any thing, Anglican I can never be again. I desire and I pray, that you may be as certain of retrieving your late unhappy step, as I am certain of never discerning any fount of grace or promise of salvation in the Church of England.

I do not say "as certain as I am certain I shall perserve [sic] in the Catholic Church," for such perseverance comes, "not of the will of the flesh, nor of the will of man," but of the electing mercy of Almighty God. But, though I cannot presume to anticipate the future, I can recall the past. I can affirm that by God's grace I have never for a moment doubted that the Roman Communion is the One Fold of Christ, ever since I entered it. . . ."[203]

On the very day of the definition, Newman told the Earl of Dunraven: "The proceedings of the Council are most serious. God will turn them to good ultimately—but I should not like to have the responsibility of their immediate authors. It has been a very anxious and painful six months."[204] Over the next several days Newman remarked in his diary on the splendid summer weather. He was back and forth to Rednal while several of the other Fathers left on holiday. The period brought various visitors, including the president of St. Edmund's College (Ware), Dr. Rymer, and Mr. and Mrs. Ambrose De Lisle. Both Frederick Rymer and Ambrose De Lisle were opponents of the definition. While De Lisle was there Newman had a long conversation with him, which must have touched on the definition. Neither of them, it would appear, had yet seen the text of the definition.[205]

OVERVIEW

There are several strands in Newman's letters on the council in the first half of 1870 that call for some brief comment at this point. All of these points will be dealt with more fully in the conclusion. Throughout this period Newman showed a great sensitivity toward the people to whom he was writing. To those close friends and associates, such as Monsell, Moriarty, and Simeon, whom he knew to be concerned by the prospect of a definition, he tried to be reassuring, but in doing so he did not hide his own misgivings and opposition. To a troubled person considering entrance into the Roman Catholic Church, he was measured and encouraging, inviting the correspondent to look carefully at his or her motives and not just at events at Rome and their possible outcome. Each letter he wrote forced him to focus his attention more sharply on his own attitudes.

The Ullathorne letter and its subsequent publication brought Newman very much into the fray. Publicly and privately, he had disavowed any

203. Newman to Edward Husband, 17 July 1870, *The Letters and Diaries*, 25:160–61.
204. Newman to the Earl of Dunraven, 18 July 1870, *The Letters and Diaries*, 25:163.
205. See Newman letter (not sent) to Ambrose De Lisle, 24 July 1870, *The Letters and Diaries*, 25:164–65.

public part in the controversy over the definition, but he did not appear in March and April 1870 to be greatly alarmed or to regret strongly his being thrust forward as a participant in the debate. The letter to Ullathorne, though frequently passionate and rhetorical, has to be taken as a true record of Newman's views. Its tone as well as its arguments show how deep-seated Newman's fears over the possibility of a definition were. It has about it in a way that no other letter from this period does an almost official character, a letter of a priest to his bishop, a letter to someone with a certain influence at the scene of the action, a letter to someone whose sense of fairness and balance he respected, whatever his misgivings about Ullathorne's being willing to stand up to Manning and the members of the ultra party.

It seems clear from the letter to Ullathorne and other letters from the same period that Newman did not simply think the definition inopportune. There is a certain mildness to that term that does not do justice to his position. Rather, he thought the definition a disastrous mistake for the times. It would in his opinion be a setback to what he saw as a growing sympathy for Catholicism as an answer to unbridled materialism and liberalism, not only among Anglican Ritualists in England but also among Christians in other parts of the world, particularly the non-Latin world. Newman feared that sincere Catholics would not be able to accept the doctrine, that the movement for the definition had taken the Church by surprise and was contrary to the history of the development of dogma, that the question was being scandalously rushed. Newman's letters show a certain going back and forth throughout this period on the papal infallibility question, now calm and accepting, now angry and uncertain. There is evidence enough that Newman, while often saying that the definition was inopportune, came very close to saying that a definition of papal infallibility (as contrasted to the Church's infallibility) would be not simply a mistake for others but a severe test of his own faith.

Despite the withdrawn position he had chosen, especially after giving up the rectorship of the Catholic University of Ireland in 1858, Newman was nevertheless in receipt of a good deal of accurate information on the council, often from firsthand sources. But his information, despite the amazing speed of the post, was inevitably at times incomplete or out of date. He appeared to be still convinced in April 1870 that a definition by acclamation was a real possibility in Rome when the promoters of the definition had already seen that there was no possibility for such a course of action. A man professedly happy to be on the sidelines, Newman was clearly eager for information from Rome and he must have occasionally regretted having so removed a part in what he saw to be—for better or worse—one of the most important episodes in the long history of the Church. Did Newman really believe that whatever he had to say would have no influence on the events of the council or the bishops gathered in Rome for it? Or did he fear this influence and the possible consequences of it?

Finally, the private notes that Newman made on the topic of papal infallibility on 20 September 1869, 12 December 1869, and 27 June 1870, however enigmatic and terse, are extremely important in evaluating his position before the definition as well as after. They set down themes that return again and again in Newman's dealings with the papal infallibility question and serve in part as a basis for his responses, private and public, to the definition that was promulgated on 18 July 1870.

The complexities that have fascinated and attracted, as well as frustrated, students of Newman are perhaps nowhere more evident than in his approach to the definition of 1870. But here also are many instances when his painstaking caution and deliberation are surprisingly cast aside.

Chapter 3

"It Is Too Soon to Give an Opinion About the Definition"

July 1870–July 1871

Newman first saw the text of the definition on 23 July. By that time Ambrose De Lisle had gone, though Dr. Frederick Rymer, president of St. Edmund's College (Ware),[1] was still with Newman, as he was until the 25th. On 24 July, Newman wrote a long letter to De Lisle which he did not send. It is the first indication of his reaction to the definition, and its third, fourth, and fifth sentences contain the famous statement that ever since has been taken as Newman's attitude after reading the text of the infallibility decree. "I saw the new Definition yesterday," he said, "and am pleased at its moderation, that is, if the doctrine in question is to be defined at all. The terms used are vague and comprehensive; and, personally, I have no difficulty in admitting it. The question is, does it come to me with the authority of an Ecumenical Council?" Though Newman did not send this letter it was printed, without its last three paragraphs, with the *Letter to the Duke of Norfolk*. At some point, probably well after he wrote it, Newman made the following annotation at the head of the letter: "My formal opinion. Letter I."

Newman continued the letter, chiefly arguing the question he had raised—"does it come to me with the authority of an Ecumenical Council?" He was still evidently concerned about the matter of a moral unanimity.[2] Certainly he must have known, or have heard some rumors, about the bishops who had absented themselves from the council's final vote:

1. The major seminary of the Westminster archdiocese.
2. Romuald A. Dibble, S.D.S., *John Henry Newman: The Concept of Infallible Doctrinal Authority* (Washington: CUA Press, 1955) 237-39. He argues that Newman had three principal reasons for initially hesitating over whether there was a necessity for Catholics to accept the definition. First, that Newman (mistakenly) believed that the pope had to make a distinct act of ratifying the decrees of a council. Dibble maintains that this requirement did not hold since the pope had actually presided over the council in person. Second, that Newman believed that a majority was not sufficient to satisfy the need for a moral unanimity. Third, that Newman, while well versed in the history of the councils of the Church,

"Were it not then for certain circumstances, under which the Council made the definition, I should receive that definition at once. Even as it is, if I were called upon to profess it, I should be unable, considering it came from the Holy Father and the competent local authorities, at once to refuse to do so. On the other hand it cannot be denied that there are reasons for a Catholic, till better informed, to suspend his judgment on its validity." Newman continued the argument that would preoccupy him and a number of other people in England and elsewhere in the months ahead. "But if the fact be so," he wrote, "that the Fathers were not unanimous, is the definition valid? This depends on the question whether unanimity, at least moral, is or is not necessary for its validity? As at present advised, I think it is; certainly Pius IV lays a great stress on the unanimity of the Fathers in the Council of Trent." And then came the question that was to involve Newman in a great deal of discussions and correspondence with Dr. Rymer, Bishop Clifford, Bishop Moriarty, and Archbishop Errington. Newman wrote: "But if I must now at once decide what to think of it, I should consider that all turned on what the dissentient Bishops now do."[3] Newman, ever careful to weigh both sides, gave the clear case

---

had an insufficient appreciation and understanding of the theology of general councils in the life of the Church.

In his recent reappraisal of the First Vatican Council, a reappraisal prompted by what he terms an "ecumenical deadlock on the papacy," Luis Bermejo, S.J., sees Newman's questioning of the moral unanimity of the conciliar fathers on the council's decision in favor of papal infallibility as an extremely important factor in Bermejo's own reappraisal of the question of whether a moral unanimity was achieved at the council, a question which he appears to answer in the negative. Bermejo lays great stress on Newman's letter (unsent) to Ambrose Phillipps De Lisle of 24 July 1870 and Newman's letter of 15 August 1870 to Frederick Rymer. See Luis M. Bermejo, S.J., *Infallibility on Trial: Church, Conciliarity and Communion* (Westminster, Md.: Christian Classics, Inc., 1992) 145, 150–51. Certainly, nagging doubts about the question of moral unanimity continued to disturb Newman well after he had given evidence of accepting the definition as binding. See, for example, his letter of 1 November 1870 to Bishop Moriarty and his letter of 13 December 1870 to Bishop Clifford.

Dibble further holds that Newman's hesitancy was largely limited to the first fourteen days after the definition (see p. 240) and that his "attitude of caution" lasted only "until definite word came from Rome through the proper ecclesiastical channels." A reading of all the letters from late July 1870 through the first half of 1871 would suggest that Dibble has simplified the problem of Newman's hesitation. It is interesting to note that while Dibble claims that too much has been made of Newman's letters from the period after the definition, he makes use of them to prove his point that any hesitancy on Newman's part was short-lived (see p. 224 and pp. 239–41, esp. n. 41 on p. 240–41, where Dibble quotes Newman's letter to Mrs. Anna Whitty of 31 August 1870). Dibble quotes from only a handful of the letters and seems to rely in his analysis of Newman's hesitancy on Newman's letters of 24 and 27 July 1870, which Newman printed as an appendix to the *Letter to the Duke of Norfolk* in 1875.

3. According to Frederick J Cwiekowski, "it was the exaggerated interpretations of the definition, . . . along with other factors—that the council was not officially concluded

for accepting the doctrine if the minority bishops did not continue their dissent as a group. "If they separate and go home without acting as a body," he said, "if they act only individually, or as individuals, . . . then I should not recognize in their opposition to the majority that force, firmness, and unity of view, which creates a real case of want of moral unanimity in the Council." Newman went on with this line of argumentation: "Again, if the Council continues to sit, if the dissentient Bishops more or less take part in it, and concur in its acts; if there is a new Pope, and he continues the policy of the present, and if the Council terminates without any reversal or modification of the definition, or any effective movement against it on the part of the dissentients, then again there will be good reason for saying that the want of moral unanimity has not been made out." Finally, Newman turned to what for him would be the highest argument beyond all others. "And further," he went on, "if the definition is eventually received by the whole body of the faithful, as valid or as the expression of a truth, then too it will claim our assent by the force of the great dictum, 'Securus judicat orbis terrarum.' "

At the conclusion of the letter Newman stepped down from his role of careful weigher of arguments and returned to the frank statements that had characterized so many of his letters during the eight months when the council was sitting. These were the sections of the letter that Newman omitted when it was printed in 1875.

> But, whatever is decided eventually about the definition of the present Council, the scandals which have accompanied it will remain, and the guilt of those who perpetrated them.
>
>   I will add that I adhere to every word of the letter which I wrote to my Bishop last January. . . . I only wish I had referred in it to the apprehension which weighs heavily upon me, that the actual tendency of the definition then in prospect will be to create in educated Catholics a habit of scepticism or secret infidelity as regards all dogmatic truth.

---

and that some were questioning the council's ecumenicity—which contributed to English hesitation in face of the council's decrees. This hesitation was, no doubt, restricted to a very small number, but Newman and some of the bishops were among them." Frederick J. Cwiekowski, *The English Bishops and the First Vatican Council* (Louvain: Publications Universitaires de Louvain, 1971) 286. Bishop Goss, who was not at the council, wrote in early August to Bishop Clifford in an effort to learn more about the position of the minority bishops, a position with which he was already in sympathy. Goss wrote: "The majority of the English B[isho]ps were opposed to the fabrication of the new article. He [Manning] says it is already of faith; but I conjecture that the decree has no force till promulgated with the other acts of the Council. It is so with a Provincial Synod. Do the opposition B[isho]ps admit the decree or do they challenge the authority of the whole Council on the score of want of liberty of action?" Archives of the Diocese of Clifton, Letters to William Clifford, Part I, Goss to Clifford, 8 August 1870, as quoted in Cwiekowski, *The English Bishops,* 293.

Nor, in saying this, do I forget that the definition, if valid, has been passed under the Presence and Aid of the Holy Ghost; for though the supernatural promise guarantees its truth, it does not therefore guarantee the Christian prudence, the spirit and temper of its promulgators.[4]

Newman had begun this letter mildly enough but he had ended with an angry flourish. He obviously did not see himself on the side of the victors and could only see the benefit of the definition and the need to accept it after elaborate and painstaking argument. He also saw his obligation to those who depended on him for encouragement, guidance, and counsel in their life of faith. The future prospects of living in the same Church as Manning, Ward, and the younger Vaughan would be unsettling for many of those who were close to him, and for himself. It is not clear why Newman did not send the letter of 24 July. Possibly he simply thought better of it. His careful temperament may well have persuaded him to think matters over again, to wait for further information. It is likely that he discussed the matter with Dr. Rymer, who was in the house, with his intimate friend, Ambrose St. John, who did not leave for his holiday until 26 July, and with his longtime friend, the distinguished Irish scholar, Dr. Charles Russell of Maynooth, who, as Newman records in his diary, came to stay at the Oratory on 27 July.[5]

Newman carefully confines his views on the definition to close friends

The first letters (at least of those extant) that Newman did send on the definition were sent to two of his oldest and closest friends, Sister Maria Pia Giberne and Father Ambrose St. John. No doubt Newman felt he could trust these two confidants to keep his thoughts to themselves and thus give him the chance to continue to weigh the issue from every side as new opinions and evidence came to him. Newman told Sister Maria Pia that Ambrose St. John, who had planned to visit her would be unable to come because of the war conditions on the Continent.[6] Newman knew that Sister Maria Pia would be disappointed and he linked that disappointment to the greater disappointment that so many were experiencing over the recent council. He began by making a half-hearted effort to put the definition, at least ideally, in a good light:

4. Newman to Ambrose De Lisle, 24 July 1870, *The Letters and Diaries of John Henry Newman*, ed. Charles Stephen Dessain and Thomas Gornall, S.J. (Oxford: The Clarendon Press, 1973) 25:164–66.

5. See Newman "Diary," *The Letters and Diaries,* 25:166.

6. France declared war on Prussia on 19 July, the day after the solemn session of the council at which the constitution on papal primacy and the infallible magisterium was formally approved.

. . . our good God is trying all of us with disappointment and sorrow just now;—I allude to what has taken place at Rome—who of us would not have rejoiced if the Fathers of the Council had one and all felt it their duty to assent to the infallibility of the Holy Father? but a gloom falls upon one, when it is decreed with so very large a number of dissentient voices. It looks as if our Great Lord were in some way displeased at us. Indeed the look of public matters generally is very threatening, and we need the prayers of all holy souls, of all good nuns, to avert the evils which seem coming upon the earth.[7]

Newman was of course in part referring to the Franco-Prussian War, but this note of apocalypticism was evidently inspired also by the Vatican Council.

Newman was more forthcoming in his letter to Ambrose St. John. This letter, which was eventually printed with the *Letter to the Duke of Norfolk*, shows Newman grappling with the question whether the doctrine had to be accepted under the present circumstances. Written on 27 July, four days after Newman had seen the text of the definition, it is in many ways a surer indication of Newman's reaction than the letter of the twenty-fourth to Ambrose De Lisle. The fact that St. John had just left on holiday the day before gave Newman the chance to put his thoughts on paper in the form of a letter to his closest friend and confidant: "I have been thinking over the subject which just now gives you and me, with thousands of others, who care for religion, so much concern." Newman's first concern was the council's lack of moral unanimity: "First, till better advised, nothing shall make me say that a mere majority in a Council, as opposed to a moral unanimity, in itself creates an obligation to receive its dogmatic decrees. This is a point of history and precedent; and of course on further examination I may find myself wrong in the view which I take of history and precedent; but I do not, cannot see, that a majority in the present Council can of itself *rule* its own sufficiency, without such external authority."

If the issue of moral unanimity was inconclusive, Newman, true to his nature, was quick to acknowledge arguments on the other side:

But there are other means by which I can be brought under the obligation of receiving a doctrine as a dogma, that is, as a part of the faith necessary to salvation.

For instance, if I am clear that it is in Scripture, . . . —or again that it is in primitive and uninterrupted tradition. . . . Or when a high probability, drawn from Scripture or tradition, is partially or probably confirmed by the Church. Thus a particular Catholic might be so nearly sure that the

7. Newman to Sister Maria Pia Giberne, 27 July 1870, *The Letters and Diaries,* 25:166–67.

promises to Peter in Scripture proved that the Infallibility of Peter is a necessary dogma, as only to be kept from holding it as such, by the absence of any judgment on the part of the Church—so that the present unanimity between Pope and 500 Bishops, even though not sufficient to constitute a formal synodal act, would at once put him in the position, and lay him under the obligation of receiving the dogma, as a dogma, i.e. with its anathema.

Although conciliar authority might be in doubt, Newman still was willing to concede an obligation of accepting the council's decision on the basis of authority "in possession":

> Or again, if nothing definitely sufficient can be brought to contradict a definition from Scripture or Tradition, the fact of a legitimate Superior having defined it may be an obligation in conscience to receive it with an internal assent. St. Alfonso lays down (with others) that, even though a legitimate Superior exceeds his power, his law is to be obeyed, for he is in possession; (unless indeed, he cannot be obeyed without great inconvenience etc.) I feel the force of this in my own case. Not to say that I have ever, since a Catholic held the Pope's Infallibility as a matter of opinion, at least I see nothing in the definition which necessarily contradicts Scripture, Tradition, or History. *I* can obey without *inconvenience;* and the Doctor Ecclesiae, whether exceeding his power or not, bids me obey. Therefore I have an obligation of accepting the definition as a dogma. In this case I do not receive it on the word of the Council, but on the Pope's self assertion.
>
> And I confess, as I said to you the other day, the fact that all along for so many centuries, the head of the Church and the teacher of the faithful and the Vicar of Christ has been allowed by God to assert virtually his infallibility, is a great argument in favour of the validity of his claim.

Before closing Newman pressed on with yet one more argument—an argument based on the divine guidance of the Church—in favor of accepting the definition:

> Another ground for receiving the dogma, still not upon the *direct* authority of the Council, or acceptance of the validity of its Act, is the consideration that the Merciful Lord would not care so little for His elect people, the multitude of the faithful as to allow their visible Head and such a large number of Bishops to lead them into error, and an error so great and so serious, if an error. This consideration leads me to accept the dogma, as a dogma, indirectly indeed from the Council, but not as from a Council, but as from the Pope and a large collection of Bishops. The question is, not whether they had a right to impose, or were right in imposing the dogma on the faithful, but whether, they having done so, I am not right, I have not an obligation, to accept it;—according to the maxim, Fieri non debuit, factum valet.

In the final paragraph, which was not printed with the rest of the letter when it was appended to the *Letter to the Duke of Norfolk,* Newman was evidently thinking of those who would seek his counsel on their obligation in face of the Vatican Council's action:

> And supposing a person says to me, "After all, I have been so opposed to the doctrine," or again, "I have so habitually considered it as a mere theological opinion, that I cannot get my mind to *act* towards it, I cannot take hold of it internally as a dogma, de fide;" I say to him "Your duty lies in observing two conditions, both of them in your power—first make an act of faith, in *all* that the Holy Church teachers [sic]—and secondly, as regards this particular doctrine, turn away from any doubt which rises in your mind about its truth. These two acts are in your power. And they are sufficient."

In the months ahead Newman would indeed use this advice for some of the people who wrote to him. It is evident from these people that some confessors and bishops in England would see Newman's view as insufficient for a true and loyal Catholic.

Newman concluded his letter to St. John with the instruction, "please keep this letter—or send it me back" and with a postscript, "Dr. Russell here, but I don't know whether he will open."[8] Newman was apparently hoping to sound out Dr. Russell on his views. Whether he succeeded is not clear. Russell left the next day and Newman went back to Rednal.

Newman expressed views similar to those that he had set down in his letter to St. John in a draft letter to another close friend. Writing on 12 August to Emily Bowles, Newman said:

> For me, the doctrine gives me no difficulty—but, as at present advised, I don't think it has been defined by the Council. I am waiting in suspense to know what the opposition Bishops think on the subject; their opinion would go a *great* way with me. The Council is not yet finished—when it is, then will be the time to judge whether the late proceeding has been a real synodal act. I don't care for the majority's threat, if they use it[,] that this act already is complete and over. I don't think it is.
>
> I had much rather take the doctrine as de fide on the Pope's self-assertion or "ipse dixit" this not[?] so tyrannical an act as the vote of the majority. There was no real moral unanimity JHN.[9]

Newman, however, decided against sending this letter to Emily Bowles and prepared a far briefer but confidential version, in which he substituted

8. Newman to Ambrose St. John, 27 July 1870, *The Letters and Diaries*, 25:167–68. In the *Letter to the Duke of Norfolk,* as reprinted in *Newman and Gladstone: The Vatican Decrees,* Alvan S. Ryan (Notre Dame, Ind.: University of Notre Dame Press, 1962) 170, Newman quoted from this letter to St. John and described it as having been written "to a friend who was troubled at the way in which the dogma was passed, in order to place before him in various points of view the duty of receiving it."

9. Draft Letter, Newman to Emily Bowles, 12 August 1870, *The Letters and Diaries,* 25:178, n. 4.

the following two sentences for what he had written in his draft: "At present I wait to see what the minority will do. If they do nothing, I shall consider it a moral unanimity in favour of the definition."[10]

Newman dissuades Father Frederick Rymer from writing publicly on the definition

In the first days of August, Newman received a paper, giving reasons why Catholics were not yet bound to accept the definition, from Frederick Rymer, who asked Newman to comment on it.[11] Rymer intended the paper for publication. After leaving the Oratory on 25 July, Rymer had written to Newman a week later, saying: "The question as to whether the recent definition on the pope's infallibility binds in conscience is—become a very important one and is likely to become every day more so."[12] Newman sent a long reply to Rymer on 3 August and he also made a number of penciled comments on Rymer's draft. Newman began his letter diffidently: "Your MS has just come and I have read it with interest. My memory is so bad that I cannot guarantee your statements of *doctrine* etc—though I *believe* them to be correct—and, as an argument, your whole paper is cogent and clear." Newman then went on to list the several difficulties that had occurred to him. First, he thought it essential that Rymer ascertain the position of the minority bishops. "I am not satisfied at your moving without knowing any thing about the views and intentions of the dissentient Bishops. Is it well for any of us to commit ourselves till we know what *they* intend to do?" Newman, attempting a middle course with regard to Rymer's plan, then went on to say: "They *may* have no intentions—but they might have a better way than ours, and we might by our act spoil or embarass [sic] theirs. I wish I knew whether Mgr. Dupanloup or Dr. Clifford had anything to say on the matter. It must be recollected that whatever line is taken against the definition may be *met,* or attempted to be met, by the violent party, when the Council meets again in October. We must take care not to *tell* our opponents what we want and what we don't."

Newman disagreed also on the use to be made of the axiom "Lex dubia non obligat" in the present instance. "St. Alfonso says," Newman wrote as he had to St. John on 27 July, "that, when a lawful authority probably goes beyond his power, the subject is bound to obey, since the ruler

10. Newman to Emily Bowles (II), 12 August 1870, *The Letters and Diaries*, 25:178.
11. On Frederick Rymer's paper and its arguments, see Cwiekowski, *The English Bishops,* 287.
12. Frederick Rymer to Newman, 1 August 1870, Archives of the Birmingham Oratory, Vatican Council file III, no. 20.

is in possession—unless the command is very onerous. *This,* I suppose, is the real issue of the case, not the Lex dubia.''

Newman considered the charge that the bishops at the council lacked the freedom necessary for a valid conciliar decision: ''Again I have some doubts whether *you* can urge that the Council was not free—what do *we* know about it? the *Bishops* themselves are the only witnesses. We must hear what *they* say and till they, as a body, (I mean the dissentients,) say so, we are premature, and intruding into their office in saying so.'' ''I do not see,'' he said, ''how we can move (*on the offensive,*) except *from* them—we can but say 'I have not yet *information enough* to accept the definition—I must suspend my judgment'—but to say that 'the Council is not free' is a positive charge.''

Finally, Newman could not agree with Rymer's use of his *Rambler* article, ''On Consulting the Faithful in Matters of Doctrine'':

> I fully agree with your 'Securus judicat orbis terrarum—the general accept-
> ance, judgment of Christendom is the ultimate guarantee of revealed truth—
> But I ought to add that according to my recollection, my paper in the
> Rambler is not in point—I think that paper was on the sensus, not the con-
> sensus, fidelium—their voice was considered as a witness, not as an authority
> or a judgment. . . . But *you* are speaking of the *ultimate* deciding power
> (securus *judicat* etc) not of the *initial* testimony, which I spoke of, in your
> remarks upon the Church diffusivè.

Having indicated these several problems in Rymer's approach, Newman was careful to conclude by saying, ''I have written all this by way of point-ing out all (possible) shoals and rocks in the way of your navigation, not as objecting with the object of opposing.''[13] But Rymer could not have missed the dissuasive thrust of Newman's letter and he continued to seek counsel before publishing his views. While a letter of Rymer to Newman on 15 August suggests that Rymer was growing impatient with Newman's extremely cautious advice on whether he should publish his views,[14] it is

13. Newman to Frederick Rymer, 3 August 1870, *The Letters and Diaries,* 25:171–72. In *On Consulting the Faithful in Matters of Doctrine,* Newman wrote: ''I think I am right in saying that the tradition of the Apostles, committed to the whole Church in its various constituents and functions *per modum unius,* manifests itself variously at various times: sometimes by the mouth of the episcopacy, sometimes by the doctors, sometimes by the people, sometimes by liturgies, rites, ceremonies, and customs, by events, disputes, move-ments, and all those other phenomena which are comprised under the name of history. It follows that none of these channels of tradition may be treated with disrespect; granting at the same time fully, that the gift of discerning, discriminating, defining, promulgating, and enforcing any portion of the tradition resides solely in the *Ecclesia docens.*'' John Henry Newman, *On Consulting the Faithful in Matters of Doctrine* (London: Collins, 1986) 63.

14. See Frederick Rymer to Newman, 15 August 1870, Archives of the Birmingham Oratory, Vatican Council file III, no. 39.

apparent from a letter to Newman from the previous week that Rymer was himself uncertain of his course. "The Tablet," he wrote, "has falsely asserted that the '*greater* and *lesser seminaries* of the diocese of Westminster have presented an address in favor of infallibility.' My difficulty is this; if I write to contradict it I shall certainly give great offence to the Archbishop and this may lead to important consequences. . . ."[15]

A few days later Rymer, having spoken with Errington and Clifford, informed Newman:

> 1. The bishops of the Minority do not consider the decree final and will not therefore try to impose it upon the faithful.
> 2. They will take no action in the matter unless some bull comes from Rome.
> 3. In the event before taking any steps they will communicate with each other so as to act in common.
> 4. The Minority is over a hundred and there seems to be no ground for asserting that *many* of them have made their submission . . .[16]

In a confidential letter of 15 August, Newman told Rymer:

> I think as follows, since you wish to know—1. Any how, I don't mean, whatever happens to be pushed out of the Church—nor do you—so that, if the worst comes to the worst, we should accept the dogma as a dogma, if the alternative was exclusion from the Sacraments.
> 2. This being the ruling principle on which we are to conduct ourselves, we should do nothing inconsistent with ultimately falling back upon it, if it must be so; and, in whatever we publish, we should see that we have not to eat our words; that we have not by bad logic to get out of a scrape etc etc.
> 3. Now *my own* lines of thought run thus. (1) As things stand, I have not information, I have not grounds sufficient for accepting the definition. The protest of 80 Bishops on the day of the voting in Session is a bar. (2) But, *supposing* that protest came to nothing, supposing its subscribers did not act in a body, and did not carry it out in their own dioceses, then I should think that the definition was valid. The bar to moral unanimity would be removed, or at least the Catholic world would have become of one mind, and I should believe on the "securus judicat orbis terrarum." But, while that bar continues, I cannot hold the dogma as a dogma by virtue of the vote in Session. Nay, even were it moved, I should think safer to believe in the "securus judicat" than on the Synodal Vote.

Yet even if moral unanimity and the universal judgment of the Church are absent, Newman saw another argument—that of papal authority:

15. Frederick Rymer to Newman, "before 6 August," Archives of the Birmingham Oratory, Vatican Council file III, no. 29.

16. Frederick Rymer to Newman, 11 August 1870, *The Letters and Diaries*, 25:172, n. 2.

(3) BUT again, even though the bar remains, and though there is not the clear and undeniable "judicium orbis terrarum", still, for myself, (and here perhaps you will not follow me) I consider the self-assertion, the ipse dixit of the Popes for 1800 years a great and imposing argument for the validity of their claims. I have said something of the kind in Loss and Gain, and somewhere else that the opposition of (e.g.) St. Cyprian to it is only the natural rising against authority of the human mind. And I confess that, if this argument were backed by the peremptory command "Believe or exclude yourself from the Sacraments," I should consider that the fact of the Pope being able by his own power of jurisdiction practically to enforce his claim of infallibility thus practically was a providential intimation that that claim was well founded, and I should receive the dogma as a dogma.

Newman concluded by questioning whether Rymer would be prudent in publishing his views: "Will you have suddenly to turn round? If not, you may publish without fear. 4. But not yet with prudence, unless you have definite and sufficient objects in view—e.g., to help and console others—to stave off the matter till the time of a New Pope etc etc. I think you should only profess to be 'waiting to see your way better.' "[17]

In a note written on a draft of this letter on 6 February 1875, shortly after the publication of the *Letter to the Duke of Norfolk,* Newman made the following comment: "These two first paragraphs, 1 and 2, were for the sake of *Dr. Rymer* I meant that *he* of course meant to secure for himself the sacraments, *he* must be 'all right behind' etc. etc."[18] In this important letter and in several others written during this period, Newman appeared to take the curious position that after all acceptance of the dogma depended on the traditional exercise of the papal office in history and the pope's power of jurisdiction, as if there had been no Vatican Council and no decision by the assembled bishops to bring the matter to its present state of contention. In the 15 August letter to Dr. Rymer, Newman looked toward a changed situation under a new pope, a change for the better, it would appear, as far as he and Rymer and others were concerned. Pius IX was seventy-eight in 1870, and Newman, as well as many others, was sure that he could not live much longer.[19] In fact he lived another eight years. But the themes of a "new Pope," and of popes going on too long crop up again and again in Newman's correspondence in the late 1860s and early 1870s. Surely the considerable effort that Newman was making to find reasons to accept the definition are indications of his own struggle as well as Rymer's.

17. Newman to Frederick Rymer, 15 August 1870, *The Letters and Diaries,* 25:186–87.
18. *The Letters and Diaries*, 25:186, n. 1.
19. The popular view (folklore?) was that no pope would reign longer than Peter whose pontificate was supposed to have lasted twenty-five years; thus, many expected Pius IX to die before his silver jubilee, June 1871.

Three days later Rymer responded to Newman's letter of 15 August. He stated his thoughts directly and showed that his focus was on the council and the minority bishops, not on the pope. "My position is I think clear and well defined," he said.

> 1. I do not and cannot *at present* accept the definition for the reason that as far as I can see the Authority of history and the past *against* it, more than counterbalance the living authority (which so long as the Minority exists is deprived of half its weight) in its favour. 2. Should the Minority yield then I should be disposed to yield with them . . . 3. I will publish nothing until it is clear that good is likely to be done to the cause of truth.[20]

On 20 August, Rymer heard from Bishop Clifford, who it would appear had seen Newman's remarks of 15 August. "My own opinion," Clifford wrote, "is that the publication now in England of such a pamphlet as you propose would be unwise. I have read Fr. Newman's remarks with much interest; they confirm me in the opinion I have expressed above."[21] Rymer apparently abandoned his plan to publish his views on the council and the definition. Some weeks later he left England for a long holiday. When he returned to England in October, he found a letter from Manning, dismissing him from his post as president of St. Edmund's.[22] Clearly his hesitancy over the definition had cost him his post.

Newman is eager to have firsthand information on the position of the minority bishops

In the midst of the correspondence with Rymer, Newman wrote directly to Bishop Clifford. Newman had just learned from Rymer that Clifford had returned to England from Rome:

> My purpose in writing was not of more importance than to express the gratitude which many Catholics must feel besides myself, at the noble stand you and other Bishops, such as Dr. Errington, have made in the Council, against a violent party. . . .
>
> For myself, I have said many Masses for those who were sustaining so ungracious and self-sacrificing a part—and now, when the end of the first stage of a great struggle is reached, I have looked with eagerness to know what they intend and recommend. Did the Bishops of the minority openly or tacitly yield now, and allow the doctrine, which has been the subject in

20. Frederick Rymer to Newman, 18 August, 1870, *The Letters and Diaries,* 25:187, n. 1.

21. Bishop William Clifford to Frederick Rymer, 20 August 1870, Archives of the Diocese of Clifton, Letters to William Clifford, Part I, as quoted in Cwiekowski, *The English Bishops,* 289.

22. See Archbishop Henry Manning to Frederick Rymer, October 1870, Archives of the Birmingham Oratory, Vatican Council file III, no. 49.

dispute, to be circulated, proclaimed, and taken for granted among Catholics, then I should think that the majority represented the whole episcopate, and that the doctrine was really defined. As at present advised, I should in that case think the definition the voice of the Church, and to come to us with a claim of infallibility.

But if on the other hand I found that there was a concerted and organized protest and stand against it, on the part of a considerable number of bishops of various countries, then I should find it difficult to determine a ground on which it was binding on my faith.[23]

Clifford responded quickly. He had no easy answer for Newman. In a letter dated 15 August, the bishop of Clifton said:

In reply to your enquiries, the position of affairs as regards the council at present seems to be as follows.

Most of the Bishops of the minority were of opinion that the only thing to be done at first is to wait the course of events. It is evident that any active steps taken at present by numbers of the minority would at once provoke action on the part of the violent party, and then schism would be the only alternative which of course is evidently wrong. On the other hand the Council is not yet concluded, the Bishops have not yet signed, and we are told to reassemble on the 11th of Nov. It seems doubtful whether we shall be able to do so. If we do not, probably some measure will be taken to supply the want of signatures, and to publish the Council. In that case the Bishops have agreed to correspond with one another before they act, so as to secure uniformity. If on the contrary they should meet in Rome, they can consult together. If in addition to all that has occurred the signatures of the Bishops were not given, grave doubts would certainly arise concerning the nature of the Council, but it would be premature for the Bishops to move in this matter at present. 1st because the time for signing has not yet come, and 2nd because it would evidently give an advantage to the violent party.

Then Clifford took up a line similar to one that Newman had followed in recent weeks:

Of course, even if the nature of the Council remained doubtful, still if the doctrines taught by it were generally accepted and believed, that would show them to be part of the teaching of the Church, and so the separate infallibility would on that ground have to be accepted as of faith. But for this also time is required. This, I think, is all I can say at present.[24]

23. Newman to Bishop William Clifford, 12 August 1870, *The Letters and Diaries,* 25:179.

24. Bishop William Clifford to Newman, 15 August 1870, Bristol Record Office, Letters to Bishop William Joseph Clifford, Bishop of Clifton, Part I, 1854–1874. (This letter with some minor differences is reprinted in *The Letters and Diaries,* 25:179–80, n. 2.) In fact, since the council never was able to reassemble, the bishops did not sign the decrees of the council.

That Clifford was under pressure from other quarters as well after his return to England is evident from a letter that Lord Acton, then in Bavaria, wrote to him on 27 July. Acton said in part:

> Several of the Bishops urged me to take advantage of the materials I have got, to write on the events of the last half year, and I have undertaken to do so. Would you have the kindness to let me have those letters of Gladstone and others, which I left in your hands?
>
> If I can do so without presumption, and without seeming to involve you in the faintest shadow of responsibility, I should like to ask you whether you could give me any other help. I have seen in the papers that the Pope opened the mouths of the Bishops before they left, in order that they might confound the mendacious opposition. Several have given me the Mss. of their speeches.
>
> If you think it right to let me have any of your speeches, notes, or counsel, I should not make a bad use of them. Would it not be well that the Memorandum on the Catholic oath should be published? Your remarks on the state of England, in reply to Manning, are only vaguely known, and it is a pity that they should not be accurately preserved. They will be of great importance in England.[25]

At the conclusion of his letter of 15 August, Bishop Clifford told Newman: "Dr. Errington who is here and goes to Liverpool tomorrow hopes to stop by Birmingham between 11 and 1:30 and to call to see you." Newman's diary for 16 August notes that "Dr. Errington called and lunched."[26] This gave Newman another chance to discuss the situation with a bishop of the minority, but no record of the conversation appears to have been kept. Newman does, however, mention his conversations with Errington in his letter to St. John of 21 August.[27]

Newman gives last-minute counsels to Father Robert Suffield before his apostasy

Newman had difficulties enough, and each day brought him some new question about the definition and its acceptance. He could not have found it easy to be involved at this time in last-minute efforts to dissuade the Dominican, Father Robert Suffield, from leaving the Church. Suffield, who was a friend of Newman's longtime friend Henry Wilberforce, had been in touch with Newman by letter and when he visited Birmingham on 13 August, Newman met with him. By that time it would appear that

25. Archives of the Diocese of Clifton, Lord Acton to Bishop William Clifford, 27 July 1870, Archives of the Diocese of Clifton, Bristol Record Office, Letters to Bishop William Joseph Clifford, Part I, 1854–74.
26. Newman "Diary," 16 August 1870, *The Letters and Diaries,* 25:188.
27. See Newman to Ambrose St. John, 21 August 1870, *The Letters and Diaries,* 25:31.

Suffield had made his decision to leave the Church. Suffield wrote a long letter to Newman on 12 August, explaining that he had for a number of years had doubts about the Catholic faith and now considered himself a Deist.[28] Undoubtedly, however, the definition of papal infallibility played some part in Suffield's decision. He certainly allowed that to appear publicly as his reason for leaving the Church. On 11 July, Suffield had been asked along with other priests in England to sign a petition in favor of the definition. His reply, which appeared in the 16 July issue of the *Westminster Gazette*, was an outright refusal. And Suffield took the occasion to say that

> knowing the deep repugnance with which, under the pressure of ecclesiastical opinion and ecclesiastical prospects, canons, priests, and bishops have signed declarations pleasing to ecclesiastical superiors and repugnant to their private opinions; knowing with an intimate and sad knowledge, that the mooting of this question has led to investigations, and then to inquiries, which have paralyzed the faith in the minds of numbers of the clergy and of the intellectual laity, and with not a few destroyed it, I must respectfully decline to sign . . .[29]

And in another letter that appeared in the *Westminster Gazette* on 6 August, Suffield maintained that the infallibility question (presumably even before its actual definition) had made him acknowledge his longstanding doubts.[30]

Newman had first thought that the definition was a primary factor in Suffield's decision, as is evident in a letter he wrote to Wilberforce on 12 August. "Of course I cannot run," he said, "with that high flying party, one of whose trophies is the unsettlement of Fr Suffield, but, thank God for undeserved mercy, I have no doubt in the Holy Catholic Roman Church, nor have had."[31] But on the following day, having received a letter from Suffield of 12 August and having just met with him, Newman told Wilberforce, "The definition of the Popes [sic] Infallibility is in no sense the ground of his change. It has been coming on ever since he was a novice."[32] Newman had gone to see Suffield "not simply in Christian charity, but in ordinary good feeling. . . ."[33] But in the tense days following so soon after the definition he was conscious, as he told Henry Wilberforce, "yet it is because of such acts of kindness towards people

28. See *The Letters and Diaries,* 25:162, n. 2.
29. 11 July 1870, *The Letters and Diaries,* 25:176, n. 1.
30. See *The Letters and Diaries,* 25:180, n. 1.
31. Newman to Henry Wilberforce, 12 August 1870, *The Letters and Diaries,* 25:180.
32. Newman to Henry Wilberforce, 13 August 1870, *The Letters and Diaries,* 25:182.
33. Newman to Henry Wilberforce, 12 August 1870, *The Letters and Diaries,* 25:180.

in doubt that I am slandered as having doubts too."[34] Newman gave Wilberforce an appreciation of Suffield's desperate position:

> I have never perhaps seen any thing so harrowing as his present state in a lodging in BM [Birmingham]—by himself—with his own thoughts, with blackness before him and misery on all sides. It is enough to turn a man mad or to kill him.
>
> "What can I do for you?" I said—but what *can* I do? What can any of us do, but pray lest we fall into temptation—take heed, lest we fall. By God's mercy no doubt has ever entered my mind—but it justly frightens one to see such a man so knocked down. My [sic] God keep us all—we have a rough time coming.[35]

Some weeks later Suffield became a Unitarian minister. He married in 1871 and died in Croyden twenty years later.

On the same day that he wrote to Wilberforce, giving this bleak assessment of Suffield's situation, Newman wrote again to Ambrose St. John, who was still away on holiday. The meeting with Suffield was much on his mind. "Do you know of Fr. Suffield's letters in the Paper?," he asked St. John. "They lead every one to think he has given up Christianity, and H. W. has written to me in great distress about it. Fr. S. maintains that it is *not* in consequence of the Definition."

Newman brought St. John up to date on other news related to the council.

> I hear that the minority Bishops are to make a stand, and the Council is not to go on. I don't vouch for this.
>
> I have heard nothing of our Bishop since the news of his delirium.[36]
>
> I can but thank God that He keeps my faith unaffected by all our troubles.

And then Newman repeated almost exactly the closing words of his letter of the same day to Wilberforce: "May God keep us all still for we have a rough time coming."[37]

Catholics troubled in conscience by the definition look to Newman for guidance

Newman's days in August 1870 were not taken up only with the greater drama following on the definition, correspondence with Rymer and

34. Ibid.

35. Newman to Henry Wilberforce, 13 August 1870, *The Letters and Diaries,* 25:182. On Newman's involvement in Suffield's case, see also his letter to Mrs. William Froude, 22 August 1870, *The Letters and Diaries,* 25:193–94.

36. Ullathorne was seriously ill on his return to England and was forced to stop in London for several weeks before going home to Birmingham.

37. Newman to Ambrose St. John, 13 August 1870, *The Letters and Diaries,* 25:181.

Clifford, meetings with Errington, and the notorious case of Robert Suffield, but also with a number of private individuals who turned to him for a word of explanation or encouragement. Some of these inquirers were close friends. Others were strangers or people that he had written to only once or twice before. Some of them were the same people who had been expressing their fears and uncertainties over the possibility of a definition for the past seven or eight months. Newman answered all of these letters patiently and carefully, if at times guardedly. The situation was uncertain not only to his inquirers but also to Newman himself. Perhaps even more than the letters to bishops and priests, these letters written to lay people, often women, are an indication of Newman's reaction to the definition and the undoubted personal distress that it caused him.

Newman was not long in hearing from those who wanted his views on the definition of infallibility and their own obligations as Catholics. The first of these letters came just days after Newman had himself seen the text of the definition. It was from Madame Jacques Blumenthal, a convert distressed by the council's action. She wrote with considerable feeling:

> I do not know what to think, I do not know whether I wake or sleep—after hearing day by day of the Bishops in opposition, of the many non-placets, after resting in the belief that we, I mean all the catholics who have never believed in the doctrine, were represented by many Bishops in the Council, there comes the news like a thunderclap that there has been an almost unanimous consent to the doctrine . . . if the Council has been all the time really pure and free and universal then how am I to get back the respect I owe it, after believing all along . . . in the tyranny and machiavelian policy and cruel force and fraud with which it has been conducted? . . . The Church cannot err I know but *can* this be her voice?[38]

Newman used strong language to begin his reply: "I think the promoters of the dogma have behaved very cruelly, tyranically, and deceitfully. . . ." He then went on to give a more positive perspective, but there is a certain half-heartedness to the effort, and it is curiously done in a series of brief statements:

> But the definition is what the Church has acted on for some centuries, and a very large body of Catholics have long held.
> God will bring His chosen people through all difficulties. Things will look brighter tomorrow. Make an act of faith in "*all* the Church teaches" etc
> Perhaps it is *necessary*, in time to come, for the seat of government to be strengthened.

38. Madame Jacques Blumenthal to Newman, 26 July 1870, *The Letters and Diaries,* 25:169, n. 2.

I don't think God would allow 530 Bishops to go wrong—and the opposition denied, not the truth of the doctrine, but its seasonableness.

"Beware of desperate steps" etc etc

Perhaps the definition will *limit* the Pope's power.

I wish this letter to be confidential, because I wish to declare my opinion only when I am obliged.[39]

The last sentence seems to indicate that Newman at some stage expected to have to make his position known in response to a request from ecclesiastical authority.

Lady Henrietta Chatterton had since February been looking to Newman for guidance and reassurance concerning the council. The definition of 18 July was a difficult moment for her, but it was made even more so by the exaggerated public remarks of members of the Ultramontane party. The immediate reason for Lady Chatterton's letter of early August appears to have been a pamphlet by Father Peter Gallwey, S.J., entitled "S. Joseph and the Vatican Council." In the pamphlet Father Gallwey wrote:

Even if the exaggerated foreboding should have its fulfilment, so that the time should come when we might expect some new definition every morning, yet so long as the watchful providence of God is pledged not to suffer any false oracle to emanate from the Apostolic See, such daily pronouncements, so far from being an evil, would be like the daily provision of manna . . . how can it be an evil to have our errors corrected, and to learn more and more of God's truth, for each truth is a foretaste of Heaven?[40]

When Newman replied to Lady Chatterton on 4 August, he had not yet seen a text of Gallwey's remarks, though he had some idea of them from Lady Chatterton's letter to him. He responded to her with great sympathy. "I grieve, as much as you can, at the news from Rome," he wrote, "because it will pain and perplex so many good people—and I think lightly of the charity of those, who seem as if they wished to increase that pain and perplexity by exaggerated statements and words of triumph." But Newman expressed some doubt to Lady Chatterton that she had quoted Father Gallwey accurately. Having put Father Gallwey's pamphlet aside, Newman gave her a reassuring view of the definition. He handled the issue straightforwardly without any reference to the position of the minority bishops or any of the other controversial points he was dealing with at the same time in his discussions with Dr. Rymer. "You must not fancy that any very stringent definition has passed," he told Lady Chatterton,

39. Newman to Madame Jacques Blumenthal, 30 July 1870, *The Letters and Diaries,* 25:170.

40. *The Letters and Diaries,* 25:174, n. 1. See a review of Father Gallwey's pamphlet in "Notice of Books," *Dublin Review,* n.s. 15 (July–October 1870) 239–40.

"on the contrary it is very mild in its tenor, and has been acted on by the Pope at least for the last 300 years. And as, during those centuries, in spite of his Infallibility being firmly held at Rome, he has done nothing extravagant, now also, when it is declared authoritatively, we may reasonably expect that all things will go on quietly as before. So I hope you will not make yourself unhappy, when it may be all for nothing."[41] No doubt Newman was being careful to take into account the needs of his correspondent in this reply. It is evident that he tried to deal with each of his many letters with an awareness of the individual who had written. Had he wanted to, Newman could have worked up a standard reply to people writing to him after the definition, but he took each case on its merits, seeing his vast correspondence as part of his priestly role. Nonetheless, there is in this reply to Lady Chatterton a certain tone of smooth assurance, of whistling in the dark, not entirely consonant with other evidence about Newman's thoughts in the first weeks following the definition.

Newman wrote again to Lady Chatterton on 6 August. In the meantime she must have sent him the exact text of Father Gallwey's remarks. When he had read them he said, "Such very incautious remarks as I read in the Pamphlet you send me are simply cruel—and I cannot say more or less," but Newman did go on, taking an approach similar to his previous letter, "I have ever held the Pope's Infallibility, since I have been a Catholic, thinking it very difficult to deny it historically, in spite of the difficulties against it, and, I repeat, I think things will go on as heretofore, even though this doctrine turns out to be legitimately defined."[42]

On the following day Newman wrote to W. J. O'Neill Daunt, who had written to him on behalf of a friend deeply disturbed by the definition. "Once more," Daunt had said on 4 August, "I solicit your christian assistance. This unfortunate dogma has had a most deleterious effect on the mind of the convert whose care I have already mentioned to you. . . . (She says) 'I have not left the Catholic assembly; they *put me out,* because I cannot believe some things which if I believed I should not believe in God as a God and Father of love, justice, compassion, pity, and long suffering goodness.' "[43] Newman in reply gave a fuller exposition of his views than he had in the letter to Lady Chatterton. As in several letters written at this time, Newman was at pains to distinguish his personal position from his appreciation of the difficulties that the definition was causing others. Indeed he had been making this distinction on the

41. Newman to Lady Henrietta Chatterton, 4 August 1870, *The Letters and Diaries,* 25:172–73.

42. Newman to Lady Henrietta Chatterton, 6 August 1870, *The Letters and Diaries,* 25:174.

43. W. J. O'Neill Daunt to Newman, 4 August 1870, Archives of the Birmingham Oratory, Vatican Council, file III, no. 26.

infallibility question since it had first been broached in earnest in the previous decade. Newman told Daunt:

> I agree with you that the wording of the Dogma has nothing very difficult in it. It expresses what, as an opinion, I have ever held myself with a host of other Catholics. But that does not reconcile me to imposing it upon others, and I do not see why a man who denied it might not be as good a Catholic as the man who held it. And it is a new and most serious precedent in the Church that a dogma de fide should be passed *without definite and urgent cause.* This to my mind is the serious part of the matter. You put an enormous power into the hands of one man, without check, and at the very time, by your act, you declare that he may use it without special occasion.

As he concluded the letter, Newman made an effort to be reassuring. "However, God will provide," he wrote. "We must recollect, there has seldom been a Council without great confusion after it. . . . The differences between those instances and this being, that now we have brought it on ourselves without visible necessity." Newman continued:

> I think it may safely be said to your friend, that the greater part of the Church has long thought that the Pope has the power which he and the Bishops of the majority have declared *is* his; and that, if the Church is the work and ordinance of God, we must have a little faith in Him, and be assured that He will provide that there is no abuse of the Pope's power. Your friend must not *assume,* before the event, that his power will be abused. Perhaps you ought not to urge her too strongly—if left to herself, your reasons may tell on her after a while, though they seem to fail at the moment.[44]

Newman saw the need for gentle persuasion and encouragement. As he had foreseen from the time the subject of papal infallibility was first seriously discussed, many people would be suddenly thrown into confusion by the definition. They needed time, a calming tone, a space to catch their breath. Arguments from authority were only likely to deepen their distress.

When Newman responded to Mrs. William Froude on 8 August, he was not quite as circumspect as he had been on the two previous days and he introduced the question of the minority's possible position from the outset:

> It is too soon to give an opinion about the Definition. I want to know what the Bishops of the minority say on the subject, and what they mean to do. As I have ever believed as much as the definition says, I have a difficulty in putting myself into the position of those who have *not.* As far as I see, no one is bound to believe it at this moment, certainly not till the end of the Council. This I hold in spite of Dr. Manning.[45] At the same time since

44. Newman to W. J. O'Neill Daunt, 7 August 1870, *The Letters and Diaries,* 25:174–75.
45. Almost certainly a reference to Manning's *ad clerum* of 3 August 1870. In *Cardinal Manning,* Robert Gray states: "Newman wisely refrained from confronting Dr. Manning

the Pope has pronounced the definition, I think it safer to accept it at once. I very much doubt if at this moment, before the end of the Council, I could get myself publicly to say it was de fide, whatever came of it—though I believe the doctrine itself.

Hints of Newman's ambiguity are evident in this last sentence.

At this point Newman still thought the council would have a further session and he told Mrs. Froude:

> I look for the Council to *right itself* in some way before it ends. It looks like a house divided against itself, which is a great scandal.
>
> And now you have my whole mind. I rule my own conduct by what is safer, which in matters of faith is a true principle of theology—but (*as at present advised,* in my present state of knowledge or ignorance, till there are further acts of the Church) I cannot pronounce categorically that the doctrine is de fide.

Despite the somewhat strained, over-careful explanations of his position, Newman made clear to Mrs. Froude that he abhorred any exaggerated notions of what the definition actually meant. In a postscript he said:

> The Pope is infallible in actu, not in habitu—in his particular pronouncements—ex Cathedra, not in his state of illumination, as an Apostle might be, which would be inspiration. I am told some wicked men, not content with their hitherto cruel conduct, are trying to bring in this doctrine of inherent infallibility, of which there is not a hint in the definition. Perhaps they would like to go on to call him a Vice-God, as some one actually did, or a sole God to us. Unless my informant was mad, I heard lately of someone (English or Irish) who said that now we ought not to pray to God at all, but only to the Blessed Virgin—God preserve us, if we have such madmen among us, with their lighted brands.[46]

The difficult consequences for those Catholics in England, especially in Manning's diocese, who found the definition a great trial to their faith were brought clearly home to Newman in a letter he received in mid-August from Mrs. Emilie Perceval, the wife of a convert clergyman. She told Newman: "And now because we cannot truly say that we embrace the new Definition of Infallibility, we are told that we are not, and could never have been, true and sincere Catholics: denied the Sacraments: considered as traitors and apostates, by those extreme Infallibilists by whom we are exclusively surrounded here." Mrs. Perceval went on in near desperate

---

directly with this view. Judging by the manner in which the Archbishop of Westminster pressed Lord Acton for a statement of submission, he would certainly have deemed Newman's *prevarication* [emphasis supplied] tantamount to heresy." Robert Gray, *Cardinal Manning: A Biography* (London: Weidenfeld and Nicolson, 1985) 236.

46. Newman to Mrs. William Froude, 8 August 1870, *The Letters and Diaries,* 25:176-77.

terms. "I entreat you," she said to Newman, "to tell me whether there is any help for us."[47] Newman replied on 15 August. As in other letters from this period he tried to be reassuring:

> The church has *acted* for 300 years on what is now defined.
>
> *If* it is defined; for I want to know what the minority do—if they do nothing,—I consider that *then* there *will* be a moral unanimity.
>
> Councils generally have been attended by much strife and incipient schism. By times things get right—securus judicat orbis terrarum—that is the rule.
>
> For myself, I have ever thought the self-assertion, the ipse dixit, of Popes for 1800 years, a great argument for the fact of their infallibility, ⟨being supreme judge⟩ vid Loss and Gain part 2 chapter 8. . . .[48]

47. Emilie Perceval to Newman, 12 August 1870, *The Letters and Diaries*, 25:185, n. 1. In a letter of 26 September to Bishop Clifford, Bishop Brown of Newport reported that the bishop of Northampton, Francis Amherst, had tried during a recent meeting to have the bishops as a body address the question of whether a priest could give absolution to someone who refused to accept the doctrine of papal infallibility. See Cwiekowski, *The English Bishops,* 286, n. 3. There is no evidence that Bishop Amherst's suggestion was taken up, or at least that any agreement on the question was reached.

That this was a vexed question is evident also from a 29 August letter of Bishop William Vaughan of Plymouth to Father Robert Whitty, S.J.:

> At this moment I am bothered with the question—Am I *obliged* to refuse absolution to a man who says, "I am quite prepared to accept and give my internal assent to the decrees of a Gen. Council—but then the Council must be complete—whereas the Council of the Vatican is still going on and incomplete—it is unsigned, etc., etc., by B[isho]ps, etc. As to what Antonelli [papal secretary of state] says—he is not my B[isho]p—nor is he infallible—it's his opinion or if you please of the whole of the Card[ina]ls but still it is only an *opinion* after all."
>
> I have no doubt you have had the difficulty discussed with a view to uniformity in the confessional—I wish you would tell me how the difficulty is got over. In many cases I fear if the answer is simply—If you do not *at once* give your interior assent you are *excluded* from the Sac[raments].
>
> The sacraments will be abandoned & the faith also—whereas when a little later it is seen that the decrees are accepted—crooked [?] minds will give way. (Archives of the Society of Jesus, Bishop W. Vaughan, Correspondence DK/3, as quoted in Cwiekowski, *The English Bishops,* 291, n. 2.)

Most likely Vaughan's inquiry of Whitty was prompted by William Maskell's canvassing of several of the English bishops on the question of absolution and the acceptance of the dogma. See pages 155-57 and 176-80 of the present study. Maskell's correspondence with several bishops is treated in detail by Cwiekowski, *The English Bishops,* 289-91.

48. Newman here is evidently referring to the following views of his character Charles Reding in the novel *Loss and Gain*: " . . . the Church of Rome has this *prima facie* mark of a prophet in Scripture, that, like a prophet in Scripture, it admits no rival, and anathematizes all doctrine counter to its own. There's another thing: a prophet of God is of course at home with his message; he is not helpless and do-nothing in the midst of errors and in the war of opinions. He knows what has been given to him to declare, how far it extends; he can act as an umpire; he is equal to emergencies. This again tells in favour of the Church of

But Newman's reply to Mrs. Perceval's problem of conscience was direct and sympathetic. "Go to some confessor," he advised, "who will not insist on your believing in the Pope's Infallibility. *Meanwhile don't set yourself against the doctrine* and don't talk with the cruel people."[49] On 19 August in a poignant response, Mrs. Perceval thanked Newman for herself and for her husband. "It has indeed been a comfort," she wrote, "to read such words of truth and soberness, after the fierce fanatical denunciations which have been singing in our ears for weeks past." Mrs. Perceval closed by saying: "We have lost all for the faith, O pray that we may not lose that too!"[50]

At the same time Newman received another anguished letter from a convert, Mrs. Priscilla Beckwith. She asked, "Am I . . . compelled to mention my dissent in Confession—and if I do, shall I be refused absolution and consequently Holy Communion?"[51] Newman replied in a brief, formulaic letter, almost as if he was devising an outline that could be filled in as needed in response to the increasing number of inquiries he was receiving about the definition and the obligation to accept it:

1. I believe the Pope's Infallibility.
2. I have [been] strongly opposed to its being defined.
3. Even tho' an article of faith it need not be *expedient.*
4. I doubt whether it is yet an article of faith.
5. Such confusion has been at other times.
6. Be calm—beware of dangerous steps.
7. Don't set yourself against the doctrine. Exclude doubts—make an act of faith in *all* teaching of the Church.
8. Choose a confessor who will absolve you. Go to communion.[52]

At the end of August Newman received yet another request for help from a convert. The exchange between Newman and Mrs. Anna Whitty, who lived in Liverpool, was to extend over several months and in contrast to the reply to Mrs. Beckwith, Newman's responses were of considerable length. His reply of 31 August to Mrs. Whitty was marked

---

Rome. As age after age comes she is ever on the alert, questions every new comer, sounds the note of alarm, hews down strange doctrine, claims and locates and perfects what is new and true. The Church of Rome inspires me with confidence; I feel I can trust her." John Henry Newman, *Loss and Gain: The Story of A Convert* (London: Longmans, Green, and Co., 1906) 225–26.

49. Newman to Mrs. Emilie Perceval, 15 August 1870, *The Letters and Diaries,* 25:185. Newman's interlinear explanations are printed in angled brackets.

50. Mrs. Emilie Perceval to Newman, 19 August 1870, *The Letters and Diaries,* 25:185, n. 3.

51. Mrs. Priscilla Beckwith to Newman, 19 August 1870, *The Letters and Diaries,* 25:189, n. 1.

52. Newman to Mrs. Priscilla Beckwith, 21 August 1870, *The Letters and Diaries,* 25:189.

"confidential." He presumably knew that Mrs. Whitty's husband was a journalist and he may have feared that his replies to her might become known when he was trying so carefully to keep his position quiet:

> It is easier to understand and feel for your distress, than to relieve it; but I will do my best.
> First as to the dogma, I doubt not you exaggerate it. For myself I have never had any difficulty in receiving it, though for the sake of others, and for many further reasons, I earnestly trusted and prayed that it might not be defined. This leads me to ask you to consider what a vast aggregation of prayers for many months had been offered in behalf of the Fathers of the Council, for their illumination, and the success of their labours—for this surely, unless we deny God's care of us, is a strong reason at first sight for believing what they have decided. To me of course, who never have had difficulty in the doctrine itself, this thought comes with great force.
> For three hundred years at least the Church has *acted* on the belief that the Pope was infallible ex cathedrâ, and no great harm has come of it; I trust that (in spite of a theological opinion having become a dogma) the future will not differ from the past.

Newman went on to treat the role of the pope in history but in doing so he somewhat begged the question. In part he appears to be talking about the pope's primacy, which he had always seen as something quite distinct from any question of his infallibility and he also deals with the teaching office of the pope in areas that he was in other circumstances very careful to say demanded a Catholic's assent but in no sense should be equated with infallibility.

> I say for three hundred years the Church has acted on the doctrine—but the doctrine itself is far older than this—indeed from the very beginning of the Church, the Pope has so intervened and interposed in all parts of Christendom, so authoritatively, so magisterially, that it is very perplexing to suppose he had no divine gift of direction and teaching.
> Don't set yourself against the doctrine, then; don't fancy consequences which may never come to pass.

Then Newman turned once more to practical directives meant to assist a troubled conscience:

> I think you should do two things—first make an act of faith *"in ALL that the Church teaches"*—and next, when doubts arise against this particular doctrine, put them away, on the ground that *perhaps* the Church teaches this doctrine, and that it is safer therefore *not* to oppose it. I say "perhaps", for considering the great number of religious Catholics who hold it, and how long it has been in the Church, there is at least a considerable probability that it is true.

Then as to Confession, I understand you to say that you have *been* to confession, told your doubts, and nevertheless got absolution. Very well— what do you require more? I don't think you need mention the subject again, *unless* you willfully allow yourself to *dwell* on the matter, and to *assent distinctly* to a doubt about the doctrine. Why need you trouble yourself about an abstract point, which for what you know will never come before you practically?

I know we are in a difficulty—I hope if we are patient, the difficulty will clear away. It is not quite certain that the dogma has passed—but it is safest and right to consider it has—and not to dwell on it. Now be of good heart, have a little faith in God's protection of the Church, and be patient and not afraid.[53]

Newman in the letter to Mrs. Whitty continued to encourage his inquirers by stressing reasons for accepting the dogma that have small bearing or only indirect bearing on the actual decision of the great majority of the council Fathers. In this instance he recalled the many prayers that had been offered by Catholics all over the world for the Fathers of the council. God would not turn aside these prayers. An accumulation of external reasons shows that it is "safest" to believe that the dogma has been passed by the council. But he continued also to emphasize a narrow interpretation of the council's decision, for "the future will not differ from the past" and so "why need you trouble yourself about an abstract point."

As some converts struggled to remain true to their Catholic allegiance, others told Newman that the definition was too much for them to accept. One of these was John Pym Yeatman, who had already expressed his doubts about infallibility to Newman earlier in the year. He told Newman on 14 August:

I feel my faith is melting away and unless I gain a new light I cannot honestly remain a "Papist"[.] I cannot accept this doctrine of Personal infallibility . . . my hope was that it was not binding upon one's conscience until signed in Council at the dissolution by all the Prelates . . .

Dr. Manning declares that it is binding already? that seems to be an assumption of the prerogatives before it is granted—or recognized.

Will you kindly direct me on this point.[54]

Newman replied at once with words that he hoped would make Yeatman see that there was no call for rash and hasty decisions:

In answer to your question I can but say, that I have not yet sufficient information about the Definition to be able to pronounce that it is binding on my conscience.

53. Newman to Mrs. Anna Whitty, 31 August 1870, *The Letters and Diaries,* 25:200–01.
54. John Pym Yeatman to Newman, 14 August 1870, *The Letters and Diaries,* 25:187, n. 3.

Since I have believed the matter of it for many years, (as I have at various times stated in print) it is not a point which concerns me very nearly. Nor really do I see that the doctrine itself, since it is drawn up in very guarded form, nor the ipse dixit of any ecclesiastical authority should drive you out of the Church. I hope not.[55]

Yeatman did in fact leave the Catholic Church for several years after the council but returned to it through the influence of his wife.

New pressures on Newman to make his views public and further questions from Anglicans on the definition

The news of the definition of papal infallibility and the discussions that followed in England and Ireland brought forth new requests to Newman to explain his position openly. One of those who approached Newman in this regard was an Irish Member of Parliament, Aubrey de Vere. De Vere's request was put to Newman by Emily Bowles, who had spoken with de Vere and William Monsell in early August about the desirability of Newman's writing something on the definition. In a letter of 12 August, Newman answered Miss Bowles by saying, "I could not undertake the thing. It is above me."[56] But in a first draft to Miss Bowles of the same day, Newman expressed the belief that de Vere was acting as an agent for Manning in this matter "directly or indirectly."[57] Newman remained silent as he had in the past, but there is at least small evidence here, confirmed more fully elsewhere, that he was sure the expression of his views would bring him again into conflict with ecclesiastical authority.

There are also indications that others outside of Newman's circle of close friends were anxious to know what Newman thought of the definition. In a letter written on the same day that Newman wrote his draft and ultimate reply to Emily Bowles, Richard Simpson said to Lord Acton:

> Newman's state of mind is to me utterly unknown. He has said that he accepted the opinion of Papal infallibility as an opinion; he has also expressed the deepest disgust at the fraud and tyranny of those who would force on the definition. I have not here his books to refer to. In one place I remember he says "How often have the Popes spoken since Trent? Once, perhaps twice." So that he would surround the act with forms which would almost preclude its exercise. Again I know a place where he explicitly denies that the Church is committed to the medieval principle of persecution & c. But his language is effusive in its exaltation of the Popes' authority & his own

55. Newman to John Pym Yeatman, 15 August 1870, *The Letters and Diaries,* 25:187.
56. Newman to Emily Bowles (II), 12 August 1870, *The Letters and Diaries,* 25:178.
57. Newman's draft of 12 August 1870 letter to Emily Bowles, *The Letters and Diaries,* 25:178, n. 4.

submissiveness, intellectually and practically. What his state of mind is now I cannot tell you either, probably.[58]

Letters also came to Newman in this period, as they had when the definition was being discussed at Rome, from Anglicans who wanted to know if Newman had now had enough of the Church of Rome. On 22 August, Henry Thomas Ellacombe, who had known Newman in his Anglican years, asked Newman what he would do in the face of the definition. In raising this question, Ellacombe gave voice to frequent and growing rumors about Newman that were whispered about in Anglican circles but also publicly voiced in the press. Ellacombe said: "I now see the question asked in the papers 'What will Dr. Newman do?'—Aye—what will he? Why—let me ask—after your wise denunciation of what was taking place at Rome! Why cannot you make up your mind to *return* to us?"[59] Newman responded by return post. His answer was blunt and gave evidence of the impatience and annoyance with which he characteristically treated reports of his return to the Anglican communion:

> Don't let impertinent Pamphleteers delude you. I am as certain that the Church in communion with Rome is the successor and representative of the Primitive Church, as certain that the Anglican Church is *not*, as certain that the Anglican Church is a mere collection of men, a mere national body, a human society, as I am that Victoria is Queen of Great Britain. Nor have I once had even a passing doubt on the subject, ever since I have been a Catholic. I have all along been in a state of inward certainty and steady assurance on this point, and I should be the most asinine, as well as the most ungrateful of men, if I left that Gracious Lord who manifests Himself in the Catholic Church, for those wearisome Protestant shadows, out of which of His mercy he has delivered me. . . .
>
> Now, disabuse your mind, my dear Friend, of this baseless imagination.

Only with the final sentence did Newman take up the matter that had particularly prompted Ellacombe's pained question. "As to your allusion," Newman wrote, "I have ever held the Pope's infallibility in matters of faith, not in conduct; and I hope still that a theological opinion will not be made unnecessarily a dogma."[60] Strangely in this letter to an Anglican, in which he strongly professed his faith in the Catholic Church, Newman shows more ambiguity with this last sentence than he does in many of the replies to Catholics in this time.

58. Richard Simpson to Lord Acton, 12 August 1870, *The Correspondence of Lord Acton and Richard Simpson,* ed. Josef L. Altholz, Damien McElrath, and James C. Holland (Cambridge: Cambridge University Press, 1971–75) 3:289.

59. Henry Thomas Ellacombe to Newman, 22 August 1870, *The Letters and Diaries,* 25:194, n. 1.

60. Newman to Henry Thomas Ellacombe, 23 August 1870, *The Letters and Diaries,* 25:195.

E. B. Pusey had corresponded with Newman on the subject of infallibility for a number of years, especially since the late 1860s when the subject became a matter of debate for Catholics on the Continent and in England. It is not surprising then to find him writing to Newman soon after the definition. In a letter of 26 August, Pusey, who like many others was looking to Newman for information, said: "I wonder whether the Council will do any thing, on its reassembling, to express the conditions of the infallibility which it has affirmed. To me some of the lesser cases seem more irreconcileable with infallibility than the great case of Honorius."[61] In his reply Newman gave Pusey what information he had, but he also took the line that he had taken with others, that the definition had in fact set careful limits on the exercise of papal infallibility and he thought further limits might still come:

> As to the Council, I don't consider the question of Infallibility quite settled— that is, it is just possible that, before the Council closes, there might be some modification, especially if there is a new Pope. And the present state of revolution, which the political world has entered upon, may suspend the further action of the Council for years. At the same time it cannot be denied that the probability is strong in favor of the permanent recognition of the dogma, pronounced, as it has been, by the Pope and so very large a number of Bishops. At least one great step has been gained towards its becoming a portion of our faith. At the same time historical facts, which are objections to its definition, must ever be elements in its interpretation. Though a Pope does all that Honorius did, he would not determine ex cathedrâ[62]

Controversy over the definition continues as Newman keeps up his private counsels and reassurances

The weather, which had been warm and sultry at the beginning of August, turned autumnlike by the end of the month. It had been a busy time for Newman. There were many visitors. The church was being repainted and arrangements for the new term of the Oratory school had to be made. Members of the community were leaving for and returning from holidays. But from the extant letters there is little doubt that the events in Rome the month before took a large part of Newman's time. Ambrose St. John was still on holiday when Newman wrote to him on 21 August. Letters to St. John are perhaps an even truer record of Newman's reaction to the definition than other letters where for various reasons he was usually inclined to speak with caution. "I have various things to say about the Definition," Newman reported to his friend,

61. E. B. Pusey to Newman, 26 August 1870, *The Letters and Diaries,* 25:197–98, n. 3.
62. Newman to E. B. Pusey, 28 August 1870, *The Letters and Diaries,* 25:197–98.

154 WHAT WILL DR. NEWMAN DO?

—but cannot recollect everything. Rymer wrote to Dr. Clifford and so did I—His answer was, that the Council was not ended—that our policy was to be perfectly quiet, lest the tyrant majority should do something more, that we must wait the turn-up of events—that the Council probably would not meet again—that the decrees ought to be signed—that if they were not, this would be additional objection against the Council in time to come. Dr. Errington called—he said the same—he said it was not a free Council. But they both implied that, putting the validity of the Acts of the Council aside, the fact of Pope [sic] and so many Bishops taking one side, if backed up by the faithful, would practically make the doctrine de fide—and that we must trust in God—and so I think myself. But to me the serious thing is this, that, whereas it has not been usual to pass definition [sic] except in case of urgent and definite necessity, this definition, while it gives the Pope power, creates for him, in the very act of doing so, a precedent and a suggestion to use his power without necessity, when ever he will, when not called on to do so. I am telling people who write to me to have confidence—but I don't know what I shall say to them, if the Pope did so act. And I am afraid moreover, that the tyrant majority is still aiming at enlarging the *province* of Infallibility. I can only say if all this takes place, we shall in matter of fact be under a new dispensation. But we must hope, for one is obliged to hope it, that the Pope will be driven from Rome, and will not continue the Council, or that there will be another Pope. It is sad he should force us to such wishes.

Newman then turned to news of the definition's effect on the English scene. He told St. John that Bishop Ullathorne was better. "Whether on account of his illness," Newman went on,

or indecision what to do about the Definition, he has not yet returned to Bm [Birmingham]. Manning has not molested Rymer, though the latter will not attend or sign the Address of Congratulation. We shall, I suppose have a Te Deum—but the Bishop has not yet spoken. Manning's Te Deum is for the Definition*s* in the plural. I think they will be cautious. People in London have wanted me to write. I declined. I should not wonder the proposal came from Manning.[63]

In this remarkable letter to St. John, Newman's anger over the definition breaks through and the apprehension he expresses is not, it would seem, simply for the sufferings of others.

Newman did not take a holiday that summer, but there were the usual short stays at Rednal. There is no clear accounting for his staying in Birmingham all through the summer, though the various repairs and redecoration were obviously on his mind in August and September. After the great flurry of letters, visits, and exchanges in August, many of them occasioned by the definition, the succeeding months were quieter, and the

63. Newman to Ambrose St. John, 21 August 1870, *The Letters and Diaries*, 25:192–93.

routines of House and School along with his regular correspondence took up most of Newman's time. But troubled converts whom Newman had tried to help continued to seek his advice.

Early in September, Newman heard again from Mrs. Whitty and he answered her saying, "I am pained to hear that your difficulties go beyond the late Definition." He told his correspondent that he did not have time for long letters, but that he would try to send replies to any questions she put to him.[64] Within the week he contradicted himself by writing again to Mrs. Whitty at some length. The principal topics in this letter deal with the nature of the papal office and the definition of papal infallibility. Newman concluded his letter of 9 September by arguing that the definition might in fact restrict the pope's power rather than intensify it:

> . . . I am not at all sure it will increase the Pope's power—it may restrict it. Hitherto he has done what he would, because its limits were not defined—now he must act by rule. I can't prophesy how it will be. Again, if terrible times are coming, this increase of his spiritual authority may be absolutely necessary to keep things together. This does not justify the way in which it has been carried at Rome—but God overrules evil for good. A heavy retribution still may await the perpetrators of the act.[65]

In this letter Newman begins to show, if still only indirectly, that he believes that the fact of the dogma must be accepted and that Catholics must find a way to live with it. He would continue to go back and forth on the issue over the next several months, but never again as strongly as he had done in late July and August 1870. Mrs. Whitty replied to Newman on 12 September that for her to accept the definition of papal infallibility would be "to put a lie upon my conscience." She returned Newman's letters to keep them from falling into the wrong hands.[66]

Archbishop Manning would no doubt have been astonished at Newman's thesis that the definition would in some sense restrict the pope's power rather than increase it. Just then the Archbishop was engaged in a dispute with the convert clergyman and noted antiquarian, William Maskell, as to whether the faithful were already obliged to accept the definition as an article of faith. As early as 3 August, Manning had written to the priests of his diocese "that the definitions of the Council require no other publication than the solemn act by which the Holy Father has already published them to the Universal Church."[67] Maskell wrote to Man-

---

64. Newman to Mrs. Anna Whitty, 4 September 1870, *The Letters and Diaries,* 25:202.

65. Newman to Mrs. Anna Whitty, 9 September 1870, *The Letters and Diaries,* 25:204–05.

66. Mrs. Anna Whitty to Newman, 12 September 1870, *The Letters and Diaries,* 25:205, n. 1.

67. See *The Letters and Diaries,* 25:205, n. 2. Maskell took the position that no obligation could be placed on the faithful until the council had come to a close.

ning to ask how the Archbishop could have stated in his letter to the clergy of the diocese that there was already a clear obligation to accept the definition. Manning, responding to Maskell through his secretary, Father W. A. Johnson, maintained that a letter of Cardinal Antonelli, the papal secretary of state, to the nuncio in Belgium, made it clear that Catholics were already bound to accept the definition. Maskell, insulted that Manning had distanced himself by replying through his secretary, wrote again to Manning on 3 September, stating that he could not accept the interpretation that Manning was placing on Antonelli's letter.[68] Maskell believed that too many questions remained unsettled for Manning to have directed his priests to teach that the doctrine was binding:

> Even if this communication from the Cardinal [Antonelli] had any claim to obedience in England it is no clearer in its language than yours of August 3rd. The doubt is as to the binding obligation, now, of the decrees of the Vatican Council; not whether some of them have been already very solemnly published. . . .
>
> If I am to take your answer as a decision that the priests in the diocese of Westminster are now to refuse absolution to all who do not at this time accept as of faith the definitions of the Vatican Council, I must own that I was unprepared for such an explanation of your circular of August 3rd. And the more so, as several English bishops have answered my question in another and different way. These bishops have been educated from early youth in very careful study of Catholic theology, and are more than one of them distinguished for exact knowledge of canon law. . . .
>
> If again your meaning really be as I have guessed it (—and it is no more than a guess—) it would seem as if we are living in England under dissimilar systems of ecclesiastical rule. In one diocese the sacraments are to be denied, in others not.

Maskell pressed his point:

> Whether the Vatican Council, up to the present day, has had entire freedom of debate; whether a decree can be of faith whilst a council is still sitting and its deliberations not ended (a point of the very gravest consequence and not to be settled by any one bishop or cardinal in the world); whether the signatures of the bishops are necessary; whether other formalities not yet completed are also essential; these are questions still open to legitimate discussion and argument, and, perhaps, to be settled only by lapse of time. That they are all open is certain from the letters of the bishops now before me, having each of them an authority, to say the least of it, no less than your own.

68. The following notice appeared in the *Tablet* on 3 September 1870: "By order of His Grace the Archbishop of Westminster the official letter from H. E. Cardinal Antonelli, upon the binding nature of the decrees of the Council, was read in every church and chapel of the Diocese on Sunday last [28 August]." *Tablet,* n.s. 4 (3 September 1870) 36:303.

A time may come, and that soon, when there will be no doubt whatever in any mind reasonable and willing to believe that the definitions of the Vatican Council are "of faith." I humbly trust that then, come when it will, I shall be, by God's grace, as ready to accept them and with the same entire obedience and interior assent as you are yourself.[69]

In a letter to his confrere, Henry Bittleston, Newman gives evidence that he knew of the Maskell controversy at this time, but only vaguely. Early in the next year he would enter into a full correspondence with Maskell concerning the latter's difficulties with the definition.

On 26 September, Newman wrote to two other converts. He proposed one of his books to Lady Chatterton as a possible help in her continuing difficulties. "It grieves me very much," Newman said, "to hear you speak of so much personal suffering on occasion of the late act of the Vatican Council. As to the agents in it, I am as deeply concerned at much that has passed as you can be—and think there are those who have a great deal to answer for. But as to the doctrine itself, which tries you so much, I do not feel with you. Did you ever meet with my Essay on Development of Doctrine? I know you like hard and dry books—else, I should not mention it to you. . . ."[70] And Newman made a further attempt to keep John Pym Yeatman, whose difficulties with the papacy had taken on a new dimension, from leaving the Catholic Church:

69. William Maskell to Archbishop Manning, 3 September 1870, *The Letters and Diaries,* 25:206. Maskell was attacked in the *Tablet* for his views: The *Tablet* treated Maskell's position with scorn and contempt, calling him a "well-to-do convert parson" (17 September 1870, p. 357). That anyone should question the obligation of Catholics to accept the definition on the basis of whether the council's decrees had been signed by the bishops appeared to the *Tablet* the height of nonsense and it went to the following lengths to make a case for its position: "For ourselves, it is impossible to conceive any way in which the teaching of the Church could be more clearly manifested or more directly brought home to the minds of the faithful. And when we call to our remembrance the first great Oecumenical Council, that of Jerusalem, presided over by illiterate fishermen, the notion of Mr. Maskell's formalities becomes puerile in the extreme. How many of the Apostles could write their names? And if, as is very possible, they did not even affix their marks to the Decrees, would Mr. Maskell hesitate about their infallibility? That a learned man, calling himself a Catholic, could have the boldness to come forward to contest the teaching of his pastors, on no better ground than the consideration of such ceremonial formalities, is a spectacle to be pondered on as a sign of the times in which we live, but one which cannot bring us to look upon them with much satisfaction." See *Tablet,* n.s. 4 (17 September 1870) 36:356–57, 363; (24 September 1870) 400; (1 October 1870) 432–33; and (8 October 1870) 453–54. See also the review of Maskell's "What Is the Meaning of the Late Definition? An Inquiry" in "Notice of Books," *Dublin Review,* n.s. 16 (January–April 1871) 216–19. The *Dublin Review* called Maskell's arguments "paltry evasions."

70. Newman to Lady Henrietta Chatterton, 26 September 1870, *The Letters and Diaries,* 25:212. It is interesting to see Newman here recommending his *Essay on Development* as an aid to someone troubled by the definition, whereas six months previously he had said to Bishop Moriarty: "Of course I do not allow, as your Eminent friend seemed to think,

Whatever be the good or the evil of the Temporal Power, it certainly seems now sure to go—and gradually, not at once, a new system must supersede the old; and one better suitable to modern times.

Let us have a little faith and patience, and we shall find that all goes well—whereas desperate acts cannot lead to good.[71]

On the same day that he wrote to Lady Chatterton and to John Pym Yeatman, Newman sent a letter of congratulation to another convert, Gerard Manley Hopkins, who had just pronounced his vows as a Jesuit. Newman had received Hopkins into the Church on 21 October 1866.[72]

During the autumn of 1870, Newman made references now and then in his correspondence to the Franco-Prussian War, which was then being fought on the Continent. He was particularly concerned about his long-time friend, Sister Maria Pia Giberne, and at one stage Newman made arrangements for her to seek refuge in England should she be forced to leave her convent in Autun. In a letter to Charlotte Wood, Newman made an unsympathetic reference to the difficulties the pope was experiencing as a result of the war: "As to Rome, I cannot think it right that the Holy Father should be protected against his own people by foreign bayonets. It is a great scandal. Any thing is better than that. When he is persecuted, he is in his proper place—not when he persecutes—but I don't say this to every one, for it would annoy most people."[73] On 20 September, the Papal States fell to the forces of Victor Emmanuel II. On 2 October, Rome was declared the capital of the kingdom of Italy and on October 20, the

---

that *anything* is a development; there are right developments and wrong ones. . . . Nor do I think with your friend that infallibility follows on Supremacy—yet I hold the principle of development." See *The Letters and Diaries,* 25:58. According to McElrath, "Acton believed that Newman was going to lead people astray with his theory of development." Damian McElrath and others, *Lord Acton: The Decisive Decade, 1864–1874: Essays and Documents* (Louvain: Publications Universitaires, 1970) 43. It is clear that Acton, Simpson, Döllinger, and other opponents of the definition mistrusted Newman's views on development of doctrine since they believed that his theories on development were a means of setting aside the historical difficulties that they saw in the way of the definition and its acceptance.

71. Newman to John Pym Yeatman, 26 September 1870, *The Letters and Diaries,* 25:213.

72. Newman's reception of Hopkins into the Roman Catholic Church is described in Norman White's full and informative biography, *Hopkins: A Literary Biography.* Once he had decided to enter the Roman Catholic Church, Hopkins's reception came about fairly quickly. On 3 August 1866 Hopkins wrote a letter to Newman asking if he could visit him at the Birmingham Oratory within the next few days. Newman was away from the Oratory and did not answer until mid-September. He asked Hopkins to suggest a date for the meeting and Hopkins chose 20 September. Newman advised Hopkins to go ahead with his reception before he completed his studies at Oxford. On 21 October Hopkins was received by Newman into the Roman Catholic Church at the Birmingham Oratory. For a description of Hopkins's reception into the Roman Catholic Church and the steps leading up to it, see Norman White, *Hopkins: A Literary Biography* (Oxford: The Clarendon Press, 1992) 136–43.

73. Newman to Charlotte Wood, 20 October 1870, *The Letters and Diaries,* 25:217.

day that Newman wrote to Charlotte Wood, the Vatican Council was prorogued indefinitely.

The definition and its consequences continue to put demands on Newman in the midst of his own private struggle

Newman had a number of visitors in late September and early October, including his nephew, John Rickards Mozley, and his longtime friends, Henry Wilberforce and Edward Bellasis. On Sunday, 9 October, Bishop Ullathorne visited Newman for the first time since his return from Rome. Newman noted the visit in his diary but there is no record of their conversation.

In mid-October, Mrs. Lavinia Wilson, who had just returned to England after a stay in Italy to find that the priests of her parish would not give the sacraments to those who had not accepted the definition, wrote begging Newman's advice. In his response Newman began by saying:

> It is a very difficult matter so to answer your sad letter as to be of real use to you—and, unless I can so write, what is the use of writing at all?
>
> I think there are some Bishops and Priests, who act as if they did not care at all whether souls were lost or not—and only wish to save souls on their own measure. If you directly asked your Confessor, whether you were obliged to receive the Pope's Infallibility, you acted imprudently—if he asked you, he was not only imprudent but cruel.
>
> . . . If I were you, I should go to a Priest, who would not make it a point to bring up this question—though I fear there are few such in London.
>
> Such unhappy times the Church has known before; nay far worse. . . .
>
> . . . When you became a Catholic, you ought to have understood that the voice of the Church is the voice of God. The Church defines nothing that was not given to the Apostles in the beginning, but that sacred deposit cannot be fully brought forward and dispensed except in the course of ages. It is not any argument against the Pope's Infallibility, that it was not defined as a truth till the 19th[74] century.
>
> Don't set yourself against the doctrine. Very little was passed, much less than its advocates wished—they are disappointed. Nothing is defined as to *what acts* are ex cathedrâ, nor to what things infallibility extends. Some people think the decree lessens the Pope's *actual* power.[75]

A few days later Mrs. Wilson replied. She told Newman that his counsel had helped to lessen her fears but she was still very troubled. She recounted

---

74. It will be recalled that in notes he wrote on 9 July 1867, Newman said: "First they have to get over the modernness of their doctrine." *The Theological Papers of John Henry Newman on Biblical Inspiration and On Infallibility,* selected, edited, and introduced by J. Derek Holmes (Oxford: The Clarendon Press, 1979) 150.

75. Newman to Mrs. Lavinia Wilson, 20 October 1870, *The Letters and Diaries,* 25:216.

a meeting she had had with Manning: "I called on the Archbishop last
week, he at once asked me where I was staying, and when I said Clapham
he at once took my address and said I shall tell F. Coffin to attend to
you. I said I don't like the Redemptorists and I told him one had refused
me absolution. He said, 'it is all vanity, you require a humiliation like
Job'; and said 'You shall go to F. Coffin mind!' I have seen enough of
F. Coffin to make me feel I would have no confidence in him. It is a great
difficulty to find a Priest even in London."[76] On 24 October, Newman
made a new effort to encourage Mrs. Wilson:

> Don't let yourself be frightened—there are many Catholics in your condi-
> tion. On the other hand, as I have said, don't set yourself against what has
> been lately decreed, for after all it is not much. . . .
>
> There has been a great deal of disturbance after any new definition of
> faith. If there was none at Trent, it must be recollected it went on for 20
> years, and good part of the trouble went before it, and the rest during it.
> The *Reformation* created the trouble—in our case, alas, an unscrupulous
> Church faction has created the trouble. We were going on quite well when
> they meddled.

76. Mrs. Lavinia Wilson to Newman, October 1870, *The Letters and Diaries*, 25:219,
n. 1. Robert Coffin, an Oxford convert, was one of the first Oratorians, but soon left to
become a Redemptorist. He became provincial of the Redemptorists in England and was
bishop of Southwark from 1882 to 1885. He issued a strong "Instruction" to the priests
of his province late in 1870, in which he made it clear that no penitent could be given absolution who did not fully accept the definition of papal infallibility and he threatened to suspend any priest in his charge who absolved such a penitent. See *Tablet*, n.s. 4 (3 December
1870) 36:721.
    Other lay people were also having their difficulties with the Redemptorists at Clapham.
Frederick Capes, a London solicitor and the convert brother of J. M. Capes, founder of
the *Rambler*, wrote to Bishop Clifford on 21 August to ask what he ought to do in view
of the Redemptorists' insistence that all must accept the dogma or be denied the sacraments.
Clifford upheld the Redemptorists by appealing to Cardinal Antonelli's letter of 11 August
to the Nuncio in Brussels. Capes, disappointed, replied to Clifford: "It appears to us that
his [Antonelli] letter simply assumes as absolutely defined, that which many among the most
pious and learned of your Lordship's Right Rev'd Brethren abroad, notoriously declare not
to have been so defined.
    It rather increases than resolves the difficulties of those who like ourselves cannot reconcile
present teaching with that of Your Lordship's predecessors among the English Episcopate."
Damian McElrath, *Richard Simpson, 1820–1876. A Study in XIXth Century English Liberal
Catholicism* (Louvain: Publications Universitaires, 1972) 138–39, referring to F. Capes to
W. J. Clifford, 21 August 1870, and quoting from F. Capes to W. J. Clifford, 1 September
1870, *Clifford Family Archives*.
    Trevor in *Newman: Light in Winter* states that "Newman was told by a lady how she
had been pressed . . . by Manning personally, who wanted her to confess at the London
Oratory. In Italy, she said, she had suffered no such moral pressure." Meriol Trevor, *Newman: Light in Winter* (London: Macmillan & Co. Ltd., 1962) 493. Trevor in her partisan
biography was very alert to the contrasts between the Birmingham and London Oratories.
Here the reference is presumably to Manning's instruction to Mrs. Lavinia Wilson to go
to the Redemptorists at Clapham for confession.

However, God overrules all things. If the whole Church accepts the late definition, then it will stand on its proper ground, universal acceptance (according to St. Augustine's maxim, 'Securus judicat orbis terrarum—' . . .). At present it is a great shame to hurry people on.

I believe very little is added to the faith of the Church by the definition. The Pope cannot do what he will more than before. I believe Bishop Brown of Newport has published a Charge, or was it in the Papers, which it is worth reading. I am told he says that the universal Church will always be able to correct an error of the Pope's. Besides, nothing is determined what is meant by ex cathedrâ. Again he is not said to be infallible in *politics,* which is what that party expressly aimed at. I heard on the first authority that the definition was brought to enable the Pope to enforce the Syllabus, and now (I am told) the Archbishop of Malines, the great Ultramontane, says that the definition does not *cover* any such use of the Syllabus, as was intended. I know that the Ultra party are much disappointed—and that they tried to introduce a stronger doctrine, and the very notion of it was scouted. Of course they talk loudly—but I am told that only a few weeks ago the Tablet criticized the Bishop of Beverley's [Robert Cornthwaite] Pastoral, as taking so tame a line—whereas, since he was very earnest on the Ultra side, you may be sure he went as far as he could. Have patience,—always think of Cowper's Poem and its moral

Beware of desperate steps—the darkest day
Live till tomorrow, will have passed away.[77]

Newman wrote in a similar vein some days later to Lady Simeon: "I pray God to forgive all those who have brought such dreadful pain on you and many others besides you. . . ." He continued:

I wish you would separate two points from each other, which ought not to be confused—the doctrine itself, and what has taken place at Rome. . . . Very little has been passed indeed—and they *know* this, and are disappointed who have been the means of passing it—but they use big words now to conceal their disappointment, and they hope by speaking big and breaking down opposition, to open the way to passing something more.

From what I heard at Rome, while the matter was going on, from almost the first authority, they hoped to get a decree which would cover the Syllabus, and they *have not* got it. They have only got *authoritatively* pronounced *that* which Fr. Ryder maintained against Mr. Ward. The whole body of theologians, Gallicans included, have always held, that what the Pope said ex cathedrâ, was true, *when* the Bishops had received it—what has been passed, is to the effect that what he determines ex cathedrâ is true

77. Newman to Mrs. Lavinia Wilson, 24 October 1870, *The Letters and Diaries*, 25:219–20. In its issue of 8 October, the *Tablet* indicated that the *Saturday Review*, its "liberalistic contemporary," found the Bishop of Newport's pastoral contradictory. "He accepts and rejects the dogma in the same breath." *Tablet*, n.s. 4 (8 October 1870) 36:463. Bishop Brown wrote to the *Tablet* to repudiate the *Saturday Review's* analysis of his pastoral. See the *Tablet,* n.s. 4 (15 October 1870) 36:529.

independently of the reception by the Bishops—but nothing has been passed as to *what is meant* by "ex cathedrâ"—and this falls back to the Bishops and the Church to determine quite as much as before. Really therefore nothing has been passed of consequence.

Again, the decree is limited to "faith and morals"—whereas what the Ultra party wished to pass was "political principles."

The present Pope cannot live long—he has lived too long—but, did he live Methuselah's age, he could not in his acts go beyond the limit which God has assigned him—nor *has* he, though he wished it.

Don't set yourself against the doctrine. Write to me again.[78]

Newman had offered to be of further assistance to Lady Simeon and he became concerned when she did not write soon again.[79] In November, Newman's urging brought a further letter from her. She was no less troubled than she had been in late October. Newman responded on 18 November. He wrote with feeling for Lady Simeon's trials. In light of the recent fall of the Papal States, he spoke of necessary changes in the papacy. He showed again, as he had several times in the past weeks, that he thought the pontificate of Pius IX had gone on too long and the Church would be better off for his departure from the scene. He wrote also in the face of Manning's recent pastoral letter on the definition, the partial occasion of Lady Simeon's scruples:

God has certainly brought upon you a dreadful weight of suffering, but He will enable you to bear it, and will bless you in it and after it. . . .

As to the immediate subject of your letter what comes upon myself with most painful force is the scandal which is involved in the whole proceeding. The Archbishop only does what he has done all along—he ever has exaggerated things, and ever has acted towards individuals in a way which they felt to be unfeeling.[80] I am speaking from the various letters I have had from strangers, since nothing has happened between him and me. And now, as

78. Newman to Lady Catherine Simeon, 1 November 1870, *The Letters and Diaries,* 25:224.

79. See Newman to Lady Catherine Simeon, 8 November 1870, *The Letters and Diaries,* 25:227.

80. Manning's Pastoral, "The Vatican Council and Its Definitions: Pastoral Letter to the Clergy," was issued in October 1870. It appeared to give an interpretation of the definition which allowed for broad claims of papal infallibility. See *The Letters and Diaries,* 25:230, n. 2. Robert Gray in his *Cardinal Manning,* an effort to present a revisionist portrait as a kind of prelude to the long-promised Chapeau-McClelland definitive account, appears to concede with regard to the definition that Manning's views were in fact exaggerated: "Manning never allowed the relatively restricted nature of the definition to moderate his joy in its accomplishment. He hastened to write a two-hundred-page pastoral (October 1870), in which he gave the decree the largest possible interpretation. Against more prudent Catholic theologians he described infallibility as being applicable to a whole corpus of issues, including dogmatic facts, papal censures, the canonization of saints and the approbation of religious orders," 235. In his pastoral Manning was unsparing in his critical comments on those

I think most cruelly, he is fearfully exaggerating what has been done at the Council. The Pope is not infallible in such things as you instance. I enclose a letter of our own Bishop,[81] which I think will show you this. . . . Therefore, I say confidently, you may dismiss all such exaggerations from your mind, though it is a cruel penance to know that the Bishop, where you are, puts them forth. It is an enormous tyranny.

For myself, I think that a new world is coming in, and that the Pope's change of position (which in spite of any temporary re-action which may come, is inevitable) will alter matters vastly. We have come to a climax of tyranny. It is not good for a Pope to live 20 years. It is anomaly [sic] and bears no good fruit; he becomes a god, has no one to contradict him, does not know facts, and does cruel things without meaning it. For years past my only consolation personally has been in our Lord's Presence in the Tabernacle. I turn from the sternness of external authority to Him who can immeasurably compensate trials which after all are not real, but (to use a fashionable word) sentimental. Never, thank God, have I had a single doubt about the divine origin and grace of the Church, on account of the want of tenderness and largeness of mind of some of its officials or rulers. And I think this will be your experience too. Bear up for a while and all will be right. What you tell me that you have ever held about the Pope's Infallibility is, I am sure, enough now. Recollect that men like the Archbishop and Mr. Ward said all the strong things they now say, *before* the Council. Such sayings did not trouble you then, why should they trouble you now?

---

who had opposed the definition and made strong claims for the acceptance of papal infallibility by virtually all Catholics throughout the Church's history:

> Now before the definition of the Vatican Council, the infallibility of the Roman Pontiff was a doctrine revealed by God, delivered by the universal and constant tradition of the Church, recognized in Oecumenical Councils, pre-supposed in the acts of the Pontiffs in all ages, taught by all the Saints, defended by every religious Order, and by every theological school except one, and in that one disputed only by a minority in number, and during one period of its history; believed, at least implicitly, by all the faithful, and therefore attested by the passive infallibility of the Church in all ages and lands, with the partial and transient limitations already expressed.
>
> The doctrine was therefore already *objectively* de fide, and also *subjectively* binding in conscience on all who knew it to be revealed.
>
> The definition has added nothing to its intrinsic certainty, for this is derived from Divine revelation.
>
> It has added only the extrinsic certainty of universal promulgation by the Ecclesia docens, imposing obligation upon all the faithful. . . .
>
> . . . the process of their opposition (the authors of Janus and others who argued before the definition against it on the grounds of scientific history) was essentially heretical. It was an appeal from the traditional doctrine of the Catholic Church, delivered by its common and constant teaching, to history interpreted by themselves.

Quoted in the *Tablet*, n.s. 4 (26 November 1870) 36:679.

81. Thought to be Ullathorne's letter to the *Birmingham Post,* 14 November 1870. See *The Letters and Diaries,* 25:230, n. 3.

They certainly spoke without authority before the Council was held; is it wonderful that (however little the Council has said) they should persevere now? Do not let phantoms frighten you or make you sad. God bless you. I will not forget you.[82]

The anguish that Newman was himself feeling at this time over the fear and perplexities of Catholics troubled by the definition is evident in an exchange of letters he had with Bishop Moriarty of Kerry in mid-autumn 1870. Moriarty had said to Newman: "I had promised myself much happiness in spending a few days with you on my way home; but I had to make all possible haste in consequence of my brother's illness. Perhaps it was all the better. I might have scandalized you, as I was not then quite over the vexation and anxiety of the previous months. I am still in pain for so many whose faith has been weakened if not utterly shattered. We must only hope that a merciful Providence has been providing needful help for many more, and for future generations." Moriarty said in addition: "I hear some yet complaining of want of liberty. This is not fair. The whole conduct of business was not what some of us had wished; but it was what the immense majority of the Council wished, and the Council can not complain of its own acts. If there was any restraint it was self-imposed. Even our absence on the last day—to which I was vehemently opposed—was the free act of the minority, and was advised, and effected by the persuasion of Mgr. Dupanloup."[83]

Newman, after so many inquiries from Catholics unsure of their faith since the definition, agreed with Moriarty on the former point, but he was not ready to accept Moriarty's point on the council's liberty. After some opening remarks about the serious illness of Moriarty's brother, Newman turned to the council:

The definition, if we are to suppose it legitimately passed, is producing most untoward effects, as far as I have experience of it,—and, when poor people ask me categorically "Is it binding?" I don't know what to say. That "securus judicat orbis terrarum," I am sure—but time has not been given yet to ascertain this, and the very cruelty of certain people, of which I complain is, that *they will not let people have time.* They would come round quietly if you gave them time—but, when you hold a pistol to their heads and say, "Believe this doctrine, however new to you, as you believe the Holy Trinity, under pain of damnation, 'THEY CAN'T.' " Their breath is taken away—they seem to say "Give me time, give me time—" And their confessors all about the country say, "No, not an hour—believe or be damned—we want to sift the Catholic body of all half Catholics."

82. Newman to Lady Catherine Simeon, 18 November 1870, *The Letters and Diaries,* 25:230–31.

83. Bishop David Moriarty to Newman, 25 October 1870, *The Letters and Diaries,* 25:223, n. 3.

I assure you this so pierces my heart. I do not know what to do—and I rise in indignation against such cruelty.

And then comes the grave retort either from themselves or from third persons, which increases the unsettlement of those whose treatment is the occasion of it "At least you Catholics are as much divided in opinion as we Anglicans—you are divided in a question of faith. We thought certainty your special boast." On this I assure you I feel quite ashamed, and know not what to say. . . .

How I wish your opinion had been followed on that last day, and not the Bishop of Orleans's. Surely it was not a free council, if the Pope lectured each Bishop so sharply as he did. He lectured you, as you told me.[84]

Here again, and in this instance three and a half months after the definition, Newman gives evidence of maintaining that acceptance of the definition is still something of an open question.

Newman is forced to deal with rumors of his defection from the Catholic Church in consequence of the definition

While debates over the meaning of the definition of papal infallibility continued in England among both Catholics and Anglicans in the autumn of 1870, stories of Newman's imminent return to the Church of England also persisted. One of these reports drew from Newman a reply that he allowed to be made public as a refutation of these rumors. The writer in this instance was Miss Alice Smith, who was about to be received into the Catholic Church. Her circumstances and the sincerity of her approach (as opposed to the baiting tactics used by other inquirers on this subject) drew from Newman an immediate and gentle reply. In her letter of 31 October, Miss Smith had said:

I am on the point of being received into the R. Catholic Church—but I have been told this afternoon,—by one who *ought* to know, that *you* are on the point of leaving it for the English Communion. It has been the perusal of your Books—which in the way of intellect,—has chiefly led me to desire this reception into the Catholic Church.

. . . may I ask you to tell *me* what to do? Shall I, or shall I not, be received into the R. Catholic Church?—Or should I let,—what I have been told is an impending Split, in her,—(Consequent on the late Council),—hinder me from doing this?[85]

Newman's reply was direct. "You have been quite right to ask me your question," he wrote.

84. Newman to Bishop David Moriarty, 1 November 1870, *The Letters and Diaries,* 25:223.

85. Miss Alice Smith to Newman, 31 October 1870, *The Letters and Diaries,* 25:225, n. 1.

And in answer I assure you that the report you speak of is utterly without foundation.

I have been a Catholic for 25 years—and through all that time the report has gone about, now subsiding and then reviving, that I am going to return to the Anglican Church; and I suppose it will go about till I die. And when I am dead, if you live till then, doubtless you will hear it asserted as if on the best authority that I died a Protestant, or at least not a Catholic. I have again and again publicly contradicted the report, but it has too tough a vitality to dread any thing I may say of it. It defies me.

I advise you by all means to become a Catholic on one condition—viz if you can say deliberately and from your heart "I believe the Holy Catholic Roman Church to be the one and only Fold of Christ and Ark of Salvation, and I believe whatever she teaches has taught or shall teach, to be the Word of God committed by our Lord to his Apostles in the beginning."

For myself, I have never had a single doubt on the subject, thank God, since I have been a Catholic; and never the slightest, however transient, wish to return to the Church of England or regret at having left it.

May God be as gracious to you.

In a postscript, Newman gave Miss Smith permission to use his reply in any way she wished.[86] Newman's letter to Miss Smith was printed in the *Tablet* on 12 November and in the *Guardian* on 16 November.[87]

Edward Husband, who had written to Newman in July expressing the hope that the definition of papal infallibility would cause Newman to return to the Anglican Church, had been pressing him for several months for permission to publish the reply that Newman had sent to him on 17 July. In that reply Newman made clear that his faith in the Catholic Church remained unshaken, but Husband thought he detected some ambiguity in Newman's position since Newman had not in his letter explicitly expressed his belief in papal infallibility. Some time after writing to Newman in July, Husband had published his letter to Newman in a pamphlet entitled *What will Dr. Newman do? A Letter to the Very Reverend J. H. Newman D.D.* The pamphlet came to Newman's attention in November when a woman, Mrs. Till of Folkestone, who had just entered the Catholic Church, wrote to Newman to say that Husband's pamphlet was deterring people who were interested in becoming Catholics from doing so. She asked Newman to write a letter to her that could be published in her local newspaper. She had seen Newman's letter to Miss Alice Smith in the *Tablet*.[88] Newman replied as follows on 19 November:

86. Newman to Miss Alice Smith, 3 November 1870, *The Letters and Diaries*, 25:225.

87. See *Tablet* (12 November 1870) 36:617. Miss Smith did not herself send the letter to the Tablet. Rather it was sent by someone to whom she had given it, who signed himself in the *Tablet* as "Ex-Parson."

88. See *The Letters and Diaries*, 25:232, n. 1.

I congratulate you on your reception and I beg to thank you for the kind thought which suggested your letter. Did I answer all the letters which are written on the subject of it, I should have no time for any thing else.

You will see this I am sure.

I do not commonly see the Tablet. You will find a letter of mine at p 1338 of the Guardian Newspaper of Nov 16.

As to the gentleman whose Pamphlet you inclose, I can not condescend to notice a person who slanders me against his better knowledge.[89]

Mrs. Till had been disappointed in her hope of having Newman write a public refutation of Husband, but she did take the last sentence from Newman's letter and quoted it in a letter she wrote to the *Folkestone Express* (26 November). Husband, who was at this time a curate at the Anglican parish in Folkestone, wrote to Newman as soon as he had seen Mrs. Till's letter in the newspaper. He said: "If you think, that my printed Letter '*slanders*' you, I will at once write to my Publisher, and request him to withdraw from sale all copies of the Pamphlet in question."[90] Newman wrote an angry response to Husband, in which he said: "You have no right to look for an excuse, for withdrawing now what you were so reckless, so unjust in publishing then. Rather publish your reasons for making it at full length; let me see what they are worth; they ought to be strong ones to have outweighed in your judgment my written contradiction of them. I challenge you to produce them." But after finishing the letter he put it in his file of letters marked "not sent." At the bottom he added the following note: "I did not send this because it would have been an excuse for his publishing my private letter, which from the first he wished to do. I sent him *no* answer, as being a dangerous man."[91]

Newman appears to accept that the Council is finished and that any hope of putting the definition in a wider context is gone

Hyacinth Loyson was in England at this time and he wrote to Newman on 21 November to assure him that he had not become a Protestant, that he still considered himself a Catholic, though he could never reconcile himself to accept "l'erreur monstrueuse que l'on nous présente aujourd hui comme un dogme et comme le fondement de tous les dogmes."[92] Newman replied three days later. He began by saying: "I am always glad

---

89. Newman to Mrs. Till of Folkestone, 19 November 1870, *The Letters and Diaries,* 25:232.

90. Edward Husband to Newman, 26 November 1870, *The Letters and Diaries,* 25:236, n. 1.

91. 29 November 1870, *The Letters and Diaries,* 25:236.

92. Hyacinth Loyson to Newman, 21 November 1870, *The Letters and Diaries,* 25:235, n. 1.

to hear from you and of you." He went on to offer Loyson the following
advice in which characteristically he appealed to the future:

> Let us be patient: the turn of things may not take place in our time; but
> there will be surely, sooner or later, an energetic and a stern nemesis of im-
> perious acts, such as now afflict us.
>   The Church is the mother of high and low, of the ruler as well as of
> the ruled. *Securus judicat orbis terrarum.* If she declares by her various voices
> that the Pope is infallible in certain matters, in those matters infallible he
> is. What Bishops and people say all over the earth, that is the truth, what-
> ever complaint we may hear against certain ecclesiastical proceedings. Let
> us not oppose ourselves to the universal voice.[93]

Newman also continued to receive requests from Catholics that he write
something for publication on the definition. In November he received a
request from Bishop Brown of Newport, whose pastoral letter on the definition he had recommended to Mrs. Wilson on 24 October. "I shall be
much obliged," Newman wrote in reply, "by the gift of your Pastoral. . . ." But Newman concluded his brief letter by turning aside
Bishop Brown's suggestion: "There is no chance of my writing on the
subject of the decree of the Council."[94]

As this decisive year in the history of the papacy drew to a close, Newman remained unmoved by the pope's position since the fall of the Papal
States. In a letter to William Monsell, he saw a connection between the
definition of papal infallibility and the pope's loss of his temporal domin-
ion: "The Pope's fall is not abrupt—every one with eyes in his head must
have been sure that it must come—and, even though there be some reaction soon, it won't last—he will gradually lose his power—nor perhaps
is it possible in the disposition of Providence that the same man should
be both infallible in spirituals and absolute in temporals. The definition
of July involved the dethronement of September."[95]

Newman's annoyance at the excesses of the Ultramontane party and
with Pius IX's pontificate are also revealed in two small incidents that
took place at this time. In early November, Charles Ruscombe Poole wrote

93. Newman to Hyacinth Loyson, 24 November 1870, *The Letters and Diaries,* 25:235.
In a letter of 11 January 1871 to Peter Le Page Renouf, Acton said: "Pere Hyacinthe writes
that Newman said to him the other day, crescit in dogma. It would be well if you would
turn over in your mind the bearings of Development on this controversy." It is not clear
from this reference if Loyson visited Newman while he was in England. Newman's letter
of 24 November does not mention development of dogma and there is no evidence of any
other letter from Newman to Loyson in this period. See McElrath, *Lord Acton: the Decisive Decade,* 104.
    94. Newman to Bishop Thomas Brown of Newport, 17 November 1870, *The Letters
and Diaries,* 25:229–30.
    95. Newman to William Monsell, 12 December 1870, *The Letters and Diaries,* 25:245.

to Newman asking for a contribution toward an offering that was to be given to Pius IX by the youth of Great Britain on 17 June 1871 to observe the occasion of the twenty-fifth anniversary of the pope's election. Newman in his reply said:

> I am by no means confident that all the Parents of our boys would like me to bring it before the School.
>
> It certainly seems to me a thing to be done at home by parents, not by schoolmasters.
>
> And the 17th of June is a great way off.[96] If the common belief is true, the Pope will not live till that day; and then the subscription and demonstration involved in it will be diverted to some other purpose at present unknown. Such things do happen.[97]

And when the Italian Barnabite, Cesare Tondini, wrote to Newman in early December to ask if he could preach in the Oratory Church in Birmingham, as he had at the Brompton Oratory, on the return of Russia to Catholic unity, Newman's refusal was full of irony and evidenced an annoyance that went beyond the immediate request and the subject of Father Tondini's cause:

> I feel the honour you do us, and the devotion you show to St. Philip in your selecting our church for the purpose of your religious and charitable object. But, if you knew Birmingham, if you knew our people here, I am sure it would not come into your mind to open here the subject of the Russian Schism.
>
> The day after tomorrow we have the subject of the Pope's Temporal Power brought before us. A Sunday or two back we had the subject of Popular Education to master. Just before that came the subject of the Vatican Council. Nor is this all. Our heads are turned by recurring proposals by Westminster Priests (zealous, good, over active men) to join in addresses, manifestations, protests, and subscriptions on many matters. We long for a little peace. Do not think me unkind if I say that we had rather prepare for the Immaculate Conception our annual Quarant' Ore, and the great Feast of Christmas, than involve ourselves in new agitations.[98]

All through the months since the council Newman had gone back and forth on the question of whether the definition had been definitively

---

96. Pius IX was elected on 16 June 1846.

97. Newman to Charles Ruscombe Poole, 7 November 1870, *The Letters and Diaries,* 25:226.

98. Newman to Cesare Tondini, 2 December 1870, *The Letters and Diaries,* 25:238. It was at this same time that a common protest was solicited from Westminster asking that the clergy and faithful of England decry the injustices visited on the pope as the result of his loss of the temporal power. In a letter of 16 November, Bishop Goss indicated to Newman his unhappiness over this initiative from the metropolitan see. See Cwiekowski, *The English Bishops,* 302, n. 1.

promulgated or awaited further action when and if the council resumed. Certainly by late autumn he was giving signs that he believed the council would never sit again and that the definition could no longer be questioned as having been finally passed. A letter written to Newman by Bishop William Clifford on 9 December must have confirmed Newman in the opinion he appears to have arrived at, however reluctantly. Clifford began by recalling the correspondence he and Newman had had just after the first session of the council ended:

> Last August on my return from Rome you were good enough to write to me some kind words relative to what had taken place in the Council.[99] In your letter you remarked: "Did the Bishops of the minority openly or tacitly yield now and allow the doctrine which has been the subject in dispute to be circulated[,] proclaimed and taken for granted among Catholics, then I should think that the Majority represented the whole Episcopate, and that the doctrine was really defined. As at present advised I should in that case think the definition the voice of the church and to come to us with a claim of infallibility."
>
> In my reply I gave you some reasons why I considered some delay necessary. That delay has confirmed the view expressed in the extract from your letter quoted above. There is now no reasonable prospect of the Bishops meeting again in Council for a long time to come, the doctrine has everywhere been openly taught without any organized stand having been made against it by the Bishops of the minority, several of whom have openly expressed their adhesion to it. As to the objections raised against the Council itself they do not seem to me to affect the real point in question. In the history of several of the Councils events are recorded which we deplore without disputing the conclusions arrived at. In this case the main fact is undisputed, that the Pope with the approval of a large majority of the Episcopate has proclaimed a certain doctrine which has then been taught throughout the church without any resistance being offered by those bishops who opposed it at the Council. Even if opposition were offered by a few Bishops, this could only result in a schism. The definition therefore must be accepted as the voice of the Church and as such, undoubtedly true.
>
> I owe this explanation to you in consequence of the remarks which I addressed to you in reply to your letter in August last. I beg of you to remember me in your prayers. . . .[100]

99. See Newman's letter to Bishop William Clifford of 12 August 1870 treated on pages 137–38 of this study.

100. Bishop William Clifford to Newman, 9 December 1870, *The Letters and Diaries,* 25:246. The approach of Bishop Clifford to the question of the necessity of accepting the definition was, it would appear from the record, a complex one. Clifford gave a strong speech against the definition at the Council on 25 May 1870. See *Collectio Conciliorum Recentiorum Ecclesiae Universae* (Arnhem & Leipzig: Société Nouvelle d'Edition de la Collection Mansi, 1927) 52:274–84. It seems fair to speculate that the consequences of this action worked to make his situation very difficult on his return to England. For the most part he favored caution. But he also at times acted with strong (though private) words against priests of

Newman's reply was brief: "I had intended before now to thank you for your kind and important letter. Let me thank you for it now. Of course one or two Bishops standing out would not interfere with the integrity of the Council. I suppose from what you say, the Austrian and Hungarian Episcopates have given in."[101] Newman's disappointment is evident. Somehow, despite all that had happened since July, he appears to have kept alive some small hope that the last word on the definition had not been said.

Even though Newman could have had little hope for further developments with regard to the necessity of accepting the definition after the

---

his diocese who were taking the position in the late summer of 1870 that no one was obliged to accept the definition. See, for example, his correspondence with Canon George Case in late August and early September in Cwiekowski, *The English Bishops*, 296–297. (It is not at all clear what the *Tablet* intended to convey when it reported in its issue of 17 September, "His Lordship, the Bishop of Clifton, has circulated through his Diocese the letter upon the binding nature of the Definition of the Vatican Council, which was officially written by H. E. Card. Antonelli to the Nuncio in Brussels" [*Tablet*, n.s. 4, 36:366]. It is clear that the *Tablet* throughout the autumn of 1870 attempted to show with each succeeding issue that all of the English bishops fully adhered to the definition.) On the other hand, when Clifford returned from Rome he ordered a Te Deum, according to Simpson, not for the definition but for his return to the diocese. (See Simpson to Acton, 12 August 1870, *The Correspondence of Lord Acton and Richard Simpson*, 3:291.) And two months later in a letter to his Vicar General, who had written to Clifford on behalf of priests of the diocese who were concerned that their bishop had not yet promulgated the dogma, Clifford showed that while he could accept the definition, he felt in its present form that it was very incomplete and that he still believed that some bishops at the council had not felt free to express their opposition. See Cwiekowski, *The English Bishops*, 298–301, quoting Clifford to Bonomi, 17 November 1870, Archives of the Diocese of Clifton, Letters to William Clifford, Part I. A week before the 9 December letter to Newman, Clifford, who was receiving urgings from Rome (as were the other bishops who had not yet adhered to the definition), wrote to Cardinal Barnabò, prefect of Propaganda, to say that he had notified the priests and people of his diocese of his acceptance. See Cwiekowski, *The English Bishops*, quoting Clifford to Barnabò, 3 December 1870, Archives of the Diocese of Clifton, Letters to William Clifford, Part I. It is interesting to note that in his letter to Barnabò of 3 December, Clifford wrote "Questo ancora ho notificato al clero ed ai fedeli della mia diocesi," yet in a letter to Bishop Brown of Newport on the following day, he said that he did not see how "formal acceptance" of the definition could be delayed, as though he himself had not yet taken definite action. See Cwiekowski, *The English Bishops*, 303 and 305. The *Tablet* in its issue of 17 December 1870 reported that the Vicar General of the Clifton diocese had read out the following during the High Mass in the cathedral on 11 December: "In consequence of some doubts having been expressed on the subject, I take this occasion of reminding *all*, in so far as it may be necessary, that the Apostolic Constitution published in the Vatican Council, which declares the Successor of S. Peter to be by divine assistance preserved from error, whenever he defines, ex Cathedra, doctrines concerning faith and morals, is binding on all Catholics. It is published on pain of anathema and any person presuming to gainsay the same thereby cuts himself off from the communion of the Catholic Church. William Bishop of Clifton." *Tablet*, n.s. 4 (17 December 1870) 36:786.

101. Newman to Bishop William Clifford, 13 December 1870, *The Letters and Diaries*, 25:246.

letter from Clifford, he continued to allow others to take their time in accepting it. On 21 December, Newman wrote again to Mrs. Lavinia Wilson about her failure to find a priest in London who could help her with her ongoing difficulties in accepting the definition. Newman's letter, full of kindness, is also revealing in other respects:

> I am glad and rejoiced to aid you as far as I can—but I am not, and never have been, or shall be, a director of souls. It is not my line. Every one has his own line. It requires a training and experience which I have not.
>
> I know none of the Brighton priests except as having accidentally met some of them; and could not give you any advice about them.
>
> As to the religious community which you are near [the Redemptorists at Clapham], evidently you make the good Fathers angry, and they give you pain—and say very sharp things to you, because they do not know what else to say. You should not go to them. They are a temptation to you and nothing else. You should choose some confessor in London or the neighbourhood in whom you can confide, and keep to him, when you have tried him thoroughly. I dare say those good fathers would not give me absolution, though I have no difficulty about the infallibility. But I don't go to them.
>
> God bless you—be of good heart. I will not forget you at Christmas."[102]

It was the Advent season. The Forty Hours Devotion was held in the Birmingham Oratory church, followed by preparations for the feast of Christmas. Snow came on the first day of winter and hung on through the closing days of the year. Newman took up his usual round of Christmas greetings. One of the first of these was to W. J. Copeland, whose gift of a Christmas turkey arrived on 23 December. In addition to the usual thanks, Newman made one small reference to the council and his celebrated letter to Ullathorne. Speaking of various Jesuits friends, Newman told Copeland, "It has struck me that, since my published dislike to their proceedings relative to the Council, they have thought they must separate themselves from me."[103] On Christmas Day, Newman sang the Mass at Dawn in the Oratory Church. Another part of his Christmas season ritual was carried out on 27 December when he wrote to Mother Mary Imelda Poole, superior of the Dominican Sisters at Stone. The community there had for a number of years sent Newman greetings on his name day,

102. Newman to Mrs. Lavinia Wilson, 21 December 1870, *The Letters and Diaries,* 25:253. It is interesting to see Newman saying that direction of souls is not his line. One wonders if this attitude was begotten out of lingering memories of the dispute between Newman and Father Bernard Dalgairns and between the Birmingham and London Oratories in the 1850s over hearing the confessions of nuns, to which Newman was adamantly opposed as being un-Oratorian. See Ian Ker, *John Henry Newman: A Biography* (Oxford: The Claredon Press, 1988) 416–19.

103. Newman to W. J. Copeland, 23 December 1870, *The Letters and Diaries,* 25:254.

the feast of St. John the Evangelist. Newman was reflecting on the events of the past year, including surely the definition of papal infallibility and the fall of the Papal States, when he wrote:

> What changes are slowly but surely coming in! a new world is rising out of the old—It may take some generations to get it into shape—as in former ages of the Church—but we should find, had we the gift of prophecy, that it was quite as happy a state for her, perhaps a happier than any of those former states which are accounted so happy. Every priest before Mass prays "pro felici statu sanctae Romanae Ecclesiae"—let us not think God's arm shortened—He has many ways of blessing us—let us have more faith than to suppose His Providence is bound up with one course of action, and that He cannot turn to good what His enemies mean for our destruction."[104]

Just before the close of the year Newman wrote a letter to Archbishop Georges Darboy of Paris, who was to lose his life several months later at the hands of the Paris Communards. Darboy had opposed the definition and was one of those who absented themselves from the council on the day the definition of papal infallibility was proclaimed. Why Newman wrote to Darboy is unclear. The original letter, written in French, is undated. It is a curious letter. Newman is almost effusive in his acceptance of the definition and he makes no mention of the part the minority played at the council. It is likely, since the letter was said to be written in excellent French, that Newman did not actually write it.[105] He may have accepted what someone else in the community wrote for him. It is hard to see a place for it in view of Newman's other correspondence on the council in the year just ending and indeed in view of his correspondence on the same subject in the year ahead. The closing sentence is particularly bombastic and consequently uncharacteristic. The letter in English translation reads:

> The doctrine of Infallibility has now been more than sufficiently promulgated. Personally I never had a shadow of doubt that the very essence of religion is protection from error, for a revelation that could stultify itself would be no revelation at all. I have always inclined to the notion that a General Council was the magisterial exponent of the Creed, just as the judges of England are the legal expounders of the statutes of our realm. Unfortunately a General Council may be hampered and hindered by the action of infidel Governments upon a weak and time-serving episcopate. It is therefore better that the individual command of Christ to Peter to teach the nations, and to guard the Christian structure of society, should be committed to his undoubted successor. By this means there will be no more of those

---

104. Newman to Mother Mary Imelda Poole, 27 December 1870, *The Letters and Diaries,* 25:257.

105. See *The Letters and Diaries,* 25:259, n. 1.

misunderstandings out of which Jansenism and Gallicanism have arisen, and which in these latter days have begotten here in England the so-called Branch Theory, by which the Catholic-minded members of a Protestant Church claim the blessings of Catholicism. When Rome spoke on this subject every misgiving vanished; for, if by some fiction those who love me will have it that I am a teacher of the faithful, I am above all a disciple of the Church, doctor fidelium, discipulus ecclesiae.[106]

Newman had in the course of 1870 written dozens of letters dealing with the council and with the definition. One of them, the letter to Bishop Ullathorne, had without Newman's wishing it been made public. Aside from that and one or two brief letters to inquirers asking about his remaining a Catholic in view of the definition, Newman had turned aside all importunings both of friends and strangers to make his views on the definition publicly known. Similar requests would continue to come his way in the new year.

Controversy over the definition continues in the new year and Newman's guidance is sought

Controversy over the definition did not subside in 1871 for Newman and for those who looked to him for guidance. A new element had entered into the debate with the fall of the Papal States in September of the preceding year. Reports of schism in Germany, centered around Ignaz von Döllinger, added as well to the drama of the situation. In the first half of 1871, Newman continued to hear from those who sought his advice in the face of doubts or distress over the definition. He was also inevitably drawn into the new controversies that arose over Döllinger's refusal to accept the definition and his subsequent excommunication. The continuing distress of many people as well as the notoriety given to Döllinger's decision brought new entreaties from Newman's friends for him to make public his own views of the definition and the obligation of Catholics to receive it.

From the second day of the new year, Newman gave evidence that the definition was still much on his mind. He made a private note that read: "As far as it is a tax upon faith it is, from its wording little enough—but considered in its effects both upon the Pope's mind and that of his people, and in the power of which it puts him in practical possession, it is nothing else than shooting Niagara."[107] Perhaps Newman made this entry because of the resumption of his correspondence on the definition with Mrs. Wil-

---

106. Newman to Archbishop Georges Darboy, end of 1870?, *The Letters and Diaries,* 25:259.
107. Newman "Note," 2 January 1871, *The Letters and Diaries,* 25:262, n. 1.

liam Froude. They had last corresponded on the subject in the weeks just after the definition. Mrs. Froude's troubles persisted. In his response, written on the same day as the note just quoted, Newman took for the most part the same tack that he had taken over the past few months with others who had written to him, that the definition was in fact very narrow and limited in its effects, but those who had promoted it had created scandal and needless anxiety for many. He added, however, to his analysis a fuller exposition of his thoughts on the end of the pope's Temporal Power, that it was an inevitable consequence of the exaltation of his spiritual office and should prove beneficial to the Church. "As little as possible was passed at the Council," Newman assured Mrs. Froude,

—nothing about the Pope which I have not myself always held—but it is impossible to deny that it was done with an imperiousness and overbearing wilfulness, which has been a great scandal—and I cannot think thunder and lightning a mark of approbation, as some persons wish to make out,[108] and the sudden destruction of the Pope's temporal power does not seem a sign of approval either. It suggests too the thought that to be at once infallible in religion and a despot in temporals, is perhaps too great for mortal man. Very likely there will be some re-action for a time in his favour, but not permanently—and then, unless the Council, when re-assembled, qualifies the dogma by some considerable safeguards, which is not unlikely, perhaps the secularly defenceless state of the Pope will oblige him to court that Catholic body in its separate nations with a considerateness and kindness, which of late years the Holy see [sic] has not shown, and which may effectually prevent a tyrannous use of his spiritual power. But all these things are in God's hands, and we are blind.[109]

In this letter Newman seems to go back again on the question as to whether the council has in fact ended and seems to hold out instead some prospect of its reassembling.

---

108. This is a reference to Thomas Mozley's (Newman's brother-in-law) account for *The Times* of the 18 July 1870 session at which the definition of papal infallibility was promulgated. Mozley wrote in his dispatch of 19 July: "The storm, which had been threatening all the morning, burst now with the utmost violence, and to many a superstitious mind might have conveyed the idea that it was the expression of Divine wrath, as 'no doubt it will be interpreted by numbers,' said one officer of the Palatine Guard. And so the *Placets* of the Fathers struggled through the storm, while the thunder pealed above and the lightning flashed in at every window and down through the dome and every smaller cupola, dividing if not absorbing the attention of the crowd." Thomas Mozley, *Letters from Rome on the Occasion of the Oecumenical Council 1869–1870* (London and New York: Longmans, Green, and Co., 1891) 2:445. The *Tablet* in its report of the same event treated the storm from another point of view: "None who heard the fury of the storm but recalled the first coming of the Holy Ghost in the sound of a mighty wind rushing through the Cenacle and preceding the great calm that fell on the Apostles." *Tablet*, n.s. 4 (30 July 1870) 36:141.

109. Newman to Mrs. William Froude, 2 January 1871, *The Letters and Diaries*, 25:262.

Some weeks later Newman wrote a very full letter to Mrs. Froude, who on behalf of a friend had asked Newman about the extent of papal infallibility. In his reply Newman made an effort to show that the history of the papacy did not contradict the definition of 1870: "As to your friend's question, certainly the Pope is not infallible beyond the Deposit of Faith originally given—though there is a party of Catholics, who, I suppose to frighten away converts, wish to make out that he is giving forth infallible utterances every day. That the Immaculate Conception was in the Depositum seems to me clear, as soon as it is understood what the doctrine is. I have drawn out the argument in my letter to Dr. Pusey." Newman pressed the point that the definition did not mean that the pope's every word or thought was infallible, and in saying this he spoke severely of the extreme ultramontanes: "A Pope is not *inspired*; he has no inherent gift of divine knowledge, but when he speaks ex Cathedrâ, he may say little or much, but he is simply protected from saying what is untrue. I know you will find flatterers and partizani such as those whom St. Francis de Sales calls 'the Pope's lackies,' who say more than this, but they may enjoy their own opinion, they cannot bind the faith of Catholics."

In closing Newman returned again to the historical analysis that characterizes most of his 5 March letter to Mrs. Froude:

> I doubt very much whether the point of the Infallibility of the Pope was clearly understood, as a dogma, by the Popes themselves at that time [Cyprian, third century]; but then I also doubt whether the Infallibility of a General Council was at that time understood either, for no General Council as yet had been. The subject was what Vincentius calls "obscurely" held. The Popes acted as if they were infallible in doctrine—with a very high hand, peremptorily, magisterially, fiercely. But when we come to the question of the *analysis* of such conduct, I think they had as vague ideas on the subject as many of the early Fathers had upon portions of the doctrine of the Holy Trinity. *They acted in a way which needed infallibility as its explanation.*[110]

Newman is drawn into William Maskell's controversy with Manning over the necessity for Catholics to accept the definition

Early in 1871, Newman was drawn into a correspondence with William Maskell, who had entered into a controversy with Manning about the obligation of Catholics to accept the definition. Newman seems to have had only vague information about the dispute when he was brought closely into it by Maskell's wife Monique, who wrote to Newman toward the end of January 1871. William Maskell had recently published a pamphlet, *What is the Meaning of the Late Definition on the Infallibility of the Pope?*

110. Newman to Mrs. William Froude, 5 March 1871, *The Letters and Diaries*, 25:297-99.

An Enquiry, and it appears that his wife sent a copy to Newman in the hope of receiving some favorable comment on it.[111] Newman replied as follows:

> Gladly would I comply with your wishes, if in so doing I could be of any service for one I so respect as I do Mr. Maskell, but I am very diffident lest I should be taking a liberty. Perhaps it will answer your purpose if I write to you.
>
> I have heard of his able pamphlets—but I have not seen them. The truth is I have been too much pained and scandalized at what happened last year in Rome, not to wish to get rid of the subject, if I could. Not that it has had any effect on my own faith, thank God. It has long been my belief that the Pope had the infallibility which he was proclaimed to have last July— and there have been great scandals at Councils before those of the Vatican. But what has been the deepest of distresses to me, has been the cruel unsettlement which the conduct of a fanatical party has brought about to so many good religious minds who had up to this time found peace and rest in the Church. . . .

Then Newman turned to the practical question, the consequences of the definition for faithful Catholics. He counseled caution and characteristically appealed to the long view:

> But under a great trial, the question is what are we to do—and I seem to see clearly that our duty is patience. Remedies spring up naturally in the Church, as in nature, if we wait for them. The definition was taken out of its order—it would have come to us very differently, if those preliminaries about the Church's power had first been passed, which, I believe, were intended. And now, if the Council proceeds, I trust that it will occupy itself in other points which will have the effect of qualifying and guarding the dogma. Even as it is, I suppose there is no doubt that the Ultra party did not effect what they wished. I am quite sure that Mr. Ward, for instance, wished a great deal more than he got. I have understood that Bishops who voted for the dogma, say that it does not cover the Syllabus—now it was *in order* to exalt the Syllabus that the doctrine was brought forward. . . .
>
> Our wisdom is to keep quiet, not to make controversy, not to make things worse, but to pray that He, who before now has completed a first Council by a second, may do so now.
>
> Can I be of any further use to you? If so, tell me.[112]

Maskell seized upon the encouragement Newman had given in the closing sentences of the letter to his wife. He wrote at once. But in doing so

---

111. See *The Letters and Diaries,* 25:277, n. 2. The beginnings of Maskell's controversy with Manning are treated on pages 155–57.

112. Newman to Mrs. Monique Maskell, 31 January 1871, *The Letters and Diaries,* 25:277–78.

he made it clear that he could not accept Newman's counsels on the need for quiet and patience:

> No one can feel more strongly than myself the difficulty of deciding whether to speak or be silent: pray believe me when I say that after reading the archbishop's pastoral,[113] I *could not* resist speaking. It seemed, God forgive me if I was wrong, an absolute duty that *someone* should speak; and perhaps the more personally insignificant the better. Anyhow; no bishop speaks and no priest. —And the world, rightly or wrongly, does hold us all as consenting to the teaching of that Pastoral. How can we wonder at it, for it comes from the chief ecclesiastic in the country.

Maskell ended by saying, "People say I am doubting and all that kind of thing.—I never had a doubt for a moment about the Catholic Faith since I was received: and the definition of the Council *confirms* me in that faith."[114]

Newman did not miss the somewhat chiding tone of Maskell's remarks on the necessity for someone to speak out. He wrote at length directly to Maskell on 12 February. He began almost apologetically:

> The truth is, that, in despair of doing good, I have put the whole subject from me, except so far as private correspondence brings it before me. I never expected to see so great a scandal in the Church. . . . I thought we had too many vigilant and hostile eyes upon it, to allow even the most reckless, tyrannical, and heartless ecclesiastics, so wounding, piercing religious souls, so co-operating with those who wish the Church's downfall. The Almighty Lord of the Church will heal over the great offence, as He has obliterated other offences. His will be done—good will come out of it—nothing has been passed, (as I think,) but what I have ever held myself, about the Pope's Infallibility—but one's natural sense of justice, of loving kindness, of large forbearance and discretion, as Christian duties, is shocked by what has taken place at Rome, and to those who thus feel the catastrophe which at once came down upon that city of God seems to be retributive.
>
> This must be my explanation for not having read your pamphlets. On reading them I can only express my deep regret that one who can write so vigorously and cogently should for so many years have been silent.

And then Newman came to the heart of the matter. He gave more clearly than he had at any time in the eventful year just past his reasons for not writing publicly on papal infallibility:

> You will say, why have not others done, what at least on this occasion you have done, when there are so much needed, words of protest, and words

---

113. Manning's *The Vatican Council and Its Definitions* of 13 October 1870.
114. William Maskell to Newman, 2 February 1871, *The Letters and Diaries,* 25:282–83, n. 4.

of guidance? For myself, my feeling is, that, did I speak, I should at once be reported to Rome, perhaps put on the Index, perhaps reproved—and thus should have made matters worse instead of better. Like you, I never have had one single doubt since I was a Catholic, that the Catholic Church is the one appointed Oracle of Truth and Ark of Salvation, but I don't therefore think the acts or the policy of every Pope, of Honorius, of Boniface VIII, or Paul IV, or (as the Jesuits would say) Clement XIV, inspired, because he is Pope, and as vast changes of one kind were necessary in the dreary time before St. Gregory VII, so equally great changes, though of another kind, may be necessary now. The loss of the Temporal Power may be (if it is ratified by time) the first step towards an emancipation, parallel though unlike, to that which Hildebrand effected.

From the past Newman turned to the present and, as was his wont, glimpsed the future. "From feeling that we can really do nothing," he wrote,

I come to think that our helplessness, and therefore that our resignation under the mighty hand of God, is the path of duty. "Be still, and see the salvation of God."[115] I have full confidence that such extravagance as marks some Pastorals is but for the moment—things will in time gradually settle down and find their level. The rationale or theory which is to be held with reference to what has been done at Rome, will come out distinctly—We cannot force things. The Council cannot force things—the voice of the Schola Theologorum, of the whole Church diffusive, will in time make itself heard, and Catholic instincts and ideas will assimilate and harmonize into the credenda of Christendom, and the living tradition of the faithful, what at present many would impose upon us, and many are startled at, as a momentous addition to the faith.

And then the hint of apology crept in again:

While I say this, I do not deny that we might have done something against it in time past, though we cannot now. It is nobody's fault—but what we have wanted, ever since Cardinal Wiseman drifted from his first policy, and took up an ultra line, has been some periodical organ of moderate views, yet unassailable in point of theology. But we have left the field open to extreme opinions and their fanatical preachers—or what is worse, we have suffered what is sober Catholic truth to become unpopular by mistakes in the opposite direction.

I do not know whether you will think what I have said in point, apropos of your letter. Anyhow I hope you will receive it as a proof of my respect for you and sympathy in what you have stated in your publications with such painful force. . . .[116]

115. Lamentations 3:26.
116. Newman to William Maskell, 12 February 1871, *The Letters and Diaries*, 25:282–84. Newman's growing appreciation of the place of the *Schola Theologorum* in the life of

Maskell replied by citing some of the evidence for his contention that the bishops of England were divided in their opinion as to whether the decrees of the council must be given full assent:

> I have had letters from some, and from people in authority, which bear me out. Especially from two of our bishops. One of them [Brown of Newport] disputes (—at least he did six weeks ago—) the title of oecumenical for the Vatican Council, because it is not finished:—the other [Clifford of Clifton] sent me a copy of a long letter which he had written (last Sept.) for the *private* guidance of his clergy, which is nearly identical with the arguments and difficulties suggested in my "Enquiry." . . . I mention these things, as they show, as it seems to me, that the decree is not so clear and decisive as Dr. Manning asserts.

Maskell continued by dealing, not altogether sympathetically, with Newman's efforts to excuse his own silence: "I have long seen and expressed to other people the difficulties which are in the way of any distinct and public expression of your own judgment. That they exist is quite certain; and no one can possibly decide of what weight they are, or how far they oblige you to be silent, except yourself. But I have gone on to say (as perhaps you feel) that silence is sometimes very eloquent."[117]

Apparently Newman made no reply to Maskell's second letter. He did not dispute the interpretation Maskell put upon his silence. While Newman in this correspondence, as elsewhere, was careful to state his own belief in papal infallibility, he made it clear that he deplored and regretted what had happened in Rome and that he had great sympathy for those who found the definition a test of their faith. Maskell in interpreting Newman's silence was, it would appear, making a statement about the seeming contradictions in Newman's position.

Newman tries to reassure doubting Catholics and hesitant converts

Even into the spring and early summer of 1871, Newman was still dealing with people who found the definition difficult to accept. As in the previous year, some of these were already Catholics, others were considering entrance into the Catholic Church. A long letter that Newman had written on 5 March was primarily intended to answer the question of Mrs. Froude's friend, Mrs. Houldsworth, who was hesitating about becoming

---

the Church comes out clearly in this letter. He was to make this position very public in 1875 in the *Letter to the Duke of Norfolk* and in 1877 in the preface to the third edition of the *Via Media.*

117. William Maskell to Newman, 15 February 1871, *The Letters and Diaries,* 25:284–85, n. 2. Maskell's reference to Bishop Clifford's position in September 1870 further complicates the picture given of Clifford in this regard on pages 170–71, n. 100.

a Catholic. She would be received into the Church by Newman in the following year. On 22 April, he told her: "Popes can err in their formal decision of *particular cases*—and these are the errors which they have often made. What the Vatican Council determines is their infallibility in broad enunciations of doctrine."[118] Some weeks later Newman, resuming their correspondence of the previous year, was again trying to reassure Mary Holmes. By this time Newman had determined his position on the definition. It could not be called into question. The council would not sit again. He moved rather to show the careful limits of the definition and to place it in a historical context, using the first centuries of the Church as an illustration. Time would bring further changes, though he and perhaps even his correspondents would not live to see them. Newman told Mary Holmes:

> As to the definition, I grieve you should have been tried with it. The dogma has been *acted on* by the Holy See for centuries—the only difference is that now it is actually *recognized*. I know this is a difference—for at first sight it would seem to invite the Pope to *use* his now recognized power. But we must have a little faith. Abstract propositions avail little—theology surrounds them with a variety of limitations, explanations etc. No truth stands by itself—as each is kept in order and harmonized by other truths. The dogmas relative to the Holy Trinity and the Incarnation were not struck off all at once but piecemeal—one Council did one thing, another a second—and so the whole dogma was built up. And the first position of it looked extreme— and controversies rose upon it—and those controversies led to the second and third Councils, and they did not *reverse* the first, but *explained* and *completed* what was first done. So will it be now. Future Popes will explain and in one sense limit their own power. This would be unlikely, if they merely acted as men, but God will overrule them. Pius has been overruled—I believe he wished a much more stringent dogma than he has got. Let us have faith and patience.[119]

Though he was not dealing directly with the subject of the definition, Newman showed the same exasperated tone about Roman authority and the same conviction that time would work more changes in its exercise in a letter he wrote at this time to Emily Bowles:

> There are those who wish Catholic women, not nuns, to have no higher pursuit than that of dress, and Catholic youths to be shielded from no sin so carefully as from intellectual curiosity. All this is the consequence of Luther, and the separation off of the Teutonic races—and of the imperiousness of the Latin. But the Latin race will not always have a monopoly of the magisterium of Catholicism. We must be patient in our time; but

118. Newman to Mrs. Houldsworth, 22 April 1871, *The Letters and Diaries,* 25:320–21. Mrs. Houldsworth's first name is not given in the *Letters and Diaries.*
119. Newman to Mary Holmes, 15 May 1871, *The Letters and Diaries,* 25:330.

God will take care of His Church—and, when the hour strikes, the reform
will begin—Perhaps it *has* struck, though we can't yet tell.[120]

At the end of May, Newman resumed correspondence with yet another
of his band of troubled souls. John Pym Yeatman was experiencing new
doubts. Newman wrote: "I grieve to find that your religious difficulty
has revived. In answer to your question, I am obliged to say, that, while
you have a clear consciousness that you reject any dogma of the Catholic
Church you cannot go to confession with the hope of gaining absolution."[121] Newman wrote more fully to Yeatman several weeks later. The
first anniversary of the definition was approaching, and Yeatman's doubts
were no less severe than they had been ten months before. By this time
Newman appears less willing than he was in the late summer and autumn
of the previous year to temper his remarks to allow his correspondents
time to accept the definition:

> No one is really a Catholic who does not believe that the Church is the Oracle
> of revealed Truth and the fold of Christ, in which, and in no other body
> of men, is salvation lodged. By the force of this definition, you cannot re-
> sist its witness about the Pope's infallibility in those things in which the
> Church is infallible, for this has been believed and acted upon by the great
> mass of Catholics for centuries.
>
> Of course one can in imagination fancy declarations of the Church which
> we could not accept, as, for instance, if the Church were to decree that there
> was no God—but we say that this will never happen. The question there-
> fore is, whether the Pope's Infallibility is a doctrine so utterly repugnant
> to common sense and history, that we may treat it as we should treat a defi-
> nition of the Church to the effect that there is no God. I don't think it is—
> Popes have virtually claimed infallibility from the first.
>
> As to the Pope being a heretic as a private person, while he is infallible
> ex cathedrâ, this is an idea quite intelligible. Balaam prophesied and preached
> the truth, yet, judging from his character, we can easily understand his throw-
> ing out, ⟨as he did,⟩ very wretched ideas to Balak in private.[122]

Newman's position on Döllinger's stand and subsequent excommunication

Certainly the most dramatic event in Europe following on the definition of papal infallibility was Döllinger's public refusal to accept the Vatican Council as an ecumenical council and his consequent refusal to accept

---

120. Newman to Emily Bowles, 30 April 1871, *The Letters and Diaries*, 25:326–27.
121. Newman to John Pym Yeatman, 25 May 1871, *The Letters and Diaries*, 25:336.
122. Newman to John Pym Yeatman, 10 July 1871, *The Letters and Diaries*, 25:355–56.
The words in the angled brackets were inserted into the copy of the letter that Newman made.
It is then likely that they were also in the original.

the definition of papal infallibility. This would lead to his excommunication in April 1871. Looking back we know that Döllinger's decision had little lasting effect upon the Roman Catholic Church. But in the months following the council the defection of one of the Church's most influential scholars caused great shock and consternation in Europe. It was not easy at the time to gauge the effects of his decision on the Church in Germany and in other parts of Europe as well. Newman was inevitably drawn into the speculation over the possible results of Döllinger's action and the debate over the legitimacy of his stand. There is no doubt that while Newman tried to be sympathetic to Döllinger's stand, he could not accept his arguments for it. In the debates at the time of the council over the exercise of the papal office in history, Newman thought Döllinger went too far and exaggerated the facts to support his own position, namely that certain popes had erred in dogmatic pronouncements intended for the whole Church. We have already seen how in April 1870, Döllinger, encouraged by Newman's letter to Bishop Ullathorne, urged Newman to take an even more public and vigorous stand against the definition. Newman had turned this request aside in a brief and formal reply. There is no doubt that Döllinger and his English protégé Lord Acton thought Newman timid and lacking in nerve, a man incapable of making a decision when bold action was called for.[123]

Döllinger had a great interest in England and used English easily. He had many English friends, including leading Anglicans. Most notable among these was William Ewart Gladstone. Early in 1871, Newman was brought into the Döllinger affair through Alfred Plummer, one of Döllinger's Anglican friends. Plummer, an English academic who had translated several of Döllinger's works into English, acted as a kind of intermediary between Newman and Döllinger during the time after the council. At the beginning of 1871, Newman told Plummer: "As to Dr.

123. McElrath describes the estrangement between Döllinger and Newman over the definition of infallibility in the following terms: "Döllinger and Newman were at cross purposes when it came to the question of development, and after 1871 Döllinger lost some of the regard which he had for the Oratorian. He deplored the idea that Newman would accept Infallibility even though Newman conceded that theoretically he might be unable to reconcile it with well-ascertained facts." McElrath, *Lord Acton: The Decisive Decade,* 43.

Further evidence of the annoyance, if not disillusion, of those associated with Döllinger toward Newman is evidenced in Sir Rowland Blennerhassett's letter of 10 April 1871 to Acton. "On my return through Birmingham," Blennerhassett recounted, "I went to call on Dr. Newman. I found him in an extremely odd state of mind. He expressed himself strongly against the Archbishop of Munich for having asked Döllinger for a declaration on the subject of Infallibility and at the same time professed his own belief in the new dogma although unable to reconcile it with well ascertained facts." Hugh A. MacDougall, *The Newman-Acton Relations: The Dilemma of Christian Liberalism* (New York: Fordham University Press, 1962) 122, quoting Blennerhassett to Acton, 10 April 1871, Blennerhassett Papers, Cambridge University Library (Add Mss. 4989).

Döllinger and others, the case is quite tragic. I wish he could see, as I do, that as little as possible has really been passed at the Council. I do not deny that the *proceedings* constitute a grave scandal—and that some one will have to answer for it—but as time goes on, the power of God will be recognized as having said to the proud waves 'Hitherto shall ye go and no further'.''[124]

When Newman wrote again to Plummer on 12 March, he had just learned from Plummer that Döllinger had been given until 15 March to accept the definition.[125] Newman, while once more expressing sympathy for Döllinger, showed, as he did in other correspondence from this period, that he believed the definition was really quite restrictive. Consequently he thought Döllinger's position too strong in view of what had actually been passed at the council. ''I deeply grieve about Döllinger,'' Newman told Plummer.

What you said was quite news to me. Of course there are propositions which the Church could not impose on us—as that God was not good—but I marvel that he should so set his judgment against so very vague a definition as that which passed the Council—In the first place it says that the Pope has the Church's infallibility, but that infallibility has never been defined or explained—then it says that the Pope is infallible, when he speaks ex cathedrâ, but what ex cathedrâ is has never been defined. Nor can it be said that this is special pleading, because the definition would not have passed unless it had been so vague—and it is an acknowledged position of the Church that ''Odiosa restringenda sunt,'' as the wording of a law. The Ultras aimed at far more, and were disappointed because they could not get more. Even Gallicans say that *under certain circumstances* the Pope is infallible. Of course I do not defend the *way* in which it was passed, but other Councils were worse.[126]

124. Newman to Alfred Plummer, 15 January 1871, *The Letters and Diaries*, 25:269.

125. A description of the Archbishop of Munich's dealings with Döllinger before the excommunication on 17 April can be found in a letter of Acton to Thomas Wetherell, 25 April 1871 in McElrath, *Lord Acton: The Decisive Decade*, 106.

126. Newman to Alfred Plummer, 12 March 1871, *The Letters and Diaries*, 25:300–1. McElrath states that ''for Newman faith was in no way dependent upon history, in fact, the two might seemingly stand in contradiction. . . . Simpson could not possibly have accepted this position in 1871.'' McElrath, *Richard Simpson*, 141. McElrath relates that Blennerhassett wrote to Acton on 4 April that although displeased with Scherr's [Archbishop of Munich] approach to Döllinger, Newman nonetheless ''professed his own belief in the new dogma although unable to reconcile it with well ascertained historical facts.'' It is evident that the letter quoted here is the same letter quoted by Hugh A. MacDougall, *The Acton-Newman Relations*, 122 (see p. 183, n. 123). McElrath gives the date of the letter as 4 April; MacDougall as 10 April. In a letter of 7 April, Newman writes to Blennerhassett about his recent visit. See *The Letters and Diaries*, 25:311. It would appear then that McElrath gives the correct date.

This letter to Plummer shows how Newman treated the subject of infallibility with shades of difference, some of them quite subtle, in this period. The responses, or more precisely the explanations of Newman's own position, were made with the recipient in mind, especially that person's theological background or understanding. In this letter to Plummer, but intended in some measure for Döllinger, Newman took a more minimalist interpretation of the doctrine than he did in most of his other letters. Newman's ability to deal sensitively with each individual person and to treat each case in its uniqueness was one of his great gifts, but it can create some uncertainty about his own position on the definition. This is not to say that Newman did not accept the definition, but his own uncertainties and struggles can at least be glimpsed in letters that at times are assertive and clear and at other times hesitant or more openly critical of the definition, or ready to view it extremely restrictively.

In early April, Plummer wrote again, giving Newman a summary of Döllinger's reply to the Archbishop of Munich. Newman answered Plummer at once. It is one of the most important expositions of Newman's thought on the definition after the council and anticipates in part the *Letter to the Duke of Norfolk*. It should, however, be noted that Newman places his chief emphasis in this letter on the infallibility of the Church, not of the pope. Newman wrote:

> You are not wrong in thinking that my heart goes along with Dr. Dollinger with extreme sympathy in this his cruel trial—and it was most interesting to me to receive your letter about him. Nay more, I will say I can hardly restrain my indignation at the reckless hard heartedness with which he and so many others have been treated by those who should have been their true brethren, and of whom the least that can be said is that they know not what they do . . . but surely some great motive is required for causing such suffering, such undoing, as has followed on the mooting of the question which is the subject of your letter.
>
> While I say all this, and feel more than I say, I must say on the other hand I neither can take Dr. Dollinger's view of it, nor do I enter into the reasons which are contained, as you report them, in his Reply. You will easily enter into my side of the controversy. *I* never should have been a Catholic, had I not received the doctrine of the development of dogmas—and, as to the present instance, I think I have said 26 years ago in my Essay on the subject, that, as the promises to Judah made by dying Jacob, were not fulfilled for many centuries, . . . so the promise "Thou art Peter etc" might belong to Peter and his successors, though there were few indications of a divine performance of it until the fourth or fifth century, or till the middle ages. I have never made the Pope's Supremacy or Infallibility my *ground* for becoming a Catholic, as men like Mr. Allies[127] have, but the doctrine

---

127. Thomas William Allies became a Catholic in 1850. He was for a time professor of history under Newman at the Catholic University of Ireland. From 1853 to 1890 he was secretary of the Catholic Poor School Committee.

has no difficulty to me, when proposed for my acceptance, more than the doctrine of purgatory or transubstantiation. . . .

What has been done is more in the style of the third, fifth, or seventh councils, which we must acknowledge as true Councils, or give up Councils altogether.

. . . I had always thought, and think still, that the infallibility of the Church is an *inference* (a necessary inference) from her prerogative that she is divinely appointed Teacher of her children, and of the world. She cannot fulfil this office *without* divine help—that is, she never can be *permitted* to *go wrong* in the truths of revelation—This is a negative proposition.—the very idea of infallibility is a negative. She teaches by human means, she ascertains the truth by human means—of course assisted by grace, but so is every inquirer; and she has *in kind* no promise of invisible grace, which a Father or a divine, or an inquirer has not—but she has this security, that, *in order* to fulfil her office, her *out come* is always true in the matter of revelation. She is not inspired—the word has sometimes been used, and in Councils especially—but, properly speaking, inspiration is positive, and infallibility is negative; and a definition may be absolute truth, though the grounds suggested for it in the definition, the texts, the patristic authorities, the historical passages, are all mistakes. In saying this, I think I speak with Bellarmine and Fr. Perrone.[128] Perhaps I am used to only one school of theology, but I never heard of any view besides that which I am drawing out.

. . . I do not know where we should be if our fundamental principle were not, that the ultimate enunciations, the upshot and outcome of the Church's deliberations are certainly true. Of course it is quite fair to say that this or that Council is not legitimate. This is a question of fact, viz whether or not the Church has spoken. Dr. D. questions this also, but I am speaking of his principles, not of his facts.

In concluding Newman appealed, as he had in several other letters in this time, to a future when the council would be completed and its imbalances set right:

Another consideration has struck me forcibly, and that is, that, looking at early history, it would seem as if the Church moved on to the perfect truth by various successive declarations, alternately in contrary directions, and thus perfecting, completing, supplying each other. Let us have a little faith in her, I say. Pius is not the last of the Popes—the fourth Council modified the third, the fifth the fourth. . . . The late definition does not so much need to be undone, as to be completed. It needs safeguards to the Pope's possible acts—explanations as to the matter and extent of his power. I know

128. The Jesuit Giovanni Perrone was a leading theologian of the Roman school. He taught for many years at the Collegio Romano. He sought refuge in England in 1848 at the time of the Roman Revolution, and returned to Rome in 1851. He admired Newman and had some sympathy for his views, which he defended at Rome. Perrone died in 1876.

that a violent reckless party, had it its will, would at this moment define that the Pope's powers need no safeguards, no explanations—but there is a limit to the triumph of the tyrannical—Let us be patient, let us have faith, and a new Pope, and a re-assembled Council may trim the boat.[129]

Six days later, on Easter Sunday, Newman wrote directly to Döllinger. The main purpose of the letter was to introduce Döllinger to a Unitarian minister, the Reverend Alexander Gordon, who had corresponded with Newman. In writing to Döllinger, Newman could not ignore the difficult and dramatic events just then surrounding him. Newman's remarks, though very brief, were full of sympathy and charity. "I hope I am not wrong," he wrote, "to intrude upon you just now, when you have so overwhelming an anxiety upon you. At least, in doing so, I am able to assure you that you are continually in my thoughts, and in my prayers. I am sure you must have many hearts, feeling and praying for you, and astonished that so true a servant and son of the Catholic Church should be so tried."[130] Döllinger was formally excommunicated by the Archbishop of Munich eight days later.

Newman was urged to take some active role in Döllinger's situation by Bishop Moriarty of Kerry, who wrote on 10 April. "Can you do any good for poor Döllinger?" Moriarty asked. "If you can not, no one can. There is something peculiarly fearful in this solitary separation. We could understand a man borne away by a party or with a party; but it looks like a passionate pride to stand up alone against the Church. . . ."[131] Newman, writing the next day, turned back Moriarty's request. He had already done all he could and he took exception to the Bishop of Kerry's characterization of Döllinger's stand as "solitary":

> I have attempted indirectly to say my say, as you wish me to do—but I don't expect with any good effect. My own position ever has been so different from D's. I should never have been a Catholic, but for the doctrine of doctrinal development, and have ever held the Pope's infallibility in rebus fidei, though I never held it as a motivum for being a Catholic, as some have; but D. sees in it nothing but the establishment of the "unum [sic] sanctam," the "mirari vos," and a thousand other strong enunications.
>
> I cannot follow you in saying he is solitary in Germany. Even in France I hear of one prominent bishop who has only stated the fact in his Pastoral, that an Apostolical Constitution, saying so and so, has been promulgated from Rome, and that every thing which comes thence demands the deference and submission of the faithful. I am told the Archbishop of Vienna [Cardinal Rauscher] has done much the same. And Bishop Hefele [of Rot-

129. Newman to Alfred Plummer, 3 April 1871, *The Letters and Diaries,* 25:308–10.
130. Newman to Ignaz von Döllinger, 9 April 1871, *The Letters and Diaries,* 25:311.
131. Bishop David Moriarty to Newman, 10 April 1871, *The Letters and Diaries,* 25:315, n. 4.

tenburg, the noted historian of the Church's councils]. Also that Cardinal Swartzenburgh [sic] [Schwarzenberg of Prague] has not promulgated the dogma, and is only kept from resigning because it would throw half Bohemia into the hands of the Russians. Also that Cardinal Hohenlo[h]e [Bavarian cardinal in curia] has not received it, though he has suffered the Roman journal to say he has, without contradicting it. Also, that a great multitude of German Catholics are making Dollinger their spokesman.

Though Newman had clearly decided by the end of 1870 that the definition of infallibility would have to be accepted in the face of the impossibility of the council's reconvening, it is interesting to note how closely he was watching events on the Continent where, at least in the spring of 1871, it appeared that some prominent bishops and numbers of Catholics were showing at best only a passive acceptance of the definition. In his letter to Bishop Clifford of 13 December 1870, Newman had appeared disappointed that the Austrian and Hungarian bishops had given their formal adherence to the definition. Since that time he must have received new information that gave him some hope that the matter was as yet otherwise. In the concluding paragraph of his letter to Moriarty, Newman showed that he still thought that the definition would cause great pain and controversy in the Church for a long time. He wrote: "It seems difficult to believe that the enforcement of the dogma will not lead to the creation on the one hand of a large body of merely nominal Catholics, and on the other to a wide spread of outward adherence and secret infidelity. This is a dreadful prospect."[132]

Newman's letter of 1 November 1870 and his letter of 11 April show some impatience with Moriarty's position after the definition. One wonders whether Newman felt that Moriarty, who had opposed the definition, had turned around too quickly without any evidence of feeling for the difficulties of others who had been against the definition and had continued their opposition (or at least endured many difficulties) after the definition. In this regard the portrait of Moriarty given by Bishop Eugene O'Connell of Grass Valley, California, in April 1870 is worth noting. O'Connell in a letter to Father William Fortune wrote: "Is it not strange that the Doctor's [Moriarty] views have undergone such a change since he taught the Doctrine *ex cathedra* for fifteen years that the Pope was infallible when addressing the Church de fide aut moribus? But age and experience mellow the fairest fruit. . . ."[133]

---

132. Newman to Bishop David Moriarty, 11 April 1871, *The Letters and Diaries,* 25:315–16.

133. Bishop Eugene O'Connell to Father William Fortune, 13 April 1870, quoted in James Hennessey, *The First Council of the Vatican: The American Experience* (New York: Herder and Herder, 1963) 187.

Some weeks later there were reports that Döllinger would come to England and would stop in Birmingham. Newman was uncertain as to his own course of action in the event that Döllinger should ask to visit him. He wrote to Bishop Ullathorne on 23 May to seek his advice:

> Report says that my friend, Dr. Dollinger, is coming to England. Now it is commonly reported also that he has been submitted to the greater excommunication by name; but this is said only on authority which in many cases has turned out, and turns out, to be untrustworthy. Will you then allow me to ask you, whether his excommunication is a fact, and, next, if so, whether you have any reason to suppose that the rules which are found in theological books about the conduct to be observed by the faithful towards heretics "non tolerati," do not apply to his case.[134]

Ullathorne replied the following day. He gave Newman the certain news that Döllinger had been excommunicated. He went on to say: "I have of course forecast the subject in the possible event of Dr D's calling on me, and what I settled for myself was this, that in the event of a call I would see him, because he might wish to consult on his position, which might involve the spirituale bonum [following an opinion of St. Alphonsus], but that I could not entertain him as a guest without violating the law, and also causing grave scandal."[135]

Some days after Ullathorne's letter, Newman wrote again to Alfred Plummer. There is no evidence that Döllinger visited Birmingham at this time, but Newman's letter does show that Döllinger and his misfortunes were still much on his mind:

> I am very glad to know that Dr. Dollinger's censure did not come directly from Rome. There is so much painful which has happened there, that it is a great relief that the responsibility of this act falls elsewhere. The longer I live, the clearer I see that there is but one Church, and that is the Roman communion—but "Iliacos intra muros peccatur et extra [Horace, Ep I, ii, 16]—and as there have been great sins committed there in the 10th and 15th centuries, so there may be acts much to be deplored, and the reproach of a later age.[136]

It is somewhat startling to find Newman in this letter implying a comparison between the papacy of Pius IX and the scandalous papacies of the tenth and fifteenth centuries. This is a further evidence of the depth of Newman's feelings about the unhappy effects of the council on the life

134. Newman to Bishop William Ullathorne, 23 May 1871, *The Letters and Diaries,* 25:334–35.
135. Bishop William Ullathorne to Newman, 24 May 1871, *The Letters and Diaries,* 25:335, n. 1.
136. Newman to Alfred Plummer, 6 June 1871, *The Letters and Diaries,* 25:341.

of the Church and on individuals such as Döllinger. Until much later in the year there would be no further mention of Döllinger in Newman's correspondence.

Newman resists efforts by his friends to have him write publicly on the definition and the defection of Döllinger

In the spring of 1871, several of Newman's friends, disturbed by Döllinger's position on the Vatican Council, made a new effort to get him to write publicly on the definition and its meaning for Catholics. As was frequently the case, the effort to persuade Newman to write on the definition began unknown to him in the correspondence or conversation of some of his close friends. Shortly after Easter, William Monsell wrote to his friend, James Hope-Scott, "I think the time has come for Father Newman to speak out." He continued:

> There are advantages and disadvantages in our position, as compared with that of Catholics of former times. The disadvantages are that acts like Dollingers [sic] have an influence far more extended than they had. The advantages that the exposure of men like Dollinger is more widely known than the exposure of e.g. Luther was. But there is only one man among us who has the ear of England.
>
> I do not think that any volume or even large pamplet [sic] is necessary. What is wanted is to show that Dollingerism is Protestantism.[137]

It is evident that Monsell, who had looked on the passage of the definition with many misgivings just before and during the council, had no sympathy for Döllinger's position. On 15 April, Hope-Scott passed on Monsell's request to Newman with the comment: "I am sure that you will do it, not only more ably, but more tenderly than any one else." He said in addition: "It is painful to me, for I have known Döllinger for many years, and have experienced much kindness from him—but I cannot relapse at his instance, into submission to private teaching, and historical investigations. I suffered from it enough in former days, and should never have become a Catholic had I thought to suffer from it again."[138] Newman's reply the next day recapitulates the several major reasons that had kept him from writing on infallibility in recent years and would keep him from doing so for several years to come:

> As to the subject of your letter, I agree with you of course, that private historical enquiry is absurd against the voice of the Church; moreover, I

---

137. William Monsell to James Hope-Scott, 13 April 1871, *The Letters and Diaries,* 25:317, n. 1.

138. James Hope-Scott to Newman, 15 April 1871, *The Letters and Diaries,* 25:317, n. 2.

don't agree with D's [Döllinger's] view of history. But as to your suggestion, your and Monsell's wishes and opinion will ever go very far with me—nevertheless in the present case I do not see my way to follow them.

1. What is the good of my having (were it so) the "ear of England" in a German question? What influence could I have on Dollinger or Germans? What help should I give to German Bishops?

2. As to England, every organ of opinion, from the Archbishop to the Tablet, is strong on the side of the definition. What evidence have I of any wide-spread distress or difficulty in clergy or laity? To write without knowledge is like prescribing without seeing the patient.

3. What reason have I for thinking that persons in authority at home or in Rome, would wish me to write? Why should I put my foot into a sea of troubles, in which I have had no part? What answer should I get, but to be told to stand out of the way?[139]

Evidently Newman felt that in any rebuttal of Döllinger's position he would have to express his views on the definition in a way that would be uncongenial to Manning and the authorities at Rome. In addition to his reply to Hope-Scott, Newman also wrote directly to Monsell. In the letter to Monsell, Newman gives an even more personal exposition of his reasons for refusing Monsell's and Hope-Scott's request:

If I wrote, *I* must write—I could not write at dictation. I must speak my mind. Nearly the whole world holds the doctrine, but that is no reason why men in authority should be tyrannical and cruel. Last year was the time to do any thing, if it was to be done. When my letter to Dr. Ullathorne, to my great astonishment, got into circulation, I had a faint hope that there might have been some expression of opinion from the laity to back up its contents—I would in that case have written strongly. I don't agree with Dollinger either as to the truth of the doctrine or the validity of its definition. The very lowest ground I should take up would be that it is a duty, as being safest, to believe it—but why is he able to take so decided a line? because he has a multitude at his back. He does not simply go by his private judgement, but by the tradition of Germany. It may be a false tradition—that is another matter; but it is sympathy which gives strength. To speak, one must have the sympathy of the many, or the sanction of men in authority. I have no confidence that a free spoken statement, such as I now should have to write, would not do more harm than good. And as for the wish of authorities, I think that they would be best pleased if I held my tongue.[140]

Monsell responded on 1 May in a new effort to convince Newman to write, especially because of the favorable effect it might have on Protestant opinion. "Both Hope-Scott and I," Monsell wrote, "fully appreciate the difficulties that are in your way. Yet the Ultras want you to come out.

139. Newman to James Hope-Scott, 16 April 1871, *The Letters and Diaries*, 25:317.
140. Newman to William Monsell, 21 April 1871, *The Letters and Diaries*, 25:318–19.

The Duke of Norfolk expresses this wish to Hope-Scott. Herbert Vaughan does so very strongly to me.''[141] It would appear that Newman's friends did not pursue the matter any further. No doubt the information that the Ultras wanted him to come out was for Newman a further reason for not complying with this new request to publish his views. Newman had left no uncertainty about his position, though curiously he revealed in the letter to Monsell of 21 April a desire to have his say and an indication that he had in fact held back only because the mandate he would have needed from numbers of lay Catholics had not been forthcoming.

Newman's distress over the consequences of the definition even spilled over again into the affairs of the Oratory school and caused him to write a severe letter in late May to his friend the young Duke of Norfolk. The Duke had written to Ambrose St. John, who was the headmaster of the school, on 26 May to ask if the Oratory school could be included among the schools in England that were planning to send addresses of respect and congratulation to Pius IX on his having reached the "years of Peter," twenty-five years as pope. The Duke hoped that the Oratory school would send not only a letter but that a group of students would go with representatives of other schools to present the letter in person to Pius IX.[142] Newman lost no time in responding:

> Fr. St. John has put into my hands your letter to him, and I answer it at once.
>
> I have all along felt that the request, which it conveys to us, is not one which it belongs to us to entertain. The answer to it rests with the parents of our schoolboys.
>
> The power of sending boys out of the country does not fall within the jurisdiction of their schoolmaster.
>
> Nor should we, as it seems to me, incur a light responsibility, even did we nothing more than recommend the taking of a boy from his studies, and occasioning him what is virtually the loss of a term; besides the unsettlement of mind which would ensue both in his own case and in that of other boys around him.
>
> Schoolboys have no place in political demonstrations.
>
> However, should you wish it, I have no difficulty in furnishing your friends with a list of the addresses of our boys' parents.[143]

141. William Monsell to Newman, 1 May 1871, *The Letters and Diaries*, 25:319, n. 2. It is interesting to see the Duke of Norfolk mentioned with the "Ultras." Gladstone certainly placed him in that group when he learned in 1874 that Newman was dedicating his reply to Gladstone's *Expostulation* to the Duke of Norfolk. See Gladstone to Döllinger, 21 December 1874 in Victor Conzemius, "Acton, Döllinger and Gladstone: A Strange Variety of Anti-infallibilists," *Newman and Gladstone: Centennial Essays,* ed. James D. Bastable (Dublin: Veritas Publications, 1978) 41.

142. See Duke of Norfolk to Ambrose St. John, 26 May 1871, *The Letters and Diaries,* 25:339, n. 1.

143. Newman to the Duke of Norfolk, 27 May 1871, *The Letters and Diaries,* 25:339.

It is doubtful that the Duke of Norfolk dared to request such a list. In any case, no students from the Oratory School were among the delegation that went to Rome in early June to be received in audience by the pope on 18 June.[144] On the same day Newman noted in his diary, "Sunday 18 June Exposition for the Pope," undoubtedly a diocesanwide day of prayer for the pope.[145]

Toward the end of June, Newman along with the Birmingham diocesan clergy and other religious priests took part in a special tribute at St. Chad's Cathedral in honor of the twenty-fifth anniversary of Bishop Ullathorne's consecration as a bishop. The address to the bishop on that occasion had been written by Newman, though it was delivered by the provost of the Cathedral Chapter. Newman made only one reference to the council in the address, and it is notable that he avoided altogether any mention of the definition of papal infallibility. Rather, it mentioned the council in terms of Ullathorne's desire to have the council deal with the need to make changes in Canon Law to bring it up to date with the needs of the time.[146]

The first anniversary of the definition was approaching. But neither in his letters nor in his diaries did Newman make any explicit reference to the 18 July anniversary. On 21 July, Lady Henrietta Chatterton, who had had so much difficulty in accepting the definition and was one of the first people that Newman had written to after it, came to visit him at the Oratory.[147] Newman continued his counsels in private.

OVERVIEW

Newman's first reaction on reading the definition of papal infallibility was almost one of relief. It was moderate enough. The promoters of extravagant views had not won out. But almost immediately he began to set down reasons against straightaway accepting the definition alongside reasons for accepting it. These arguments relayed to friends such as Ambrose St. John are evidence of Newman's own struggle. There was a hope that the outcome was not yet final, but at the same time he appeared to be rehearsing for himself as well as for others various reasons for accepting the definition. His efforts to find reasons for adherence to the definition went at times to surprising lengths, for example, since the pope was the supreme voice and lawgiver in the Church, it would be prudent to accept the definition on his authority alone.

144. See *The Letters and Diaries,* 25:339, n. 4.
145. Newman "Diary," 18 June 1871, *The Letters and Diaries,* 25:345.
146. See *The Letters and Diaries,* 25:457–58, appendix 1. While this had certainly been one of the aims of the council and was a subject of interest to many bishops, including Ullathorne, the revision of the Code of Canon Law was in fact delayed until 1917.
147. See Newman "Diary," Friday, 21 July 1871, *The Letters and Diaries,* 25:359.

It is clear that Newman's hopes that the final word had not been spoken on the definition of papal infallibility were initially buoyed up by his contacts with bishops of the minority and others who maintained that the question of a lack of a moral unanimity among the bishops was still an open one and that this and other questions remained to be resolved in the next session of the council. Newman's conversations and correspondence with Bishop Clifford, Archbishop Errington, Bishop Moriarty, and Dr. Rymer gave him some reason for hope in this regard. Newman wavered in this hope, now surer, now pessimistic, almost from week to week through the month of August and into early September. But later in the year he had all but given up on it. More and more of the minority bishops, including Bishop Clifford, had formally adhered to the definition, and from October it was clear that the council had been prorogued indefinitely.

As Newman had feared all along, the definition was a cause of great consternation to many Catholics. By early August 1870, he was already in receipt of anguished letters in this regard. These too played a part in upsetting his initial equanimity over the definition. Characteristically he still favored caution insofar as the binding character of the definition was involved, but he also expressed anger over the definition and those who had promoted it at the council. Against a background of triumph and insistence on the part of Manning, Ward, the *Tablet*, and others who had favored the definition, Newman maintained that troubled Catholics should be dealt with gently and patiently. No one should be hurried and bullied into submission. Time was needed. In the heightened aftermath of the council, he kept firmly to this course in the advice he gave to those who sought his help. Newman relied also on his deep knowledge of Church history to assure his correspondents that there had always been controversy following the councils of the Church, and subsequent councils had often to fill out and put into truer focus the enactments of their predecessors.

The demands upon Newman to speak out publicly on the definition continued after its promulgation, and his friends, especially, became more insistent in this regard after the excommunication of Döllinger in April 1871. By that time it was evident that the definition must be accepted by all Catholics, but they hoped that Newman could clear the air by promoting a moderate view. Newman refused. He had had enough difficulties with ecclesiastical authority over the past decade. He thought it would be foolhardy for him to venture forth into the public arena in the highly charged and partisan atmosphere that was still evident in England in the months just after the definition. And he feared also that Manning was behind some of the attempts to get him to express his views publicly. He evidently thought that his own presentation on the definition, the view that he had taken in so many letters over the past nine months, would be out of step with the ecclesiastical authorities "at home" and "in Rome."

Some Anglican observers were sure that Newman had finally had enough of the Church of Rome. He vigorously denied that his convictions about the Roman Catholic Church had changed. He would not look back.

Chapter 4

"We Could Not Have a More Unfavourable Time for Getting into Controversy"

August 1871–August 1874

A year had passed since the definition. In August, Newman was a good deal freer than he had been the previous year just after its passage. He went back and forth frequently to Rednal where he was supervising some improvements in the property. He had also had a chance to spend two days in Derby visiting with members of his family.

Though discussion over the council had certainly died down from what it had been a year before, even this visit to his Anglican relatives did not allow Newman to escape thoughts on the council and its aftermath. He told Sister Maria Pia Giberne of his visit to Derby in a letter of 16 August: "They were very curious to know about Catholics—as to their conversion, humanly speaking, as regards my relations and friends, that is, all Anglicans, there is not a chance. The Definition of the Pope's Infallibility seems to have settled the matter once for all. There was a great yearning for unity. Now apparently it has all ceased. They seem to think it is like a child crying to have the moon; a thing which cannot be."[1]

On 9 August, Newman wrote to Lord Acton, a rare occurrence in this period. His principal reason for writing was to ask Acton if he knew anything about conditions (in terms of travel) in Rome, but he could not avoid some mention of Döllinger's situation, however indirect. "You may understand how keenly distressed I am," Newman wrote, "about what is going on in Germany as regards religion. The prospect of taking a middle line there seems so forlorn and hopeless; no one could feel more grieved than myself at the proceedings of the Council—but the question is, in the present state of things what is to be done."[2]

---

1. Newman to Sister Maria Pia Giberne, 16 August 1871, *The Letters and Diaries of John Henry Newman,* ed. Charles Stephen Dessain and Thomas Gornall, S.J. (Oxford: The Clarendon Press, 1973) 25:383.

2. Newman to Lord Acton, 9 August 1871, *The Letters and Diaries,* 25:375. It would appear that Acton did not respond to Newman's letter. See *The Letters and Diaries,* 25:375, n. 2.

Through the rest of August and September the subject of papal infallibility is absent from Newman's correspondence. There is, however, a reference in the diaries on 14 September to the visit of William Maskell. Newman notes that he had not seen Maskell for twenty years but records nothing of what they discussed.[3] It is likely that the principal purpose of Maskell's visit was to discuss his long-standing dispute with Manning over the correct interpretation of the definition and what Catholics were obliged to believe about the pope's infallibility in consequence of it. The dispute between Maskell and Manning had taken a new turn in July 1871 when Manning at a diocesan Synod had spoken unfavorably to those present about Maskell's pamphlet, *What is the Meaning of the Late Definition of the Infallibility of the Pope?*[4] It is possible that when Maskell visited Newman on 14 September he had not yet learned of Manning's remarks. When Maskell heard that Manning had spoken in public about his pamphlet, he resumed his earlier correspondence with the Archbishop. In the letter "he stated that he fully accepted the Definition, in the fair interpretation of its meaning, but not the interpretation put forward by high ecclesiastical authority."[5] Afterwards Maskell met twice with Manning and in the course of these meetings the Archbishop accepted Maskell's position, and Maskell in turn agreed to destroy any remaining copies of his pamphlet. Newman was drawn into this new exchange between Maskell and Manning when Maskell sent him copies of the letters he was writing to Manning. Newman was ready with advice. On 14 October he told Maskell:

> I thank you very much for letting me see your letters to the Archbishop. They are very important ones, and the result is very satisfactory. I suppose he has not committed himself to one single word in writing. This makes it more necessary that you should have a formal copy of what he *said* to you. I wish you had written him a letter, rehearsing to him his own admissions. E.g. you say to me, "I am perfectly satisfied that the highest authority in England knows and allows my position." Perhaps you *did* write thus to him in a *third* letter to clinch the whole matter—any how, I could have wished you had done so. But now of course you should let well alone, and do nothing more.[6]

Maskell knew Newman well enough by now to know that behind the facade of his careful courtesy he was in fact suggesting that Maskell write again to Manning to get a written statement of their agreement. On 17 October, Maskell did write a new letter to Manning, and the Archbishop

3. Newman "Diary," 14 September 1871, *The Letters and Diaries,* 25:399.
4. See *The Letters and Diaries,* 25:414, n. 1.
5. Ibid.
6. Newman to William Maskell, 14 October 1871, *The Letters and Diaries,* 25:414.

then responded in writing with an acceptance of Maskell's account of their meeting.[7] Manning's letter of 20 October was as follows:

> In my last note I said that the Definition of the Infallibility of the Head of the Church ascribes to him whatsoever has been believed by all Catholics of the infallibility of the Church.
>   The infallibility of the Church is of faith.
>   The *extension* of that infallibility is not yet defined, and is therefore matter of Theology.
>   The same is true of the Head of the Church.
>   His infallibility is of faith.
>   The *extension* of his infallibility is matter of Theology. . . .
>   The Council intended not to touch the *extension* of his infallibility.
>   You are, therefore, free *debita reverentia,* to regard this as matter of Theology.[8]

Maskell sent a copy of Manning's letter to Newman. Newman was not persuaded that Manning had in any significant way retreated from his belief in the very full scope of the pope's infallibility that had characterized his statements and pastoral letters before the council and his pastoral letter of 13 October 1870.[9] He was, Newman thought, only biding his time. Newman not surprisingly glimpsed a different future. On 22 October, Newman returned the correspondence that Maskell had shared with him. "The Archbishop's letters quite confirm," he said,

> what I had conjectured. So much so, that I do not need (thank you) to avail myself of your leave to copy them.
>   He and his are looking out for a definition of Council [sic] *extending* the province of infallibility of the *Church,* over politics, science, etc etc. Not a word more will be said about the *Pope's* Infallibility—for (since he has the *same* infallibility as the Church's) *his* infallibility will be extended indirectly, when such a decree is passed about the *Church.*
>   *Whether* it *will* be ever, depends on the will of God. Great changes may take place in the policy of Rome, if we have two or three short Pontificates.
>   If such a decree ever is passed, then doubtless God will give greater personal gifts to his Vicar—such as Popes hitherto have not had. Perhaps too

7. See *The Letters and Diaries,* 25:416, n. 3.

8. Archbishop Manning to William Maskell, 20 October 1871, *The Letters and Diaries,* 25:420, n. 2.

9. Newman would also most likely have known that Manning in his sermon on the fall of the Papal States, "Rome, the Capital of Christendom," given toward the end of the previous year, had said: "When the world persecutes, persecution purifies." And the happy result of this persecution that Manning foresaw, he expressed as follows: "We shall have among us fewer bad Catholics, worldly Catholics, lax Catholics, and *liberal* Catholics." He went on, "Nominal Catholics are our weakness and vexation, our scandal and our shame, sometimes our greatest danger." *Dublin Review* (quoting "Rome, the Capital of Christendom," 13), n.s. 16 (January–April 1871) 208.

so great a change may be accompanied by the throwing open of St. Peter's Chair to all nations—also to an "extension" of the College of Cardinals, etc etc and many other extensions which will trim St. Peter's boat.[10]

While Newman was engaged in this correspondence with Maskell, Bishop Clifford of Clifton visited Newman on 16 October. As usual, only the fact of the visit is recorded in Newman's diary, but it is interesting to speculate on whether Newman's letter to Maskell of the twenty-second might reflect something of his conversations with Bishop Clifford the week before. It was also in mid-October that Newman wrote again to Lady Simeon. The definition and its acceptance were still obviously very much on her mind. Newman gave her the latest information he had on its acceptance by various individual bishops and hierarchies that had been opposed to the definition:

> Archbishop Kenrick [of St. Louis] has accepted the Dogma—but I can easily understand a man in authority, though accepting it, refusing to disturb people who, if brought to confront it, might have a difficulty. I suspect the Hungarian Bishops stand out. It is difficult to get at the truth. Meanwhile how Döllinger will be able to stand his ground, is to me a mystery. His ground is intelligible, if he could keep it—but, he will be lifted off his footing by the wave of Anti-catholic opinion, unless he gains the shore, before it is too late. So at least it seems to me. I find the Bishop of Orleans quite confirms the view I took myself—that other definitions are necessary, and were intended, and will be added, if we are patient, to reduce the dogma to its proper proportions and place in the Catholic system. This is just what took place in the history of the 5th century, as regards the doctrine of the Incarnation.[11]

It is not clear what Newman, a year after the definition, meant by saying of Döllinger—"his ground is intelligible, if he could keep it. . . ."

A year later the definition still has a significant place in Newman's life

Concern over Döllinger's position and support for it was raised by an Anglican correspondent of Newman's in early November. He saw a par-

10. Newman to William Maskell, 22 October 1871, *The Letters and Diaries*, 25:420.
11. Newman to Lady Catherine Simeon, 15 October 1871, *The Letters and Diaries*, 25:415. In his depiction of Kenrick's acceptance, Newman appears to take a position similar to Acton's on Kenrick, though Acton's view was harsher. On 30 December 1871, Acton in a letter to Ward said: " . . . Kenrick of St. Louis has made an explicit declaration of acquiescence, without by any means accepting the doctrine. . . . No doubt the position of such men is illogical, deceptive, and unsound. But I don't think that in every case they are insincere." Damian McElrath and others, *Lord Acton: The Decisive Decade, 1864–1874* (Louvain: Publications Universitaires de Louvain, 1970) 108. Acton thought the same

allel between Newman's position in the Oxford Movement and Döllinger's current stand. Dr. Malcolm MacColl wrote:

> The Ultramontanes seem to me to have treated him much in the same way in which you were treated at Oxford. . . . German Catholicism has not deserved this treatment. I went from Germany to Italy this year, and I compared as diligently as I could the two phases of Catholicism. The one seemed to me a reality, a living, energising body; the other a corpse. . . . The prevailing feeling among educated Italians with respect to the dogma of infallibility was one of gladness that the Church of Rome had made such a fool of herself. And this quiescent sneering scepticism seems preferable at Rome to the manly piety of such a man as Dr. Döllinger.[12]

Though Newman ignored MacColl's comparison of his role in the Oxford Movement to Döllinger's stand following the Vatican Council, he did not disagree in the slightest with MacColl's analysis of German and Italian Catholics and Rome's attitude toward them. In fact he went further. He likened the position of some of the English bishops to the attitudes of Italian Catholicism. It was a harsh estimate that shows Newman's continuing belief that Manning's ultramontane orientation was detrimental to the life of the Catholic Church in England. Newman said to MacColl:

> I think, certainly, Dr. Dollinger has been treated very cruelly. And I fear your account of the Italian Catholics is true; for other persons make the same contrast between them and the Germans. Every consideration, the fullest time should be given to those who have to make up their minds to hold an article of faith which is new to them. To take up at once such an article of faith may be the act of a vigorous faith; but it may also be the act of a man who will believe anything because he believes nothing, and is ready to profess whatever his ecclesiastical, that is, his political party requires of him. There are too many high ecclesiastics in Italy and England, who think that to believe is as easy as to obey—that is, they talk as if they did not know what an act of faith is. A German who hesitates may have more of the real spirit of faith than an Italian who swallows. I have never myself had a difficulty about the Pope's Infallibility—but that is no reason I should forget Luke xvii. I.[13]

---

of Schwarzenburg, Simor, Place, MacHale, Darboy, and Clifford. See Acton to Simpson, 23 February 1872, *The Correspondence of Lord Acton and Richard Simpson,* ed. Josef L. Altholz, Damian McElrath, and James L. Holland (Cambridge: Cambridge University Press, 1975) 3:302–3.

It is interesting here to see Newman still following the position of the Hungarian bishops, a matter he had mentioned in several letters over the past year.

12. Malcolm MacColl to Newman, 10 November 1871, *The Letters and Diaries,* 25:430, n. 2.

13. Newman to Dr. Malcolm MacColl, 11 November 1871, *The Letters and Diaries,* 25:430. Luke 17:1—"It is impossible but that offences will come: but woe unto him, through whom they come!"

Despite this harsh view of Italian Catholicism, Newman two weeks later in a letter to Alfred Plummer declared that an Italian (not "Roman") view of Döllinger's position that had appeared recently in an English newspaper corresponded with his own view of Döllinger's stand:

> Did you see a letter to the Guardian,[14] some months ago, written by (I think) Mr. Skinner? giving the *Italian* view of Döllinger, (I don't mean the *Roman*)? that he is *wrong* in making the worst of the definition instead of making the best. I notice it because, as far as I understood it, it is just the one which approves itself to myself. Why should one play into the hands of extreme men, by putting a gloss upon the Council's words, which serves to reconcile them to (by undoing) the defeat which I sincerely believe they had in the actual definition?[15]

As the year ended, Newman wrote several letters dealing with reflections on the papacy and the papal teaching office. One of these letters was to the poet, Matthew Arnold, who had written to Newman several times since 1868. Replying to the most recent letter from Arnold on 3 December, Newman presented again his views on the future of the papacy and also made a rather rare observation on current socio-political events:

> Perhaps la Mennais will be a true prophet after all. It is curious to see the minute tokens which are showing themselves of the drawings of the Papal policy just now in the direction of the democracy. Of course the present Papacy is (humanly speaking) quite unequal to such a line of action—but it was the policy of Gregory VII [1073-1085]—and, though we may have a season of depression, as there was a hideous degradation before Gregory, yet it may be in the counsels of Providence that the Catholic Church may at length come out unexpectedly as a popular power. Of course the existence of the Communists makes the state of things now vastly different from what it was in the middle ages.[16]

Writing to Canon Walker of Scarborough at the end of December, Newman made a brief year-end review of some ecclesiastical trouble spots, but his primary focus was on the present papacy and its difficulties following the capture of Rome by the armies of Victor Emmanuel. Newman was not only unsympathetic to the pope's plight but seemed to blame Pius IX for his misfortunes:

14. It would appear that Newman was mistaken about the source of the story he had read. See *The Letters and Diaries,* 25:438, n. 2.

15. Newman to Alfred Plummer, 25 November 1871, *The Letters and Diaries,* 25:438.

16. Newman to Matthew Arnold, 3 December 1871, *The Letters and Diaries,* 25:442. It is not clear what Newman meant by "the minute tokens which are showing themselves of the drawings of papal policy just now in the direction of democracy." Certainly Newman believed that increasing evidence of a vibrant Catholicism in places such as Australia, Canada, and the United States could not be ignored by Rome.

Don't you think, if it is pious to criticize, that the Pope, to be consistent
with his antecedents, ought to have left Rome, when the Italians came? The
dignified course is to say to his people "It is your lookout—I don't want
to force myself on you. I am not your tyrant or conqueror, but your Father." And it *is* the fault of his people that the Italians came in. Do you
mean to tell me, that, if they had stood out and rallied around him against
the battalions of Victor Emmanuel, every man in England would not have
taken part with the weaker, and applauded him and them? I think he is in
a false position, remaining in Rome. Of course he might 20 years ago have
made terms—but he took the "Non Possumus" line. That line, I think, required him to shake the dust off his sandals, and to have left Rome. Now
people pity him, or contemn him—and he has to bear numberless insults.

Newman turned from Rome and the pope to the present difficulties of
Döllinger and his followers: "The Old Catholics may form a sect," he
said, "but what Dollinger *hoped* to do was to bring about a reform *in*
the Church, not to make a sect."[17]

And in the same month Newman dealt once again with the definition
and its effects upon an Anglican who was giving serious thought to becoming a Catholic. Newman wrote to Sir William Cope on 10 December:

Divine Providence has allowed the act of last year for some good purpose,
and we must submit to His Will. For myself, I see the doctrine implied in
the conduct of the Roman see [sic], nay of the Catholic Church, from the
first, but I am not of course blind to the difficulties in detail which it has
to encounter. The dogma seems to me as mildly framed as it could be,—or
nearly so. That the Pope was infallible in General Council, or when speaking *with* the Church, all admitted, even Gallicans. They admitted, I think
I may say, that his word ex cathedrâ was infallible, if the Bishops did no
more than keep silence—All that is passed last year, is, that in some *sense*
he may speak per se, and his speech may be infallible—I say in some sense,
because a bishop who voted for the dogma tells me that at the time an explanation was given that in one sense the Pope spoke per se, and in another
sense not per se.[18]

All these questions are questions for the theological school—and theologians will as time goes on, settle the force of the wording of the dogma,
just as the courts of law solve the meaning and bearing of Acts of Parliament.

I don't think it should interfere, whatever perplexity it may cause, with
the great fact that the Catholic Church (so called) is the Church of the Apostles, the One fold of Christ.

17. Newman to Canon John Walker of Scarborough, 28 December 1871, *The Letters
and Diaries,* 25:454–55.

18. Bishop Vincent Gasser of Brixen was a leading theologian of the council. On 11
July 1870, he gave an exposition on behalf of the deputation *de Fide* on the whole subject
of papal infallibility. See Cuthbert Butler, O.S.B., "Bishop Gasser's Exposition," *The Vatican
Council* (London, New York, and Toronto: Longmans, Green, and Co., 1930) 2:134–44,
esp. 135–36 where Gasser deals with the question, "In what sense is the Pope's infallibility
personal?"

I have written as my course of thought has taken me, without premeditation—hoping, if what I have said is worth nothing else, it will at least show I have not forgotten your anxieties.[19]

In the event Cope did not enter the Catholic Church, though both of his children did. He continued, however, a cordial correspondence with Newman in the years ahead.

At the very end of the year, Emily Bowles wrote to Newman to say that she had received a letter from W. G. Ward. In the letter Ward explained why he had found it necessary but at the same time personally distressing to take public positions against Newman, for example, his opposition to Newman's establishing an Oratory in Oxford. Speaking of Newman, Ward told Miss Bowles: "To me he is beyond all comparison the most attractive person I ever came across." He continued: "Indeed at a certain period of my Catholic life, to my unspeakable surprise it appeared to me (and does still) as clear as day that I had to choose between submitting my intellect to *Fr Newman* on the one hand or to *Pope and Bishops* on the other. To my mind it is perfectly clear that I should have committed formal mortal sin if I had adhered to his views under my *existing state of mind*."

Ward explained his opposition to Newman's having any role at Oxford "because of his surpassing power of influencing young men united with what I must consider the unsoundness and disloyalty of various of his views." He said of his determined opposition to Newman in this matter that "there is no one act of my life on which I look back with so much gratitude to God than having been able to take part in so *sacred a cause*."[20]

Newman agreed to read Ward's letter, but it would appear that Miss Bowles did not send it on to him until the following summer. "As to Ward," Newman wrote to Emily Bowles on 26 December,

I will gladly accept from you his Letter of Criticism. But you must [not] expect me to answer it. I have waited 20 years, and then the criticisms on me by Protestants were set right—and so in due time God will clear me from the charges of Catholics—⟨I have made various attempts to answer criticisms—but they have been simply *put aside* (not weighed). The time is not come, I suppose,⟩ but the errors of fact, the ignorances of the fact and the imputing of motives, have been such, not to say the simple lies, that they make me sick to think of—and I am not going to spoil Christmas by bringing them up before me.[21]

19. Newman to Sir William Cope, 10 December 1871, *The Letters and Diaries*, 25:447.
20. W. G. Ward to Emily Bowles, 22 December 1871, *The Letters and Diaries*, 25:452, n. 1.
21. Newman to Emily Bowles, 26 December 1871, *The Letters and Diaries*, 25:452–53. The editors of *The Letters and Diaries* use angled brackets to indicate interlinear explanations made by Newman.

It is probably just as well that Newman had not yet seen Ward's letter to Miss Bowles. Earlier in December in a letter to Miss Bowles, Newman professed to have no unkind feelings against Ward because his opposition to Newman had at least been open and straightforward. But after his kind remarks he added the following advice for Miss Bowles: "You must not hate theologians, but theologists."[22] The reference is unclear, but it seemingly had something to do with the continuing controversy over the definition and with Ward's position in that debate. That there remained considerable disagreement between Newman and Ward on a whole range of issues facing the Church, including papal infallibility, is evident from a long article, "The Definition of Papal Infallibility," that had appeared in the first issue of the *Dublin Review* for 1871. In the course of the unsigned article (almost surely by Ward), the author wrote: "But now how stand facts. The very first utterances of the Council set forth the intellectual evils prevalent among Catholics. Is it counted among those evils, that certain persons try to force 'extreme views' on their co-religionists? that there exists some 'insolent and aggressive faction,' which labours to make the Church's intellectual yoke heavy and almost insupportable? There is no hint of the kind ever so distant. . . ."[23] Distinct aim had been taken at Newman.

A further passage from the same article is evidence of the very different approach with which Newman and Ward treated the aftermath of the definition in the Catholic world:

> The Catholic's reason for knowing that this article was revealed by God, is the Definition of the Council; but the historical argument for its truth is irrefragable. . . .
>
> We are of course well aware, that a large number of historical objections have quite recently been raised against the dogma, by various Catholic opponents of its definition: nor does the fact of the Definition having been issued make it less important that these arguments should be answered. Doubtless the vast majority of these writers hold now with divine faith that very verity against which they then argued; while the few remaining (if indeed there are any such) have ceased to *be* Catholics.[24]

Even though, following the definition, the *Dublin* was somewhat thrown off guard because the extent of the pope's infallibility had not been defined, it came in time to insist again on its former line, that *ex cathedra* decisions were hardly a rarity in the Church.[25] When after a few years it became evident that the council would not be resumed and that

22. Newman to Emily Bowles, 9 December 1871, *The Letters and Diaries,* 25:446.

23. *Dublin Review,* n.s. 16 (January–April 1871) 200–01. Page 201 is misnumbered in the January issue as page 205.

24. Ibid., 196–97.

25. See for example *Dublin Review,* n.s. 23 (July–October 1874) 22.

the extent of papal infallibility would remain undefined, the *Dublin* thought the problem could easily be solved by the pope's pronouncing *ex cathedra* on the extent of infallibility.[26]

Early in the new year Newman would turn seventy-one. It had been nearly twenty-two years since the founding of the Birmingham Oratory. The passage of time had caused many changes in the life of the community. We get a glimpse of life in the Oratory at the end of 1871 in a letter that Newman wrote to Bishop Ullathorne in response to a request from the bishop that the Oratorians provide a priest, presumably one Sunday a month, for a Mass at the nearby home of the Little Sisters of the Poor. Newman replied directly and with just a hint of annoyance:

> We have ever [sic] wish to help them—but, after considering the matter very carefully, we are obliged to say that at present it is out of our power to do so. We have seven out of nine Masses bespoken every Sunday, and considering that most of us now are not young, we must have a reserve for the chance of indisposition on the part of some of us. . . .
>
> Of course, when your Lordship sees your way to relieve us of the Jail and Asylum, which we know you are anxious to do, the question would come before us under new circumstances.[27]

On his name day, 27 December, Newman noted in his diary that he had sung the High Mass.[28] And on the following day he thanked Mother Mary Imelda Poole, Prioress of the Dominican sisters at Stone, for that community's feast day greetings.[29] The customary rituals and remembrances that marked the passage of each year had been kept.

The pressure on Newman continues in the new year

Instead of a lessening of discussion about the definition, 1872 brought new occasions for Newman's having to deal with the subject, including his first major public statements on the issue since the letter to Ullathorne had found its way into the newspapers in the spring of 1870. Through Alfred Plummer, Newman engaged in a new exchange with Döllinger. There were also fresh reports that Newman was disappointed and bitter as a Catholic, and this particularly in consequence of the definition. And even two years after the Vatican Council had ended, there were further

26. See ibid., 25.

27. Newman to Bishop William Ullathorne, 23 December 1871, *The Letters and Diaries*, 25:451. Only two novices were received into the Birmingham Oratory from the mid-1860s until the late 1870s, and one of them was fifty when he entered. See Meriol Trevor, *Newman: Light in Winter* (London: Macmillan & Co., Ltd., 1962) 535.

28. See Newman "Diary," 27 December 1871, *The Letters and Diaries*, 25:453.

29. See Newman to Mother Mary Imelda Poole, 28 December 1871, *The Letters and Diaries*, 25:453–54.

efforts by Newman's friends to get him to write a pamphlet or essay on the definition. No doubt these fresh attempts were in part inspired by the fact that Newman did write several letters to the press in the late summer of 1872, dealing with or touching on the definition and his acceptance of it.

Early in 1872, Newman's thoughts turned to the difficulties he had had with ecclesiastical authority since his first years as a Catholic. The occasion for these recollections was a letter to Emily Bowles of 8 January. Newman wanted to be sure that in his letter of 26 December 1871, he had told Miss Bowles that he would "*not* answer Ward," referring to Ward's letter to Miss Bowles of 22 December. Newman confessed to Miss Bowles that one of his "lifelong infirmities" was "to put one word for another" and that another evidence of this infirmity was his tendency to leave out negatives in sentences. He then went on to give a recital of his difficulties with Church leaders in England and Rome, particularly the frustration of his plans to found an Oratory at Oxford. He saved his parting shot for officials of the Roman Curia. "And I suppose too," he wrote, "that they have so much experience of tricky men, men with an object etc that they cannot understand a person who is straightforward."[30]

The first evidence in the new year that difficulties over the definition continued a year and a half after its passage was a further letter of Newman to Lady Chatterton. Despite several letters and a visit to Newman in the previous summer, Lady Chatterton had, it would appear, not yet found the resolution to her doubts and distress. Newman did not lose patience with her but continued painstakingly to respond to the questions she raised:

> Ever since I have been a Catholic, I have heard on all sides a profession of belief in the Pope's Infallibility. Before I was a Catholic, I was informed that the point had been decided, in the Jansenist controversy, as long ago as Innocent XI's Bull Unigenitus. My own reading before I was a Catholic strongly impressed me with the belief that as early as the 5th century St. Leo acted as no Pope could have acted unless he was infallible. Long before that, in the 3rd century, Pope Dionysius claimed to act and was obeyed, in matters in which he could not have acted unless he had been generally considered infallible. Of course it is a difficult thing to determine when it is that he acted ex cathedrâ—and whether a particular subject is one in which, from its nature, he is infallible—but these difficulties in detail do not interfere with the abstract truth.[31]

Newman continued his correspondence with Lady Chatterton through the rest of the year. When he wrote to her in May, he expressed happiness

    30. Newman to Emily Bowles, 8 January 1872, *The Letters and Diaries*, ed. Charles Stephen Dessain and Thomas Gornall, S.J. (Oxford: The Clarendon Press, 1974) 26:7–8.
    31. Newman to Lady Henrietta Chatterton, 27 February 1872, *The Letters and Diaries*, 26:33.

that she had begun writing a novel. There is just a suggestion in his letter that he saw this as a helpful occupation that would turn her mind from religious doubts and controversies.[32] It would appear that Lady Chatterton visited Newman again late in the year.[33]

Newman sees the definition as having created new difficulties concerning higher education for English Catholics

In 1872, the consequences of the definition also had an effect on Newman's attitude toward an issue that he had for a number of years been involved in, sometimes passionately so. This was the question of higher education for the Catholic laity in England, the matter that had largely inspired his outburst to Emily Bowles in the first days of 1872 over how he had suffered at the hands of ecclesiastical authority. In the 1860s, several efforts of Newman to establish some kind of Catholic presence for students at Oxford were thwarted by Church authorities in London and Rome. Newman was in favor of permitting Catholics to attend Oxford and Cambridge since he believed it was the only viable option at the time. In 1871, a committee had been set up under the auspices of the hierarchy to deal with the question of higher education for Catholics. Several of the members of the committee were friends of Newman and one of them, Canon J. Spencer Northcote, corresponded with Newman in an effort to have his advice on various plans that were under consideration. Newman, sorely disappointed over the suppression of his earlier efforts in regard to higher education for Catholics, replied coolly to Northcote's inquiries on behalf of the committee. Interestingly, while there can be no doubt that five years earlier he had wanted some Catholic establishment at Oxford, directly involved with students, and would not have ruled out a Catholic college there, he considered this an impossibility in 1872 in consequence of the definition. It is difficult to say how much his disappointment over the treatment he had received in his efforts to establish a Catholic presence at Oxford affected the strongly negative reply that he sent to Canon Northcote on 7 April. Ostensibly it was the matter of the definition that led him to take such a strong stand against any possible new efforts at founding a Catholic college at Oxford. Newman did make it clear, however, that he was still in favor of allowing Catholics to attend Oxford and Cambridge, but at the existing Protestant colleges. What was needed, according to Newman, was a strong mission staffed by the Jesuits for the spiritual needs of Catholics at the universities.[34] Newman told Northcote,

32. See Newman to Lady Henrietta Chatterton, 14 May 1872, *The Letters and Diaries*, 26:88.
33. See 10 November 1872, *The Letters and Diaries,* 26:199.
34. See 9 April 1872, *The Letters and Diaries,* 26:60–62.

. . . though I could not advocate, hitherto I should have been quite able to acquiesce in any plan for a Catholic College at Oxford, and that, on the reasons you so lucidly and powerfully draw out; I should have been able *till lately*, but I confess I am in great doubt just now.

And for this reason:—the antagonism between the Catholic Church and Oxford has become far more direct and intense during the last two years. From all I read and hear it seems to me that the Anglican Church and the University are almost or quite in a whirlpool of unbelief, even if they be as yet some distance from the gulf and its abyss. On the other hand there are the decrees of the Vatican Council.

The two main instruments of infidelity just now are physical science and history; physical science is used against Scripture, and history against dogma; the Vatican Council by its decrees about the inspiration of Scripture and the Infallibility of the Pope has simply thrown down the gauntlet to the science and the historical research of the day. . . .

In former times it was by the collision of Catholic intellects with Catholic intellects that the meaning and the limit of dogmatic decrees were determined; but there has been no intellectual scrutiny, no controversies as yet over the Vatican definitions, and their sense will have to be wrought out not in friendly controversy, but in a mortal fight at Oxford, in the presence of Catholics and Protestants, between Protestant Professors and Tutors and a Catholic College. I do not see how this conflict is to be avoided, if we go to Oxford. Ought we to go before we are armed? Till two years ago, Trent was the last Council—and our theologians during a long 300 years had prepared us for the fight—now we are new born children, the birth of the Vatican Council, and we are going to war without strength and without arms. We do not know what exactly we hold—what we may grant, what we must maintain. A man who historically defends the Pope's infallibility must also originate a polemic—can he do so, as being an individual, without many mistakes? but he makes them on the stage of a great theater.

. . . till Catholics agree in sentiment, they cannot really agree in action.[35]

Newman continued to correspond with Canon Northcote on the subject of Catholic higher education through April. He gave a particularly revealing indication of his irritation with the subject and showed also one of the principal reasons for his annoyance at the close of a letter on 17 April. Speaking of both the clergy and the laity, Newman wrote: "There is no reason why both should not be well educated for their respective duties in life; but, for want of a clearer account of the matter, I am inclined to think that the Archbishop considers only an ignorant laity to be manageable."[36] A few days later, Newman, in a long letter to Lord

35. Newman to Canon J. Spencer Northcote, 7 April 1872, *The Letters and Diaries,* 26:59–60. There is evidence to suggest that Northcote showed some of his correspondence with Newman on the question of higher education to Manning. See *The Letters and Diaries,* 26:71, n. 3.

36. Newman to Canon J. Spencer Northcote, 17 April 1872, *The Letters and Diaries,* 26:66.

Howard of Glossop, in which he continued to support not a college at Oxford but a strong mission run by the Jesuits, voiced, but from a somewhat different angle, his conviction that the definition of 1870 was a major obstacle in the way of a successful Catholic college at Oxford:

> Then again a Catholic college with its Tutors etc professes intellectual Catholicity on the face of it, as a Mission does not. It is a direct challenge to Protestants. On the other hand it is at this very time prophesied at Oxford, that the principles of Catholics necessarily hinder them from following out the higher exercises of reason. Now we have lately had an ecumenical Council. Councils have generally acted as a lever, displacing and disordering portions of the existing theological system. Not seldom have they be[en] followed by bitter quarrels in the Catholic body. Time is necessary to put things to rights. When Trent was the last Council, we enjoyed the stability and edification of three hundred years. A series of the ablest divines had examined, interpreted, adjusted, located, illustrated every sentence of the definitions. We were all of us on sure ground, and could speak with confidence, after Suarez, Lambertini, and a host of others. Now, as regards the force, limits, and consequents of the recent definitions, we have as yet nothing better to guide us, from the necessity of the case, than the Dublin Review and the Civiltà Cattolica. We have yet to learn what is precisely meant by "inspiration," as applied to a book, and in what cases and under what conditions the Pope is infallible. Not to say that the Council is not yet finished. We could not have a more unfavourable time for getting into controversy.[37]

The result of the various soundings and inquiries over Catholic higher education in England was the founding in 1872 of Manning's ill-fated Catholic University in Kensington.[38]

Newman and Döllinger correspond through Alfred Plummer but succeed only in deepening their disagreement

Some weeks later Newman welcomed to the Oratory a German priest, Franz Brentano, a Professor at Würzburg. The weather was cold and

37. Newman to Lord Howard of Glossop, 27 April 1872, *The Letters and Diaries,* 26:76–77. Here it is interesting to see Newman take the view that the council was not finished, a position he appeared to have given up several months after the definition.

38. In a rare instance of sympathy for Newman, Robert Gray states: " . . . as Newman well knew, it was Manning's illiberalism which made him quite unsuited to run a university." Robert Gray, *Cardinal Manning: A Biography* (London: Weidenfeld and Nicolson, 1985) 257. Newman refused Manning's invitation to be a member of the Senate of the new college, giving as his reason its association with London University, "a body which has been the beginning, and source, and symbol of all the liberalism existing in the educated classes for the last forty years." See Newman to Archbishop Henry Manning, 24 November 1873, *The Letters and Diaries,* 26:390. For a treatment of the commission on higher education established by the bishops, see Vincent McClelland, *English Roman Catholics and Higher*

dreary as if setting the tone for Brentano's visit.[39] Brentano was in doubt
over his remaining a priest because he found great difficulty in accepting
the definition of papal infallibility. He believed especially that the Fathers
of the council had not been free. Evidently friends of Brentano in Germany had recommended that he visit Newman while he was on a trip to
England. Brentano came to Birmingham early in May and stayed about
two weeks.[40] Acton kept Döllinger informed of Brentano's progress
through England. On 6 May, he reported: "Brentano ist bei Newman.
Ich weiss nicht mit welcher Aussicht."[41] Newman reported in letters written in Latin to Brentano's friends in Germany that he had been unable
to help Brentano see his way to accepting the definition and that he had
left Birmingham to visit Anglicans of the High Church party at Oxford.
Newman wrote on 16 May: "Nullis argumentis meis, nullis fratrum me-
orum, commovebatur, ut ab hac opinione vel latum unguem discederet.
Hoc vespere nobis valedixit, iter faciens in Oxoniam."[42] And in his diary
for the same day Newman recorded: "candles at breakfast Dr Brentano
left dark, rain."[43] Brentano, brother-in-law of Peter le Page Renouf, left
the Catholic Church and became for a time professor of philosophy in
Vienna. He died in 1916. No doubt Acton felt justified in his belief that
Brentano's visit to Newman would be useless when he reported to Döllinger on 16 June: "Er hat von Newman nur Ausflüchte und vage Sen-
timentalitäten gehört."[44]

A month later Newman's attention was drawn again in the direction
of the Continent when Alfred Plummer asked Newman, "if I may bear
any words of yours to either Hyacinthe [Loyson] or Döllinger. You know,
I think, how much they value any thing from you. . . ."[45] Newman
responded the very next day. He was quite willing to send greetings to
Loyson and Döllinger, but he took the occasion of his reply to Plummer
to say how he disagreed with Döllinger's position. "Of course you may
say every thing which is kind and sympathetic from me to Dollinger and
Fr Hyacinth," Newman said straightaway. "The former at least of them
has been cruelly dealt with—and a nemesis is likely to come for it. But

Education, 1830–1903 (Oxford: At the Clarendon Press, 1973) 245–66. Both Newman's and
Ambrose St. John's views were sought by the commission.

39. See Newman "Diary," 3 May 1872, *The Letters and Diaries*, 26:82.

40. See Acton to Döllinger, 17 June 1872, *Ignaz von Döllinger: Briefwechsel, 1820–
1890* (hereafter cited as *Briefwechsel*), ed. Victor Conzemius (Munich: C. H. Beck'sche Verlagsbuchhandlung, 1971) 3:72.

41. Acton to Döllinger, 6 May 1872, *Briefwechsel*, 3:70.

42. Newman to German Doctor of Theology, 16 May 1872, *The Letters and Diaries*,
26:90.

43. Newman "Diary," 16 May 1872, *The Letters and Diaries*, 26:89.

44. Acton to Döllinger, 17 June 1872, *Briefwechsel*, 3:72.

45. Alfred Plummer to Newman, 16 June 1872, *The Letters and Diaries*, 26:120, n. 2.

I should not be honest, if I implied even by my silence that any thing but evil could come of their present position. Their associates are not like them, and they will either find themselves alone or with those from whom they will dissent more than from those whom they have left.'' Newman continued his arguments on historical grounds:

> You will say that Dollinger is an historian and has a right to go by facts. But more than an historian is necessary in this case—he is not (speaking under correction) a philosophical historian. I was struck with this especially in the work of his which Oxenham translated.[46] He does not throw himself into the state of things which he reads about—he does not enter into the position of Honorius, or of the Council 40 years afterwards. . . . How can he defend the 3rd General Council [Council of Ephesus], and yet quarrel with the Vatican, I cannot make out—but perhaps by this time the very force of logic, to say nothing of philosophy, has obliged him to give up Councils altogether. Certainly if their Acta are to be the measure of their authority, they are, with few exceptions, a dreary, unlovely phenomenon in the Church.
>
> However, I have said all this for yourself, to explain how it is that, though I am sincerely afflicted that so great a man should be lost to us, though I feel the scandal and the reproach which it is to us, and though I am indignant at the way in which he has been treated and am much distressed in his distress, still I think he has taken a wrong course, and has got the Catholic world against him—and whatever be the sins, the intrigues, the cruelties of individuals, Securus judicat orbis terrarum.[47]

Plummer wrote again several weeks later. He had conveyed to Döllinger the arguments that Newman had raised against his position. Döllinger had in turn disagreed with Newman's reading of the early councils. Plummer reported:

> I told him what you say about the third Council. For a moment he did not seem to see how the remark applied. I ventured to say that I believed your meaning to be, that at Ephesus there was all the violence and intrigue which disfigured the Vatican Council, and yet the third Council is accepted. The cases are not parallel, he said. No doubt Cyril and others behaved badly and the proceedings were irregular; but the Council of Ephesus imposed nothing on the Church. It merely confirmed a foregone conclusion; it condemned a doctrine which had already been rejected by the bulk of the Church. It did not alter the existing state of things one iota. . . .[48]

In the same letter Plummer relayed to Newman Döllinger's personal reaction to the message Newman had sent to him through Plummer. "I gave him your kind message," Plummer said,

46. Ignaz von Döllinger, *The First Age of Christianity and the Church,* trans. Henry Nutcombe Oxenham, 3rd ed. (1st ed. appeared in 1866) (London: William H. Allen, 1877).
47. Newman to Alfred Plummer, 17 June 1872, *The Letters and Diaries,* 26:120.
48. Alfred Plummer to Newman, 14 July 1872, *The Letters and Diaries,* 26:120, n. 4.

and I believe I may say with certainty that he is quite as much pained to think that you are not with him, as you can be to think that he is not with you in this great trial. Forgive me if I venture to add that I believe he is more surprised at your position than you seem to be at his. If I interpret what you have said of him aright, you think his position as a historian not altogether unnatural and to a great extent intelligible, though a grievous mistake. Though he has never, so far as I remember, said so to me in as many words,—I believe he is fairly puzzled to know how one who is in uprightness and ability what he knows you to be could think and say what you thought and said of the Dogma before it was passed and yet can defend it now.[49]

The letter to Ullathorne still loomed large in Newman's dealings with the definition after the council despite his own efforts to put it to one side as a passionate outburst that he had at a certain moment felt impelled to make privately to his bishop. In his reply to Plummer five days later, Newman attempted, as he had often since the council, to show that his writings and public utterances, as far back as his Anglican years, revealed a consistent attitude of accepting papal infallibility. He began: "Give my best love to Dr. Dollinger, and tell him, not that I was *surprised,* but sorry that he was separated from me, and that he has no cause for being more than sorry, not surprised, that I should be separated from him. His message about being surprised at me is not a 'Tu quoque,' because *I* was not surprised at *him*—but it is a proof that the most excursive of readers and the most accurate of memories sometimes are at fault—"

After this exercise in elegant courtesy, Newman pressed on in defense of himself and his consistency in the matter of infallibility. "I have for these 25 years spoken *in behalf* of the Pope's infallibility," he insisted.

> The other day a review (I forget what) observed with surprise that even in my article on la Mennais in 1838 I had tacitly accepted the Pope's infallibility.[50] I think I have spoken *for it* in my Essay on Development of Doctrine

49. Ibid., 138-39, n. 3. On 26 June, Plummer had met with Döllinger in Munich. In the course of their conversation Plummer relayed to Döllinger what he understood to be Newman's view of the definition: "He [Newman] is able to accept it by making it mean as little as possible; and he thinks that you [Döllinger] are making a great mistake in making it mean so much. You are playing, he says, into the hands of the Jesuits in contending that their interpretation of the dogma is the right one. The true course is to consider that the dogma means next to nothing." Alfred Plummer, *Conversations with Dr. Döllinger 1870–1890,* Introduction and Notes by Robrecht Boudens, with collaboration of Leo Kenis (Leuven: University Press, 1985) 25-26.

50. The *British Critic* (October 1837), reprinted as "Fall of de la Mennais," John Henry Newman, *Essays Critical and Historical* (London, New York, and Bombay: Longmans, Green, and Co., 1907) 1:138-72.

in 1845.[51] In 1850 I have introduced the Pope's Infallibility several times into my lectures at the Birmingham Corn Exchange.[52] In 1852 I introduced it most emphatically and dogmatically into my lectures delivered at the Rotundo at Dublin. In 1856 I spoke of it in a new Preface I prefixed to the new Edition of my Church of the Fathers—and in 1868 I reprinted the passage from my Dublin Lectures in a collection of passages made by a Roman Jesuit Father on the dogma, in an Italian translation.[53]

This is quite consistent, in my way of viewing it, in my being most energetic against the *definition*. Many things are true which are not points of faith, and I thought the definition of this doctrine *most inexpedient*. And, as St. Paul, though inspired, doubted whether his words might not do harm to his Corinthian converts, so do I now fear much lest the infallible voice of the Council may not do harm to the cause of the Church in Germany, England, and elsewhere.

What I said in the private letter to my Bishop, to which Dr D. alludes, was that the definition *would unsettle men's minds*. This anticipation has been abundantly fulfilled. I said moreover expressly that it would be *no* difficulty to *me*, but that it was making the defence of Catholicism more *difficult*. And as proof that all of this is the true view of my position, *I have never been called on*, as Gratry was, *publicly* to accept the doctrine—*because I had never denied it*.[54]

The attempt at a long-distance dialogue between Newman and Döllinger did not work. In the future Newman would send greetings through Plummer and say how sad (but insupportable) Döllinger's position was. But there would be no further efforts toward a real exchange of views. When he was raised to the cardinalate in May 1879, Newman hoped to visit Döllinger on the return journey from Rome. The precarious state of his health, aggravated by the damp of Rome, made this plan impossible.[55]

51. John Henry Newman, *An Essay on Development of Christian Doctrine* (London, New York, and Bombay: Longmans, Green, and Co., 1906) 78–92.

52. John Henry Newman, *Lectures on the Present Position of Catholics in England* (London, New York, and Bombay: Longmans, Green, and Co., 1908) 334–35, 338.

53. See the passage from the Dublin Lectures on page 219 of this chapter.

54. Newman to Alfred Plummer, 19 July 1872, *The Letters and Diaries*, 26:138–39. When told of Newman's letter, Döllinger said: "Fifty Newmans living all at once, and all working to explain and pare down the dogma, would not have any appreciable effect on the working of the dogma." Plummer, *Conversations with Dr. Döllinger*, 66–67.

Auguste Gratry, a member, though not always happily, of the Oratory of France, was from 1863 professor of theology at the Sorbonne. He died in 1872.

55. Sheridan Gilley says that any hope of Newman's reconciling Döllinger was dashed "by a public letter in which the German historian declared 'That he [the Pope] makes Newman a Cardinal, a man so infinitely above the Romish *vulgus praelaticum*, is only conceivable when the true views of the man are unknown in Rome. If Newman had written in French, Italian, or Latin, his books would long since have been on the Index.' " Sheridan Gilley, *Newman and His Age* (London: Darton, Longman, and Todd, 1990) 403.

*Newman marshals evidence of what he sees as his long held views
on papal infallibility*

Newman's letter to Döllinger makes for the first time a rather careful
catalogue of past statements of his which he saw as evidence of his consistent acceptance of papal infallibility well before the Vatican Council.
It is not altogether clear why Newman waited until after the council to
marshal these citations, though he had certainly referred to one or other
of them over the past several years. But what made him, two years after
the definition, look into the matter with such precision? It is fair to speculate that events in Germany as well as questions over the definition, questions that still came to him from a whole host of people with continuing
regularity, made Newman decide that the disputes were bound to go on
for some time and that a careful search of his past writings would be of
use in answering both friendly and hostile queries. Certainly at the conclusion of the letter Newman's references to the Church in "Germany,
England, and elsewhere" indicate that he thought the controversy over
the definition was far from over. It is also not altogether idle to wonder
if Newman had some fear that a time would come when he would have
to give an account of his position on the definition to those in authority.
The final sentence of the letter to Döllinger with its reference to Auguste
Gratry might be taken as some evidence of this. Certainly Newman's dealings with William Maskell and others who were known by those in
authority to be questioning or hesitant, as well as Newman's continuing
denunciations of the tactics of some of those who had promoted the definition, must have been known to Manning and others, however ostensibly private Newman's correspondence on these matters. It is also worth
noting that on another occasion Newman denounced the use that had been
made of the quotation from his Dublin Lectures in the collection edited
in 1867[56] by Valerian Cardella, "a Roman Jesuit Father." He felt that
he had been tricked into doing this and regretted the appearance of his
quotation in this highly ultramontane collection.[57] Why, in fact, did he
appear to wait until the council was sitting and during the controversies
that followed it to gather this information on his long held views on papal
infallibility? It is surprising to see how little use, how few references were
made to this material by Newman in the years just before the council when
the controversy over papal infallibility was beginning to grow, and it should
be recalled that in his February 1868 correspondence with John Stanislas
Flanagan Newman not only said "I dare say I have not been consistent

56. Newman makes reference to the passage he sent to Father Cardella in "1867 or
1868." In fact, it was in 1867 that Cardella's *Ommagio Cattolico ai Principi degli Apostoli*
was printed at Rome.
57. See pages 239–40 of this chapter, Newman's letter of 24 August 1873 to John Wallis.

or logically exact in what from time to time I have said about the extent
& subject matter of the Church's Infallibility, for it is a very large question and I have never set myself formally to answer it," but he also went
on to say with regard to his writings on, *not papal,* but the Church's infallibility: "So much on what I have said in my Essay on Development
& in the Apologia; I don't recollect having said any thing on the subject
elsewhere."[58] Whatever Newman's reason for listing these citations from
his writings, they were to be put to a further use two months later when
for the first time since the publication of the letter to Ullathorne he made
public statements on the definition.

In the midst of his indirect exchange with Döllinger, Newman was also
making comments on the position of Döllinger's protégé, Lord Acton,
relative to the definition. These occurred in a letter Newman wrote on
6 July to his friend of many years, Frederic Rogers, who had been created Lord Blachford the previous year. Blachford had come to know Acton in the House of Lords and had spoken very positively of him to
Newman. He planned to invite Acton to dinner when Newman was to
be in London on 8 and 9 July. Newman said in reply: "I shall be most
happy to meet at dinner anyone you please, especially Lord Acton—but
I suppose Monday morning, when you get this, will be late for an invite.
I have had the greatest liking for Acton ever since I knew him near 20
years ago; but, alas, we have never quite hit it off in action. And now
I don't know where he stands as regards this sad Vatican question. There
is only one locus standi—and I think in time he will see that; but mind,
I shall *rejoice* to meet him—."[59]

It appears that Newman did not in fact see Acton at Lord Blachford's
house. He records in his diary for 8 July, "Liddon etc. to dinner," but
in a letter to Ambrose St. John on 14 July, in which he gives an account
of his stay in London, Newman does not mention Acton among those
he met there.[60] And in his letters to Döllinger on 12, 14, and 20 July, Acton
does not mention having seen Newman.[61]

Newman spent two weeks in July on holiday in Scotland, mostly at
the home of his friend of many years, James Hope-Scott. On his return
to Birmingham on 27 July, he became involved in matters related to the
Oratory school, including the launching of an appeal for funds on 15 August. Most of the members of the community were away when on 23 Au-

58. Newman to John Stanislas Flanigan, 15 February 1868, *The Theological Papers
of John Henry Newman On Biblical Inspiration and On Infallibility,* selected, edited, and
introduced by J. Derek Holmes (Oxford: The Clarendon Press, 1979) 154 and 156.
59. Newman to Lord Blachford, 6 July 1872, *The Letters and Diaries,* 26:131.
60. Newman "Diary," 8 July 1872, *The Letters and Diaries,* 26:133, and Newman to
Ambrose St. John, 14 July 1872, *The Letters and Diaries,* 26:134.
61. See Döllinger to Acton, *Briefwechsel,* 3:84–87, 3:87–89, 3:90–91.

gust a young priest from the London Oratory, Father Frederick Antrobus, came to visit. Newman with some amusement recalled the visit for Ambrose St. John, who was in Switzerland. "Father Antrobus of the London Oy called just now," Newman wrote, "with a letter to you from Fr. Gordon and a relic—wishing to be hospitably entertained. I was civil—but said we were in such confusion and so few that we could do nothing for him. I took him over the Church and House—but I thought his dining with us, Wm [Neville] reading, Thomas [Pope] waiting, and I eating, would be a scandal."[62] After this pleasant interval, there were very soon new problems to be faced.

Newman at last breaks his silence, though carefully and guardedly

Three letters of Newman's appeared in major English publications in the late summer of 1872. All of them dealt in some way with the definition, but the cause for one of them was unrelated to the reason for the other two. *The Times* on 6 September 1872 carried an article that dealt with the St. Bartholomew's Day Massacre and papal infallibility. The article stated that no pope had ever denounced the massacre and that as a consequence of the definition of papal infallibility it would be impossible for any pope ever to do so. In fact, the article went on, no Catholic sincere in his commitment to his faith, could possibly decry what had happened on 24 August 1572. *The Times* said: "We certainly should be surprised to find any Roman Catholic, except one Liberal to laxity, ready to admit that the act was a crime, or even a mistake." *The Times* then asked rhetorically of Catholics, "who disavows the deed?"[63] Somewhat surprisingly Newman took up the challenge. His letter, written on 9 September, appeared in *The Times* on 13 September. It read as follows: "You have lately in your article on the Massacre of St. Bartholomew's day, thrown down a challenge to us on a most serious subject. I have no claim to speak for my brethren; but I speak in default of better men.[64] Newman continued:

> No Pope can make evil good. No Pope has any power over those external moral principles which God has imprinted on our hearts and consciences. If any Pope has, with his eyes open, approved of treachery or cruelty, let those defend that Pope, who can. If any Pope at any time has had his mind so occupied with the desirableness of the Church's triumph over her enemies, as to be dead to the treacherous and savage acts by which that tri-

---

62. Newman to Ambrose St. John, 23 August 1872, *The Letters and Diaries,* 26:153.

63. See *The Letters and Diaries,* 26:163, n. 3.

64. No protest against the article appeared in *The Times* until 10 September. Two days of silence following the article was thought to be a long period of silence in the letters page of *The Times!*

umph was achieved, let those who feel disposed say that in such conduct he acted up to his high office of maintaining justice and showing mercy. Craft and cruelty, and whatever is base and wicked have a sure *nemesis*, and eventually strike the heads of those who are guilty of them.

Whether, in matter of fact, Pope Gregory XIII had a share in the guilt of the St. Bartholomew massacre, must be proved to me, before I believe it. It is commonly said in his defence, that he had an untrue, one-sided account of the matter presented to him, and acted on misinformation. This involves a question of fact, which historians must decide. But, even if they decide against the Pope, his infallibility is in no respect compromised. Infallibility is not impeccability. Even Caiphas prophesied; and Gregory XIII was not quite a Caiphas.[65]

Newman had spoken clearly and directly. No one, it would appear, wrote to *The Times* to challenge Newman's statements. Letters from several leading laymen were also eventually printed, but Newman's was the only one from an ecclesiastic.[66]

Newman's second letter was written to the *Guardian* on 12 September. It arose from a more complex set of circumstances than did his response to the bombastic piece in *The Times*. Controversy in the Church of England between the High Church party, represented especially by E. B. Pusey, and the Low or Broad Church mentality continued apace throughout most of the nineteenth century. And there were frequent disputes among High Churchmen themselves over what issues should be fought for and which made the subject of compromise. In 1872, a controversy arose in the High Church party over a proposal in the Anglican Church to move the Athanasian Creed from its accustomed place in the Prayer Book, a place that assured its frequent recitation through the Sundays of the year, to a position in the back of the book. In effect the recitation of the Athanasian Creed would no longer be the custom. Pusey opposed this, and there was even some fear that he and others would leave the Anglican Church, this dispute being so to speak the last straw. Newman was certainly aware of the controversy and had corresponded with several Anglicans on it.[67] On 11 September, the *Guardian* published a let-

65. Newman to the Editor of *The Times*, 9 September 1872, *The Letters and Diaries,* 26:163–64. See also *The Times* (13 September 1872) 3. Derek Holmes maintains that Newman's September 1872 letter to *The Times* played a part in paving the way for the acceptance accorded to his *Letter to the Duke of Norfolk* in 1875. See Derek Holmes, "Liberal Catholicism and Newman's *Letter to the Duke of Norfolk," Clergy Review,* 60 (1975) 505–06.

66. The *Tablet* in its issue of 21 September 1872, n.s. 8, vol. 40, printed Newman's and several of the other letters. See 372–74.

67. See for example Newman to William Bright, 15 March 1872, *The Letters and Diaries,* 26:44–45, and Newman to H. P. Liddon, 18 April 1872, *The Letters and Diaries,* 26:66. See also Newman to Frederick George Lee, 5 April 1872, *The Letters and Diaries,* 26:55–56.

ter by John Moore Capes, a High Churchman who had become a Catholic in 1845 and had served for a time as editor of the *Rambler,* but who left the Catholic Church in 1858. Capes's letter was an effort to dissuade Pusey from leaving the Anglican Church over the removal of the Athanasian Creed from its traditional place. But he went further. "The little finger of the Pope is heavier than the loins of English Kings and Bishops," Capes said. "And as for this proposition to relegate the Athanasian Creed to the more hidden sections of the Prayer-book, we may rest assured that if Rome thought that its public or private recitation in the smallest degree tended to lessen the Papal authority, it would vanish absolutely from the office books of the Roman Church." Then out of the blue Newman's name was brought in. "And here," Capes continued,

> I cannot but introduce a name still dear to Dr. Pusey, and regarded with sincere respect by many Churchmen of all schools. We all know how Dr. Newman felt the enforcement of the dogma of Papal Infallibility. There were published a few sentences of the expressions of intense distress which were wrung from him, when he foresaw the imposition of a doctrine which would cut up the historical basis of his faith by the very roots. At the same time, as he then avowed, he himself contrived, by some mysterious subtleties, to accept the tyrannical and false decree. But it was evident that it was only by putting a terrible force upon his previous convictions that he could bring himself to submit as he has submitted; and the strain upon his principle of absolute obedience to Rome was plainly such as he had never contemplated when he left the English communion. Yet what is the submission that may now be asked by those who threaten secession, in comparison with the submission which Dr. Newman has thus forced upon himself? Clearly he yielded to the inevitable; and it is not for any of us to suggest that his yielding was not absolutely sincere, and, to his own satisfaction, logically consistent with his previous creed. Why cannot Dr. Pusey do the same, in a far less serious matter? Why cannot he also yield to the inevitable? What is the disuse of a single Creed in public worship, in comparison with the imposition of a new theory as to the grounds of belief in all creeds and articles of faith?[68]

Lee, an Anglican clergyman and distant relative of Newman, was distressed about the possible elimination of the Athanasian Creed from the Prayer Book. Newman in his response said that what Anglicanism needed was a strong, central force, "a pope" whether this be the body of bishops or the majority of a designated committee was not important. "It must be such," he wrote, "as to compel all members to one mode of action as they already would agree . . . in one faith." He continued: "This is what reconciles me to the definition at this time of that primitive tradition (as I consider it) that the Holy See, when speaking as such, i.e. the Pope ex cathedrâ, is infallible—At this time a strong force is needed to bind men together. It is not time for the practical tolerance of a hundred opinions."

    68. John Moore Capes to the *Guardian,* 11 September 1872, *The Letters and Diaries,* 26:166, n. 2.

Newman responded at once with a letter to the *Guardian*. As in the past, he had been provoked to speak out, and his inhibitions gave way in the face of a blatant attack on his religious convictions:

> I cannot allow such language as Mr. Capes uses of me in yesterday's *Guardian* to pass unnoticed, nor can I doubt that you will admit my answer to it. I thank him for having put into print, what doubtless has often been said behind my back; I do not thank him for the odious words which he has made the vehicle of it.
>
> I will not dirty my ink by repeating them; but the substance, mildly stated is this,—that I have all along considered the doctrine of the Pope's Infallibility to be contradicted by the facts of Church history, and that, though convinced of this, I have in consequence of the Vatican Council forced myself to do a thing that I never, never, fancied would befall me when I became a Catholic—viz., forced myself by some unintelligible quibbles to fancy myself believing what really after all in my heart I could not and did not believe. And that this operation and its result have given me a considerable amount of pain.
>
> I could say much and quote much from what I have written, in comment upon this nasty view of me. But, not to take up too much of your room, I will, in order to pluck it up "by the very roots" (to use his own expression), quote one out of various passages, in which long before the Vatican Council was dreamed of, at least by me, I enunciated absolutely the doctrine of the Pope's Infallibility. It is my Discourse on University Education, delivered in Dublin in 1852. It runs as follows:
>
> "Deeply do I feel, ever will I protest, *for I can appeal to the ample testimony of history to bear me out,* that, in questions of right and wrong, there is nothing really strong in the whole world, nothing decisive and operative, but the voice of him, to whom have been committed the keys of the kingdom and the oversight of Christ's flock. That voice is now, as ever it has been, a real authority, *infallible* when it teaches, prosperous when it commands, ever taking the lead wisely and distinctly in its own province, adding certainty to what is probable and persuasion to what is certain. Before he speaks, the most saintly may mistake; and after it has spoken, the most gifted must obey. . . . If ever there was a power on earth who had an eye for the times, who has confined himself to the practicable, and has been happy in his anticipations, whose words have been deeds, and whose commands prophecies, such is he in the history of ages who sits on from generation to generation in the Chair of the Apostles as the Vicar of Christ and Doctor of His Church. . . . Has he failed in his successes up to this hour? Did he, in our fathers' day, fail in his struggle with Joseph of Germany and his confederates; with Napoleon—a greater name—and his dependent kings; that, though in another kind of fight, he should fail in ours? What grey hairs are on the head of Judah, whose youth is renewed like the eagle's, whose feet are like the feet of harts, and underneath the everlasting arms?"— pp. 22–28.

This passage I suffered Father Cardella in 1867 or 1868 to reprint in a volume which he published at Rome. My reason for selecting it, as I told him, was this—because in an abridged reprint of the Discourses in 1859 I had omitted it, as well as other large portions of the volume, as of only temporary interest, and irrelevant to the subject of University education.

I could quote to the same purpose passages from my *Essay on Development,* 1845; *Loss and Gain,* 1847; *Discourses to Mixed Congregations,* 1849; *Position of Catholics,* 1851; *Church of the Fathers,* 1857.

Newman concluded:

I underwent then no change of mind as regards the truth of the doctrine of the Pope's Infallibility in consequence of the Council. It is true I was deeply, though not personally, pained both by the fact and by the circumstances of the definition; and, when it was in contemplation, I wrote a most confidential letter, which was surreptitiously gained and published, but of which I have not a word to retract. The feelings of surprise and concern expressed in that letter have nothing to do with a screwing one's conscience to profess what one does not believe, which is Mr. Capes's pleasant account of me. He ought to know better.[69]

There are some problems with the passage from the Dublin Lectures that Newman chose as the principal evidence for his long held conviction on papal infallibility. It is certainly in many ways the strongest passage of the several that he cites in the letter to the *Guardian.* Nonetheless, it is not meant to be a closely argued statement. It is highly rhetorical, the kind of thing that could be used in a talk or sermon but not in a carefully written exposition. Newman himself would surely have been the first to ask the meaning of the words "a real authority, infallible when it teaches, prosperous when it commands, ever taking the lead wisely and distinctly in its own province, adding certainty to what is probable and persuasion to what is certain." This is not the language of theology, and Newman would very likely have decried such language if it had appeared in some piece by Ward in the *Dublin Review* in the late 1860s as a defense of the pope's infallibility. And this passage is very unlike some of the sentiments he expressed about the exercise of papal authority in various letters from 1870 and afterwards. It is also to be noted that all of the passages that

69. Newman to the *Guardian,* 12 September 1872, *The Letters and Diaries,* 26:166–68. The acting Editor of the *Guardian* let it be known that he thought Newman would have done better to keep silence in the face of Capes's charge. "We can understand," the editor said, "his outburst of 1864, when Mr. Kingsley's remarks brought him once more into vivid contact with the *infandum dolorem* of past years, but now, we might have thought, he could have entered more calmly into personal controversy under the great shadow of the Infallibility in which he believes." See *The Letters and Diaries,* 26:212, quoting the *Guardian* (18 September 1872) 1165. (The passage from the Dublin Lectures *[Discourse on University Education]* was not reprinted in *The Idea of a University* [1873] [1902]).

Newman used in defense of his long held view on infallibility were written before 1860, even the passage used in Father Cardella's collection in
1867.

One other point in the letter is also curious. This is Newman's saying
that he was deeply, though not personally, pained by the definition and
the proceedings that led up to it. While it is certainly true that Newman
was strongly concerned about the pain that the definition caused in the
lives of the many people who sought his help, a fair reading of the record
would indicate that he experienced deep personal pain in addition.

Because the *Pall Mall Gazette* printed some extracts from Capes's letter to the *Guardian,* Newman wrote also to that publication. Newman's
letter of 13 September appeared the next day. In the main it is a summary
of his letter to the *Guardian,* but there are some variations which give
further insights into Newman's position:

> You have inserted in your columns of yesterday [12 September] some re-
> marks made on me by Mr. Capes, which, to use a studiously mild phrase,
> are not founded on fact. He assumes that I did not hold or profess the doc-
> trine of the Pope's Infallibility till the time of the Vatican Council, whereas
> I have committed myself to it in print again and again, from 1845 to 1867.
> And, on the other hand, as it so happens—though I hold it as I ever have
> done—I have had no occasion to profess it, whether in print or otherwise,
> since that date. Any one who knows my writings will recollect that in so
> saying I state the simple fact. The surprise and distress I felt at the defini-
> tion was no personal matter, but was founded on serious reasons of which
> I feel the force still.[70]

70. Newman to the *Pall Mall Gazette,* 13 September 1872, *The Letters and Diaries,*
26:169. Capes made a public reply to Newman's letter to the *Pall Mall Gazette.* He wrote:
"Dr. Newman says that I was in error when I implied that he did not personally hold the
doctrine of Papal Infallibility before it was decreed by the Vatican Council. I need hardly
say that I much regret the mistake. At the same time, Dr. Newman makes an admission
which confirms the force of my argument, drawn from his examples, as against Dr. Pusey.
He says that the definition caused him 'surprise and distress,' founded upon reasons of which
he still feels the force. What more than this can Dr. Pusey feel, in the present condition
of the English Church? But further Dr. Newman must pardon me if I add that his state
of mind is, to my understanding, perfectly incomprehensible. How can he, as a private Christian, venture to feel distress when the infallible authority chooses its own time for putting
forth its claims to the Church and the world? Surely, the belief which permits a man to
be thus distressed must be singularly unreal, and can have little hold upon the depths of
his spiritual nature. In fact, according to Dr. Newman's view, Infallibility has made a serious mistake in the time and means which it has chosen for proclaiming the message of God
to man. We are asked to believe that for 1800 years the infallible authority never informed
Christians where they were to go for teaching, and then at last chose the wrong season for
making the announcement. The mere statement of such a theory appears to me to carry
with it its own refutation." Quoted in the *Tablet,* n.s. 8 (21 September 1872) 40:374. Newman was not drawn out again.

In his letter to the *Pall Mall Gazette* of 13 September 1872, Newman wrote that with regard to his position on papal infallibility before the Vatican Council he had "committed" himself "to it in print again and again, from 1845 to 1867." He continued: "And, on the other hand, as it so happens—though I hold it as ever I have done—I have had no occasion to profess it, whether in print or otherwise, since that date."

The question of Newman's long held views on the definition that he publicly declared and then supported with his past writings requires some extended comment in light of the by no means uniform position that Newman took on papal infallibility in the years between 1865 and 1875, especially in the years just prior to the council. In the period before the council he said that he had never given great study to the question, that he had never been "consistent" in his study of it, that he had held the doctrine "vaguely." Yet in the late summer of 1872 he essayed to give a clear view on papal infallibility and to show that he had held it for a quarter century.

As has been shown, the passage that Newman chose to use from his Dublin Lectures in the letter of 12 September to the editor of the *Guardian* is highly rhetorical. At the end of the same letter he instances five other works as evidence of his longstanding views and his consistent approach to the topic. In the several drafts of his letter to the *Guardian* which he wrote before deciding on the final version that he did send, he gave full quotations from these other writings but in the end decided not to quote the passages but simply to list the works in which they appeared. Whether he thought the letter long enough and the passage from the Dublin Lectures a sufficient witness to his views or whether he sensed that the other passages were not as clear as he would like them to be cannot be determined. Several of the writings were, like the Dublin Lectures, first given as talks and most if not all of the writings he listed in the letter to the *Guardian,* had an immediate and largely apologetic purpose. They were not intended to be searching and rigorously theological expositions of the Church's teaching on papal infallibility. Rather, they were aimed more at serving as parts of a whole and much fuller exposition of the chief tenets of Catholic belief.

Newman in the letter to the *Guardian* listed the five works which he believed to be evidence of the profession of his belief in papal infallibility in chronological order, beginning with the *Essay on Development* in 1845 and concluding with the new preface to "The Church of the Fathers" (*Historical Sketches,* Volume II) in 1857.

From the *Essay on Development* Newman in his draft letter appealed first to the following passage: "Whatever objections may be made to this or that particular *fact, . . .* on the whole[,] I consider *that a cumulative argument* rises from them in favour of the active and the *doctrinal* authority of Rome, much stronger than any argument which can be drawn from the same era [pre-Nicene] for the doctrine of the Real Presence."[71] The next passage Newman cited was from the section of the Essay entitled "Papal Supremacy."[72] It reads: " . . . it is impossible, if we may so speak reverently, that an infinite Wisdom, which sees the end from the beginning, in decreeing the rise of an universal Empire, should not have decreed the development of a sovereign *ruler.*"[73] Newman in the drafts of his letter to the *Guardian* then went on to say "to this must be added the . . . probability in particular in favour of the existence, in *some* quarter, of an *infallible authority in matters of faith.*"[74] He then resumed his line of thought by again quoting directly from the *Essay on Development:* "And, on the other hand, as the counterpart of these anticipations, we are met by certain announcements in Scripture, more or less obscure, and needing a comment, and claimed by the Papal See as having their fulfillment in itself. Such are the words 'Thou art Peter' etc. 'Feed my lambs' etc. . . . 'Strengthen thy brethren.' "[75]

In the *Essay on Development* Newman speaks much more directly to the infallibility of the Church. The authority of the pope and the obedience due to him are certainly upheld, and his role in the Church is equated with the Apostles, particularly St. Peter, but the word "infallibility" with reference to the pope is generally avoided. What is more clearly described in the *Essay* is the primacy of the Roman See, its premier position, recognized certainly from the fourth century onwards in the Church. In Chapter II, Section 2 ("An infallible developing authority to be expected") of the *Essay,* Newman wrote: "Next, all Catholics agree in two other points, not, however, with heretics, but solely with each other: first, that the Pope with General Council cannot err, either in framing decrees of faith or general precepts of morality; secondly, that the Pope when determining anything in a doubtful matter, whether by himself or with his own particular Council, *whether it is possible for him to err or not, is to be obeyed by all the faithful.*"[76]

In 1877, when Newman prepared a new edition of the *Essay on Development* he carefully added the following footnote to this passage: "[Seven years ago, it is scarcely necessary to say, the Vatican Council determined that the Pope, *ex cathedrâ,* has the same infallibility as the Church. This does not affect the argument in the text.]"[77] Although not

---

71. *Essay on the Development of Christian Doctrine* (London, New York, and Bombay: Longmans, Green, and Co., 1906) 25–26. Newman supplied the emphases in his draft letter. They are not in the original.

72. Ibid., ch. IV, sect. 3.

73. Ibid., 155.

74. *The Letters and Diaries,* 26:167, n. 2.

75. *The Letters and Diaries,* 26:168, n. 2, quoting *Essay on Development,* 156.

76. Ibid., 87.

77. Ibid.

cited in his draft letter to the *Guardian,* the closest that Newman does come to an explicit statement about papal infallibility is also found in Chapter II, Section II of the *Essay on Development,* where Newman writes: "Thus, what conscience is in the system of nature, such is the voice of Scripture, or of the Church, or of the Holy See, as we may determine it, in the system of Revelation. It may be objected, indeed, that conscience is not infallible; it is true, but still it is ever to be obeyed. And this is just the prerogative which controversialists assign to the See of St. Peter; it is not in all cases infallible, it may err beyond its special province, but it has in all cases a claim on our obedience."[78]

Again, the principal point made is the *obedience* to the pope's decisions required of the faithful. It is also interesting to see Newman speaking here of controversialists assigning the prerogative. Newman was always so careful to distinguish between controversialists and theologians, especially in his own case.

Next in chronological sequence came Newman's novel *Loss and Gain,* a somewhat unlikely source from which to make a theological citation, no matter the apologetic and didactic purpose of the work overall. The strongest passage on the papal office and the one that Newman used in his draft letter to the *Guardian* avoids the assignment of infallibility to the pope. In this passage we find Charles Reding, in his discussion with Mr. Highfly, saying:

> The Popedom is the true Apostolate, the Pope is the successor of the Apostles, particularly of St. Peter. . . . And hence Catholics call him the Vicar of Christ, Bishop of Bishops, and the like; and, I believe, consider that he, in a pre-eminent sense, is the one pastor or ruler of the Church, the source of jurisdiction, the judge of controversies, and the centre of unity as having the power of the Apostles, and especially of St. Peter.[79]

Moving further along the line, Newman found evidence for his long held views on papal infallibility in one of his *Discourses to Mixed Congregations,* given in 1849. Referring to a Catholic believer, Newman asserts: "He knows whose vessel he has entered; it is the bark of Peter. . . . The greatest of the Romans . . . said . . . 'Caesarem vehis etc.' What he said in presumption, we can repeat in faith of that boat, in which Christ once sat and preached."[80]

Here too rhetoric rather than doctrinal enunciation is to the fore, and again papal primacy is chiefly underscored.

---

78. Ibid., 86.

79. *Loss and Gain: The Story of a Convert* (London, New York, and Bombay: Longmans, Green, and Co., 1906) 393-94.

80. *Discourses Addressed to Mixed Congregations* (London, New York, and Bombay: Longmans, Green, and Co., 1906) 245.

Newman's other fairly clear statements on papal infallibility in the years before the Vatican Council are found in *Lectures on the Present Position of Catholics in England* and in "The Church of the Fathers," found in *Historical Sketches,* Volume Two. In Lecture Eight of *The Present Position of Catholics,* Newman selected the following passage to use in his draft of the letter to the *Guardian* of 12 September: "Here, too, is vividly brought out before you what we mean by Papal infallibility, or rather what we do not mean by it: you see how the Pope was open to any mistake, as others may be, in his own person, true as it is, that whenever he spoke *ex cathedrâ* on subjects of revealed truth, he spoke as its divinely-ordained expounder."[81] Here the phrase "subjects of revealed truth" would be open to further analysis. Later in the same lecture Newman said: "Popes, then, though they are infallible in their office, as Prophets and Vicars of the Most High, and though they have generally been men of holy life, and many of them actually saints, have the trials, and incur the risks of other men. Our doctrine of infallibility means something very different from what Protestants think it means."[82]

While Newman does speak clearly here about the pope's infallibility, his chief purpose in this passage is to show that Catholics do not claim that the pope is impeccable. In the 1857 preface to "The Church of the Fathers," found in the second volume of *Historical Sketches,* Newman wrote:

> And in like manner, the dissatisfaction of Saints, of St. Basil, or again of our own St. Thomas, with the contemporary policy or conduct of the Holy See, while it cannot be taken to justify ordinary men, bishops, clergy, or laity, in feeling the same, is no reflection either on those Saints or on the Vicar of Christ. Nor is his infallibility in dogmatic decisions compromised by any personal and temporary error into which he may have fallen, in his estimate, whether of a heretic such as Pelagius, or of a Doctor of the Church such as Basil. Accidents of this nature are unavoidable in the state of being which we are allotted here below.[83]

Newman's reference to papal infallibility "in dogmatic decisions" is almost in the nature of an aside. It is certainly not a clear indication of his views on the matter. Again, he also stresses that the pope too is subject to human frailties.

One further passage that Newman culled from his earlier writings at this time is taken from Lecture Eleven of his *Difficulties of Anglicans.*

81. *Lectures on the Present Position of Catholics in England* (London, New York, and Bombay: Longmans, Green, and Co., 1908) 334–35.

82. Ibid., 338.

83. *Historical Sketches,* (London, New York, and Bombay: Longmans, Green, and Co., 1906) 2:xiii.

It reads: "The faultiness of this passive state of mind is detected, whenever a new definition is promulgated by the competent authority. Its immediate tendency as exhibited in a population, will be to resist it, simply because it is new, and they recognise nothing but what is familiar to them. . . ."[84] It can immediately be asked what Newman meant by the "competent authority." The authority, whether of an ecumenical council or of the pope alone, is not specified.

While Newman in 1872 seems to have made a careful search in his previous public writings for his treatment of papal infallibility, directly or indirectly, it is interesting that he appears not to have gone through a similar exercise in the notes he made in 1866 and 1867 for himself, as he considered a second reply to Pusey, and eventually for Ignatius Ryder. It is curious too that the latest of his public writings that Newman could appeal to for support of his position of consistency on papal infallibility came in 1857. What held him back from writing publicly on the subject from 1857 until the *Letter to the Duke of Norfolk* in 1875? Certainly it is fair to speculate that the rise and prominence of the Ultramontane party in England from the late 1850s played some part in his favoring caution on the topic of papal infallibility. Certainly too the very bruising encounters he had had with Church authority beginning in the late 1850s with his withdrawal from the Catholic University of Ireland and continuing in the 1860s with his delation to Rome over the *Rambler* article, *On Consulting the Faithful in Matters of Doctrine,* and with the sad and trying setbacks he experienced in his hopes for an Oratory to be established at Oxford must have played a part in his decision to keep silent on the great question of the pope's infallibility. Why was it only after the definition and its evident acceptance by the Church diffusive that he decided in the summer of 1872 that it was time to return to those earlier writings of fifteen and twenty years ago as a defense against those who charged him with hesitance or at best lukewarmness toward the definition promulgated at the council two years before?

Despite the letters to the *Guardian* of 12 September and to the *Pall Mall Gazette* the next day, Newman's involvement with the press was hardly over. The very day that he wrote to the *Pall Mall Gazette,* another newspaper, the *Echo,* made some comments on Newman's letter to *The Times* of 9 September, written in response to that paper's piece on the St. Bartholomew's Day Massacre and papal infallibility. The *Echo* said of Newman's position:

> In short, Dr. Newman's definition of Infallibility is just such and no more than would apply to our Statute Book of English Law. The "Infallible"

84. *Certain Difficulties Felt by Anglicans in Catholic Teaching* (London, New York, and Bombay: Longmans, Green, and Co., 1908) 1:351.

Pope makes the law of the Roman Church just as do the three Estates of our realm, just as does the Czar by a Ukase, or the Sultan by a Hatt. Dr. Newman does not claim for the Bulls of the Supreme Pontiff any absolute Truth, or Right, or Freedom from Error, which he would deny to English, Russian, Turkish, or any other law. We expected no less from a mind so clear as his.[85]

It would appear that when Newman did not respond to the *Echo,* its editor, Arthur Arnold, wrote to Newman in the hope of eliciting a letter for publication. In this instance Newman decided not to make a public response, though he did write to Arnold to express his strong disagreement with the *Echo's* interpretation of his letter to *The Times.* Newman wrote to Arnold on 20 September:

> The *Echo* has on various occasions treated me and my writings with great kindness, and I am glad to have an opportunity, such as this, of acknowledging my sense of it to the Editor.
>
> As to the questions which you ask me in your letter of yesterday, I am obliged to say that I cannot follow you in your interpretation of what I lately wrote to the Times. And again I hope you will excuse me, if I do not write a letter for publication, stating my dissent from it. The Duke of Wellington said that a great country could not have a little war; nor can a great theological question have a short answer. If I began, I should get into a controversy, and should almost be committing myself to a treatise. You can easily fancy that, at my age, and after so many things to weary my mind, I shrink from writing on any serious subject.
>
> I certainly do hold that the Supreme Pontiff has a gift which no Czar or Sultan has—and to which, as far as I know, Czar and Sultan never made claim. A Ukase or a Hatt is a command or an ordinance, I suppose—but the subject matter of the Pope's infallibility is a truth, and truth in the province of religion and morals. The Pope is not infallible in his acts or his commands. Pope Honorius made a great mistake, when he advised a certain course of policy as regards a certain heterodox opinion. But, we should contend, he did *not* enunciate, and *could not formally* enunciate, a doctrine which was heterodox—not because he had a sort of inspiration by being Pope, but that a Providence is over the Church which would hinder a Pope (at the last moment) from teaching, propounding to be believed, an error. Revelation, in its very idea, is a revelation of truth—and it is a revelation not for the first century alone, but for all times. Who is its keeper and interpreter, or oracle, in centuries 2, 3, 4 as the Apostles were in the first? We do not want, nor do we recognise in St. Peter, an impeccable man, but a sure teacher of the truth. The Popes take his place. St. Peter erred in deed, and was reproved by St. Paul at Antioch—but when he spoke as the minister of heaven, he, as well as St. Paul (as in their Epistles) spoke truth and nothing but truth. We do not want more than this, viz. truth—but we do

85. *The Letters and Diaries,* The *Echo,* 13 September 1872, 26:172, n. 3.

want as much. We can blame a Pope's actions, while we believe in his formal enunciations of Christian doctrine.[86]

As if to prove his point "nor can a great theological question have a short answer," Newman wrote again to Arnold two days later. He was concerned that his first letter had not adequately explained his position. He said in the second letter:

> I have no confidence I brought out my meaning adequately in my letter to you. I recollect, on reading it over, I noticed clauses which might have been expressed better—for instance, in the last two lines, written along the page, I recollect I seemed to confuse inspiration with "adsistentia"—the Apostles were inspired—the Pope is not. What he "defines" or explains in Catholic doctrine is gained by him by human means such as the advice of theologians etc.,—but in the last step, a Divine Hand is over him, keeping him *in tether*, so that he cannot go beyond the truth of revelation. He has no habit on [or] what is called "donum infusum" of infallibility, but when he speaks *ex cathedra* he is restrained *pro re nata, pro hac vice.*
>
> I am told those [there] are highfliers who say much more than this, and there are those, learned men, who wish to bring in a higher doctrine—but Perrone, whose book is the theological hand book for students in this day, says "Nec enim sive Romani Pontificis, sive concilii oecumenici infallibilitas media excludit ad veritatem de qua agitur assequendam, quippe, non per modum infusi doni, sed per modum praesidii, sive ut ajunt adsistentiae, Deus illam promisit" t. 2, p. 451, Ed. 1841.
>
> Again, "*Nunquam* Catholici docuerunt donum infallibilitatis a Deo ecclesiae tribui per modum inspirationis" ibid. p. 253.
>
> Again, the recent definition says that the Pope has *that* infallibility which the Church has—but as Perrone says above "*Never* have Catholics taught that the gift is an inspiration."
>
> I think I have unintentionally shown you in these last sentences, to which I have been led on, how difficult it is to do justice to the subject in a few words.[87]

Again Newman had begged off giving a full exposition of his views, relying instead on disjointed fragments and scattered quotations from his earlier writings. And yet he seems to be arguing against himself and his use of discrete statements from the past when he says to Arthur Arnold, "how difficult it is to do justice to the subject in a few words." In the mid-September 1872 correspondence occasioned by the several newspaper items he took a long step toward the *Letter to the Duke of Norfolk,* a work of 120 pages.

---

86. Newman to Arthur Arnold, 20 September 1872, *The Letters and Diaries,* 26:172–73.
87. Newman to Arthur Arnold, 22 September 1872, *The Letters and Diaries,* 26:173–74.

New questions on the definition continue to be put to Newman by friends and strangers

Newman continued in this period to devote a great deal of time to giving advice and encouragement to people who found the doctrine of infallibility hard, if not impossible, to accept. In June 1872, he began a correspondence with a young Anglican clergyman, J. H. Willis Nevins. Nevins had for a time been a Catholic but left the Church over the definition. In a letter of 3 June to Newman, he stated: "I see nothing *unreasonable* in the Infallibility of the Pope—but it seems opposed to History." He was particularly disturbed by the case of Pope Honorius. In the same letter Nevins said: "I am now an Anglican Clergyman. I never renounced Rome when I came back and I hold all Catholic doctrine save the Vatican Decree, where then am I?"[88] Newman treated him with great kindness. In his reply of 4 June, Newman, speaking of Nevins's difficulties over the definition, wrote: "I grieve to hear of your mental suffering. Do you really mean to say that you know what happened a thousand or fifteen hundred years ago so intimately and accurately, that on the ground of your knowledge you can separate from the Church?"[89] Nevins replied a few days later that he did not understand what Newman meant. Newman began his second letter to Nevins by saying: "I wish you would tell me where you learn your *fact* that 'Honorius taught heresy ex cathedrâ.' It is your *inference* from certain historical facts—not a fact—and *my* inference is the other way. *I* say, from the facts of history, that he did *not* teach heresy ex cathedrâ." Newman went on to say:

> For myself, I never would believe, I *said* "I never would believe—that the Church would pass the Pope's infallibility, *till* I actually found that it had passed it." But I said this, not as not holding the doctrine, for I have long held it, but as thinking the historical evidence in its favour not so strong that the Church would think it safe to pass it. Consequently I can quite understand a man saying "there is not evidence strong enough for my believing it (*on* evidence)" but I cannot understand a man logically saying "there is evidence sufficient for my rejecting it (when the Church has affirmed it)."[90]

There was a new letter from Nevins on 14 June and a further reply from Newman two days later. In this letter Newman devoted considerable time to the question of Honorius.[91] Nevins found Newman's position, that Honorius was not "in his own person" heretical but rather "that he originated or promoted heresy," so acceptable that he asked Newman

88. J. H. Willis Nevins to Newman, 3 June 1872, *The Letters and Diaries,* 26:105, n. 1.
89. Newman to J. H. Willis Nevins, 4 June 1872, *The Letters and Diaries,* 26:105.
90. Newman to J. H. Willis Nevins, 12 June 1872, *The Letters and Diaries,* 26:111–12.
91. See Newman to J. H. Willis Nevins, 16 June 1872, *The Letters and Diaries,* 26:117–18.

if he could publish the letter of 16 June. Newman, as he had in similar instances since July 1870, refused. He told Nevins:

> I am glad you are pleased by my remarks—and you are quite at liberty to test the correctness of them, as you have the opportunity. I believe them substantially sound.
>
> But by no means can I let you print them—The Duke of Wellington used to say "England could not have a *little* war"—nor can so great a subject as the Pope's infallibility. Every link in the argument must be drawn out with authorities.
>
> Moreover, I could not write on the subject, without speaking of what others have said on it—of the Vatican Council—and of certain of its chief actors. I feel very deeply the cruelty and the unscrupulousness of certain men—I could not get myself to do the thing by halves.
>
> I agree with you, that, since you have taken so grave a step, as to separate yourself from the Church, it will not mend matters to return on an impulse. You must take your time about it.[92]

Newman now nearly two years after the definition gives two reasons why he cannot write: the subject is too large, too intricate; and he cannot write without strong words against some of the leaders of the movement for the definition. He fears that he will stir up new trouble for himself on either or both accounts. Nonetheless, the letter of 16 June to Nevins is a model of pastoral sensitivity. Newman has put himself in Nevins's place. He has full sympathy for his difficulties. He so characteristically takes the view with respect to Nevins's situation that no one can be rushed or bullied into believing. Time is everything.

Newman wrote again to Nevins toward the end of 1872 in a new effort to help him with his religious difficulties:

> "If there is a Church, the Oracle of God and Ark of Refuge, it is that Church called Catholic and in communion with Rome." "But there *is* such a Church." I think, if a man believes firmly both the conditional proposition, and the minor, "there *is* such a Church"—this involves a conviction as regards the Catholic Roman Church, which is sufficient for assent, or rather, which makes assent a duty. This I rejoice to think is your case.
>
> But I would add, Has not some principle of rashness or hastiness, or some argumentative imagination, led to your leaving the Catholic Church. If so, it seems to me your duty to try your assent to yourself thus—I assent, *though* it involves the belief of the Pope's Infallibility, of the eternal separation of the impenitent from God, of the Church's gift of miracles, of the inspiration of all Scripture etc. etc.[93] Do not let any of these doctrines re-

---

92. Newman to J. H. Willis Nevins, 20 June 1872, *The Letters and Diaries,* 26:121-22.

93. Nevins had told Newman of other doubts about Catholic teaching beyond the teaching on papal infallibility.

main as (in some sense) temptations to you to plague you afterwards—of course God alone can give us perseverance—and no one can prophesy of himself that he will persevere to the end—but bring the matter before God and beg Him to perfect your resolutions.[94]

Nevins returned to the Catholic Church in 1873, only to become an Anglican again in 1886. He died an Anglican ten years later.

In addition to Nevins, Newman dealt in 1872 with others who approached him for the first time with questions on the doctrine of papal infallibility. Richard Francis Littledale, an Anglo-Catholic clergyman, first wrote to Newman in 1864, sending him a copy of his pamphlet, *Unity and Rescript. A Reply to Bishop Ullathorne's Pastoral against the A.P.U.S.*[95] In mid-September 1872, Littledale wrote to Newman consequent upon Newman's letter to *The Times* on the St. Bartholomew's Day Massacre. He evidently took issue with Newman's view of Gregory XIII's attitude toward the Massacre and went on to press Newman on the question of papal infallibility. Newman replied on 15 September:

> I will but say one thing—viz that to consider Gregory's act or acts of which you speak as a dogmatic *statement* on morals, such as constitute a definition ex cathedrâ, appears to me one of the least logical ideas, to use your words, that ever entered into the mind of a learned and able man. It shocks my common sense—and, speaking under correction, I think it would shock the common sense of most men, certainly of Catholic theologians.
>
> Allow me to say you really have not got hold of what we mean by the Pope's Infallibility, and what *we* hold by the idea, not what you hold by it, must be the starting point of any fruitful controversy.[96]

And Newman told Littledale two days later:

> Without implying that I am necessarily opposing your view of our doctrine, I will say this:—
>
> Infallibility is not a *habit* in the Pope, or a state of mind—but, as the decree says, that infallibility which the Church has. The Church when in Council and proceeding by the strictest forms enunciates a definition in faith and morals, which is certainly true. The Church is infallible *then, when* she speaks ex cathedrâ—but the Bishops out of Council are fallible men. So the Pope is infallible *then, when* he speaks ex cathedrâ—but he has no habit

94. Newman to J. H. Willis Nevins, 26 November 1872, *The Letters and Diaries,* 26:208–09.

95. Association for the Promotion of the Unity of Christendom. In 1880 Littledale wrote *Plain Reasons against joining the Church of Rome,* which brought a response from Ignatius Ryder.

96. Newman to Richard Francis Littledale, 15 September 1872, *The Letters and Diaries,* 26:169–70.

of infallibility in his intellect, such that his *acts cannot but* proceed from it, *must* be infallible *because* he in [is] infallible, *imply, involve,* an infallible judgment. He in [is] infallible *pro re natâ, when* he speaks ex cathedrâ— not except at particular times and on grave occasions.

Nay further than this, even on those grave questions the gift is negative. It is not that he has an inspiration of truth, but he is simply guarded from error, circumscribed by a divine superintendence from transgressing, extravagating beyond, the line of truth. And his definitions do not come of a positive divine guidance, but of human means, research, consulting theologians, etc etc It is an "adsistentia" not an "inspiratio—"an aid *eventual,* in the event, and does not act till the event, not in the *process*—and an adsistentia, as I have said, *pro re natâ.* His words would be infallible one moment, not the next.

Newman then quoted the same sentences from Perrone's *Praelectiones Theologicae* that he would use in his reply to Arthur Arnold, the editor of the *Echo,* five days later. He ended the letter to Littledale with the following explanation of papal infallibility: "It is an external not an internal aid."[97] Much of what Newman said about the actual exercise of papal infallibility in the 17 September letter to Littledale, he would say with more precision and expansion in the *Letter to the Duke of Norfolk.*

It was also around this time that Newman answered a letter from W. E. Gladstone's sister, Helen, on papal infallibility. Helen Gladstone had become a Catholic in 1842. For many years she lived in Germany where she devoted her life to various charitable activities. She wrote to Newman on 20 September 1872 from Cologne. She said in part: " . . . it is under the pressure of great anxiety that I venture to ask counsel of the one upon whose judgement and upon whose undeviating truth I have learnt to place thorough confidence, such as I know not how to place elsewhere."[98] Newman answered two days later. Though his letter is not extant, he left the following note:

> answered Sept. 22 that she need not believe in the Temporal Power or aid its restoration; that the Syllabus is not de fide that, if she said to herself "I distinctly and positively believe the Pope is fallible in definition of doctrine," she could not properly omit such a state of mind in confession— But, if she said, "I believe in the Church's infallibility, I wish to believe the Vatican Council to be a true Council, I am not *sure* that the Pope's infallibility is not contained in the Scripture promises to St. Peter" she need not mention it in confession.

97. Newman to Richard Francis Littledale, 17 September 1872, *The Letters and Diaries,* 26:171. The editor of *The Letters and Diaries* indicates some doubt as to whether this letter was written to Littledale.

98. Helen Gladstone to Newman, 20 September 1872, *The Letters and Diaries,* 26:175, n. 1.

She ought not to set herself against the definition. Of course the *fact* of the definition increases the pope's power, but *the thing defined* is very moderate.[99]

By late 1872, the stories and rumors about Newman's opposition to the definition and his consequent disaffection with the Catholic Church had also found their way to North America. In November 1872, Thompson Cooper, an English journalist and a convert, sent Newman clippings from a long letter that had appeared in the *Cincinnati Commercial* and in other newspapers in the United States. The letter had in fact been written from London by a Unitarian lecturer, Moncure D. Conway. Cooper was anxious to have from Newman a denial of Conway's assertions. Newman drafted a response on 23 November:

I thank you for sending me the article in an American Paper, entitled "Father Newman under a cloud." It is easier to set down what statements in it are false, than to discover which are simply true. I will note some of the more prominent falsehoods relating to myself, as my eye runs down the column.

1. It is false that there was any "correspondence between Dr. Dollinger and Father Newman with regard to the ultimate authority in the Church," or on any subject, "the year preceding the promulgation of the dogma," or in any year.

2. It is false that "Father Newman," then or at any time "expressed the opinion that infallibility could only be said to reside in the voice of the entire clergy assembled in a Council," or that it did not reside in the voice of the Pope.

3. It is false both that "this correspondence was never published," and that it was published, because there never was any correspondence to publish.

4. It is false (to the best of my knowledge or belief) that "at the same time," or that any time "Father Newman preached a very singular discourse" or any discourse, which was "submitted to the Pope," or that any discourse of his was the "cause" of any cloud "which has come over him."

5. It is false that, in any sermon, written or preached, he spoke of "the Massacre of St. Bartholomew," or of "Galileo's demonstration of the motion of the earth"; or "dealt with" such charges against the Church, or spoke of "its Popes and Cardinals having been guilty of many personal sins."

6. It is false that any "Archbishop" or any "Editor" of any periodical was led by any such sermon "to represent to the Pope the necessity" of "the new dogma", because there was no Sermon at all and no correspondence at all.

7. It is false, that "when the new dogma was promulgated, Fr. Newman hesitated a long time, but finally resolved to give a reluctant adhesion";

---

99. Newman "Note," 22 September 1872, *The Letters and Diaries,* 26:175.

for his published works show, that he has held its truth for the last twenty
years.[100]

Over the next several days Newman thought better of what he had put
down in this draft and on 26 November he sent Cooper a far briefer reply. Only points 6 and 7 of the draft were in part kept. It appears that
Newman decided, as he had in previous instances since the definition, that
to respond carefully to Conway's assertions was to give to them a seriousness they did not merit. Phrases in the reply are, nonetheless, obscure
as though Newman saw the difficulty of dealing with partial truths and
with possibilities which he had no certain knowledge of but also had no
reason to think unlikely. It was not, however, his duty to attempt to speak
for others, including "Catholic Archbishops," who might well have dealt
inimically with his past writings or sermons. But he appreciated Thompson Cooper's positive purpose in writing and was kind, though matter
of fact, in his reply:

> I thank you for your friendly letter. After carefully considering both it and
> its inclosure, which is a tissue of untruths, I have decided to take no notice
> of it, on the ground that any one else is able to answer it as I am.
>   In such a case there is no call upon me to undertake my own defence.
>   If the question were one of matter which I knew and others did not know,
> then there might be the duty incumbent on me of answering it in detail;
> but on the contrary it relates to the private thoughts and doings of persons
> at a distance from me which have never been brought to light on the one
> hand, and on the other to writings of my own, which have long passed out
> of my own keeping.
>   Other men, not less than I, have the means of determining whether, in
> my publications of the last 20 years, I have affirmed or denied the Pope's
> Infallibility; I not more than other men, have the means of determining
> whether Catholic Archbishops or Editors have been troubled in their secret
> hearts, or impelled to confidential correspondence, by aught contained in
> those publications.[101]

In many ways Newman appears in this carefully considered letter to be
backing away from the strong assertions about the history of his belief
in papal infallibility that he had taken in public and private letters two
months previously.

Continuing controversy over the definition as well as rumors of Newman's disagreement with it had kept alive the hope among Newman's
friends that he would write publicly on the subject. Some time in late Oc-

100. Newman to Thompson Cooper, 23 November 1872, *The Letters and Diaries,* 26:204.
Draft letter not sent. The discourse mentioned under no. 4 was very likely Newman's sermon, "The Pope and the Revolution," given on 7 October 1866.
    101. Newman to Thompson Cooper, 26 November 1872, *The Letters and Diaries,* 26:208.

tober or early November 1872 there was a new plea from Bishop Moriarty and Aubrey de Vere. Perhaps they had been encouraged to think that Newman would write a full exposition of his views after the three public letters in September. Newman responded to Bishop Moriarty on 5 November:

> You and Aubrey de Vere pay me a great compliment in wishing me to undertake so difficult a subject—but I don't expect to write any thing again—if I do, it will be something I can do, not what I can't.
> The Pope's Infallibility is a question of *fact,* and a thesis for *historians*—not a pure revealed doctrine—and to prove it within compass of a pamphlet or a Letter such as that which I wrote on the Immaculate Conception is, I hold, an impossibility. The utmost that could be said against the Immaculate Conception was that great authorities in past times had opposed it—but this is only the least that can be urged against the Pope's Infallibility. There is no historical question about the Blessed Virgin. No act of hers can be brought forward in the last 1800 years of a sinful character—but half a hundred can be brought forward by an adversary in behalf of the fallibility of Popes, and have to be answered. How can this be done popularly?

Newman saved his strongest words for the concluding paragraph:

> I doubt not that both De Vere and your Lordship have been led, from your kindness towards me, to hope that I could do something against that dreadful growth of Indifferentism among Catholics which will be, and is already, the fruit of the transactions at Rome in 1870. But it is impossible. I am not saying a word against the dogmatic authority of the doctrine of Papal Infallibility—but, if Popes cannot teach falsehood ex cathedrâ, they can extra cathedram do great evil, and have so done before now. I suppose Liberius and Honorius are instances in point. If they, why not Pius?[102]

Toward the close of 1872, Newman prepared a memorandum about what form written remembrances after his death should take. He began the document by saying, "I don't wish my life written—because there is so little to say. This is the case with most Lives—and in consequence the writers are forced to pad. . . . Moreover, in the Apologia I have virtually written my life up to 1845—and there is little or nothing to say since. Little or nothing—for if anything is attempted other men's toes will be trod upon, and the Life will be answered and a controversy ensue. . . ." Newman then went on to show how collections of letters from various periods or events in his life might be published. One category that he excepted from publication were the letters "which cannot be touched upon without getting into controversy." He included in these the difficulties

102. Newman to Bishop David Moriarty, 5 November 1872, *The Letters and Diaries,* 26:198.

with the London Oratory, the troubles in founding the Catholic University in Ireland, the *Rambler* affair, and the translation of the Scriptures.[103] Newman did not include the controversy over the definition of papal infallibility, though the last category on the list of five controversial topics was "etc etc." "These collections [the five cases listed], Newman said, "I make with the view of their being used, and only used, *in defence*—i.e. if enemies make misstatements or impute motives, these collections are authorities to refer to."[104] Over the next several years Newman spent a considerable amount of time arranging his letters, including copies of his letters that he asked friends to return to him.

The position of the Irish bishops against Gladstone on Catholic higher education is seen as a consequence of the Vatican Council

By 1873 controversy over the definition was beginning to abate, at least if Newman's correspondence can be taken as a gauge. In early 1873 there was a lively dispute in Ireland and England over Gladstone's proposed Irish University Bill.[105] The bishops of Ireland, led by Cardinal Cullen, were adamantly against its passage since they believed it forfeited the rights of Catholics to their own educational institutions altogether separate from colleges under government or nonsectarian sponsorship. Gladstone had painstakingly worked out a compromise plan that gave the Church a large say in higher education in Ireland but as part of a state system. Archbishop Manning made efforts to get Cardinal Cullen to see the wisdom of Gladstone's bill. Inevitably, Newman was drawn into the debate because of his past experience with the Catholic University of Ireland, but he refused to make public his views on the question, saying that he was too removed from the situation. Or as he told a group of students of the Catholic University who wrote asking him to speak out against the Bill,

103. In 1857, Cardinal Wiseman asked Newman to undertake a translation of the Bible, but when Newman had agreed, nothing more was heard from Wiseman on the subject. See Richard J. Schiefen, *Nicholas Wiseman and The Transformation of English Catholicism* (Shepherdstown. W.Va.: The Patmos Press, 1984) 242.

104. Newman "Memorandum on Future Biography," 15 November 1872, *The Letters and Diaries,* 26:200–01.

105. The Irish episcopate, led by Cardinal Cullen, thought that Gladstone's bill on university education continued the discriminatory pattern that they had opposed since the mid-1840s. They were against a "mixed system" of education in which Catholics and Protestants were educated at state-sponsored institutions and they looked instead for government funding for the Catholic University of Ireland. See E. R. Norman, *Anti-Catholicism in Victorian England,* vol. 1 of *Historical Problems: Studies and Documents,* ed. G. R. Elton (New York: Barnes & Noble, Inc., 1968) 1:86; see also John Morley, *The Life of William Ewart Gladstone* (London: Macmillan and Co., Ltd., 1903) 2:436–45; and Emmet Larkin, *The Roman Catholic Church and the Home Rule Movement, 1870–1874* (Chapel Hill and London: The University of North Carolina Press, 1990) 157–78.

"it is fourteen years since I was across St. George's Channel, and any words of mine would not be worth much more, as regards an Irish question of 1873, than would have been a political Tract of one of the seven Sleepers on his waking from his long slumber at Ephesus."[106] Quite apart from the complex arguments over the merits or flaws of Gladstone's scheme, there was a prevalent feeling that the definition of papal infallibility was a factor in the controversy, all the more so after the Irish Bishops condemned Gladstone's bill on 28 February 1873. This was the first political dispute involving the Catholic Church in England and Ireland since the definition, and many saw the Irish bishops' position as evidence that the Church would accept no compromises but would insist on its absolute independence in matters related to the State. However inexact, there was a feeling in England that the Irish bishops were simply carrying out the policies of the pope. In the latter part of 1872, the Anglican Bishop of St. David's in Wales, Connop Thirlwall, published a "Charge," in which he alleged that the definition of papal infallibility had meant a sea change "in the position of every Roman Catholic throughout the world, and in the relation of every political society to the Church of Rome. As there can be no political question of the slightest moment that does not bear upon faith and morals, or both, the Papal infallibility implies a claim of absolute sovereignty over the whole range of thought and action."[107]

This was precisely the kind of misunderstanding that Newman had feared, but in a letter to Alfred Plummer he acknowledged what appeared to him some relationship between the Irish bishops' position and the definition of 1870. On 21 February 1873 he wrote: "I am always glad to hear about Dollinger, much as I grieve at what he has felt it a duty to do. He knows more of the Bishop of St. D's charge than I do—but I think it plain the Irish University Bill has been affected by the Vatican decrees. As it stands, I don't see how Cardinal Cullen can accept it without great inconsistency. . . ."[108] The eventual failure of Gladstone's bill in the House of Commons led to the downfall of his government, and many would say this defeat led him to write his famous *Expostulation* in the following year.

But for the present there was still the occasional stranger seeking Newman's guidance in the face of doubts over the definition. In the first months of 1873, Newman wrote twice to Henry Tenlon of Montreal. In his second letter, written on 23 March, Newman, though replying at some length,

106. Newman to George Fottrell, 24 February 1873, *The Letters and Diaries,* 26:261.
107. J. J. Stewart Perowne, ed. *Remains Literary and Theological of Connop Thirlwall, Bishop of St. David's* (London, 1877) 2:300. See *The Letters and Diaries,* 26:259, n. 1. Gladstone in his *The Vatican Decrees In Their Bearing on Civil Allegiance: A Political Expostulation* (London, 1874) would take a similar position on the broad claims over the State that the definition gave to the Roman Catholic Church.
108. Newman to Alfred Plummer, 21 February 1873, *The Letters and Diaries,* 26:258–59.

evidenced a certain impatience. He wondered if Tenlon was more interested in engaging him in controversy than in having Newman help him in his doubts:

> My belief is that you have not got hold of Catholic principles, and that the views you take of theological truth would have led you in the fifth century to take the part of Eutyches and the Monophysites against Pope St. Leo and the main body of Catholics.
>
> It is simply impossible I can to any good purpose answer your difficulties, unless we agree in principles, and it is to principles that I directed your attention in my letter. I could do nothing else.
>
> You refer to Drs. Milner and Trevern.[109] They were holy men and able writers, but neither of them converted me, nor am I bound by their unguarded language. They wrote as they did from their ignorance of ecclesiastical history.
>
> It is evident you mistook my position when you first wrote. I am as grieved as any man can be at the scandals which have accompanied the act of 1870—and in my letter to my Bishop which was stolen from his custody and published, I expressed, what I still feel. But I have distinctly insisted on the Pope's Infallibility in most of my books for the last 28 years, and, if you knew them better, you would have from the first seen that I could only reply to you on the definite principles which I laid down in my letter.
>
> To recur to your illustration,[110] a case like yours must be treated with alternatives. There is no way of getting right soon. I may feel very angry with those who have inflicted such a wound on you, but we must take things as they are. Almighty Wisdom directs the passions or the craft of men, even Bishops, to Its own purposes. If you look at the history of the Councils, you will find they have generally two characteristics—a great deal of violence and intrigue on the part of the actors in them, and a great resistance to their definitions on the part of portions of Christendom.
>
> I am quite perplexed why you have written to me your second letter. It looks as if you liked to exercise me in controversy. If so, I must refer you to my published works. You speak of your opinions being 22 years old— my own principles have been the growth of a continuous 40 years—and to meet you in the way you seem to wish, I should have to turn into the shape of letters to you some volumes I have written. If you ask for one particular volume in which the principles are stated on which alone I can teach or controvert, I refer you to my Essay on Development of doctrine [sic], published in 1845.[111]

109. John Milner, *The End of religious controversy in a friendly correspondence between a religious society of Protestants and a Catholic divine* (Philadelphia, 1823); and Jean François Marie Le Pappe de Trevern, *Discussion amicale sur l'Eglise anglicane et en général sur la réformation, redigée, en forme de lettres, écrites en 1812 et 1813; Par un licencié de la Maison et Société de Sorbonnes* (Londres: R. Juligné, 1813).

110. Tenlon had used the analogy that he was approaching Newman as one would approach a medical doctor.

111. Newman to Henry Tenlon, 23 March 1873, *The Letters and Diaries*, 26:280-81.

It is interesting to note that Newman in his reply to Tenlon said that he had "distinctly insisted on the Pope's Infallibility in most of my books for the last 28 years. . . ." On the evidence this appears to be an exaggeration, however uncharacteristic.

Newman shows his unhappiness with the course of the Church's life in England under Manning

When in the late spring of 1873 Newman was invited by the bishops of England and Wales to participate in the fourth Provincial Synod, he begged off in a brief letter of 13 June to Manning: "I feel the honour done me by the Episcopal meeting of Low week [sic] in asking me to be present at the Provincial Synod of next month.

I trust, however, that Your Grace and the other Bishops will be so kind as to allow me to decline it, as they did in 1856 and 1859. I wish to plead my age, and my total ignorance of Synodal matters."[112] It is fair to speculate that an unstated reason for Newman's declining this invitation was his continuing lack of trust in Manning.

In the summer of 1873, Newman had a chance to express his feelings on both the definition and the course of Catholicism in England over the past fifteen years. Again, mistrust of Manning, though indirectly stated, had a part in his remarks. The occasion was a letter from the secretary of the Catholic Union, inviting him to membership of that association. Newman replied to John Wallis on 24 August in a letter marked "private":

> I feel the great kindness of your letter—also, the self-denial on your part which has led you to accept such irksome and thankless duties as your secretariship to the Catholic Union involves, also the seeming ungraciousness on my own in not yielding to the reasons which you put before me in behalf of my becoming a member of it. However my reasons against now yielding are such as these.
>
> It is now some years since I came to the conclusion that I should never find myself taking part in any large religious association of any kind. Westminster must be its head quarters in England and I have an utter distrust of Westminster. Many years ago I was asked to join the Academia.[113] I said

---

112. Newman to Archbishop Henry Edward Manning, 13 June 1873, *The Letters and Diaries,* 26:326.

113. The Academia, founded by Cardinal Wiseman in 1861, was meant to bring together leading Catholics in England to discuss theological, philosophical, and historical topics. Manning was its chief organizer. When it became apparent that a primary aim of the Academia would be support for the pope's temporal power, Newman, who had at first agreed to join, told Manning in a letter of 21 June 1861: "I find the Cardinal Archbishop (for Cardinal Antonelli is out of my sight) is taking strong measures on the question of the Temporal Power. . . . Should his Eminence put out any matter, bearing on the same question in the same way, in *his Inaugural Address on the 29th,* I certainly will not remain a member of

I would wait till I was sure that the Pope's Temporal Power and similar objects were not the real aim of a Society which professed to be of a general literary and theological character—and I think the event has proved I had reason for waiting. Six years ago there was a lay address to the Pope. A prominent layman, now dead, would not give his name to it, because he thought it covertly advocated the Pope's infallibility—and the event proved he was not very far from the mark.[114] At the same time a Jesuit Father got up a volume of testimonies from living writers to the Pope's Infallibility. I like a fool, gave him a passage of my own, since I had ever held the doctrine—but I saw afterwards the meaning of the project when the question of the Definition was suddenly mooted in the Council, a measure which I had never wished.[115] Seeing is believing—this Union must be tested by its fruits, and that takes time. . . . I do recollect the caution given by the old head of Lincoln to his bursar, when our own Head in a frank and liberal spirit proposed to him some arrangement between the two colleges, "Take care, Mr. Radford, be on your guard, Mr. Radford, Copleston is a deep man, a long headed man, Mr. Radford, he will take you in Mr. Radford."[116]

In September, Newman was approached by a recent convert to Catholicism whose problem he told her was impossible for him to solve. Miss Rowe[117] evidently felt that there were reasons which compelled her to take communion in the Anglican Church. Newman told her that even the pope could not give such a permission, though rare permissions had been given for Catholics to join in "praying" with Anglicans. Newman's reply to Miss Rowe on 16 September gives some insight into the diffidence with which he approached the frequent calls he received from people in religious difficulties. It was a true apostolic work for him, but he did it with hesitation: "I have always a great anxiety in writing on religious subjects to persons I do not really know—for written words are but an imperfect vehicle of thoughts—they may lead to misconceptions on both sides of the correspondence, and this is a serious risk when the subject is religion." After telling Miss Rowe that she still had "a great deal to learn about the Catholic Faith," Newman closed this long letter by touching upon

---

the Academia." Newman to Henry Edward Manning, 21 June 1861, *The Letters and Diaries,* ed. Charles Stephen Dessain (London: Thomas Nelson and Son, Ltd., 1969) 19:519.

114. See Newman to Sir John Simeon, 2 June 1867, *The Letters and Diaries,* ed. Charles Stephen Dessain and Thomas Gornall, S.J. (Oxford: The Clarendon Press, 1973) 23:245. Newman wrote: "I don't see what you could have done but decline to sign the Address. . . . A lay Address should be written by laymen—else, it loses all its meaning and force. This on the contrary was not an Address to the Pope from the laity, but a formula presented for lay signature by the Archbishop."

115. This was the passage from the Dublin Lectures that Newman sent to Father Valerian Cardella, S.J., in 1867.

116. Newman to John Wallis, 24 August 1873, *The Letters and Diaries,* 26:355–56.

117. Newman to Miss Rowe, 16 September 1873, *The Letters and Diaries,* 26:364. No first name for Miss Rowe is given in *The Letters and Diaries.*

the definition: "Mr. Huntingford[118] says 'Almost all the ablest Bishops protested against' (the Infallibility of the Pope) *as untrue; all* have accepted it *as true.*' I *simply and utterly deny this.* I believe there were very few who did not hold the Infallibility—but they thought the proclamation of the doctrine highly inexpedient at that time. Has not what has taken place in Germany since [the Kulturkampf], been a proof that they had good reason for so thinking? And now, be of good heart—be brave—call upon God—and fear nothing."[119] In a letter some weeks later, Newman offered encouragement to Miss Rowe: "You have gained the 'Pearl of great price'. You must thank God, and pray and resolve that you never will let it go." And in a postscript he said: "If you ever come this way, I should be *most glad* to see you—Write to me again, if you have occasion or wish."[120]

Newman had experienced great personal trials of his own in 1873. In the spring two of his dearest friends among the lay converts, Henry Wilberforce and James Hope-Scott, died within days of each other. Newman preached at both funerals with great difficulty. In a letter to R. W. Church on 2 May, Newman repeated words that Hope-Scott's daughter had just written to him: "He loved you so." And Newman continued: "I know he did, and I loved him. His death was most 'peaceful and calm.' So was H. Wilberforce's—so was Bellasis',[121] as sunny as his life. May I be as prepared as they when my time comes."[122] Newman cannot but have felt the passage of the years. Not surprisingly, when he was asked by the Jesuit Matthew Russell to write a piece for an Irish periodical, he replied in November 1873: "I am now too old for such engagements, and suppose I shall not write any thing more, except under some unforeseen and urgent stress of duty."[123] A year later the unforeseen and urgent stress of duty would make its claim.

Events on the Continent have repercussions for English Catholics

In December 1873, Archbishop Manning gave a speech to the Academia of the Catholic Religion, in which he denounced the Kulturkampf that had been going on in Prussia since the May Laws of 1873. In the course of his talk entitled, "Caesarism and Ultramontanism," Manning said, "the vindication of the liberties of the Church in their highest and

118. An Anglican clergyman, rector at Barnwell St. Andrews.
119. Newman to Miss Rowe, 16 September 1873, *The Letters and Diaries*, 26:366–67.
120. Newman to Miss Rowe, 23 October 1873, *The Letters and Diaries*, 26:379.
121. Edward Bellasis, who also died in 1873.
122. Newman to R. W. Church, 2 May 1873, *The Letters and Diaries*, 26:303. Newman dedicated the *Grammar of Assent* to Bellasis.
123. Newman to Matthew Russell, S.J., 6 November 1873, *The Letters and Diaries*, 26:382.

most sacred form is Ultramontanism."[124] He said in addition: "Obedience to the Church is liberty; and it is liberty, because the Church cannot err or mislead either men or nations. If the Church were not infallible, obedience to it might be the worst of bondages. This is Ultramontanism or the liberty of the soul divinely guaranteed by an infallible Church; the proper check and restraint of Caesarism, as Caesarism is the proper antagonist of the sovereignty of God."[125] Newman was appalled by these sentiments and decried them in a letter early in the new year to William Monsell, who had just given up his seat in Parliament in the face of a strong challenge from a candidate for the Irish Home Rule party and had been named a peer with the title, Lord Emly:

> I fully think with you, indeed I had said it, that the Archbishop of W. was wantonly insisting on the abstract, when he might have made a good fight, if he had kept to the concrete. I can't understand. Perhaps Cardinals in petto must so act.[126] He seems to be desirous of providing matter for Lord Russell's meeting.[127] I suppose he has a notion that Englishmen like outspoken men; and that they will respect Catholics, if they are bold—but that does not solve the diffculty to me. As the Pope has been putting arms against him in the hands of the Prussians, so, as it seems to me, is Manning putting arms into the hands of English Protestants—it is incomprehensible.[128]

Some days later Newman took up again with the newly-named Lord Emly a discussion of the Church's relationship to the State. In his brief remarks he was anticipating the subject that would have him so fully occupied by the end of the year:

> I find I did not answer all the remarks you made in your last letter; so I add a word or two to what I wrote.
>   Some one or other must have the decision practically as to what matters fall within the province of faith and morals, and what do not. Why not then the Church? is it not natural that she should know the extent of her own powers? is it not most unnatural that any one else should have the power of deciding for her . . . ?

124. *The Letters and Diaries*, ed. Charles Stephen Dessain and Thomas Gornall, S.J. (Oxford: The Clarendon Press, 1975) 27:4, n. 2.
125. *Dublin Review*, n.s. 22 (January–April 1874) 410, quoting Manning's *Caesarism and Ultramontanism*, 2nd ed. (London, 1874) 25. For the reaction in England caused by Manning's talk, see Walter L. Arnstein, *Protestant versus Catholic in Mid-Victorian England: Mr. Newdegate and the Nuns* (Columbia and London: University of Missouri Press, 1982) 187–88.
126. Ever since the council, it had been rumored that Manning would soon be named a cardinal. This did not occur until March 1875.
127. In consequence of Manning's *Caesarism and Ultramontanism*, Earl Russell, the former Prime Minister, had held a public meeting in support of Bismarck and his policies.
128. Newman to William Monsell, 5 January 1874, *The Letters and Diaries*, 27:4–5.

Take the parallel of nations—Some things indeed you can refer to arbitration—but it is a common saying that "a nation is the sole keeper of its own honour and judge of what is necessary for maintaining it." Every nation draws lines for *itself*—The Pope does no more than this. . . . The Church has never held out in defence of its full rights. It has always fought in order to compromise—as England and France, each on its own side, might do. Each is infallible, but each gives way.

As to absolving subjects from their allegiance, that involves a question, not of faith, but of obedience; nay, hardly of obedience, for I am not obliged to give up my allegiance to my sovereign, because the Pope gives me leave to do so. . . . and did such times recur,[129] I do not see why English Catholics (I speak under correction) might not hold meetings, and, not denying the Pope's power (for surely in certain cases he has the power) respectfully declare that they do not mean to avail themselves of the privilege which he offers them. But perhaps I am writing inconsiderately.[130]

In part, Newman in this response was alluding to the situation in Germany where the Church was suffering under severe restrictions imposed by the State, but he was also obviously disagreeing with Manning's high claims for the Church over the State. However, Monsell's questions about the relationship between Church and State may also have been prompted by his own personal situation. He had been forced to resign the seat he had held in Parliament for twenty-seven years because of the rise in Ireland of the Home Rule party. The leadership of the Church in Ireland was divided on the issue of Home Rule and on the legitimacy of the various kinds of agitation in favor of it.

Newman's distress over events in the Church was evident also early in January 1874 when he wrote to Charlotte Wood: "You know how strongly the present Pope has spoken in behalf of invincible ignorance[131]—and I suppose there never was the time, since the Church was, when there were more formidable arguments against joining the Church, and more plausible reasons for remaining in the communion in which a man is born. I think we have great scandals which weigh us down—but it is God's will for some great purpose which we shall know hereafter."[132]

In the following month, one of those from whom Newman received greetings on his seventy-third birthday was Alfred Plummer. Newman in his letter of appreciation to Plummer took the occasion to say: "Is not the new move of getting an episcopal succession for the Old Catholics contrary to the policy which Döllinger intended? and can he come into

---

129. Pope Pius V in excommunicating Elizabeth I, 25 February 1570, purported to release her Catholic subjects from allegiance to her.

130. Newman to William Monsell, 14 January 1874, *The Letters and Diaries,* 27:10–11.

131. Encyclical letter to the Bishops of Italy of 10 August 1863.

132. Newman to Charlotte Wood, 7 January 1874, *The Letters and Diaries,* 27:7.

it? I thought he recognized the duty, nay necessity, of communion with Rome, and only denied the fact that the Vatican decrees were legitimate and valid, or that the disunion was more than accidental and temporary."[133] Döllinger, who was shown this letter by Plummer, said in reply to Plummer: "With regard to what Newman says you are quite right. The Old Catholics don't separate themselves from the Church of Rome, don't anathematize other members of it, but exercise the inalienable right of necessity and self-help, just as was done also in the primitive Church of the first centuries." Plummer translated Döllinger's words for Newman and passed them on to him on 9 April.[134]

Shortly after Easter, Newman's thoughts were turned again to events affecting the life of the Catholic Church in Germany. Newman was responding to Mrs. Meadows.[135]

> It is quite sad, as you say, to think of the sufferings of the Swiss and German Catholics—but still they cannot be long, please God—there must be some compromise, as in former times of the Church, when the Holy See has inflicted interdicts. To me such trials and greater have been so long a matter of anticipation that perhaps I do not feel them now, as keenly as I ought. They are the will of God, and the Holy Father must have foreseen them before the Vatican Council, and must have deliberately considered that that Council was worth the sacrifice, and that these trials of the faithful were seasonable.[136]

After writing this letter Newman decided not to send it. Perhaps he thought his remarks on both the definition and Pius IX too strong to send to someone that may at best have been only casually known to him. Mrs. Meadows did, however, visit Newman in the autumn of the following year.[137]

Newman's role as counselor to troubled souls continues

The long and highly theological correspondence between Newman and J. H. Willis Nevins began again in June. Nevins had by this time returned to the Catholic Church, though Newman had had to write to Nevins's father, an Anglican clergyman, in the hope of getting him to accept his son's decision, to which he was strongly opposed. Nevins had been reading some of Newman's Anglican works and he had come away with doubts about the infallibility of ecumenical councils. He did not think that the

133. Newman to Alfred Plummer, 21 February 1874, *The Letters and Diaries,* 27:20.
134. See *The Letters and Diaries,* 27:20, n. 2.
135. No first name is given in *The Letters and Diaries.*
136. Newman to Mrs. Meadows, 13 April 1874, *The Letters and Diaries,* 27:51.
137. See Newman "Diary," 30 October 1875, *The Letters and Diaries,* 27:373.

bishops who met in the early councils would have taken the position that councils were infallible. He did not see how infallibility either of a council or of the pope could be said to be of apostolic origin. On 19 June, Newman told him:

> In answer to your question I should say, that, as I understand the subject, the doctrine of the Church's infallibility is primarily an inference, grounded on the Church's office of *teaching*.
>
> How could the Church be the organ of revelation and teach gospel truth without a security given to it that it should be preserved from *error* in its teaching? that is, without infallibility *so far,* infallibility in its guardianship and transmission of what the Apostles preached? The Church is the columna et firmamentum veritatis—Now is this possible, unless it is guarded from going wrong, kept straight in all its formal utterances?
>
> The question of the times, places, modes of its teaching is a further and after question—Our Lord said, "When two or three, are gathered together" etc. At first sight, then, meetings short of a General Council would seem formal organs of the Church's teaching. And when this question was disposed of by the logic of facts, and it was understood that the assemblage must be ecumenical, still what conditions were necessary to constitute it ecumenical, would be a further question—as, for instance, what place the Holy See had in it, and then at length the still further question whether the fact of the Holy See's supremacy in jurisdiction did not in itself go on to suggest another mode by which the Church taught, that is, the Holy See's prerogative of formal teaching, (in other words, its infallibility or inerrancy in doctrine), even apart from an Ecumenical Council.
>
> All these were questions of detail; and, as the infallibility of the Pope was not determined till just now, and even now the formal conditions of the occasions when his teaching is infallible are not yet determined, so in the fourth century the formal conditions of an Ecumenical Council, that is, the conditions which constitute a General Council to be ecumenical and to have and to be exercising the office of teaching, were not ascertained with that precision which in the sequel enabled the Catholic world of the 16 [sic] century, as a whole, without hesitation or delay to call the Council of Trent ecumenical. Accordingly, an interval, greater or less, past [sic], before certain of the early Councils were recognized as ecumenical and infallible. Pope Gregory speaks of four, though he ought to have said six; and a parallel delay, more or less, occurred in the recognition of the second and third—and of the first. . . .
>
> This is how I should answer your difficulty.[138]

Nevins's reply to this letter caused Newman to think that Nevins had not understood him. Newman wrote from Rednal on 25 June:

> Somehow I don't think I have made you see the drift of my letter.
> You ask—"Must not the idea or doctrine that Ecumenical Councils were

138. Newman to J. H. Willis Nevins, 19 June 1874, *The Letters and Diaries,* 27:79–80.

to be inspired or infallible, have been taught by our Lord to his Apostles?''
I answer—No, it need not. Then you say, "If not, can we claim *Divine* guidance for what, unless of divine institution, becomes merely an *ecclesiastical*
regulation?''

I answer, "the infallibility and immutability" of the decrees of Ecumenical Councils need not be, cannot be, an *institution*, it is a *doctrine*,—and
no doctrine is a regulation.

It is, as I answered you, a doctrine *derived from,* a *consequence* of, an
Apostolical and Divine doctrine, viz. that the Church is the *authoritative
teacher.* She cannot teach without infallibility—that is the first deduction—a
General Council is an act of her teaching—this is a second deduction. This
is what is often called development of doctrine. It is no where said e.g.,
by the early Fathers, that Mary was without sin—but they say that She is
the second Eve, and that also she is the contrary to Eve in not having fallen;
from which the Church, under the gift of infallibility, deduces her sinless-
ness. And this deduction nevertheless might not seem necessary to Catholic
believers on the first blush of the matter—and so much more might the infallibility of certain assemblies of Bishops, and what was necessary for them
to come up to the idea of their being infallible, and the fact of the Nicene
Council having come up to that idea, require to sink into the minds of the
Nicene generation before it was thoroughly received.

I don't think we get a right view of infallibility (as negative far more
than positive) till we *begin* with the idea of *teaching.*[139]

Newman would not hear again from Nevins until the following year. At
that time he would use Newman's two letters of June 1874 in writing to
Gladstone to say that Newman's position in the *Letter to the Duke of Norfolk* was inconsistent with the June letters. Nevins sent Newman a copy
of Gladstone's reply.[140]

At the end of the summer the usual routine of the Oratory community took over. Various members of the community went on holiday, including Ambrose St. John, who went to Scotland. Newman kept him in
touch with news of the house and school. In the middle part of August,
Newman was ill for a number of days, but by 21 August he felt his strength
returning. In late August, Catherine Ann Bathurst, one of the people in
Newman's life who most depended on his guidance and counsel, visited
him. Miss Bathurst wrote Newman a letter after that visit in which she
asked Newman, "how to answer those who say they have been thrown
back by the Vatican Council, and that new doctrines are taught Etc."[141]
Newman answered some days later. He said: "Your question about the

139. Newman to J. H. Willis Nevins, 25 June 1874, *The Letters and Diaries,* 27:84.
140. See *The Letters and Diaries,* 27:237–38, n. 2.
141. Catherine Ann Bathurst to Newman, 26 August 1874, *The Letters and Diaries,* 27:116,
n. 5.

Vatican Council is too vague for me to be able to answer it—put down distinctly your difficulties, and I will do my best to clear them up."[142]

Four years after the definition Newman was still involved with the subject of papal infallibility. Over the past nine years he had dealt with the subject in various notes, memorandums, and well over one hundred letters. All of this was to serve him in good stead for the great challenge on the subject of papal infallibility that would come his way in the autumn of 1874.

OVERVIEW

In the later part of 1871, Newman was still receiving letters from people seeking advice in their personal distress over the definition. Newman's responses remained considerate, but they had also a more measured quality as time passed. Newman made less frequent reference to the manner in which the definition had been passed at the council. But he remained impatient, even angry, with correspondents who he thought were trying to bait him into saying intemperate things. He was annoyed too, but resigned, when confronted with continuing rumors that he intended to leave the Roman Church in consequence of the definition.

That Newman still considered the definition a difficulty for the life of the Church, especially in England, was shown in his opposition to Manning's plans for higher education for Catholics. Newman was opposed to the founding of the Catholic University in London and refused to have any role in it. He maintained still that Catholics should be permitted to attend Oxford and Cambridge, but practically he did not think this altogether possible or wise since he believed that the definition would put Catholics too much on the defensive at a time when sincere Christians should be joining together to do battle against religious liberalism and indifferentism.

Newman, however, continued to keep his views private and to resist the urgings of friends to speak publicly on the definition. He was shocked, even scandalized, by the public stand that Döllinger had taken in Germany and he viewed the rise of the Old Catholic movement with sadness. Though Döllinger separated himself from the Old Catholics, still, Newman believed, they were an inescapable consequence of Döllinger's defiant public attitude toward Rome and the Vatican Council.

Newman's decision not to write publicly on the definition was surprisingly breached in small but significant ways in the late summer of 1872

---

142. Newman to Catherine Ann Bathurst, 11 September 1874, *The Letters and Diaries,* 27:116. It appears that Miss Bathurst took Newman up on this invitation but that he became too absorbed in responding to Gladstone to answer her new queries. See 27 May 1875, *The Letters and Diaries,* 27:300.

when he wrote letters to *The Times,* to the Anglican newspaper, the *Guardian,* and to the *Pall Mall Gazette.* In the first instance, Newman was disturbed by what he believed to be *The Times's* reckless words on the unlimited power of the pope, but in the other two instances the challenge was more personal, a new public insinuation that Newman had not deep down accepted the definition of papal infallibility or, if he had, he was simply buckling under to ecclesiastical authority. The coincidence of *The Times* piece and the *Guardian* piece coming within days of each other gave Newman the fortunate opportunity to show on the one hand the limits of papal authority and on the other his own acceptance of the definition of papal infallibility.

And yet on close scrutiny the writings cited by Newman in the letter to the *Guardian* do not appear to justify his strong statements on the clarity of his position on papal infallibility in the quarter century between his entrance into the Roman Catholic Church and the definition of 1870. The passage from his *Dublin Lectures* that Newman appealed to in his letter of 12 September 1872 to the editor of the *Guardian* was omitted by him when a somewhat shortened version of the *Lectures* was published in 1859. Newman's justification for removing the passage on papal authority was that it was "of only temporary interest, and irrelevant to the subject of University education."[143] And from the early 1860's onwards as the debate on papal infallibility became more intense and partisan, Newman steadfastly kept clear of any public statements on the matter, most notably in his decision not to write a second letter to Pusey in 1867. It is interesting to see Newman saying in a letter to Arthur Arnold on 20 September 1872 that "a great theological question" cannot have "a short answer," and yet he himself defends the consistency of his "longheld" views on papal infallibility by calling scattered quotes from his writings from the 1840s and 1850s.

In 1873 and 1874, there is a noticeable decrease of letters dealing with the definition in Newman's correspondence but the subject still came up regularly. Clearly it would not go away.

143. Newman to the Editor of the *Guardian,* 12 September 1872, *The Letters and Diaries,* 26:167.

Chapter 5

"But, If I Am to Write, I Will Say My Say"

August 1874–January 1875

In late August 1874, Newman had been ill for several days and with his energies at a low point he thought, as he had from time to time in the past thirty years, of his contributions to his adopted Church and judged them of little consequence. He had been a useless servant.[1] Absorbed in this bleak meditation, he had small, if any, reason to expect that one of the great challenges of his life lay just ahead. In fact, the scene, all unknown to him, was already being set. The defeat of the Liberals in November 1873 ended Gladstone's ministry. (He carried on as caretaker prime minister until January 1874.) Though he was to continue for another year as the leader of his party in opposition, Gladstone after his defeat began to lose interest in politics and he turned not surprisingly to the other great interest of his life, religion. There is little doubt that his effort to solve the issue of higher education in Ireland with all of its religious implications was a major factor in Gladstone's downfall. That he should spend what he thought to be the closing days of his political career reflecting on religion and the State, and more precisely the Roman Catholic Church

---

1. On 30 August 1874, Newman wrote in his private notes, "I have so depressing a feeling that I have done nothing through my long life—and especially that now I am doing nothing at all. Anglicans indeed rather think more of what I have written than they did, if I may judge from letters I receive—but, as to Catholics, they would not deny that I have done some good service towards bringing Anglicans into the Church, nay am perhaps doing so still; but, as to the great controversies of the day, about the divinity of Christianity & c., they think I am passé—at least this, (perhaps rather,) that I have taken a wrong line in respect to them. At least I think the Jesuits do. They would think my line too free and sceptical, that I made too many admissions & c. On the contrary I *cannot* at all go along with them—and, since they have such enormous influence just now, and are so intolerant in their views, this is pretty much the same as saying that I have not taken, and do not take, what would popularly be called the Catholic line." *John Henry Newman: Autobiographical Writings,* ed. and intro. Henry Tristram of the Oratory (New York: Sheed and Ward, 1956) 270.

Newman describes his intestinal illness and feelings of depression in a letter of 26 August 1870 to Ambrose St. John. See *The Letters and Diaries of John Henry Newman,* ed. Charles Stephen Dessain and Thomas Gornall, S.J. (Oxford: The Clarendon Press, 1975) 27:111.

and the State, did not surprise interested observers. What did startle them was the vehement attack on the Roman Church with which he began these reflections. Gladstone had been considering the theme of the Catholic Church and the State since the definition of papal infallibility, but his absorption in political affairs had kept him from focusing his attention on it. His defeat—which he certainly blamed on the Irish bishops and their failure to support him on the Irish education issue—lessened his political responsibilities and freed him from concerns that were, or would be, beyond his control.

The first result of Gladstone's meditation on ecclesiastical questions came in October 1874 with the publication in the *Contemporary Review* of his "Ritual and Ritualism." While this piece was concerned with Church and State issues, it dealt primarily with an Anglican controversy.[2] But buried within the article, almost like the warning shot that comes before direct aim, was a sentence that greatly angered and alarmed members of the English Roman Catholic community, particularly Gladstone's Roman Catholic political colleagues, and especially those of his own party.[3] The offending sentence, which dealt with Gladstone's thoughts on "the effort to Romanise the Church and people of England," ran as follows:

> But if it had been possible in the seventeenth or eighteenth centuries, it would still have been impossible in the nineteenth; when Rome has substituted for the proud boast of *semper eadem* a policy of violence and change of faith; when she has refurbished and paraded anew every rusty tool she was fondly thought to have disused; when no one can become her convert without renouncing his moral and mental freedom, and placing his civil loyalty and duty at the mercy of another; and when she has equally repudiated modern thought and ancient history.[4]

To close observers and even some casual onlookers, the reference to converts to the Roman Church was immediately understood. Gladstone had been deeply distressed when Lord Ripon, who had been a close friend and

2. On the Public Worship Bill sponsored by the Disraeli Ministry in 1874, and opposed by Gladstone, see Walter Arnstein, *Protestant versus Catholic in Mid-Victorian England: Mr. Newdegate and the Nuns* (Columbia and London: University of Missouri Press, 1982) 182–84. For a discussion of the ritualist movement in the Church of England, see Horton Davies, *Worship and Theology in England, 1850–1900* (Princeton, N.J.: Princeton University Press, 1962) 4:114–31, and Owen Chadwick, *The Victorian Church: Part II* (New York: Oxford University Press, 1970) 2:308–25.

3. See William Monsell to Ambrose De Lisle, no date, 1874, as quoted in Edmund Sheridan Purcell and Edwin Phillipps De Lisle, *The Life and Letters of Ambrose Phillipps De Lisle* (London: Macmillan & Co., Ltd., 1900) 2:55. Monsell wrote of Gladstone: "I had a correspondence with him on his article in the Contemporary, and pointed out the evils which must follow from his course. He answered me kindly, but he set at nought my warnings."

4. See *The Letters and Diaries,* 27:122, n. 3.

a member of his government, was received into the Roman Catholic Church on 7 September 1874 at the Brompton Oratory.[5] But the vehemence of this statement spoke also of other angers and hurts, of fury reined in and finally released. The troubles with the Irish bishops were a factor, and so indeed was the definition of papal infallibility four years previously.

It is not entirely clear when Newman became aware of Gladstone's essay in the *Contemporary Review* and his furious blast at Roman Catholics. Though the issue was dated October, it must have been in circulation before the end of September. This is evident from a letter that William Monsell wrote to Newman on 1 October, in which Monsell takes it for granted that Newman has already read "Ritual and Ritualism." Newman had returned to Birmingham on the day that Monsell wrote to him. He had been on holiday for ten days. It had been a time of vigorous physical activities and visits to his Anglican relatives, and Newman appears to have completely recovered from the illness and depression of late August-early September.[6] He returned home fully restored, and it seems that this respite played a part in helping him to endure, even survive, the several strenuous difficult months ahead.

Newman's first known reference to Gladstone's article comes in a letter to Lord Blachford written on the day after his return to the Oratory. Newman was responding to a letter from Blachford that he found waiting on his return:

> As to the other perplexity, which only concerns him, in common with others, the rubric reformation question, I don't think Gladstone's article throws any light upon it, for it does not touch the real difficulty, while he has offended us by one sentence in it very deeply. It seems strikingly rude to Lord Ripon, and I hope it will have the effect of making some Catholic or other speak out. Gladstone's excuse is,.I suppose, the extravagance of Archbishop Manning in his "Caesarism,"[7] and he will do us a service, if

5. When Gladstone heard of Lord Ripon's impending reception into the Catholic Church, he wrote as follows to Lady Ripon on 21 August 1874: "How is it possible that such news can be true." Quoted in Hugh A. MacDougall, *The Acton-Newman Relations: The Dilemma of Christian Liberalism* (New York: Fordham University Press, 1962) 130–31.

The conversion of the Marquis of Ripon, the son of Viscount Goderich, prime minister of England, 1827–1828, caused a sensation in London. *The Times,* anticipating Gladstone's language in his *Expostulation,* said in its edition of 5 September 1874 that a statesman taking the course that Ripon had just taken "forfeits at once the confidence of the English people. Such a step involves a complete abandonment of any claim to political or even social influence in the nation at large, and can only be regarded as betraying an irreparable weakness of character. To become a Roman Catholic and remain a thorough Englishman are—it cannot be disguised—almost incompatible conditions." *The Times* (5 September 1874) 9.

6. Newman "Diary," 20 September–30 September 1874, *The Letters and Diaries,* 27:118, 120–22.

7. On 23 December 1873, Manning delivered an address entitled "Caesarism and Ultramontanism" to the Academia of the Catholic Religion. The address was published under

he gives us an opportunity of speaking. We can speak against Gladstone, while it would not be decent to speak against Manning. The difficulty is, *who* ought to speak. For me to speak would do no good, even if I were the person to speak, which I am not.[8]

Not surprisingly, Newman's first reaction was to excuse himself from responding to Gladstone and also, not surprisingly, he laid a good deal of the blame for Gladstone's outburst on Manning. In the weeks ahead Newman would change his position on who should respond, but not on Manning's responsibility for the controversy. It was a theme that would recur in his letters over and over in the weeks ahead and indeed it would be a factor, however delicately disguised, in his eventual response to Gladstone.

Newman put under pressure to respond to Gladstone's parenthesis

On the very day that Newman wrote to Lord Blachford, he received the letter from Monsell already mentioned. Only a day back from his holiday, he was being drawn by his closest friends into the thick of the battle. The pressures on him were intense from the first. Monsell wrote to ask Newman's advice on a draft of a letter to Gladstone that he had prepared in response to Gladstone's insult to Catholics in "Ritual and Ritualism." "You have of course read Gladstone's rhetorical invective against Catholics," Monsell began.

> I think I have a right to call him to account for it.
> I shall be very much obliged to you if you would tell me 1st whether

---

the same title in 1874. Manning's principal target was Bismarck and the anti-Catholic Falk Laws that were then being put into place in Prussia, but Manning also used the occasion to identify true Catholicism with Ultramontanism and to hold up Boniface VIII's *Unam Sanctam* as the Catholic Church's operative statement on the ultimate supremacy of the spiritual power over the temporal. While acknowledging a role for the State in daily life, Manning at the same time espoused such a high interpretation of the Church's rights, that the State was left with little practical autonomy. Readers such as Newman were particularly alarmed by such statements as the following: "Obedience to the Church is liberty; and it is liberty because the Church cannot err or mislead either men or nations. If the Church were not infallible, obedience to it might be the worst of bondage. This is Ultramontanism, or the liberty of the soul divinely guaranteed by an infallible Church; the proper check and restraint of Caesarism, as Caesarism is the proper antagonist of the sovereignty of God," and "The natural antagonist of Caesarism is the Christian Church, with all its liberties of doctrine and discipline of faith and jurisdiction; and the vindication of these liberties of the Church in their highest and most sacred form is Ultramontanism. Therefore, the world hates it. Therefore it now rails against it in all its tones and with all its tongues. 'Divus Caesar' and 'Vicarius Christi' are two persons and two powers and two systems, between which there can be not only no peace, but no truce." "Caesarism and Ultramontanism," Henry Edward Manning, *Miscellanies* (New York: The Catholic Publication Society, 1877) 523 and 550.

8. Newman to Lord Blachford, 2 October 1874, *The Letters and Diaries,* 27:122–23.

you think I ought to write. 2ndly Should I or not mark my letter private. 3rd Do you approve of a letter to this effect?

I am sure you will not be annoyed with me for telling you with what great astonishment and pain I have read your charges against Roman Catholics.

I say Roman Catholics, because as you well know every sincere Roman Catholic would reject with indignation the assertion that his Creed differs one iota from that accepted by the most recent convert.

The accusation of renouncing our mental and moral freedom and placing our civil loyalty and duty at the mercy of another is at least as grave and as offensive as any contained in the Durham letter.[9] The quarter your charges come from enhances the pain they give to multitudes of your fellow countrymen.

If you will descend from the abstract to the concrete you will find no difficulty in testing the truth of your words. Ask yourself only whether, not to speak of myself who have been in close connection with you for 27 years, Lord O'Hagan or the O'Conor Don,[10] or the

9. Letter of Lord John Russell following upon the restoration of the Roman Catholic hierarchy in 1850 and Wiseman's famous pastoral issued "Out of the Flaminian Gate." In his letter, written to the bishop of Durham on 4 November 1850 and published in *The Times*, Russell said: "Even if it shall appear that the ministers and servants of the Pope in this country have not transgressed the law, I feel persuaded that we are strong enough to repel any outward attacks. The liberty of Protestantism has been enjoyed too long in England to allow any successful attempt to impose a foreign yoke upon our minds and consciences. No foreign prince or potentate will be at liberty to foster his fetters upon a nation which has so long and so nobly vindicated its right to freedom of opinion, civil, political, and religious." And in his conclusion Russell referred to "a nation which looks with contempt on the mummeries of superstition, and with scorn at the laborious endeavours which are now making to confine the intellect and enslave the soul."

Although strongly anti-Catholic in this letter, Russell in fact aimed his chief fury at the Ritualist movement in the Church of England. The Durham Letter can be found in E. R. Norman, *Anti-Catholicism in Victorian England,* vol. 1 of *Historical Problems: Studies and Documents,* ed. G. R. Elton (New York: Barnes and Noble, Inc., 1968) 159–61.

In its November 1874 issue, the *Month* carried an article on Gladstone's "Ritual and Ritualism," which it entitled "Mr. Gladstone's Durham Letter." In an evident reference to the Old Catholic movement in Germany, it said that Gladstone's parenthesis "smells of Bonn and Munich and Dr. Döllinger," and further on the article stated: "Whatever Mr. Gladstone may mean, his language, we take the liberty of telling him, is the language of vituperation, insult, and calumny." *Month,* n.s. 3 (November 1874) 22:268, n. 1, and 268–69. Gladstone made a note in his diary on 31 October to show that he had read the *Month's* essay on "Ritual and Ritualism" See "Note," 31 October 1874, *The Gladstone Diaries,* ed. H.C.G. Matthew (Oxford: The Clarendon Press, 1982) 8:539.

Commenting on the affinities between Russell's action in 1850 and Gladstone's a quarter century later, E. R. Norman says: "The similarity also, . . . is an interesting indication of a virile tradition [of no-popery] even in most unexpected carriers." Norman, *Anti-Catholicism in Victorian England,* 81.

10. The O'Conor Don, Charles Owen O'Conor, was the Liberal M.P. for County Roscommon, 1860–1880. Lord Thomas O'Hagan, appointed Lord Chancellor of Ireland in 1868, was the first Catholic to hold that office since the time of James II.

Duke of Norfolk have ever exhibited any want of mental or moral freedom, and whether the thought that they were less loyal and dutiful than you are would not be dismissed by any as calumnious.

These men are not lukewarm or insincere in their religion, and no general description of it can be true that does not include them. I know that injustice is repugnant to your mind and I feel sure that when you find that your statements are groundless you will not hesitate to withdraw them.

After setting down his draft, Monsell continued his letter to Newman: "If you think I ought to write you would oblige me very much by making any changes you like in this, or by telling me what sort of letter I should substitute for it.

" . . . If I can get away on Saturday could you receive me at the Oratory?"[11]

Newman's immediate reply was welcoming and encouraging:

It is quite necessary that some one should answer that sentence of Gladstone's—and you are the proper person to do it. And the sketch you have sent me, is just what will be telling. I hope you will make it a pamphlet; indeed you can't help doing so. You will be forced to bring out your meaning when you speak of abstract and concrete, after the manner of your letter to me some months ago.[12] You must not conceal from yourself that really you will be answering, not Gladstone, but Archbishop Manning. He ought to be answered and this is the opportunity—and you, as not being under his jurisdiction, have a great advantage, which an English Catholic has not. . . .[13]

You will be doing Lord Ripon a great service, who must feel Gl.'s attack to be cruel, since he cannot condescend to reply to it."[14]

Newman experiences frustration as he attempts a reply to Gladstone

Monsell came to Birmingham the next day and stayed until Monday, 5 October.[15] There is no record of the conversations that he had with Newman, but it is clear that before 7 October, Newman had himself decided to try his hand at a reply to Gladstone. There can be little doubt then that Monsell had tried to persuade Newman that he should answer Glad-

11. William Monsell to Newman, 1 October 1874, *The Letters and Diaries,* 27:123–24.

12. This very likely refers to the correspondence on Church and State issues in January 1874. See pages 242–43.

13. Monsell, by this time a member of the House of Lords, was Irish and had previously represented Limerick in the House of Commons for twenty-seven years.

14. Newman to William Monsell, 2 October 1874, *The Letters and Diaries,* 27:124.

15. See Newman "Diary," 3 October 1874, *The Letters and Diaries,* 27:125, and 5 October 1874, 27:127.

stone. Monsell had been among that group of Newman's friends who over the past four years had been urging him to speak publicly on the definition of papal infallibility and the various controversies that had continued in England as a consequence of it. In his diary for 7 October, Newman wrote: "In these weeks attempted in vain to write on Gladstone's parenthesis in the *Contemporary*."[16] There would be a complex sequence of starts and stops before Newman was finally on the way to his celebrated reply to Gladstone. These starts and stops had as much to do with Newman's reluctance to becoming engaged in public controversy with Gladstone (and Manning) as they did with his uncertainties about what tone and form a reply to Gladstone should take. The weekend conversations with Monsell were clearly the starting point of his attempts.

Monsell did go ahead and send his contemplated letter to Gladstone. No doubt this was another result of his weekend visit to Newman. In his reply to Monsell of 6 October, Gladstone suggested that someone from the Catholic side should publicly make counter-arguments to his position, and there is little doubt that Gladstone had Newman in mind. At the same time Gladstone sent Monsell a copy of a letter that he had just sent to Lord Ripon. In it Gladstone said that the Vatican Decrees "bind you to *believe* whatever the Pope decrees *ex cathedra*. . . . Besides this, you are bound by the Council to obey whatever the Pope orders or requires to be obeyed, *ex cathedra* or not."[17] Monsell sent this correspondence on to Newman.

Newman soon gave evidence that Gladstone's letters to Monsell and Ripon as well as his polite challenge for some Catholic to reply had strongly affected him. Though he says in his diary that from 7 October he was attempting "in vain" to reply to Gladstone, it is clear from his correspondence that the subject of Catholic allegiance since the definition of 1870 was very much on his mind. Ample evidence of this is found in his long letter to Monsell of 9 October. "Your packet," he began, "came last night, and I lost not a minute in attending to it, and now return its inclosures." Newman continued, referring to Gladstone: "He confuses between dogmatic universal definitions, which are to be received on faith, whether they relate to religion or to morals, with directions, orders, commands about particular facts and matters of conduct."

Having clearly isolated this basic misunderstanding in Gladstone's position, Newman then went on to argue against Gladstone's overall posi-

16. Newman "Diary," 7 October 1874, *The Letters and Diaries,* 27:129. It appears that Newman made this note well after 7 October, as seems to be the case with a number of his diary entries in this period.

17. *The Letters and Diaries,* 27:132, n. 1. Gladstone notes his letter to Monsell in his diary on 6 October. Two days earlier he had recorded: "Wrote to Ld. Ripon: a stiff letter in answer to one from him." *The Gladstone Diaries,* 4 and 6 October 1874, 8:533.

tion as revealed both in the article in the *Contemporary Review* and in
his letter to Lord Ripon:

> Thus, as to a universal doctrine in morals, the Pope might certainly declare
> and promulgate to the Catholic world that "taking interest for money is
> against the natural law," and every Catholic would be bound to believe it;
> but then an Ecumenical Council might do this quite as well, and with the
> same obligation upon Catholics; and it is about as likely that a Pope should
> so decree as that a Council should. Moreover, there is a traditional opinion
> against taking interest, coming down from early times; if, in spite of this,
> it is unlikely, for reasons natural and supernatural, that a Pope or a Coun-
> cil should define the immorality of taking interest to be a revealed truth,
> how much less likely is it, that doctrines which have not the advantage of
> a tradition, should be made *de fide,* whether by Pope or Council?
>
> Nothing to my mind is more unlikely than such an evolution at Rome
> of a new moral doctrine; especially in the field of politics, considering how
> the Catholic Church has been found to get on so well with every form of
> government.
>
> However, I grant that such a definition, if made, and the consequent
> obligation to believe its truth, would in consistency affect the conduct of
> every individual Catholic. He would not take interest for his money— But
> then it must be recollected that this is no *new* possibility, and G. insists on
> the *alteration* which has been made in a Catholic's duties by the Vatican
> decree. Any Ecumenical Council might have brought such a possibility into
> effect for the last 1800 years, and the chance of its being carried out by
> a Pope is too vague and remote to form a ground of his declamation against
> us.
>
> And now, secondly and on the other hand, for particular utterances or
> for commands of the Holy See, concerning facts or points of conduct or
> lines of action. Here, still more precisely, things remain just as they were
> before the Vatican decree. There is no addition whatever in it to the Pope's
> power. Not a word is said in it about practical obedience to the command
> of a Pope. The duty remains what it was in the time of Bellarmine. It re-
> mains what it was in Elizabeth's reign, when her Catholic subjects with great
> zeal took part in the defence of their country against an Armada blessed
> by the Pope.

Newman, continuing to build up his argument, moved from the past
to the immediate present:

> And so now in other matters. If, on occasion of a general election, the Pope
> in a letter to the Bishops of Ireland bade all Catholics every where to vote
> for the conservative candidate, and a particular Catholic felt it in his con-
> science a duty to vote for the liberal in his own borough or county, having
> reason to know that the Pope was misinformed, that the conservatives were
> hollow in their professions and would injure Catholic interests, and that
> the man he wished to support was honest, straightforward, both just and

generous to Catholics and their true friend, in spite of his liberal opinions, I conceive he would be committing no sin, though he voted in opposition to the Pope's command.

Or again, supposing the Prince of Wales became a Catholic, and the Pope bade Catholic members of Parliament to accept him as their king, in spite of their oath to the contrary, it would be their duty, while the nation enforced the oath, and they were in the House, to refuse that allegiance that was demanded of them.[18]

In two respects then I consider G. to be wrong—1. in supposing that the particular precepts or commands of the Pope to be infallible, whereas only general propositions on religion and morals are such, not propositions on matters of expedience, but about things intrinsically good or evil, right or wrong, and therefore few and rare, and at best only indirectly bearing on the conduct of individuals.

2. next in supposing that, as regards such particular commands bearing on conduct, the Vatican Council has said so much as one word whereas it leaves the Pope's power in this respect just as it found it.

Lastly, if it be said that, putting aside formal commands, it is impossible a Catholic should not be influenced in his political acts by the Pope's wishes, or by what he knows will be for the advantage of the Catholic religion, I answer

1. this is no *new* difficulty, and it is on the change of a Catholic's duties since the Council on which G. replies and insists.

2. it applies to all class interests—e.g. Anglican members of Parliament support the Church of England, dissenters oppose it—men sent in by the Railway interest or the publican interest support those interests respectively.[19]

Though replying to Gladstone's brief statements in "Ritual and Ritualism" and in his letter to Lord Ripon, Newman is clearly anticipating further arguments that Gladstone would soon make in his *Expostulation.* But despite the fact that he sets out a response to Gladstone very fully in this letter to Monsell, Newman made it evident all through October that he could not hit on a way to answer Gladstone publicly. It was only with Gladstone's *The Vatican Decrees in Their Bearing on Civil Allegiance: A Political Expostulation* that he would feel confident that he at last had a clear enough presentation of Gladstone's case to attempt to make a cogent and compelling reply.

Newman finished his long letter to Monsell by inviting Monsell to ask for fuller arguments if he thought them necessary and by giving him leave

18. In his first letter to Newman following the publication of the *Letter to the Duke of Norfolk,* Gladstone was to correct Newman on this point, telling him that there was no oath involved but rather it was simply a matter of Statute Law. See *The Letters and Diaries,* 15 January 1875, 27:192–93.

19. Newman to William Monsell, 9 October 1874, *The Letters and Diaries,* 27:132–34. This letter to Monsell includes a number of points that Newman would make in the *Letter to the Duke of Norfolk.*

to use what he had said in whatever way Monsell thought best. Newman made it clear that he was deferring to Monsell because he had a far greater knowledge and understanding of the world of affairs than did Newman. Newman would return to this theme, his lack of knowledge of the great world, in the weeks ahead as he struggled to reply to Gladstone. Newman also sent Monsell some remarks, presumably in answer to Gladstone, written by Ignatius Ryder, made, as Newman said, "independently of me, but agreeing with me closely."[20]

There was also a postscript to the letter, and the last sentence of it introduced a subject to which Newman would give much attention in his efforts to reply to Gladstone and in his eventual reply. Newman wrote, "I should leave Dr. Doyle and the Bishops of 1829 to themselves—." When Bishop James Doyle of Kildare and Leighlin and the other Irish bishops, as well as the four English Vicars Apostolic, were asked in the late 1820s in the discussions preparatory to the Catholic Emancipation Act, whether papal infallibility was an article of faith and would therefore compromise Catholic allegiance to the State, the bishops replied in the negative. Gladstone was to make much of this in arguing that the definition of 1870 had cut the ground from under the Catholic position of 1829, partly in consequence of which the civil liberties of Catholics had been granted.[21] It was Gladstone's position that the Emancipation Act had been secured on false grounds, if not through the deceit of the Catholic side, and this led Monsell to worry that Gladstone might actually seek a repeal of the Emancipation Act or the enactment of some restrictions on it.[22]

Monsell had already replied to Gladstone's letter of 6 October by saying that the Vatican Decrees had changed nothing as far as the allegiance of Catholics was concerned and he had appealed to Newman's *Essay on the Development of Christian Doctrine* to make his case.[23] Newman supported Monsell in the first argument, but he was unhappy with Monsell's attempts to use the *Essay on Development* in responding to Gladstone.[24]

20. Whether at any time Newman thought of letting Ryder answer Gladstone in his stead, as had been the case with Ryder's reply to Ward in 1867, is not known.

21. See *The Letters and Diaries*, 27:134, n. 1. The position of the Irish and English bishops in the three decades leading up to the Emancipation Act was to play a large part in the ensuing controversy between Gladstone and his Catholic opponents. According to Odo Russell in a despatch to the Earl of Clarendon during the Vatican Council: "Some English and Irish bishops, but I do not think more than three or four of them, have founded their petition against Infallibility on the repeated repudiation of that doctrine by their predecessors at the time of the Emancipation Act." Russell to Clarendon, 20 March 1870, in N. Blakiston, ed., *The Roman Question: Extracts from the Despatches of Odo Russell from Rome, 1858-70* (London: Chapman and Hall, 1962) 410.

22. See William Monsell to Newman, 11 October 1874, *The Letters and Diaries*, 27:141, n. 1.

23. See *The Letters and Diaries*, 27:136, n. 2.

24. See 12 October 1874, *The Letters and Diaries*, 27:136. It is interesting to see how throughout the long controversy over papal infallibility Newman at times showed a certain

Monsell over the next several days continued to ask for Newman's advice, including advice as to whether he should publish his recent correspondence with Gladstone. Newman was against this, as he made clear in a letter to Monsell on 15 October. He also showed again that he was not entirely happy with Monsell's replies to Gladstone, especially since he felt that Monsell had tried to employ too many arguments instead of keeping to one clear, consistent line. And Gladstone in answering Monsell had changed the ground of his own argument by saying that his remarks in the *Contemporary Review* were not meant to include converts who like Monsell had entered the Roman Church before the definition of papal infallibility. In his letter of 15 October, Newman appeared to have come to the view that responses, public or private, to Gladstone would not be useful. Rather, he suggested to Monsell that a protest from prominent Irish Catholics might be more effective. "But I am led," he wrote, "to throw out a suggestion, which, if feasible in the present serious disunion of Irish MPs etc [over the Home Rule question], you must yourself already have thought of. Could you get a short and telling protest signed by the leading Catholics of Ireland headed by Lord Fingall, Lord Gormanston, Lord OHagan etc etc." But he immediately stepped back from his proposal and, taking refuge in his recurring theme, he said, "Excuse my ignorance of the *lie* of things." Newman concluded this letter with an interesting postscript that shows how much he had begun to look into the Catholic position at the time of the Emancipation. "The strongest thing I have seen on the Ante-Emancipation representations," he told Monsell, "is a passage in an Irish Catechism in which it is said of Papal Infallibility 'This is a Protestant calumny.' "[25]

Even though Newman seems to have come to the conclusion by 15 October that a public reply to Gladstone was not a good idea, his diary shows that he was continuing to attempt his own reply to Gladstone in the third week of October, but that by the end of that week he seems to be on the verge of giving up. Across the pages of his diary from 20 to 23 October,[26] he records his failure and the fact that he has told Monsell that he could not find a way forward. But it would appear that he did not actually tell Monsell of his decision until 4 November. It would also

---

reluctance, if not touchiness, over efforts to show a consistency between his *Essay on Development* and the definition but at other times used it as an explanation of how the definition of papal infallibility had in 1870 entered into the life of the Church.

25. Newman to William Monsell, 15 October 1874, *The Letters and Diaries,* 27:141–42. The catechism was Stephen Keenan's *Controversial Catechism: or Protestantism Refuted and Catholicism Established* (Edinburgh, 1846). See *The Letters and Diaries,* 27:142, n. 2.

26. See Newman "Diary," *The Letters and Diaries,* 27:143 and 143, n. 2. In a letter to Lord Blachford on 25 October, Newman appears pessimistic about his ability to frame an adequate reply to Gladstone: "As to *my* writing, I have not vigour or nerve now to do what, if done, should be done well." *The Letters and Diaries,* 27:145.

appear that Monsell was not even aware of Newman's efforts to frame a reply to Gladstone until late in October.

Despite his rather dissuasive letter to Monsell on 9 October, Newman returned to encouraging him to write a public response to Gladstone in a letter of 27 October marked "confidential." His renewed encouragement to Monsell may have been the result of his own failure to find a way to respond to Gladstone. Nonetheless, it is in the 27 October letter to Monsell that Newman gives the first indication apart from the entries in his diary that he has himself considered a reply to Gladstone. Interestingly, he does not say directly that he has already made an effort, rather he gives the impression that he is planning a reply. "I knew you were well employed," Newman told Monsell in an obvious reference to Monsell's efforts to reply to Gladstone, "but I could not help being impatient. And in my impatience I thought of writing something about Gladstone myself. It would be written theologicè, and therefore not in any way meddle with your own. But I cannot tell whether I shall be *able* to do it—a failure would be terrible—and I do not in consequence consider it begun till it is finished. Therefore I want it kept secret—only one or two of our Fathers know what I am at."[27]

Monsell was overjoyed to learn that Newman was contemplating a reply and he wrote at once to encourage him. "For the last three years," he said, "I have been longing that you should do what you now propose doing."[28]

Gladstone's Expostulation *suddenly opens up for Newman an entirely new possibility for a public reply*

It appeared that Newman was at last close to breaking his long silence. Events over the next few days moved with dizzying speed. Although Newman notes in his diary for 29 October that "about this time Mr. Gladstone's Expostulation came out,"[29] this entry was probably made some days later, as is most likely the case also with the entry of 4 November, "Began to attempt an answer to Mr. G's expostulation."[30] Gladstone's *The Vatican Decrees in Their Bearing on Civil Allegiance: a Political Expostulation* was published on 5 November. Newman had advance word of it in a letter of 2 November from Ambrose Phillipps De Lisle, who had just come from spending several days with Gladstone at his country home, Hawarden Castle.[31] Gladstone had asked De Lisle to send a proof

27. Newman to William Monsell, 27 October 1874, *The Letters and Diaries,* 27:145–46.
28. William Monsell to Newman, 28 October 1874, *The Letters and Diaries,* 27:146, n. 1.
29. Newman "Diary," 29 October 1874, *The Letters and Diaries,* 27:146.
30. Newman "Diary," 4 November 1874, *The Letters and Diaries,* 27:147.
31. Gladstone noted in his diary on 28 October: "I gave him [De Lisle] my MS. to read, & we had a great deal of conversation on it & on kindred topics" (Gladstone, *Diaries,* 29

copy of his *Expostulation* to Newman, but this did not reach Newman until the 6th. However, De Lisle must have given some idea of Gladstone's argument, because when Newman replied on 4 November, agreeing to read Gladstone's pamphlet, he said to De Lisle: "He seems to me to have said some very unjustifiable, cruel things in his Paper, but I fear we shall have great difficulty in making every thing clear and satisfactory to the Protestant mind."[32] Gladstone had arranged for his *Expostulation* to be sent to Newman with the possible purpose of eliciting a response from him. De Lisle had suggested to Gladstone that it would be good to send a copy of his pamphlet to Newman since "it was very desirable in the interests of Peace and Truth that a satisfactory answer should be given from a moderate Point of view."[33]

A further evidence that Newman probably did not see Gladstone's *Expostulation* before 6 November is had from his letter of 4 November to William Monsell. Newman began: "Various concurrent causes have led me this morning to give us [up] my pamphlet. And I think *you* had better wait awhile before you publish."[34] Here Newman was still speaking of his on again-off again efforts to answer publicly Gladstone's "Ritual and Ritualism" and Monsell's determination to do the same. It is evident that Newman was worried that a new wave of anti-Catholicism was building up in England,[35] Gladstone's "parenthesis" in the *Contemporary Review*

October 1874, 8:539). Lord Acton was also at Hawarden in the days just before the publication of Gladstone's *Expostulation*. See ibid., 29 and 30 October 1874, 539. In a letter to Richard Simpson on 4 November, Acton, having just come from Hawarden, wrote: "Objections to detail were attended to, but to all political, spiritual, and other obvious arguments against publication he was deaf." Josef Altholz, Damien McElrath, and James C. Holland, eds. *The Correspondence of Lord Acton and Richard Simpson* (Cambridge: Cambridge University Press, 1975) 3:319. And in a letter to Döllinger on 25 November 1874, Acton said of his visit to Gladstone in late October, "I found De Lisle at Hawarden and stayed for two days. I realised that the manuscript was written with a certain acrimony and made objections in detail." Ignaz von Döllinger, *Briefwechsel 1820–1890* (hereafter cited as *Briefwechsel*), ed. Victor Conzemius (Munich: C. H. Beck'sche Verlagsbuchhandlung, 1971) 3:133. The translation from the German is found in Victor Conzemius, "Acton, Döllinger, and Gladstone: A strange variety of Anti-Infallibilists," James D. Bastable, *Newman and Gladstone: Centennial Essays* (Dublin: Veritas Publications, 1978) 46.

32. Newman to Ambrose De Lisle, 4 November 1874, *The Letters and Diaries*, 27:147–48.

33. Ambrose De Lisle to Newman, 2 November 1874, *The Letters and Diaries*, 27:147, n. 4. In a letter to Lord Granville on 2 November 1874, Gladstone said that he knew his pamphlet would infuriate Manning and his camp but that "the moderate men" would "only be embarrassed if they are too timid to do their duty. My wish is to help them in doing it." Damian McElrath, *The Syllabus of Pius IX* (Louvain: Publications Universitaires de Louvain, 1964) 236, quoting Agatha Ramm, ed., *The Political Correspondence of Mr. Gladstone and Lord Granville, 1868–1876* (London, 1952) 2:458.

34. Newman to William Monsell, 4 November 1874, *The Letters and Diaries*, 27:148.

35. Newman and Monsell were not the only ones who feared a new campaign in England of no-popery in the autumn of 1874. There were even those who feared that some kind of

being just one manifestation of the new mood that Newman sensed. He said to Monsell:

> When the University Bill was thrown out in 1873, the Times gave a hint that, since there was need of a cry, perhaps a party might be formed on the "No-popery." And I don't think they have forgotten it. You know better than I as being a politician, but the unanimity of the House against the unhappy Ritualists seemed to me at the time the first step of a move against *us* and an omen of its success.
>
> Since then, Lord Ripon's conversion must have sunk deeply into the Protestant mind, though there is an affectation of making light of it.
>
> Might they not pass a registration of religious houses, a limitation of their numbers, a visitation of them etc (suffering the Act in its extreme points be a dead letter in Ireland)?
>
> And now I am told, I have not seen it, Ward has come out with a strong attack in the Dublin to the tune of the Unam Sanctam of Boniface the VIII![36]

Newman seeks advice as he struggles to answer Gladstone

That Ward and Gladstone were much on Newman's mind on 4 November is also apparent from a letter he wrote to Dr. Russell of Maynooth. It is unclear in this letter whether Newman is referring to the advance word of Gladstone's arguments in his *Expostulation* that De Lisle had passed on to him. Since on the same day he had told Monsell that he was giving up on any reply to "Ritual and Ritualism," it is unlikely that he would be asking Russell for advice that would aid him in replying to the piece in the *Contemporary Review*. Newman, however, in his letter to Russell makes no direct references to Gladstone or any of his writings. The themes that he takes up with Russell are certainly themes that he was to treat in the *Letter to the Duke of Norfolk*. All that can be safely concluded is that Newman was preoccupied with the theme of papal authority and the civil allegiance of Catholics and wanted to be ready if it became necessary for him to speak publicly on this issue.[37] In his letter to Russell, Newman posed three questions:

---

anti-Catholic legislation would be drawn up, imitating, though in a milder way, Bismarck's Kulturkampf. See Norman, *Anti-Catholicism in Victorian England,* 81. See also Hilary Jenkins, "The Irish Dimension of the British Kulturkampf: 1870–1875," *Journal of Ecclesiastical History,* 30 (July 1979) 361–62, who writes, "Liberal sympathy with the anti-Catholic campaign in the German Empire had been expressed at a meeting in London earlier in 1874 which congratulated William I and his chancellor on their action."

36. Newman to William Monsell, 4 November 1874, *The Letters and Diaries,* 27:148–49. The article by Ward was most likely his "The Sovereignty In Modern States—The Count de Chambord and the Pope's Civil Princedom." See *Dublin Review,* n.s. 23 (July–October 1874) 259–312.

37. Dessain appears to be trying to sort out the confusion of Newman's intentions in the opening days of November when he writes: "Even before he saw the pamphlet Newman

1. Could the Pope, now that he is infallible *teacher,* teach, and thereby make matter of faith, that "he is infallible in his acts as Supreme Legislator"? Fessler[38] says that, whereas he has the Supremacy in four respects, of which teaching and legislation are two, the Vatican Council made a point of declaring his Infallibility only in teaching.

2. Fr. Liberatore speaks to the effect of the "Unam Sanctam." He says that the Pope is sovereign over Kings, that they are his vassals (he does not use the word)—that, did he bid a King to use his material force against another King, that King would be bound to obey him etc etc I see these statements in a Protestant print, but suppose they are correct. For myself I have no difficulty in such saying for I have said the like in my Oxford Sermons forty years ago—but could the Pope make them part of the faith of the Church? I suppose he could.

I will add a third—Could not the Pope, if he pleased, make St. Alfonso's Homo Apostolicus, by the prerogative of his infallibility, part of the faith? I suppose he could.[39]

A third letter of 4 November deals with the same matters that Newman took up that day with Monsell and Russell, especially the latter. Here there is evidence to suggest that Newman had given up any thought of replying to Gladstone because of Ward's piece in the October issue of the *Dublin.* In fact, the questions to Russell may indicate that Newman, having given up on responding to Gladstone, was thinking instead of a reply to Ward, or at least of having something ready when enquiries came to him about Ward's latest assertions. As has already been seen, Ignatius Ryder had set down some thoughts on "Ritual and Ritualism," which Newman had sent to Monsell, and certainly Newman was referring to Ryder in his letter of 27 October to Monsell when he said that only one or two Fathers in the house knew of his efforts to frame a reply to Gladstone's parenthesis. When Newman wrote on 4 November, Ryder was in London where he had gone for the wedding of his sister, Beatrice, to R. H. Froude. The wedding had been suddenly postponed when Froude became ill. "Soon after you went yesterday," Newman told Ryder,

---

realised it would be his duty to answer this renewed denunciation of the mental and moral slavery of Catholics and especially converts." Introduction, *The Letters and Diaries,* 27:xxiii–xxiv.

38. Joseph Fessler, *The True and False Infallibility of the Popes: A Controversial Reply to Dr. Schulte,* trans. Ambrose St. John (London: Burns and Oates, 1875).

39. Newman to Dr. Russell of Maynooth, 4 November 1874, *The Letters and Diaries,* 27:149–50. The *Homo Apostolicus* is St. Alphonsus Liguori's influential manual of moral theology, translated into Latin from the Italian original, *Istruzione e practica per un confessore* (1757).

Macaulay says of this letter, that Newman wrote to Russell "to clear up difficulties in his own mind about the extent of papal infallibility." Macaulay terms these difficulties of Newman, "remarkably strange doubts and anxieties." Ambrose Macaulay, *Dr. Russell of Maynooth* (London: Darton, Longman, and Todd, 1983) 305.

I gave up my pamphlet—and this morning my resolution was confirmed. Here is Ward, I am told, firing away in defence of the Unam Sanctam— then it occurs to me, even though now Gosselin's line is possible, yet surely the Pope might make half a dozen propositions de fide, such as are contained in Fr. Liberatore's work.[40] And then again, though he has as yet only infallibility in teaching, yet might he not, by virtue of that infallibility, declare his legislation unerring and belief in it de fide? A Catholic will say, he cannot unless it be true, but I am thinking of Protestants.[41]

Newman ever alert to all sides of a question had come up with difficulties that he knew would be hard to deal with in a reply intended for Protestants. These difficulties caused him to give up his plan of writing, but he could not get them out of his mind and so wrote on the same day to Dr. Russell of Maynooth. That Ward's article in the *Dublin* may have had a part in his decision not to go on is possible, but from the letter to Ryder it almost appears that Newman was using it as a confirmation after the fact of the wisdom of his decision. All of this is very difficult to sort out. There seems to be no way out of the conflicting evidence, and it may be no more than a case of groping for a solution to suggest that Newman had already written to Monsell, Russell, and Ryder on 4 November before later in the day deciding to answer Gladstone, as he notes in his diary. But the principal reason for Newman's decision to give up on a reply to Gladstone's piece in the *Contemporary Review* may well have been the news that he had received from De Lisle the day before of Gladstone's new pamphlet.

The weeks since his return from holiday had been a time of intense activity and frustration for Newman. He had tried without success over many days to answer Gladstone's comments on Roman Catholic loyalty to the State and he had given counsel to Monsell and others in their own efforts to answer Gladstone. At the same time he kept up a very full correspondence, including the usual necessity of refuting some misrepresentations about his Catholic life that had appeared in print. In this regard he told the editor of the *Echo* on 21 October: "I lose no time in contradicting the report, which was admitted into your columns yesterday, that before now I have asked and been refused admittance into the Society of Jesus."[42] In the first days of October, he had also to deal with the con-

---

40. Matteo Liberatore, a Jesuit, wrote *La Chiesa e Lo Stato,* published in 1871. Jean Gosselin, a French Sulpician, wrote a work dealing with the pope's authority over rulers. He took the position that the pope's authority over sovereigns was a product of history and not a matter of doctrine. His book, written in 1839, was translated into English in 1853 as *The Power of the Pope during the Middle Ages, or an Historical Inquiry into the Origin of the Temporal Power of the Holy See, and the Constitutional Laws of the Middle Ages relating to the Deposition of Sovereigns.* See *The Letters and Diaries,* 27:150, n. 3.

41. Newman to Ignatius Ryder, 4 November 1874, *The Letters and Diaries,* 27:150–51.

42. Newman to the Editor of the *Echo,* 21 October 1874, *The Letters and Diaries,* 27:144.

tinuing and increasingly unhappy position of Döllinger. In a letter to Alfred Plummer on 6 October, Newman spoke almost with anger of Döllinger's present stand, which he had made at the Reunion Conference held at Bonn from 14–16 September.[43]

> As to Dr. Dollinger I shall always think and hear of him with interest, and I may say, with affectionate solicitude—and am obliged to you for telling me about him—but also I must say frankly that what the Papers have lately told me of him has filled me with dismay, and I am prepared to hear any thing, however dismal, of him. He is not an Anglican getting nearer to the truth, but a Catholic receding from it. It is not a yearning after unity which made him turn from Rome, such as has made Liddon[44] and others journey to Bonn. I do not see what is to save him, anymore than Bishop Reinkens,[45] (who has *already* gone the whole hog,) from giving up all Councils and Creeds, and falling back upon a private-judgment induction from the works of St. Irenaeus or St. Cyprian, of Origen or Tertullian, as the ultimate standard of Christian Truth. And then, since such a standard is sure to be no standing point, he must, if he lives long enough, give up dogma altogether, or at least his party must (as Bishop R. already) and then how long will they be separate from Renan?"

And Newman concluded, "Excuse this polemical letter, but Dr. Dollinger forces me to write it."[46]

43. The conference, the inspiration principally of the Old Catholics, brought together Anglicans and Orthodox Christians with a view to discussing Church unity. Döllinger was the guiding force at the conference. See the description of the first Bonn conference in Alfred Plummer, *Conversations With Dr. Döllinger 1870–1890,* intro. and notes by Robrecht Boudens, with the collaboration of Leo Kenis (Leuven: University Press, 1985) 99–116. Gladstone, though invited, did not attend, but the Congress's effects on his writings against the Vatican Council in the months ahead cannot be underestimated. It is clear, however, that "Ritual and Ritualism" was written before the Congress, since Gladstone notes in his diary on 10 September, "Corrected revise of Art. on Ritualism." *The Gladstone Diaries,* 10 September 1874, 8:524.

44. H. P. Liddon, an Anglican of the High Church party, who attended the Reunion Conference.

45. Joseph Hubert Reinkens was the former rector of the University of Breslau. He was excommunicated by the Roman Catholic Church in 1872, and was consecrated as the first bishop of the Old Catholic Church the following year.

46. Newman to Alfred Plummer, 6 October 1874, *The Letters and Diaries,* 27:128–29. The position of Döllinger was to play a large part in the ensuing controversy, although Döllinger did not, as some thought at the time, have a direct part in Gladstone's *Expostulation.* This is clear from Gladstone's letter to Döllinger of 1 November 1874, in which he writes: "Had the facts been before me when I was in Munich, I should have desired to consult you largely." *Correspondence on Church and Religion of William Ewart Gladstone,* selected and arranged by D. C. Lathbury (New York: The Macmillan Company, 1910) 2:59. But Gladstone, after seeing Döllinger in Munich in the early part of September, came away newly-moved by his solitary stand. In a letter to his wife, written at this time, Gladstone said: " . . . and it makes my blood run cold to think of his [Döllinger] being excommunicated

On 6 November, Newman, having looked over the draft of Gladstone's pamphlet that De Lisle had sent him, immediately returned it. "I feel your kindness," he said "in obtaining for me a sight of Mr. Gladstone's powerful Pamphlet. . . ." Newman went on, "I am not at all sorry that he is publishing such an expostulation as this is; it must turn to good. Today's papers say that Archbishop Manning is going to have a great meeting, and to bind us all to certain propositions. I cannot think it possible that at such a meeting he can ignore Mr. Gladstone's demand upon him for an expression of civil allegiance, or that he will not notice Mr. Gladstone's appeal to the declaration on that point of the English and Irish Bishops in 1826."

In his letter of 4 November to De Lisle, Newman had reacted to Gladstone's *Expostulation* on the basis of what De Lisle had told him. Now, after reading it, he gave his first direct comments:

> For myself, I consider he is misled in his interpretation of the ecclesiastical acts of 1870 by judging of the wording by the rules of ordinary language. Theological language, like legal, is scientific, and cannot be understood without the knowledge of long precedent and tradition, nor without the comments of theologians. Such comments time alone can give us. Even now Bishop Fessler has toned down the newspaper interpretations (Catholic and Protestant) of the words of the Council, without any hint from the Council itself to sanction him in doing so. To give an instance of what I mean: —Broad statements, standing by themselves, are open to large exceptions;— thus, St. Cyprian and St. Augustine, as the succession of great ecclesiastical authorities since, have said "Out of the Church is no salvation;" yet Pius the IX, and perhaps he the first Pope, has made in addition the large exception to that principle, of invincible ignorance. Obedience to the Pope in like manner has, in the writings of theologians, important limitations.

Newman concluded, "But the subject is too large for a letter."[47] De Lisle showed Newman's letter to Gladstone. It was also seen by Lord Acton, who on account of it wrote to Newman for the first time in a long while.

Newman already convinced that he must reply to Gladstone is urged to the task by his friends

The scene was at last set. Most of the players were in place—Monsell, De Lisle, Ryder, Ward and Manning, Gladstone, Döllinger, and Acton.

---

in his venerable but, thank God, hale and strong old age." Quoted in Morley, *The Life of William Ewart Gladstone,* 2:513.

Döllinger did have a direct role in the preparation of Gladstone's *Vaticanism,* issued late in February 1875.

47. Newman to Ambrose De Lisle, 6 November 1874, *The Letters and Diaries,* 27:152–53. Newman was to give a prominent part to the role of the *Schola Theologorum* in the *Letter to the Duke of Norfolk.*

The moment had come for Newman to take the part that his friends, and even his critics, had been expecting him to take over the past four years. He was finally ready. On the following day, 7 November, Newman wrote to Monsell, who, having received Newman's letter of the 4th, was deeply disappointed that Newman was giving up on a reply to "Ritual and Ritualism." "Your letter has just come," Newman told Monsell in reply. "I *could not* have answered Gladstone's parenthetic, sweeping declamation. It had no points. And Ireland became a great difficulty—But his today's pamphlet, I can answer—at least I shall try and will tell you when I fail, or else go to press."[48] That Newman went immediately to work on a reply to Gladstone is evident from an entry in his diary on 9 November. The suggestion of confidence in his letter to Monsell three days previously is, however, absent. Newman recorded: "[began to attempt an answer to Mr. Gladstone's expostulation] but in vain   plucking every morning what I had done the day before."[49]

The pressure on Newman to reply to Gladstone was immediate and intense, as is shown in a letter of 9 November from Lady Georgiana Fullerton.[50] When Newman replied to her on the next day, it is evident that he was feeling this pressure and that it was having its effect in keeping him from carrying forward his first determination to reply, even the conviction that he could. Newman told Lady Fullerton:

> I have been very touched, and I may say frightened too, by your and Mr. Fullerton's joint request.
>
> It is not as if I were ten years younger—but, as old men throw about their limbs or throw out their voice, so I, though I may have thoughts in my mind, and feel as if I had something to say, have the greatest difficulty in saying it.
>
> Then in this case the Papers seem almost to have superseded the necessity of writing against Mr. Gladstone by their own remarks, and one is tempted to say Let well alone, especially since it is painful to write against such a man.
>
> And I have heard too that our Bishop is going to write, and I should not like, as it were, to jostle with him.[51]
>
> But my great difficulty would be my little knowledge of the world at large, Protestant and Catholic. I have my own answers to Mr. Gladstone, which satisfy myself, but I have no confidence in my ability to see what

---

48. Newman to William Monsell, 7 November 1874, *The Letters and Diaries,* 27:153.

49. Newman "Diary," 9 November 1874, *The Letters and Diaries,* 27:155.

50. Lady Fullerton was moved to write to Newman after reading Lord Acton's provocative and, to many Catholics, traitorous letter in *The Times* the same day.

51. Ullathorne wrote two replies to Gladstone's *Expostulation.* The first in the form of a pastoral letter, "The Döllingerites, Mr. Gladstone, and the Apostates from the Faith," appeared in November 1874; the second, "Mr. Gladstone's *Expostulation* Unravelled," appeared in January 1875.

would satisfy others—and then comes the most anxious thought that unless I really succeed, I shall do the Catholic cause harm. A failure would be deplorable—Protestants would say, Now we know all that can be said—and we see how little that is.

You are so good as to speak of prayers for me. If I might ask for some, my intention would be this—that I might write, if it was my duty—but not write if I was to fail in it.[52]

Newman avoids in this letter any indication that he is actually at work on a reply. This he would keep a close secret, apart from Monsell, members of the Oratory community, and a handful of others, until he had finished the eventual reply in late December. The letter to Lady Fullerton is notable for three points it makes. First, it is clear that Newman had no doubt that whoever else replied from the Catholic side, his would beget the most expectation. Second, Newman was to say in the weeks ahead, as he had already to Monsell in October, that his innocence of worldly affairs, of the political world especially, made it difficult to reply to someone like Gladstone who had spent his life in politics. And finally, Newman would say over and over again that he was simply too old to undertake such a task, or at least to carry it through to completion. There is no doubt that he worried about the toll such an effort would take on his health.

It is clear that the pressure on Newman was great. Gladstone's pamphlet was an immediate sensation. Before the year was out 145,000 copies were in print.[53] Though the newspapers were somewhat critical,[54] the general populace greeted Gladstone's pamphlet with enthusiasm.[55] Leading members of the Catholic community believed that a fully elaborated re-

52. Newman to Lady Georgiana Fullerton, 10 November 1874, *The Letters and Diaries,* 27:155-56.

53. Gladstone was obviously elated by the success of his pamphlet. He noted in his diary for 27 November, "Today Mr. Murray reports 52,000 sold: 20,500 more printed. Every post brings me a mass of general reading . . . : and all my time is absorbed. But the subject is well worth the pains." *The Gladstone Diaries,* 27 November 1874, 8:546. The *Month* in its January 1875 issue remarked that Gladstone's *Expostulation* had sold more copies than the serialised works of Dickens. See p. 14. There is evidence to suggest that Gladstone's writings against the Vatican Council gave him more royalties than any of his previous publications. See "Introduction," H.C.G. Matthew, ed., *The Gladstone Diaries* (Oxford: The Clarendon Press, 1986) 9:lxxxv.

54. Norman sums up the reaction of the newspapers with two comments: "The English press, taken as a whole, was certainly not wildly in favour of Gladstone's publication," and "in Ireland the press was almost unanimously hostile." Norman *Anti-Catholicism in Victorian England,* 96.

55. A few cautionary notes must be made on this point. The sensation was probably more immediate than lasting, a topic for the moment that engaged the popular attention in the closing weeks of 1874 and the first weeks of the new year. The number of pamphlets sold supports the sensational effect of Gladstone's charge, but numbers sold does not of course equate with numbers read. By the time Newman's response came out in January,

sponse from the Catholic side was imperative, and many of these same Catholics believed that Newman was the only one who could do it. When Newman wrote to Ambrose De Lisle on 15 November, it was clear that De Lisle was one of those expecting that Newman would reply to Gladstone, but Newman did not offer him much encouragement. "Excuse a short letter," he said. "You know it won't do to write unless one writes *well*. It would do more harm than good. I will write if I can, but I am not sure I can. And any how, if I write, I am sure kind friends will expect too much of me and will be disappointed. I could not write any thing long.''[56] In his reply the following day, De Lisle showed that not only he but Gladstone also was looking forward to Newman's reply. "I hear constantly from Mr. Gladstone," De Lisle reported, "and I am sure his object is truth and justice. He too is looking forward earnestly to what you have to say on this very important subject.''[57] On the same day that De Lisle wrote, Newman responded to a request from Bishop Brown of Newport that he write a response to Gladstone's *Expostulation*. Newman answered: "I was much flattered by your letter this morning—but I fear I am too old to undertake what you wish me to do. It ought to be done well, if done at all.''[58] But Brown was persistent and in a reply to Newman written the following day he suggested that another member of the Oratory community might write the actual reply, but with assistance from Newman. And then in a telling comment, he added, "What is taking place would not now be afflicting religion, had your sentiments, in which I fully concurred, been allowed the consideration by the Vatican Council which they merited.''[59]

---

the controversy was already moving from a popular one to what E. R. Norman has called "a wholly theoretical one" whose "participants were mostly priests and journalists." Norman, *Anti-Catholicism in Victorian England*, 97. Arnstein makes the same point when he writes: "The most immediate repercussions of Gladstone's pamphlet proved to be literary. . . .'' Arnstein, *Protestant Versus Catholic*, 194.

John Morley in his early but still solidly reliable biography of Gladstone treats the reaction to the *Expostulation* in England well when he writes: "Whether the excitement in the country was more than superficial; whether most readers fathomed the deep issues as they stood, not between catholic and protestant, but between catholic and catholic within the fold; whether in fastening upon the civil allegiance of English Romanists Mr. Gladstone took the true point against Vaticanism—these are questions that we need not here discuss." "But here, as always," Morley continues, "he was a man of action, and wrote for a specific though perhaps fugitive purpose." Morley, *Life of Gladstone*, 2:518 and 519.

56. Newman to Ambrose De Lisle, 15 November 1874, *The Letters and Diaries*, 27:156.

57. Ambrose De Lisle to Newman, 16 November 1874, *The Letters and Diaries*, 27:156, n. 3.

58. Newman to Bishop Brown of Newport, 16 November 1874, *The Letters and Diaries*, 27:156.

59. Bishop Brown of Newport to Newman, 17 November 1874, *The Letters and Diaries*, 27:157, n. 1.

In the same week Newman received a letter that was to play a very prominent part in his decision to reply to Gladstone. It was from the young Duke of Norfolk. Norfolk had already spoken to Father Ambrose St. John to the effect that he hoped that Newman would reply. At that time he had not yet had the chance to read Gladstone's full text. When he had, he wrote a long letter directly to Newman on 15 November. "I cannot keep myself from writing to you about Gladstone's pamphlet," he began. "On my journey down here . . . ," Norfolk, who was on his way to France, continued,

> I have read it through at my leisure and I am more fully impressed with the feeling that an immense amount of good would be done if you would write an article in reply.
>
> It is not merely that an article coming from you would be, you must forgive my saying this, so very much better in itself than one coming from anybody else but it will be read by an immeasurably larger number of people will have more weight with them and will be more readily acquiesced in by them. . . .
>
> What I feel myself is that there are in all probability many in England outside the Church who if they could be got to see that in a way very different from that which he means Gladstone is in a measure right and that it is quite true that God has given us his Church to teach and guide us and that as the teaching and guidance is from Him it must be obeyed and followed even if necessary at the cost of our national feelings, and if it could be shown them at the same time how their proper loyalty and patriotism is not impaired but made sacred by their accepting and acting up to this belief, I feel tolerably sure that they would hail such a ray of light in their present darkness. . . .
>
> I hope that you will not think that I am taking a great liberty in writing all this. I would not have written but that I heard every one hoping for an answer from you and saying that it was from you that the answer should come and now that I have read the pamphlet I feel it myself even stronger than before.[60]

Newman waited a week before replying, most likely because when he first received the Duke's letter he still had great doubts about his ability to complete a reply. A week later this had changed, and in fact Newman felt confident enough on 22 November to tell Norfolk that he was attempting to write a reply. Thus the Duke of Norfolk was taken into that circle of friends who actually knew that Newman was working on a response to Gladstone. In his reply to Norfolk marked "confidential," Newman said:

> Father Ambrose gave me your message. I am acting upon it. A number of friends wrote to me as you did,—but it is the toughest job I ever had,

and I have a great anxiety lest after all, when it is done, it should not do its work.

What you say is *very* good and true, and it pleased me very much to read it—I wish I could do it in the way you sketch out—I doubt if I can. I shall not conceal any thing—and think with you that some things he says are true—and are good, though in a different sense from what he means, but you must recollect things are taking a political turn, and I fear men would say, if I spoke as I should like, We don't want your preaching, it is quite enough for us you cannot contradict Gladstone.

Pray don't tell any one that I am writing. I might get into great embarassment [sic], if the Pope knew it.[61] My age is an excuse always, when the question is asked—and certainly I feel that a more vigorous man would be better for the work. You must give me your prayers.[62]

And besides the urging of friends, there was another kind of pressure, even more intense—public expectation aroused by the newspapers. In the 14 November issue of the London *Echo*, the lead article, following a reply to Gladstone that had just come out from Monsignor Thomas Capel,[63] said: "We take away the impression that if Mr. Gladstone's pamphlet is to be answered at all, it can only be by John Henry Newman."[64] It is apparent from a letter that Newman wrote to Arthur Arnold, the editor of the *Echo,* on 19 November that Arnold had approached Newman about his agreeing to a serialised response to Gladstone that would appear in the pages of the *Echo*. Newman responded: "I am sorry to say that the difficulty I feel in writing at all in answer to Mr. Gladstone tells still more against availing myself of your flattering offer to receive what I might write into your columns. It is impossible to answer him briefly—he has touched on so many subjects, none of which ought to be shirked. And in a daily Paper they never would be got through. Not to say, that an answer ought to be a whole—and not published in small advances, which have to be read in connection with each other."[65] Another public reference at this time to a possible reply to Gladstone from Newman was made in a far more negative and troubling way. In its issue of 16 November,

61. Norfolk was then in France on his way to Rome. See *The Letters and Diaries,* 27:159, n. 1. It is not clear why Newman feared the pope's knowing of his effort to respond to Gladstone. It is perhaps one more evidence of Newman's fear of ecclesiastical censure if he expressed his full views on the definition of 1870.

62. Newman to Duke of Norfolk, 22 November 1874, The Letters and Diaries, 27:158–59.

63. A pamphlet by Capel, "Reply to Right Hon. W. E. Gladstone's Political Expostulation," was published in December. He also wrote several letters to *The Times* in November, and one of these was undoubtedly the cause of the comment in the 14 November issue of the *Echo*. Capel was the rector of Manning's ill-fated Catholic University in Kensington. He was dismissed by Manning after several personal and financial scandals, and ended his days as a priest in California where he died in 1911.

64. The *Echo,* 14 November 1874, *The Letters and Diaries,* 27:157, n. 2.

65. Newman to Arthur Arnold, 19 November 1874, *The Letters and Diaries,* 27:157.

the *Liverpool Daily Post* made a statement that went well beyond the present matter and whether Newman would be drawn into it:

> There was an expection [sic] in some quarters that Dr. J. H. Newman would interfere in the controversy which Mr. Gladstone's pamphlet has raised, but I have reason to believe that there is no likelihood of his being drawn into it. He never disguised his aversion to the proclamation of the doctrine of Infallibility, and the Ultramontane party know that he is but a half-hearted believer in their opinions. It is in fact understood that at one time he was on the point of uniting with Dr. Dollinger and his party, and that it required the earnest persuasions of several members of the Roman Catholic Episcopate to prevent him taking that step.[66]

One can only speculate about the pressure that Newman must have felt from such a statement, but it is likely that it was strong. The *Liverpool Daily Post* had added a new element to his quandary—if he did not answer Gladstone, some sections of the Catholic Church in England would conclude that Newman was in substantial agreement with him, and precisely because he was not wholehearted in his acceptance of the definition of papal infallibility. In his reply to the *Liverpool Daily Post* of 19 November,[67] Newman avoided any mention of Gladstone and his pamphlet. He spoke directly and bluntly to one point only:

> I beg you to do me the favour of allowing me to contradict absolutely the assertion of one of your correspondents that "at one time I was on the point of uniting with Dr. Dollinger and his party, and that it required the earnest persuasions of several members of the Roman Catholic Episcopate to prevent me from taking that step."
>
> This statement, in both its clauses, and from beginning to end, is utterly and ridiculously false.
>
> And it is a crime in an anonymous writer to make allegations against another, of a nature to damage him in the eyes of his brethren, without a tittle of evidence to bear them out.[68]

It is clear from Newman's correspondence during the first three weeks of November that the controversy caused by Gladstone and his possible role in it was taking up most of his time. That he was anxious and frustrated is evident from his letters and his diary entries. Finally on 23 November a sudden change occurred. That morning, while saying the Mass of the feast of St. Clement, he prayed specifically for his efforts to reply to

---

66. *Liverpool Daily Post*, 16 November 1874, *The Letters and Diaries*, 27:157, n. 3.
67. Published 21 November.
68. Newman to the Editor of *The Liverpool Daily Post*, 19 November 1874, *The Letters and Diaries*, 27:157–58. It is interesting to note that while avoiding any mention of Gladstone, Newman also passed over the references to his "aversion" to the definition and the estimate of Ultramontanes of his views on it.

Gladstone.[69] And later that day it would appear that he began at last to reply in earnest. In his diary he noted, "Monday 23 November 1874 [plucking every morning what I had done the day before] till today, when I suddenly began my first section (Introductory Remarks)."[70]

Newman after several vain attempts at last conceives a plan that he will carry through to completion

Not surprisingly, Newman first announced his success to Monsell. Though there was still a note of defeat, there was also a hint of confidence.

> You must be very impatient to hear from me. You may be sure, however, I should have written, had I any thing to say. For 5 or 6 weeks I have been at it for perhaps 5 or 6 hours a day, and have produced nothing. I have written quires, but not pleased myself and begun again. Gladstone is so rambling and slovenly, it is so difficult to follow him with any logical exactness. I can't get a plan. Today I have begun on a new arrangement of matter (for matter I have more than enough) and at present I am satisfied with it—but my great fear is that in two or three days I shall see it won't do. I ought to be in society and hear what people say and how they take the pamphlet. It is no good doing it, if it is not readable. I am fidgetty lest you should not like what I say about the University Bill, and about Ireland.

And mention of Ireland led Newman to think back to another anxious time he had had twenty-two years before: "Before now, I have been quite as much posed, and lost even more time—specially with my Dublin Lectures—and in both cases for the same reason, that I was addressing classes etc whom I don't know. I am not a politician."[71] Monsell was immediately reassuring. "I am grieved," he wrote to Newman on 25 November, "to hear that your great and good work is giving you so much trouble. Pray do not fear Irish University questions, or difficulty of appreciating

---

69. See Newman to Lady Georgiana Fullerton, 18 December 1874, *The Letters and Diaries,* 27:176, and Newman to William Monsell, 31 December 1874, *The Letters and Diaries,* 27:180.

70. Newman "Diary," 23 November 1874, *The Letters and Diaries,* 27:159. A similar note appears in the diary for 29 November. See Newman "Diary," 29 November 1874, *The Letters and Diaries,* 27:162. It would appear that during this period Newman filled in some diary entries at a later time. He himself clearly took 23 November as his real starting point for the *Letter to the Duke of Norfolk.* It is possible that the twenty-third was the day that he was at last sure of his plan for his first section and that six days later he actually began to fill it out in writing. This would also appear to be borne out by the letter to Monsell on 23 November. A further complication comes from Newman's sure tone about his effort in his letter to Norfolk on 22 November.

71. Newman to William Monsell, 23 November 1874, *The Letters and Diaries,* 27:159.

the views of those you don't mix with. Very competent judges, such as John O'Hagan,[72] think your Irish works the best you ever produced."[73]

For several days there was almost a daily correspondence between Newman and Monsell as Newman's work gathered purpose and speed and as he looked to Monsell for help in the area of politics where he felt so inadequate. In a brief letter of 24 November, Newman posed two questions to Monsell. His first question was "Did the British Government in Pitt's time [1801, the year of the Legislative Union of Great Britain and Ireland] or in Peel's [1829, the year of the Catholic Emancipation Bill], or any other, *apply direct* to Rome or to any authorised representative of Rome, on the question of Infallibility, as it did to Bishop Doyle etc." And second, "Are the Catholics allowed to present themselves by Delegacies to the Throne, i.e. the presence of the Sovereign, as the Three Denominations [Presbyterians, Baptists, and Congregationalists] are, and the Quakers?"[74] Monsell replied two days later. "The British Government," he wrote, "never applied to Dr. Doyle on the subject of Papal Infallibility. His utterances on the subject were 1st his evidence before the Committee of Lords and Commons in 1824–1825. 2ndly His letters to Lord Liverpool. . . . Mr. Pitt did not so far as I know even ask any question on the subject. He did address three questions to the Catholic universities of Europe—not to Rome. None of those questions had reference to Papal infallibility."[75] Newman wanted to be certain that he was on solid ground. In a letter of 27 November, he largely repeated his earlier question to Monsell, whether the British government in the time of Pitt or Peel had made "*direct* application" to Rome "to ascertain the state of things on the *Pope's Infallibility*.'"[76]

Though he had a plan for going on and was hard at work on it, a week later Newman was still worrying over whether the English government at the end of the eighteenth century or in the late 1820s had sought some assurance from the Holy See that the question of papal infallibility was not a matter of Church doctrine. For the third time in a matter of days he wrote to Monsell on this point:

. . . what I want to know is, whether either in Pitt's time or Peel's there was any *direct* application to, or negociation with the Pope or with any for-

72. A respected Irish lawyer, who as a young man had served under Newman on the faculty of the Catholic University.
73. William Monsell to Newman, 25 November 1874, *The Letters and Diaries,* 27:159, n. 4.
74. Newman to William Monsell, 24 November 1874, *The Letters and Diaries,* 27:159–60.
75. William Monsell to Newman, 26 November 1874, *The Letters and Diaries,* 27:160, n. 1.
76. Newman to William Monsell, 27 November 1874, *The Letters and Diaries,* 27:161.

mal representative of his, as there was with the foreign Universities, and with Bishop Doyle.

I mean can I say, "Why did you go to Dr. Doyle? Why didn't you go to the Pope? If you had gone to headquarters,[77] *he* would have told you that he could not pledge himself that the dogma of Infallibility would never be defined, or on the other hand he would have been bound by his engagement, had he pledged himself.[78]

Monsell, with just the slightest hint of impatience, answered Newman the next day. He said: "So far as I know, and I have diligently enquired, neither in Pitts or Peels[sic] time was there any direct application to or negotiation with the Pope or any formal representative of his."[79]

On the last two days of November, Newman responded to further requests that he answer Gladstone by saying that the task was beyond him. He was still not at all ready to make public the fact that he was hard at work on a reply. On 2 December, he had his first section ready for the printer. He sent it off to B. M. Pickering, who had served as his publisher since 1873. Newman took extra precautions to ensure that the fact he was writing would not get out prematurely:

I hope to send you five packets of copy tomorrow evening (Thursday).

You will see, the corrections are in my handwriting. Perhaps it would be well not to have a Catholic printer.

I should have my name on the title page, but I don't want it known that I am writing. Till I finish, I don't consider I am sure to publish—but I am more sure than I was a week ago.

Would a week before publication be sufficient for advertising?

I shall do my best to keep the Press supplied with copy.[80]

That Newman was at last confident of finishing his project was evident in a letter he wrote the next day to the Duke of Norfolk. The letter was very brief, an evidence that Newman was absorbed in his task. "Will you let my Pamphlet take the shape of a letter addressed to you?" And there was a postscript, "I wish I could be quick about it."[81] That Newman was heavily engaged in his task is also apparent from two letters that he wrote on 4 December. The first, written to Malcolm MacColl, read only, "Don't think me rude if I don't write an answer to your letter at

77. Newman was to repeat this point, using the word "headquarters" in the *Letter to the Duke of Norfolk*. Gladstone seized on this word in his *Vaticanism* and charged Newman with having given the game away by showing that the only authentic answer would have had to come from Rome.

78. Newman to William Monsell, 6 December 1874, *The Letters and Diaries*, 27:165.

79. William Monsell to Newman, 7 December 1874, *The Letters and Diaries*, 27:165, n. 4.

80. Newman to B. M. Pickering, 2 December 1874, *The Letters and Diaries*, 27:163.

81. Newman to Duke of Norfolk, 3 December 1874, *The Letters and Diaries*, 27:164.

once. I am more busy than I have been for ten years, and I am not sure that my health will stand it."[82] And to John Shortland, a convert priest of the diocese of Plymouth, Newman, after a brief letter of thanks for a book that Shortland had promised to send him, added the following postscript: "Do you never come this way? I am nearly always here and at leisure, tho' at this moment I am most seriously busy."[83] And in the midst of all this feverish activity, it appears that Newman was finding it difficult to write because of a sprained thumb.[84]

Acton caught up in difficulties with Manning over Acton's public replies to Gladstone asks Newman's help

But despite his absorption in the work of responding to Gladstone and his anxiety over it, there were still matters that Newman could not set aside or deal with hurriedly. In the first week of December, he was drawn into a long correspondence with Lord Acton. The reason for that correspondence was also Gladstone's *Expostulation*. Acton, however, was not approaching Newman in an effort to encourage him to reply to Gladstone. Rather, he was seeking advice from Newman on the consequences of the public replies that he had himself made to Gladstone in the pages of *The Times*. Acton's first letter to *The Times* appeared on 9 November. With reference to Gladstone's statements about the position of the Irish and English bishops prior to the Emancipation Act, Acton said: "Your indictment would be more just if it was more complete. If you pursue the inquiry further, you will find graver matter than all you have enumerated, established by higher and more ancient authority than the bishops half-a-century ago. And then I think you will admit that your Catholic countrymen cannot fairly be called on to account for every particle of a system which has never come before them in its integrity, or for opinions whose existence among divines they would be exceedingly reluctant to believe." Acton then gave examples from papal history of instances where popes had exceeded their authority with regard to the state. He also asserted that Archbishop Fénelon had only outwardly accepted the pope's authority when in 1699 Pope Innocent XII condemned certain sections of Fénelon's *Explications des maximes des saints*. And bringing the matter from the past to the present, he said: "It is not the unpropitious times only, but the very nature of things, that protect Catholicism from the consequences of some theories that have grown up within it."[85] In a second letter published in *The Times* on 24 November, Acton concluded by saying:

82. Newman to Malcolm MacColl, 4 December 1874, *The Letters and Diaries,* 27:164.
83. Newman to John Shortland, 4 December 1874, *The Letters and Diaries,* 27:165.
84. Ibid.
85. Acton's first letter to *The Times* is printed in *The Vatican Decrees In Their Bearing on Civil Allegiance: A Political Expostulation by the Right Hon. W. E. Gladstone, M.P.*

I know that there are some whose feelings of reverence and love, are, un-happily, wounded by what I have said. I entreat them to remember how little would be gained if all that came within the scope of my argument could be swept out of existence—to ask themselves seriously the question whether the laws of the Inquisition are or are not a scandal and a sorrow to their souls. It would be well if men had never fallen into the error of suppressing truth and encouraging error for the better security of religion. Our Church stands, and our faith should stand, not on the virtues of men, but on the surer ground of an institution and a guidance that are divine. Therefore I rest unshaken in the belief that nothing which the inmost depths of history shall disclose in time to come can ever bring to Catholics just cause of shame or fear. I should dishonour and betray the Church if I entertained a suspicion that the evidences of religion could be weakened or the authority of Councils sapped by a knowledge of the facts with which I have been dealing, or of others which are not less grievous or less certain because they remain untold.[86]

The letters that Acton wrote to *The Times* made his position public. It is evident from Acton's letter of 4 December to Newman that Manning was not happy with Acton's statements and began to press him on the question of whether he did in fact accept the definition of 1870. Manning

---

With the Replies of Archbishop Manning and Lord Acton (New York: D. Appleton and Company, 1874) 78–84.

86. Lord Acton to *The Times,* 21 November 1874, *The Letters and Diaries,* 27:166, n. 2. Acton's main point in answer to Gladstone was that popes had tried to interfere with the civil allegiance of Catholics in the past but that Catholics, especially English Catholics, had ignored such papal directives. They had acted thus before the council. They would continue to do so. The council had changed nothing.

Acton's primary concern was with the history of the papacy and what he believed to be unwarranted, even immoral, political acts on the part of various popes. These he called Ultramontanism. Intent on a historical exposition, Acton touched the definition of infallibility only obliquely. He professed to be a layman neither interested nor versed in theological precision. Acton, according to Conzemius, had a "moral, non-theological view of infallibility." "Acton, Döllinger, and Gladstone: A strange variety of Anti-Infallibilists," James D. Bastable, ed., *Newman and Gladstone: Centennial Essays* (Dublin: Veritas Publications, 1978) 50.

Acton's letters to *The Times* caused a furor among Catholics nearly as great as Gladstone's *Expostulation.* Not only was Manning disturbed but leading moderate and liberal Catholics as well. Ambrose De Lisle in a letter to Gladstone on 14 November 1874 said: "If Lord Acton had announced his secession from the Barque of Peter, I should understand the line he is taking better than I do." Purcell and De Lisle, *De Lisle,* 92. Richard Simpson in a letter to Acton on the day the letter was published reported the reaction of the wife of Peter Le Page Renouf. "Mrs. Renouf," he wrote, "protests against your letter—It is, she says, as if you were waiting to say all the disagreeable things you could against the Vatican decrees. . . ." *The Correspondence of Lord Acton and Richard Simpson,* 3:319. And Lady Georgiana Fullerton in a letter to Newman on 9 November, already mentioned, said: "This morning I have read poor Acton's letter in *The Times.* It has made me very unhappy and I thank God with all my heart that his mother is not alive to witness his betrayal of the Church." Quoted in MacDougall, *The Acton-Newman Relations,* 132.

maintained that even though Acton did not live in his diocese, he was obliged to respond to him since the letters to *The Times* had been published
in the Archdiocese of Westminster and had given scandal there.[87] Acton
for reasons that are not entirely clear turned to Newman for advice on
how to answer Manning and his own bishop, James Brown of Shrewsbury, who had also asked Acton for a clarification of his views on the
definition of 1870. In his long letter of 4 December, Acton told Newman:

> I shall give myself a day or two to answer. I will try to explain my position
> to you, if I may do so without presuming too much. The decrees have never
> been a difficulty to me not because I have examined them and found that
> they approved themselves to my judgment, but because, be they what they
> may, I am sure it will be all right, and if it is not evidently all right now,
> that is not my business. I take it that no interpretation holds that it is in-
> consistent with tradition, and with former decrees. And if one does not see
> how the new and the old can be reconciled, time will show it, and the new
> will be digested and assimilated, and will be worked into what was there
> before. I feel no impulse to do this as well as I can for my own satisfaction,
> or to choose an interpreter. Indeed I have felt no more curiosity to read
> these decrees through than those of Trent, and know about them both only
> casually, very imperfectly, and partly at second hand. Therefore, just as
> I have kept aloof from the Germans, who think that they ought to raise
> their voice and hand against the Council, I have gone through no process
> of study, comprehension and argument with respect to the several proposi-
> tions it lays down. I take them in the raw state, without the least resistance,
> subject to the process they have to go through, and to the law of interpreta-
> tion which upholds the continuity and consistency of doctrine; but I do not
> guess what the process will effect, and do not attempt to apply the law my-
> self. I am in the same position with regard to hundreds of canons of former
> Councils; and I daresay you know how little most of us, native Catholics,
> care to master details.
>
> If therefore I am asked whether I accept the decrees with definite un-
> derstanding and inward conviction of their truth, I cannot say yes or no.
> But this is the question which the Archbishop—taking his letter [to Acton]
> and pastoral together[88]—wants an answer to. I certainly cannot satisfy him.

87. Manning wrote seeking Ullathorne's advice the day Acton's first letter appeared
in *The Times*. "Is it possible," he asked "for the Bishop of Shrewsbury [the diocese in which
Acton had his official residence] and myself to allow Lord Acton's letter in *The Times* of
to-day to go unnoticed?" Shane Leslie, *Henry Edward Manning: His Life and Labours*
(London: Burns, Oates, and Washbourne, Ltd., 1921) 247. And when Manning remained
dissatisfied with letters that he received from Acton concerning Acton's acceptance of the
council, he sought further advice from Ullathorne: "Can I in conscience allow him to receive the Sacraments in London?" Ibid., 7 December 1874, 232.

88. Manning had written a pastoral letter on the obligation of Catholics to accept the
definitions of the Immaculate Conception and papal infallibility. The letter had been read
in all the churches of the archdiocese on 29 November 1874. It read in part: "Events which

I hope you will understand that, in falling under his censures, I act from no spirit of revolt, from no indifference, and from no false shame. But I cannot accept his tests and canons of dogmatic development and interpretation, and must decline to give him the only answer that will content him, as it would, in my lips, be a lie.

I have tried to avoid the crisis as long as I could, and have given every opening I could find for the archbishop to content himself. It is quite natural that he, on the other hand, should force on a catastrophe. In the last ten years I have collected a very considerable mass of historical materials, and I must try to avail myself of them. At every step I should be sure to encounter the same difficulties as now and I cannot make any concession to danger without treason.

Acton concluded by asking Newman's advice and even suggesting a visit to Newman at the Oratory. Acton summed up his long letter by putting his difficulty in the form of a question: "Should you think ill, spiritually, of a penitent refused the sacraments without having denied or even disbelieved the Decrees?"[89]

It would appear that Newman told Acton that it would not be possible to have a face to face conversation, but Newman did reply to Acton with at least two letters written around 5 or 6 December. Unfortunately we have only Acton's replies. Acton expressed his gratitude to Newman, but it is evident that he did not find his replies altogether helpful. In a letter of 7 December to Newman, Acton said: "My present impression is that 'to adhere to the doctrines' implies belief in them. No bishop that I have consulted has ever told me that it would be right to go as far as that. They say the decrees are legitimate, but they do not admit that they are true."[90] And in a letter to Newman two days later, Acton, referring to his 9 Novem-

---

unhappily are notorious induce us to make known to the faithful, lest any should be misled by the words or example of one or two who still profess to be Catholic, that whosoever does not in his heart receive and believe the doctrine of the Immaculate Conception and the doctrine of the infallibility of the Vicar of Jesus Christ, as they have been defined by the supreme authority of the Church, does by that very fact cease to be a Catholic." *Tablet,* n.s. 12, 5 December 1874, 726. Lady Blennerhassett reported this in a letter to Döllinger several days later: " . . . on the first Sunday of Advent, in London a pastoral letter of Manning was read out, which you have probably seen. He declared that the opponents of the Immaculate Conception and the Vatican Decree would be excluded from the Church. Lord Acton was himself in the church of the Jesuits in London at the reading of this letter. The *Tablet* said that he who placed such a great value on the communion of the Church, nevertheless had for years not been going to the sacraments." Lady Blennerhassett to Döllinger, 3 December 1874, *Briefwechsel,* 4:584. English translation provided for the author by the Rev. Joseph F. Wimmer, O.S.A.

89. Lord Acton to Newman, 4 December 1874, *The Letters and Diaries,* 27:167.

90. Lord Acton to Newman, 7 December 1874, *The Letters and Diaries,* 27:168. Acton is referring here principally to his correspondence with various bishops who had formed the minority at the council, particularly Bishop Clifford of Clifton.

ber letter in *The Times* and Newman's reservations about it, wrote: "I cannot understand why you think what I said of the Popes gratuitous. The papal power was the very thing in question, and we were in danger of such declarations of its harmlessness as the bishop of Orleans gave of the Syllabus. It is the presumption in favour of papal acts, the tenderness for papal examples, that is the difficulty for Catholicism." Acton did not disguise his annoyance even in his conclusion to the letter. "I sometimes ask myself," he said, "whether there is not here a point of fundamental difference which makes my efforts vain to understand the position of other Catholics."[91]

Basic differences in temperament and approach worked once more to keep Acton and Newman estranged. In the event Acton was never pressed for a declaration from Manning. He did, however, at the end of 1874 indicate to Bishop James Brown of Shrewsbury that he could accept the Vatican Decrees, and it would appear that Newman's advice in the letters of early December played some part in the adherence that Acton sent to his bishop.[92]

Newman is absorbed in his task as rumors grow that he is preparing to answer Gladstone

Newman also took time from his writing in the first part of December to enter into correspondence with Bishop Clifford of Clifton. Again, the cause for the correspondence was Gladstone's *Expostulation*. Clifford had published a reply in the form of a pastoral letter on 25 November.[93] He

91. Lord Acton to Newman, 9 December 1874, *The Letters and Diaries,* 27:168.

92. See *The Letters and Diaries,* 27:168, n. 1. See also Simpson to Acton, ? January 1875, *The Correspondence of Lord Acton and Richard Simpson,* 3:332–33. This appears to be a letter that Simpson proposed for Acton as a reply to Manning's continuing inquiries. That Acton satisfied Bishop Brown of Shrewsbury at the end of December would appear to be borne out by the following remarks in a letter of Lady Blennerhassett to Döllinger: "For four weeks Lord Acton and Bishop Brown exchanged letters, with the result that Bishop Brown now is satisfied with a declaration of obedience and does not wish to mix into 'historical' questions, and for the moment at least, these two gentlemen are in unity, but a spark can still cause a fire, and a letter from Newman will soon appear on this matter." Lady Blennerhassett to Döllinger, 27 December 1874, *Briefwechsel,* 4:587.

In fact, however, Acton may well have been saved from a Roman censure by the publication of Newman's *Letter to the Duke of Norfolk* in mid-January 1875. Manning may have decided that it would not be wise to act publicly against Acton in the face of the largely harmonious atmosphere created among the various Catholic parties in England by Newman's *Letter.* It appears that Manning decided to accept the reconciliation of Acton with Bishop Brown of Shrewsbury as evidence of Acton's position and set aside his concern over the scandal Acton had caused in his archdiocese. Acton, nonetheless, continued for months afterwards to fear a Roman condemnation. See Lady Blennerhassett to Döllinger, April 1875, *Briefwechsel,* 4:600.

93. "Catholic Allegiance," Clifton, 25 November 1874. Gladstone was not impressed with Clifford's pastoral letter. In a letter to Döllinger on 8 December 1874, Gladstone wrote:

sent a copy to Newman, who thanked him on 2 December. Although Newman's letter is not extant, it is clear from Clifford's response three days
later that Newman had asked the bishop's advice on a point that he wanted
to deal with in his reply to Gladstone. Bishop Clifford responded:

> The question you ask "Could the Pope by virtue of his infallibility as su-
> preme teacher declare himself infallible as supreme Legislator? for Legisla-
> tion comes into the domain of morals," seems to me to have received a
> negative solution in the Bull "Unam Sanctam." Boniface VIII therein says
> "Si deviat terrena potestas judicabitur a potestate spirituali, sed si deviat
> spiritualis minor a suo superiore, si vero suprema a solo Deo." As the Bull
> had previously declared that the suprema potestas in the church is the Pope,
> these words seem clearly to establish two things 1st That from the Pope's
> sentence there is no appeal in all matters that come within the domain of
> the church, and 2ndly That though the Pope's authority as Legislator and
> judge is supreme it may possibly go astray. Boniface could not have said
> salvâ fide, "Si erraverit supremus doctor." If he was able in a Bull of the
> authority of the Unam Sanctam to say salvâ fide, "Si deviat suprema
> potestas" no future Pope can declare the supposition heretical.
>
> I have said that the authority of the Pope is supreme in all that relates
> to the domain of the Church—for this is really all that the Bull states, and
> I have been surprised to see how frequently during the present controversy
> the Bull Unam Sanctam has been quoted both by Catholics and by Protes-
> tants, as asserting authority for the Pope over Kings in purely temporal mat-
> ters; where it does nothing of the kind. . . .[94]

Newman expressed his thanks to Clifford for his interpretation of the
Unam Sanctam, but Newman very politely told Clifford that he thought
Fessler's interpretation of the *Unam Sanctam* in his *The True and False
Infallibility of the Popes* needed to be taken into account in answering
Gladstone and those who stood with him. Newman told Clifford on 15
December:

> You must have thought it very rude in me not to have answered your letter
> before now, but it has not been from not feeling its value, and having been
> much interested in it. It is very clear and good, I mean your comment on
> the Unam Sanctam, just as your Pastoral is, which I hear, as I dare say
> you do, as being of great service to troubled minds in the unexpected ad-
> venture of Mr. Gladstone's attack upon us.
>
> The only question which struck me about your explanation of Boniface
> VIII was how to reconcile it directly with Fessler's interpretation of the
> Bull—not that this concerns yours directly, but in the presence of different

---

"Bishop Clifford has replied in the tone of a gentleman and a Christian. I think his argument fails entirely. . . ." *Correspondence on Church and Religion of William Ewart Gladstone,* 260.

94. Bishop William Clifford to Newman, 5 December 1874, *The Letters and Diaries,*
27:173, n. 1.

interpretations of a document which is so commonly brought against us, our enemies, as the Pall Mall Gazette, seize the opportunity of saying sharp things against us. I think Fessler's ground is that the formal definition at the end of the Bull is informal in its wording, and thus escapes being de fide. Is it not possible to combine this view with yours which is so especially good and clear? It ought certainly to be given to the public; if so, I hope it will not be the only subject which you will put into the publication. It is very few persons who with competent knowledge can write so clearly.

At the end of his letter Newman gave another glimpse to a close friend of the toll that his own response to Gladstone was exacting. "I am writing," he said, "without full possession of my wits; for I am dreadfully overworked just now, and that has been one reason of my silence. So many persons write to me wishing me to answer Gladstone, but it is a very wearisome occupation for an old man."[95]

And there were personal intrusions involving friends that Newman could not ignore. As so often at this time, they brought sadness. In the first part of December, Newman learned that the eldest son of his closest friend from his undergraduate days was gravely ill.[96] John Edward Bowden, the son of John William Bowden, was a priest of the London Oratory. The elder Bowden had died in 1844, but Newman remained on close terms with his family, especially his widow, Elizabeth Swinburne Bowden. When Newman learned by telegram on 14 December of Father Bowden's death that same day, he wrote immediately to his mother. "For myself," Newman said, "I have been thrown back to the time when we lost his dear Father, and then again to that early time when he and I lived at Trinity almost entirely in each other's company. My best love to dear Emily.[97] I shall be saying (please God) masses for you and her when I have satisfied our duties toward John."[98]

95. Newman to Bishop William Clifford, 15 December 1874, *The Letters and Diaries,* 27:172-73. It would appear from Newman's words, "if so, I hope it will not be the only subject which you will put into the publication," that Clifford was planning another publication beyond his pastoral letter.

Fessler in *The True and False Infallibility of the Popes,* 81-82, held that only the final sentence of the Unam Sanctam was a *de fide* definition and that "the definition itself asserts only the Catholic doctrine of the Primacy of the Roman Pontiff; for if the Pope has been appointed by God to be the Head of His Church, and if every one who cares for the good of his soul must belong to the Church, then it follows he must be subordinate to the Pope as the Head of the Church (*subesse Romano Pontifici*)." It was then for Fessler a spiritual not a temporal primacy.

Because Ambrose St. John's translation of Fessler explicitly says of the final sentence of the *Unam Sanctam,* "These words and only these words, are the definition *de fide* of the Bull Unam Sanctam," it would appear that Newman was in error on the question of *de fide* in his letter to Clifford of 15 December.

96. See Newman to R. W. Church, 10 December 1874, *The Letters and Diaries, 27:170.*

97. Mrs. Bowden's younger daughter.

98. Newman to Elizabeth Swinburne Bowden, 14 December 1874, *The Letters and Diaries,* 27:172.

But for the most part in the first half of December, Newman's correspondence was taken up with his work on a response to Gladstone and in answering the continuing letters that urged him to the task. Although he had begun to make arrangements with his publisher on 2 December and though he wrote in his diary on 9 December, "and went to press about this time," Newman still kept his work a secret except for a gradually increasing, but still very small, circle of close friends. In a letter on 8 December to Charles Appleton, the editor of the *Academy,* who hoped that Newman would write a reply to Gladstone for publication in his journal, Newman said:

> I have been paid the compliment by several persons, of their wishing me to insert in their publications something on the subject of Mr. Gladstone's Pamphlet. I have been obliged to decline the opportunity they have given me—and in like manner I cannot avail myself of your offer.
>
> Indeed my difficulty is one which would tell against writing on the subject in any form. A few paragraphs would be utterly insufficient in answer to a pamphlet which brings in so many subjects with such extreme or rather heroic disregard of the meaning and drift of the documents or facts which he introduces—and I am too old to write a volume. The only chance of my writing would be my coming to the conclusion that I could say what is necessary in a moderately sized Pamphlet.[99]

And on the same day Newman wrote again to the editor of the *Echo,* Arthur Arnold. "No one has any authority to say I am writing against Mr. Gladstone," he began. "Many friends press me—but it would be no good writing, unless I satisfied myself—and, even if I did that, it still would not follow that I should be satisfying other people. There are many things which you can neither avow nor deny (as the old question, Had you the wickedness to knock so and so down) and which it would take a volume to explain, and I am too old to write a volume. And then it would not be pleasant to make things worse, instead of making them better, as would be the case if I wrote a weak pamphlet." Newman must have felt somewhat guilty about leaving the impression that a response from him was not at all a sure thing and so he concluded, "This is about how I stand."[100]

Although Newman continued his efforts to keep his project a secret, there was little doubt in the public arena that he was in fact about to issue a reply. That Newman himself was aware of this is clear from a letter that he wrote on 10 December to his longtime friend, R. W. Church, the Dean of St. Paul's. "I am writing against time, and my old fingers will not move quick," Newman told Church.

> I am most dismally busy. *Don't tell,* for I wish nothing said from me as yet, but I am *trying,* as the Papers repeat, to answer Gladstone, but I don't

99. Newman to Charles Appleton, 8 December 1874, *The Letters and Diaries,* 27:168–69.
100. Newman to Arthur Arnold, 8 December 1874, *The Letters and Diaries,* 27:169.

like to commit myself till I have actually done. I have had so many urgent requests, asking me to do so. And I feel I must do so, if I can, for my own honour. I grieve indeed that he should have so committed himself—I mean by charging people quite as free in mind as he is, of being moral and mental slaves. I never thought I should be writing against Gladstone! but he is as unfair and untrue, as he is cruel. It is a marvel. I think men like W. G. Ward have in part to answer for it—but he should have had clearer notions of what we hold and what we don't, before he sent 100,000 of his pamphlets through the country.

I thought I should be in peace for the remainder of my life—and now I am in controversy again.[101]

When the young Baron Von Hügel wrote to Newman from Cannes on 13 December, he appears to have had no doubt that Newman was about to issue a response to Gladstone's *Expostulation.* Speaking for himself and his wife, he said:

We have read most of the newspaper criticisms on, and answers to, Mr. Gladstone—I suppose his pamphlet is a good thing, inasmuch as it is the occasion of the question being thoroughly discussed and sifted—But I for one, and all who will read you with me, must, I am sure be grateful to him, for making you take up your pen—I need not say how eagerly, almost feverishly, I am looking forward to the publication of your reply. I have no doubt, that it, like your other books, will be to me a fresh starting point, intellectually, and an additional link in the chain of the many helps and enlightenments that binds me to you.[102]

Newman, his pamphlet all but completed, at last breaks the news to his friends

By mid-December Newman was at last ready to let the news of his writing in reply to Gladstone get out. But there was a last minute difficulty that he had to solve before he could do so. In a letter from Rome, written on 3 December, the Duke of Norfolk showed reluctance to having Newman's letter addressed to him. He was uneasy about letting his name be put forward in such a public controversy and he asked Newman, "Why do you not address it to Gladstone himself?"[103] In his response of 12 De-

---

101. Newman to R. W. Church, 10 December 1874, *The Letters and Diaries,* 27:169–70. On the same day, Döllinger in a letter to Lady Blennerhasset wrote: "What will Newman do? They will probably hound him so long, until he makes his pronunciamento. What he wrote to Acton *sub sigillo,* he will probably not say openly. I would love to know. I am sure many thousands are waiting to hear a word from him—but if the trumpet gives an uncertain sound?" *Briefwechsel,* 10 December 1874, 4:586. The original is in German.

102. Baron Von Hügel to Newman, 13 December 1874, *The Letters and Diaries,* 27:189–90.

103. Duke of Norfolk to Newman, 3 December 1874, *The Letters and Diaries,* 27:170–71, n. 3.

cember, Newman was apologetic, but he persisted by renewing his original request:

> I fear I have been very inconsiderate and would not for the world urge you—but I was misled by the great interest you showed in the prospect of my writing.
>
> But you do not see my position. I am too old to stand up to my man as some champion, for by standers to see which hit hardest, I am too old to give my opinion unasked, when no duty compels me.
>
> I cannot write at all, except in the form of a letter, and he who is good enough to let me address him, must also be good enough to let me say, that he was one of those who asked me to write. Any one, without leave at all, may write to the Duke of Norfolk, but it would not become me so to act; and, unless I said in what I wrote that you had led me by your initiative to think of writing to you, how could I write to you at all?
>
> Would it relieve your difficulty, if I said that those who have asked me to write are answerable, not for *what* I wrote, but for *my writing*?
>
> But I know how good your judgment is—and be sure that I shall quite understand you, if you should feel there is no way possible way [sic] of getting over the difficulty.[104]

On 17 December the Duke consented.[105] Two days later Newman expressed his gratitude. He wrote in addition: "I am not, as you fancy, pay-

---

104. Newman to Duke of Norfolk, 12 December 1874, *The Letters and Diaries,* 27:170–71.

105. See Duke of Norfolk to Newman, 17 December 1874, *The Letters and Diaries,* 27:177, n. 1. Gladstone makes it clear in a letter to Döllinger, written on 21 December, that he knew that Newman was about to come out with a response and that it would be in the form of a letter to the Duke of Norfolk. Gladstone spoke of Newman's effort in vaguely disparaging tones. He wrote: "The latest news in our Vatican controversy is that seemingly after several changes of mind, Dr. Newman is going to publish. The form is a letter to the Duke of Norfolk: a bad sign as the Duke is a thorough-paced Ultramontane, whom his religion has ever diverted from the politics of his family into Toryism. I am afraid that the pamphlet will bring out more of the weak side of Dr. Newman than of the strong one." Victor Conzemius, "Acton, Döllinger, and Gladstone," quoting Gladstone papers, British Museum, in Bastable, *Newman and Gladstone,* 41.

By mid-December, Gladstone was already contemplating a reply to those Catholics who had answered his *Expostulation.* See *The Gladstone Diaries,* 12 December 1874, 8:550. But he was obviously annoyed that Manning and Newman had not yet spoken. He realized that he could not go forward significantly without what he believed would be the chief replies from the Catholic side. At one point he seems to have given credence to a wild rumor that Manning had gone to Rome for consultation and would write his reply from there. See Damian McElrath, *The Syllabus of Pius IX,* 290. Manning was in fact at Rome around this time as is clear from the letter Lady Blennerhassett wrote to Döllinger on 3 December. See *Briefwechsel,* 4:585. But there is no evidence at all to suggest that his reply to Gladstone, published in February 1875, had either support or advice from the Roman authorities.

As he waited impatiently, Gladstone decided to fill the time by preparing a review of *Discorsi del Sommo Pontefice Pio IX.* See *The Gladstone Diaries,* vols. 8–9, from 14 November 1874 to 3 January 1875. This highly critical review appeared anonymously in the January issue of the *Quarterly Review.* Its authorship was almost immediately known.

ing you a compliment in asking, but you are doing me a great favour in granting.

"It will be a great satisfaction to me, in the last thing probably I shall write, to end my say with the great House of Norfolk on my tongue."[106]

The final obstacle had been removed. On 18 December, Newman broke his silence at last. He wrote thirteen letters that day, at least seven of them dealing with his reply to Gladstone, and most of these were addressed to people who had urged him over the past six weeks to reply.[107] The first letter Newman wrote was to Lady Georgiana Fullerton:

> I have just decided to advertise an answer to Mr. Gladstone—and, as in duty bound my first letter announcing my intention is to you. You must say a prayer for me, for I am sadly knocked up, and can hardly write a line.
>
> Up to St. Clement's day, I did nothing but write and cast what I had written aside—but from that day I have begun and gone on without any interruption or undoing. I have done my best, and God must be merciful enough to accept my intention.[108]

Newman wrote in a similar vein to Bishop Brown of Newport, Father Reginald Buckler, O.P., Father Henry Coleridge, S.J., and Dr. Charles Russell of Maynooth. Newman's letter the same day to Charles Bowden was intended primarily to assure the Bowden family of prayers for Father John Edward Bowden, but Newman was so much taken up with his reponse to Gladstone that even here he could not pass over it:

> After finishing my Masses for dear John, I began Masses for you, your Mother and Emily. Please God, I shall continue them once a week—Will you tell your Mother this. I am so knocked up, or I would write to her.
>
> This is the 13th letter I have written this afternoon—and I am nearly run over by the printer.

Newman continued in a postscript, "Your two letters were most welcome to me. . . . Do excuse me if I have not said so before—but my brain is in such a whirl, that I cannot well tell, what I have written and what I have not."[109]

Newman wrote also to the two journalists who had asked him to write an answer to Gladstone for publication in their newspapers. To Arthur Arnold he said: "At length I have determined to publish—and I write, by the first post after giving directions to advertise, to tell you." In a postscript Newman tried to explain to Arnold why he had not told him of

---

106. Newman to Duke of Norfolk, 19 December 1874, *The Letters and Diaries,* 27:177.

107. Of the *extant* letters from 18 December, all in fact mention Newman's reply to Gladstone.

108. Newman to Lady Georgiana Fullerton, 18 December 1874, *The Letters and Diaries,* 27:176.

109. Newman to Charles Bowden, 18 December 1874, *The Letters and Diaries,* 27:175.

his project in his letter ten days previously. "I hope you understood," Newman said, "that when I spoke (as I think I did in my last letter) of not being able to 'satisfy' myself, I did not mean that Mr. Gladstone's Pamphlet affected *me* personally, but that I could not write any thing that came up to what I wished to be able to write."[110] In his letter to Charles Appleton, Newman revealed something of the difficulty of steering a middle course he had felt in answering Gladstone: "I am heartily obliged to you for your wish to have it [Newman's pamphlet] in your columns, but, when you see it, you will understand how impossible it would have been to cut it into pieces—for the subject is so complicated, that, as the successive issues proceeded, I should have been called alternately a bad Catholic or a red-hot ultramontane." And then Newman added a somewhat disingenuous further reason for his refusal of Appleton's invitation: "However, the real reason why I could not comply with your proposal was, that I had already been permitted by the Duke of Norfolk to put his name on my title page."[111] Appleton had made his request to Newman on 7 December. The Duke of Norfolk's consent to Newman was given in a letter of 17 December.

In this series of short, quick letters Newman had cleared away a large part of his backlog of correspondence. There were still a number of other letters that had accumulated over the past several weeks that needed to be answered. But most of these required longer, more detailed replies, and they would have to wait until after Christmas. On 21 December, Newman noted in his diary, "finishing the pamphlet by this day, making altogether 4 weeks."[112] As was his custom Newman sang the Mass at Dawn on Christmas Day. On his name day, two days later, there was snow and this seasonal weather lasted into the new year.[113] On the same day, in his customary Christmas greeting to W. J. Copeland, Newman's response to Gladstone was very much on his mind. "My task is nearly finished," he told his friend of forty years. "You know I am writing on Gladstone's pamphlet. I could not help doing so."[114]

110. Newman to Arthur Arnold, 18 December 1874, *The Letters and Diaries,* 27:174.
111. Newman to Charles Appleton, 18 December 1874, *The Letters and Diaries,* 27:174.
112. Newman "Diary," 21 December 1874, *The Letters and Diaries,* 27:177. McElrath may be rushing things a bit when he writes: "The Diary records that he finished the pamphlet on the twenty-first of December." *The Syllabus of Pius IX,* 274, n. 1. In fact, the diary entry as given in *The Letters and Diaries,* 27:177 reads: "finishing the pamphlet by this day, making altogether 4 weeks." And this entry must be read against Newman's letter of 31 December 1874 to Miss Munro in which he says: "I am beginning slowly to lessen the heap of unanswered letters which crowd my table. . . . I have been busy with my Pamphlet and it is still upon my hands . . . and which makes me anxious—for I have spoken out." 31 December 1874, *The Letters and Diaries,* 27:181. While the writing may have been finished by 21 December, Newman was at least correcting proofs a week later.
113. See Newman "Diary," 27 December 1874, *The Letters and Diaries,* 27:177.
114. Newman to W. J. Copeland, 27 December 1874, *The Letters and Diaries,* 27:177.

One of the last letters of the year was to William Monsell. There is in it a note of satisfaction, of a hard, wearying effort over:

> Let me begin by wishing you and all yours a happy new year which will have begun, when you receive this letter.
>
> I have owed you a letter a long time, but I hope you have excused me by reason of my present work.
>
> Your passages from Dr. Troy[115] were most apropos—and of great service to me.
>
> When I last wrote, I said I had just begun *again,* as a last chance—It proved satisfactory to me—and from that time I went on without a stop. That morning I had said to myself "I have not said Mass for my attempt," and so I then did so. It was St. Clement's day too. And, as I say, from that time I went straight on.

And then Newman finished with a flourish. He had come to the end of a difficult task. He would not look back. "I am very bold—and cannot be surprised if I make some people very angry," he said. "But, if I am to write, I will say my say."[116] Despite his almost defiant tone, Newman knew at the same time that the consequences of his pamphlet could bring even more anxious times for him than the months spent in writing it. He looked ahead to the coming year, but uncertainly. In a postscript to a letter to Mrs. Wilson, written also on 31 December, Newman said, "Don't forget to say a Hail Mary, for the success of my Pamphlet."[117]

His pamphlet finished, Newman is fearful of the reaction to it, especially from ecclesiastical authority

Early in the new year Newman's thoughts were still very much on his answer to Gladstone and on prayers for its success. On 4 January he said to Mrs. Edward Bellasis:

> I trust you give my forthcoming pamphlet a good prayer now and then. You must not expect too much from it, and must recollect there is a party of men in the Church who have been dissatisfied with every thing I have done, who will be sure not to be pleased with my new work. I call it a work, but it is not more than a large pamphlet of 150 pages closely printed. As to Mr. Gladstone, his attack upon us is most strange. I think he has long been chafed by the extravagant things some Catholics have said, and at last his accumulated irritation has burst forth.[118]

115. John Thomas Troy was archbishop of Dublin from 1786 to 1832.

116. Newman to William Monsell, 31 December 1874, *The Letters and Diaries,* 27:179–80.

117. Newman to Mrs. Wilson, 31 December 1874, *The Letters and Diaries,* 27:181. No first name is given in *The Letters and Diaries,* but it may have been Mrs. Lavinia Wilson, with whom Newman had previously corresponded.

118. Newman to Mrs. Edward Bellasis, 4 January 1875, *The Letters and Diaries,* 27:182.

On the same day Newman, in a long letter to Malcolm MacColl, spoke harshly of some of those Catholics who had said "extravagant things." Newman had owed a letter to MacColl since early December. In a letter of 8 December, MacColl had spoken of some of the antipathy toward Newman in various Catholic circles in London. MacColl's letter may have been a goad to keep Newman at his task, determined, if he must, to say his say. "You know it is not against the Church of Rome as such, that I feel irritated," MacColl had said,

> but against that hard narrow spirit in it which has been so prominent in London during the last few years, under the influence of Archbishop Manning, Dr. Ward and Monsignor Capel. To give you an instance of what I mean. I was talking lately on these matters with one of the leading members of that party, and I quoted you against him on a point which he appeared to me to be pushing to an extravagant length. His answer was: "You must not accept Father Newman as an authority. The fact is, Newman was 45 years of age when he became a Catholic. At 45 years of age it is next to impossible to change, and Newman has not changed. He is but a badly tinkered Catholic now."
>
> It is this pedantic Pharasaic spirit which repels one, and which, I know, repels Mr. Gladstone also. . . .[119]

Newman's response on 4 January 1875 was strong, his anger evident. His pamphlet against Gladstone was the end of the long silence he had kept since his letter to Bishop Ullathorne had become public nearly five years before. "As to Mr. Ward," Newman began,

> you can tell me nothing more extravagant about his view of me than I know already. He has told my friends that I am in material heresy, that he would rather not have men made Catholics than have them converted by me, and that he accounts it the best deed of his life that he hindered my going to Oxford by the letters he sent to Rome etc. He is so above board, and outspoken, that he is quite charming. It is the whisperers, and I have long suffered from them, whom (as Dickens says) I "object to". But both whisperers and outspeakers had received a blow over the knuckles from Fessler's pamphlet, which has the Pope's approbation, and simultaneously with its being known in this country I have been afforded an opportunity,[120] at

119. Malcolm MacColl to Newman, 8 December 1874, *The Letters and Diaries*, 27:183, n. 1.

120. It is evident on reading the *Letter to the Duke of Norfolk* that Newman made considerable use of Fessler. The fact that Ambrose St. John was translating Fessler into English at the same time Newman was writing his *Letter* is not altogether coincidental, and there can be no doubt that St. John and Newman discussed Fessler during this period. Newman's *Letter to the Duke of Norfolk* was published on 14 January 1875. St. John dated his translation of Fessler 10 January 1875. The publication, however, probably took place some days or weeks later. That St. John's translation appeared shortly after Newman's *Letter* can be shown from a letter Newman wrote a week after St. John's death to Bishop Francis Amherst

the earnest wishes of my friends and strangers, by answering Mr. Gladstone
to break a silence which I so long have observed.

In saying this, you must not suppose that my direct reason for writing
was to protest against men like Mr. Ward—Time will answer them without
me—but it so happens, that the intense indignation, which Mr. Gladstone
has excited among Catholics, has led to their being very pressing with me
to come forward, as otherwise I should never have done. Of course I may
make mistakes as well as others, but it is well for the world to be told that
those wild views, which have been put forward as the sole and true Catholic ones, are not what they pretend to be.

As to Mr. Gladstone's letter, I think it quite shocking. I should not have
thought it possible that a statesman could be so onesided. With you I agree
most fully that "he wears his heart upon his sleeve" but that does not seem
to make an excuse for charges so serious, so inaccurate and so insulting.

Newman concluded with a reference to the imminent publication of
his pamphlet. "I suppose," he said, "I shall be out in a week or ten
days."[121]
Over the next several days Newman wrote few letters. Very likely his
time was taken up with reading proofs of his pamphlet.[122] By 9 January,
Newman had completed his task and had time again to tackle his correspondence. He turned once more to letting his friends know the latest
progress on his response to Gladstone. With Bishop Clifford he also took
up points from their correspondence in the previous month:

> I got my Pamphlet off my hands yesterday—and have told the publisher
> to send you one of the first copies.
>
> Father Ryder tells me that the Unam Sanctam is in part taken from St.
> Thomas, who says (contr. error. Graec. p. 25. 1787) "ostenditur, quod
> subesse Romano Pontifici sit de necessitate salutis," the words of the Bull—
> and, that those words relate only to spiritual subjection is plain from the
> two authorities, to whom he refers, Cyril and Pseudo-Maximus.
>
> I should have said to you in the letter I wrote to you some time ago that
> there is a Bull of Boniface's five years before the Unam Sanctam[123] which
> should be looked at in connexion with it. . . .

of Northampton. Newman said: "That translation of Fessler, to which, as also to my Pamphlet you so kindly refer, was the additional weight which overcame him. I did not know
at the time, but he told me afterwards he had worked at it six hours a day, to bring it out
as soon as possible after my Letter. He went through it again most conscientiously for the
second edition." Newman to Bishop Francis Amherst, 2 June 1875, in *The Letters and Diaries,* ed. Charles Stephen Dessain and Thomas Gornall, S.J. (Oxford: The Clarendon Press,
1977) 31:94*.

121. Newman to Malcolm MacColl, 4 January 1875, *The Letters and Diaries,* 27:183.
122. See ibid., 183.
123. *Clericis Laicos,* 1296.

The questions which Mr. Gladstone opens in his Pamphlet are so many and so large, that of course what I myself have written only goes a certain way in answering him.[124]

On the same day Newman wrote also to Ambrose De Lisle and to Mrs. Henry Wilberforce to announce the imminent publication of his pamphlet. In the letter to Mrs. Wilberforce, Newman explained why he had been at last persuaded to write on the subject of the pope's infallibility:

I did not think I should ever write any thing more; but, much as I wished to escape, I could not help answering Mr. Gladstone; so many friends and strangers asked me—and then I felt something was due to my own character—for *could* I allow that I was instrumental in bringing a number of persons into a Church in which they lost their mental and moral freedom and were bad subjects of the State? to have been silent would have been to acknowledge the accusation was well founded, and to have thereby implied that I had made a false step in becoming a Catholic and would retrace it if I could.[125]

Two months previously Ambrose De Lisle, acting at Gladstone's behest, had drawn Newman into the controversy that the *Expostulation* was about to arouse. Now Newman informed him, "the pamphlet went out of my hands yesterday—and I suppose will be made public property in a few days." Newman told De Lisle that he was satisfied that he had handled his response to Gladstone as well as he could. "I have gone," he said, "into most of the subjects which come into controversy—and have all through said all that I think—so, I am not sure to please every one—perhaps not, in all things any one. But I have done my best—and must leave it to a Higher Power to determine its value."[126] Newman was evidently still concerned about the reception of his pamphlet in high places. At the moment he was concerned particularly about the reaction of his own bishop. Ullathorne had followed his November pastoral letter in response to Gladstone with a pamphlet that had just come out in the early days of January. Newman had not known of Ullathorne's plan to publish a pamphlet and he evidently feared that his own reply to Gladstone could in its timing be seen to be upstaging his bishop and he also feared that things he had said in his pamphlet might be at odds with Ullathorne's approach.[127] On 14 January, Newman noted in his diary, "My Pamphlet

124. Newman to Bishop William Clifford, 9 January 1875, *The Letters and Diaries*, 27:185.
125. Newman to Mrs. Henry Wilberforce, 9 January 1875, *The Letters and Diaries*, 27:186.
126. Newman to Ambrose De Lisle, 9 January 1875, *The Letters and Diaries*, 27:185.
127. See ibid. Ullathorne's pamphlet, "Mr. Gladstone's *Expostulation* Unravelled," was well received and some people at the time judged it the best of the Catholic replies. Even Gladstone was appreciative, writing in his diary, "Read Ullathorne's (able) Reply. . . ." *The Gladstone Diaries*, 16 January 1875, 9:6. In an undated letter, probably written in early

published.''[128] That same day he took a copy to Bishop Ullathorne's residence where he left it with a brief note of explanation. "When I was first pressed to write," he told the bishop, "my answer was that you were going to write. Then when your Pastoral about Mr. Gladstone came to us, and I heard of no other purpose of yours, I thought you had said all you meant to say—and I had no reason sufficient to resist the wish of so many.''[129] His duty to his bishop satisfied, Newman returned to the Oratory to await the verdict of the wide world on his labors of the past three months.

Gladstone's Expostulation

A brief look at Gladstone's *Expostulation* and a somewhat more extended commentary on Newman's response will be useful at this point toward understanding the effect that the controversy had on Catholics and others in England. It should also help to make clearer the part that Newman's *Letter* played in this time of his life, coinciding as it did with his seventy-fourth birthday, and his role in England and in the English Catholic Church in its immediate aftermath.

There is little doubt that the subjects which Gladstone treated in his *The Vatican Decrees in Their Bearing on Civil Allegiance: A Political Expostulation* had long been on his mind. The precipitating cause for his deciding at last to sit down and put his views on paper appears to have been the reaction to his parenthesis in "Ritual and Ritualism.''[130] Although

---

January 1875, William Monsell said to Ambrose De Lisle: "How good the Bishop of Birmingham's letter was. Coming out at the same time, as Newman's, I fear few have read it. Tho' indeed those who have read Newman require to meet nothing else." Purcell and De Lisle, *Life and Letters of Ambrose De Lisle,* 2:56. According to Dom Cuthbert Butler, "Of the three principal replies to Gladstone—Manning's, Newman's, Ullathorne's—Ward in the *Dublin* pronounced the last to be the 'much more direct and sustained reply'." *The Life and Times of Bishop Ullathorne, 1806–1889* (London: Burnes, Oates, and Washbourne, Ltd., 1926) 2:100.

128. Newman "Diary," 14 January 1875, *The Letters and Diaries,* 27:187.

129. Newman to Bishop William Ullathorne, 14 January 1875, *The Letters and Diaries,* 27:189.

130. While it is clear that the defeat of the Irish University Bill had a part in Gladstone's parenthesis in "Ritual and Ritualism" and in his *Expostulation,* there were a number of other reasons for Gladstone's deciding in 1874 to speak out so strongly against the definition of 1870: (1) the treatment of Döllinger by the Roman Church; (2) Gladstone's belief that his attack might serve to goad and to rally the moderate Roman Catholics to speak out against Manning and Ward; (3) detestation of what he viewed as political ultramontanism and his belief that this party was determined on a war in Europe to restore the pope's temporal authority; (4) an effort to appeal to the Protestant temper of the English nation and to show for political purposes, the Liberal Party's as well as his own, that he was neither a crypto-Catholic nor an ardent Catholic sympathizer as some of his opponents in the Ritualist controversy had tried to portray him; (5) Gladstone's belief that the Vatican Council

written only six to eight weeks later, the *Expostulation* was intended to
be Gladstone's considered reaction to the storm he had raised by his
parenthesis, especially his charges against the mental and moral freedom
of English Roman Catholics. The *Expostulation* is, however, anything but
a calm exposition. It is full of fury, exasperation, and invective. Gladstone repents not at all of the tone he had taken in his parenthesis. He
claims at the outset that he will treat his subject historically, but his exposition is in fact hardly dry and scientific. Rather, his rhetoric is heightened and he resorts frequently to sarcasm. By all accounts Gladstone had
a popular audience in mind, and the eventual sale of nearly 150,000 copies
of his pamphlet bears this out. Despite its easy, fluent style, its verbal fire-
works and practiced scorn, it is difficult to believe that the pamphlet would
in fact have been the type of thing that appealed to "the man in the
street."[131] It is in the end more an exposition for England's rulers, its
aristocratic and educated leader class. There is of course no way of knowing how many of the people who purchased the pamphlet ever read it,
or got beyond the first few pages.

Gladstone began by calling attention to the newly aggressive attitude
of the Roman Church, an aggression manifested in England by the reception of various prominent converts into its ranks. In view of this more
determined Roman activism and in view of the proceedings of the recent
council in Rome, Gladstone considered it was time for the people of
England, "who fully believe in their [Roman Catholics] loyalty, . . . to
expect from them some declaration or manifestation of opinion, in reply
to that ecclesiastical party in their Church who have laid down, in their
name, principles adverse to the purity and integrity of civil allegiance."[132]

At the outset Gladstone promised to avoid all religious bigotry, a pledge
that a fair reading of his pamphlet would indicate was not kept.[133] Early
on also he introduced the name of Newman, almost as if to be sure to
draw him out, a public reference being more likely to do this than his
behind-the-scenes suggestions to Newman conveyed through De Lisle and
others:

---

had dashed any hopes of Christian unity; (6) and in the case of the *Expostulation* alone,
the hurt and anger he felt over the negative reaction to his September article in the *Contemporary Review*.

131. H.J.T. Johnson, "The Controversy Between Newman and Gladstone Over the Question of Civil Allegiance," *Dublin Review* 217 (October 1945) 176, states: "But to the great
majority of English men and women of all classes Mr. Gladstone's attack on the decrees
of the Vatican Council was naturally devoid of even passing interest."

132. W. E. Gladstone, M.P., *The Vatican Decrees In Their Bearing On Civil Allegiance:
A Political Expostulation* (hereafter cited as *Expostulation*), *Newman and Gladstone: The
Vatican Decrees*, intro. by Alvan S. Ryan (Notre Dame, Ind.: University of Notre Dame
Press, 1962) 7–8.

133. *Expostulation*, 9.

To aim the deadly blows of 1854 and 1870 at the old historic, scientific, and moderate school, was surely an act of violence; and with this censure the proceeding of 1870 has actually been visited by the first living theologian now within the Roman Communion, I mean, Dr. John Henry Newman; who has used these significant words, among others: "Why should an aggressive and insolent faction be allowed to make the heart of the just sad, whom the Lord hath not made sorrowful?"[134]

Specific mention was also made of Döllinger. Gladstone made no secret of his admiration for the great German historian and he spoke out against the brutal penalty of excommunication that had been inflicted on him by the Catholic authorities.[135]

Gladstone devoted a large portion of his pamphlet to a rehearsal of the assurances that had been given by the Irish and English bishops in the three decades leading up to Catholic Emancipation, that Roman Catholics were not obliged to believe in papal infallibility nor in a sweeping papal power that could interfere with the civil allegiance of Roman Catholics in the two countries. Gladstone gave particular emphasis in treating this subject to public statements of Bishop Doyle of Kildare and Leighlin in the decade just prior to the Emancipation Act.[136] Gladstone's point in this exposition was to suggest with a great sense of injury and grievance that had it been known that the Roman Church would forty years later make the pope's infallibility *de fide*, civil restrictions against Catholics might never have been removed. It was this line of argument that made many Catholics in England and Ireland fear that Gladstone was actually considering, or at least planting the seed for, new national legislation aimed at curbing some of the rights that the Catholic Church in England and Ireland had now come to take for granted.

The Vatican Council, Gladstone contended, had dramatically changed the position of the Roman Catholic Church in England. That Church had gone on the offensive, from a peaceable body largely concerned with its own internal life to an external force claiming a large power and arena for its activities. "The Pope's infallibility," Gladstone wrote,

when he speaks *ex cathedrâ* on faith and morals, has been declared, with the assent of the Bishops of the Roman Church, to be an article of faith, binding on the conscience of every Christian; his claim to the obedience of his spiritual subjects has been declared in like manner without any practical

134. *Expostulation,* 15. The reference here is, of course, to Newman's letter to Ullathorne of 28 January 1870, *The Letters and Diaries,* 25:18–20.

135. *Expostulation,* 21.

136. H.J.T. Johnson comments that "most reassuring was the rhetorical question of Bishop Doyle to Lord Liverpool: 'My lord, what have we Catholics to do with Popes?' " "The Controversy Between Newman and Gladstone Over the Question of Civil Allegiance," *Dublin Review* 217 (October 1945) 174.

limit or reserve; and his supremacy, without any reserve of civil rights, has been similarly affirmed to include everything which relates to the discipline and government of the Church throughout the world. And these doctrines, we now know on the highest authority, it is of necessity for salvation to believe.[137]

It is evident from this statement that Gladstone had taken at face value the position of the extreme Ultramontane party, and it was precisely this line in Gladstone's pamphlet that made Newman realize, even in some sense welcome, that Gladstone had provided him with an indirect way of answering Manning and the Westminster circle.

Not only the precise words of the definition of papal infallibility but the whole tenor of the Constitution *Pastor Aeternus* had, Gladstone argued, given the Church's official sanction to the pope's all-embracing powers and claims. The phrase *ex cathedra* was in Gladstone's view not a limit on the pope's authority but in its vagueness exactly the reverse. Sweeping too was the phrase "faith and morals"; morals, in particular, Gladstone took to mean every endeavor and activity of human life. The Vatican Council had made clear according to Gladstone that "absolute and entire Obedience" to the pope was now the rule for Roman Catholics and that the decisions of the pope were "unappealable and irreversible."[138] To bolster his argument that the Roman Church had of late embarked on a new and dangerous course, Gladstone spent several pages dealing with *Quanta Cura* and the *Syllabus of Errors*. He selected eighteen propositions from the *Syllabus* to show that the Roman claims of papal sovereignty over the State were not from the distant and disputed past.[139]

---

137. *Expostulation,* 32.
138. See *Expostulation,* 37–38.
139. See *Expostulation,* 16–18. Gladstone's English translation of these eighteen propositions was criticized by a number of his opponents for its looseness. He did, however, provide the Latin text in the first appendix to his *Expostulation.* The fourteenth of the propositions listed by Gladstone, "Or that marriage, not sacramentally contracted, (*si sacramentum excludatur*) has a binding force," was to have a life of its own in the reaction to Gladstone's pamphlet. Gladstone's major opponents in this dispute were Father Henry Coleridge, S.J., and Richard Simpson. Newman was drawn into the dispute after Gladstone in his *Vaticanism* made the point concrete by citing a case in which the Holy See had declared that a marriage between two Protestants, one a Scottish nobleman, in the chapel of the English Embassy in Brazil could not be recognized as valid since the decrees of the Council of Trent had been promulgated in Brazil. This interpretation appeared to imply that the Catholic Church took to itself the authority to declare on the validity of Protestant marriages. Newman in his "Postscript," 220–23, to the *Letter to the Duke of Norfolk* attempted to answer Gladstone on this point, but the matter was so tangled that Newman did not entirely succeed in making his point. Dr. Charles Russell disagreed with Newman's handling of the matter in his "Postscript." See Dr. Charles Russell to Newman, 8 April 1875, *The Letters and Diaries,* 27:270, n. 3. In any case, the incident in Brazil and the Roman judgment on it gave Newman another of those occasions to make a barbed comment about the practices of the Roman Curia.

And he intimated that should the council convene again it would declare the *Syllabus* as coming within the scope of *de fide* teaching.[140]

And why had the Roman Church suddenly decided to embark on this new course at the Vatican Council? To Gladstone the answer was clear. The chief aim of the council's action was neither theological nor ecclesiastical but political, and precisely, the restoration of the pope's temporal power.

To support this view Gladstone turned to the public statements of Archbishop Manning. He reached back to a statement of Manning's from 1861 to show that the archbishop had long held that support for the temporal power was essential to the Roman Catholic faith.[141] The importance of Manning's statements over the years came not only from his position since 1865 but also from his undoubted leadership of the Ultramontane party in England, which by 1874, had become according to Gladstone, "the sole legitimate party of the Latin Church."[142] As evidence of his indictment of Manning's views, Gladstone quoted extensively from the archbishop's recent "Caesarism and Ultramontanism" (1874) to support his contention that the Roman Church claimed supremacy over the State and that Catholics made this claim not simply in view of the Vatican Decrees but also in view of the authority of the *Unam Sanctam* and the *Syllabus of Errors*.[143] Speaking of "Caesarism and Ultramontanism," Gladstone concluded: "But the whole pamphlet should be read by those who desire to know the true sense of the Papal declarations and Vatican decrees, as they are understood by the most favoured ecclesiastics. . . ."[144]

In an effort to demonstrate the practical consequences of the definition of 1870 in the life of the English nation, Gladstone turned to the defeat of the Irish University Bill of 1873, a defeat which, as has been shown, he clearly attributed to the Irish bishops and their influence over those

---

In a letter to Mrs. William Froude on 9 March 1875, Newman said, "I cannot be sorry if the case is brought out, for they must be made to feel at Rome that they, as others, are exposed to the public opinion of the world—but we shall have to suffer." *The Letters and Diaries,* 27:246.

140. See *Expostulation,* 42.

141. *Expostulation,* 53. In 1860 and 1861, Manning preached a series of sermons which strongly favored the pope's temporal power. According to Purcell, Manning's "zeal" on the subject of the temporal power "outran his discretion or knowledge." In fact, some of Manning's statements in these sermons even alarmed Rome, and there was for a time a threat that the published sermons would be placed on the Index. These sermons also brought Manning into conflict with Gladstone, who supported the Italian nationalists. See Edmund Sheridan Purcell, *Life of Cardinal Manning, Archbishop of Westminster* (New York and London: Macmillan & Co., 1896) 2:152–69.

142. *Expostulation,* 50.

143. See ibid., 54.

144. Ibid., 54.

Irish members of Parliament who had voted with the Conservatives to bring down his government on this question.[145]

In his summary Gladstone's tone became heavily sarcastic. It is almost as if he wanted to be sure to have his greatest impact on those readers who would find his long arguments from papal and other ecclesiastical documents too tedious and would then skip over them in the hope that everything they needed to know could be found in the last few pages. Speaking of Roman Catholic "aggression" in England as shown by its recent converts, Gladstone wrote: "The conquests have been chiefly, as might have been expected, among women; but the number of male converts, or captives (as I might prefer to call them), has not been inconsiderable."[146] And how had this servitude been evidenced? Gladstone said: "Too commonly, the spirit of the neophyte is expressed by the words which have become notorious: 'a Catholic first, an Englishman afterwards'."[147] And then like a man delighting in his own clever rhetoric, Gladstone saved his meanest barb for converts from among the aristocracy: "If the Pope does not control more souls among us, he certainly controls more acres."[148]

In his conclusion Gladstone resorted to bombast, including an appeal to his fellow citizens to remain undeterred in their mission to civilize the world. "It is not then for the dignity of the Crown and people of the United Kingdom to be diverted from a path which they have deliberately chosen, and which it does not rest with all the myrmidons of the Apostolic Chamber either openly to obstruct, or secretly to undermine."[149] And a few sentences further on he repeated this theme in a slightly different form: ". . . a strongheaded and soundhearted race will not be hindered, either by latent or by avowed dissents, due to the foreign influence of a caste, from the accomplishment of its mission to the world."[150]

Newman's Letter to the Duke of Norfolk

The *Letter to the Duke of Norfolk* gave Newman, as he said in a letter to William Monsell, the chance at last to "say my say." Newman, following a brief preface, divided his response to Gladstone into ten sections: "Introductory Remarks," "The Ancient Church," "The Papal Church," "Divided Allegiance," "Conscience," "The Encyclical of 1864," "The Syllabus," "The Vatican Council," "The Vatican Definition," and a brief

145. See ibid., 60.
146. Ibid., 61.
147. Ibid.
148. Ibid., 62.
149. Ibid., 65.
150. Ibid., 66.

"Conclusion." It will be especially important to follow Newman in his remarks on the definition of 1870.

In his preface Newman expressed a theme common to his letters during the period when he struggled to find a way to answer Gladstone and even after he had found a way forward. Addressing the Duke of Norfolk, he said "You consented with something of the reluctance which I had felt myself when called upon to write; for it was hard to be summoned at any age, early or late, from a peaceful course of life and the duties of one's station, to a scene of war."[151] Newman then went quickly to two points that would play a significant part in the close to one hundred fifty pages to follow. The first was meant especially for Gladstone: it was the *Schola Theologorum,* Newman insisted, that was competent to determine the acts of the council, and this would require time. The second was intended for those Catholics who, in Newman's view, by exaggerating the meaning of the Vatican Decrees had in part caused Gladstone to make his charges. Rash interpreters in their instant and polemical pronouncements should not be allowed to usurp the province of careful theological inquiry. These latter were those who, in Newman's famous and provocative phrase, "having done their best to set the house on fire, leave to others the task of putting out the flame."[152] It is this double purpose running through Newman's *Letter* that has caused one commentator to remark that "the perspective of Newman's *Letter to the Duke of Norfolk* is that of a third party to a battle royal over the meaning of Vatican I."[153]

Newman began his "Introductory Remarks" with Gladstone's great question, "Can Catholics be trustworthy subjects of the State? has not a foreign Power a hold over their consciences such, that it may at any time be used to the serious perplexity and injury of the civil government under which they live"[154] Newman took as one of the principal motives for Gladstone's having decided to raise this question the defeat of the Irish University Bill in 1873 and his belief that this was largely owing to the influence of the Irish bishops on the Irish members of Parliament. Using his experience of Irish higher education matters, Newman spent some time in these opening remarks giving a history of the Irish bishops' attitude on the need for government funding for Catholic higher education, and he went on to assert that the real reason for the bishops' opposition to

151. John Henry Newman, *A Letter Addressed to His Grace the Duke of Norfolk on the Occasion of Mr. Gladstone's Recent* Expostulation (hereafter cited as LDN), *Newman and Gladstone: The Vatican Decrees,* intro. by Alvan S. Ryan (Notre Dame, Ind.: University of Notre Dame Press, 1962) 75.

152. LDN, 76.

153. Paul Misner, *Papacy and Development: Newman and the Primacy of the Pope* (Leiden: E. J. Brill, 1976) 150.

154. LDN, 78.

Gladstone's bill was nationalism rather than any ecclesiastical motive, especially one involving the interference of the pope. Though he brought Ireland very much to the fore at the outset of his reply to Gladstone, Newman has been accused, as has Gladstone also, of having shied away from Irish questions. In Hilary Jenkins's view this was a serious flaw in the famous exchange.[155] Newman was, however, extremely diffident about questions that he regarded as political and he made a decision to avoid these questions as much as possible in the hope of achieving his main goal, a clear statement that the political allegiance of Catholics had not changed as a consequence of the Vatican Definition.

From a defense of the Irish bishops' position on university education, Newman turned to the several responses elicited from the Irish and English bishops (Vicars Apostolic) by the English government in the period 1790 to 1829 on whether papal infallibility was a dogma of the Catholic Church and whether the pope could in fact supersede the command of the government in the case of English and Irish Catholics. In both instances the bishops had largely answered in the negative, and this was especially so in the case of the testimony that Bishop James Doyle had given to a parliamentary committee in 1826. Newman contended that the bishops had correctly expressed the teaching of the Church at that time and that, in any case, if the Government had wanted the most authentic answer on these points, it should have applied to "head-quarters," [156] that is, the Roman authorities for the answer. Here, as in several other places, Newman fell into something of a trap. Gladstone would charge him with having vindicated the central claim of his *Expostulation* and his subsequent *Vaticanism,* that Rome for a Catholic had the only answer to every question. Newman's dilemma is highlighted here as so often in the letter: he provided on the one hand instances from history to show that Catholics had not been united in believing that papal infallibility was a dogma of faith, while he feared on the other that in the present controversies among Catholics he would be seen to be espousing only a half-hearted belief in the definition and the pope's position in the Catholic Church as a consequence of it.

In his main exposition Newman began with a historical approach, starting with the Church in the first five centuries. He contended that the Church from the first had made clear its claim to be entirely independent of the State. Indeed, he pointed out in an indirect but unmistakable allusion to his own experience of religious conversion, it was the "likeness in political action" of the present day Roman Church to "the Church of the first centuries, that has in our time attracted even to her commun-

155. Hilary Jenkins, "The Irish Dimension of the British *Kulturkampf:* 1870–75," *Journal of Ecclesiastical History* 30 (July 1979). See for example 376.

156. LDN, 86.

ion, or at least to her teaching, not a few educated men, who made those first centuries their special model."[157] And in the same section he made an unfavorable comparison between the Erastianism of the Anglican Church and the political and spiritual independence of the Church of Rome.[158]

Newman continued his historical review by turning next to the "Papal Church," the Church which from the fourth century through the nineteenth had recognized in the pope the head of the Christian communion and its ultimate authoritative voice. Newman began this section by maintaining that it was in the fourth century that the scattered hierarchy came to recognize in the pope the supreme authority over the Church, a recognition that had been present only indistinctly in the first centuries of the Church's history. "I say then," Newman wrote, "the Pope is the heir of the Ecumenical Hierarchy of the fourth century, as being, what I may call, heir by default. No one else claims or exercises its rights or its duties."[159] This was a statement that was to cause Newman difficulties after the publication of his pamphlet, especially with the Roman authorities but even with some sympathetic commentators, and Newman would feel obliged to return to this point in the "Postscript" that he published to the *Letter to the Duke of Norfolk*.[160] After this rapid survey of the history of the early Church, Newman concluded that the position and authority of the pope was integral to the faith of Catholics. "I say," he wrote, "we cannot help ourselves—Parliament may deal as harshly with us as it will; we should not believe in the Church at all, unless we believed in its visible head."[161]

But as Newman came forward in history he did not gloss over the fact that individual popes had lived disreputable and unworthy lives. He clearly distinguished the office from some of those who had held it. "I am not bound," he wrote, "to defend the policy or the acts of particular Popes, whether before or after the great revolt from their authority in the 16th century."[162] Even though Newman was careful to point out that far more of the popes had lived holy lives, this admission of papal turpitude was another point that would not sit well with the censors in Rome.[163] At the close of the section on the Papal Church, Newman ridiculed Gladstone's

157. Ibid., 94.

158. Ibid., 92.

159. Ibid., 98.

160. See letter of Cardinal Franchi to Bishop Ullathorne, 22 October 1875, *The Letters and Diaries,* 27:408, appendix 1. See comment on Newman and the role of bishops as teachers of the faith on page 394 in ch. 6 of this study.

161. LDN, 99.

162. Ibid., 105–06.

163. See Cardinal Franchi to Bishop Ullathorne, 22 October 1875, *The Letters and Diaries,* 27:408, appendix 1.

charges against the present pope, charges made, Newman said, at the very time when it should have been evident to everyone that the beleaguered Pio Nono was bereft of all political power and temporal authority.[164] Newman, warming to his task as a controversialist, used scornful words to decry what he saw as Gladstone's immoderate language and its intended popular appeal. "Surely, in the trial of so august a criminal," Newman said with reference to Pope Pius IX, "one might have hoped, at least, to have found gravity and measure in language, and calmness in tone—not a pamphlet written as if on impulse, in defence of an incidental parenthesis in a previous publication, and then, after having been multiplied in 22,000 copies, appealing to the lower classes in the shape of a sixpenny tract, the lowness of the price indicating the width of the circulation.[165]

From this selective survey of history, Newman turned next to the heart of the dispute, that Catholics by reason of the pope's authority over them could not give that undivided allegiance to the State which was required of every citizen toward the lawfully constituted government. In dealing with this question, Newman divided his response into two separate but related points, "Divided Allegiance" and "Conscience." Newman began by charging that Gladstone had misread for his own purposes the third chapter of *Pastor Aeternus* and had made it appear that the word "absolute" with regard to the obedience owed to the pope had been used.[166] Further, Newman took Gladstone to task for misrepresenting the words *regimen* and *disciplina* with respect to the pope's rule over the Church. Newman pointed out that *regimen* and *disciplina* were hardly meant to convey some unbridled power of the pope over the most minute details of every Catholic's life, but rather that they referred to the Church's unity with respect to its internal life—its "divine worship, sacred rites, the ordination and manner of life of the clergy, the order of ecclesiastical regimen, and the right administration of the temporal possessions of the church."[167] Newman clarified this point further by stating: "The Pope tells us that all Catholics should recollect their duty of obedience to him, not only in faith and morals, but in such matters of regimen and discipline as belong to the universal Church, 'so that unity with the Roman Pontiff, both of communion and of profession of the same faith being

164. LDN, 107.
165. Ibid., 106–07.
166. Ibid., 111. The dogmatic constitution *Pastor Aeternus* speaks of *veraeque obedientiae*. See Cuthbert Butler, *The Vatican Council* (London, New York, and Toronto: Longmans, Green, and Co., 1930) 2:284, appendix. However, the conciliar debate had frequently focused on the pope's exercise of infallibility as "absolute" (as well as "personal" and "separate").
167. LDN, 118.

preserved, the Church of Christ may be one flock under one supreme Shepherd'.''[168]

After dealing with Gladstone's misreading of the Vatican Council, Newman took up the allegiance of Catholics toward the State. He began surprisingly by advocating a method of overcoming points of contention between England and the pope that seems somewhat inconsistent with his fairly negative views on the pope's Temporal Power. "As to the duty of the Civil Power," he wrote, "I have already intimated in my first section, that it should treat the Holy See as an independent sovereign, and if this rule had been observed, the difficulty to Catholics in a country not Catholic, would be most materially lightened.''[169]

Like many Englishmen of his time Newman had a fascination with the American Civil War and, in an effort to build his case against Gladstone's suspicious attitude toward Catholic allegiance, he drew an analogy between English Catholics and those Americans, favorable to the Union, who continued to live freely in England despite the British government's partiality toward the Confederacy. From this topical but perhaps dubious example, Newman moved to more solid ground when he gave three very concrete examples of how a Catholic should act when faced with conflicting demands on his or her allegiance. If the government should require English Catholics to attend Protestant services each week and the pope forbade this, then Catholics would be obliged to follow the pope's command. If on the other hand, a member of Parliament or the Privy Council had taken an oath to support the Protestant succession to the throne, the pope would have no authority to contravene this oath. Nor would an English Catholic fighting for England in what he believed to be a just war be obliged to follow the pope should the pope order English Catholics to withdraw from the fighting forces. But all of this was in the end, Newman insisted, so highly hypothetical. He wrote: "I say, *till* the Pope told us to exert ourselves for his cause in a quarrel with this country, as in the time of the Armada, we need not attend to an abstract and hypothetical difficulty: —then and not till then.''[170]

Newman summed up his treatment of allegiance to Church and State with a strong, clear statement that led easily to his subsequent section on conscience:

---

168. Ibid., 119.
169. Ibid., 120.
170. Ibid., 122. John Finnis believes that the two examples that Newman gives to show when a citizen has an obligation to obey the State rather than the pope "scarcely instantiate a clear-cut contradiction between papal orders and faith or morals, and today seem highly problematical." "Conscience in the *Letter to the Duke of Norfolk,*" *Newman after a Hundred Years,* ed. Ian Ker and Alan G. Hill (Oxford: The Clarendon Press, 1990) 406.

When, then, Mr. Gladstone asks Catholics how they can obey the Queen and yet obey the Pope, since it may happen that the commands of the two authorities may clash, I answer, that it is my *rule,* both to obey the one and to obey the other, but that there is no rule in this world without exceptions,[171] and if either the Pope or the Queen demanded of me an "Absolute Obedience," he or she would be transgressing the laws of human nature and human society. I give an absolute obedience to neither. Further, if ever this double allegiance pulled me in contrary ways, which in this age of the world I think it never will, then I should decide according to the particular case, which is beyond all rule, and must be decided on its own merits. I should look to see what theologians could do for me, what the Bishops and clergy around me, what my confessor; what friends whom I revered: and if, after all, I could not take their view of the matter, then I must rule myself by my own judgment and my own conscience.[172]

But what is meant by conscience? In answering this question, Newman wrote what many commentators believe to be the most enduring result of the celebrated exchange. "It seems, then," he begins the section on conscience, "that there are extreme cases in which Conscience may come into collision with the word of a Pope, and is to be followed in spite of that word."[173] Having begun decisively, Newman continued by calling conscience "the voice of God,"[174] the aboriginal Vicar of Christ,"[175] and he sharply distinguished it from the popular meaning of the nineteenth century that had come to view conscience as "the right of self-will."[176] Using the classic definition of St. Thomas, Newman said, "Conscience is the practical judgment or dictate of reason, by which we judge what *hic et nunc* is to be done as being good, or to be avoided as evil." "Hence conscience," Newman concluded, "cannot come into direct collision with the Church's or the Pope's infallibility; which is engaged only on general propositions, or the condemnation of propositions simply particular."[177] Newman moved his argument forward briskly but with deft, sure strokes:

> Next, I observe that, conscience being a practical dictate, a collision is possible between it and the Pope's authority only when the Pope legislates, or gives particular orders, and the like. But a Pope is not infallible in his laws, nor in his commands, nor in his acts of state, nor in his administration,

171. Here Gladstone would say that Newman was hedging the issue.

172. LDN, 125. Consistent with his view, expressed throughout the response to Gladstone's *Expostulation,* that the *Schola Theologorum* must always be consulted, Newman quoted here from Bellarmine and Kenrick to show that in some cases Catholics may disobey the pope.

173. LDN, 127.

174. Ibid., 128.

175. Ibid., 129.

176. Ibid., 130.

177. Ibid., 134.

nor in his public policy. Let it be observed that the Vatican Council has left him just as it found him here.[178]

And then in an effort to make his point concrete, Newman gave particular examples from history, a device that he turned to often in his response to Gladstone. After giving several examples from the early centuries of Church history, Newman continued:

> And, to come to later times, was Gregory XIII. [infallible], when he had a medal struck in honour of the Bartholomew massacre? or Paul IV. in his conduct toward Elizabeth? or Sextus V. when he blessed the Armada? or Urban VIII. when he persecuted Galileo? No Catholic ever pretends that these Popes were infallible in these acts. Since then infallibility alone could block the exercise of conscience, and the Pope is not infallible in that subject-matter in which conscience is of supreme authority, no dead-lock, such as is implied in the objection which I am answering, can take place between conscience and the Pope.[179]

Pressing his argument on the primacy of conscience forward, Newman stated that even in the case of an erroneous conscience, conscience is supreme over the pope's command. The person in this situation is responsible for being in error, but he or she is obliged to follow his or her conscience.[180]

Once more in the presentation of his argument, Newman reverted to theological authorities to show that cases exist in which the pope may be disobeyed. And he concluded this section with the famous statement that has come to be seen as the sum of his whole argument in the *Letter to the Duke of Norfolk.* "I add one remark," he said almost as though casually. "Certainly, if I am obliged to bring religion into after-dinner toasts, (which indeed does not seem quite the thing) I shall drink,—to the Pope, if you please,—still, to Conscience first, and to the Pope afterwards."[181]

---

178. Ibid.

179. Ibid., 135. Again, Newman's excursions into papal history were to upset some of the critical readers of his *Letter.*

180. LDN, 137.

181. Ibid., 138. John Finnis in his essay, "Conscience in the *Letter to the Duke of Norfolk,*" *Newman after a Hundred Years,* is somewhat critical of Newman's treatment of conscience in the *Letter.* See for example 406, 412-13, and 417. Concerning Newman's famous toast, Finnis writes: "At the end of a penetrating exposition of the Christian philosophy of conscience, and of this century's philosophical explorations of the corrupt consciousness engendered by corrupt societies, the Episcopalian philosopher recalls Newman's toast, and drily adds: 'Were we obliged to bring morality into toasts, we should not refuse to drink to conscience; but we should beg to drink to a truthful consciousness first,' " 418, quoting A. Donegan, *The Theory of Morality* (Chicago and London, 1977) 142. After quoting Donegan, Finnis goes on to add: "For our generation, Donegan's toast expresses better than Newman's the essential premiss, and something of the spirit, of the *Letter,*" 418.

Since Gladstone, in his effort to show that the modern papacy had advanced the arguments for its supremacy well beyond the teachings of Trent, had quoted heavily from *Quanta Cura* and the *Syllabus of Errors,* Newman was obliged to bring these two Roman documents into his response. Here again he no doubt sensed a trap, to answer Gladstone effectively was surely to disturb the more determined Ultramontanes, including the ecclesiastical authorities. Newman did not shy away from the topic, devoting nearly thirty pages to the Encyclical and the attached *Syllabus.* He took an interesting tack in his opening remarks on *Quanta Cura*, attempting to disarm his opponents by saying that all the evils of the modern world opposed by the present papacy had in fact been the position of the English people just fifty years before when "Tory principles" had been in the ascendant. He professed to be himself a Tory in his own sympathies, in the sense of Toryism as "loyalty to persons."[182] But, alas, the world had changed rapidly and an institution as old as the papacy needed time to catch up with its advances. While bringing himself into a position of apparent sympathy with the pope, Newman had just before this remark already marched off in another direction. He wrote: "Though I profess to be an admirer of the principles now superseded, in themselves, mixed up as they were with the imperfections and evils incident to everything human, nevertheless I say frankly I do not see how they could possibly be maintained in the ascendant."[183] He took this point further by ever so subtly referring to a theme that had appeared often in his letters after the council, "Pius is not the last of the Popes," the Church will go on: "The Pope has denounced the sentiment that he ought to come to terms with 'progress, liberalism, and the new civilization.' I have no thought at all of disputing his words. I leave the great problem to the future. God will guide other Popes to act when Pius goes, as He has guided him."[184]

Newman answered the charge that the pope in *Quanta Cura* had condemned all liberty of thought and conscience by showing that any society, including England, must place some restrictions on the untrammeled liberty of each individual in the common society:

> The very idea of political society is based upon the principle that each member of it gives up a portion of his natural liberty for advantages which are greater

182. Ibid., 143–44. On this point Derek Holmes writes: "But in spite of strong Tory influences on Newman and his temperamental affinity with such views, the evidence of his rejection of Toryism is overwhelming." "Factors in the Development of Newman's Political Attitudes," Bastable, *Newman and Gladstone,* 82. And writing of Newman and Gladstone, David Nicholls says: "Both men were conservative by temperament and liberal by conviction. Although Newman was by reputation the more conservative, a good case could be made for the reverse judgment." "Gladstone, Newman, and the Politics of Pluralism," Bastable, *Newman and Gladstone,* 28.

183. LDN, 142.

184. Ibid., 143.

than that liberty; and the question is, whether the Pope, in any act of his which touches us Catholics, in any ecclesiastical or theological statement of his, has propounded any principle, doctrine, or view, which is not carried out in fact at this time in British courts of law. . . . I repeat, the very notion of human society is a relinquishment, to a certain point, of the liberty of its members individually, for the sake of a common security. Would it be fair on that account to say that the British Constitution condemns *all* liberty of conscience in word and in deed?[185]

Newman concluded by attempting to put *Quanta Cura* on seemingly reasonable ground: "Who is it who would force upon the world a universal? All that the Pope has done is to deny a universal, and what a universal! a universal liberty to all men to say out whatever doctrines they may hold by preaching, or by the press, uncurbed by church or civil power."[186]

In treating the *Syllabus*, Newman moved quickly to put it outside the bounds of a dogmatic statement. In fact, he said, it did not even come with the authority of the pope but only with the authority of his secretary of state, Cardinal Antonelli. Speaking of the pope, Newman went on to say that the *Syllabus* certainly had indirectly his extrinsic sanction; but intrinsically, and viewed in itself, it was nothing more than a digest of certain errors made by an anonymous writer. Newman continued: "I do not speak as if I had any difficulty in recognizing and condemning the Errors which it catalogues, did the Pope himself bid me; but he has not as yet done so, and he cannot delegate his *Magisterium* to another."[187] And driving the point home, Newman said finally of the *Syllabus of Errors:* "But we can no more accept it as *de fide,* as a dogmatic document, than other index or table of contents."[188]

Having put the *Syllabus* at a remove, Newman spent time looking at some of Gladstone's objections to its various propositions. Newman, as other expositors of the *Syllabus* before him, took the reader back to the encyclical or allocution to which the separate numbers of the *Syllabus* refer. He attempted to show that each statement in its original context had a particularity and narrowness that was not at all apparent to the reader of the general, often sweeping, condemnations of the *Syllabus*. Here one

185. Ibid., 144–45.

186. Ibid., 148.

187. Ibid., 151. Ward took strong exception to both Newman's and Fessler's views on the *Syllabus*. "Notwithstanding the authority of Mgr. Fessler and F. Newman," Ward wrote in the *Dublin*, "we still venture to hold with much confidence that the issuing of the *Syllabus* was an ex cathedra Act." *Dublin Review,* n.s. 24 (January–April 1875) 341–42. And later in the same essay, Ward wrote: "F. Newman objects . . . that the Syllabus 'has no mark or seal upon it, which gives it a direct relation to the Pope'; but we would submit, that the mere fact of its transmission by his command was the most unmistakable of marks and seals." Ibid., 343.

188. LDN, 155.

wonders if Newman spent time with this exercise not because he himself
found it persuasive but because he could not simply pass over the prominence that Gladstone had given to the *Syllabus* in his *Expostulation*. Newman's defense is somewhat strained, for he surely realized that the compiler
of the *Syllabus* would not have been unhappy to see the tone and tenor
of each statement taken at face value. The Roman atmosphere of the 1860s
had created this document, which Rome itself had to some degree been
forced to softpedal after the outcry against it, both outside and within
the Church. Newman himself acknowledged that some of the vociferous
reactions against the *Syllabus* had been caused by some of its more perfervid Catholic expositors and "persons in high station."[189]

Newman concluded his treatment of the *Syllabus* by saying that it was
very much an internal Church document, intended for the bishops and
not the public prints.[190] It was a technical document that could only be
unravelled by the careful and patient work of theologians and canonists.[191]
In explaining the work of theologians in the exposition of official ecclesiastical pronouncements, Newman took critical aim at the state of theology in his day when he said "indeed a really first-rate theologian is rarely
to be found."[192] Newman had frequently deplored the weakening of the
great European theological schools, which he saw as in part a consequence
of the French Revolution and Napoleonic Wars. He would return to this
topic several weeks later in a letter to Lord Blachford.[193]

Before leaving the subject of the *Syllabus* altogether, Newman, perhaps to show that he had found the task of trying to make the *Syllabus*
look reasonable an extremely disagreeable occupation, had harsh words
for both the compiler of the *Syllabus*, "the flourishing fellow who writes
the briefs,"[194] and indeed for the Roman Curia. First he said, "Another
circumstance, which I am not theologian enough to account for, is this,—
that the wording of many of the erroneous propositions, as they are drawn
up in the *Syllabus*, gives an apparent breadth to the matter condemned
which is not found in the Pope's own words in his Allocutions and Encyclicals."[195] And then taking dead aim, he concluded his treatment of the
Syllabus with the following flourish:

> Now, the Rock of St. Peter on its summit enjoys a pure and serene at-
> mosphere, but there is a great deal of Roman *malaria* at the foot of it. While

189. Ibid., 162.
190. Ibid., 166.
191. Ibid., 163.
192. Ibid., 164.
193. See Newman to Lord Blachford, 5 February 1875, *The Letters and Diaries,* 27:212–13.
194. See Lord Blachford to Newman, 29 January 1875, *The Letters and Diaries,* 27:211–12,
n. 2, and Newman's reply, 5 February 1875, *The Letters and Diaries,* 27:211–13.
195. LDN, 163.

the Holy Father was in great earnestness and charity addressing the Catholic world[196] by his Cardinal Minister, there were circles of light-minded men in his city who were laying bets with each other whether the Syllabus would "make a row in Europe" or not. Of course it was the interest of those who betted on the affirmative side to represent the Pope's act to the greatest disadvantage; and it was very easy to kindle a flame in the mass of English and other visitors at Rome which with a very little nursing was soon strong enough to take care of itself.[197]

Not surprisingly, the Roman authorities did not miss the point, and this section of Newman's *Letter* was criticized for being "troppo irreverente."[198]

Newman came last to the Vatican Council and the definition of 1870. He had chosen to deal separately and beforehand with the civil allegiance of Catholics, though Gladstone had made his charge against Catholics precisely in light of the council and what was to him the sea change that it had caused in the constitution of the Catholic Church. As he had done in the section treating the *Syllabus*, Newman began his exposition on the council from a very personal point of view. He made reference to the recent letter in a Liverpool paper which had said that he had been on the verge of joining with Döllinger. He denied again the truthfulness of this statement, but his chief purpose in bringing it up was to set the stage for the very personal remarks that would follow. He knew that stories of his opposition to the definition had been current before, during, and since the council. Indeed his opposition had become dramatically evident when his letter to Bishop Ullathorne had become public in the late winter of 1870. Newman knew also that for his own credibility in answering Gladstone, he would have to deal with both public and private reports on his position with regard to the definition: "But the explanation of such reports about me is easy. They arise from forgetfulness on the part of those who spread them, that there are two sides of ecclesiastical acts, that right ends are often prosecuted by very unworthy means, and that in consequence those who, like myself, oppose a mode of action, are not necessarily opposed to the issue for which it has been adopted."[199] This was certainly meeting the issue head-on, in fact daringly so. But Newman was not finished. He chided the ultramontanes for creating problems by their intransigent views:

> What I felt deeply, and ever shall feel, while life lasts, is the violence and cruelty of journals and other publications, which, taking as they professed

196. This appears to be a slip since Newman just above had taken pains to show that the *Syllabus* was a document intended for bishops and theologians.

197. LDN, 166.

198. See letter of Cardinal Franchi to Bishop Ullathorne, 22 October 1875, *The Letters and Diaries,* 27:409, appendix 1.

199. LDN, 167.

to do the Catholic side, employed themselves by their rash language (though, of course, they did not mean it so), in unsettling the weak in faith, throwing back inquirers, and shocking the Protestant mind. Nor do I speak of publications only; a feeling was too prevalent in many places that no one could be true to God and His Church, who had any pity on troubled souls, or any scruple of "scandalizing those little ones who believe in" Christ, and of "despising and destroying him for whom He died."

It was this most keen feeling, which made me say, as I did continually, "I will not believe that the Pope's Infallibility will be defined, till defined it is."[200]

Having made clear his position during the council, Newman went immediately to his stance just after the solemn session of 18 July 1870. As evidence of his attitude at that time, he quoted, nearly in their entirety, the two important letters he had written on 24 July and 27 July 1870. While these letters certainly tended toward acceptance of the definition, it will be recalled that they are not in every respect explicit and unequivocal. It is somewhat surprising that Newman decided to use them in this first full exposition of his views following the council. Newman's courage in this regard may have enhanced his ability to gain a hearing from his Protestant audience, but Rome, in its review of the *Letter to the Duke of Norfolk,* found Newman's views in the 24 July 1870 letter "ereticale,"[201] particularly his statement: "On the other hand, it cannot be denied that

200. Ibid., 167–68.
201. Cardinal Franchi to Bishop Ullathorne, 22 October 1875, *The Letters and Diaries,* 27:409, appendix 1. In the *Letter to the Duke of Norfolk,* Newman did, however, omit the three final paragraphs of his letter of 24 July 1870: "But, whatever is decided eventually about the definition of the present Council, the scandals which have accompanied it will remain, and the guilt of those who perpetrated them.

I will add that I adhere to every word of the letter which I wrote to my Bishop last January, and which to my great surprise got into circulation. I only wish I had referred in it to the apprehension which weighs heavily upon me, that the actual tendency of the definition then in prospect will be to create in educated Catholics a habit of scepticism or secret infidelity as regards all dogmatic truth.

Nor, in saying this, do I forget that the definition, if valid, has been passed under the Presence and Aid of the Holy Ghost; for though the supernatural promise guarantees its truth, it does not therefore guarantee the Christian prudence, the spirit and temper of its promulgators."

And he also omitted the last paragraph of the 27 July letter: "And supposing a person says to me, 'After all, I have been so opposed to the doctrine,' or again, 'I have so habitually considered it as a mere theological opinion, that I cannot get my mind to *act* towards it, I cannot take hold of it internally, as a dogma, de fide;' I say to him 'Your duty lies in observing two conditions, both of them in your power—first make an act of faith in *all* that the Holy Church teachers [sic]—and secondly, as regards this particular doctrine, turn away from any doubt which rises in your mind about its truth. These two acts are in your power. And they are sufficient.' " *The Letters and Diaries,* ed. Charles Stephen Dessain and Thomas Gornall, S.J. (Oxford: The Clarendon Press, 1973) 25:166, 168.

there are reasons for a Catholic, till better informed, to suspend his judgment on its validity."[202]

By printing these two letters Newman had engaged the issue directly both with regard to his own personal position at the time of the council and the external controversy that surrounded the conciliar debates. Having acknowledged this personal and public controversy, he did not try to explain away the disagreements that had taken place within the council, among the conciliar Fathers themselves. There had been sharp disagreements surrounding the Church's councils in the past, Newman pointed out. He cited especially the controverted history of the Council of Ephesus and he appeared to say that at Ephesus [431 A.D.] doctrinal errors had been introduced which were put right by the Council of Chalcedon [451 A.D.].[203] And returning again to a point he had made several times in letters just after the definition of papal infallibility, Newman showed that succeeding councils not infrequently completed the work of their immediate predecessors. In making this point, he was careful, perhaps too obviously so, to state that he did not himself foresee the need for a further council to complete the work of the Vatican Council:

> There is nothing of course that can be reversed in the Vatican definitions; but, should the need arise, (which is not likely,) to set right a false interpretation, another Leo [Council of Chalcedon] will be given us for the occasion; "in monte Dominus videbit."
>
> In this remark, made for the benefit of those who need it, as I do not myself, I shelter myself under the following passage of Molina, which a friend has pointed out to me:—". . . Moreover, it belongs to the later Councils to interpret and to define more exactly and fully what in earlier Councils have been defined less clearly, fully, and exactly. (*De Concord. Lib Arbit* & c., XIII. 15, p. 59.)"[204]

The *Tablet* in a generally very positive review of the *Letter to the Duke of Norfolk* was evidently uneasy about the 27 July letter to Ambrose St. John, but the reviewer put the best construction on it by taking the view that Newman did not himself believe what he had written but from his great kindness was trying to find a way to help someone who had strong reservations about accepting the definition. See *Tablet,* n.s. 13 (20 February 1875) 235. Newman had not revealed the name of the recipient of the 27 July 1870 letter in the *Letter to the Duke of Norfolk*. Had the *Tablet* known it was intended for Newman's colleague, Father St. John, it may well have been less generous in interpreting Newman's motives.

202. LDN, 169.

203. Cardinal Franchi in his 22 October 1875 letter called Newman's views on the Council of Ephesus "erronee." *The Letters and Diaries,* 27:409, appendix 1. Newman felt it necessary to clarify his views on the Council of Ephesus in his "Postscript."

204. LDN, 173–74. Newman had, of course, several times told correspondents over the past four and a half years that the Vatican Council would be completed and clarified by a subsequent council.

Newman turned next to Gladstone's charge that the Roman Church in enacting the definition of papal infallibility had repudiated the history of the Church, especially the history of the first centuries. Newman was aware that this was the position of Döllinger and his circle and he knew of Döllinger's strong influence on Gladstone's views. Unlike Manning, who had attacked Döllinger bitterly in his first response to Gladstone,[205] Newman wrote of the great Munich scholar with restraint, and even sympathy. He could not, as he had shown since the time of the council, accept Döllinger's view of Church history: "I will never say a word of my own against those learned and distinguished men to whom I refer. No: their present whereabout, wherever it is, is to me a thought full of melancholy. It is a tragical event, both for them and for us, that they have left us. It robs us of a great *prestige*; they have left none to take their place. I think them utterly wrong in what they have done and are doing; and, moreover, I agree as little in their view of history as in their acts."[206]

Historical evidence was according to Newman an important but not at all the determinate factor in the belief of Catholics. "For myself, I would simply confess," he wrote, "that no doctrine can be rigorously proved by historical evidence; but at the same time that no doctrine can be simply disproved by it."[207] Newman continued, "He who believes the dogmas of the Church only because of History, is scarcely a Catholic."[208] And finally he drove home his point: ". . . in all cases the immediate motive in the mind of a Catholic for his reception of them is, not that they are proved to him by Reason or by History, but because Revelation has declared them by means of that high ecclesiastical *Magisterium* which is their legitimate exponent."[209] Newman did concede that the definition of

---

205. In his first response to Gladstone, a letter to *The Times* of 7 November 1874, Manning wrote of Döllinger: "The Empire of Germany might have been . . . peaceful and stable if its statesmen had not been tempted in an evil hour to rake up the old fires of religious disunion. The hands of one man, more than any other threw this torch of discord into the German Empire. The history of Germany will record the name of Dr. Ignatius von Döllinger as the author of this national evil. I lament not only to read the name, but to trace the arguments of Dr. von Döllinger in the pamphlet [Gladstone's *Expostulation*] before me." Manning's letter is printed in *The Vatican Decrees in Their Bearing on Civil Allegiance* (New York: Catholic Publication Society, 1875) 9–10.

206. LDN, 176. The *Tablet* expressed mild disapproval of Newman's treatment of Döllinger. See *Tablet,* n.s. 13 (20 February 1875) 235. But W. G. Ward was practically apoplectic. "On no other question of the day," he wrote, "do we find ourselves so irreconcilably at issue with F. Newman, as on his view of the Döllingerites. . . ." "Mr. Gladstone and His Catholic Critics," *Dublin Review,* n.s. 24 (January–April 1875) 456, footnote.

207. LDN, 177.

208. Ibid.

209. Ibid., 178. Ward was critical of Newman's scant attention to the historical basis for the definition of papal infallibility. He wrote: "Now, for ourselves, we follow the large majority of Catholic theologians, in holding that there is a superabundance of direct histor-

1870 and the definition of the Immaculate Conception in 1854 were exceptional moments in the Church's long history, but they came with the authority of the Church's highest magisterium, the pope acting in concert with the college of bishops:

> As to the ecclesiastical Acts of 1854 and 1870, I think with Mr. Gladstone that the principle of doctrinal development, and that of authority, have never in the proceedings of the Church been so freely and largely used as in the Definitions then promulgated to the faithful; but I deny that at either time the testimony of history was repudiated or perverted. The utmost that can be fairly said by an opponent against the theological decisions of those years is, that antecedently to the event, it might appear that there were no sufficient historical grounds in behalf of either of them—I do not mean for a personal belief in either, but—for the purpose of converting a doctrine long existing in the Church into a dogma, and making it a portion of the Catholic Creed. This adverse anticipation was proved to be a mistake by the fact of the definition being made.[210]

In his *Expostulation,* Gladstone had written: "For there is no established or accepted definition of the phrase *ex cathedra.* . . ."[211] Newman had certainly tended toward the same opinion just after the Vatican Council and he had seen this imprecision as a deliberate decision of the Fathers of the council, an indication by them that they had not in the end favored the extreme ultramontane position.[212] But in his response to Gladstone, Newman could not ignore the term *ex cathedra,* especially in treating Gladstone's claim that the Catholic Church had repudiated history. The case of Pope Honorius was too elusive without some defining limits, such as the use of the phrase *ex cathedra.* Newman used at this point the council's criteria for an *ex cathedra* statement: the pope had to speak "as exercising the office of Pastor and Doctor of all Christians, defining, by

---

ical evidence for Papal infallibility, quite independently of the Vatican Definition." "Mr. Gladstone and His Catholic Critics," *Dublin Review,* n.s. 24 (January–April 1875) 462. Ward continued by invoking again the *majority* position against Newman. He said " . . . Mr. Gladstone's words produce the impression, that Catholics in general agree with F. Newman in considering the historical evidence to have been inadequate at an earlier period; whereas the great majority of Catholics by no means agree with F. Newman in this opinion." Ibid., 463–64.

210. LDN, 178–79.
211. *Expostulation,* 34.
212. See for example Newman to Mrs. Lavinia Wilson, 20 October 1870, *The Letters and Diaries,* 25:216; Newman to Mrs. Lavinia Wilson, 24 October 1870, *The Letters and Diaries,* 25:219–20; Newman to Lady Catherine Simeon, 1 November 1870, *The Letters and Diaries,* 25:224; Newman to Alfred Plummer, 12 March 1871, *The Letters and Diaries,* 25:301; and Newman to Lady Henrietta Chatterton, 27 February 1872, *The Letters and Diaries,* ed. Charles Stephen Dessain and Thomas Gornall, S.J. (Oxford: The Clarendon Press, 1974) 26:33.

virtue of his Apostolical authority, a doctrine whether of faith or morals for the acceptance of the universal Church."[213] Using this definition, Newman concluded that Honorius did not speak *ex cathedra,* because he could not fulfill the above conditions of an *ex cathedra* utterance, if he did not actually *mean* to fulfill them.[214] It is evident that Newman was straining somewhat in his efforts to say something convincing on the notoriously slippery case of Pope Honorius. This is especially obvious when he writes: "What resemblance do these letters of his, written almost as private instructions, bear to the 'Pius Episcopus, Servus Servorum Dei, Sacro approbante Concilio, ad *perpetuam rei memoriam,*' with the 'Si quis huic nostrae definitioni contradicere, (quod Deus avertat), praesumpserit, *anathema* sit' of the 'Pastor Aeternus'?"[215] Newman has here leapt somewhat breathlessly over a millenium. With his second defense of Honorius, Newman is somewhat more convincing. The letters of Honorius, he said, were not a definitive decision; rather they were the preparation for a decision. In such preparations the pope is not guaranteed freedom from error. Newman then concluded: "For these two reasons the condemnation of Honorius by the Council in no sense compromises the doctrine of Papal Infallibility. At the utmost it only decides that Honorius in his own person was a heretic, which is inconsistent with no Catholic doctrine; but we may rather hope and believe that the anathema fell, not upon him, but upon his letters in their objective sense, he not intending what his letters legitimately expressed."[216] Newman did not come out of this tangle with complete success. He had not made his point convincingly and he had intimated that Honorius was in some sense a heretic, a point that did not go down well in Rome.[217] The Fathers of the Vatican Council had deliberately decided not to have the definition look back retrospectively to past papal decisions. Perhaps Newman would have done better simply to point this out rather than tackle the impossible history of Pope Honorius.

Newman ended his section on the Vatican Council by quoting an Anglican authority whose views seemed to support the Catholic Church's position that in the course of time the Church's reflections on the Scriptures would lead to new and deeper insights that would come to be part of the Christian faith. Speaking of the Bible, Bishop Butler of Durham had written: "Nor is it at all incredible that a book, which has been so long in the possession of mankind, should contain many truths as yet undiscov-

213. LDN, 179.
214. Ibid., 180.
215. Ibid.
216. Ibid., 181.
217. Letter of Cardinal Franchi to Bishop Ullathorne, 22 October 1875, *The Letters and Diaries,* 27:409, appendix 1.

ered."[218] In the Vatican definition, Newman said, the Catholic Church had after centuries of reflection on three passages of Scripture—Matthew 16:16-19, Luke 22:32, and John 21:15-17—moved to a "definitive recognition of the doctrine thus gradually manifested to her."[219]

In his analysis of the definition itself, Newman began by maintaining that the Church had always been careful not to extend what must be believed on divine faith but rather "to contract, as far as possible, the range of truths and the sense of propositions, of which she demands an absolute reception."[220] Here again he forgot Gladstone for the moment and spoke to some of his fellow Catholics:

> A few years ago it was the fashion among us to call writers, who conformed to this rule of the Church [those who held that the Church was careful to demand belief only in what is necessary for salvation], by the name of "Minimizers;"[221] that day of tyrannous *ipse-dixits,* I trust, is over: Bishop Fessler, a man of high authority, for he was Secretary General of the Council, and of higher authority still in his work, for it has the approbation of the Sovereign Pontiff, clearly proves to us that a moderation of doctrine, dictated by charity, is not inconsistent with soundness in the faith.[222]

After invoking Bishop Fessler, and more so Pius IX, in a view he had long and tenaciously held, Newman was ready to go on. The infallibility of the head of the Church participates in the infallibility of the Church. The apostles in establishing the Church were *inspired*; those who come after them in the office of teaching the faithful are *assisted* in preserving the faith precisely because God watches over the Church to preserve it in the truth. The pope, not being inspired as the apostles were, is limited in his teaching office by certain definite conditions, defined by the Vatican Council. Newman then treated again the meaning of *ex cathedra*. He wrote of the pope: "He speaks ex cathedrâ, or infallibly, when he speaks, first, as the Universal Teacher; secondly, in the name and with the authority of the Apostles; thirdly, on a point of faith and morals; fourthly, with the purpose of binding every member of the Church to accept and believe his decision."[223]

---

218. LDN, 182.

219. Ibid.

220. Ibid., 183.

221. It will be recalled that Newman, writing to Pusey on 22 March 1867, was not happy to be called a "minimizer" and delivered in that letter "a sort of Sermon against Minimism and Minimists." *The Letters and Diaries,* ed. Charles Stephen Dessain and Thomas Gornall, S.J. (Oxford: The Clarendon Press, 1973) 23:99.

222. LDN, 183–84. This comment probably irked Manning, whose pastorals on infallibility did not receive papal approval.

223. LDN, 187.

After dealing with the meaning of *ex cathedrâ,* Newman continued with his presentation on the careful limits of papal infallibility. He wrote: "But since the process of defining truth is human, it is open to the chance of error; what Providence has guaranteed is only this, that there should be no error in the final step, in the resulting definition or dogma."[224] Newman gave added emphasis to the restricted nature of the pope's infallibility by quoting, in a footnote, from Fessler: "The Pope is not infallible as a man, or a theologian, or a priest, or a bishop, or a temporal prince, or a judge, or a legislator, or in his political views, or even in his government of the Church."[225]

Gladstone had almost gleefully proposed that the second member in the phrase "faith and morals" gave the pope a sweeping power over even the most minute aspects of a Catholic's life. Newman responded by showing that the word "morals" with regard to the pope's power was in fact used very narrowly. "As regards the precepts concerning moral duties, it is not in every such precept that the Pope is infallible."[226] And he continued:

> It may be added that the field of morals contains so little that is unknown and unexplored,[227] in contrast with revelation and doctrinal fact, which form the domain of faith, that it is difficult to say what portions of moral teaching in the course of 1800 years actually have proceeded from the Pope, or from the Church, or where to look for such. Nearly all that either oracle has done in this respect, has been to condemn such propositions as in a moral point of view are false, or dangerous, or rash; and these condemnations, besides being such as in fact, will be found to command the assent of most men, as soon as heard, do not necessarily go so far as to present any positive statements for universal acceptance.[228]

Newman gave a topical example to illustrate his point that the pope's infallibility involved matters of universal importance, not particular situations: ". . . orders which issue from him for the observance of particular countries, or political or religious classes, have no claim to the utterances

---

224. Ibid., 189.

225. Ibid., 187.

226. Ibid., 191.

227. Ian Ker points out that Newman was "writing before the acute ethical problems raised by advances in medical knowledge" and that he could make this statement "with blissful lack of prescience." *John Henry Newman: A Biography* (Oxford: Clarendon Press, 1988) 688. John Finnis appears to take a similar view. See "Conscience in the *Letter to the Duke of Norfolk*" where Finnis, commenting on Newman's statement in the *Letter* [192] "that the Church's infallible teachings are 'such as in fact, will be found to command the assent of most men, as soon as heard' " is "another sign of his distance from our age," 416.

228. Ibid., 192.

of his infallibility. If he enjoins upon the hierarchy of Ireland to with-
stand mixed education, this is no exercise of his infallibility."[229]

Coming to his conclusion, Newman repeated again, even more insistently, his exposition of the very limited meaning of papal infallibility.
As in other instances in the *Letter to the Duke of Norfolk,* he had a double purpose: to show to Protestants the restricted nature of the definition
of 1870 and to upbraid certain Catholics for their exaggerated accounts
of the pope's power, both before and after the Vatican Council. "The
infallibility, whether of the Church or of the Pope, acts principally or solely
in two channels, in direct statements of truth, and in the condemnation
of error. The former takes the shape of doctrinal definitions, the latter
stigmatizes propositions as heretical, next to heresy, erroneous, and the
like. In each case the Church, as guided by her Divine Master, has made
provision for weighing as lightly as possible on the faith and conscience
of her children."[230] Newman said in addition: "From these various con-
siderations it follows, that Papal and Synodal definitions, obligatory on
our faith, are of rare occurrence; and this is confessed by all sober theologians."[231]

Newman had kept a long silence. This was his chance to speak out.
He pressed his point further, almost relentlessly: "To be a true Catholic
a man must have a generous loyalty towards ecclesiastical authority, and
accept what is taught him with what is called the *pietas fidei,* and only
such a tone of mind has a claim, and it certainly has a claim, to be met
and to be handled with a wise and gentle *minimism.* Still the fact remains,
that there has been of late years a fierce and intolerant temper abroad,
which scorns and virtually tramples on the little ones of Christ."[232]

In his brief restrospective conclusion, Newman expressed his regret
for having to enter into public controversy with Gladstone, but he felt
himself compelled by Gladstone's charges to break "a long silence on a
subject deeply interesting to me," and to defend his own honor.[233] Newman responded one last time to Gladstone's principal complaint, that
Catholics had a divided allegiance in consequence of the Vatican Council. He argued that the Pope's infallibility "bears upon the domain of
thought, not directly of action, and while it may fairly exercise the theo-

229. Ibid.
230. Ibid.
231. Ibid., 196.
232. Ibid., 197. These last few words were said to have deeply troubled W. G. Ward and
caused him to consider whether his writings had been so heedless of the faith of others.
But in the October 1875 issue of the *Dublin Review,* he pronounced Newman's "wise and
gentle minimism" a fundamental "mistake." See "F. Newman on Ecclesiastical Prudence,"
Dublin Review, n.s. 25 (July–October 1875) 299.
233. LDN, 199.

logian, philosopher, or man of science, it scarcely concerns the politician."[234] Nothing had practically changed in the life of the Catholic Church since 1870. "But there is no real increase," Newman wrote of the pope's authority; "he has for centuries upon centuries had and used that authority, which the Definition now declares ever to have belonged to him. Before the Council there was the rule of obedience, and there were exceptions to the rule; and since the Council the rule remains, and with it the possibility of exceptions."[235]

Before closing Newman confessed that he had had many fears about entering into such a public controversy, but especially the fear of giving a response to Gladstone different from the responses of other Catholics. But in the end he had concluded that this was a false anxiety, since he believed that all Catholics were united in matters of faith and differences of opinion in other than matters of faith would in fact have the happy effect of showing that the Church left a good deal to the private opinion of Catholics.[236] Having introduced indirectly the great maxim of St. Augustine, "in dubiis, libertas," Newman addressed his last remark neither to Gladstone, nor to his Protestant audience. "For the benefit of some Catholics," he wrote, "I would observe that, while I acknowledge one Pope, *jure divino,* I acknowledge no other, and that I think it a usurpation, too wicked to be comfortably dwelt upon, when individuals use their own private judgment, in the discussion of religious questions, not simply 'abundare in suo sensu,' but for the purpose of anathematizing the private judgment of others."[237]

Newman finished the *Letter to the Duke of Norfolk* with a profession of faith and a ready willingness to submit all that he had said to the Church's judgment.

OVERVIEW

Newman had returned from his September holiday mentally and physically restored. He was in many ways more ready for a major task than he had been in several years. The vehemence of Gladstone's comments on Catholics in the *Contemporary Review* shocked him, and though the urgings of Monsell played a part in Newman's deciding to respond to Gladstone, it is clear that Newman himself felt that he must be the one to answer Gladstone. Throughout his life Newman had done his best work in response to explicit challenges. Gladstone's insult to Catholics had deeply

234. Ibid.
235. Ibid., 200.
236. See ibid., 201. Newman was no doubt especially apprehensive in this regard because Manning, aside from fairly brief letters to newspapers, had not yet spoken. His response followed Newman's by three weeks.
237. LDN, 203.

offended Newman. He hesitated momentarily because of his regard for Gladstone, out of fear for his health in his seventy-fourth year, and from a longstanding reluctance to have to deal publicly with the definition of papal infallibility. All of these inhibitions kept Newman from finding a way in October to respond to Gladstone's brief but sweeping aside in "Ritual and Ritualism." But the appearance of the *Expostulation* changed things considerably. Gladstone had developed his arguments in a popular pamphlet of seventy pages and he had given Newman, as well as other leading Catholics, ample material on which to base a counterargument.

At first, Newman found Gladstone's presentation so diffuse and uneven that he could not hit on a way to develop a sustained, logical reply. A good part of November was spent in discarding plans and drafts, and Newman more than once decided that the whole thing was beyond him. But it is clear that even in these moments of frustration and doubt Newman held strongly to his belief that there must be a Catholic reply to Gladstone and that it must be a reply that gave the moderate Catholic position on the Vatican Council. He remained deep down convinced that only he could do it. By the end of November he had found a plan and a way forward, and on 14 January 1875 *A Letter Addressed to His Grace The Duke of Norfolk on Occasion of Mr. Gladstone's Recent Expostulation* was published. Newman had at last had his say.

Why Newman chose in late 1874 to do something that friends and strangers had been urging on him to no avail since July 1870, and even before, must remain something of a mystery. Time had tempered things, as he had himself foreseen. Some of the heat had gone out of the debate over papal infallibility in the four intervening years. Moderate voices, such as Fessler's, had gained a hearing in the Church, and even the approbation of the pope. There can be no doubt that Newman strongly believed that Fessler had provided a shelter for the views he would express in the *Letter to The Duke of Norfolk*. Newman also clearly felt that Gladstone's *Expostulation* gave him what would surely be his last opportunity to write on a major topic of his day. In a sense he must have decided to throw caution to the winds, if that can ever be said of Newman. Almost seventy-four, he must have felt less concerned than previously about difficulties with Rome and Archbishop Manning. It was unlikely that another such opportunity would come his way. He had always maintained that he was a controversialist and not a theologian. Indeed, he had turned aside entreaties to speak publicly about papal infallibility by invoking this definition of himself. Gladstone had let loose a storm of controversy and Newman, the controversialist, could not keep from entering the fray one last time.

Chapter 6

"There Is a Time to Keep Silence and a Time to Speak"

January 1875–December 1875

The reaction, overwhelmingly favorable, that followed after Newman's pamphlet was published made his life nearly as busy as it had been during the two months in which he wrote it. His correspondence in the last half of January was extremely heavy. There had been nothing to compare with it in the past several years. Daily the post brought letters of support and congratulation from Catholics and Anglicans—intimate friends, distant acquaintances, and strangers. Newman, it would appear, tried to respond to all of them. Nearly the whole of his surviving correspondence for the rest of January and for February is taken up with the subject of his answer to Gladstone.

At the very time the *Letter to the Duke of Norfolk* was published, Gladstone was stepping down as leader of the Liberal Party. It was not an easy time for him. Though the future would prove him decidedly wrong, he believed that his long political career had come to an end. Nonetheless, he lost no time in acknowledging the publication of Newman's pamphlet. Writing from London, but intending to leave for Hawarden, his country home, he said:

> Your letter to the Duke of Norfolk was published yesterday morning; and you may from the newspapers of this morning perceive that yesterday was a busy day with me, for I had to fold my mantle and to die.[1] I have *therefore* only read as yet rather less than half of your letter. The simple and sole purpose of these lines is to thank you for the genial and gentle manner in which you have treated me, and the evident unwillingness you have shown to fasten upon me censures which you not unnaturally think that I deserve.

1. Trevor appears to take Gladstone's "for I had to fold my mantle and to die" as a reference to the success of Newman's pamphlet and its complete triumph over Gladstone's *Expostulation*. See Meriol Trevor, *Newman: Light in Winter* (London: Macmillan & Co., Ltd., 1962) 515. Gladstone's remark was a reference to his resignation as leader of the Liberal Party.

In what yet remains to me of this the one battle of my life on the religious field, I shall have I believe to defend in full my propositions and even my "vehement rhetoric" but I shall thankfully recollect that your spirit has been able to invest even these painful subjects with something of a golden glow and if I am bad I shall be less bad than I should have been had you not set me a good example of what I am sure must have been a severe self control.

This is really all I had to say, and my small sheet forbids a large infliction.

But in fact Gladstone could not resist a comment or two on points that Newman had made and so he closed by saying: "But I may notice with regard to your p. 51 that there is no oath, it is simply a matter of Statute Law:[2] and with regard to myself that I have slidden through some momentary remission of watchfulness into an egregious error by admitting that the Popes have in the main contended for their dogmatic infallibility for near 1000 years.[3] It should have been for their absolute Supremacy. Of course I had the Decretals[4] in mind."[5]

Newman on his side kept up the careful courtesies, responding to Gladstone by return of post. He avoided any direct comments on Gladstone's arguments or his own in response, though he did speak very directly of his reasons for writing. "I thank you for your forbearing and generous letter," Newman began.

It has been a great grief to me to have had to write against one, whose career I have followed from first to last with so much (I may say) loyal interest and admiration. I had known about you from others, and had looked at you with kindly curiosity, before you came up to Christ Church, and, from the time that you were launched into public life, you have retained a hold on my thoughts and on my gratitude by the various marks of attention which every now and then you have shown me, . . . ; and I could not fancy my ever standing towards you in any other relation than that which had lasted so long.

What a fate it is, that, now when so memorable a career has reached its formal termination, I should be the man, on the very day on which it

2. Newman had mistakenly said that members of Parliament and of the Privy Council *took an oath* not to accept a successor to the throne who had become a Catholic.

3. Gladstone retracted this remark in his *Vaticanism,* calling it a "loose assertion." See William Ewart Gladstone, *Vaticanism: An Answer to Reproofs and Replies* (New York: Harper Brothers Publishers, 1875) 38. He was evidently aware that he had hurt his argument against papal infallibility by making it. See Acton to Döllinger, 30 December 1874, in *Ignaz von Döllinger, Briefwechsel 1820–1890* (hereafter cited as *Briefwechsel*), ed. Victor Conzemius (Munich: C. H. Beck'sche Verlagsbuchhandlung, 1971) 3:138–39.

4. From late antiquity through the medieval period, popes frequently asserted their power through decretals. These came to be recognized by the medieval canonists as having binding force and as being the highest expressions of papal authority.

5. William Ewart Gladstone to Newman, 15 January 1875, *The Letters and Diaries of John Henry Newman,* ed. Charles Stephen Dessain and Thomas Gornall, S.J. (Oxford: Clarendon Press, 1975) 27:192–93.

is closed, to present to you, amid the many expressions of public sympathy which it elicits, a controversial pamphlet as my offering:—but I could not help writing it. I was called upon from such various quarters; and my conscience told me, that I, who had been in great measure the cause of so many becoming Catholics, had no right to leave them in the lurch, when charges were made against them as serious as unexpected.

I do not think I can be sorry for what I have done, but I never can cease to be sorry for the necessity of doing it.[6]

On the following day Gladstone, writing from Hawarden Castle, thanked Newman for his letter and also for a copy of his pamphlet, which Gladstone found waiting him on his arrival. Speaking of Newman's pamphlet, Gladstone said: "Since I wrote from London I have finished it and I desire to extend to the 131 pages what I then said of 50 or 60."[7] The rest of his letter was taken up with two comments. The first dealt with Döllinger. Gladstone thanked Newman for his irenic reference to Döllinger in the *Letter to the Duke of Norfolk*. Gladstone had seen Döllinger in Munich several months before. Having known Döllinger for twenty-nine years, Gladstone professed to have come away from his recent visit with a new "sense of his extraordinary meekness, and total self-abnegation."

Gladstone's second comment went directly to a major point in the controversy that he had begun in September and which Newman had now

6. Newman to William Ewart Gladstone, 16 January 1875, *The Letters and Diaries,* 27:193.

7. There is evidence to show that Gladstone in fact thought Newman's response to him contained several major weaknesses. In a letter to Döllinger written a few days after his two letters of thanks to Newman, Gladstone wrote with great severity against Newman's arguments: "Newman has the highly elastic Theory of Development which, like Dido's cowhide, can embrace vast expanses of the world of spirit, always geared towards providing new information. A touch with this magic wand will turn the worst and impurest materials into pure gold." Victor Conzemius, "Acton, Döllinger, and Gladstone: A Strange Variety of Anti-infallibilists," in James D. Bastable, ed., *Newman and Gladstone: Centennial Essays* (Dublin: Veritas Publications, 1978) 42. And in a further letter to Döllinger, written just after the publication of *Vaticanism,* Gladstone wrote of Newman: "In my opinion, if he had professed will and character enough, he ought to have been at this moment on the same standing-ground with you, engaged in the same noble conflict for the truth. You are a better friend to 'Rome' than he is. He lulls it in its deadly lethargy, you strive to alarm it into repentance, and such alarm I think gives one the only hope." Ibid., 44. Döllinger did not like Gladstone's reference to him as Rome's "better friend."

J. Derek Holmes in "Cardinal Newman and the First Vatican Council," *Annuarium Historiae Conciliorum,* 1 (1969) 396, maintains that Gladstone was not convinced by Newman's arguments. And Josef L. Altholz in "The Vatican Decrees Controversy, 1874–1875," *Catholic Historical Review* 57 (January 1972) 601, writes: "Gladstone professed to be satisfied, after these replies [from the Catholic respondents to the *Expostulation*], that the English Catholics had given adequate assurances of their loyalty; but he refused to admit that his argument had been refuted." On the other hand, Robert Gray in *Cardinal Manning: A Biography* (London: Weidenfeld and Nicolson, 1985) 248, says that Gladstone "admitted the effectiveness" of Newman's reply.

joined. Gladstone after reading Newman's reply had evidently seen a need to shift the grounds of his argument, or at least to draw attention to what he thought had been a misapprehension of his meaning, and he gave hint that he was already making plans to do this in a new publication. He told Newman:

> It will be my first duty I think (if I write again) as regards your book, to maintain that I have made *no* charge (see p. 1) against the Roman Catholics of England. My charges are against what the Germans call Vaticanismus. Then against its authors and promoters whom I cannot affect to treat as innocent. Next come its receivers. Then those who think they receive but do not. Then those who reject. I think I have made no charge at all except against the first of these four classes. Against any but Vaticanists I have no charge to make at all; nor do I admit all to be Vaticanists who would give themselves the name, or not deny it included them. Any appearance at variance with this must be due to my clumsiness. The spirit in which you have written will be a good *daimon* at my elbow.[8]

Newman did not have to wait long for other reactions to his pamphlet. By the end of January he had been overwhelmed with supportive letters. Public comment was also largely favorable. Though Newman's pamphlet was not the success among the general populace that Gladstone's appears to have been, it was appreciatively received by numbers of thoughtful people, both Catholic and Anglican.[9]

Newman is gratified by the overwhelmingly favorable reaction to his pamphlet

The Times in its second leader of 15 January commented favorably on the *Letter to the Duke of Norfolk* on the day after its publication:

> In a controversy which is changing its ground from day to day, and which seems to put now and then its foremost men in the awkward predicament of forgetting what they started with, there is a certain comfort in finding one who is always the same. Dr. Newman enjoys the secret of perpetual youth. He is the same in the Oratory as he was at Littlemore and still earlier at the College which owes to him one of its wondrous successive developments. . . . The Roman Catholic Church of the early Martyrs and primi-

---

8. William Ewart Gladstone to Newman, 17 January 1875, *The Letters and Diaries,* 27:194.

9. In a letter to Ambrose Phillipps De Lisle, an Anglican clergyman, the Reverend Frederick George Lee, "mentioned the fact that fifteen thousand copies of Newman's *Letter to the Duke of Norfolk* had already been sold, as evidence of how great an interest was taken in the subject of it, two days after publication." Edmund Sheridan Purcell and Edwin De Lisle, *Life and Letters of Ambrose Phillipps De Lisle* (London: Macmillan and Co., Limited, 1900) 2:56–57.

tive Fathers, the Church that won universal power by its weakness and awed despots by its strength. . . . It is to Dr. Newman the Church of the humble, the poor, the many and the believing. . . .

The Times was, however, not as generous in its reaction to Newman's dealing with the practical political questions involved, but it was ready to excuse him on this point as not being a politician.[10] Five days later the Pall Mall Gazette was also laudatory and in fact was somewhat at odds with The Times on whether Newman had satisfactorily dealt with the practical political issues. In an article entitled, "Dr. Newman on Catholic Allegiance," it said: "As to the practical question—if ever there was one—between Mr. Gladstone and the Roman Catholics, we consider it closed by this reply of Dr. Newman's." The article went on to say: "The statesman has written like a narrow and bitter sectary, and the ecclesiastic has answered like an enlightened statesman."[11] The Spectator also had words of praise, but it was not ready to take Newman as the authentic voice of Roman Catholicism in England. It believed that the ultramontane party, if it remained true to its position, might well bring the Catholic Church in England into conflict with the government at some future time.[12]

Undoubtedly, the reaction that was most gratifying to Newman were those letters that came from his close friends, especially those who had stood by him with their sympathy and support in the controversies involving the papacy over the past decade. Lady Georgiana Fullerton, writing on 18 January, told Newman: " 'A Letter to the Duke of Norfolk' will relieve anxious minds and I earnestly hope rally to the Church some of those on the brink of apostasy."[13] In his reply the next day, Newman showed that he was no less anxious since the publication of his pamphlet than he had been in writing it. "Your letter, just received, is one of those which have been an immense relief to me," Newman began.

> On such and so many subjects as I have had to treat, it is impossible that I should not come into collision with the opinions of others, and, what is

10. The Times said: "Dr. Newman is where he was, in the Wilderness, in the Catacombs, in the Colosseum, in all the Churches of all the Saints, among Fathers, Annalists, and the great intellects who gave their lives to the solution of the earth's greatest problems; but he is not on the stage of British politics, nor need we wish him there." The Times (15 January 1875) 9.

11. The Letters and Diaries, 27:191, footnote 1, quoting the Pall Mall Gazette (20 January 1875) 10–12.

12. See also Baron von Hügel to Newman, 26 January 1875, The Letters and Diaries, 27:191–92. The letter mentions the disappointment among some Catholics with the Spectator's position. See the Spectator (16 January 1875) 70–71.

13. Lady Georgiana Fullerton to Newman, 18 January 1875, The Letters and Diaries, 27:197, footnote 1.

far more anxious a thought, run the risk, in the case of delicate points, of saying what might be said better or more exactly. The certainty of mistakes is the penalty one pays for engaging in controversy at all—but, if we waited till we could do things perfectly, nothing would be done. So I repeat what I have said to you before, that I have done my best, and no one can do more than that—and I pray God that what you anticipate as the good effect of what I have written may come true.[14]

Several days later Newman received a letter from Emily Bowles, who said:

I never can be glad enough that you have spoken and that strongly about those who have made Our Lord's yoke heavy on His little ones—crushing and trampling on them, without the least remorse—nay with joy.[15] The last time I saw Mr. Ward and I said something to him about the sufferings of some (which I had witnessed) about the Vatican Decrees—he said he *rejoiced*—and always should rejoice that such non-believers should be cut off. He is in a terrible state about the Letter—and yet I agree with Louy Ward[16] that if he met you face to face he would burst into tears and you would come to more understanding than now seems possible.[17]

14. Newman to Lady Georgiana Fullerton, 19 January 1875, *The Letters and Diaries,* 27:197.

15. This is a reference to Newman's remark in the *Letter to the Duke of Norfolk,* "Still the fact remains, that there has been of late years a fierce and intolerable temper abroad, which scorns and virtually tramples on the little ones of Christ." John Henry Newman, *A Letter Addressed to His Grace the Duke of Norfolk on the Occasion of Mr. Gladstone's Recent Expostulation* (hereafter cited as LDN) in *Newman and Gladstone: The Vatican Decrees,* "Introduction" by Alvan S. Ryan (Notre Dame, Indiana: University of Notre Dame Press, 1962) 197. This statement was said to have caused W. G. Ward to have scruples about his course and tactics over the years. In a letter to Ignatius Ryder, Ward spoke of his reaction on reading this passage in Newman's *Letter:* "Do you remember Warren Hastings saying that when he heard Burke's speech he for the moment thought himself a monster. Apply the parable and remember how enormously JHN has always influenced my mind." Wilfrid Ward, *William George Ward and the Catholic Revival* (London and New York: Macmillan and Co., 1893) 232–33. But if he did in fact have doubts, he soon set them aside. See Trevor, *Light in Winter,* 516–17. In an article entitled "F. Newman On Ecclesiastical Prudence" that appeared in the July 1875 issue of the *Dublin Review,* Ward wrote: "The thesis which we are opposing (be it remembered)—whether or no F. Newman intends to maintain it,—is this; that any Catholic offends against charity, who presses any ex cathedra utterance on the acceptance of his brethren, as being obligatory in any sense more stringent, than the widest and most indulgent interpretation which prevails among theologically instructed Catholics. This is the thesis, which we understand F. Newman to maintain; and in virtue of which (as we apprehend his meaning) he rebukes us for 'scorning and virtually trampling on the little ones of Christ,' " *Dublin Review,* n.s. 25 (July–October 1975) 289.

16. Louisa Simeon Ward, the daughter of Newman's friend, Sir John Simeon, married Richard Ward, a former pupil of the Oratory School, in 1872. Richard Ward was the son of F. R. Ward and was not related to W. G. Ward.

17. Emily Bowles to Newman, 23 January 1875, *The Letters and Diaries,* 27:204, footnote 5.

In his reply, Newman expressed satisfaction over the reception given to his pamphlet and the hope that he would not suffer for it in high places. About Ward he was not as sanguine as Miss Bowles. Referring to the *Letter to the Duke of Norfolk,* Newman said:

> I call it success because I have had such satisfactory letters from St. Beuno's, the Bishop of Plymouth, from Maynooth, from Archbishop Errington etc. It has been, as you may suppose, a great anxiety to me, because I felt bound in duty to speak out, yet thought I might be putting myself in opposition to influential people, if I did. At Stonyhurst[18] too they are satisfied with it. I don't see that the Archbishop can say any thing against it; but the chance is he will engage himself chiefly with Lord Acton.
>
> I wrote to Ward, saying how I wished he would live in peace with me and others—he answered that he desired it of all things, but that faith was a greater thing than peace, and it was a great grief to him that I would not take his views. Every thing would go right, if I did.[19]

As he showed in the letter to Miss Bowles, Newman was particularly pleased with the kind treatment given to his pamphlet by the Jesuits in England. He had felt a certain reserve on the part of some Jesuits after the publication of the *Grammar of Assent* and after various of his public remarks about the Society during the Vatican Council, especially those expressed in his letter of 28 January 1870 to Bishop Ullathorne. One of the first letters of congratulation Newman received was from Father Henry Coleridge, the editor of the *Month.* Writing on 18 January, he said: "*Deo gratias* I *think* all our Fathers that I have seen are quite delighted—and I hope there will be nothing anywhere to mar its success."[20] Newman began his reply the following day by saying:

> Your letter is a great relief to me. You may fancy I am anxiously expecting how Catholics will take my Pamphlet—and it is a comfort to find you do not expect that your own circle will find any serious fault with it. Of course on such a subject or so many such subjects as I have had to treat, I cannot expect to say every thing in the best way or without mistakes, and still less without coming into collision with the opinions of others; but, if I have done what is substantially serviceable, I should have cause to be thankful.

18. St. Beuno's in Wales was the theologate for the English province of the Society of Jesus; the bishop of Plymouth was William Vaughan (1814–1902), uncle of the future cardinal archbishop of Westminster but decidedly more cordial towards Newman; Maynooth, just outside of Dublin, was the most prestigious of Ireland's seminaries; Archbishop Errington (1804–86) had been for a time coadjutor archbishop of Westminster under Wiseman; Stonyhurst was a well-regarded Jesuit secondary school in Lancashire.

19. Newman to Emily Bowles, 24 January 1875, *The Letters and Diaries,* 27:204.

20. Father Henry James Coleridge, S.J., to Newman, 18 January 1875, *The Letters and Diaries,* 27:196, footnote 1.

It has been a great trial to me even physically—and at one time I was afraid
I should break down—but I have been carried through it.[21]

Further evidence that the Jesuits thought highly of Newman's pamphlet comes in a letter that Father Thomas Harper of Stonyhurst sent to
William Gowan Todd. The letter was shown to William Monsell, who sent
it to Newman before the end of January. Father Harper was lavish in his
praise for the *Letter to the Duke of Norfolk* and he described for Todd
the reaction to it in the Jesuit communities at Stonyhurst. "I look upon
it," he said,

> as Newman's *chef-d'oeuvre*. It is gigantically grand, built up on a sound,
> accurate, deep Theology; and what strikes me perhaps most of all, he seems
> to have written it with one eye raised to God, the other fixed on his pen. . . .
> There is not one sentence in it, (on a first perusal), to which I could not
> heartily subscribe; unless it be perhaps the question of Honorius.
>
> There is a *furore* here about it. Our Rector (Fr. Purbrick)[22] is very much
> of the same mind as myself. It is to be read at once in both Refectories;
> here at the College, and over at the Seminary. . . .
>
> There was only *one* passage in the dear Giant's *brochure* that I did not
> like, nay LOVE; it was where he says it will probably be his last publica-
> tion. . . . We can't spare him. We shall want ere long lots more of pails
> of water to out fresh fires.[23]

And a further evidence of Jesuit reaction came from Father James
Jones, who wrote to Newman on 21 January. Father Jones, rector and
professor of moral theology at St. Beuno's, the Jesuit theologate in
Wales,[24] said:

> I am sure you will bear with me when I say that your name was dear to
> me even before you became a Catholic, and that this feeling has been in-
> creased by every work that has since come from your hand, and by none
> more than this last. . . .
>
> I cannot help saying that I sympathise very much in your aversion to
> extravagance and intolerance in matters where the Church has left us free
> to form our own judgement. . . .

21. Newman to Father Henry James Coleridge, S.J., 19 January 1875, *The Letters and
Diaries,* 27:196.

22. Father Edward Purbrick was provincial of the English Province of the Society of
Jesus from 1880 to 1888 and was provincial of the Maryland-New York Province from 1897
to 1901.

23. Father Thomas Harper to William Gowan Todd, 17 June 1875, *The Letters and
Diaries,* 27:204, footnote 3.

24. Father Jones was later provincial of the English Province and a year before his death
in 1893 was named assistant to the general of the Society of Jesus.

I would gladly speak of the great theological light I have obtained in each section of your letter, and of the encouragement to thorough loyalty to the Church and the Pope that breathes in every page of it. . . .[25]

Newman showed himself especially grateful to have this endorsement from a theologian, unsure, as he sometimes professed himself to be, of his theological competence. "Great as the weariness of writing has been," Newman confessed to Father Jones,

my anxiety has been quite as great a trial. I have never considered theology my line or my forte, and have not written on it except when obliged. Under these circumstances you may think how exceedingly gratified I have been to receive your letter. It is a great thing to have cause to believe, that on the whole I have been prospered in what I have written. Please, sometimes say a prayer for an old man. . . .[26]

In the first days after the publication of his *Letter,* Newman heard from another theologian, Dr. Russell of Maynooth. While Russell's letter was also largely laudatory, typically he indicated some reservations, though he did not at this point spell them out. Writing on 18 January, Russell said: "There are a few things which will be criticised, no doubt; and one or two in which I should not myself fully agree; but as a whole it is admirable. . . ."[27] Spending what must have been long hours at his writing desk in these days, Newman again replied immediately. He used an extended image to describe his anxieties over writing his pamphlet and the reaction to it, an image that he was to employ several times in the weeks ahead:

It is a great kindness in you to write to me, for you may easily suppose I am like a man who has gone up in a balloon, and has a chance of all sorts of adventures, from gas escapes, from currents of air, from intanglements in forests, from the wide sea, and does not feel himself safe till he gets back to his fireside. At present as I am descending, I am in the most critical point of my expedition. All I can say is that I have acted for the best, and have done my best, and must now leave the success of it to a higher power. Under these circumstances of course your letter is a great encouragement to me.[28]

In addition to his gratitude for the reaction of the Jesuits and for Dr. Russell's praise, Newman was also buoyed up by the letters of thanks he received from representatives of the old Catholic families of England.

25. Father James Jones to Newman, 21 January 1875, *The Letters and Diaries,* 27:200, footnote 1.

26. Newman to Father James Jones, 22 January 1875, *The Letters and Diaries,* 27:200-1.

27. Dr. Charles Russell to Newman, 18 January 1875, *The Letters and Diaries,* 27:199, footnote 1.

28. Newman to Dr. Charles Russell, 19 January 1875, *The Letters and Diaries,* 27:198-99.

These descendants of Catholics who had suffered persecution and the in-
dignities of penal times had always found Newman's moderate approach
to issues far more congenial than the more combative brand of Catholicism favored by the Westminster circle, and they showed this once more
in their appreciation for the *Letter to the Duke of Norfolk*.[29] Daniel Noble,
who described himself in a letter to Newman as "an Old Lancashire Catholic from Preston," wrote: "So far as I know, unbending faith and the
observance of religious duty were not less marked in my early days (half
a century ago) than now; when the subjective manifestations of our faith
in devotion had probably a form in greater correspondence with our national temperament and habit of thought."[30] Newman's reply was brief,
but it was clear that he had not missed Noble's principal point. "It is very
kind in you to write to me," he said, "and it is very pleasant to me to
get such letters. Of course my pamphlet has caused me much anxiety—
but the letters I have received from various quarters have re-assured me,
and yours has a value of its own from the circumstances under which you
give your testimony."[31] Newman heard also from Canon Thomas Cookson, the Provost of the Liverpool Chapter and a member of an old Catholic
family, who in a letter of 20 January, in which he thanked Newman for
answering Gladstone, said in addition: "I hope the reproach will not be
fruitless, which you have given to some among ourselves, whose language
on Papal claims is usually high-flown, and not always accurate, and as
a matter of course confirms the opinion of the governing class and of Protestants generally that they encroach upon civil rights."[32]

That Newman's pamphlet was a success beyond Catholic circles is evident from letters he received from Anglican friends and acquaintances,
though these letters were understandably more tempered in their enthusiasm than those from Catholics. In a letter of 20 January, Canon
H. P. Liddon, a leader of the Ritualist party in the Church of England,
thanked Newman for the kind references that he had made in the *Letter*

29. In a letter to Professor Mayor, written on 9 December 1874, Gladstone lamented
what he saw as the decline of the recusant Catholic families and the ascendancy of the
Ultramontanist party in their place: "It is impossible not to feel objectively and historically,
a strong interest in the *old* Anglo-Roman body. Suffering from proscription, and in close
contact everywhere with an antagonistic system, it refused all extremes, and remained loyal
in adhesion, devout in religious duty, and moderate and rational in theological colour. All
this is gone, and replaced by what Tennyson might call its 'loathsome opposite.' " *Correspondence on Church and Religion of William Ewart Gladstone,* selected and arranged
by D. C. Lathbury (New York: The MacMillian Company, 1910) 2:61.

30. Daniel Noble to Newman, 17 January 1875, *The Letters and Diaries,* 27:199, footnote 2.

31. Newman to Daniel Noble, 20 January 1875, *The Letters and Diaries,* 27:199.

32. Canon Thomas Cookson to Newman, 20 January 1875, *The Letters and Diaries,*
27:202, footnote 2.

to the Duke of Norfolk to the sad difficulties of the Ritualists, which had led to the recent passage by Parliament of the Public Worship Regulation Act. While expressing his thanks, Liddon did, however, feel the necessity of saying: "There is, of course, much in your Letter, as to which I cannot follow you; but I never think of this without regret, or of yourself without deep gratitude and affection."[33]

Robert Charles Jenkins, an Anglican clergyman who had corresponded with Newman for several years, thought that Gladstone's four years of silence since the Vatican Decrees, which Newman had pointedly noted in his pamphlet, was less regrettable than the failure of leading Roman Catholics in that period to challenge the exaggerated statements of Archbishop Manning.[34] Newman did not turn aside the complaint Jenkins had made:

> I agree with you that Mr. Gladstone is not to be blamed for waiting four years before he wrote his Pamphlet. The Preacher says, "There is a time to keep silence, and a time to speak", and I say the same of myself.
>
> Qui s'excuse, s'accuse. I do not know anyone, of such name, [who] had formally and publicly addressed us in 150,000 copies with an accusation and a challenge, before Mr. Gladstone. As to our own people one has said a strong thing about the Syllabus—another about the Vatican Council, but one cannot make a dozen answers to a dozen provocations, and it is the part of wise and patient men to wait, till the proper opportunity arrives. I have written under 10 heads—they are all apropos of Mr. Gladstone. I have to thank him for enabling me by so comprehensive an indictment to say all that had at this time to be said.

Newman concluded his defense by reaching back into his past to the Tractarian disputes at Oxford in the 1830's. He wrote:

> I have but acted upon the rule I thought it a duty to observe forty years ago—
> "Not so"—He said, "hush thee, and seek
>   With thoughts in prayer and watchful eyes,
>   My seasons sent for thee to speak,
>   And use them as they rise".[35]

On 18 January, Newman wrote to R. W. Church, the Dean of St. Paul's, to express his belated greetings for the new year. He recounted something of the strain the work of responding to Gladstone had caused him. "It is not pleasant," Newman said, "to make these experiments on

33. H. P. Liddon to Newman, 15 January 1875, *The Letters and Diaries,* 27:195, footnote 1.

34. See Robert Charles Jenkins to Newman, 18 January 1875, *The Letters and Diaries,* 27:198, footnote 1.

35. Newman to Robert Charles Jenkins, 19 January 1875, *The Letters and Diaries,* 27:198. The verse is from Newman's "A Word In Season," *Verses on Various Occasions* (London, New York, Bombay: Longmans, Green, and Co., 1903) 87.

my strength, and I never forget how many of my friends have ended with paralysis.''[36] Church replied several days later. He spoke appreciatively of the *Letter to the Duke of Norfolk*: ''I have read with great interest and sympathy what so occupied you. I wish it had not been necessary to write: but it is an example of controversy, both in tone and thoroughness, which it is pleasant to learn from.''[37]

From the time when Newman had attempted to answer Gladstone's parenthesis in ''Ritual and Ritualism'' and through the difficult weeks of writing the *Letter to the Duke of Norfolk,* he had bemoaned the fact that he suffered from the disadvantage of not knowing the world of affairs, of his trying to answer Gladstone from the distant, almost alien world of Birmingham and the Oratory. In the event, leading public men also considered his pamphlet a success and wrote to Newman to express their admiration. John Pope Hennessy, who had served in Parliament and as a colonial governor, told Newman on 16 January that the ''letter to the Duke of Norfolk is the only thing we can talk about in this club at present; and indeed in other clubs and in society generally it seems to be one of the two absorbing topics of the moment.''[38] Newman's longtime friend Lord Blachford wrote at length on 29 January. He wrote mainly in appreciation of Newman's *Letter,* but he touched too on related topics:

> I have long been intending to write to you to say with how much admiration and interest—and may I add occasional amusement I read your pamphlet. I am very sorry that you and Gladstone have so fallen across each other—and I suppose his recent article on the Pope[39] (which I have not seen myself) is more painful and annoying to you than anything that has gone before. He has always been something of an Italo-maniac—and now he seems to be almost Prussianizing.
>
> I think my impressions of what you have done are 1. that it was an effective rebuke to ''vehement rhetoric.'' 2. that though a Roman Catholic may be—and may even be *in virtue of his religion*—a better subject and truer patriot in fact than many a loyal Protestant yet that you do not and cannot get rid of the fact (I suppose you would have no difficulty in admitting this) that he is *liable* to have his duty to his Country interfered with by an external authority to an extent differing in kind from the case of the

36. Newman to R. W. Church, 18 January 1875, *The Letters and Diaries,* 27:194.

37. R. W. Church to Newman, 22 January 1875, *The Letters and Diaries,* 27:194, footnote 4.

38. John Pope Hennessy to Newman, 16 January 1875, *The Letters and Diaries,* 27:202, footnote 2. The other topic of conversation in London was Gladstone's resignation.

39. This was Gladstone's anonymous review in the January issue of the *Quarterly Review* of *Discorsi del Sommo Pontefice Pio IX.* It was a decidedly critical appraisal of Pius IX's speeches. According to Walter Arnstein: ''. . . *The Times* dismissed the subjects of the pope's recent speeches as too trivial to warrant such careful attention.'' Walter Arnstein, *Protestant versus Catholic in Mid-Victorian England: Mr. Newdegate and the Nuns* (Columbia: University of Missouri Press, 1982) 196.

average Englishman. 3. that you showed clearly that this state of things had no substantial connection with the Vatican decrees and furnished no reason whatever for throwing doubt on the loyalty theoretical or practical of individual Catholics except under trying circumstances which do not exist and are not likely to occur—or unless they caricature the obligatory doctrines of their Church.

I think in the eyes of an English statesman unaffected by theology—the case of the English Catholics would mainly suffer by its Irish connexion[40]— and that he would view your Church's theory as formidable, mainly because it—or some easy development of it—is calculated to give such advantage and obstinacy to Irish disaffection. Of course it might conceivably be turned the other way . . . but the chances are against this.[41]

As reaction to the *Letter to the Duke of Norfolk* began to come in, Newman was also eager to have comments from members of the hierarchy, particularly his close friends among the bishops. He was grateful for the immediate and favorable reactions of Bishop William Vaughan of Plymouth[42] and Bishop Thomas Brown of Newport. On 21 January, Newman received the wholehearted endorsement of Archbishop Errington. But at the same time Errington was concerned about possible Roman reaction to portions of Newman's pamphlet. It will be seen that the concern he expressed turned out to be entirely correct. "What I imagine will be most likely to affect the susceptibilities of Rome, in your letter," Errington wrote,

will be the theory of the *heirship* of Rome to the claims exercised in earlier times *by* the dispersed hierarchy, (*by* Rome—*through* the dispersed hierarchy would be their formula I should think). It could not however be called

---

40. Earlier in the same letter *The Letters and Diaries* prints this word as "connection".

41. Lord Blachford to Newman, 29 January 1875, *The Letters and Diaries*, 27:211, footnote 2. Concerning Lord Blachford's remarks about Ireland, it should be noted that some commentators suggest that what Blachford thought nearly impossible actually turned out to be the case, that the papacy, especially under Leo XIII, took the side of the English government against the Irish nationalists. This was especially true with the Roman condemnation of the Plan of Campaign in 1888. Archbishop Walsh of Dublin, far more a nationalist than Cullen had been, and the majority of the Irish bishops opposed Rome's decision and were eventually successful in having Rome modify its position. See Emmet Larkin, *The Roman Catholic Church in Ireland and the Fall of Parnell, 1888-1891* (Chapel Hill: University of North Carolina Press, 1979) 3-4 and 18-20. See also Patrick Corish, *The Irish Catholic Experience: A Historical Survey* (Wilmington, Delaware: Michael Glazier, Inc., 1985) 227. The Irish bishops in this period were opposed also to the establishment of diplomatic relations between the Holy See and Great Britain, since they feared that the government would put pressure on the Irish bishops through a nuncio in London. See, for example, Larkin, 137-38.

42. Vaughan had issued a reply to Gladstone in the form of a pastoral letter in December 1874. Döllinger was disappointed that Vaughan, who had been opposed to the definition during the council, had joined Manning in attacking Döllinger's position. See Döllinger to Lady Blennerhassett, 10 December 1874, *Briefwechsel*, 4:586.

in question that historically speaking the distinction between the working of the hierarchy in early days and in later times was just as you describe, and that externally the distinction between the ancient Church and the Papal Church as given by you really existed, though the antithesis conveyed in the titles of the 2d ["The Ancient Church"] and 3d ["The Papal Church"] sections may not be acceptable, as favoring the notion of a real difference.[43]

The following week Newman received congratulations on his pamphlet from Bishop Clifford. After writing to Newman, Errington had met with Clifford, and they had discussed the concern that Errington had brought up to Newman on 21 January. Clifford began by expressing his belief that Newman's pamphlet would do great good in England. He thought this would be achieved "by quieting disturbed consciences, and allaying the ill feeling raised against us amongst Protestants by Mr. Gladstone, but it will also I am sure help in no small degree to cheque the overbearing spirit which exists amongst some of us, and of which you justly complain." Clifford went on to give his own views on the question that Errington had raised. The bishop of Clifton thought that Newman had stated the matter accurately. He held that Newman's argument did not

imply that the Pope has received the powers he now possesses from the Hierarchy of the 4th century, but that whereas in the 4th century certain powers (distinct from the Primacy) derived from Christ and the Apostles were still held not only by the Pope but by the Hierarchy, since that time all other Bishops have from various causes lost those powers, the Pope alone retaining his, hence the powers which in the 4th century were claimed by many can now be claimed by the Pope alone, and must be claimed by him otherwise they would be lost to the Church.

Clifford ended by saying, "I see nothing offensive in this view." But Clifford did have a question of his own on something Newman had said in his pamphlet. It is evident that Clifford felt that Newman had been too expansive in one of his references to papal infallibility. Clifford asked: "Is it correct to say that any *precept* of the Pope is infallible?" And then Clifford answered his question. "The Council strictly confines itself to *definitions*," he said. "It may be said that a definition in matter of morals is a precept. This is true indirectly but not directly, and I think the distinction is important, 'as limiting the scope of infallibility.' "[44] Newman overwhelmed with correspondence related to his pamphlet would wait a week before responding to Clifford.

43. Archbishop George Errington to Newman, 21 January 1875, *The Letters and Diaries,* 27:214, footnote 2.

44. Bishop William Clifford to Newman, 28 January 1875, *The Letters and Diaries,* 27:213, footnote 2 and 214, footnote 2.

By the end of January Newman was feeling a great deal of relief and satisfaction over the reaction to his letter. He must have been particularly gratified by the Marquis of Ripon's letter of 26 January. Ripon expressed his thanks to Newman for sending him a copy of the pamphlet:

> I lose no time in thanking you very much for your kindness in thinking of me; and I hope you will allow me at the same time to express my gratitude to you for your complete vindication of the loyalty and unimpaired allegiance of English Catholics.
>
> It almost seems an impertinence on my part to say with what deep satisfaction I have read your "Letter"; and it is with a feeling difficult to describe that I find myself writing to one, who has, though unknown to himself, exercised a great influence over me for 30 years, and whose works have tended more than any other human cause to bring me to the Catholic Church.[45]

That the accumulation of gratitude and praise pleased Newman is apparent from the letters he sent at this time to several among his close circle of friends. On 23 January, Newman reeled off the names of those who had congratulated him for Ambrose St. John, who was away from the Oratory: "I have had excellent letters from Bishop Vaughan of Plymouth, Archbishop Errington, Fr. Jones, Dr. Russell, Provost Cookson, Provost Render, Allies, Sir George Bowyer, Mr. Pope Hennessy etc."[46] Three days later Newman told William Monsell, "The Tablet too is good,"[47] and in his letter of 29 January, thanking Mrs. William Froude and her daughter, Isy, for their words of gratitude, Newman said, "I should not like names or places mentioned, but for yourself I say that I have letters of approval from Bishops Brown, Clifford, Errington, and especially your own, Dr. Vaughan; from St. Beuno and Stonyhurst, from the Dominicans of Newcastle and of Campden, from Maynooth, Provosts Cookson and Render, and various priests."[48]

But in both the letter to William Monsell and to Mrs. Froude Newman showed that he had not been lulled by his success into thinking that he had achieved a complete victory. He was by nature realistic, and time, especially the past thirty years, had reinforced this side of his personality. In the letter to Mrs. Froude, Newman wrote: "As you and he [Mrs. Froude's son, William] say, we must wait to see what Archbishop Manning says. . . ." Newman was already anticipating what Manning's difficulties would be, but he had hopes that the appearance that same

45. Marquis of Ripon to Newman, 26 January 1875, *The Letters and Diaries,* 27:223, footnote 4.

46. Newman to Ambrose St. John, 23 January 1875, *The Letters and Diaries,* 27:202.

47. Newman to William Monsell, 26 January 1875, *The Letters and Diaries,* 27:205.

48. Newman to Mrs. William Froude, 29 January 1875, *The Letters and Diaries,* 27:208.

month of Ambrose St. John's translation of Fessler's *Die wahre und die falsche Unfehlbarkeit der Päpste* would make Manning think twice of publicly challenging Newman. "The section on the Syllabus is the most opposed, I am told, to Archbishop Manning," Newman informed Mrs. Froude, "and in it I am sheltered by Fessler, whose book is sanctioned by the Pope."[49] At the same time Newman did not forget Ward. As he said in his letter of the 26th to Monsell, "Ward, I suppose, will protest."[50] Newman had tried to be conciliatory to Ward in a letter that he wrote on 18 January. In it he acknowledged that he expected Ward to have difficulties with his pamphlet. Ward was not moved and in fact he found all sorts of reasons for being offended by Newman's letter, even to the point of minutely analysing Newman's closing, "with much affection, yours most sincerely," and finding it lacking in warmth.[51] In a reply written several days later, Ward was uncompromising. He said to Newman: "Your chief charge against me is that I 'make my own belief the measure of the belief of others.' As these words stand they do not convey to me any definite idea." Ward continued: "It has always appeared to me that a Catholic thinker or writer ought to aim at this: viz., so to think and write, as he judges that the Holy See (interpreted by her official Acts, and due regard being had to individual circumstances) would wish him to think and write." Ward closed by appealing to his high doctrine of the Roman magisterium. "I have thought," he said in an obvious reference to Newman's letter to him, "that the 'peace and unity,' which as you so truly say are the 'privilege and duty of Catholics,' are to be sought in one way and no other viz., in increasing among us all an *ex animo* deference, not only to the definitions but to the doctrinal intimations of the Holy See."[52] Ward would eventually join in the general praise for the *Letter to the Duke of Norfolk* but never without finding parts of it regrettable, if not censurable.

Unfavorable Roman reaction to his pamphlet is unknown to Newman

In several of his letters after the publication of the *Letter to the Duke of Norfolk,* Newman showed his concern that his pamphlet would be dis-

49. Ibid.

50. Newman to William Monsell, 26 January 1875, *The Letters and Diaries,* 27:206.

51. See Wilfrid Ward, *The Life of John Henry Cardinal Newman* (London: Longmans, Green, 1912) 2:407.

52. *The Letters and Diaries,* January (?) 1875, 27:204–05, footnote 5. Ward dealt with the *Letter to the Duke of Norfolk* in the January and April 1875 issues of the *Dublin Review.* In his first notice he wrote: "After having been bewildered by Mr. Gladstone's wild and reckless declamation, it is a real refreshment to study F. Newman's cautious and well-

pleasing to ecclesiastical authorities, especially those at Rome. The reaction from high places was not long in coming. It would appear, however, that Newman was unaware of it and of the correspondence it occasioned between officials of the Curia and Archbishop Manning and Bishop Ullathorne. On 3 February, the prefect of Propaganda, Cardinal Alessandro Franchi, said in a letter to Manning that while the first part of Newman's reply to Gladstone was a triumph, the second part contained propositions

---

weighed statements. The very remarkable view of his pamphlet, which appeared in the Pall Mall Gazette of Jan. 20th, is one sample of the effect produced by this contrast on the mind of non-Catholic Englishmen." *Dublin Review,* n.s. 24 (January–April 1875) 215.

In the April issue in an essay entitled "Mr. Gladstone and His Catholic Critics," Ward said of Newman: "As regards the last-named great writer, we must frankly say that there are two or three passages of his pamphlet containing statements with which we cannot concur; and two or three passages (the same or other) in which we cannot altogether sympathize with his tone: but no one of the three [Newman, Manning, and Ullathorne] has spoken more nobly in behalf of the highest Catholic truths and interests, nor grappled more closely and more successfully hand to hand with the common enemy." *Dublin Review,* n.s. 24, 454–55.

In the October 1875 issue of the *Dublin Review,* Ward continued to treat the *Letter to the Duke of Norfolk* with muted praise: "As regards indeed one or two of the matters we have been discussing with him [Newman], we cannot profess to consider them of small amount. Still, after taking them into account, we are confident that the permanent effect of the letter to the Duke of Norfolk will be almost exclusively for good; and that it will be found, as time goes on, to have conferred, both on the Catholic and non-Catholic world, benefits of a really important and lasting character." *Dublin Review,* n.s. 25 (July–October 1875) 307.

Ward was most critical of Newman's gentle reference to Döllinger, of his views on the noninfallible character of the Syllabus, of the small place Newman gave to the need to build up an arsenal of historical arguments to support the definition of papal infallibility, and of Newman's criticisms of the extravagant and intemperate language of some English Catholics in the controversies surrounding the definition.

There can be little doubt that Ward felt trapped somewhat by Fessler's *True and False Infallibility* and the approbation that Pius IX had given to it. The availability of an English translation just at this time was certainly a constraint on the expression of his full views. In the April 1875 issue of the *Dublin Review,* Ward spoke of Fessler's treatise with words of grudging praise: "He is dealing throughout with an opponent [Dr. Schulte], who had put forth an incredible tissue of misstatements on the purport of the Vatican Definitions; and it was not to be expected that, in exposing these intolerable falsehoods, Mgr. Fessler would trouble himself to consider carefully the comparatively minute points of difference between Catholic and Catholic. Indeed, to say the truth, he does not impress us as ever having examined these points of difference with any kind of care; contending as he was on a far larger scale, in defence of what is common Catholic ground. On *this latter* ground he has justly earned imperishable gratitude from children of the Church, and hearty gratulation from the common Father of all the faithful: and sorry indeed should we be, if anything we have said were taken as implying that we do not heartily unite in that gratitude, and submissively sympathize with that gratulation." *Dublin Review,* n.s. 24 (January–April 1875) 340.

But in the July issue of the *Dublin,* as the public controversy began to die down, Ward in an article, "The Purport of Bishop Fessler's Treatise," had obviously had enough of

that could be disturbing to the faithful. Franchi asked for Manning's advice on the matter.[53] Two days later Franchi wrote in a similar vein to Bishop Ullathorne. Franchi asked Ullathorne for a confidential but candid reaction to the concern of the prefect that Newman's pamphlet contained propositions on the papacy and on the Vatican Council that would cause scandal among Catholics. In addition, Franchi asked for Ullathorne's advice on how to overcome the difficulties that he found in Newman's pamphlet.[54]

Manning replied to Franchi on 6 February. He strongly advised that the Holy See take no public action against Newman. He gave twelve reasons for urging this. Among the points that Manning made was his belief that Newman's work had had a positive effect on Protestants and indifferent Catholics. If it was in some ways inexact, this would certainly have no effect upon the vast majority of English Catholics, who accepted the teaching on papal infallibility and were devoted to the Holy See. Manning also told Franchi that the *Letter to the Duke of Norfolk* was the first time that Newman had publicly defended the infallible magisterium of the pope. Though Manning's points were at times repetitive, the sum of them made it very clear that he felt that any action by the Holy See would cause far worse problems than those which might occur because of a lack of precision in some words or phrases found in Newman's pamphlet.[55] Manning had every reason to believe that his response to Franchi had been accepted when he heard some days later from Father Henry O'Callaghan, the rector of the English College in Rome: "The H. Father said to me this morning that he understood you were afraid that he was going to condemn Fr Newman, but that he had no such intention, though he would

---

being chided with the authority of Fessler. He wrote: "A notion has got abroad among some Catholics, that Mgr. Fessler's treatise was partially directed against a certain Catholic ultra party, which is supposed to exist, and to defend an exaggerated interpretation of the Vatican Definition. And from this supposition it is inferred, that the Pope, by complimenting the treatise, expressed his own special approbation of the more moderate line taken by the Bishop, as contrasted with that of the aforesaid contemporary ultras. We must maintain in reply that there is not so much as the vestige of a foundation, for any part of this theory. . . ." *Dublin Review,* n.s. 25 (July–October 1875) 83. And later, in the October 1875 issue, Ward in his essay "F. Newman On Ecclesiastical Prudence" felt sure enough to put Fessler at an even greater remove when he said "the treatise has really no special authority whatever, and there is no reason for supposing that the Holy Father ever read a word of it." Ibid., 294.

53. See Cardinal Alessandro Franchi to Archbishop Henry Edward Manning, 3 February 1875, *The Letters and Diaries,* 27:401, Appendix I. Cardinal Franchi's letter is in Italian.

54. Cardinal Alessandro Franchi to Bishop William Bernard Ullathorne, 5 February 1875, *The Letters and Diaries,* 27:404, Appendix I. In this instance Cardinal Franchi wrote in Latin.

55. Archbishop Henry Edward Manning to Cardinal Alessandro Franchi, 9 February 1875, *The Letters and Diaries,* 27:401–02, appendix I. Manning wrote in Italian, a language in which he was completely at home.

wish that some friend might let Newman know that there were some objectionable passages in his pamphlet. He had heard, he said, that good had been effected by it, and that the notion of Newman's opposition to the Pope was completely dispelled."[56]

Ullathorne replied to Franchi in a long Latin letter. In part, he took the same tack as Manning had, that Newman's pamphlet had done immense good for the Church in England and he illustrated this point by citing the favorable reactions of the *Tablet,* the *Month,* and the *Dublin Review.* Ullathorne explained that Newman's arguments had to be looked at in the context of Protestant England, and it had to be understood that Newman had made an effort to reply to Gladstone on the historical grounds that Gladstone had chosen and not on the grounds of theology. Ullathorne maintained that Newman's pamphlet evidenced a very strong belief in the pope's infallibility and that this should put to rest the unfounded whisperings that had since 1870 gone about concerning Newman's dissatisfaction with the definition of papal infallibility. Like Manning, Ullathorne told Franchi that he thought that any move against Newman would destroy all the gain that Newman's pamphlet had achieved for the Catholic Church in England.[57]

56. Rev. Henry O'Callaghan to Archbishop Henry Edward Manning, 16 February 1875, *The Letters and Diaries,* 27:403, Appendix I. According to Purcell, Pius IX's generally positive reaction to Newman's pamphlet was never conveyed to Newman. See Edmund Sheridan Purcell, *Life of Cardinal Manning, Archbishop of Westminster* (New York and London: Macmillan & Co., 1896) 2:486, footnote 1. There is also no evidence that Manning ever congratulated Newman on his reply to Gladstone. Perhaps he never read it. In a letter to Ullathorne on 15 January 1875, Manning wrote: "I have not yet read Dr. Newman's pamphlet, and I have not done so that I may be clear of seeming in any way to refer to what he has said, if in anything, which I hope is not likely, there were a divergence. I am glad to say this to you, that he also may know it, if ever there were need." Shane Leslie, *Henry Edward Manning: His Life and Labours* (London: Burns Oates & Washbourne Limited, 1921) 247. Nor is there any evidence that Newman wrote appreciatively to Manning after the Archbishop's answer to Gladstone appeared in February 1875. It is interesting to note that Manning in his reply to Gladstone mentioned the earlier replies of Bishops Vaughan, Clifford, and Ullathorne, but not Newman's. See Purcell, *Life of Cardinal Manning,* 2:480–81. In a letter of 18 June 1875, Manning credited Newman with having caught Gladstone out in "mistranslations," but nothing more. Ibid., 488.

57. Bishop William Bernard Ullathorne to Cardinal Alessandro Franchi, *The Letters and Diaries,* undated, 27:404–06, appendix I. In a letter to Newman, written on 22 February 1875, Malcolm MacColl reported: "I know nothing in English history like the revolution which the public mind of England has undergone in your case. At a party at which I happened to be present some days after your Letter to the Duke of Norfolk came out an Ultramontane expressed an ardent wish that your pamphlet might be put on the Index; whereupon a strong 'Protestant' retorted that 'Rome would not dare to offer such an affront to *England.*' The remark expresses the true feeling of the public. They have come to regard you as an English possession of which they are proud." Malcolm MacColl to Newman, 22 February 1875, *The Letters and Diaries,* 27:240, footnote 2.

Newman is exhausted after the hard effort of replying to Gladstone,
but his health and buoyant spirits soon return

For the time being the situation quieted down. Already it was apparent that Rome was having second thoughts about any action against Newman, but the matter would drag on until the end of the year. As February began, he was still receiving many expressions of congratulation for his pamphlet. The strain of the work of writing the response to Gladstone and the heavy correspondence afterwards had their effect in late January when Newman became ill with a serious cold, the worst, by his own testimony, that he had had in many years.[58] He was so ill that for several days he was confined to his room, unable to offer Mass and to participate in the daily routines of the house.[59] In the first ten days of February he managed a few long letters, including letters to Lord Blachford and Bishop Clifford on the 5th, but he was not able to leave the house until a week later.

Newman's illness had kept him from answering Bishop Clifford's letter of 28 January. In his response a week later, Newman began by thanking Clifford for his kind remarks on his pamphlet and for his defense of Newman's statement in it, "the Pope is heir of the Ecumenical Hierarchy of the 4th century." Newman said: "It is very kind of you to bring out what certainly is a vindication of me. I have myself, I think, given another, which seems to be recognized and accepted in the *Month* of February[60] when it speaks of my insisting on 'the manner in which, *to the merely historical eye, and without consideration* of what is involved in Christian *theology* on the subject, the Papal Church became the heir of the rights etc. etc. of the Ancient Church'." Newman then took up another of Clifford's observations on his pamphlet. Here Newman was not entirely ready to concede the bishop of Clifton's point. "As to your Lordship's remark about 'Precepts'," Newman wrote,

> I should like extremely to take what I understand to be your view, that the Pope is not infallible in precepts as precepts—but that his general categori-

58. See Newman "Diary," 27 January 1875, *The Letters and Diaries,* 27:206.
59. See Newman "Diary," 2 February 1875, *The Letters and Diaries,* 27:209.
60. In its "Commentaries on Public Affairs," the February 1875 issue of *The Month* (4 [23]) said: "The chapters on the Ancient Church and the Papal Church are instances of the power possessed by Dr. Newman of giving history in its principles and characteristic lines and yet in a small space. The absolute independence of attitude of the early Church, the almost dominant position of the Church after the conversion of the Empire, and then the manner in which, to the merely historical eye, and without consideration of what is involved in the Christian theology on the subject, the Papal Church became the heir of the rights, privileges, prerogatives and duties of the Ancient Church, and how its position was necessary for the formation and rule of Christian Europe—all these things have never been more clearly summed up in a few pages as here," 225.

cal enunciations (which *are* infallible), such as would be "lotteries are sinful," have *indirectly* a preceptive force, and in *this* way some of his precepts may be *called* infallible. I think I have heard of some theologians who have taken this view—but what weighed with me was Bellarmine, who, if I am not mistaken, distinctly states that the Pope is infallible, in praeceptis morum, if they are about things which are in se bona vel mala, if they are addressed to all, and on points necessary for Salvation.

But it is a further question of course, whether the Vatican Council has *defined* the Pope's infallibility in praeceptis morum, and I am very glad you have started [sic] it. Certainly the infallibility is made in the Pastor Aeternus to attach to "doctrina" only.[61]

Whether Newman and Bishop Clifford ever came to a meeting of minds on their long-running disagreement on the extent to which papal infallibility could be said to extend to questions of moral precepts is not clear. Newman had steered a careful course on this point in the *Letter to the Duke of Norfolk* by saying that while the pope's infallibility did extend to the area of moral precepts, it would in practice be hard to give an example of such since questions of morality were so much bound up with natural law that papal definition in this area would be redundant.

Illness had also kept Newman from replying to Lord Blachford's letter of 29 January. At the end of his long reply on 5 February, Newman asked Blachford to forgive him both his penmanship and ungrammatical sentences. "But you must ascribe it to my cold," Newman explained. Newman covered a range of topics in his reply to Blachford, who had obviously touched on subjects that Newman had given a great deal of thought to in the past decade and a half. He had treated some of them, but indirectly, in his *Letter to the Duke of Norfolk*. His letter to Blachford allowed him the chance to speak more bluntly. "Of course I was much interested with your remarks on my Letter," Newman began, "which you can fancy I was most reluctant to write. But I was bound to write from my duty to those many men who had been more or less influenced in their conversion by my own conversion—and whom I fancied saying to me, 'Is this what you have let us in for?'" After this very revealing glimpse at his reason for carrying the struggle to reply to Gladstone through to completion, Newman went on to speak gratefully of the Catholic response to what he had said. "And I certainly have had my reward on the other hand from old Catholics, from Bishops, Jesuits, Dominicans, and various clergy, who have with one voice concurred in what I have written, as a whole and in its separate parts," Newman told Blachford.

He turned next to Gladstone's recent review of some speeches of Pius IX. "I don't see that Gladstone's article in the Quarterly (tho' I have not

61. Newman to Bishop William Clifford, 5 February 1875, *The Letters and Diaries,* 27:213–14.

seen it yet) touches me, as certainly it does not personally affect me.''[62] And then Newman showed why he understood what Gladstone had said did not affect him. In fact he appeared to agree largely with what Gladstone had said. "If in private," Newman wrote, " 'the Pope's lackies' (as St. Francis de Sales calls them) butter the Pope, and he, an old cruelly treated man allows it, and Gladstone comes down upon the Don Pasquales (is not that the name?)[63] who publish all this to the world, I leave Don P. to answer Gladstone, and consider it no business of mine. The Catholic Church has its constitution and its theological laws in spite of the excesses of individuals.[64] In his letter of 29 January, Blachford had shown that he had not missed that Newman's pamphlet, while in the main a reply to Gladstone, was also concerned with the extravagant language of some Catholics in England. Indeed, in referring to this aspect of Newman's pamphlet, Blachford used the celebrated words, "an insolent and aggressive faction," from Newman's letter, written exactly five years before, to Bishop Ullathorne. Blachford believed that Newman in his attempts to deal with Catholic exaggeration had taken a very minimizing stance toward the doctrine of papal infallibility and he professed to be surprised by this:

> Your representation of papal decisions as throwing out a kind of rough material to be hammered into shape (sometimes very unlike its original one) by the "Schola Theologorum minimizantium" presented to my mind a curious picture which I do not quite know what to make of.
>
> I do not mean that these things seemed the most *valuable* parts of your pamphlet but in reading them I felt like travelling in a foreign country with new sights and circumstances.[65]

Newman in his response to Blachford offered guidance for the journey:

> It is this, which, if I understand your letter, is a novel idea to you—and it is this, which Acton *means* (I consider) though he is unlucky in his lan-

---

62. *Quarterly Review* (January 1875), 266–304. See *The Letters and Diaries,* 27:211, footnote 3.

63. The editor of the Pope's speeches was Don Pasquale de Franciscis.

64. Newman to Lord Blachford, 5 February 1875, *The Letters and Diaries,* 27:211-12.

65. Lord Blachford to Newman, 29 January 1875, *The Letters and Diaries,* 27:212, footnote 1. Blachford likened reading Newman's *Letter* to travel in a foreign country. Malcolm MacColl made a similar point in his letter to Newman of 22 February 1875, when he wrote: "I always find myself in a different atmosphere when reading what you write. . . ." *The Letters and Diaries,* 27:240, footnote 2. Here a comment of a present-day theologian speaking not of the First Vatican Council but of the Second seems very apt. In his essay, "Tides and Twilight: Newman Since Vatican II," Nicholas Lash writes of Newman: "Before the council [Vatican II], still an occasionally suspect stranger, an outsider to the neo-scholastic world. After the council, its godfather and our guide into the strange territory that now lay before us." *Newman after a Hundred Years,* ed. Ian Ker and Alan G. Hill (Oxford: Clarendon Press, 1990) 454.

guage, as not being a theologian, when he says it is no matter what Councils or Popes decree or do, for the Catholic body goes on pretty much as it did, in spite of all—the truth being that the Schola Theologorum is (in the Divine Purpose, *I* should say) the regulating principle of the Church, and, as lawyers and public offices (if I may speak thus coram te) preserve the tradition of the British Constitution, in spite of King, Lords, and Commons, so there is a permanent and sui similis life in the Church, to which all its acts are necessarily assimilated, nay, and, under the implied condition of its existence and action, such acts are done and are accepted.[66]

Newman continued by speaking bluntly of the state of theological learning in the Catholic Church in England and of the frustration of steps he had tried to take to begin to remedy the situation:

I think, when you were here last, I said to you our great want just now was theological schools, which the great French Revolution has destroyed. This has been the occasion of our late and present internal troubles. Where would Ward have been, if there had been theological Schools in England? Again, the Archbishop is not a theologian, and, what is worse, the Pope is not a theologian, and so theology has gone out of fashion. This is the only reason which made me regret not going to Oxford—and this is why Ward did

66. Newman had given an important emphasis to the *Schola Theologorum* in the *Letter to the Duke of Norfolk* and he repeats this underscoring of the role of theologians (the prophetical office) in this letter to Blachford. (Newman also touches on this topic in a letter to Isy Froude of 28 July 1875, which will be treated later in this chapter.) Newman would develop his views on the role of theologians two years later in the preface to the third edition of the *Via Media*: "I say, then, theology is the fundamental and regulating principle of the whole Church system. It is commensurate with Revelation, and Revelation is the initial and essential idea of Christianity." *The Via Media of the Anglican Church* (Longmans, Green, and Co., 1901) xlvii–xlviii. Misner sees Newman's giving priority to theologians as a shift from his earlier emphasis on the supremacy of the regal or ruling office in the Church. Misner traces the beginning of this shift to a letter that Newman wrote to William Brownlow shortly before Brownlow's reception into the Catholic Church in November 1863: "Newman had put church authority, what he now called the regal office of the church, on a pedestal during his long fight against state supremacy over the church and against undue trust in reason where religion was concerned. In his preface to the third edition of the *Via Media* he pulled it down from its pedestal and bade it take its place in the arena with 'theology' and 'devotion.' With this he gave the underpinnings of much that he had formerly written about the church a mighty shake." Paul Misner, *Papacy and Development: Newman and the Primacy of the Pope* (Leiden: E. J. Brill, 1976) 173. Newman was moved, in Misner's opinion, to make this significant shift in his views because of the dominance of the Ultramontane party in the 1860s and 1870s. See ibid. In addition to the letter to Brownlow another important letter in Newman's growing appreciation of the place of the *Schola Theologorum* in the Church was written exactly two years later in a letter of 9 November 1865 to Henry Oxenham, in which Newman says of the *Schola* that without it, "the dogma of the Church would be the raw flesh without skin—nay a tree without leaves. . . ." *The Letters and Diaries of John Henry Newman,* ed. Charles Stephen Dessain (London: Thomas Nelson and Sons Ltd., 1972) 22:98–99. On Newman's views on the role of theologians in the life of the Church, see also Lee H. Yearley, *The Ideas of Newman: Christianity and Human Religiosity* (University Park and London: The Pennsylvania State University Press, 1978) 77–81.

all he could at Rome, and successfully, to hinder me going. I don't profess
to be a theologian, but at all events I should have been able to show a side
of the Catholic religion more theological, more exact, than his.

From unhappy thoughts about his hopes for an Oratory at Oxford nearly
a decade before, Newman brought the discussion of theology back to the
present moment:

> Where there is such a lack of theological science, I must not take it for granted
> as yet that I am out of the wood, for I may still receive some cuff from
> the political ultra-devotional party—but I don't think it can be very bad.
> This I may say for my comfort—the only great school now going is the Jesuit
> School, and they have always been for me—not always, I suppose, agree-
> ing with me (about that I know nothing) tho' *often* agreeing, but always
> taking my part and backing me up, (I don't include the Civiltà party, about
> which there is some mystery) but all the Jesuits I have come across for thirty
> years. My Grammar of Assent did not go in their groove, and I suppose
> they did not like it, but that did not alter their uniform line of conduct to-
> wards me.

Newman concluded his long letter by addressing Blachford's comments
on Catholic allegiance and particularly Catholic allegiance with regard to
Ireland, an area that Blachford believed could possibly put Catholics in
opposition to the English State, and with papal approval. Newman disagreed on both the general and particular points:

> Of course Religion always interferes with the State. You will say that the
> peculiarity of the Catholic Religion is that the moving power of interfer-
> ence lies in a foreigner—but I question whether a strong English party, as
> the Puritans, may not be even more formidable, though foreigners are al-
> together excluded—the bond of esprit de corps will be far more intense,
> and the principle of loyalty to each other being an external bond as strong
> as loyalty to the Pope. Moreover, the Pope can be approached and negotiated
> with, but Charles I would have found it difficult to treat with the Puritan
> conscience and Puritan mutual comaradaria.
>   It is through the Pope that Ireland would be kept from using religion
> for political purposes—but neither England or Ireland will at present suf-
> fer such a thing to be said.[67]

Some Newman critics do not join in the positive reaction

Newman had been especially critical of Ward in his letter to Blachford. Despite Newman's attempt to reach a more cordial relationship with
Ward two weeks previously, Ward had just given Newman new cause for
annoyance in the pages of the *Dublin*. In a comment in the January issue

---

67. Newman to Lord Blachford, 5 February 1875, *The Letters and Diaries*, 27:212–13.

of the *Dublin Review* on Ullathorne's "Mr. Gladstone's Expostulation Unravelled," Ward had made it appear that Ullathorne held that the *Syllabus* was an *ex cathedra* pronouncement, whereas Newman in his pamphlet took an opposite view. Ullathorne protested Ward's assertion. He said that he had not spoken of *ex cathedra* pronouncements with regard to the *Syllabus*.[68] Though at first Newman had felt that Ullathorne might not have been altogether pleased with the *Letter to the Duke of Norfolk,* Ullathorne's protest to Ward made it clear that Newman had not lost his bishop's confidence. Ullathorne had not allowed Ward to place him in opposition to Newman. When the bishop of Birmingham made his defense known to Newman, Newman despite his illness, hastened to thank Ullathorne. "I was of course pleased to receive your letter," Newman wrote on 1 February, "for I certainly thought that Mr. Ward had not given a right sense to your words. He seems to find it difficult to take a straightforward view of any thing. And it is very considerate in you to send your letter to the Papers."[69] Ward apologized to Ullathorne on 3 February. In his defense he explained that he had been in an anxious state for some time. Ullathorne sent Ward's letter to Newman, who thanked him for sight of it in a letter of 9 February. Referring to Ward, Newman said:

> I wrote to him some weeks ago on the publication of my Pamphlet a letter, which I meant to be kind, by way of softening what I had said of him, and he returned me a friendly answer. I have said nothing in my Pamphlet so severe as I have said to himself in these latter years again and again, and since what I said to him produced no effect, but he went on saying the same things in the Dublin as strongly or more strongly, it was clearly a question of opposing *principles* on his side and mine, and, as he had in so many words or their equivalents called me a material heretic, I called him a doctrinal Novatian. I know perfectly well how affectionate his feelings are towards me, and I may truly say I never have borne him illwill and felt towards him any resentment for a moment, but have always expressed my admiration, to himself as to others, of his perfect frankness and sincerity. He has never whispered against me—he has spoken out as a man, and he had a right to do so. But I have a right to speak too, and they who play at bowls must expect rubbers.[70]

Newman made one further attempt to use the publication of his response to Gladstone's *Expostulation* as a means of reaching a more

68. See Bishop William Bernard Ullathorne to Newman, 31 January 1875, *The Letters and Diaries,* 27:209, footnote 1. Bishop Ullathorne's letter of 1 February to the *Dublin Review* is found in the April 1875 issue, n.s. 24 (January–April 1875) 530.

69. Newman to Bishop William Bernard Ullathorne, 1 February 1875, *The Letters and Diaries,* 27:209.

70. Newman to Bishop William Bernard Ullathorne, 9 February 1875, *The Letters and Diaries,* 27:216.

amicable relationship with Ward. In the generous view of Ward that he had expressed to Bishop Ullathorne and in this further effort to put aside his many difficulties with Ward, Newman was perhaps moved by Ward's admission to Ullathorne that he was in an anxious and nervous state. When Ward in the January issue of the *Dublin Review* spoke in the main approvingly of Newman's pamphlet, Newman wrote him on 15 February to say, "During the last day or two I have seen your January Dublin, and I thank you very much for the generous and frank way in which you speak in approval of what I have written, not only at other times, but in the present controversy with Mr. Gladstone."[71] Ward, perhaps as a consequence of his declining health, was showing signs at this point of wearying of the Ultramontane battle. Indeed, he had told Ullathorne in early February that he intended to use his remaining energies in the struggle against atheism. He would turn over the editorship of the *Dublin Review* to his son, Wilfrid, in 1878.

But Ward remained in early 1875 the leading proponent of the Ultramontane cause and members of the party still looked to him as their champion. When Father Paul Bottalla, a Liverpool Jesuit, found to his surprise that the *Tablet* would not accept some unfavorable observations he had written on Newman's pamphlet,[72] he turned to Ward in the hope of finding a forum for his views. In his letter of 25 February, Bottalla told Ward:

> I send you an Article of critique on Dr. Newman's pamphlet. You are one of the few in England who can judge with great independence of the correctness of my remarks. The *Tablet's* Editor, to whom I had sent this article for publication, returned it to me, accompanied with a very kind letter, in which he stated that though he would have been pleased to insert it in the columns of his paper, many in London had advised him not to publish any critique on that pamphlet. I answered that many also of the Clergy and the Laity had invited me to write that article, and I had let it be preceded by two others of review and praise of the pamphlet, in order to show that I did not intend to take the side of opposition against Dr. Newman, but only the defense of the pure Catholic doctrine. . . . I think that it is not a prudence to hold our tongue, when Protestants may in future times avail themselves of the principles of Dr. Newman against the Catholic Church. I feel confident that we will perfectly agree in our judgments. I have received many congratulations for this critique from those who are able to judge in the matter, and who were informed of the author of the critique in question.[73]

71. Newman to William George Ward, 15 February 1875, *The Letters and Diaries,* 27:223.

72. See Trevor, *Newman: Light in Winter,* 518.

73. Father Paul Bottalla, S.J., to William George Ward, 25 February 1875, *The Letters and Diaries,* 27:403, Appendix I.

When Newman had written to Lord Blachford on 5 February, he had spoken of the general esteem in which the Jesuits had held his writings. He excepted only the Civiltà. Obviously he had overlooked the determined Father Bottalla, or had judged his opposition of little consequence.

Newman is elated by positive reaction in unexpected quarters, especially from those in high places

The *Tablet's* largely positive reaction to the *Letter to the Duke of Norfolk* is surely one of the best evidences of the overall success of Newman's pamphlet in the Catholic community and an indication that Father Bottalla may have been guilty of some overstatement when he told Ward that he had written his critique at the urging of "many" Catholics, priests and lay people. The editor of the *Tablet* in 1875 was George Eliot Ranken. Herbert Vaughan, while retaining ownership, had given up editing the *Tablet* and had turned his attention to the founding of the Mill Hill Fathers.

The *Tablet* carried three generally laudatory notices of the *Letter to the Duke of Norfolk*. While expressing some reservations, the editor spoke in expansive, almost lavish tones. In its first notice on 23 January 1875, the *Tablet* said: "The arguments of this remarkable *Letter* are so unanswerable that we are inclined to doubt with *The Times* whether Mr. Gladstone will attempt to grapple with them." The writer went on to say: " . . . and while we gratefully acknowledge the immense assistance which Father Newman's gentle moderation has been to so many sensitive consciences, we must beg of his large heart to make allowances for us when we conscientiously believe that some souls are helped by strong language which we have now and then thought it our duty to use." And finally in a mood of acknowledging sinfulness that grace may more abound, the editor said: "And even if our indiscretion did 'set the house on fire,' it is a gain rather than a loss to find that Father Newman is more than equal to the 'task of putting out the flames.' This *Letter* is not likely to go through so many editions as the pamphlet to which it is a reply; but it is likely to live in English literature long after Mr. Gladstone's Expostulation is buried in oblivion."[74]

In its final notice on 20 February 1875, the *Tablet* expressed the hope that Newman before his death would "enrich our literature with many more such unanswerable defences of our holy faith."[75] Even before the third notice, Newman wrote to the editor of the *Tablet* to express his thanks:

74. *Tablet,* n.s. 45 (23 January 1875) 104–05.
75. *Tablet,* n.s. 45 (20 February 1875) 236.

I have waited before writing you, lest I should be premature in doing so. Now I may safely act upon the impulse which I have felt since your first notice on January 23 last of my Letter to the Duke of Norfolk.

Let me then return to you my best thanks for the generous reception you have given that Letter. I use the word "generous" with a definite meaning, and as implying, as its correlative on my part, my great gratification, and, I may say, gratitude.

I trust too that the tone of your remarks upon me may impress on outsiders that there are not those serious differences of opinion between Catholics which they are so ready to believe.[76]

And even Herbert Vaughan, who was travelling in America when Newman's pamphlet was published, showed his positive reaction in a letter to Lady Herbert of Lea.[77]

There can be little doubt that the reaction to his pamphlet that most pleased Newman was Cardinal Cullen's single but very positive sentence on it in his Lenten Pastoral Letter. In this letter, issued in early February, Cardinal Cullen wrote: "The grounds on which this statesman founded his expostulation have been admirably answered by the venerable Dr. Newman, for many years the great and pious and learned rector of the Catholic University, whom Ireland will ever revere, and by the illustrious Archbishop of Westminster, and equally so by his suffragans."[78] Newman first saw Cullen's pastoral letter on 14 February. His letter of thanks to Cullen was written the same day, which was also the First Sunday of

76. *The Letters and Diaries,* Newman to the Editor of the *Tablet,* 15 February 1875, 27:222. Newman's letter to the *Tablet* was printed in the 27 February issue, n.s. 45, 269.

77. See *Letters of Herbert Cardinal Vaughan to Lady Herbert of Lea,* ed. Shane Leslie (London: Burns, Oates, 1942) 267. Before his death Cardinal Vaughan destroyed his personal papers. The letters that he wrote over a long period of time to Lady Herbert are one of the few surviving records of his personal thoughts and reactions to the events of his time.

78. *The Letters and Diaries,* 27:220, footnote 4. It is clear from a letter of Cullen of 17 January 1875 to Monsignor Tobias Kirby, rector of the Irish College in Rome, that Cullen was concerned about Newman's *Letter* when he first read of it in the *Times.* He was particularly doubtful about the following statement in Newman's conclusion: ". . . for the benefit of some Catholics, I would observe that, while I acknowledge one Pope, *jure divino,* I acknowledge no other, and I think it a usurpation too wicked to be comfortably dwelt upon, when individuals use their private judgment, in the discussion of religious questions, not simply 'abundare in suo sensu,' but for the purpose of anathematizing the private judgment of others." LDN, 203. Cullen told Kirby, "This seems a hit at Dr. Manning," and while he found the *Letter* to have many positive aspects, he instructed Kirby to "get someone to examine the document" and to bring it to the attention of Cardinal Franchi, the prefect of Propaganda. See James Bastable, "Gladstone's *Expostulation* and Newman," in Bastable, *Newman and Gladstone,* 20–21, quoting from the Kirby Papers, no. 29, Pontificio Collegio Irlandese, Rome. While it is clear that the *Letter to the Duke of Norfolk* would have come to the attention of Propaganda from various sources, Cullen's instruction to Kirby, coming as it did from a cardinal, was surely one of the most influential and, to the curial mind, persuasive.

Lent, the day on which Cullen's letter was read from the pulpits of the archdiocese of Dublin. It is clear that Newman was overwhelmed by Cullen's comment, especially since he had not heard from him since early in 1862 when Newman had corresponded in stiff terms with Cullen over the ownership of the University Church in Dublin.[79] In stating his gratitude Newman wrote:

> I have this morning received your Eminence's Pastoral, and have read with gratification and thankfulness the very kind and gracious approval which in the course of it you express of my recent Pamphlet in reply to Mr. Gladstone. Since its publication I have been fortunate in receiving many encouraging and friendly letters from Bishops and theologians, but not any commendation that I have received has given me such heartfelt pleasure as your Eminence's notice of me. After receiving it, I do not require any additional praise from any one whether here or in Ireland.[80]

Newman's letter brought from Cullen a reply in which he expressed in even stronger terms than in his pastoral his appreciation for Newman's response to Gladstone and his own esteem for Newman himself. Writing on 19 February, Cullen said:

> I was very happy to receive your letter and to learn from it that the few words I said about your labours and your sacrifices for Ireland were gratifying to you. I can assure you that our people and clergy are not forgetful of the services you rendered us, and that they continually speak of you with feelings of gratitude and respect. I must add that they were delighted with the powerful logic and eloquence with which you refuted Mr. Gladstone's charges against the Vatican Council and the Pope. Indeed many think that that statesman has done us a great service by giving you and his Grace Dr. Manning an opportunity of putting the catholic case in so admirable a light.
>
> I trust that God will give you health and strength to labour in his cause for many years to come, and to shed lustre on the church by the splendour of your writings.
>
> As to myself I am well, but I celebrate the 25th year of my episcopate next Thursday, and am fast advancing in the evening of life. Be so good as to say a prayer for me on this occasion.

And in closing, Cullen wrote: "Wishing you every happiness I remain with great esteem. . . ."[81]

79. See Archbishop Paul Cullen to Newman, 28 February 1862, *The Letters and Diaries of John Henry Newman,* ed. Charles Stephen Dessain (London: Nelson, 1970) 20:158–59. Newman evidently forgot this unhappy correspondence when he told Ambrose De Lisle on 14 February 1875 that he had not had "a word" from Cullen since "I left Dublin in 1858. . . ." See *The Letters and Diaries,* 27:221.

80. Newman to Cardinal Paul Cullen, 14 February 1875, *The Letters and Diaries,* 27:220.

81. Cardinal Paul Cullen to Newman, 19 February 1875, *The Letters and Diaries,* 27:221.

In a letter written to Ambrose Phillipps De Lisle on 14 February, the same day as his letter of thanks to Cullen, Newman makes very evident his reasons for being so encouraged by the cardinal's positive reaction to his pamphlet. At the same time he tried to reassure De Lisle, whose own response to Gladstone in the *Union Review* had got him into difficulty with his bishop, Edward Bagshawe of Nottingham. Bishop Bagshawe had condemned what De Lisle had written.[82] In the midst of his own success, Newman showed sympathy for the difficulties of those who had stood by him for so many years. "I am deeply grieved at what you tell me," Newman began his letter to De Lisle. "It is simply shocking—but it really must not discourage you. Be of good heart—there is nothing more to come. It is impossible you can be touched. The Bishop of C.," Newman said referring to Clifford of Clifton, who had approved De Lisle's article in manuscript, "is a good Roman theologian, and knows when a book is safe and when it is not."

And then Newman continued with news that he was evidently excited to share with his friends, but which he also believed had a message for De Lisle in his troubles:

> I have had a most gratifying good fortune this morning and it concerns you in your present distress—for you have not said nearly such strong things as I have, and if I am safe, much more you. Cardinal Cullen, from whom I have not had a word since I left Dublin in 1858, in his just published Lent Pastoral speaks of me thus: —"The grounds on which this statesman (Gladstone) founded his expostulation have been admirably answered by the venerable Dr. Newman, for many years the rector of the Catholic University, whom Ireland will ever revere, etc." Now considering that Dr. C. is a Cardinal, that he is a good theologian, that he has ever been prominently trusted at Rome, and is a personal friend of the Pope's, it is impossible he should use those words of me if there was anything in my Pamphlet which would call for animadversion from Rome—and I repeat, if I am safe, much more you.
>
> Therefore, however painful the occurrence is, put it aside.[83]

82. "The Council of the Vatican In Its Bearings on Civil Allegiance," which appeared in the February 1875 issue of the *Union Review*. De Lisle at age 65 and a Catholic for fifty years was deeply distressed by Bagshawe's criticisms. Bagshawe, who had been a priest of the London Oratory, had been named bishop of Nottingham only the year before. There were rumors current that he had been imposed on the diocese by Manning, the *terna* of the cathedral chapter having been set aside. De Lisle sought help from Newman and from Bishop Clifford in responding to the bishop of Nottingham's charges. De Lisle had consulted Clifford, who was a distant relative, before publishing his article, and this undoubtedly played some part in Bishop Bagshawe's decision to confront De Lisle. In a long letter to Newman on 13 February, De Lisle set out his side of the controversy and in passing spoke of Bagshawe as "young, indiscreet and violent." Purcell and Edwin De Lisle, *Life and Letters of Ambrose Phillipps De Lisle,* 2:59. Several pieces of important correspondence dealing with De Lisle's troubles with Bishop Bagshawe are found in Purcell and De Lisle, 57–67.

83. Newman to Ambrose De Lisle, 14 February 1875, *The Letters and Diaries*, 27:221–

Newman continued his efforts to encourage De Lisle when he wrote again
several days later: "I hear many accounts of priests etc who like your article, and not one of readers who dislike it. To me the question is, first
is the *scope* and substance of the whole good? secondly is the tone and
object good? and thirdly the opinions in it, do they transgress that liberty
which the Church allows? This is what I think most candid men would
ask and would answer in the affirmative."[84] Before the end of the month,
De Lisle had reached an agreement with his bishop, and the charges
brought against him were pursued no further.[85]

The day after receiving Cullen's praise for his pamphlet, Newman went
up to London for a visit to Lord Coleridge that he had postponed earlier
in the month when he was ill.[86] While he was there he saw among others
Father Henry Coleridge, the brother of his host, Dean Church, Canon
Oakeley, and Lord Ripon. When Newman returned to Birmingham on
18 February he came down no doubt encouraged by the congratulations
on his pamphlet that had been personally expressed to him during his visit
to London. These were simply face to face confirmations of the expressions of thanks that continued to come to him by letter all through the

---

22. See also Newman to Lord Charles Rynne, 22 February 1875, *The Letters and Diaries,*
27:231.

While Newman clearly meant to encourage De Lisle with news of Cullen's favorable words
on the *Letter to the Duke of Norfolk,* De Lisle did not see what particular bearing Newman's good fortune had on his own difficulties. In a letter of 15 February to Bishop Clifford,
De Lisle, speaking of Newman's letter of the previous day, said: "This letter is of course
very satisfactory to me to get but it reminds me of a story I could tell you, which I must
reserve till we meet again, for it is too long for a letter, but which tends to prove that because one man escapes a danger, another is not always equally fortunate."

And further in the same letter De Lisle, fearing that the matter would be taken to Rome,
makes an interesting and amusing comment on why he thinks the dispute is likely to be taken
that far: "An enraged and disappointed 'Party,' such as that to which Dr. B.[agshawe] does
not *scruple* to declare 'that he belongs,' will want a victim to save its own honor, and as
Rome neither knows nor cares for the Position I hold among the Landed Aristocracy of
England or its most ancient Feudal Families, or for my connexions, *Friendships,* and acquaintances, the heads of the 'Party' there may possibly think me a convenient, and not
a *dangerous* victim, and sacrifice me accordingly. . . ." Purcell and Edwin De Lisle, *Life
and Letters of Ambrose De Lisle,* 2:61.

84. Newman to Ambrose De Lisle, 19 February 1875, *The Letters and Diaries,* 27:224.

85. See De Lisle to Bishop Bagshawe, 22 February 1875, in Purcell and Edwin De Lisle,
Life and Letters of Ambrose De Lisle, 2:66–67. See also Newman to De Lisle, 25 February
1875, *The Letters and Diaries,* 27:234.

86. One of the reasons for this visit appears to have been a drawing of Newman that
Lady Coleridge was doing. She had planned to come to Birmingham in November to work
on it, but Newman was too busy with his pamphlet. See Newman to Miss Holmes, 9 January 1875, *The Letters and Diaries,* 27:186. The drawing by Lady Coleridge is found on the
front of the dust cover of Bastable's *Newman and Gladstone: Centennial Essays* and Gilley's *Newman and His Age,* and as the frontispiece in Ker's *John Henry Newman: A Biography* and Trevor's *Newman: Light In Winter.*

month of February. In a number of cases those who customarily sent him
birthday greetings took the occasion of his seventy-fourth birthday on 21
February to congratulate him also on his answer to Gladstone. One of
those who combined congratulations with birthday greetings was Gerard
Manley Hopkins. In his response on 21 February, Newman wrote:

> I thank you sincerely for your friendly letter on my birthday. It is a pledge
> to me that you sometimes think of me in your prayers, which I need very
> much.
>   You can easily understand what anxiety the writing of my late Pamphlet
> gave me. I had heard it had been read in your Refectory,[87] which I accounted
> a great honour.[88]

And in a letter to Mrs. Wilson on the same day, Newman said:

> I thank you most sincerely for your congratulations both upon another birth-
> day and upon my recent Pamphlet. The latter, as you may suppose, has
> given me much anxiety as well as thought. I had to state my own belief and
> views so as at once to answer Mr. Gladstone and yet to satisfy both Catho-
> lics and Protestants,—and though, as time goes on, some of my details may
> be questioned by these persons or those, I do not think that the general satis-
> faction which I have given will be reversed, and I feel very thankful that
> I am able to indulge this anticipation."[89]

In his reply to Mrs. Wilson, Newman had said that one of the great
challenges he had faced in writing his answer to Gladstone was his need
to gain the attention and respect of both Catholics and Protestants at the
same time. In January, Newman had received several encouraging indications of the success his pamphlet had had among those who were not
Catholics. These continued in February. In a letter to Newman of 5
February, Alexander Fullerton said, "How truly we rejoice to hear from

---

87. Newman's letter was read at St. Beuno's College, but at recreation not in the refectory.
Newman was probably misled in this by the letter of Father Thomas Harper to William Gowan
Todd. Monsell had sent Newman a copy of this letter. See p. 326.

88. Newman to Gerard Manley Hopkins, 21 February 1875, *The Letters and Diaries,*
27:227. Around this time Gerard Manley Hopkins made the following entry in his note-
book: "In the autumn of 1874 Mr. Gladstone brought out his Expostulation with Catholics
upon the Vatican decrees and Syllabus. Many good answers appeared and were read in the
refectory—by Lord Robert Montagu, Pope Hennessy, Dr. Ullathorne, Mgr. Capel, Dr. Manning, the last two the least interesting. But Dr. Manning's was more interesting towards
the end and dignified throughout. Dr. Newman's we read in recreation. This came out about
the beginning of the year. Simcox reviews it interestingly in the *Academy.*" *The Note-Books
and Papers of Gerard Manley Hopkins,* ed. Humphry House (London & New York: Oxford University Press, 1937) 216.

89. Newman to Mrs. Lavinia Wilson, 21 February 1875, *The Letters and Diaries,* 27:228.

all quarters such a consoling account of the influence that your answer to Gladstone has exercised not only on Catholic minds but upon the *Intellectual* protestant minds of this country."[90] Some time soon after the publication of the *Letter to the Duke of Norfolk,* the Earl of Denbigh told Newman, "Your pamphlet has already led several into the One Fold. I have never heard but one opinion of it, from Protestants or Catholics that it was *crushingly successful* as an answer to all Mr. G.'s charges."[91] An independent witness to the success of Newman's pamphlet beyond the Catholic community is given in a letter written by William Palmer at the beginning of February to T. W. Allies:

> It certainly is a most effective answer; if anything can move honest Protestants or mitigate their prejudices that ought to do so. And there is not one word in it to offend or repel them. . . . His complete openness and his independence going as far as it is possible for Catholicism to go ought to make him all the more authoritative and persuasive for Protestants for whom he writes. . . . I do not suppose that any permanent effect will be produced by Gladstone's Expostulation on any body; but I do expect that many minds will be permanently influenced by F. Newman's answer.[92]

Newman gratified by reaction to his pamphlet from Ireland, America, and the Continent

Since the position of Catholics in Ireland toward the English government had played a part in the controversy, Newman was especially gratified to receive indications that the Catholic community in Ireland, particularly the bishops, had judged his pamphlet successful. The reaction of Cardinal Cullen and its effect upon Newman have already been noted. Newman's closest friend among the Irish bishops, Bishop Moriarty of Kerry, expressed his gratitude in a very candid letter to Newman on 24 February: "Many thanks for the coup de grace you have given to the faction who would allow none to be Catholics but Dublin Reviewers and Tablet Editors. They have taken the castigation meekly. Strange that while the tenor of Moral Theology, at the present time, is so lenient as to be nearing laxity, these men should be making the obligations resulting from the obedience of faith so excessively stringent. You and Dr. Fessler have *shut them up.*" Moriarty obviously believed that Newman's real

90. Alexander Fullerton to Newman, 5 February 1875, *The Letters and Diaries,* 27:215, footnote 1.

91. Earl of Denbigh to Newman, late January or early February 1875, *The Letters and Diaries,* 27:230, footnote 2.

92. William Palmer to T. W. Allies, 1 (?) February 1875, *The Letters and Diaries,* 27:209, footnote 1 bis. There are two footnotes marked "1" on the same page.

success had been against the Ultramontane party and that Gladstone, for whom Moriarty had a great deal of personal sympathy and regard, was simply the occasion for this rout of the papalist party. The bishop of Kerry wrote: "I thank you too for treating poor Gladstone gently. May we not attribute his present position to disappointed good will? Perhaps he had a hope of union, and that it seemed to him that by the Vatican Council inter nos et vos chaos magnum firmatum est. I cannot be angry with him for thinking as I thought myself."[93]

Further evidence of Newman's success with the Irish bishops came in a letter from Dr. Russell of Maynooth. Writing on 5 February, Russell reported to Newman, "I met a large body of bishops and clergy [at the funeral of Archbishop Leahy of Cashel], and I was quite happy in the unanimity of approval and admiration." Russell went on to report reaction from another quarter that was obviously of concern to Newman. Russell told Newman that "Lord O'Hagan in a letter written before his return reported the same of those he met in Rome and specially of Mgr. Nardi,[94] who had reviewed it in the *Voce della Verità.*" "In fact," Russell concluded his report, "the more the Letter is read, and the more closely it is studied the better people are pleased with it."[95]

Newman was also gratified to receive expressions of thanks from ordinary Catholics in Ireland, people only distantly known to him. One of these, Miss Alice Augnier, confessed to Newman, "I felt a fear, that you were not an Irish born Catholic and might be wanting in that real loyalty and devotion to the Holy Father, but, O thank God, you have come out of the combat a true Catholic, true to the Church, true to the liberty of the Children of God. . . ."[96] Newman in his reply said: "Your letter is a very kind one, and I thank you most sincerely for the great charity you

93. Bishop David Moriarty to Newman, 24 February 1875, *The Letters and Diaries,* 27:237, footnote 1.

94. Monsignor Francesco Nardi, an official of the Roman Curia who was somewhat conversant with English affairs, had visited Newman in 1851 and in 1867. Nardi contributed his own pamphlet to the controversy initiated by Gladstone's *Expostulation.* It appeared early in 1875 under the title, "Sul tentativo anti-cattolico in Inghilterra e l'opusculo dell Sig. Gladstone." Gladstone made an entry on Nardi's pamphlet in his diary for 16 January 1875. See *The Gladstone Diaries,* ed. H. C. G. Matthew (Oxford: Clarendon Press, 1986) 9:6. Gladstone also notes one other Italian publication in the Vatican Decrees controversy. This was the pamphlet of the Oratorian Father Alfonso Capecelatro. Capecelatro's pamphlet, "Gladstone e gli effetti de Decreti Vaticani," appeared in the spring of 1875 and was referred to by Gladstone in his diary on 8 April 1875. See ibid., 28. Capecelatro, who became Vatican Librarian in 1893 and a cardinal in 1895, published a two-volume work in 1859 entitled, *Newman e la religione cattolica in Inghilterra.*

95. Dr. Charles Russell to Newman, 5 February 1875, *The Letters and Diaries,* 27:215, footnote 2.

96. Miss Alice Augnier to Newman, 1 February 1875, *The Letters and Diaries,* 27:210, footnote 1.

have shown me in your prayers. It is really a wonderful charity, for what have I done to have a claim upon you? and I pray God may return to you a ten-fold blessing as a reward for it.''[97]

In February, Newman also received letters that showed appreciation for his pamphlet beyond England and Ireland. Archbishop John Baptist Purcell of Cincinnati wrote at the beginning of February to assure Newman that the unkind reaction of James McMaster, the decidedly Ultramontane and frequently vitriolic editor of the *New York Freeman's Journal,* was untypical of the overall reaction in the United States. The venerable archbishop declared:

> Thank you from my heart for all your admirable writings in defence of Catholic truth. Thank you for your most able, and, it ought to be most satisfactory reply to Mr. Gladstone.
>
> Our sense of its great merits is imperfectly expressed in this week's Catholic Telegraph [Catholic newspaper in Cincinnati]. And now we are shocked by the tirade of a violent, half crazy, and it is said, drunkard's abuse of that noble Championship of our rightful allegiance to the Church and to the State, by McMaster of the New York Freeman's Journal. You disregard the persecution which foolish, or even wicked, men seek to make you suffer for your advocacy of justice and truth, but on earth as in Heaven your reward is great indeed. An humble individual who enjoyed your edifying supper at the Oratory in Birmingham and heard one of your pious instructions, should probably ask pardon for this intrusion on your precious moments; but he could not bear his own reproaches if he did not make the amende for an American journalist's violence.
>
> Go on, Dear Dr. Newman, in the warfare until death, if necessary for the truth—In caelo quies.[98]

From the French Jesuit Henri Ramière, Newman received a letter in praise of his pamphlet, though Ramière did have some reservations on several points of Newman's letter. (Ramière had expressed these reservations in an article on Newman's letter for the February issue of *Etudes Religieuses.*) These had largely to do with the authority of the *Syllabus,* Newman's treatment of disreputable popes, and the tactics of the majority at the Vatican Council. On one point particularly Newman was, however, grateful for Father Ramière's support. That was Newman's assertion that the papacy was the ''heir by default'' of the episcopate of the fourth century. As has already been seen, Newman had been criticized on this point, including the reservations expressed by Archbishop Errington. Newman was happy to have the endorsement of Ramière on this controverted point and, in fact, he quoted from Ramière when dealing with this question in

97. Newman to Miss Alice Augnier, 3 February 1875, *The Letters and Diaries,* 27:210.
98. Archbishop John Baptist Purcell to Newman, 5 February 1875, *The Letters and Diaries,* 27:229, footnote 2.

his "Postscript" to the *Letter to the Duke of Norfolk*.[99] On 28 February, Newman told Ramière: "I thank you very much for your kind letter and the kind tone of the remarks you have made on my recent reply to Mr. Gladstone. You do me great honour where you praise me, and show great gentleness and considerateness where you feel it your duty to criticize me. In the next edition of my Pamphlet I shall not fail to keep before me your valuable observations.[100]

Newman responds to praise from Anglicans

At the end of February, Newman wrote to two Anglicans who had praised his pamphlet. Along with his letter of 25 January, Canon Robert Jenkins had sent a copy of his pamphlet "The Privileges of Peter and the Claims of the Roman Church." It was only at the end of February that Newman had a chance to respond to this correspondent of many years:

> I did not answer your letter of January 25, because I am weighed down with correspondence, and am obliged to delay my acknowledgements whenever a matter is not urgent, but I was very much pleased with it and now, though tardily, thank you for it. The decrees of Popes have a side on which all Catholics are agreed, but there is a side on which they admit of a variety of interpretations—just as the Council of Nicaea settled once for all the question of our Lord's divinity, leaving open the question how that divinity stood in relation to 'The word was made flesh'. And now in the first definition there are many open questions; and partizans of the Pope, as if to compensate for his temporal losses, wish to close them in favour of the extremest sense of them. At the same time, when it is asked what has actually been passed at the Vatican Council, I do not think it is more than I have stated in my Pamphlet.[101]

Typically, Newman was more forthcoming in his exchanges with interested Anglicans than he was with many Catholics.

Newman was especially gratified by the "long most affectionate letter" he received from his dear friend of many years, W. J. Copeland.[102] Copeland saw sections of Newman's pamphlet as the logical outcome of Tract 90,[103] written thirty-four years previously. "The 'minimising' argu-

---

99. See "Postscript" to the *Letter to the Duke of Norfolk,* 212–13.

100. Newman to Father Henri Ramière, S.J., 28 February 1875, *The Letters and Diaries,* 27:239.

101. Newman to Canon Robert Jenkins, 25 February 1875, *The Letters and Diaries,* 27:234–35.

102. W. J. Copeland to Newman, 26 February 1875, *The Letters and Diaries,* 27:235, footnote 3.

103. Tract 90, written by Newman and published on 27 February 1841, showed that the forty-nine articles of Anglicanism were certainly open to a Catholic interpretation. New-

ment of the Letter," Copeland wrote, "is in striking contrast with the language in high quarters, and in most wonderful and beautiful harmony,—at the other end of the chapter, with the whole spirit and principle of Number 90. . . ." Copeland believed that remarks made by his brother on Newman's *A Grammar of Assent* could easily be applied also to the *Letter to the Duke of Norfolk*. Copeland's brother had written: "Newman has very carefully avoided the use of the theological vocabulary, and in this avoidance will arise much misunderstanding. The writing of N like that of Shakespeare will admit of neither paraphrase nor translation, and those who cannot read it in the *true original* had better not read it at all,—I mean, by the true original not only the English language 'established in these realms,' but that pure and reformed branch of it to which Newman and nobody else belongs."[104]

February had been a month of contrast for Newman. He had been very ill at the beginning of the month, the winter weather had been hard with frequent and heavy snow. He had received many good wishes on his birthday, but even this occasion found him in a pensive and melancholy mood. He told Miss Holmes that

> a birthday is a very sad day at my age—or rather I should say a solemn day. When I call it sad, it is when it brings before me the number of friends who have gone before me—though this is a most ungrateful sadness, since I have so many affectionate and anxious friends left, who are so good to me. I think what makes me low, is the awful thought that where my departed friends are, there I must be—and that *they* can and do rejoice in their trial and judgment being over, whereas I am still on trial and have judgment to come. The idea of a judgment is the first principle of religion, as being involved in the sentiment of conscience—and, as life goes on, it becomes very overpowering. Nor do the good tidings of Christianity reverse it, unless we go into the extreme of Calvinism or Methodism with the doctrine of personal assurance. Otherwise, the more one has received, the more one has to answer for. We can but throw ourselves on the mercy of God, of which one's whole life is a long experience.[105]

But there had also been the very full visit to London when he had been received so warmly by his friends, Catholic and Anglican. And each day of February had brought new evidences of the success of the *Letter to*

---

man wrote that his purpose was to demonstrate that "while our Prayer Book is acknowledged on all hands to be of Catholic origin, our Articles also, the offspring of an uncatholic age, are, through God's good providence, to say the least, not uncatholic, and may be subscribed by those who aim at being catholic in heart and doctrine." *Via Media*, 2:271–72. For a discussion of Tract 90 and its stormy aftermath, see Ker, *John Henry Newman*, 216–27.

104 W. J. Copeland to Newman, 20 February 1875, *The Letters and Diaries*, 27:235, footnote 3.

105. Newman to Miss Mary Holmes, 21 February 1875, *The Letters and Diaries*, 27:226–27.

the Duke of Norfolk and new expressions of esteem for its author. It is interesting to contrast the letter written on 21 February to Miss Holmes with a letter the following day to Mrs. William Froude. In the second letter Newman is obviously delighted by the success of his pamphlet and is glad for the opportunity to share this delight with a close and sympathetic friend:

> I send you a lot of letters—you will see they are very confidential and I very immodest in sending them—twenty-two including Dr. Cullen's Pastoral. This is the most important testimony I have had, as being in print and read in all the Dublin Churches. He never would so have done, unless he meant to sanction the *substance* of my Pamphlet. Dr. Purcell's . . . is very important too—It shows there will be some opposition to me in the United States—and doubtless in England too, for someone is moving against me, as regards portions of my Pamphlet, in a Catholic Liverpool paper [Father Paul Bottalla, S.J.]—but I trust they will not be able to do anything to hurt my views and arguments in the estimation of Protestants, by anything like a bold opposition to them.

In the same high spirits Newman then recounted for Mrs. Froude some recent developments on the Continent which he obviously believed would strengthen those forces of moderation that he had championed throughout his years as a Catholic, but especially since the first clamors over the Temporal Power fifteen years before. "I hear good news from France," Newman wrote.

> M. Veuillot is giving up the Universe—some say from bad health, others because he finds his position a very ticklish one. In Italy too, Father Curci, *S.J.* is leaving the staff of the Civiltà and wishes to set up a moderate periodical at Florence, having published a paper in which he plainly announces that it is a dream to fancy that the temporal power can be restored in these times, and that the Church must go back to Apostolic times. Other "moderate organs of religious opinion," I am told, are struggling into light in Italy.[106]

Gladstone keeps the controversy going with further public writings

It could not have escaped Newman while he was writing his answer to Gladstone and after he had finished it that Gladstone might decide to carry the controversy forward by another publication. Newman told Lord Blachford on 5 February that he did not see Gladstone's review of Pius IX's speeches in the January *Quarterly* as having any bearing on the controversy that he and Gladstone were engaged in, and consequently there was no need for him to take it into account. In fact, from the tone of

---

106. Newman to Mrs. William Froude, 22 February 1875, *The Letters and Diaries,* 27:229–30.

Newman's letter to Blachford and many other evidences it would seem that Newman was at least in partial agreement with Gladstone on the extravagances of the pope's speeches. For example, in a letter to Mrs. John Podmore on 12 February, Newman said of the collection of the pope's speeches, "I wish the volume, from what I hear of it, had never been published."[107] But in a letter of 6 February to Charles Russell, Newman showed that he would not be surprised by a more direct reply from Gladstone to his Catholic critics. Newman was already anticipating what Gladstone would say:

> As to Gladstone, if he writes, I think he will say that he has been quite misunderstood; that he did not speak of the great masses of English, nor again of Irish, Catholics—indeed, that he had expressly excepted them from the subjects of his animadversion in various passages of his Pamphlet—that he was glad to find that he had elicited from them the patriotic spirit of which he was already sure—but his words held good still, against those at whom they were originally aimed—that I myself had pointed out who they were—that I had spoken of them as extravagant and tyrannous, and as having set the house on fire—those are the objects of his attack—that the Pope is at their head—therefore he calls them 'Vaticanists—' that nothing has been made good by me or anyone else to dislodge him from this position, which is the position he originally took up—that what is witnessed in England is witnessed all over Europe—that the tomes of theologians are not the appropriate depots or loci for appeal in this matter, but the Ultramontane newspapers—that it has been all along notorious that Rome was cautious, logical, unassailable in *doctrine*—but the present question was as to the *political* use or rather abuse of her doctrine etc etc.
>   This I really think will be his line.[108]

Newman in this very prescient review of what he thought Gladstone was likely to say next was no doubt, as any controversialist would (but especially one who saw the several sides of most questions), simply setting down some of the points that he had realized in the course of writing his pamphlet might well be open to challenge. He did not have long to wait to see if his surmises had been correct. In the third week of February, Gladstone published his *Vaticanism, an Answer to Replies and Reproofs.*[109] As is clear from its title, it was more than a reply to New-

107. Newman to Mrs. John Podmore, 12 February 1875, *The Letters and Diaries,* 27:219.
108. Newman to Dr. Charles Russell, 6 February 1875, *The Letters and Diaries,* 27:215–16.
109. De Lisle on 17 February had sent Newman a proof copy of the conclusion to Gladstone's *Vaticanism.* See *The Letters and Diaries,* 27:224, footnote 1. Newman in his reply to De Lisle on 19 February wrote: "There is nothing in Gladstone's conclusion (which is written in a religious tone, as one would expect) to throw light upon the probable contents of the pages that preceded it. So one must wait patiently. He ought to have *proved* a good deal in what goes before to assume so much in the peroration." *The Letters and Diaries,* 19 February 1875, 27:224.

man. Rather, it was meant as an answer to the many Catholic critics of
Gladstone's *Expostulation*. From the Catholic side there had been over
twenty public replies. *The Times* in its review of 25 February was again
not altogether sympathetic. Newman was inclined to see very little in Gladstone's *Vaticanism* that he himself need take note of. By 26 February,
Newman had concluded that all that was called for from him was a postscript to his original *Letter*. He said as much to Gladstone in a letter thanking him for sending a copy of *Vaticanism*. Newman did not pass over
Gladstone's new tribute to him in *Vaticanism* nor the fact that Gladstone,
though in most gentle tones, appeared to say that the greatness of Newman's life was largely synonymous with his Anglican years. "Of course
I feel very much the extreme kindness of the language which you use concerning me," Newman wrote, "and quite understand how grievous it must
be to you, that a person like me, who was doing his best to serve the Anglican Church, should have been led to throw of[f] his allegiance to it and
to become its opponent."

But Newman had a different view, one that overrode any concerns
of courtesy and measured words. He continued: "On the other hand stands
the fact, that from the time I took that step, close on 30 years ago, I never
have had a moment's misgiving in my conviction that the Catholic Roman
Church comes from God, and that the Anglican is external to it, or again
in my sense of the duty which lay upon me to act on that conviction."

And those blunt words aside, Newman returned to the occasion for
his letter to Gladstone. "I am glad," he wrote, "to be able to consider
that only a part of your pamphlet is directed against me, and that what
I have to say in reply can be conveniently contained in a Postscript in my
letter to the Duke of Norfolk." Newman closed with an unexpected reference to Cardinal Cullen's approbation of his pamphlet, as though this
was the only evidence he needed that he had been successful in his original reply to Gladstone: "It is a great satisfaction to me that Dr. Cullen,
who I hope you do not think is disrespectful to you, takes such a favourable
view of my Letter."[110]

By most estimates Gladstone's *Vaticanism* was considered a clearer,
more reasoned presentation than his *Expostulation*. He was certainly more
careful in his argumentation, and it is evident that *Vaticanism* is more
the product of planning and preparation than was the case with the *Expostulation*, which gives evidence of having been written hastily and in
the heat of the moment. Gladstone was to be sure assisted in the preparation of *Vaticanism* by having before him the various replies and objec-

---

110. Newman to William Ewart Gladstone, 26 February 1875, *The Letters and Diaries*,
27:236. Gladstone's relations with Cullen at this point were difficult to say the least, and
he cannot have been happy to have Newman's appealing to Cullen as evidence of the success of the *Letter to the Duke of Norfolk*.

tions to his *Expostulation.* These rejoinders no doubt helped him to focus his presentation on several clearly defined lines of argumentation. While the tone of *Vaticanism* is higher than that of the *Expostulation,* Gladstone could not resist again mean-spirited sarcasm, and this is especially evident in his concluding remarks. And at times he strains badly in an effort to score a telling point, for example, when he says of the pope:

> He has only to use the words, "I, *ex cathedrâ* declare," or the words, "I, in the discharge of the office of pastor and teacher of all Christians, by virtue of my supreme Apostolic authority, define as a doctrine regarding faith or morals, to be held by the Universal Church, and all words that follow, be they what they may," must now and hereafter be as absolutely accepted by every Roman Catholic who takes the Vatican for his teacher, with what in their theological language they call a divine faith, as must any article of the Apostles' Creed.[111]

Gladstone began his *Vaticanism* by saying that he had not meant to impugn the faith and loyalty of English Roman Catholics but rather his arguments had been aimed at the partisans and abettors of the papal system, a system whose primary aim was political and to which he applied the designation "Vaticanism." Gladstone singled out by name Newman, Clifford, and De Lisle as English Roman Catholics whose loyalty and motives were unimpeachable.[112] And he took his remarks much further in the case of Newman by speaking appreciatively of Newman's writings and decrying the great loss that Anglicanism had sustained in Newman's decision to enter the Roman Church. Indeed, he gave a kind of backhanded compliment to Newman by lavishly praising the works of his Anglican years, as though nothing of similar consequence had followed. "But has he outrun, has he overtaken," Gladstone wrote of Newman, "the greatness of the 'History of the Arians' and of the 'Parochial Sermons,' those indestructible classics of English theology."[113] In addition, Gladstone thanked Newman for a number of points that Newman had made in the *Letter to the Duke of Norfolk,* points that Gladstone took to be confirmatory of his own position or helpful in making it clear that not all Roman Catholics accepted the exalted claims of the Ultramontane or Vaticanist party in the Roman Church. For example, Gladstone thanked Newman for stating "that a definition by a general Council, which the Pope approves, is not absolutely binding thereby, but requires a moral unanimity, and a subsequent reception by the Church."[114] But Newman's admissions

111. W. E. Gladstone, *Vaticanism: An Answer to Reproofs and Replies* (New York: Harper Brothers Publishers, 1875) 72.

112. Ibid., 11.

113. Ibid., 10.

114. Ibid., 10.

and clarifications aside, Gladstone feared that the poison of the Vaticanist system was working its way through the whole of the Roman Church and that in time it would completely eradicate the healthy views of what Gladstone, speaking of Newman, De Lisle, and Clifford, termed "this minority."[115] "Even in those parts of Christendom," Gladstone wrote, "where the decrees and the present attitude of the Papal See do not produce or aggravate open boils with the civil power, by undermining moral liberty they impair moral responsibility, and silently, in the succession of generations if not even in the lifetime of individuals, tend to emasculate the vigor of the mind."[116]

From this sweeping and provocative charge, Gladstone moved to his next section to illustrate just what he had in mind when he spoke of the emasculation of the vigor of the mind. In his treatment of the *Syllabus,* Gladstone did not back down an inch, and in fact McElrath maintains he was more insistent in declaring that the *Syllabus* was an *ex cathedra* statement than he had been in the *Expostulation.*[117] Gladstone indicated that he could willingly accept the *Syllabus* of Dr. Newman, but unfortunately this was not the *Syllabus* as proposed by those whom Gladstone in his "Introduction" had called "the veiled prophets behind the throne."[118] In a comment reminiscent of those made to Newman by some of his Anglican friends after their own reading of his *Letter,* Gladstone said: "Now, when I turn to the seductive pages of Dr. Newman, I find myself to be breathing another air, and discussing, it would seem, some other Syllabus."[119] And then in another somewhat backhanded compliment to Newman, Gladstone made a comment that would soon go the rounds, no doubt to Newman's discomfit if not embarrassment. Gladstone wrote: "If we had Dr. Newman for Pope, we should be tolerably safe, so merciful and genial would be his rule."[120]

Gladstone stuck to his guns in maintaining that the Syllabus had condemned freedom of speech and of the press. In the conclusion of his section on the *Syllabus,* he gave this summary:

The result then is:

1. I abide by my account of the contents of the Syllabus.
2. I have understated, not overstated, its authority.

115. Ibid., 11–12.
116. Ibid., 14.
117. See Damian McElrath, *The Syllabus of Pius IX* (Louvain: Publications Universitaires de Louvain, 1964) 293–94.
118. Gladstone, *Vaticanism,* 5.
119. Ibid., 25.
120. Ibid. Robert Gray in *Cardinal Manning,* 248, is wrong to say that Gladstone said this in a letter to Manning. Here Gray followed Shane Leslie, *Henry Edward Manning: His Life and Labours,* 248, too trustingly, though it is true that Leslie's treatment of this reference to Newman is rather confusingly stated.

3. It may be ex cathedra; it seems to have the infallibility of dogma: it unquestionably demands, and is entitled (in the code of Vaticanism) to demand, obedience.[121]

In his third section, "The Vatican Council and the Infallibility of the Pope," Gladstone appeared to have Manning chiefly in mind. But he also disputed Newman's views on the position of Manning's predecessors[122] on the pope's infallibility. As has already been mentioned, Gladstone took Newman to task on this point for saying that if the English government in the 1820s had really wanted to know the Roman Church's position on papal infallibility, "why did they not go to head-quarters?"[123] In *Vaticanism,* Gladstone turned this question on its head by saying, "In all seriousness I ask whether there is not involved in these words of Dr. Newman an ominous approximation to my allegation that the seceder to the Roman Church 'places his loyalty and civil duty at the mercy of another?'"[124]

Gladstone conceded in *Vaticanism* that he had overstated his case by giving the impression that papal infallibility was a very recent theological position of the Roman Church, but he made his concession grudgingly by saying, "It is an opinion held by great authorities that no pontiff before Leo X attempted to set up the infallibility of the Popes as dogma," and, "I do not deny to the opinion of Papal infallibility an active, though checkered and intermittent life exceeding six centuries."[125]

In the fifth section of his new pamphlet, Gladstone addressed the topic "The Vatican Council and Obedience to the Pope." Once more he brought Newman to the fore:

> Dr. Newman says there are exceptions to this precept of obedience. But this is just what the Council has not said. The Church by the Council imposes Aye. The private conscience reserves to itself the title to say No. I must confess that in this apology there is to me a strong, undeniable smack of Protestantism. To reconcile Dr. N's conclusion with the premises of the Vatican will surely require all, if not more than all, "the vigilance, acuteness, and subtlety of the Schola Theologorum."[126]

In his sixth section, "Warrant of Allegiance According to the Vatican," Gladstone spent much of his time arguing that the popes had not in any sense repudiated their claim to be able to set aside civil rulers. The State, Gladstone insisted, was put in the position of having to deal with a power "dwelling beyond its limits, and yet beyond the reach of its

121. Gladstone, *Vaticanism,* 27.
122. The vicars apostolic.
123. LDN, 86.
124. Gladstone, *Vaticanism,* 29.
125. Ibid., 39.
126. Ibid., 50.

arm.''[127] The definition of 1870 had made absolutely clear the Roman Church's position on the supereminent authority of the pope over all matters spiritual and temporal. Then, according to Gladstone, "the infallible, that is virtually the divine title to command, and the absolute, that is the unconditional duty to obey, were promulgated to an astonished world.''[128] Here is a good example of Gladstone carried away by the cleverness of his own rhetoric.

In his seventh section, "On the Intrinsic Nature and Conditions of the Papal Infallibility Decreed In the Vatican Council," Gladstone said that "popery" had once been a mean term of prejudice and discrimination used against Catholics but that since the Vatican Council there was simply no other word to use to describe the Roman Church. Gladstone professed to be not at all convinced by his critics' arguments that he had given an extravagant interpretation to the meaning of papal infallibility as defined by the council:

> Whatever was formerly ascribed either to the Pope, or to the Council, or to the entire governing body of the Church, or to the Church general and diffused, the final sense of the great Christian community, aided by authority, tested by discussion, mellowed and ripened by time—all—no more than all, and no less than all—of what God gave, for guidance, through the power of truth, by the Christian revelation, to the whole redeemed family, the baptized flock of the Saviour in the world; all this is now locked in the breast of one man, opened and distributed at his will, and liable to assume whatever form . . . he may think fit to give it.[129]

Gladstone poured a like scorn on Newman's careful distinction between the *inspiratio* which the apostles enjoyed and the *assistentia* given to Peter's successors:

> It is indeed said by Dr. Newman, and by others, that this infallibility is not inspiration. On such a statement I have two remarks to make. First, that we have this assurance on the strength of his own private judgment; secondly, that if bidden by the self-assertion of the Pope, he will be required by his principles to retract it, and to assert, if occasion should arise, the contrary; thirdly, that he lives under a system of development, through which somebody's private opinion of today may become matter of faith for all the to-morrows of the future.[130]

Surely Gladstone used the phrase, "system of development," deliberately, and with some degree of malice.

127. Ibid., 62.
128. Ibid., 63.
129. Ibid., 73.
130. Ibid., 74.

Gladstone thought that his Catholic opponents had tied themselves in knots in their efforts to explain the meaning of "ex cathedra," or to point out that its meaning had been left deliberately vague. At the end of this section, Gladstone wrote: "Decrees *ex cathedra* are infallible; but determinations what decrees are ex cathedra fallible; so that the private person, after he has with all docility handed over his mind and freedom to the *Schola Theologorum,*[131] can never certainly know, never know with 'divine faith,' when he is on the rock of infallibility, when on the shifting quicksands of a merely human presumption."[132]

Gladstone saved his most hard-hitting language for his "Conclusion." He began his final remarks by taking into account his critics' comments on the strong language of his *Expostulation.* He was initially unrepentant about the language he had used. "The cause of it," he said, "may be that for the last thirty years, in this country at least, Ultramontanism has been very busy making controversial war upon other people, with singularly little restraint of language; and has had far too little of the truth told to itself."[133] He professed, however, to "have always entertained a warm desire that the better elements might prevail over the worse in that great Latin communion which we call the Church of Rome," and he spoke with admiration for some of its great figures, Thomas à Kempis, Colet, More, and Pascal and "for the Church of some now living among us, of whom none would deny that they are as humble, as tender, as self-renouncing, and as self-abased . . . as the most 'Evangelical' of Protestants by possibility can be."[134] And he went on to speak glowingly of the English Catholic body that had survived since Elizabethan times and of all that it had endured: "Amid all these cruel difficulties,[135] it retained within itself these high characteristics: it was moderate; it was brave; it was devout; it was learned; it was loyal."[136]

Kind words spoken, Gladstone returned to the attack. It was his duty, he wrote, to warn of the dangers of Ultramontanism that dominated the Roman Church and "to produce, if possible, a temper of greater watchfulness; . . . to warn my countrymen against the velvet paw, and smooth and soft exterior of a system which is dangerous to the foundations of civil order, and which any one of us may at any time encounter in his daily path. If I am challenged, I must not refuse to say it is not less dangerous, in its ultimate operation on the human mind, to the foundations

131. Here again Gladstone takes Newman as his chief opponent.
132. Gladstone, *Vaticanism,* 78.
133. Ibid., 80.
134. Ibid., 82.
135. One of the difficulties instanced by Gladstone was that those English Catholics' reasonable aspirations for the measures that would have secured relief were mercilessly thwarted and stifled by those popes whom they loved too well. See *Vaticanism,* 83.
136. Gladstone, *Vaticanism,* 83.

of that Christian belief, which it loads with false excrescences, and strains even to the bursting.[137] And finally there was one last great oratorical outpouring, aimed to be sure at the Roman system but clearly in its repetition of the word "developed" aimed also at Newman:

> But in the Churches subject to the Pope, clerical power, and every doctrine and usage favorable to clerical power, have been developed, and developed, and developed, while all that nurtured freedom, and all that guaranteed it, have been harnessed and denounced, cabined, and confined, attenuated and starved, with fits and starts of intermittent success and failure, but with a progress on the whole as decisively onward toward its aim as that which some enthusiasts think they see in the natural movement of humanity at large. At last came the crowning stroke of 1870. . . .[138]

Newman decides that only a brief reply to Gladstone's Vaticanism is called for from him

After reading Gladstone's *Vaticanism,* Newman turned at once to his new task. He had determined on a brief reply and seems to have experienced nothing of the anguish and uncertainty that had plagued him when he had started out on his first reply to Gladstone in October and November of the previous year. On the same day that he wrote to Gladstone to thank him for *Vaticanism,* Newman apologized for a hurried letter to W. J. Copeland, "but I am called off by a Postscript I must write to my 'Duke of Norfolk' by G's Vaticanism. . . ."[139] However, by early March it is clear that Newman had decided to take his time. The "Postscript" would appear in the fourth edition to the *Letter to the Duke of Norfolk,* and Newman must have known that this would not come out for several weeks. A kind of calm entered his life in March, and he was able to return at a measured pace to the projects he had had to set aside five months before. In a letter of 6 March to Malcolm MacColl, Newman provides a glimpse of the course of his days at this time. "I should have answered your letter before this," he began, "had I not been so busy. Not that I have done a great deal, but when the time is taken out of the day which my Priesthood and our Rule, and meals, and exercise, and the weariness of old age exact, little time is left for work or letters."[140] Newman was responding to a letter that MacColl had written some days before, in which he told Newman of the effect that he believed the *Letter to the Duke of Norfolk* was having in the great world. MacColl wrote:

137. Ibid., 84.
138. Ibid., 86.
139. Newman to W. J. Copeland, 26 February 1875, *The Letters and Diaries,* 27:235.
140. Newman to Malcolm MacColl, 6 March 1875, *The Letters and Diaries,* 27:240.

I know nothing in English history like the revolution which the public mind
of England has undergone in your case. At a party at which I happened
to be present some days after your Letter to the Duke of Norfolk came out
an Ultramontane expressed an ardent wish that your pamphlet might be put
on the Index; whereupon a strong "Protestant" retorted that "Rome would
not dare to offer such an affront to *England*." The remark expresses the
true feeling of the public. They have come to regard you as an English possession of which they are proud.

MacColl added of Newman's pamphlet, "it gives me a view of the doctrine quite different from that with which Ward and Archbishop Manning have made me familiar. . . ."[141] However unwittingly, MacColl,
in recounting the conversation he had heard and in underscoring it with
his own contrast between Newman on one side and Manning and Ward
on the other, had pointed out one of the paradoxes of Newman's Catholic life, especially in the years following the publication of the *Apologia*.
In other circumstances Newman would have dealt bleakly with this situation and its consequences for him, but he was at this point obviously
cheered by the success of his pamphlet, and in his reply to MacColl on
6 March he touched on it as a secondary theme. Once more Newman took
the long view, looking to the lessons of the past and his hopes for the
future:

> One of the incidental disadvantages of a General Council, is that it throws
> individual units through the Church into confusion and sets them at vari-
> ance, so far as an age is educated, so it was at the first, the third, the sixth,
> and the seventh. The consequence is schism and heresy. I am neither sur-
> prised then at the rise of the Alt-Catholics on one side, nor at the ex-
> travagances of Dr. Ward etc. on the other. Of course no one can write
> without mistakes, and in details my recent Pamphlet doubtless may be rightly
> criticised by Catholics, but it is my great comfort and happiness to find it
> has been generally accepted by all shades of Catholic opinion both in England
> and Ireland, as substantially unexceptionable, and, as time goes on I think
> this will be felt more and more.[142]

It was in these good spirits that Newman in the month of March considered his further reply to Gladstone.

Newman's almost relaxed attitude toward the need to respond to Gladstone's *Vaticanism* is revealed in several letters that he wrote to friends
during March. In general, he made it very clear that he had had his say
and was satisfied with it. Further controversy, Newman believed, was unnecessary and would soon weary those who had found the exchange be-

---

141. Malcolm MacColl to Newman, 22 February 1875, *The Letters and Diaries,* 27:240,
footnote 2.

142. Newman to Malcolm MacColl, 6 March 1875, *The Letters and Diaries,* 27:240.

tween himself and Gladstone of interest. In addition, he thought that Gladstone without cause had so shifted the course of his arguments that it was impossible to pin him down. In his letter of 6 March to Malcolm MacColl, Newman, while acknowledging that Gladstone had been most gracious to him, despaired of finding a way to deal with the new points raised by Gladstone in his *Vaticanism*: "Nothing of course can be kinder than Mr. Gladstone's language about me, it is of a character indeed to frighten me. As to his argument, I feel about it so far as it concerns me, what I felt about his first pamphlet that it is most difficult to find what he means to be his reasons for the definite and specific positions which he takes up against me, and, while I am waiting for them or looking about for them in the jungle in which they lie, I find he suddenly proclaims himself victor and marches off to another point." And not forgetting Mac-Coll's deep admiration for Gladstone, Newman continued: "I hope I don't seem ungrateful to him in your eyes for thus speaking, for I really do believe one reason of this appearance in his controversial method, is his great desire to deal tenderly with me; but in consequence it has cost me some trouble to do justice to his arguments. However, I have no thought of provoking the controversy, though in the next edition of my letter I shall add a Postscript making two or three remarks on his "Vaticanism", in defence of what I have said."[143]

Two days later Newman gave further reasons why he had decided that a full-scale reply to Gladstone's new pamphlet was not called for from him. He thought especially that Gladstone in taking up the question of whether papal infallibility had been the constant teaching of the undivided Church was taking the controversy to ground that had been gone over again and again, particularly at the time of the Vatican Council. Newman viewed this tack as sheer polemic. Further, he decided that Archbishop Manning was the real, if not sole, target of Gladstone's *Vaticanism,* and he would make this point emphatically to several of his correspondents in the days ahead.[144] In a letter to Ambrose De Lisle on 8 March, Newman makes his overall position extremely clear:

> I should not think of writing a new pamphlet, first because Protestants are tired of the controversy and we ought to let well alone.

143. Ibid.

144. It is difficult to follow Newman in his belief that Manning was more the object of Gladstone's *Vaticanism* than he himself. Gladstone cites Newman far more than Manning in the course of his exposition, and while it is true that some of these citations are sympathetic references, many of them (there are twenty-five in all) are not. *Vaticanism* was in large measure a response to all those who had answered the *Expostulation*. Certainly Gladstone considered Newman's the chief reply. In his recent study of Newman, Ian Ker repeats Newman's view of the matter: "As for Gladstone's *Vaticanism* . . ., Newman had no intention of trying to answer the burden of the argument, which was directed against Manning rather than himself." Ker, *John Henry Newman,* 691.

Secondly, because Mr. Gladstone says little against my Pamphlet, and confesses that he has little to say against those special points which I proposed to maintain. The first was our civil loyalty—the second our moral freedom. He has not answered what I have said about the ancient Church, or Divided Allegiance or Conscience. He has not, much less, attempted to refute my arguments about the Encyclical, or the Syllabus. He has said only very little against my two concluding chapters. All I need say will go into a P.S. of the next edition of my Letter.

Instead of answering me, partly from kindness to me, partly from policy, he has gone off in an attack on Archbishop Manning, on the question whether the dogma of the Pope's Infallibility was always held—and I think he is triumphant in his denial of it—but that is nothing to me. I only had to account for the Bishops seeming to break faith with Mr. Pitt's or Mr. Peel's government, and this point I shall further observe upon in my P.S. But to go to the Council of Constance etc. would be to enter into the general controversy between Catholics and Protestants, in which each party has its own texts and its own facts, and has had them, and flourished them, for the last 300 years. Gladstone says nothing new—our writers have our answers to all he says. And the general public would be soon sick of such an interminable conflict. Indeed, even now, before things have gone this length, I don't think a new pamphlet from me would pay its expenses.[145]

The realistic and eminently practical sides of Newman are interestingly evident in this last sentence.

The following day, Newman repeated the same arguments against his having to mount a full reply to Gladstone in a letter to Mrs. William Froude. "To go into the Council of Constance," he insisted again, "is merely to take up the old trite controversy which has been gone through time out of mind by the two parties, each having its cut and dried answers and rejoinders." But, Newman having told MacColl and De Lisle in the previous days, that he had determined on a brief postscript of two or three points, appeared in his letter to Mrs. Froude unsure of just what points he needed to make. He told Mrs. Froude: "In a new Edition of my letter I shall add a Postscript—but I should really like to be enlightened as to *what* I have to answer; for G. only denies what I have said for the most part, without giving reasons why."[146]

145. Newman to Ambrose De Lisle, 8 March 1875, *The Letters and Diaries,* 27:243. In a letter to Ullathorne on 2 March, Manning takes a similar line to Newman's on the public's attitude towards the continuance of the controversy. Manning wrote: "People are annoyed with Gladstone, not for attacking us, but for breaking the peace and making politics impossible. They would be quickly and still more annoyed with us if we kept the controversy alive. They do not think that we are beaten, and they would not endure to think that we had beaten him." Leslie, *Henry Edward Manning: His Life and Labours,* 248. Ambrose Macaulay, *Dr. Russell of Maynooth* (London: Darton, Longman, and Todd, 1983) 307, appears to support the view that the controversy had run out of steam when he writes of *Vaticanism:* ". . . Gladstone's reply to Newman fell flat."

146. Newman to Mrs. William Froude, 9 March 1875, *The Letters and Diaries,* 27:245.

Newman resists DeLisle's urging that he write a full reply to Gladstone and dissuades DeLisle from the same course

While these several letters written in the first days of March show that Newman's friends were interested in his reaction to Gladstone's *Vaticanism* and were wondering what he would do in consequence of it, there is no evidence to suggest that Newman was put under the kind of external pressure to reply that he had experienced in the weeks after Gladstone's *Expostulation*. The only proponent of a very full reply from Newman appears to have been Ambrose De Lisle. Over the course of several days in mid-March, Newman and De Lisle exchanged letters dealing with the necessity, as De Lisle saw it, of preparing a thorough and detailed reply to Gladstone's second pamphlet. De Lisle, while hoping that Newman would also make an extensive reply to Gladstone, was at work on his own answer. He had obviously got the impression, probably from Newman's letter to him of 8 March, that Newman thought a full reply to Gladstone on his part or anyone else's was a waste of time. At the beginning of his letter to De Lisle on 10 March, Newman tried to assure De Lisle that he had not meant to give this impression: "You must not stop writing in answer to Mr. G. for anything I have said. Recollect I only profess to notice in my P.S. what he has said against *me*."

From a further letter that Newman wrote to De Lisle two days later it was evident that De Lisle remained concerned that Newman had not given his endorsement to his plan to write an extensive reply to Gladstone. In his letter of 12 March, Newman still started off on a dissuasive note:

> When I said "don't let me hinder you", or some such words, I meant let me not hinder your doing what I am doing, viz replying to Mr. Gladstone's remarks as directed against *oneself*. This is all that I am doing. The greater part of his Pamphlet is against what the Archbishop has said—and I should not like to interfere with the Archbishop's quarrel; perhaps he would not thank me for the way in which I did it. And in like manner; if you will allow me to say it, I doubt whether you should interfere with what does not concern you personally.[147]

For a moment Newman seemed to relent from his negative tone, but he soon resumed his cautions and dissuasions:

> But if you meant to spread your sails and launch out into the deep, then think what an endless controversy it is—and how can you ever expect one single reader of the Union Review to take our view of the Council of Constance and of its significance in Catholic questions? I think we, I mean the Church, has had to be piloted thro' very difficult straits and shallows with

---

147. Newman to Ambrose De Lisle, 10 March 1875, *The Letters and Diaries*, 27:246. Newman may have been recalling the difficulties that De Lisle's first reply had caused with Manning and with the bishop of Nottingham.

hidden rocks and without buoys and light-houses with next to no human means; and, though her Divine Guide has taken care she should not suffer material damage, and she has escaped in every peril, yet she has not much more than escaped; and it is natural and not very difficult for rival ship-builders and shipowners to maintain that she has suffered. Three centuries have taught us that a case may be made against us, and tho' we have the right on our side, it is God's will that an opportunity and a call is left for faith.[148]

This extraordinary reflection shows Newman, ever the realist, affirming that there are too many grey areas in life and perforce in the history of the Church. There will be no complete triumphs while we see through a glass darkly. Enough has been said in the present controversy for people to make up their minds. To carry on would simply continue the fruitless polemic of the past. If De Lisle is determined on a further reply, he must narrow his focus to one or two central issues and leave aside the dozens of other questions. From a letter written the following day it would appear that De Lisle had decided to follow Newman's advice. He would try to show that the Church had always had a general acceptance of the doctrine of papal infallibility and to this end he would quote the following from the Creed of Pius IV [1563], "Ecclesiam *Romanam* matrem et *magistram* omnium ecclesiarum agnosco."[149] On 14 March, Newman wrote briefly to say "thank you very much for your sketch of your second article in the Union Review. It seems likely to be a very good one. Certainly the word 'Magistra' is very strong."[150] Evidently, Newman still did not have a great deal of enthusiasm for De Lisle's plan. When, however, De Lisle's article was published in the May issue of the *Union Review*, Newman seemed to be satisfied with it.

Newman's correspondence following on his Letter to the Duke of Norfolk *continues as do the rumors that he had not accepted the definition*

In early March, Newman's pace had slowed, but he was still faced with a few remaining letters that had come in over the past several months, and the post continued to bring new letters occasioned by his controversy with Gladstone. On 9 March, Newman told John Finlayson, who had written deploring the absence of a theological faculty at London University: "You must not suppose I did not read your letter of Novr 21 with great interest because I did not answer it. But I was at the time quite oc-

148. Newman to Ambrose De Lisle, 12 March 1875, *The Letters and Diaries,* 27:248.
149 *The Letters and Diaries,* 13 March 1875, 27:249, footnote 1. See also Purcell and Edwin De Lisle, *Life and Letters of Ambrose Phillipps De Lisle,* 2:51–52.
150. Newman to Ambrose De Lisle, 14 March 1875, *The Letters and Diaries,* 27:249.

cupied with writing a pamphlet I have since published, and for a month put my letters aside. Then the arrears of answers to them were great—indeed I am only now emerging from them. For they kept still increasing from the arrival of fresh letters, if not in number, yet in weight."[151] And two weeks later Newman said in a letter to Lady Henry Kerr:

> I am very grateful to Lord Henry for taking so warm an interest in my Pamphlet and so kindly wishing to write me about it. Indeed I owe great thanks to the mercy of Providence, that I was carried so well through it, for it was a great responsibility to write and had it not succeeded, the world [would] have said, Now we know the utmost that can be said for Catholics, and we see how little there is to say. But, thank God, I succeeded, and I have had many good friends such as Lord Henry and you, to tell me so. And I have felt with a great consolation and delight, that probably it was the prayers of dear souls, who have been taken away from us, who helped me.[152]

Though the hectic activity occasioned by his reply to Gladstone was certainly dying down in March, there were still consequences from his *Letter,* aside from acknowledging congratulations, that Newman had to deal with. His friend, Bishop Moriarty, had heard criticisms of Newman's treatment of a culpably erroneous conscience in his reply to Gladstone. In a letter of 6 March to the bishop of Kerry, Newman repeats for Moriarty the exact words from his pamphlet that are in dispute. This is curious since it gives the impression that Moriarty, who wrote to Newman on 3 March, had still not seen Newman's pamphlet but had only heard reports of it. Newman defended what he had said and asked in some exasperation, "How can I express it more clearly?" He closed by saying, "I am publishing a Postscript to my letter—so I can easily express myself more clearly, if I have a need to do so."[153]

Newman also dealt with his treatment of conscience in the *Letter to the Duke of Norfolk* when he wrote three days later to George Sherston Baker,[154] a barrister and former pupil of the Oratory School:

> As to the question of conscience, neither Gladstone nor any other Protestant would deny that law must give way before it, when it is the *personal* suggestion of the individual and dictates to act thus or that. What they accuse Catholics of is, of in every case ruling our conscience by the command of the Pope or of our Confessor, so that conscience ceases to be a tribunal within us, and to fall under the notion of a natural right of man. "Instead

---

151. Newman to John Finlayson, 9 March 1875, *The Letters and Diaries,* 27:244–45.

152. Newman to Lady Henry Kerr, 22 March 1875, *The Letters and Diaries,* 27:252. This last reference is obviously meant to include James Hope-Scott, Lady Henry Kerr's brother.

153. Newman to Bishop David Moriarty, 6 March 1875, *The Letters and Diaries,* 27:241.

154. The dates given for George Sherston Baker, 1814–75, in vol. 27 of *The Letters and Diaries* are those for his father Henry Sherston Baker. George Baker's dates are 1846–1923. The correct dates for both father and son are given in vol. 21 of *The Letters and Diaries.*

then of being what *we* mean by conscience" they say, "it is nothing else than the command of a political party, external to England, which makes use of a sacred name for its own purposes." This is the representation which I had to meet, and I think have met in my letter—by showing that after all, whatever our duties to the Pope, there are cases in which conscience may come into collision with his word, and in which conscience must be followed, not he.[155]

This letter to George Sherston Baker is important as showing that Newman meant emphatically what he had said about conscience and papal directives in his *Letter to the Duke of Norfolk* and that later claims that he has been incorrectly read on this point cannot be maintained.

Though his correspondence was largely taken up with the controversy with Gladstone, Newman did not escape at this time the usual rumors about his belief in the Roman Catholic Church and its teachings, particularly the definition of 1870. In this instance the matter was put before him in a very unusual form. Someone unknown to Newman wrote to him on 15 March to tell him the following:

> The counsel of my confessor superadded to a promise by me some little time ago to a dying man is the cause of this letter.
> Mr. H. Savage late Catholic Publisher etc of N'castle on Tyne told me before his death that I ought to tell you that Mr. R. Suffield formerly a well known priest of the order of St. Dominic is constantly in the habit of saying to people: "*that though he does not wish it to go farther, you yourself had told him during a stay he made with you previous to his* (fall), *that were you not so advanced in years and had you not so many people looking up to you, you would leave the Catholic Church.*"
> Pardon me Revd and dear Father for having even second hand placed such rubbish before you. But very soon after Father Suffield's apostasy, he said the same words to *me*. . . .[156]

This was the kind of letter Newman was sure to lose no time in answering. He wrote immediately and with a suggestion of shock:

> Thank you for your letter just received. It is the first time that the statement about me contained in it or any thing like it has been reported to me. I deny it at once in toto;—in as strong language as I can. I never used any such words to any one as it attributes to me, and I never had a thought or wish, of which such words would be even the distorted expression. It never came into my head to think or say that "were I not so advanced in years," or "had I not so many people looking up to me, I should leave the Catholic Church." I can have used no words to anyone, which [could] have given him any sort of excuse for a statement which is simply untrue.[157]

155. Newman to George Sherston Baker, 9 March 1875, *The Letters and Diaries,* 27:244.
156. J. Millage to Newman, 15 March 1875, *The Letters and Diaries,* 27:249, footnote 2.
157. Newman to J. Millage, 16 March 1875, *The Letters and Diaries,* 27:249–50.

Manning named a cardinal; Newman is courteous
but keeps his distance from Manning's circle

March also brought the news that Archbishop Manning after ten years at Westminster had been named a cardinal, an appointment which had been anticipated both by friends and opponents of Manning since the close of the Vatican Council. In fact, the several-year delay between July 1870 and Manning's nomination caused many to wonder why one of the chief promoters of papal infallibility had not been very quickly honored by Pius IX. There was much speculation at the time and there has been much since. In his recent biography of Manning, Robert Gray says: "This promotion came surprisingly late; it had been expected almost from the moment when Manning became an Archbishop. But his high-handed conduct at the Vatican Council—*troppo fanatico* was the verdict of Rome—had left him enemies among the Cardinals, and Pius IX may have been wary of immediately overruling this opposition by conferring a favour that might seem like a quid pro quo for the infallibility definition."[158]

Newman sent his congratulations to Archbishop's House on Holy Saturday, 27 March, while Manning was still in Rome where the consistory had been held twelve days before. His tone was formal but on the whole gracious:

> I beg you to accept the congratulations of myself and this house on your recent promotion. It must be a great gratification to you to receive this mark of the confidence placed in you by the Sovereign Pontiff. And it must be a source of true pleasure to your brother and his family and your other relatives and friends.
>
> And as regards the Protestant world it is striking to observe the contrast between the circumstances under which you return invested with this special dignity and the feelings which were excited in England twenty-five years ago on occasion of the like elevation of your predecessor, Cardinal Wiseman.
>
> That the temporal honours, to which you have attained may be the token and earnest of those which come from God above, is the sincere prayer of yours affectly John H. Newman.[159]

Manning showed his appreciation by sending Newman his first letter of thanks on the day of his return to England, 5 April:

158. Gray, *Cardinal Manning*, 254–55. It should, however, be recalled that the number of cardinals in this period was fixed at seventy and as a consequence only a small number of cardinals were named from late 1870 through early 1875. Another leading proponent of the definition, Archbishop Dechamps of Malines, was also named a cardinal in 1875. And Bishop Pie of Poitiers, also an ardent proponent, was named a cardinal only under Leo XIII in 1879.

159. Newman to Cardinal Henry Edward Manning, 27 March 1875, *The Letters and Diaries*, 27:254. While the overall tone of the letter is cordial, the conclusion is perhaps pointed.

I came home this morning at 7 o'clock: and found your letter among many others. But I answer it first; that I may assure you how much I feel the kindness which prompted you to write. Accept my affectionate thanks: and thank also your Fathers who have united with you. You have touched the points which in the last weeks have been in my mind. I had so great a fear lest any thing should hinder the benevolence which has been sensibly growing in public opinion towards us, that I wrote to the Holy Father saying that I could not judge or decide in such a case.

But the just and kindly way in which those who are not Catholic have written has greatly relieved this anxiety.

I pray God, as you promise me to do, that nothing of this world may stand between God and my soul.

Your note has brought back the memories of many happy days, and of the many benefits I owe you.

Believe me, My dear Newman, Always affectly yours Henry E. C. Abp. Westm.[160]

It is interesting to speculate on what part Newman's response to Gladstone may have contributed to the cordial reception given in England to the news of Manning's appointment. In any case, this exchange of letters was the first evidence of amicability since Newman had informed Manning of the death of John Keble in April 1866. In the spring of 1879, Newman would himself be receiving congratulations on his being named a cardinal by Pius IX's successor.

At this very time when Newman and Manning had achieved some degree of cordiality in their relationship, Newman was declining an invitation extended by Monsignor Thomas Capel, one of Manning's circle, to preach at the inauguration of the Catholic University at Kensington. Manning, it would appear, had approved of Capel's plan to ask Newman to preach.[161] Newman used as his excuse his disapproval of London University to which the Kensington institution would be loosely connected, but he could not resist a reference to his thwarted plans eight years previously to establish an Oratory at Oxford. In his letter of 23 March, turning down Capel's invitation, Newman said:

Nor am I unmindful of the important fact that the English Bishops, who thought residence at Oxford and Cambridge dangerous to Catholic youth, are tolerant of the course of studies pursued at the London University; but I could not preach (for you) without being at liberty, if I chose, to speak against any such recognition as I fear you concede to that University, an institution which has been the great champion and example of mixed education now for 50 years, and which through all that time I have on that

160. Cardinal Henry Edward Manning to Newman, 5 April 1875, *The Letters and Diaries,* 27:254–55.

161. See *The Letters and Diaries,* 20 March 1875, 27:253, footnote 1.

ground shrunk from. I think you will feel that I ought not to go out of my way to incur so real a difficulty.[162]

Capel persisted, sending Newman a telegram on the 29th to announce that he was coming in person to Birmingham to ask Newman to reconsider. Newman answered Capel the same day, telling him in barely polite terms to stay home.[163] In fact, Capel did call on Newman the following day,[164] but to no avail. Manning's cardinalate was one thing, but Newman was not ready to forget all the troubles he had had from Westminster in Manning's ten years there.

Newman completes his Postscript to his Letter to the Duke of Norfolk

By the end of March, Newman had finished his postscript to the *Letter to the Duke of Norfolk*. He had in the end taken his time despite the signs of hurrying to do his postscript that he had shown a month before. On Easter Monday he told Emily Bowles: "Thank you for your affectionate Easter greetings which I return with all my heart. Gladstone has said so little against my Pamphlet, that my new Postscript is very short. There is a writer in the Spectator who is dealing with his remarks in the 'Vaticanism' against the Cardinal's Pamphlet."[165]

162. Newman to Monsignor Thomas Capel, 23 March 1875, *The Letters and Diaries,* 27:253.

163. See Newman to Monsignor Thomas Capel, *The Letters and Diaries,* 29 March 1875, 27:257.

164. See Newman "Diary," *The Letters and Diaries,* 30 March 1875, 27:258.

165. Newman to Emily Bowles, 29 March 1875, *The Letters and Diaries,* 27:256–57. The writer in the 13 March issue of the *Spectator* brought evidence to bear to show that Gladstone was wrong in saying that the Relief Act of 1791 had been secured when the bishops gave assurances that Catholics were not obliged to accept the infallibility of the pope. See *The Letters and Diaries,* 27:257, footnote 1.

The timing of Newman's "Postscript" is somewhat complicated by the fact that Father Dessain in his introduction to vol. 27 of the *Letters and Diaries,* p. xvi, states: ". . . Newman answered [Gladstone] in a matter of fact postscript, published early in March, to *A Letter to the Duke of Norfolk,* and added to the fourth and subsequent editions." The date given for the completion of the "Postscript" is perhaps a misprint that should read *early April.* See Newman's letters to Moriarty (6 March, 241), De Lisle (8 March, 243), Mrs. Froude (9 March, 245), De Lisle (12 March, 248), Bowles (29 March, 256–57), Simpson (30 March, 259). More important perhaps is the letter of 5 April to Emily Bowles. It is the first evidence that the "Postscript" has actually appeared in print. Newman wrote: "Soon after my Pamphlet came out, I saw I was rash in having given my own idea of the numbers voting at Ephesus, and in the second Edition I cut them out. Now I send two copies of the 4th edition to you, in the P.S. of which you will find a note on the subject." *The Letters and Diaries,* 5 April 1875, 27:267. See also letter to Lord Blachford, *The Letters and Diaries,* 11 April 1875, 27:272.

Newman dated his "Postscript" as of 26 February 1875, but the evidence cited suggests that this is the day he began work not the day he finished.

Newman also made a reference to the completion of his postscript in a letter the next day to Richard Simpson, who had written to him on 27 March. Simpson, whose not always easy relationship with Newman had continued for nearly twenty years, was full of praise for Newman's *Letter to the Duke of Norfolk:*

> I ought to have written three months ago to thank you for the most kind and generous mention which you made of me in your reply to Gladstone, more especially as I know that you disapproved of the way I spoke of some Popes in the context of the passage in my life of Campion to which you refer. But the charity you show to men in difficulties is boundless, and you will like to know, is often most efficacious. Tomorrow Admiral Hall the Secretary of the Admiralty makes his first communion—His difficulties were removed by your pamphlet. Schollaert, an old friend of Montalembert and Vicepresident of the Belgian chamber writes to me "Gladstone's fault may be termed 'felix culpa', since it made our beloved and Rev. Father Newman write his loyal and learned reply. Never the 'fortiter in re, suaviter in modo' got a brighter and fairer application. The chapter on 'Conscience' will remain in English literature as a pattern of both eloquence and honesty."[166]

In his reply Newman, after expressing concern about reports he had heard of Simpson's poor health, not surprisingly made mention of Acton. "I wish I heard something about Lord Acton," he wrote. "There were unpleasant words used of him in both Protestant and Catholic papers, when Gladstone's pamphlet came out, and then all notice of him ceased."[167] Newman concluded with a reference to the imminent publication of his "Postscript." He said: "I am now bringing out a new edition of my own with a short Postscript, short because Gladstone in his Vaticanism says comparatively little about me, turning instead with fury upon the Cardinal."[168] It would appear that this was Newman's last correspondence with Simpson, who died the following year.

Newman's response to Gladstone's *Expostulation* was nearly 130 pages; his "Postscript" following Gladstone's *Vaticanism* ran just over twenty. The *Letter* was a sustained, carefully constructed piece of writing, careful in its style as much as in its argument. The "Postscript" was more prosaic and practical in its approach, in the words of Father Dessain, "mat-

---

166. Richard Simpson to Newman, 27 March 1875, *The Letters and Diaries,* 27:258.

167. In a letter of 13 April 1875 to an unknown correspondent, Newman defended Acton as a good Catholic, while decrying his November 1874 letters to *The Times,* to which this correspondent had apparently strongly objected. Newman wrote: "I do not think you should say what you say about Lord Acton. He has ever been a religious, well-conducted, conscientious Catholic from a boy. In saying this, I do not at all imply that I can approve those letters to which you refer. I heartily wish they had never been written." *The Letters and Diaries,* 13 April 1875, 27:277.

168. Newman to Richard Simpson, 30 March 1875, *The Letters and Diaries,* 27:258-59.

ter of fact."[169] After two introductory paragraphs, it was divided into nine separate sections, each of them responding to points in Gladstone's *Vaticanism* or to specific criticisms that Newman had received from other readers of his *Letter*. At times the points are almost technical in presentation, for example, those dealing with the somewhat tedious question as to whether the Catholic Church recognized the validity of marriages between two (baptized) Protestants in countries, such as England, where the decrees of Trent had never been introduced.[170]

In his first section Newman felt obliged to return once more to the controverted question of what had been said by the Irish and English bishops to the British government in the decades leading up to the Emancipation Act of 1829. Gladstone in his *Vaticanism* had seized upon Newman's question as to why the English government had looked for an answer from the bishops instead of going to Rome, to "head-quarters." Obviously then, Gladstone had concluded triumphantly, Rome had all the answers, the local bishops had no authority. Newman responded somewhat curiously. He said that the Gallican tradition was in the late eighteenth and in the early nineteenth century dominant among Irish and English clerics. They could not then have been expected to have answered other than they did but "with the Ultramontane [position] stood Rome itself."[171] Newman then continued in a line more consistent with the argumentation of his *Letter*: "It never can be said then that this opinion, which has now become a dogma, was not perfectly well known to be living and energetic in the Catholic communion, though it was not an article of faith, and was not spoken of as such by Catholics in this part of the world during the centuries of persecution."[172]

And he concluded his response on this point by stating, in perhaps the most memorable section of his "Postscript":

> But it is no change surely to decide between two prevalent opinions; but, if it is to be so regarded, then change has been the characteristic of the church from the earliest times, as, for instance, in the third century, on the point of the validity of baptism by heretics. And hence such a change as has taken place, (which I should prefer to call doctrinal development,) is in itself a positive argument in favour of the Church's identity from first to last; for a growth in its creed is a law of its life.[173]

Newman's fourth point was more a response to Archbishop Errington and others (and, though unknown to Newman, to his Roman censors) than to Gladstone. Newman dealt here with the criticisms of his

169. *The Letters and Diaries,* Introductory Note, 27:xvi.
170. See "Postscript," LDN, 220–23.
171. Ibid., 209.
172. Ibid., 211.
173. Ibid., 212.

statement that the pope was the "heir by default" to the hierarchy of the fourth century. Newman conceded that he had been inexact in his choice of words, though he believed that the misunderstanding had come in part because he had been speaking historically, not theologically.[174] To set matters right Newman explained: "I did not mean to deny that those prerogatives were his from the beginning, but merely that they were gradually brought into full exercise by a course of events, which history records."[175]

Gladstone maintained that Newman had gained nothing by showing that the pope was bound by the moral and divine law, by the commandments of God, by the rule of the Gospel, since in the end the pope remained "the judge without appeal." In the fifth section of his "Postscript," Newman relied again on Cardinal Turrecremata in an effort to turn aside Gladstone's persistence on the point that Catholics gave unlimited authority to the pope. Newman gave the quote as follows: "Were the Pope to command any thing against Holy Scripture, or the articles of faith, or the truth of the Sacraments, or the commands of the natural or divine law, he ought not to be obeyed, but in such commands to be ignored."[176]

And when Gladstone said that Newman had an almost Protestant attitude in his exposition of what was left to the individual Catholic's freedom as far as papal statements were concerned, and especially his contentions that there are always exceptions to general statements, Newman replied: "I willingly endure to have about me a smack of Protestantism, which attaches to Cardinal Turrecremata in the 15th century, to Cardinals Jacobatius and Bellarmine in the 16th, to the Carmelites of Salamanca in the 17th, and to all theologians prior to them; and also to the whole Schola after them, . . . and so down to St. Alfonso Liguori the latest Doctor of the Church in the 18th, and to Cardinal Gousset and to Archbishop Kenrick in the 19th."[177]

Gladstone had replied to Newman's treatment of the *Syllabus of Errors* by citing Catholic authors who maintained that the *Syllabus* was in fact an infallible pronouncement. Newman answered by taking Fessler as his guide: "I do not know what Fessler himself says of it more than that it is to be received with submission and obedience. I do not deny another's right to consider it in his private conscience an act of infallibility, or to say, in Mr. Gladstone's words, p. 35, 'that utterances *ex cathedrâ* are not the only form in which Infallibility can speak;' I only say that I have a right to think otherwise."[178]

174. See ibid., 212.
175. Ibid., 212.
176. Ibid., 214.
177. Ibid., 215.
178. Ibid., 218.

Gladstone had seized upon statements that Newman had made, immediately after the definition of 1870, in the two letters he had used in the appendix to the *Letter to the Duke of Norfolk* to show what his views were at the time, especially his statement that a moral unanimity was needed before a definition could be considered valid and that reception by the Church was necessary before a definition could be considered *de fide*. Newman interestingly backed away somewhat from these letters, saying that he did not stand by each and every point made in them but had used them to show that his general line just after the definition was that it should be accepted as binding on all Catholics.[179] In any case, Newman continued, moral unanimity among the Fathers was no longer of any moment since the definition made it clear that the pope alone had the authority to make *ex cathedra* pronouncements binding on the faith of all Catholics.[180] As to "subsequent reception by the Church," Newman answered: "I said that by the 'Securus judicat orbis terrarum' all acts of the rulers of the Church are 'ratified. . . .' In this passage of my private letter [letter of 24 July 1870] I meant by 'ratified' brought home to us as authentic. At this very moment it is certainly the handy, obvious, and serviceable argument for our accepting the Vatican definition of the Pope's Infallibility."[181]

When Gladstone, having noted Newman's (and Fessler's) minimalist interpretation of the definition, retorted that this result seemed hardly worth bringing bishops to Rome from the four corners of the earth, Newman responded by saying that the council had not been called to define papal infallibility and that the real reasons for its convocation had been hindered by the outbreak of war in Europe. "The Council," Newman said, "is not yet ended."[182]

It was all well and good, Gladstone had said, to assert that the pope was not inspired as the apostles had been, but surely the power that the pope now had would allow him to stand Newman's assertion on its head. Newman did not back down. "I can only say to so hypothetical an argument," he wrote, "what is laid down by Fessler and the Swiss bishops,[183] that the Pope cannot, by virtue of his infallibility, reverse what has always been held; and that the 'inspiration' of the church, in the sense in which the Apostles were inspired, is contrary to our received teaching."[184]

179. See ibid., 223.
180. See ibid., 224.
181. Ibid., 224.
182. See ibid., 226–27. It is interesting to see Newman here go from a minimalist defense of the definition to a minimalist view of the First Vatican Council, a council that has loomed so large in the life of the Church for over a century, the successor Vatican Council notwithstanding. Noteworthy too is his declaration that "the Council is not yet ended."
183. Pastoral Letter of the Swiss Bishops, June 1871. See Cuthbert Butler, *The Vatican Council* (London: Longmans, Green, & Co., 1930) 2:218–19.
184. "Postscript," LDN, 228.

Newman's last words in his *Postscript* were written with the same double object in view that had characterized his whole participation in the controversy, a response to Gladstone and a response to Catholic Ultramontanism. Gladstone had said that Newman lived "under a system of development, through which somebody's private opinion of today may become matter of faith for all the to-morrows of the future." "I think he should give some proof of this", Newman answered,

> let us have one instance in which "somebody's private opinion" has become *de fide*. Instead of this he goes on to assert (interrogatively) that Popes, e.g. Clement XI. and Gregory II. and the present Pope, have claimed the inspiration of the Apostles, and that Germans, Italians, French have ascribed such a gift to him; —of course he means theologians, not mere courtiers or sychophants, for the Pope cannot help having such, till human nature is changed. If Mr. Gladstone is merely haranguing as an Orator, I do not for an instant quarrel with him or attempt to encounter him; but, if he is a controversialist, we have a right to look for arguments, not mere assertions.[185]

Newman, his duty done, refuses to enter into further controversy over the definition

Newman had known a great deal of satisfaction in March. He had quickly decided that a full-scale reply to Gladstone's *Vaticanism* was not demanded on his part, and having made this decision, he proceeded calmly to prepare his brief reply. In April, the aftermath of his *Letter* continued, but he was finally free of pressing correspondence and the need to concern himself directly with any debate continued by Gladstone or other principals in the discussion. At the beginning of April, Newman began an extended correspondence with his nephew, John Rickards Mozley, then professor of mathematics at Owens College in Manchester. The correspondence had its origin in the *Letter to the Duke of Norfolk*, particularly the passage where Newman dealt with the disreputable and indefensible conduct of some of the popes. Mozley asked how a Church which claimed to have divine guidance could have initiated or tolerated so many acts that appeared to be evil and refused afterwards, for example, in the nineteenth century, to disown them. The first of Newman's five long letters to Mozley was written on 1 April. Newman began by saying to his nephew, "You open a subject too large to be dealt with in one letter: but I shall be able to get a certain way in it today."[186] In summary, Newman, in a letter that went on for several pages, took the following position:

185. Ibid.
186. Newman to John Rickards Mozley, 1 April 1875, *The Letters and Diaries*, 27:259.

> But leaving the highest and truest outcome of the Catholic Church, and descending to history, certainly I would maintain firmly, with most writers on the Evidences, that, as the Church has a dark side, so (as you do not seem to admit) it has a light side also, and that its good has been more potent and permanent and evidently intrinsic to it than its evil. . . . If in the long line there be bad as well as good Popes, do not forget that long succession, continuous and thick, of holy and heroic men, all subjects of the Popes, and most of them his direct instruments in the most noble and serviceable and most various works, and some of them Popes themselves . . . all of whom, as multitudes besides, in their day were the life of religion.[187]

When John Mozley replied immediately, Newman took up his side of the correspondence again on 4 April. In this letter Newman touched on several points of papal history—the Inquisition, the St. Bartholomew Day Massacre, the bad government of the Papal States—that had come up again and again in the past decade during debate over the papacy and the papal teaching office. He did not shy away from the difficulties, but at the same time he stuck to the defense of the Catholic Church he had made in his first letter to John Mozley: "You see all along I have kept to my purpose of describing *my own* view of the difficulties of Catholicity on which you fasten, instead of attempting to deal with them controversially. The temporal prosperity, success, talent, renown of the Papacy did not make me a Catholic, and its errors and misfortunes have no power to unsettle me. Its utter disestablishment may only make it stronger and purer, removing the very evils which are the cause of its being disestablished."[188] In the third letter in this series, written on 21 April, Newman, while again acknowledging the human side of the Catholic Church, continued to see the Church as integral to the survival of Christianity: "Still, if it is a great work to preserve Christianity in the world, this I think the Church has done and is doing; and at this moment Christianity would be dying out in all its varieties, were the Catholic Church to be suppressed."[189] Newman on 16 May, distressed by the serious illness of Ambrose St. John, asked to be excused from answering John Mozley's latest letter. Eventually he concluded the correspondence on 3 December in a letter gentle in tone but unyielding in its presentation of Roman Catholicism as singular among the Christian Churches in having preserved the ethical system introduced into the world by the first Christians.[190] In 1899 Mozley published the correspondence in the September issue of the *Contemporary Review*.[191]

187. Ibid., 27:262–63.

188. Newman to John Rickards Mozley, 4 April 1875, *The Letters and Diaries*, 27:267.

189. Newman to John Rickards Mozley, 21 April 1875, *The Letters and Diaries*, 27:284.

190. See Newman to John Rickards Mozley, 3 December 1875, *The Letters and Diaries*, 27:385–89.

191. See *The Letters and Diaries*, 27:259, footnote 1.

Over the past ten years Newman had had to deal again and again with questions related to the papal office and the definition of papal infallibility. This continued after the *Letter to the Duke of Norfolk,* at times in consequence of it but also quite apart from it, except to the extent that the publication of his *Letter* had perhaps kept his name before the public as the leading Catholic controversialist in England. After the controversy with Gladstone, he began to show that he had had enough of the subject. The April issue of the *Contemporary Review* contained an article on the seventeenth-century Jesuit Louis Maimbourg and his defense of Gallicanism against claims of papal infallibility.[192] The editor of the *Contemporary Review,* James Knowles, sent a copy of the April issue to Newman and pointed out the piece entitled "A Jesuit Father on Papal Infallibility."[193] Newman thanked Knowles on 7 April but went on to say with evident exasperation:

> . . . I very much doubt whether any thing new can be said either for or against the Pope's Infallibility. Maimbourg, who was not the only Jesuit, I believe, who wrote against it, (though these others did not leave the Society) is not equal to Bossuet, and his arguments from the case of Liberius, of Vigilius, of Honorius etc etc are the usual topics which are urged and repelled to and fro in controversy ad infinitum. I believe there is nothing in Maimbourg which is not, according to my recollection, answered in such a work as Ballerini's.[194] It would be difficult for a Catholic, who is even moderately well read in it, to throw his mind into so hackneyed a subject; whether the public too is not just now tired of the subject, you are a better judge than I can be.[195]

When Newman was asked in mid-April what the role of the bishops was in a definition *de fide* as a result of the Vatican Council, he replied almost curtly, as though weary of the whole debate. In a letter of 15 April to Thomas Edwards, he wrote:

> Up to 1870, what was of faith was that infallibility lies in the voice of Pope and Bishops together. The question which followed, what if Pope and Bishops differ? might be answered in three ways, in fact there is no act of infallibility, 2 infallibility lies with the Bishops by themselves—3. Infallibility lies in the Pope by himself. In the Council of the Vatican, the third answer has been made de fide. In saying this I do not mean to imply that the

192. Maimbourg, who in 1682 wrote *Traité historique de l'établissement et des prérogatives de l'Eglise de Rome et ses evêques,* was forced to leave the Jesuits after his book had been published.

193. See *The Letters and Diaries,* 27:268, footnote 1.

194. *De Vi ac Ratione Primatus Romanorum Pontificum et de ipsorum Infallibilitate in definiendis Controversiis Fidei* (Verona, 1766).

195. Newman to James Knowles, 7 April 1875, *The Letters and Diaries,* 27:268.

Pope and Bishops ever will disagree, though a portion of the Episcopate may disagree with the Pope.

a difference not in fact but an hypothesis.[196]

When Edwards several months later continued to press the matter and to charge Newman with having been discourteous, Newman did not hide his exasperation.[197] His letter to Edwards is not extant, but he wrote a summary of his reply as follows: "It is no omission of 'ordinary courtesy' to decline to enter into controversy with a stranger. I answered your question in two letters, when I thought you a bonâ fide inquirer; now I have a clear view that you are nothing else than a controversialist." And in response to Edwards's determination to come to Birmingham and meet with Newman, Newman said: "Should you take the illadvised step of coming here, you will find me as resolved not to engage in conversation as in correspondence."[198]

Though avoiding public controversy, Newman, as always, is ready to counsel troubled Catholics and sincere inquirers

Though Newman by April 1875 shows that he has had enough of public controversy and dealings with strangers on topics related to the papal office, he continued to respond, even in considerable detail, to the same questions raised by close friends. In an important letter to Isy Froude, written on 24 April, Newman dealt fully with questions that she had raised about papal infallibility. This letter and its sequel are a notable exposition of Newman's views after a decade of debate and controversy. There is no doubt that that debate, however draining, had sharpened and crystallized his views:

> As to your first question, I should say that the word "infallibility" has never been ascribed to the *Church* in any authoritative document till the Vatican Council—and it has been not unfrequently urged as an objection (and I think by myself in print in former days) that the Church's "infallibility" was not de fide.[199] Yet the Church acted *as* infallible and was accepted as infallible from the first. What was the case with the Church was the case with the Pope. The most *real* expression of the doctrine is, not that he is infallible but that his decisions are "irreformabilia" and true. So that the question did not arise in the mind of Christians in any formal shape "is he infallible,

196. Newman to Thomas Edwards, 15 April 1875, *The Letters and Diaries,* 27:277–78.

197. See Thomas Edwards to Newman, 12 August 1875, *The Letters and Diaries,* 27:278, footnote 1.

198. Newman to Thomas Edwards, mid-August 1875, *The Letters and Diaries,* 27:278, footnote 1.

199. "Lectures on the Prophetical Office of the Church," *The Via Media,* 1:195–201.

and in what and how far?'' for all they felt was that what he said was "the Voice of the Church", "for he spoke for the Church", "the Church spoke in him", and what the Church spoke was *true*. And accordingly his word was (to use a common phrase) "taken for Gospel", and he meant it "for Gospel", he "laid down the law", and he *meant* to "lay down the law"— he was *sure* he was right, no one had any *doubt* he was right—he was "the proper person to speak and to settle the matter." This (with whatever accidental exceptions) was his and the Christian world's feeling in the matter; as any ordinary man now (bigotted Protestant, if you will acting from prejudice) says "I know I am right",—so the Pope would say "I know it is so, and it is my duty to tell the flock of Christ so", *without analyzing* whether it was a moral certainty, or an inspiration or a formal limited infallibility, or whatever other means which was the ground of his unquestioning and his absolute peremptoriness. Honorius then or any other Pope of those times, when he chose, *acted* as infallible and was *obeyed* as infallible, without having a clear perception that his ipse dixit arose from a *gift* of infallibility.

But again, at least the *Church* acted as infallible from the first, e.g. in Councils etc—Now the Pope ever acted in company *with* the Church, sometimes before the hierarchy, sometimes after, sometimes simultaneously with, the hierarchy. He always showed, as the *voice* of the Church. The Vatican Council has decided that he is not only the instrumental and ministerial head or organ of the Church, not only has a power of veto, not only is a co-operating agent in *de fide* decisions, but that in him lies the root of the matter, that his decision, viewed separate even from the Bishops, is gospel.

Before the Vatican Council, even Gallicans allowed that the Pope was infallible, *supposing* the Bishops accepted his decision—and at least *that* Honorius would feel, supposing him led to make any ex cathedrâ decision, so that I *deny* your correspondent's words, "he could not in the 7th century actually intend to exert that infallible authority, which has been dogmatically defined in the 19th." Yes, he could, and though he might not be clear as to the *conditions* of infallibility, though he might take for granted, or implicitly expect, and *be sure* of, the concurrence of the Bishops of the world with him as a condition of the act being infallible.

The account I have given of the Council of Ephesus in "Theodoret" in Historical sketches [sic] is a further illustration of what I have tried to bring out here.[200]

I might have taken a higher ground, for long before the Vatican Council, though not perhaps in the time of Honorius, Popes have realized to themselves their own infallibility, and from the first, as we see in the history of St. Victor, St. Stephen, St. Dionysius, in the Ante-nicene times,—they have acted as if their word was *law,* without making nice distinctions.

When your correspondent says "Previous to the Vatican Council no doctrines defined only by the Pope are absolutely to be received", I remark on the contrary there was such an agreement in fact between Pope and

200. *Historical Sketches* (London, New York, Bombay: Longmans, Green and Co., 1906) 2:347–52.

Bishops that, when he *taught* and was followed by the world (as took place) it was impossible to discuss whether the Bishops concurred by an act of independent judgment or by an act of submission to him. *Practically* the Pope has taught dogmatically from the first, e.g. it is not at all clear that Leo's famous Tome against Eutyches is an act of infallibility; but what *is* clear is that it had the effect of turning a great mass of Bishops right round, as if he were infallible, and making them with him in the Council of Chalcedon use the words definitive of the two natures in One Person, which he had in his Tome forced upon them. He has been from the first, (where history is minute enough for the purpose,) the beginning and the end, he has had the first and last word, of every definition. You understand me, I am bringing out my view, without stopping to notice objections or opposite statements.[201]

After ten years of debate, often rancorous, over papal infallibility, Newman had begun this summary of the topic in the hope of satisfying questions raised by Isy Froude's correspondent. He had tired before he could finish and would conclude his presentation in a further letter to Isy Froude three months later. The considerable effort that Newman so frequently went to in dealing with questions raised by sincere inquirers shows again his great pastoral sensitivity. The letter itself appears to give a very high doctrine of papal authority—"that in him lies the root of the matter, that his decision, viewed separate even from the Bishops, is gospel"— and to give a very sure reading of the exercise of this authority through history, centuries before the definition of 1870. Much of what Newman says in this letter to Isy Froude seems incompatible, or at least inconsistent, with what he had written on the subject of the pope's authority in the previous decade, especially in his correspondence on the subject. It has to be noted that Newman toward the end of the letter to Isy Froude makes an important and not untypical qualification, "You understand me, I am bringing out my view, without stopping to notice objections or opposite statements."

The letter was ultimately intended for a friend of Isy Froude's who was considering entrance into the Roman Catholic Church and for this reason should not perhaps be overestimated in the history of Newman's thought on the subject of papal infallibility. Clearly, Newman had this in mind as he wrote. The matter of papal infallibility had for now been settled. There would be no further council. Pius IX was still reigning. Someone about to enter the Church should have full knowledge of the present situation. It would be unfair to offer speculation and possibilities of future councils, future popes, and more refined teachings on the papal office. But it must be recognized that Newman was at this point in his life concerned more and more with a growing religious liberalism that,

201. Newman to Isy Froude, 24 April 1875, *The Letters and Diaries,* 27:286-87.

he believed, would end up in indifferentism. Increasingly in this period he came to see the need for an authoritative, universal voice. This had always been an important theme for Newman. Before the Vatican Council he had looked to the Church as the universal guide. After the council and in view of the definition, he began more to emphasize the pope's role as the universal voice.

Yet ever one to see the several sides of any question, he would in a further letter to Isy Froude, written three months later, give a prominent place to the role of theologians in the Church's system and to "the passive infallibility of the whole body of the Catholic people."[202] Just two years later in the preface to the third edition of the *Via Media,* Newman would publicly make known his strong views on the role of the *schola theologorum* in the life of the Church. All of this recalls the comments made by Newman in the 1860s when the matter of papal infallibility began to be controverted in England. Then he told several of his correspondents that he had never been logical or consistent in his attitude toward papal infallibility. Even after the definition Newman continued to take views on the issue that are not consonant with something he had said the day, the week, the month before. He continued to explore and to search in faith and in hope.

Newman and continuing debate over the pope's temporal power

In addition to papal infallibility, the other prolonged debate surrounding the papacy in the past decade had been the question of the pope's temporal power. By 1875 realistic hopes on the part of advocates of the temporal power of seeing the pope restored as a civil ruler were waning. Nonetheless, some determined voices continued. One of these was the American Father Isaac Hecker, founder of the Paulists and editor of the *Catholic World.* At the end of March, Hecker, then in Rome, had asked the English publisher, B. M. Pickering, to send Newman a copy of Hecker's new pamphlet, "An Exposition of the Church in view of Recent Difficulties and Controversies and the Present Needs of the Age." Strongly ultramontane articles had for some years appeared in the pages of the *Catholic World.* These were the work of Orestes Brownson with whom Hecker, certainly not an Ultramontane prior to the Vatican Council, was frequently in disagreement. However, in his pamphlet, Hecker, whose views had undergone a change since the council, took a strongly Ultramontane stance.[203] Newman showed his regret for this, and in his

202. Newman to Isy Froude, 28 July 1875, *The Letters and Diaries,* 27:336–38.

203. Hecker had gone to the council opposed to the definition of papal infallibility and was a close associate of two determined North American opponents of the definition, Archbishop Kenrick of St. Louis and Archbishop Connolly of Halifax. After the council, Hecker

letter of thanks to Hecker he dealt not with the definition of 1870 but with the pope's temporal power and the growth of the Church in the time ahead:

> . . . I do not see that you start from the right point in your contemplation of the future. The main point, the one point (as far as I have the means of knowing) which the Holy Father has insisted on as the condition of a prosperous state of the Catholic Religion, is, not an effusion of Divine Influences,[204] whether among Catholics or in the circumjacent Protestantism and infidelity, but the maintenance of the Temporal Power. He has again and again declared that His Temporal Power is *necessary* for the well being of the Church, and, when English Catholics have wished to use a milder word, they have not been allowed to do so. They have not been even allowed to use the qualification of "in the present state of things" as a shelter for holding that the present state is changing, and the necessity of the Temporal Power in consequence ceasing. The Temporal Power then being a first principle at Rome, and the prospective movement of the races of Europe and America being, as you say, "expansive and popular," I do not see how Catholicity is likely to "attract, as regards those races," sympathy and cheerful co-operation. I believe firmly that the Lord of the Church will make a way out of the difficulty, but I do not see how. Of course I have theories of my own, but they would as little approve themselves to you, as those of M. Veuillot and others approve themselves to me.

Newman did not relent even in his closing. "I am grieved," he wrote, "to observe the line that the Catholic World has taken for some years."[205]

Newman receives general praise for his Postscript; after his success he experiences one of the greatest trials of his life

The first reaction to Newman's "Postscript" came on 8 April in a letter from Dr. Russell of Maynooth. Russell said: "I have just read your

---

traveled for several years in Europe and he conceived a theory of evangelization, which gave a central and dominant role to the papacy.

204. Hecker saw the Catholic world as more open to the inspiration of the Spirit as a consequence of the definition of papal infallibility. Hecker's pamphlet is reprinted as appendix III, 230–74, in William L. Portier, *Isaac Hecker and the Vatican Council*, Studies in American Religion, vol. 15 (Lewiston, New York: The Edward Mellen Press, 1985). See also David J. O'Brien, *Isaac Hecker: An American Catholic* (New York and Mahwah, N.J.: Paulist Press, 1992) 269–86. O'Brien gives the title of Hecker's pamphlet as "An Exposition of the Church in View of Recent Difficulties and Controversies and the Present Needs of the *Church*," whereas *The Letters and Diaries*, 27:271, footnote 1, gives the conclusion of the title as "The Present Needs of the Age."

205. Newman to Father Isaac Hecker, 10 April 1875, *The Letters and Diaries*, 27:271–72. See David O'Brien's comment on Newman's letter to Hecker in *Isaac Hecker: An American Catholic*, 275. In a letter to his confrere, Abraham Hewit, Hecker said that Newman "appears a little soured." Ibid.

"Postscript" with the utmost delight. It is a *complete* answer, and will clinch the hold which your "Letter" took of the public mind."[206] Newman had also sent a copy of his "Postscript" to Lord Blachford. When Blachford thanked Newman on 9 April and spoke appreciatively of the effects of the *Letter to the Duke of Norfolk,* especially on Anglicans, Newman responded on 11 April with a long letter that looked back over the past several months and recorded his pleasure in the success of his letter, particularly its favorable reception by Catholics:

> I sent you my P.S. mainly to elicit a letter from you, not on its subject, but for the sake of a letter. As to my Pamphlet, what you say of its success agrees, to my surprise as well as my pleasure, to what I hear from others. What surprises me most is its success among my own people. I had for a long time been urged by friends to write—but I persisted in saying that I would not go out of my way to do so. When Gladstone wrote, I saw it was now or never, and I had so vivid an apprehension that I should get into a great trouble and rouse a great controversy around me, that I was most unwilling to take up my pen. I had made a compact with myself, that, if I did write, I would bring out my whole mind, and especially speak out on the subject of what I had in a private letter called "a violent and aggressive faction"—So that I wrote and printed, I may say, in much distress of mind. Yet nothing happened such as I had feared. For instance, Ward is unsaying in print some of his extravagances,[207] and a priest who with others has long looked at me with suspicion and is a good specimen of his class, writes to me "I hope everybody will read it and re-read it. . . . I may also congratulate you that you have carried with you the Catholic mind of England, and made us feel but one pulse of Ultramontane sympathy beating in our body— May God give you length of days etc."[208] In Ireland Cardinal Cullen spoke of me in the warmest terms and in his Lent Pastoral, read in all the Churches of his Diocese, and my friend Dr. Russell of Maynooth, who had been frightened at the possible effect of some of my pages, wrote to me, after being present at a great gathering of Bishops and priests from all parts of Ireland, on occasion of Archbishop Leahy's funeral, that I had nothing to fear, for there was but one unanimous voice there, and that was in my favour.
>
> Of course as time goes on "the clouds may return after the rain"—but anyhow I have cause for great thankfulness—and I trust now I may be allowed to die in peace. Old age is very cowardly—at least so I find it to be.[209]

Blachford in his letter to Newman thought that in his "Postscript" Newman had weakened his case for resisting a pope's order to a Catholic

---

206. Dr. Charles Russell to Newman, 8 April 1875, *The Letters and Diaries,* 27:270, footnote 3.

207. See *Dublin Review* n.s. 24 (January–April 1875) 454–55.

208. Letter of Canon Thomas Longman, Birmingham, 7 April 1875. See *The Letters and Diaries,* 27:273, footnote 3.

209. Newman to Lord Blachford, 11 April 1875, *The Letters and Diaries,* 27:272–73.

to resign from the army in a war that the Catholic believed to be just by quoting Canon Henry Neville, a former professor of theology at Maynooth. Neville had written, "It is a trite principle, that mere ecclesiastical laws do not bind, when there would be a very grave inconvenience in their observance."[210] Blachford thought that Neville by using the word "inconvenience" trivialized the high and courageous duty that Newman seemed to be invoking when he spoke of a Catholic's conscience overruling the pope's command in a civil matter. Newman defended Canon Neville and showed how useful an ally he thought him to be:

> As to Canon Neville's passage, you must recollect what a strong thing it is to tell the party spirit, and the enthusiasm, and the sentiment unreasoning and untheological, of Catholics, that the Pope is *ever* to be disobeyed—not to speak of the political partizans of his cause and the tyranny of newspaper Editors. To quote a Maynooth Professor who could say the Pope need not be obeyed in the critical case of an English war against him, that his command was to be resisted on *any* motive, for *any* reason, that this was the *rule* in such a case, was to possess a great ally, who would block any attack, any annoyance, which my words might have caused. Recollect the contract under which soldiers are bound, holds as soon as it is found to be lawful. And Canon Neville's argument secures its legality. Nor did I mean at all, as the Saturday [Review] thinks to *withdraw* my *own* ground.

Newman concluded this review of his success by recording one further triumph: "The Jesuits, as usual, have stood my friends. One of them only, Fr. Bottalla, without the sympathy of the body, has made in a Liverpool Paper, five charges against me—but we have stood to our guns, and all but silenced him."[211] Two days later, Newman spoke more briefly, but in similar terms, of his elation over the reaction to his *Letter*. Writing to Lord Henry Kerr, he said: "And thank you for what you say of my Pamphlet; it has been both a labour and a trouble of mind to me, but I have

210. See "Postscript," 213–14. Neville published a reply to Gladstone's *Expostulation* entitled *A few comments on Gladstone's Expostulation* (1875). Gladstone noted in his diary on 25 February 1875 that he had read Neville's reply. See *The Gladstone Diaries,* 9:16.

It is interesting to see how much Newman valued a Maynooth professor's opinion for the success that he believed it would secure for his position on obedience to the pope from the Ultramontane party. Cardinal Cullen considered Maynooth a hotbed of Gallicanism and worked actively against the institution, for example, by promoting the ill-fated theology faculty at the Catholic University in Dublin and by working against the promotion of Maynooth professors to the episcopate. See Corish, *The Irish Catholic Experience,* 199 and 201–03.

211. Newman to Lord Blachford, 11 April 1875, *The Letters and Diaries,* 27:273–74. Newman's phrase "we have stood to our guns" is perhaps remarkable. It may in fact be simply a question of style used by a writer who even in the most casual letters gives frequent evidence of not simply writing but *hearing* what he is writing. On the other hand, Newman rarely if ever referred to himself in the first person plural and one can speculate that the "we" is an indication of how confident he felt after the *Letter to the Duke of Norfolk,* that its success had gathered to him a following, that he no longer felt the odd man out.

been abundantly recompensed, I am thankful to say, by its reception by all parties—those in the Church as well as those outside it—And I have many letters from friends, which like yours, are the best of consolations to me. . . ."[212]

On 16 April, Newman wrote to congratulate Miss Emily Buchanan on her reception into the Catholic Church, a step she had finally made up her mind to take after reading the *Letter to the Duke of Norfolk*. Newman began: "I am very glad to receive from you the tidings of your conversion, and am thankful to God both for it and for the circumstances under which it occurred." But Newman, no doubt thinking of his own life as a Catholic and of many of those he had led into the Catholic Church, went on to speak not only of the happy occasion but also of the trials Miss Buchanan could expect in consequence of it:

> God has been very gracious to you—and you may feel confident that He who has done so much for you will do still more. You must guard against your spiritual enemy, who will try to use you against yourself. After a time of excitement, perhaps of spiritual exultation, such as often is the attendant on conversion, there is often in turn a season of re-action, from the mere weariness of the mind, as we are apt to feel in the parallel case of bodily exertion. Then a despondency comes on, and then is our enemy's time to suggest difficulties or murmurings. And the shorter has been the process of conversion, the more severe is likely to be this reverse. If such happens to you, you must be brave, and call on God to help you, and go straight forward in spite of all difficulties, and cherish a sure trust that your Lord and Saviour will in His own time bring your trial to an end.[213]

Newman in the time of his new success did not forget his duties to others, as is also shown in a letter of 9 April to Charles Bowden, whose brother John had died in December. "I meant before this, certainly before the Easter week was out," Newman told Charles Bowden,

> to have asked about your Mother and Sister. I hope they are getting over the shock of their great loss. I don't write to them, for I could not expect they would be able to tell me about themselves.
> I trust I am nearly out of the wake of the Gladstone Controversy—but the number of private letters it has demanded of me has been great.[214]

The controversy had all but ended by the last days of April. But the calm that had returned to Newman's life proved to be short-lived. On 25 April, Ambrose St. John began to show signs of serious illness. This was to last over several weeks until his death a month later. The advice that

212. Newman to Lord Henry Kerr, 13 April 1875, *The Letters and Diaries,* 27:276.
213. Newman to Miss Emily Buchanan, 16 April 1875, *The Letters and Diaries,* 27:278.
214. Newman to Charles Bowden, 9 April 1875, *The Letters and Diaries,* 27:269.

Newman had given to Miss Buchanan on perseverance in trials would be needed by Newman himself in the coming months and the sympathy that he had shown to the Bowden family and so many others would be returned to him by hundreds of friends and strangers in the days just ahead.

In the first part of May, as Ambrose St. John's illness took various turns, now better, now worse, Newman was able to spare some time for his correspondence. On 7 May, he wrote a letter of congratulation to Mrs. Maxwell-Scott on the birth of her first son. "I rejoice to have a letter from you," Newman began. "I said Mass for you when I heard what was to happen, and should have said more, had I not been interrupted by the good news. You may be sure I have not forgotten at this season dear Papa [James Hope-Scott]. I think it owing to his and Serjeant Bellasis's prayers for me, that I have got through my answer to Mr. Gladstone so well."

In his diary for 2 May, Newman had recorded: "Splendid wonderful weather I never recollect such a May."[215] He surely had this in mind as he continued his letter to Mrs. Maxwell-Scott:

> I rejoice to find that you are a half convert to Spring. For myself, even as a boy, I preferred it to Autumn; but all men, as time advances with them, I think turn their faces to it rather than to autumn [sic]. I do not call you as yet a very old lady, but the time will come, when you will want the support of that Divine Promise of restoration in the midst of decay, of which Spring is the emblem and pledge.
>
> I was beginning to enjoy it now, when I have been afflicted by a very serious sorrow. I don't wish it told, lest it should be exaggerated—but I ask your prayers for my dearest friend, Father St. John, who has suffered what is very like a sunstroke and is suddenly thrown out of work.[216]

On the same day Newman noted in his diary, "he received communion" and after Ambrose St. John's death he added, "his last."[217]

In a letter the next day, Newman thanked Ambrose Phillipps De Lisle for a copy of his article, "On the Perpetual Belief of the Catholic Church of Christ concerning the Office and Authority of St. Peter," which appeared in the May issue of the *Union Review*. Though Newman had had much advice about De Lisle's plans to respond to Gladstone's *Vaticanism,* when the article appeared he was too distracted by Ambrose St. John's illness to give it more than cursory notice. He told De Lisle:

> You must not be angry with me for having delayed my acknowledgements of your letter and article. We are in much anxiety or rather distress about Fr. St. John. . . .
>
> It has put me into great confusion and I seem to lose my reckoning of time and every thing else.

215. Newman "Diary," 2 May 1875, *The Letters and Diaries,* 27:291.
216. Newman to Mrs. Maxwell-Scott, 7 May 1875, *The Letters and Diaries,* 27:292.
217. Newman "Diary," 7 May 1875, *The Letters and Diaries,* 27:292.

I have not read the whole of your article, which came this morning—what I have read I think spirited, eloquent and forcible. I wish I could believe that Mr. Gladstone would lay to heart what you say—but the suspicion of tyrannical conduct and double-dealing at Rome seems to absorb his whole mind.[218]

Despite his daily anxiety over Ambrose St. John's condition, Newman also took the time in this period to deny once more that he was in any sense doubting with regard to the Catholic Church or dissuasive toward those individuals seeking to enter into communion with it. In a letter of 11 May, Newman told Clarence Woodman, an American Episcopalian clergyman:

> I never dreamed of "advising English Churchmen in doubt of their faith and almost persuaded to be Catholics, not to make any change." This is a report which has been going about these thirty years, and I have to contradict it as a matter of routine about once a quarter, sometimes in print. But lies have a wonderful vitality, like weeds, and I suppose are self sown, or rather sown, by the evil spirit, and find soil amongst human hearts for a large growth.
>
> I have lately been led to speak of my own belief in the Catholic Church in the Postscript of my letter on Mr. Gladstone's Pamphlet.
>
> All I can say to those who are looking towards the Church, by way of warning is "count the cost." Recollect you must believe whatever the church does or shall teach you, for she is the Oracle of God. Hoping I have removed one obstacle in the way of your conversion by this letter, and praying God to prosper you on your way.[219]

Woodman was reassured by Newman's response and became a Catholic two months later. Having entered the Paulists, he was ordained a priest in 1879.

On 8 May Ambrose St. John was moved to Ravenhurst, about a mile and a half from the Oratory. From that time Newman was constantly back and forth between the Oratory and Ravenhurst. He was, however, at the Oratory on the night of 24 May when he was awakened and told that his friend of more than thirty years was dying. By the time he arrived at Ravenhurst, Ambrose St. John had died. After the funeral on 29 May, Newman's time was taken up for weeks answering more than one hundred letters of condolence. It was one of the most difficult periods of his long life. Indeed, on 13 June he said in a letter to Miss Holmes: "This is the greatest affliction I have had in my life, and so sudden."[220] And to Lord Blachford he wrote: "Sometimes I have thought that like my Patron Saint, St. John I am destined to survive all my friends."[221]

---

218. Newman to Ambrose De Lisle, 8 May 1875, *The Letters and Diaries,* 27:292–93.
219. Newman to Clarence Woodman, 11 May 1875, *The Letters and Diaries,* 27:295–96.
220. Newman to Miss Mary Holmes, 13 June 1875, *The Letters and Diaries,* 27:319.
221. Newman to Lord Blachford, 31 May 1875, *The Letters and Diaries,* 27:305.

*Newman denies yet another report that he is on the verge of leaving
the Church; he resumes his important correspondence to Isy Froude
on the papal office*

Toward the end of July, Newman turned again to topics that had engaged him before Father St. John's illness and death. He assured yet another inquirer that he had no intention of leaving the Catholic Church
and he directed his correspondent's attention to the following sentences
from the "Postscript" to the *Letter to the Duke of Norfolk:*

> From the day I became a Catholic to this day, now close upon thirty years,
> I have never had a moment's misgiving that the communion of Rome is
> that Church which the Apostles set up at Pentecost, which alone has "the
> adoption of sons, and the glory, and the covenants, and the revealed law,
> and the service of God, and the promises", and in which the Anglican com-
> munion, whatever its merits and demerits, whatever the great excellence of
> individuals in it, has, as such, no part. Nor have I ever for a moment since
> 1845 hesitated in my conviction that it was my clear duty to join that Catholic
> Church, as I did then join it, which in my own conscience I felt to be di-
> vine. Persons and places, incidents and circumstances of life, which belong
> to my first forty-four years, are deeply lodged in my memory and my affec-
> tions; moreover, I have had more to try and afflict me in various ways as
> a Catholic than as an Anglican; but never for a moment have I wished my-
> self back; never have I ceased to thank my Maker for His mercy in enabling
> me to make the great change, and never has He let me feel forsaken by Him,
> or in distress, or any kind of religious trouble.[222]

Several days later Newman resumed the correspondence with Isy
Froude that he had had to put aside three months before. He dealt again
with the office of the pope in the Church and responded at length to the
questions she had raised on this subject in her letter to him. And in this
second letter to Isy Froude, Newman continued to uphold the critical place
of the theological schools in the life of the Church as he had done in the
Letter to the Duke of Norfolk and as he would again do in the Preface
to the third edition of the *Via Media.* "I am not sure," Newman wrote,

> that you apprehend my answer to your first [question] which was, I think,
> to this effect. "Did not the Pope exert his infallible voice in early times?
> but if so, must he not have known himself infallible, and did he?" I think
> I answered thus—He never acted by himself—he acted in General Council,
> or in Roman Council, or with the concurrence or co-operation of some local
> Council, or with his own counsellors and theologians, never by himself—
> nor to this day has he acted by himself—Now in cases of this kind, the ques-
> tion always arises, what was, and in what lay, the *essence* of the act—for

---

222. Newman to J. B. Robertson, 23 July 1875, *The Letters and Diaries,* 27:333–34. See
"Postscript," 205–6. The wording in the "Postscript" is slightly different.

instance, the Holy Eucharist is a *sacrifice*—but to this day it is an open question, *what* is the act of sacrifice, what is the *constituting* act, which *is* the sacrifice. The common opinion is that the act of consecration is the act of sacrifice—but Bellarmine, I think, held that it is the Priests [sic] communion—While another opinion is that the whole action from the consecration to the communion is sacrificial. I believe also it is allowable to consider that it cannot be determined, but that the whole canon, must be viewed as one indivisable act (per modum unius is the theological phrase) and that we *cannot* analyze it, as schoolmen wish to do.

The condemnation of Nestorius illustrates what I would say—his doctrine is first condemned by the Alexandrians—then by his own people of Syria—then the Pope sends round to the principal sees of Christendom who do the same—Upon this the Pope sends him notice he must recant within ten days or he will excommunicate him—After this the General Council is called and his condemnation passed—on which the Emperor banishes him. Now where in what lay the infallible voice? if they had been asked, I suppose they could not have told—viz whether it lay in the whole process as being the result of it, or in the Council or in the Pope, or again, taking the Pope by himself, while they would understand that an infallible decision followed on his voice. Still they would not be able to say whether he spoke by his own intrinsic absolute authority, or as the voice and organ of the whole Church, who spoke through him.

This too must be considered—that the *infallibility* of the Church (or of the Pope) is, as far as I know, a novel phrase. The infallibility of the Church has never been defined as a dogma (except indirectly in the late Vatican Council). The form which the doctrine took was to say that the point in dispute, when once decided, was "irreformable", it was settled once for all—it was part of the Catholic faith—Therefore attention was centred in the *thing* not in the person—and, though of course it could not be settled for good in one certain way, *unless* the parties settling it were infallible, this view of the subject did not prominently come before the Pope or the Bishops. This is what I have meant to say on your first question.

Your second, I think, was this:—"If the *Schola* Theologorum decides the meaning of a Pope or a Council's words, the Schola is infallible, not *they* or *he*".

In answer to this I observe that there are no words, ever so clear, but require an interpretation, at least as to their extent. For instance, an inspired writer says that "God is love"—but supposing a set of men so extend this as to conclude "*Therefore* there is no future punishment for bad men?" Some power then is needed to determine the general sense of authoritative words—to determine their direction, drift, limits, and comprehension, to hinder gross perversions. This power is virtually the *passive infallibility* of the whole body of the Catholic people. The active infallibility lies in the Pope and Bishops—the passive in the "universitas" of the faithful. Hence the maxim "Securus judicat orbis terrarum." The body of the faithful never can misunderstand what the Church determines by the gift of its active infallibility. Here on the one hand I observe that a *local* sense of a doctrine, held in this or that country, is not a "sensus universitatis"—and on the other hand the schola theologorum is one chief portion of that universitas—and it acts with great force both in correcting popular misapprehensions and narrow views of the teaching of the active infallibilitas, and, by the intellectual investigations and disputes which are its very life, it keeps the distinction clear between theological truth and theological opinion, and is the antagonist of dogmatism. And while the differences of the School maintains [sic] the liberty of thought, the unanimity of its members is the safeguard of the infallible decisions of the Church and the champion of faith.

And then in a closing sentence, Newman, perhaps looking back over the public controversy of the past year as much as to his letters to Isy Froude, said: "I wonder whether I have made myself clear."[223]

In this second letter to Isy Froude, Newman backs away somewhat from the more narrowly papalist view of the Church's teaching authority that he took in the letter of 24 April. In the July letter, he underscores the role of theologians and the whole body of the faithful. He shows that there are many matters left open to discussion, even in such important areas as the "constituting act" of the eucharistic sacrifice. Theological writing and discussion work with the passage of time toward greater precision and understanding of what initially are broad enunciations. The body of the faithful possess a "passive infallibility," an ingrained sense of what is true and to be held. The active infallibility of the pope and bishops in declaring formally what the Church has always and everywhere believed cannot run counter to the passive infallibility of the whole body of believers. And it is noteworthy that while Newman in the April letter to Isy Froude spoke rather narrowly of the pope and the exercise of the papal office in history, here he speaks of the active infallibility that lies in "the Pope *and Bishops.*"

When he had written to Isy Froude in April, Newman was still in the aftermath of the *Letter to the Duke of Norfolk*. The *Letter to the Duke of Norfolk* was a moderate exposition of the Roman Church's teaching on papal infallibility. Despite a daring thrust here and there, it was overall a careful statement, a suitable declaration of his views for a public audience. The 24 April letter to Isy Froude shares to some degree in this caution and balance. Three months later, Newman had begun to move beyond the restraints of the *Letter to the Duke of Norfolk*. His letter of 28 July is less cautious, a slightly different approach from what he decided was necessary in the *Letter to the Duke of Norfolk*. He was already on his way to the more innovative and daring position he would take two years later in the preface to the third edition of the *Via Media*.

Newman was in generally good health in the late summer of 1875. He had taken on himself many of the duties, especially pastoral duties, that

223. Newman to Isy Froude, 28 July 1875, *The Letters and Diaries*, 27:336–38.

had been Ambrose St. John's.[224] He spent several days in London in the first part of August, visiting friends and consulting a specialist on hearing problems. He was frequently at Rednal in August and September. Controversy over, he resumed the preparation of a new edition of *The Arians of the Fourth Century*.[225] And in September, he resumed an earlier practice, preaching at Mass.

Disputes concerning the papacy had continued for more than a decade. For the most part Newman, despite the urgings of friends, had stayed in the background. With the *Letter to the Duke of Norfolk* he had had his say and it had been accepted. Nearing seventy-five, Newman returned, perhaps more than ever, to the daily routines and familiar patterns of the Oratory.

Manning and Ullathorne dissuade the Roman authorities from censuring Newman for his Letter to the Duke of Norfolk

Despite dissuasive letters from Manning and Ullathorne, and it would appear from Cardinal Cullen,[226] the Roman authorities at the end of the summer of 1875 were still intent on some kind of censure of Newman's *Letter to the Duke of Norfolk,* if not a public censure, then at least some private words of admonishment from Ullathorne. On 22 October, the prefect of Propaganda, Cardinal Franchi, sent Ullathorne a list of eleven points in the *Letter to the Duke of Norfolk* that Rome found irreverent, erroneous, or even outright heretical. The points singled out had largely to do with Newman's treatment of the papal office in the first four centuries, his comments on scandalous popes, and his views on the non-dogmatic character of the *Syllabus of Errors.* Ullathorne was urged by Franchi to confer with Newman and to ask that he find some way to correct the alleged errors in his future writings.[227] Ullathorne was to act as though the points raised came directly from him and was not to reveal the role of the Roman authorities in their preparation. Ullathorne replied on 2 December. He recalled the hurt that had been done to Newman when Propaganda in 1867 had sent Ullathorne secret instructions suggesting how he might dissuade Newman from his plans to take part directly in the work of the Oratory then being considered for Oxford. In his letter of 2 December, Ullathorne made it clear to Propaganda that he would not again participate in such a procedure. If the Congregation had anything to say

224. See William Neville to John Hungerford Pollen, 5 September 1875, *The Letters and Diaries,* 27:350–51, footnote 2.

225. See Newman to B. M. Pickering, 7 August 1875, *The Letters and Diaries,* 27:340.

226. See editor's comments, *The Letters and Diaries,* 27:411, Appendix I.

227. See Latin letter of Cardinal Franchi and attached list of censurable items in Italian, *The Letters and Diaries,* 22 October 1875, 27:407–09, appendix I.

to Newman, it should deal with him directly. Further, Ullathorne said that secret instructions would inevitably become public and harm the Church in England. Finally, Ullathorne pointed out that some of the censurable points listed by the Congregation had in fact been clarified in the "Postscript" to the *Letter to the Duke of Norfolk.*[228] There the matter ended, whether through the persuasiveness of Ullathorne's letter or Roman weariness of the subject is not clear.

OVERVIEW

The reaction to the *Letter to the Duke of Norfolk* left Newman with a satisfaction and serenity that he had seldom known in his Catholic years. According to Meriol Trevor, "Of all Newman's writings, except the *Apologia,* this was the most immediately successful. It completely reversed the public attitude."[229] Newman for a decade had feared entering publicly into the debate in England over papal infallibility. Several times he had seemed on the verge of doing so but found reasons in the end to abandon his plans. There can be little doubt that this restraint weighed heavily on Newman, especially when he had continually to turn down the entreaties of some of his closest friends to write on the subject. The aftermath of the *Letter to the Duke of Norfolk* was for Newman a time of exhilaration and relief. The success of his pamphlet clearly delighted him. And what he had feared most over the years, the reaction of ecclesiastical authority, turned out in the event to be largely appreciative. Newman seemed genuinely surprised to receive the public support of Church authorities such as Cardinal Cullen of Dublin. The news of Cullen's reaction took him by surprise, and he lost no time in exuberantly telling close friends this piece of good news. Most commentators would agree that what gave Newman the greatest sense of accomplishment after the publication of the *Letter to the Duke of Norfolk* was its positive acceptance by the Roman Catholics of England and Ireland.[230] He had a sense of being accepted at last, not just as a prominent voice among Catholics, but as their defender and champion. Had Newman known of the suspicions and complaints of Rome about his pamphlet, his sense of success may have been tempered or dashed, but Manning in an unlikely role and the sympathetic Ullathorne kept the Roman censors at bay.

The death of Ambrose St. John in May came as a heavy blow to Newman in this period of elation and success. It was easily the greatest sorrow that Newman had known in forty years. He felt St. John's loss deeply, but he was able after a few months to resume his accustomed routine in

228. See Latin letter of Bishop William Bernard Ullathorne, *The Letters and Diaries,* 2 December 1875, 27:409–10, Appendix I.
229. Trevor, *Newman: Light In Winter,* 515.
230. See, for example, Ker, *John Henry Newman,* 690.

the Oratory and even to take on new duties. It is hard to estimate how much the success of the *Letter to the Duke of Norfolk* helped Newman in overcoming his great loss, but one can speculate that his sense of being accepted in the public life of the Church and the nation enabled him to go on in this period, the immediate prelude to the great honors that would come his way in the next several years. And it is of interest to speculate further on how much the success of the *Letter to the Duke of Norfolk* encouraged Newman in 1877 to tackle the subject of the theology of the Church and the role of theologians in the Church in the preface to the third edition of the *Via Media,* one of Newman's most important and enduring essays.

Conclusion

"For a Growth in Its Creed Is a Law of Its Life"

Newman, however cloistered his life at the Birmingham Oratory from the late 1850s, struggled with the issue of papal infallibility in a real arena. The question was alive and immediate, a pressing, clamorous public debate, not a remote and careful disputation among schools and theologians. This was already true before the Vatican Council. It became even more so with the opening of the council and in its aftermath. The debate went from journals to the council to consciences within a short time. It is evident that Newman was less than happy to be placed in the position of having to deal with the public ramifications of this issue, since he was by his own admission more a controversialist than a theologian.[1] He had looked forward in his sixties to a quiet time and he saw his views as having little chance of success in the English Catholic atmosphere of the period.

In 1867, he told his close friend, Henry Wilberforce, "for myself I have never taken any great interest in the question of the limits and seats of infallibility"[2] and seven months later in a letter to the former Oratorian, John Stanislas Flanagan, Newman said: "I dare say I have not been consistent or logically exact in what from time to time I have said about the extent & subject matter of the Church's infallibility, for it is a very large question and I never have set myself formally to answer it."[3] The letter

1. See Newman to William George Ward, 18 January 1866, *The Letters and Diaries of John Henry Newman,* ed. Charles Stephen Dessain (London: Thomas Nelson and Sons, Ltd., 1972) 22:157. In the midst of the Tractarian debates nearly twenty-five years previously Newman had taken a more jaundiced view of the worth of controversy. In a letter to Robert Belaney on 25 January 1841 Newman had written: "Controversy too is a waste of time—one has other things to do. Truth can fight its own battle." And two weeks before he had said to Frederic Rogers: "I declare I think it is a rare thing, candour in controversy, as to be a Saint." See Ian Ker, *John Henry Newman: A Biography* (Oxford: Clarendon Press, 1988) 203.

2. Newman to Henry Wilberforce, 21 July 1867, Georgetown University, Special Collections, Newman Collection, A283. See also *The Letters and Diaries,* ed. Charles Stephen Dessain and Thomas Gornall, S.J. (Oxford: Clarendon Press, 1973) 23:275.

3. See *The Theological Papers of John Henry Newman on Biblical Inspiration and On Infallibility,* selected, edited, and introduced by J. Derek Holmes (Oxford: Clarendon Press, 1979) 155.

to Wilberforce is an indication of the reluctance with which Newman approached the subject of papal infallibility, a reluctance which in many ways he never overcame all through the long controversy. The subject had been thrust on him at a time in his life when his true interests and energies lay elsewhere. And while the opening sentence of Newman's letter to Flanagan speaks of "the Church's infallibility," Newman was really speaking more narrowly of the pope's infallibility. He spoke of never having been "consistent or logically exact" on the subject, and in many ways this was to continue until he formally and finally set down his views in the *Letter to the Duke of Norfolk* at the end of 1874. It was not an issue, Newman believed, that could be dealt with hurriedly through agitation and pressure. It needed time, reflection, measured deliberation. The consideration of the question at the council was, Newman thought, the consequence of a polemic. Indeed the infallibilist party claimed that the issue was only moved forward at the council because of Maret, Dupanloup, and Döllinger, forgetting the part played on their own side by Manning, Veuillot, and the *Civiltà Cattolica*.

One of Newman's chief fears was that the party of dogmatists would be favored in their dogmatism by the definition of papal infallibility, which they would then use to give a kind of legitimacy by extension to their own views in the Church. As a result, Newman and his allies would be further shunted aside, their views further discredited. There were then practical and "political" consequences for Newman, who had always acknowledged a role for ecclesiastical politics, though he readily granted that it had at times its disedifying, even ugly, side.[4]

The decade of the 1860s, despite the success of the *Apologia,* which was more successful among Anglicans than Catholics—was still a period of bruising encounters with Catholic ecclesiastical authority for Newman. This was particularly true in the Oxford Oratory proposals, in which despite the generally supportive role of Bishop Ullathorne, Newman was thwarted by the maneuvering of Manning and Talbot at Rome. And despite the apparent rehabilitation that Rome had allowed to Newman after Ambrose St. John and Henry Bittleston[5] had gone there in 1867 to try to set things right, Newman was still suspect, a "badly tinkered" con-

4. In a letter of 10 June 1863 to Lady Chatterton Newman said: "And it is a further fact, that our Lord distinctly predicted these scandals as inevitable; nay further, He spoke of His Church as in its very constitution made up of good and bad, of wheat and weeds, of the precious and the vile. One out of His twelve Apostles fell, and one of the original seven deacons. Thus a Church, such as we behold, is bound up with the very idea of Christianity." *The Letters and Diaries,* ed. Charles Stephen Dessain (London: Thomas Nelson and Sons, Ltd., 1970) 20:465.

5. Henry Bittleston was received into the Roman Catholic Church in 1849 and joined the Birmingham Oratory the following year. He left the Oratory in 1879 and served as a parish priest until his death in 1886.

vert. His *Apologia* and the *Letter to Pusey* were not favorably received by Manning, Ward, and Talbot. And there is even the telling incident in 1869 when the usually sympathetic Ullathorne questioned Ambrose St. John closely about what Newman was writing as rumors went the rounds that he would soon publish a new and major work. Ullathorne was somehow of the opinion that Newman should not be writing for publication unless expressly asked to do so by the pope.[6] Even the *Grammar of Assent,* published soon after the opening of the Vatican Council, was accepted in Catholic circles with a certain reserve, though its subject matter was not directly related to the debate over papal infallibility. It is clear that Newman at this period in his life dreaded any further battles with his ecclesiastical superiors. He made this almost pathetically clear in 1866 when he told his friend and confidante, Emily Bowles: "You don't know me, when you suppose I 'take heed of the motley flock of fools.' No it is *authority* that I fear."[7]

It was in this less than congenial atmosphere that the controversy over papal infallibility became intense. It is not altogether surprising then to find Newman holding back in 1867 from his second reply to Pusey on the role of the pope in the Church and hesitating over responding to the extravagant statements of W. G. Ward in the *Dublin Review.* There can be little doubt that Newman was relieved to have Ignatius Ryder step forward to answer Ward. With Newman's blessing and support, Ryder took on the difficult task. It was, Newman thought, a job for a younger man, a time for a fresh voice.[8]

In the months leading up to the council, it is clear that Newman was apprehensive about the possibility of the Vatican Council's defining papal infallibility. In the late summer of 1869, he actively aided and counseled his friend, William Monsell, in Monsell's efforts to make Döllinger's views in opposition to papal infallibility available to bishops in the English-speaking world. He made it evident in letters to friends and inquirers that he hoped that no definition would be passed. Just weeks before the opening of the Vatican Council, Newman said to Mrs. William Froude: "Hitherto nothing has been ever done at Councils but what is *necessary;* what is the necessity of this?" And in the same letter Newman used words that tellingly describe his own personal attitude to the question: "It is making the system more miraculous—and it is like seeking a bodily cure by miracle, when human means are at hand."[9] He spoke at times almost with

---

6. See Newman to William Monsell, 26 April 1869, *The Letters and Diaries,* ed. Charles Stephen Dessain and Thomas Gornall, S.J. (Oxford: Clarendon Press, 1973) 24:245 and 245, footnote 1.

7. Newman to Emily Bowles, 16 April 1866, *The Letters and Diaries,* 22:215.

8. See Newman to William George Ward, 30 April 1867, *The Letters and Diaries,* 23:197.

9. Newman to Mrs. William Froude, 21 November 1869, *The Letters and Diaries,* 24:377.

certitude in saying that no definition would result from the council's deliberations. It would appear that these were Newman's own views rather than simply calming words for his correspondents.

Newman fearful over the council's outcome

In September 1869, before the council opened, Newman made private notes to show why he was opposed to the definition of papal infallibility. In these notes he recorded his own belief in the doctrine but expressed the view that its definition would gain nothing for the Church. It would instead arouse only new controversies and contentions. Three months later, as the council convened, Newman took a similar line but went further by implying that his own "vague" views on papal infallibility helped to make the doctrine credible to him and he believed that what was true of himself was also true of others. As he told J. F. Seccombe at this time, he accepted papal infallibility "as being pious to hold or agreeable to general sentiment" and because others whom he knew held it.[10] Precision and definition would needlessly provoke and challenge those who held the doctrine "vaguely." The resulting controversies would last long into the future, and the Roman Church, turned in on itself through this intramural strife, would repel people who would otherwise have been attracted to its claims and witness. The Church would be derided as outdated and irrelevant to the modern world. For these reasons Newman in half a prayer, half a cry wrote at the end of his 12 December 1869 private notes: "Save, the church, o my Fathers, from a danger as great as any that has happened to it."[11]

By the end of January 1870, Newman was so alarmed by the rumors he was hearing out of Rome about a possible definition that he wrote in searing terms to his bishop to express his own disquiet and dismay: "I am continually asking myself whether I ought not to make my feelings public; but all I do is to pray those great early Doctors of the Church, whose intercession would decide the matter, Augustine and the rest, to avert so great a calamity."[12] When Newman's letter to Ullathorne became public in March, he was suddenly and without warning thrust forward into the debate over infallibility. He was like a man in constant motion, quenching one fire, only to have the flames leap up again in another place. The reaction to his letter was various. Those in fear of the definition were relieved that Newman had revealed his own forebodings; other Catholics

10. Newman to J. F. Seccombe, 14 December 1869, *The Letters and Diaries,* 24:390.
11. Newman, 12 December 1869, *The Letters and Diaries,* 24:378, footnote 1.
12. Newman to Bishop William Bernard Ullathorne, 28 January 1870, *The Letters and Diaries,* ed. Charles Stephen Dessain and Thomas Gornall, S.J. (Oxford: Clarendon Press, 1973) 25:19.

were scandalized that a priest of his prominence should say such forceful things against the proceedings at Rome. In Anglican circles and in the wider nation, reports about Newman's leaving the Roman Church gained new vitality and attention. Despite this unexpected public scrutiny and the need to deal with the several distinct groups and issues that rose up in consequence of it, Newman in the end appeared to be relieved that his letter to Ullathorne had got out. He had not wished it, but all the better since he could claim that he had acted responsibly by writing in confidence to his bishop. In the circumstance no one could accuse him of trying to rally opposition to the definition, of using his prominence in the English Catholic Church to gather a party in opposition to the definition around himself. In a sense Newman was able to have it both ways. But the consequences of the letter to Ullathorne were lasting, and in the years ahead Newman had constantly to defend what he had decided to say to Ullathorne in the opening weeks of the council. Döllinger, after his break with the Roman Church in 1870, and Gladstone used the letter to Ullathorne to suggest that Newman had been inconsistent, even cowardly, in his acceptance of the definition of July 1870.

The late winter and spring of 1870 were clearly for Newman an anxious time as reports out of Rome of the increased likelihood of a definition gathered strength. The heightened rhetoric of the famous letter to Ullathorne often continued in letters to close friends and, surprisingly, even at times in letters to strangers or distant acquaintances. "There are right developments and wrong ones," Newman told Bishop Moriarty on 20 March,[13] and in a letter to Bishop Goss some days later he wrote that "a majority has no right to vote away the right of their fellow-Bishops."[14] He spoke also of a need for a moral unaminity among the Fathers of the council in a letter to Bishop Ullathorne in early June, "for how could we take as the voice of the Council, which is infallible, a definition which a body of Bishops, of high character in themselves, and representing large masses of the faithful, protested against?"[15]

He continued to be shocked by what he considered the haste of the proceedings at Rome and what he believed to be a careless disregard for the consciences of sincere Catholic people. Charity and patience were everything. They were tests that evidenced the truth and rightness of things. They distinguished the life of the Church from human society and secular political processes. "The Church moves as whole," Newman told Father Whitty on 12 April, "it is not a mere philosophy; it is a communion; it not only discovers, but it teaches; it is bound to consult for charity,

13. Newman to Bishop David Moriarty, 20 March 1870, *The Letters and Diaries,* 25:58.
14. Newman to Bishop Alexander Goss, 1 April 1870, *The Letters and Diaries,* 25:76.
15. Newman to Bishop William Bernard Ullathorne, 6 June 1870, *The Letters and Diaries,* 25:138–39.

as well as for faith."[16] And further in the same letter Newman said, "we need that this should be done in the face of day, in course, in quiet, in various schools and centers of thought, in controversy. This is a work of years."[17]

By the end of June, as the news from Rome brought clear indications that a decision in favor of the definition would not be long in coming, Newman kept up his attitude of opposition. "It seems to me a duty, out of devotion to the Pope and charity to the souls of men, to resist it, while resistance is possible."[18] The previous day in another letter, Newman wrote, "There are truths which are inexpedient," and "for myself, I refuse to believe that it can be carried, till it actually is."[19] In a private memorandum dealing with the definition that he wrote on 27 June, Newman said "inopportune means 1. uncharitable 2. unecclesiastical—a false step."[20] These notes are similar in tone to those he made in September and December of the previous year, but there is about them more of a sense of resignation, of looking toward ways of dealing with the sure consequences of what was about to happen in Rome. "Two subjects," Newman wrote as if preparing for what would come, "1. Councils have been scenes of violence etc. 2. they have been followed by long disputes and schisms."[21]

But all through this period Newman also gave indications that he would accept the council's decision. It would be a hard effort, but he had made his decision a quarter century ago to live and die in the Catholic faith. It was his home. In the event, he would ask for the grace to accept what the Church believes and teaches. "Councils have ever been times of great *trial*," Newman said to Mrs. F. R. Ward early in July, "and this seems likely to be no exception."[22] Several days earlier Newman told Mrs. Wilson, "to myself, with many others, it is the Presence of our Lord in the Blessed Sacrament which is the relief and consolation for all the troubles of ecclesiastical affairs."[23] He continued, "It is but rational in you to put away your doubts, and to trust Him unreservedly. I pray God to enable you to do this. . . ."[24]

16. Newman to Father Robert Whitty, 12 April 1870, *The Letters and Diaries,* 25:93.

17. Ibid., 94–95. This statement recalls the famous passage in the last chapter of the *Apologia* where Newman speaks of the long playing out in the medieval Church of the conflict of ideas before authority was at length ready, and even then almost with reluctance, to interpose itself decisively. See John Henry Newman, *Apologia Pro Vita Sua,* standard ed. (Garden City, N.Y.: Doubleday & Co., Image Books Edition, 1956) 251.

18. Newman to Francis Wackerbarth, 28 June 1870, *The Letters and Diaries,* 25:153.

19. Newman to W. J. O'Neill Daunt, 27 June 1870, *The Letters and Diaries,* 25:150.

20. Newman "Memorandum," *The Letters and Diaries,* 25:151.

21. Ibid.

22. Newman to Mrs. F. R. Ward, 9 July 1870, *The Letters and Diaries,* 25:158.

23. Newman to Mrs. Wilson, 3 July 1870, *The Letters and Diaries,* 25:156.

24. Ibid., 157.

Newman, disturbed by the definition,
gives himself over to counseling friends and strangers

When the news of the definition came, Newman was from the account of those who were with him disturbed and disheartened.[25] But when he saw the text of the definition a few days later, he wrote the sentence that has been used again and again to characterize his attitude as one of acceptance and even satisfaction. "I saw the new Definition yesterday, and am pleased at its moderation," Newman wrote in a letter intended for Ambrose De Lisle but which in the end he did not send. He went on, however, with more than a trace of ambiguity in words that are less frequently quoted or hurried over, "that is, if the doctrine in question is to be defined at all. The terms are vague and comprehensive; and personally, I have no difficulty in admitting it. The question is, does it come to me with the authority of an Ecumenical Council?"[26]

This question was to play a large part in Newman's life over the course of the next six weeks and it was to continue, though in a less urgent form, well into the following year. Having said that he personally could accept the definition if the Church so required, Newman put his private thoughts and concerns to one side and entered with vigor into the question of what was required of his fellow Catholics, especially those whom he knew to be troubled and in anguish at the prospect of having to accept the definition as part of their Catholic faith.

Newman did not miss the point that the vast majority of those who asked for his advice were deeply committed and sincere Catholics. They had thought the matter through for months and even years and they had followed the deliberations of the council with alarm and consternation. The practical tactic that Newman took was to throw himself into technical questions concerning the council and its proceedings. Was a moral unanimity needed? What would the minority bishops, most of whom had left Rome before the solemn session of 18 July, do? Were the signatures of the bishops required before the definition could be considered binding? Was there not reason to wait until the council reconvened to see what further actions would be taken to place the definition in a larger context? Until all these questions had been answered, could it be said that the Church had accepted the definition, that the great maxim of St. Augustine, "Securus iudicat orbis terrarum," had been fulfilled?

Newman was suddenly active on many fronts—consulting, meeting, making further inquiries, giving advice and counsel. He spent a great deal

25. See Wilfrid Ward, *The Life of John Henry Cardinal Newman* (London: Longmans, Green, and Co., 1912) 2:307.
26. Newman to Ambrose Phillipps De Lisle (not sent), 24 July 1870, *The Letters and Diaries,* 25:164.

of time consulting his friends among the bishops, especially Errington and Clifford, and seeking the opinion of people whose theological ability he respected, such as Russell and Rymer.

But even in the midst of these activities Newman returned to his own personal acceptance of the definition. It was as if he could separate his own approach out from the larger discussion, to deal with it almost as if it had no relation at all to the questions in which he was so actively involved. These private thoughts came especially in letters to intimates such as Ambrose St. John. Newman fell back for the most part on the argument from authority. Did the legislator have the power to command his obedience, quite apart from the controversies surrounding the council and other technical points? And did not the pope have a universal authority that had to be accepted, quite apart from the decision of the bishops which led one into theological and canonical thickets on questions of moral unanimity and the ratification of the council's decisions? These private struggles led Newman to take the curious stand that prescinding from both the moral unanimity of the bishops and the acceptance of the Church diffusive, " . . . I should consider that the fact of the Pope being able by his power of jurisdiction practically to enforce his claim of infallibility thus practically was a providential intimation that the claim was well founded, and I should receive the dogma as a dogma."[27]

Newman made an effort to find a way out of his own personal difficulties by invoking the principles of moral theology, especially those enunciated by St. Alphonsus Liguori. He told Ambrose St. John:

> . . . if nothing definitely sufficient can be brought to contradict a definition from Scripture or Tradition, the fact of a legitimate Superior having defined it may be an obligation in conscience to receive it with an internal assent. St. Alfonso lays down (with others) that, even though a legitimate Superior exceeds his power, his law is to be obeyed, for he is in possession; (unless indeed, he cannot be obeyed without great inconvenience etc) I feel the force of this in my own case. Not to say that I have ever, since a Catholic held the Pope's Infallibility as a matter of opinion, at least I see nothing in the definition which necessarily contradicts Scripture, Tradition, or History. *I* can obey without *inconvenience;* and the Doctor Ecclesiae, whether exceeding his power or not, bids me obey. Therefore I have an obligation of accepting the definition as a dogma.

And finally the rather startling conclusion to this exercise in moral theology: "In this case I do not receive it on the word of the Council, but on the Pope's self-assertion."[28]

---

27. Newman to Frederick Rymer, 15 August 1870, *The Letters and Diaries,* 25:186.
28. Newman to Ambrose St. John, 27 July 1870, *The Letters and Diaries,* 25:168.

The tension between the more active role that Newman was taking in August 1870 to ascertain the force of the definition and his private, more personal attitude toward its acceptance is apparent in this unexpected approach to the question of the necessity for accepting the definition. It would be naive to suggest that this was not for him a time of testing of his faith. He had spent too much energy and effort in the last decade, and especially in the preceding months, disputing the need for a definition of papal infallibility and decrying exaggerated notions of the papal office to allow for a calm and ready acceptance of what had happened at Rome. He, as much as his inquirers, needed time, time to shift and adjust to something he had strenuously opposed, however unexpected, even moderate, the actual decision when measured against his own and others' deep fears through the preceding years.

And underlying all the ambiguity of this time, now confident that the definition was not yet binding, now resigned to accepting it out of motives of simple faith and obedience, there was certainly his fear of having to make some public declaration. What would he say if called upon to do so? How would he find a formula true to himself, consistent with his known opposition, and true to those many people who relied on him, a number of whom had taken strength from his own opposition to the definition and his view, expressed as late as the end of June of 1870, that the definition might never come about.[29] He had a public place in the life of the Roman Catholic Church in England, however much he himself had tried at times to avoid it or, as was more often the case, the ecclesiastical authorities had worked to keep him from having such a role. His letter of 28 January to Bishop Ullathorne was a very fresh event that had had an impact on many people in England, Catholics and Anglicans. It is doubtful that Newman had known a more trying time in his life as a Catholic. The previous difficulties, and they were many, had in the end been on the level of ecclesiastical politics and human relations in the Church. However exasperating and discouraging, these Newman saw for what they were. They did not and could never touch the core of the faith. They were an unavoidable part of the life of the Church in the human here and now. But this was a challenge of a different order and for a man just short of seventy, a man settled and secure in a way of life that now through two decades he had come to rely on and expect. He grasped the full implications of his position. If he spoke his every word would be hung on, examined, and dissected by opponents as well as friends. By his own admission he had never taken a great interest in the subject of papal infallibility, his views on it had never been consistent, and he had held it only vaguely. When the moment that he had feared finally came, he realized how unpre-

---

29. See Newman to W. J. O'Neill Daunt, 27 June 1870, *The Letters and Diaries,* 25:150.

pared he was for any public role and shrank from it, preferring to deal with the matter privately and within a close, tight circle of friends and sincere inquirers whom he could not turn aside. Characteristically he told people troubled by the definition that time was everything. He more than once gave evidence in this period that he saw this approach as the only solution for his own difficulties as well. There is a time to speak and a time to keep silent, Newman was fond of saying, and for four years he would favor the latter course.

The intricate lengths to which Newman went in his efforts to establish grounds for accepting the definition may in large measure have been out of concern for the troubled consciences of others, but they say something also, however indirectly, however unacknowledged, about his own personal struggle, about the shock and offense to his own faith. More than anything else it was the process, the method that deeply troubled Newman's own faith rather than the teaching on papal infallibility as such. For all of his knowledge of history, the decision of the Vatican Council was a heavy blow for him. How could the divinely guided Church fall prey to what seemed to him little better than political agitations and maneuverings? However conversant he was with the story of such tactics at councils in the first centuries of the Church, it was quite another matter to be confronted with the real live unfolding of such events and to know firsthand some of the chief actors in them.

It is not clear why Robert Suffield after his apostasy told others that Newman in August 1870 had said to him in their face to face meeting that age and the example he must give to those who looked up to him kept him from leaving the Roman Catholic Church after the definition of papal infallibility.[30] And it is not clear why Newman five years later made the annotation on his 15 August 1870 letter to Frederick Rymer that the first two paragraphs of that letter were meant for Dr. Rymer, "that *he* of course meant to secure for himself the sacraments, that *he* must be all right behind."[31] But each of these pieces of evidence, though slight and in the first case very likely unreliable, may offer some glimpse into the man behind the careful letters and arguments of this time and tell something of the crisis that he himself experienced, a crisis that in time he mastered as he had done so often in the past. "For years past," Newman told Lady

30. See J. Millage to Newman, 15 March 1875, *The Letters and Diaries,* ed. Charles Stephen Dessain and Thomas Gornall, S.J. (Oxford: Clarendon Press, 1975) 27:249, footnote 2.

31. *The Letters and Diaries,* 25:186; footnote 1. The first two paragraphs of the 15 August letter to Rymer read: "I think as follows, since you wish to know—1. Any how, I don't mean, whatever happens to be pushed out of the Church—nor do you—so that, if the worst comes to the worst, we should accept the dogma as a dogma, if the alternative was exclusion from the Sacraments.

Catherine Simeon in November 1870 in terms reminiscent of his July 1870 letter to Mrs. Wilson, "my only consolation personally has been in our Lord's Presence in the Tabernacle. I turn from the sternness of external authority to Him who can immeasurably compensate trials which after all are not real, but (to use a fashionable word) sentimental. Never, thank God, have I had a single doubt about the divine origin and grace of the Church, on account of the want of tenderness and largeness of mind of its officials or rulers. And I think this will be your experience too. Bear up for a while and all will be all right."[32] Newman would make very clear in private letters in the years after the council, and most notably in the *Letter to the Duke of Norfolk*, that it was the final statement of a dogmatic definition, not what led up to it, that mattered and was of faith. He had perhaps come to appreciate this fact more fully and personally in the weeks just after the definition.

In the autumn of 1870, it became clear that the council would not soon meet again. At the same time more and more bishops of the minority gave their public adherence, however tortuous in some cases, to the definition. Bishop Clifford made his acceptance clear in early December, and in the first months of the following year Archbishop Errington was the last of the English bishops to declare his adherence to the definition. Newman appeared to be genuinely disappointed at Clifford's decision,[33] though he himself had already been showing signs for weeks that he thought it vain to hope for a new session of the council and some bold new action on the part of the bishops who had opposed the definition.

Newman's letters in the months immediately after the definition give enough evidence of his anger to cast serious doubt on some of the accounts of his easy and faith-filled acceptance of the definition. It was not a tranquil time for him. He was angered by reports of confessors threatening their penitents, by what he believed to be Manning's and Ward's exaggerated interpretations of the definition, by the maneuverings of certain members of the majority at the council. He was angry too at Pius IX for his determined championing of the definition. Newman showed small sympathy for the plight of the pope after the troops of Garibaldi overran the city of Rome in September 1870. Rather he looked forward eagerly, almost with defiance, to a new pope and a new council. Pius IX had gone

---

2. This being the ruling principle on which we are to conduct ourselves, we should do nothing inconsistent with ultimately falling back upon it, if it must be so; and, in whatever we publish, we should see that we have not to eat our words; that we have not by bad logic to get out of a scrape etc etc."

32. Newman to Lady Catherine Simeon, 18 November 1870, *The Letters and Diaries*, 25:231.

33. See Newman to Bishop William Clifford, 13 December 1870, *The Letters and Diaries*, 25:246.

on too long. A new council was needed to set things right, to put the definition in its proper perspective.

In the months after the definition, Newman continued to counsel
Catholics troubled in conscience by the definition. He believed that faithful Catholics had an obligation to accept the definition. But those who
needed time should not be bullied and threatened. They should make an
act of faith in all that the Church teaches. They should not give in to doubts
about the definition but should accept it trustingly. Newman was generous and untiring in his advice to those who were troubled by the definition. He was angered that confessors in England treated such people sternly
and unyieldingly. A Catholic who had made an act of faith in the Church's
teaching authority need not confess doubts about the definition unless he
or she had willfully dwelt on them. Confessors should not demand of a
penitent a declaration of adherence without that person's having raised
the subject of the definition and his or her hesitation or unwillingness to
accept it. Newman felt a deep obligation to these troubled people and particularly the converts among them, who had given up so much by way
of family ties and chances of success in the great world to enter the Roman
Church. He appreciated the pain of those who asked his counsel far more
than those who had long been advocating the definition and had been
elated by its promulgation He had come by a different route that gave
him a sympathy and compassion for those who found the passage hard
and rough.

Newman refuses to make public his views of the definition and looks to a future council that will put the definition in its proper context

Newman was resolute in his decision not to write or say anything publicly on the definition unless obliged to do so. He made this clear to Bishop
Brown of Newport in November 1870[34] and he gave some glimpses into
his reasons for such a determined stand when he told William Maskell
in February 1871: "For myself, my feeling is, that did I speak, I should
be at once reported to Rome, perhaps put on the Index, perhaps
reproved—and thus should have made matters worse instead of better."[35]
And in a scarcely disguised and deeply felt complaint, Newman gave a
further and telling reason to his friend, William Monsell, for his having
held back from writing publicly: "When my letter to Dr. Ullathorne, to
my great astonishment, got into circulation, I had a faint hope that there
might have been some expression of opinion from the laity to back up

34. See Newman to Bishop Thomas Brown, 17 November 1870, *The Letters and Diaries*,
25:230.
35. Newman to William Maskell, 12 February 1871, *The Letters and Diaries*, 25:284.

its contents—I would in that case have written strongly." Newman then went on to disavow any sympathy for Döllinger and his stand, but he more than implied that Döllinger had found it possible to take a bold and public course because he had backing and support in Germany. "It is," Newman continued, "sympathy which gives strength. To speak, one must have the sympathy of the many, or the sanction of men in authority. I have no confidence that a free spoken statement, such as I should now have to write, would not do more harm than good. And as for the wish of authorities, I think they would be best pleased if I held my tongue."[36]

In the fall of 1871, Newman was still fearful that Manning was trying to extend the meaning of the definition. This encouraged Newman in his conviction that other definitions and precisions of the teaching on papal infallibility were necessary and in fact had been intended but had not come about owing to the postponement of the council. He was glad to learn that Bishop Dupanloup had expressed similar views.[37] But try as he would to take the long view, looking to a future council and trusting that in time theologians would "settle the force of the wording of the dogma, just as the courts of law solve the meaning and bearing of Acts of Parliament,"[38] Newman was still, over a year after the definition, angry at the way the proponents of the definition were using their authority to insist that Catholics accept the definition unreservedly, heedless of their struggles and efforts to remain true to the teachings of the Church. "There are too many high ecclesiastics in Italy and England, who think that to believe is as easy as to obey—that is, they talk as if they did not know what an act of faith is," Newman told Malcolm MacColl in November 1871.[39]

One of the consequences of the definition that Newman had feared was the weakening of the defense of Catholicism against both Protestants and unbelievers. He thought that the claims of Catholicism would no longer receive a favorable hearing from inquirers and that Catholics would be put on the defensive in discussions with Protestants.[40] It must be remembered that this was an age that valued an apologetic, almost militant approach to matters of faith. Catholics themselves would be seen as divided, and their proud boast of unity would be undermined, their charge against Anglicans of having no sure body of teaching and rule of faith would be turned back on them. Anglicans would gladly point to disagreements among Catholics since the council. Newman insisted that his fears had

36. Newman to William Monsell, 21 April 1871, *The Letters and Diaries,* 25:318–19.

37. See Newman to Lady Catherine Simeon, 15 October 1871, *The Letters and Diaries,* 25:415.

38. Newman to Sir William Cope, 10 December 1871, *The Letters and Diaries,* 25:447.

39. Newman to Malcolm MacColl, 11 November 1871, *The Letters and Diaries,* 25:430.

40. See Newman to Bishop David Moriarty, 1 November 1870, *The Letters and Diaries,* 25:223.

in large measure been fulfilled and when he was asked in early 1872 to join other Catholics in England in supporting Manning's plans for a Catholic university, he not only refused to associate himself with the project but lamented that the better, though not ideal, approach, making provision for Catholics at Oxford and Cambridge, had been dashed because of the definition. "Now we are new born children," Newman told Canon Northcote in April 1872,

> . . . and we are going to war without strength and without arms. We do not know what exactly we hold—what we may grant, what we must maintain. A man who historically defends the Pope's infallibility must almost originate a polemic—can he do so, as being an individual, without many mistakes? but he makes them on the stage of a great theatre.

"Till Catholics agree in sentiment," Newman said in the same letter, "they cannot really agree in action."[41]

In the summer of 1872, Newman echoed the same theme in a letter to Alfred Plummer, who at times served as his go-between with Döllinger. Döllinger still could not understand how Newman had said such severe things in his January 1870 letter to Bishop Ullathorne and yet had apparently accepted the definition without even a murmur of protest or dissent. Newman responded by saying: "What I said in the private letter to my Bishop, to which Dr D. alludes, was that the definition *would unsettle men's minds*. This anticipation has been abundantly fulfilled. I said moreover expressly that it would be *no* difficulty to *me*, but that it was making the defence of Catholicism more *difficult.*"[42]

Newman breaks his silence in brief public letters but refuses again his friends' entreaties to give a full exposition of his views

Two years after the definition, Newman continued to tell his inquirers that the definition had not been a difficulty for him. He had accepted it, and this, he told Plummer in the letter mentioned above, was why he had never been called on publicly as others had to express his belief in the dogma.[43] When in the late summer of 1872, Newman for the first time since the definition wrote publicly of his views on it, he continued to say what he had said in private, that he deplored the way the definition had come about but that he himself accepted it and in fact had always held it. He attempted to demonstrate this by citing various of his Catholic writ-

41. Newman to Canon J. Spencer Northcote, 7 April 1872, *The Letters and Diaries,* ed. Charles Stephen Dessain and Thomas Gornall, S.J. (Oxford: Clarendon Press, 1974) 26:59–60.

42. Newman to Alfred Plummer, 19 July 1872, *The Letters and Diaries,* 26:139.

43. "I have for these 25 years spoken *in behalf* of the Pope's infallibility," Newman told Plummer in his 19 July letter. Ibid., 139.

ings and lectures, especially from the 1850s. In some sense Newman had to acknowledge that he deplored the proceedings of the council, since his letter to Ullathorne had made that so clear. But the writings Newman cited did not in every case support his position that he had long held a belief in papal infallibility. At times they dealt with the infallibility of the Church or with the primacy of the pope or were rhetorical statements more suited to public speeches than careful points of theological exposition. And Newman gave no explanation as to why he had nothing to appeal to beyond 1857. The one instance that he did have was actually an excerpt from his 1852 Dublin Lectures, and this he later regretted allowing the Roman Jesuit Father Cardella to use in 1867, in what Newman considered afterwards to be a piece of shameless infallibilist propaganda.

Despite the unabated urging of friends, Newman would not go beyond the letters he wrote to the *Pall Mall Gazette* and the *Guardian*. The subject, he continued to insist, was beyond him. It would require a large work. As England, according to the Duke of Wellington, could not have a little war, so a great theological question could not be handled in a pamphlet or a letter.[44] Exactly two years later he would change his views on this point that he had so insistently held, but then unexpected circumstances had, as in the past, provided him with the "call" that always inspired his best work. Already in a brief letter to *The Times* in September 1872, he had anticipated one of the major themes of the *Letter to the Duke of Norfolk*. "No Pope can make evil good," he wrote. "No Pope has any power over those eternal moral principles which God has imprinted on our hearts and consciences."[45]

Newman sees his obligation to reply to Gladstone's Expostulation

It is interesting to speculate on whether Newman would ever have spoken publicly on papal infallibility had not Gladstone in the late summer and early autumn of 1874 thrust the subject into the public consciousness, first with his article "Ritual and Ritualism" and then with his more extended treatment of the topic in his six-penny pamphlet, *The Vatican Decrees In Their Bearing on Civil Allegiance: A Political Expostulation*. Perhaps Newman would have waited to deal with the subject in his preface to the third edition of the *Via Media* in 1877. It would have had a logical place there in his brief but important treatment of the teaching or prophetical office in the Church, and especially the role of theologians as teachers of the faith.[46] Yet there is a good chance that he would have

44. See Newman to Arthur Arnold, 20 September 1872, *The Letters and Diaries*, 26:173.

45. Newman to the Editor of *The Times*, 9 September 1872, *The Letters and Diaries*, 26:163.

46. In the preface to the third edition of *The Via Media*, Newman states tersely and directly: "I say, then, theology is the fundamental and regulating principle of the whole

continued his long silence, leaving the topic to be pieced together strand by strand after his death from his surviving letters and writings. Gladstone's acidulous attack on the loyalty of English Catholics was, however, simply too public and pervasive, its influence strong, at least in the upper reaches of the political and ecclesiastical life of England. Newman could not forgo the challenge, for to have done so would have left in the lurch many people, known and unknown to him, whom he had influenced to enter the Roman Church. There was a deep personal challenge as well. "To have been silent," Newman told Mrs. Wilberforce early in 1875, "would have been to acknowledge the accusation was well founded, and to have thereby implied that I had made a false step in becoming a Catholic and would retrace it if I could."[47] There can be no doubt that Gladstone was looking for an answer from Newman. Certainly that was not his sole purpose, but a response from Newman was the one reply to his charges that he most anticipated and desired.

Newman wanted to reply to Gladstone as soon as he had seen the offending "parenthesis" from "Ritual and Ritualism" in the first days of October 1874. He had, however, many fears, most of which he had rehearsed in one way or another over the past four years. He was too old, the topic was too large, he risked ecclesiastical censure, he had small knowledge of politics and public life. As a result, he openly encouraged William Monsell to take up the task, while secretly he tried again and again all through October to find his own way forward. This most likely would never have come but for the greatly changed situation of Gladstone's more extended exposition, appearing at the beginning of November. Now Newman knew he must reply and though he had many doubts and made many false starts through three anxious weeks, he kept at it till at last a breakthrough came on 23 November. Sometime later Newman told Monsell: "That morning I had said to myself 'I have not said Mass for my attempt,' and so I then did so. It was St. Clement's Day too. And, as I say, from that time I went straight on."[48] For several weeks more he would keep his work a close secret, sharing it with only a few intimates. For a man of his age and careful, deliberate habits, both intellectual and personal, the work must have been a severe strain. Indeed Newman made frequent reference to the toll the work was taking and his fear that his health would altogether fail. He especially feared a disabling stroke. By 18 December, he was at last so confident of finishing that he was ready to make the secret of his project known to a wider circle of friends, particularly those who had begged him to reply to Gladstone. On that day he wrote at least

---

Church system." *The Via Media of the Anglican Church,* 3d ed. (London: Longmans, Green, and Co., 1901) xlvii.

47. Newman to Mrs. Henry Wilberforce, 9 January 1875, *The Letters and Diaries,* 27:186.
48. Newman to William Monsell, 31 December 1874, *The Letters and Diaries,* 27:179–80.

eight letters to let friends and several editors know what he was writing. But beyond this he wished the secret kept, even going to such lengths as to suggest to his publisher, B. M. Pickering, that the job of typesetting the first installment would best be given to a Protestant printer. By the end of December the work was done. In early January, Newman was busy with reading the proofs, and on 14 January the *Letter to the Duke of Norfolk,* a closely printed pamphlet of one hundred-thirty pages, was published.

Newman had maintained a long silence on the subject of papal infallibility. His *Letter to the Duke of Norfolk* had in some respects many audiences and many purposes. There were three chief ones: Gladstone and Protestant England, Manning and the Ultramontanist Party in the English Roman Catholic Church, Döllinger and his followers on the Continent. This several-headed task was difficult to accomplish, and a writer of lesser power would surely have failed. In some rather minor ways these several focuses were occasionally to trip Newman up and lessen the force of his answer, but in the main he handled the three principal tasks brilliantly, and a number of lesser ones besides.

Newman argued his case chiefly from history, though he was careful to say, with Döllinger especially but also Gladstone in mind, that anyone who believed the claims of the Catholic Church solely because of history was scarcely a Catholic.[49] Newman gave a masterful, succinct survey of the history of the papacy, beginning with the assertion that the pope was the heir to the ecumenical hierarchy of the fourth century and coming up to his own day with the theologians of the Roman School and the definition of 1870. He made sure also in what was essentially a popular work not to overwhelm his readers with theory and theology. He dealt with practical questions and examples to show that the allegiance of English Catholics to the State had in no sense changed as a consequence of the Vatican Council. An English Catholic had the same obligations to the State on 18 July 1870 as he or she had had the day before. The dilemmas of conscience that Gladstone had foreseen for English Catholics were so unlikely that almost no response was called for. But Newman knew that popular prejudices had been aroused, and careful reasoning was needed to set things right. In certain instances a Catholic would be obliged to obey the pope and turn aside the claims of the State, in other instances the opposite would be true. But above all the individual's conscience was supreme. Neither the Church nor the State could demand something that ran counter to a person's conscience.

49. *A Letter Addressed to His Grace the Duke of Norfolk on Occasion of Mr. Gladstone's Recent Expostulation* (hereafter cited as LDN), as reprinted in *Newman and Gladstone: The Vatican Decrees,* intro. Alvan S. Ryan (Notre Dame, Ind.: University of Notre Dame Press, 1962) 177.

Before tackling the definition of 1870 and showing what it meant and did not mean, Newman had to clear the ground by treating the encyclical *Quanta Cura* and the *Syllabus of Errors*. Though he had held back from saying that *Quanta Cura* and the *Syllabus* were infallible, Gladstone had insisted that Roman Catholics were obliged to accept the "binding force" of the encyclical and *Syllabus* and that the Vatican Council had, if this were possible, only strengthened the place of *Quanta Cura* and the *Syllabus* in the faith of the Roman Church. Gladstone used the *Syllabus* to assert that the pope's power in the Church, both as teacher and ruler, was so sweeping that it knew no bounds in the civil as well as the ecclesiastical order. Perhaps this was the hardest of Gladstone's challenges for Newman to handle. He was somewhat caught here between Gladstone and Manning. Newman showed that the *Syllabus* was not infallible. It had not been in 1864, and the definition of 1870 could not in any sense be read backwards to make it so in consequence of the council. But it is clear in this section that Newman felt obliged to take a careful path, and the result, especially in light of the furor that the *Syllabus* had caused in England and on the Continent,[50] lacks the force of other sections of his reply. Further, Newman maintained that the *Syllabus* was simply an index and one that had not come from the pope, perhaps not even from the cardinal secretary of state, but from some compiler in the Curia. The so-called "condemned propositions" had no meaning apart from the original papal statements from which they had been culled, and there the unprejudiced reader would find that they lost the sweeping certainty and ferocity assigned to them by commentators, such as Gladstone, unskilled in reading Roman documents.

Newman's chief object in the section on the Vatican Council's definition of papal infallibility was to show that it was in fact moderately worded and hardly patent of the extravagant interpretations that Protestants as well as some Catholics had put forth as the council's teaching. Here Newman was obviously grateful for the path that Fessler had blazed for him. Fessler, Newman was quick to point out, had received the commendation of Pius IX for his exposition of "true" and "false" infallibility. The role that Fessler's book played in Newman's response to Gladstone was indeed a large one, and it could even be suggested that he might still have kept his silence had it not been for Fessler's book and its acceptance in high places.

"A Pope," Newman wrote, "is not infallible in his laws, nor in his commands, nor in his acts of state, nor in his administration, nor in his

---

50. Derek Holmes states that "between 1864 and 1870, the dogmatic significance of the *Syllabus* became the crucial issue in the debate between Ultramontanes and Liberal Catholics." J. Derek Holmes, "Liberal Catholicism and Newman's Letter to the Duke of Norfolk," *Clergy Review* 60 (1975) 498.

public policy. . . . Let it be observed that the Vatican Council has left him just as it found him here."[51] Gladstone had contended that the word "morals" in the actual definition of the pope's infallibility covered every facet, no matter how minute, of human life. Newman insisted that the word "morals" was hardly so large and all-embracing as Gladstone claimed. Newman showed that the meaning of the word "morals" was in fact very restricted. "The field of morals," Newman countered, "contains so little that is unknown and unexplored, in contrast with revelation and doctrinal fact, that it is difficult to say what portions of moral teaching in the course of 1800 years actually have proceeded from the Pope, or from the Church, or where to look for such."[52] Most papal statements in the area of morals had been meant for particular situations and did not then fulfill one of the primary requisites for an infallible statement, that it had to be addressed to the universal Church.

In answer to Gladstone's charge that what was meant by *ex cathedrâ* had not been spelled out by the council and therefore the pope's power to make dogmatic statements binding on all Catholics knew no limits, Newman showed that the words had in fact been precisely delineated, that the pope's power to speak infallibly was limited and carefully circumscribed, "viz., the proposition defined will be without any claim to be considered binding on the belief of Catholics, unless it is referable to the Apostolic *depositum,* through the channel either of Scripture or Tradition. . . ."[53] It is interesting to see Newman taking this position so surely and calmly, since in the first year after the definition he had said on several occasions that the meaning of *ex cathedrâ* had not been spelled out by the council and that as a result Catholics were free to continue to hold different opinions on its meaning and need not accept the fulsome claims of the ultramontanists on the meaning of the definition and its extent.[54] It is difficult to know when and how Newman's views on this point changed. Here again he may have been influenced by Fessler.

Ever since the definition, but especially when it became clear that the Vatican Council would not meet again, Newman had told his correspondents that future councils would be needed, not to rescind the definition of papal infallibility but to put it in proper perspective through further definitions and conciliar declarations. There was ample precedent for this

51. LDN, 134.
52. LDN, 192.
53. LDN, 190.
54. See, for example, Newman to Mrs. Lavinia Wilson, 24 October 1870, *The Letters and Diaries,* 25:220, Newman to Lady Catherine Simeon, 1 November 1870, *The Letters and Diaries,* 25:244, and Newman to Alfred Plummer, 19 March 1871, *The Letters and Diaries,* 25:301.

in the life of the Church, especially in the early centuries. In the *Letter to the Duke of Norfolk,* Newman, quoting the sixteenth century Jesuit theologian, Luis de Molina, said:

> And, whereas by disputations, persevering reading, meditation, and investigation of matters, there is wont to be increased in course of time the knowledge and understanding of the same, and the Fathers of the later Councils are assisted by the investigation and definitions of the former, hence it arises that the definitions of later Councils are wont to be more luminous, fuller, more accurate and exact than those of the earlier. Moreover, it belongs to the later Councils to interpret and to define more exactly and fully what in earlier Councils have been defined less clearly, fully, and exactly.[55]

Perhaps the two overriding themes of Newman's *Letter* were its insistence on moderation in the life of the Church and the role of the theological schools in hammering out over time the precise meaning of dogmatic definitions. In many ways they were one and the same theme, since Newman believed that theologians had the task of limiting and putting into context dogmatic definitions, of ensuring that exaggerated and far-reaching interpretations did not get the upperhand in the life of the Church. Not only was the definition when considered carefully a moderate statement, but the whole tenor of the Church's life must be one of moderation, of a "wise and gentle minimism." "The Church, as guided by her Divine Master," Newman wrote, "has made provision for weighing as lightly as possible on the faith and conscience of her children."[56] In his last major work Newman had returned to a theme that had characterized his life through fifty years. And given the chance, as he had told Monsell at the end of December 1874 "to say my say," he felt bold enough to save one of his final salvos for those in the English Catholic community who had pressed for the definition and demanded its immediate acceptance afterwards, those who in his estimation had substituted rigidity and coercion for compassion and understanding. "Still the fact remains," he wrote, "that there has been of late years a fierce and intolerant temper abroad, which scorns and virtually tramples on the little ones of Christ."[57]

Newman overjoyed by the widespread positive response to his Letter

Newman, despite his bold and certain tone, was still very apprehensive about the reception of his pamphlet, especially by Church authori-

55. LDN, 173–74.
56. LDN, 192.
57. LDN, 197.

ties. Even as the first evidences of its success among Catholics as well as Protestants reached him, he continued to fear some reproving word from Rome or Westminster. Once he had received the news in mid-February of Cardinal Cullen's brief but favorable remarks in his Lenten pastoral, he put these fears aside. Cardinal Cullen was trusted in Rome as a theologian and a sound churchman, Newman reasoned, and he was a man who weighed his words. Newman was not to know that there had been reservations in Rome about his *Letter* and that even Cullen had had a part in them. Nor was he to know that Ullathorne and Manning had dissuaded the Roman authorities from acting against him. Manning quickly realized that Newman's pamphlet had been positively received by Protestant England, that it had been an important success for the Catholic Church. All of this could be lost if Rome were seen to be challenging the venerable and revered Dr. Newman.

Practically all of Newman's letters in the early months of 1875 are taken up with the *Letter to the Duke of Norfolk*. So many expressions of gratitude had come in that Newman was forced to put nearly all other correspondence aside. In several of his letters he made important additions by way of commentary or explanation on points he had raised in the *Letter to the Duke of Norfolk*.[58] In a letter to Isy Froude on 24 April, Newman gave a brief statement of what he believed the pope's teaching authority to be as a consequence of the Vatican Council:

> The Vatican Council has decided that he is not only the instrumental and ministerial head or organ of the Church, not only has a power to veto, not only is a co-operating agent in *de fide* decisions, but that in him lies the root of the matter, that his decision, viewed separate even from the Bishops, is gospel.[59]

Here Newman proposed a very strong theory of the papal office, one that appears at odds with many of his pre-conciliar as well as post-conciliar statements. It could be that he felt the correspondence with Isy Froude, which was ultimately intended for a friend of hers who was considering entry into the Roman Church, demanded a clear, unequivocal statement without qualifications, such as the expectation of further teachings on the subject from future councils. Or it could be that Newman had definitely decided that the matter was now closed, at least for a time, and that there was no purpose both for his correspondents and himself to spend time on what might have been or on some future and distant possibility.

---

58. See Newman to Lord Blachford, 5 February 1875, *The Letters and Diaries,* 27:211–13, Newman to Canon Jenkins, 25 February 1875, *The Letters and Diaries,* 27:234–35, and Newman to John Rickards Mozley, 1 and 4 April 1875, *The Letters and Diaries,* 27:259–67.
59. Newman to Isy Froude, 24 April 1875, *The Letters and Diaries,* 27:286–87.

Newman concludes that only a brief "postscript" is called for from him after Gladstone's Vaticanism

At least from December 1874, Gladstone was planning a reply to the responses to his *Expostulation*. There had already been considerable reaction, and he was supremely confident of more. He was particularly eager to have the replies of Newman and Manning. He was impatient when they were slower in coming than he had anticipated, Newman's appearing in January 1875 and Manning's in February. Very soon after Manning's reply was published, Gladstone entered the fray again with his *Vaticanism: An Answer to Replies and Reproofs*. The reaction was far more subdued than had been the case with his *Expostulation*. The public was wearying of the subject, as Manning and Newman had correctly gauged. Some thought Gladstone too obsessed with the topic. Newman's friend Lord Blachford, called Gladstone "an Italo-maniac."[60]

When Ambrose Phillipps De Lisle thought that a further, full-scale reply was needed, Newman was cool to the suggestion. He had said enough and it had been by most accounts well-received, even a triumph. Besides, he concluded, perhaps a little too conveniently, that Gladstone in his *Vaticanism* had gone more after Manning than after him. Newman did finally decide on a brief response, in part to answer some points in Gladstone's *Vaticanism* but also to clarify or fill out certain points that had been criticized by readers of his pamphlet from within the Catholic community. Newman's "Postscript" of just over twenty pages appeared in late March. He made nine separate points, most of them handled in two or three pages. Perhaps his most important point in response to Gladstone came in the first section where Newman turned back Gladstone's assertion that the definition of papal infallibility was so novel and recent that even the English and Irish bishops of the early decades of the nineteenth century had not held it. Newman responded briefly, summarizing a lifetime of study and inquiry into the councils of the Church by stating that "change has been the characteristic of the church from the earliest times. . . . And hence such change as has taken place, (which I should prefer to call doctrinal development,) is in itself a positive argument in favour of the Church's identity from first to last; for a growth in its creed is a law of its life."[61]

Newman responded to various Catholic readers, including unknown to him members of the Roman Curia, who had challenged his statement that the pope was the "heir by default to the ecumenical hierarchy of the fourth century" by saying that he had not been speaking "theologically,

---

60. See Lord Blachford to Newman, 29 January 1875, *The Letters and Diaries*, 27:211, footnote 2.
61. "Postscript," LDN, 212.

but historically, nay looking at the state of things with 'non-Catholic eyes.' " This is one of the several instances where Newman's multiple task made it hard to gain success on every front. To avoid any misapprehension about what he had intended in his reference to the place of the pope in the early Church, Newman wrote: "I did not mean to deny that those prerogatives were his from the beginning, but merely that they were gradually brought into full exercise by a course of events, which history records."[62]

Newman would take up the topic of papal infallibility later in the year in an important letter to Isy Froude on 28 July. Here his approach was very different from his letter to her of 24 April. Then he had put the pope's authority first and foremost; just three months later he took up a former line, putting forward reservations and qualifications on the pope's teaching authority in the Church. In some sense then Newman had returned yet once more to the very nuanced statements that had characterized his writings on papal infallibility a decade before when the great controversy began to play a part in his life, a part which grew larger and more absorbing as time went on.

The death of Ambrose St. John in May 1875, coming so soon after the success of the *Letter to the Duke of Norfolk*, was a cruel blow for Newman. It was the one great trial of his old age. As for the contentious subject of papal infallibility, which had loomed so large in his life for a decade, it was now behind him. He had had his say. Inquirers, sympathetic or hostile, could look to that record. He had won a new acceptance in Catholic eyes. There would be no need to prove again that he was a loyal Catholic, an accepted and respected member of the Church he had embraced at Littlemore on a rainswept autumn night thirty years before.

62. Ibid.

A Postlude

In February 1866, Newman had said in a letter to Father Henry Coleridge, "Yet I may be challenged to write till I am obliged to write."[63] That challenge did not come for nine years, or perhaps it is more correct to say that Newman fended off the challenge for nine years. The *Letter to the Duke of Norfolk* is the culmination of Newman's decade-long struggle with the question of the pope's authority in the Church. It was an issue that for him simply would not go away. Newman's journey on the question of papal infallibility from 1865 to 1875 is circuitous and indirect. In part, this is the result of his theological method, which is more historical and inferential than logical and deductive; in the words of Ian Ker, "Newman's theological method is so markedly unscholastic."[64] In part, it is the result of his personality, which was careful, tolerant, and given to second thoughts. The story is often complex, at times baffling, frequently frustrating. Just when things seem on the verge of falling into place, Newman goes back to an earlier position or moves off, all unexpectedly, in a new direction. On Newman's approach to the question of papal infallibility, Avery Dulles has written: "He writes as if caught between two mindsets, unable to chose between them. He is torn by two sets of fears. . . . Thus he is at one moment the ally of Döllinger and at the next moment the admirer of Cardinal Dechamps and the papalists. He wavers and sometimes contradicts his own previous statements."[65] The central question comes down to this: why did Newman decide in late 1874 that he could write publicly and at length on papal infallibility? The challenge of Gladstone's *Expostulation* is clear, but there is more to it than that.

---

63. Newman to Father Henry James Coleridge, S.J., 28 February 1866, *The Letters and Diaries,* 22:167.

64. Ian Ker, *The Achievement of John Henry Newman* (Notre Dame, Indiana: University of Notre Dame Press, 1990) 96. Another contemporary Newman scholar has remarked on Newman's approach to theology: "The reason for Newman's disavowal [that he was a theologian] was that he was never comfortable with the Scholastic theology of his day; the reason why theologians today feel much more comfortable with Newman (and have ignored most of his scholastic contemporaries) is that his theology, rooted in the Bible and the patristic tradition, was presented in a way that still speaks to the hearts as well as the minds of his readers." John T. Ford, review article of Ker, *The Achievement of John Henry Newman* in *The Catholic Historical Review,* vol. 77, no. 2 (April 1992) 314.

65. Avery Dulles, S.J., "Newman on Infallibility," *Theological Studies* 51 (1990) 449.

Before late 1874, despite the urgings of many people and despite at times his own frustration at having to continue his silence, Newman simply could not have written. Given his temperament, his fears, his uncertainty, it was not a possibility. What changed his mind? Why did he at last decide that he could and should speak out openly?

Perhaps the simplest way to put it is that by the end of 1874 Newman believed that the "securus iudicat orbis terrarum" had in fact been achieved. Several important events from the conclusion of the council in July 1870 until Gladstone's challenge in November 1874 had led Newman to believe that everything had settled down and that the time had come for him to make his views known.

First, over the course of 1870–1871, it was clear that the minority bishops had accepted the definition and further that the Vatican Council had been prorogued indefinitely. The chances of the council's reconvening faded away. At the same time the pontificate of Pius IX, despite popular expectations, continued. Thoughts of a new council and a new pope had to be set aside. Second, the great falling away of Catholics from the faith as a result of the definition did not take place. By 1874 it was clear that Döllinger was in an isolated position and that the Old Catholic movement in northern Europe had failed to attract followers. In England the Roman Church continued to gain converts, especially among Anglicans. The celebrated conversion of the Marquis of Ripon in 1874 is just one evidence of this. Many of Newman's fears had simply not been borne out over time.

In late 1874, as Newman surveyed what had taken place in the four years since the council, he was approaching his mid-seventies. Characteristically, he was still capable of taking the long view. This was particularly evidenced by his continued insistence on the role of the *schola theologorum*. Time would resolve any lingering disputes over papal authority. Changes would in time come, but nearing seventy-four he had no great expectation of living to see them. Many of his closest friends had already died. Newman saw the need for husbanding his energies for what he could still do. His future was decidedly foreshortened. He lived now, perhaps more so than ever before, in the present. Hopes and expectations need not be put aside, but the reality of the current situation had to be faced. He counseled those who sought his advice to follow the same course. He gave practical advice for living as a Catholic in the 1870s. His letter of 24 April 1875 to Isy Froude is one evidence of this. It takes a highly papalist view that seems incompatible with Newman's earlier views and, to some extent, with the "wise and gentle minimism" of the *Letter to the Duke of Norfolk,* written just four months before.

It must also be recalled that Newman had throughout his life decried the dangers of liberalism in religion. He believed that liberalism would lead in time, especially among educated people, to the abandonment of all religious belief. It is not surprising that this took a stronger hold on him in his old age. The danger of religious liberalism was to be the central theme of his *biglietto* speech in May 1879, when he became a cardinal. Not infrequently after the council, Newman had thought about the need which current intellectual and social movements had created for a strong voice in religious matters. Though he deplored what had happened at the Vatican Council, he increasingly came to view the council's definition on papal infallibility as evidence of God's guidance of the Church in an uncertain time. The definition of papal infallibility gave the Church a strong, universal voice that would be more and more needed in the coming battle between the claims of believers and the proponents of scepticism and indifference. Newman's own fears and convictions forced him, though perhaps reluctantly, to this position.

Yet Newman in old age was still fully capable of surprise. As always, even in the midst of disappointment and foreboding, optimism and great hope were never entirely absent for him. The *Letter to the Duke of Norfolk* was in 1875 a moderate, centrist position on papal infallibility. A century later, despite the efforts of various commentators of one or other persuasion, it holds its place as a centrist statement, eschewing the extremes. Early in the *Letter to the Duke of Norfolk,* Newman wrote: "None but the *Schola Theologorum* is competent to determine the force of Papal and Synodal utterances, and the exact interpretation of them is a work of time."[66] In a second letter to Isy Froude, written in July 1875, Newman stepped away from the more papalist position of his April 1875 letter to her. He advanced again the role of theologians; he saw the need for more than one school of theological opinion; he emphasized the passive *infallibility* of the whole body of believers; and he highlighted the place of *the bishops along with the pope* in the exercise of the Church's active infallibility. In the preface to the third edition of the *Via Media*, Newman would intensify and underscore all that he had been saying about the role of theologians in his private notes and in letters over the past decade.

During and after the Vatican Council Newman tried to reassure those who looked to him for guidance by recalling that most of the Church's major councils, especially the earliest councils, had been characterized by rancor and division, not only during their sitting but for a generation or more afterwards. In fact this was not the case with Vatican Council I. To be sure, Döllinger and the Old Catholic movement looked at first to be fulfillments of Newman's frequently-stated prediction on councils and their aftermaths. But in a matter of a few short years after the conclusion

66. LDN, 76.

of Vatican Council I, it was clear that the Old Catholic movement had gained only a small number of adherents. Fairly quickly it became no more than a footnote to the history of Vatican I. In a very limited sense the rise of Modernism at the end of the nineteenth and in the early years of the twentieth century can be seen as a consequence of Vatican I. Its leaders and major proponents certainly regarded the council as an unhappy development in the life of the Church. Their concerns, however, were far broader and deeper than a simple opposition to Vatican I and the definition of papal infallibility. But, if anything, the sad history of Modernism revealed the power and strength that the pope and Roman curia had gained not just in Europe but in the Church worldwide since the definition of the pope's infallibility nearly four decades earlier. Rather than causing deep and pervasive division in the Church, Modernism succeeded only in heightening the pope's universal authority and his complete pre-eminence over the Church's episcopate, which quickly took up the rooting out of Modernism in its own particular territories. The rout of Modernism was a great success for the papacy, which under the pontificate of Leo XIII had already gained new authority and this continued and grew under Pius X. Catholics everywhere triumphantly and militantly vied with each other in exalting the pope and his place in the Church. The *Schola Theologorum* was purged of dissidents, and the theology of the Roman school gained control over theological learning the world over. It is hard to see Newman completely at peace with these developments. Is this the "long view" he had anticipated? Or was Newman's "long view" more one of a century or two rather than a few decades?

In addition to seeing controversy and contention as the fairly normal consequences of the Church's councils,[67] Newman in the years leading up to Vatican I, but especially afterwards, recalled for his troubled correspondents that one council had often to be followed by another or even by several councils before its teaching was put into its proper perspective and its true meaning shown in the life of the Church. Newman believed that a further council or councils would refine and put into its proper perspective the definition of papal infallibility. He encouraged those to whom he wrote to have this same hope. Certainly Newman saw such future councils as all the more necessary given the abrupt conclusion to Vatican I occasioned by the outbreak of the Franco-Prussian War in July 1870 and the fall of the Papal States two months later.

Nearly a century after Newman had encouraged inquirers to look with hope toward future councils, Pope John XXIII convened the successor council to Vatican I. Two questions, neither of them open to an easy an-

---

67. Newman excepted Trent, saying that in that instance the divisions and disputes had gone on for a long period before the council.

swer, obviously arise. Was Vatican Council II the further council or the beginning of a further series of councils that Newman had expected and predicted? And while he certainly had evidenced no expectation that his own writings would have a place in any future council's deliberations, was Newman in fact an influence on Vatican Council II?

The answer to the first question—was Vatican Council II the council that Newman had looked forward to and hoped for—is positively answered by Father Charles Stephen Dessain, the foremost authority on Newman in our time, who shortly after the close of Vatican Council II said that at that council "the tides of clericalism, creeping infallibility, narrow unhistorical theology and exaggerated Mariology were thrown back, while that which Newman stood for was brought forward—freedom, the supremacy of the conscience, the Church as a communion, a return to Scripture and the fathers, the rightful place of the laity, work for unity, and all the efforts to meet the needs of the age, and for the Church to take its place in the modern world."[68] Certainly this is a formidable list of the achievements of Vatican II that Newman would have rejoiced over. It solidly places Father Dessain among those who proclaimed Newman nearly a century after his death, "the absent Father of Vatican Council II."

Father Dessain sees the influence of Newman in this vigorous listing of many of the chief accomplishments of Vatican Council II, but perhaps only two of them have a direct relation to Newman's expectations after Vatican I and its definition of papal infallibility—the turning back of "creeping infallibility" and the displacement of a "narrow unhistorical theology."

It is to be sure a risky venture to bring a man as complex and multifaceted as Newman forward a hundred years. Attempts to draw sure conclusions about his attitude toward the constitutions and decrees of Vatican Council II are very uncertain at best. It has often been pointed out that an understanding of Newman the person, so much engaged in and influenced by the questions of his own times, is vital to an understanding of his thought. Newman in the Church of the 1960s would almost certainly have been a very different person from the Newman of the 1860s. And surely Father Dessain would have been the first to acknowledge the risk in attempting to picture Newman as completely at home with the enactments of Vatican II, and yet he believed that that council's overall thrust and direction would have pleased Newman very much.

The question whether Newman would have been gratified by the outcome of Vatican II is of course different from the question whether Newman had a real influence on the council. Father Dessain's coupling of the

68. Nicholas Lash, "Tides and Twilight: Newman since Vatican II," 460, in *Newman after a Hundred Years,* ed. Ian Ker and Alan G. Hill (Oxford: Clarendon Press, 1990), quoting C. S. Dessain, "Newman's Spiritual Themes" (Dublin: 1977) 30.

council's achievements with "things that Newman stood for" would appear to suggest that he saw Newman in some sense as being a direct influence on Vatican Council II.

A rather different view is, however, presented by Bishop Basil Christopher Butler, O.S.B., who like Newman was an Oxford graduate and an Anglican before becoming a Roman Catholic. Bishop Butler took part in the Second Vatican Council as the Abbot President of the English Benedictine Congregation. Speaking in 1966, just a year after the conclusion of Vatican II, Bishop Butler maintained that Newman's influence on the council "was not deep or determinative."[69] Nicholas Lash in his important essay "Tides and Twilight: Newman since Vatican I" stands with Bishop Butler.[70] He believes that Newman's influence on the proceedings of Vatican II was not large. Lash does not treat the question of whether Newman would have seen in Vatican II the successor and completion of Vatican I, the future council that Newman in the 1870s had looked forward to and predicted. For Lash there is a further question to be asked that goes beyond the matter of Newman's direct or indirect influence on Vatican II and whether Newman's hopes following Vatican I were in fact fulfilled by what took place at Rome from 1962 to 1965.

Lash in a sense looks beyond these questions, at least by implication, toward a further possibility, the influence and role of Newman in the Church after Vatican II and in the Church as it moves toward Vatican Council III. The Second Vatican Council opened up in Lash's words "Newman's accessibility to the Catholic imagination."[71] In some respects this is a shocking conclusion, especially because Newman since his death has been such an admired figure in the Church, and this not only after Vatican II but in the seventy-two years between Newman's death and the opening of that council. In so many ways in the time between his death and the Second Vatican Council, Newman had become chiefly a hero for a militant and triumphalist Catholicism, a prized convert, a coveted trophy gained and set out for display. But, in fact, Newman in this period was in many ways more revered than read, more admired than understood. He was seen as a great spiritual figure, a religious founder, the author of religious verse, hymn texts, and devotional prayers. He was regarded by some as an authority on Catholic higher education because of his *The Idea of a University*. But only a small and somewhat rarefied group of specialists in England, North America, and perhaps especially on the Continent, seriously studied his writings because they saw in Newman a deep

---

69. Lash, "Tides and Twilight," 449, quoting B. C. Butler, "Newman and the Second Vatican Council," in J. Coulson and A. M. Allchin, eds., *The Rediscovery of Newman: An Oxford Symposium* (London, 1967) 245.

70. See Lash, "Tides and Twilight," 449.

71. Lash, "Tides and Twilight," 450.

and innovative theologian and philosopher of religion. To a certain extent the association of Newman's name, whether correctly or not, with some of the leading Modernists, may have played some part in keeping Newman the theologian an outsider, not altogether reliable and safe. As a result, more than being acclaimed as a profound and seminal religious thinker, Newman's place in the intellectual life of Catholicism prior to Vatican II was more that of a brilliant English stylist and Catholic apologist. For many, even well-educated Catholics, knowledge of Newman was largely confined to an acquaintance with the major biographical events of his life and with excerpts from the *Essay on Development, The Idea of University,* the *Apologia,* the *Dream of Gerontius,* and a sampling of his sermons. The *Letter to the Duke of Norfolk* also had a place on this list, but in some respects it was viewed with suspicion. For although Newman in the winter of 1875 had succeeded in calming the controversy over papal infallibility, the moderate position he had espoused came over time to be superseded in the main by the very exaggerated claims he had done battle against. This was true not only in England but in the Roman Catholic Church worldwide. While the *Letter to the Duke of Norfolk* was held up as a classic by Catholic apologists, its overall intent and message were often, and at times deliberately, lost sight of.

As mentioned above, perhaps the truest course is suggested by Nicholas Lash—to bring Newman from Vatican I through Vatican II to Vatican III. "It is only in recent decades," Lash maintains "that Catholic theology, at least in its approved and erudite forms, has begun . . . to think historically, after three centuries of captivity to more 'classicist' and rationalist modes of procedure. It is accordingly only in recent decades that Newman has come to be seen less like a stranger and more like a doctor of the Church."[72]

Though the questions of Newman's influence on Vatican II and whether he would have seen in that council the needed completion of Vatican I cannot now be answered with surety and satisfaction, Nicholas Lash's comment speaks to the value of Newman's voice in the important theological questions that the Roman Catholic Church faces at the end of the twentieth century. Perhaps a third Vatican Council, sometime early in the next century, will provide clearer answers about Newman's influence on its deliberations and his satisfaction with its outcome than has been the case with Vatican II. A hoped-for Vatican Council III may well bring to completion and put in its true place the definition of papal infallibility at Vatican I.

Three decades after the opening of Vatican Council II, the place of the papal office in the teaching authority of the Roman Catholic Church

72. Ibid.

continues to be a matter for lively, even contentious, study and discussion. At the same time the authority of diocesan bishops, and more so of national conferences of bishops, in the teaching of the faith for their dioceses and territories are also subjects of debate and the source of disagreement. In addition, efforts aimed at Christian unity, inspired and fostered by Vatican Council II, have necessarily had to grapple with discussions of the Petrine ministry in the Church, especially as that ministry is exercised in the pope's office of teacher of the universal Church. This has become an issue of paramount importance to other Christian Churches, particularly those Christian Churches that have entered into formal dialogues and conversation with the Roman Catholic Church in the quest for Christian unity. These dialogues have struggled, and at times have appeared to falter, over the meaning for Roman Catholics of papal primacy, but even more the exercise of papal infallibility. At the same time historical and theological probings into questions connected with the exercise of the pope's office in the Church have brought longstanding dialogues almost to an impasse over this issue alone, though it would be wrong to suggest that it is in all cases the sole point of contention or even necessarily the most vexatious one. Lastly, there is the continuing debate, a debate that grows increasingly intense in the Roman Catholic Church, over the role of theologians in the Church's teaching mission both in the areas of dogmatic and moral theological issues.

On all of these questions Newman's is very much a voice worth heeding, even though his positions are not necessarily spelled out in the precise terms of today's debate. As will have become clear in the preceding pages of this study, one cannot go to Newman expecting a systematic and well laid out discussion on these complex questions. Some of them he did discuss in his writings, others he treated only in passing. And though he has discussed, or at least touched on all of these issues—papal primacy, papal infallibility, the role of bishops in the *ecclesia docens*, and the role of theologians in the Church's ongoing life—in his formal writings, some of his most important and lasting statements on these distinct but related issues are found scattered throughout his vast body of correspondence. These letters also deserve new study and attention. Even Newman's struggles with these questions, his hesitations, his inconsistencies, his at times incomplete probings have relevance in the present discussions. The reader will soon discover that rather than diminishing the figure of Newman, they add luster to it. They reveal a vital human person, struggling to keep faith alive and vibrant in an uncertain and contentious time, ever conscious that we see now through a glass darkly, and continually pleading for a wise and gentle minimism until that time has passed away.

Bibliography

PRIMARY SOURCES

Archives

Birmingham, England. Archives of the Birmingham Oratory.
Bristol, England. Bristol Record Office. Letters to Bishop William Joseph Clifford, Bishop of Clifton. Part I, 1854–1874; Part II, 1875–1892.
Washington. Georgetown University. Special Collections, Newman Collection.

Printed Sources

Acton, John Dalberg. *The Correspondence of Lord Acton and Richard Simpson.* Edited by Josef L. Altholz, Damian McElrath, and others. 3 vols. Cambridge: At the University Press, 1971–1975.
Collectio Conciliorum Recentiorum Ecclesiae Universae. Edited by Ludovicus Petit and Joannes Baptista Martin. Tomus Decimus Tertius, 49. Tomus Decimus Quintus, 51. Tomus Decimus Sextus, 52. Sacrosancti Oecumenici Concilii Vaticani, Acta. Arnhem and Leipzig: Société Nouvelle d'Edition de la Collection Mansi, 1923 and 1927.
Döllinger, Ignaz von. *Briefwechsel 1820–1890.* Edited by Victor Conzemius. 4 vols. Munich: C. H. Beck'sche Verlagsbuchhandlung, 1963–1985.
Gladstone, William Ewart. *Correspondence on Church and Religion of William Ewart Gladstone.* Selected and arranged by D. C. Lathbury. New York: The Macmillan Company, 1910.
―――――. *The Gladstone Diaries.* Edited by M.R.D. Foot and H.C.G. Matthew. 9 vols. Oxford: The Clarendon Press, 1968–1986.
Hansard's Parliamentary Debates. Third Series. Volume 200 (16 March 1870–29 April 1870).
Hopkins, Gerard Manley. *The Note-Books and Papers of Gerard Manley Hopkins.* Edited by Humphry House. London and New York: Oxford University Press, 1937.
Mozley, Thomas. *Letters from Rome on the Occasion of the Oecumenical Council 1869–1870.* 2 vols. London and New York: Longmans, Green, and Co., 1891.
Newman, John Henry Newman. *Autobiographical Writings.* Edited by Henry Tristram of the Oratory. New York: Sheed and Ward, 1956.
―――――. *The Letters and Diaries of John Henry Newman.* Edited by Charles Stephen Dessain and others. Vols. 1–6, Oxford: The Clarendon Press, 1978–

1984; vols. 11–22, London: Thomas Nelson and Sons, Ltd., 1970–1972; vols. 23–31, Oxford: The Clarendon Press, 1973–1977.

_____. *The Theological Papers of John Henry Newman on Biblical Inspiration and on Infallibility*. Selected, edited, and introduced by J. Derek Holmes. Oxford: The Clarendon Press, 1979.

Plummer, Alfred. *Conversations With Dr. Döllinger 1870–1890*. Introduction and notes by Robrecht Boudens, with collaboration of Leo Kenis. Leuven: University Press, 1985.

Russell, Odo. *The Roman Question: Extracts from the Despatches of Odo Russell from Rome, 1858–1870*. Edited by Noel Blakiston. London: Chapman and Hall, 1962.

Vaughan, Herbert Cardinal. *Letters of Herbert Cardinal Vaughan to Lady Herbert of Lea, 1867–1903*. Edited by Shane Leslie. London: Burns and Oates, 1942.

Newman Works

Newman, John Henry. *A Letter Addressed to His Grace the Duke of Norfolk On Occasion of Mr. Gladstone's Recent Expostulation* (London: B. M. Pickering, 1875) as reprinted in *Newman and Gladstone: The Vatican Decrees*. Introduction by Alvan S. Ryan. Notre Dame, Ind.: University of Notre Dame Press, 1962.

_____. *An Essay in aid of a Grammar of Assent*. London, New York, and Bombay: Longmans, Green, and Co., 1906.

_____. *An Essay on the Development of Christian Doctrine*. London, New York, and Bombay: Longmans, Green, and Co., 1906.

_____. *Apologia Pro Vita Sua*. Garden City, N.Y.: Doubleday and Company, Image Books Edition, 1956.

_____. *Certain Difficulties Felt by Anglicans in Catholic Teaching*. 2 vols. London, New York, and Bombay: Longmans, Green, and Co., 1907–1908.

_____. *Discourses Addressed to Mixed Congregations*. London, New York, and Bombay: Longmans, Green, and Co., 1906.

_____. *Essays Critical and Historical*. 2 vols. London, New York, and Bombay: Longmans, Green, and Co., 1907.

_____. *Historical Sketches*. 3 vols. London, New York, and Bombay: Longmans, Green, and Co., 1903–1908.

_____. *The Idea of A University Defined and Illustrated*. London, New York, and Bombay: Longmans, Green, and Co., 1907.

_____. *Lectures on the Present Position of Catholics in England*. London, New York, and Bombay: Longmans, Green, and Co., 1908.

_____. *Loss and Gain: The Story of a Convert*. London, New York, and Bombay: Longmans, Green, and Co., 1906.

_____. *On Consulting the Faithful In Matters of Doctrine*. London: Collins, 1986.

_____. *Sermons Preached on Various Occasions*. New edition. London: Longmans, Green, and Co., 1898.

_____. *Verses on Various Occasions*. London, New York, and Bombay: Longmans, Green, and Co., 1903.

_____. *The Via Media of the Anglican Church*. 2 vols. Third edition. London: Longmans, Green, and Co., 1901–1908.

Newman, John Henry, and others. *Tracts for the Times* (1833–1841). 6 vols. London: J.G.F. and J. Rivington, reprinted from the bound editions of 1840–1842. First AMS edition. New York: AMS Press, Inc., 1969.

Contemporary Books, Pamphlets, and Articles

"Commentaries on Public Affairs." *Month* 4 (23) (February 1875).

Döllinger, Ignaz von. *The First Age of Christianity and the Church*. Translated by Henry Nutcombe Oxenham. Third edition. London: William H. Allen, 1877.

Fessler, Joseph. *The True and False Infallibility of the Popes: A Controversial Reply to Dr. Schulte*. Translated by Ambrose St. John. London: Burns and Oates, 1875.

"F. Ryder and Dr. Ward." *Dublin Review*, n.s. 9 (July–October 1867).

Gladstone, W. E. *The Vatican Decrees In Their Bearing on Civil Allegiance: A Political Expostulation by the Right Hon. W. E. Gladstone, M. P. With the Replies of Archbishop Manning and Lord Acton*. New York: D. Appleton and Company, 1874.

_____. *The Vatican Decrees In Their Bearing on Civil Allegiance: A Political Expostulation* as reprinted in *Newman and Gladstone: The Vatican Decrees*. Introduction by Alvan S. Ryan. Notre Dame, Ind.: University of Notre Dame Press, 1962.

_____. *The Vatican Decrees In Their Bearing on Civil Allegiance: A Political Expostulation*. New York: Catholic Publication Society, 1875.

_____. *Vaticanism: An Answer to Reproofs and Replies*. New York: Harper Brothers Publishers, 1875.

Gosselin, Jean. *The Power of the Pope during the Middle Ages, or an Historical Inquiry into the Origin of the Temporal Power of the Holy See, and the Constitutional Laws of the Middle Ages relating to the Deposition of States*. Translated into English in 1853.

Knox, Thomas Francis. *When Does the Church Speak Infallibly or The Nature and Scope of the Church's Teaching Office*. Second edition, enlarged. London: Burns, Oates, and Co., 1870.

Manning, Henry Edward. "Caesarism and Ultramontanism" in *Miscellanies*. New York: The Catholic Publication Society, 1877.

_____. *The Vatican Council and Its Definitions: A Pastoral Letter to the Clergy*. New York: Sadlier, 1871.

Milner, John. *The end of religious controversy in a friendly correspondence between a religious society of Protestants and a Catholic divine*. Philadelphia, 1823.

"Mr. Gladstone's Durham Letter." *Month* 3 (November 1874).

"Notice of Books." *Dublin Review*, n.s. 15 (July–October 1870).

_____. *Dublin Review*, n.s. 16 (January–April 1871).

Perowne, J. J. Stewart, ed. *Remains Literary and Theological of Connop Thirlwall, Bishop of St. David's.* London, 1877.

Trevern, Jean François Marie Le Pappe de. *Discussion amicale sur l'église anglicane et en général sur la réformation, redigeé, en forme de lettres, écrites en 1812 et 1813; par un licencié de la Maison et Société de Sorbonnes.* Londres: R. Juligné, 1813.

Ward, W. G. "Catholic Controversies." *Dublin Review,* n.s. 12 (January–April 1869).

————. "F. Newman on Ecclesiastical Prudence." *Dublin Review,* n.s. 25 (July–October 1875).

————. "Mr. Gladstone and His Catholic Critics." *Dublin Review,* n.s. 24 (January–April 1875).

————. "The Sovereignty In Modern States—The Count de Chambord and the Pope's Civil Princedom." *Dublin Review,* n.s. 23 (July–October 1874).

————. "A Brief Summary of the Recent Controversy on Infallibility Being a Reply to the Rev. Father Ryder on His Postscript." *Dublin Review,* n.s. 11 (July–October 1868), appendix to July issue.

————. "A Letter to the Rev. Father Ryder On His Recent Pamphlet by William George Ward, D.Ph." *Dublin Review,* n.s. 9 (July–October 1867), appendix to July issue.

————. "A Second Letter to the Rev. Father Ryder." *Dublin Review,* n.s. 10 (January–April 1868), appendix to April issue.

————. "The Encyclical and the Syllabus." *Dublin Review,* n.s. 4 (January–April 1865).

Contemporary Newspapers and Periodicals

The *Dublin Review*
The *Month*
The *Tablet*
The *Times.*

SECONDARY SOURCES

Altholz, Josef L. *The Liberal Catholic Movement in England: the "Rambler" and Its Contributors 1848–1864.* London: Burns and Oates, 1962.

————. "The Vatican Decrees Controversy, 1874–1875." *Catholic Historical Review* 57 (January 1972).

Arnstein, Walter L. *Protestant Versus Catholic in Mid-Victorian England: Mr. Newdegate and the Nuns.* Columbia and London: University of Missouri Press, 1982.

Aubert, Roger. *Vatican I.* Paris: Editions De l'Orante, 1964.

Bastable, James D., ed. *Newman and Gladstone: Centennial Essays.* Dublin: Veritas Publications, 1978.

Bermejo, Luis. *Infallibility on Trial: Church, Conciliarity and Communion.* Westminster, Md.: Christian Classics, Inc., 1992.

Butler, Cuthbert, O.S.B. *The Life and Times of Bishop Ullathorne 1806–1889*. 2 vols. New York: Benziger Brothers, 1926.

_____. *The Vatican Council: The Story Told From Inside In Bishop Ullathorne's Letters*. 2 vols. London, New York, and Toronto: Longmans, Green, and Co., 1930.

Chadwick, Owen. *Newman*. Oxford and New York: Oxford University Press, 1983.

_____. *The Victorian Church*. Part II. New York: Oxford University Press, 1970.

Chirico, Peter. *Infallibility: The Crossroads of Doctrine*. Kansas City: Sheed, Andrews, and McMeel, 1977.

Corish, Patrick. *The Irish Catholic Experience: A Historical Survey*. Wilmington, Del.: Michael Glazier, Inc., 1985.

Cwiekowski, Frederick J., S.S. *The English Bishops and the First Vatican Council*. Louvain: Publications Universitaires de Louvain, 1971.

Davies, Horton. *Worship and Theology in England, 1850–1900*. Princeton, N.J.: Princeton University Press, 1970.

De Leonardis, Massimo. *L'Inghilterra e la Questione Romana 1859–1870*. Milan: Vita e Pensiero, 1980.

Dessain, Charles Stephen. *John Henry Newman*. Second edition. Stanford, Calif.: Stanford University Press, 1971.

Dibble, Romuald A., S.D.S. *John Henry Newman: The Concept of Infallible Doctrinal Authority*. Washington: CUA Press, 1955.

Dulles, Avery, S.J., "Newman on Infallibility," *Theological Studies* 51 (1990).

Fenton, Joseph. "John Henry Newman and the Vatican Definition of Papal Infallibility." *American Ecclesiastical Review* 111 (October 1945).

Ford, John T., C.S.C. "Infallibility: A Review of Recent Studies." *Theological Studies* 40 (June 1979).

_____. Review of *The Achievement of John Henry Newman* by Ian Ker. In *The Catholic Historical Review* 76 (April 1992).

Gilley, Sheridan. *Newman and His Age*. London: Darton, Longman, and Todd, 1990.

Goulder, M., and others. *Infallibility in the Church*. London: Darton, Longman, and Todd, 1968.

Gray, Robert. *Cardinal Manning: A Biography*. London: Weidenfeld and Nicolson, 1985.

Hasler, August Bernhard. *How the Pope Became Infallible: Pius IX and the Politics of Persuasion*. Garden City, N.Y.: Doubleday and Company, 1981.

Hastings, Adrian, ed. *Bishops and Writers: Aspects of the Evolution of Modern English Catholicism*. Wheathamstead-Hertfordshire, 1977.

Hennessey, James, S.J. *The First Council of the Vatican: The American Experience*. New York: Herder and Herder, 1963.

Holmes, J. Derek. "Cardinal Newman and the First Vatican Council." *Annuarium Historiae Conciliorum* 1 (1969).

_____. "Liberal Catholicism and Newman's Letter to the Duke of Norfolk." *Clergy Review* 60 (1975).

_____. *More Roman than Rome: English Catholicism in the Nineteenth Century*. London: Burns and Oates; Shepherdstown, W.Va.: Patmos Press, 1978.

————. "A Note on Newman's Reaction to the Definition of Papal Infallibility," *Spode House Review,* occasional papers 3 (1976).

————. *The Triumph of the Holy See.* Shepherdstown, W.Va.: Patmos Press, 1978.

Jenkins, Arthur Hilary, ed., *John Henry Newman and Modernism. Cardinal-Newman Internationalen Studien* 14. Sigmaringendorf: regio Verlag Glock und Lutz, 1990.

Jenkins, Hilary. "The Irish Dimension of the British Kulturkampf: 1870–1875." *Journal of Ecclesiastical History* 30 (July 1979).

Johnson, H.J.T. "The Controversy Between Newman and Gladstone." *Dublin Review* 217 (October 1945).

Kelly, J.N.D. *The Oxford Dictionary of Popes.* Oxford, New York: Oxford University Press, 1986.

Ker, Ian. *The Achievement of John Henry Newman.* Notre Dame, Ind.: University of Notre Dame Press, 1990.

————. *John Henry Newman: A Biography.* Oxford: The Clarendon Press, 1988.

Ker, Ian and Alan G. Hill, eds. *Newman after a Hundred Years.* Oxford: The Clarendon Press, 1990.

Klausnitzer, Wolfgang. *Päpstliche Unfehlbarkeit bei Newman und Döllinger: ein historisch—systematischer Vergleich.* Innsbruck: Tyroliaverlag, 1980.

Küng, Hans. *Infallible? An Inquiry.* New York: Doubleday, 1971.

Larkin, Emmet. *The Roman Catholic Church in Ireland and the Fall of Parnell, 1888–1891.* Chapel Hill: University of North Carolina Press, 1979.

————. *The Roman Catholic Church and the Home Rule Movement in Ireland, 1870–1874.* Chapel Hill and London: The University of North Carolina Press, 1990.

Leslie, Shane. *Henry Edward Manning: His Life and Labours.* London: Burns, Oates, and Washbourne, Ltd., 1921.

Liddon, Henry Parry. *Life of Edward Bouverie Pusey.* 4 vols. London and New York: Longmans, Green, and Co., 1893–1897.

Lord Acton: The Decisive Decade: Essays and Documents. Edited by Damian McElrath and others. Louvain: Publications Universitaires, 1970.

MacDougall, Hugh A. *The Acton-Newman Relations: The Dilemma of Christian Liberalism.* New York: Fordham University Press, 1962.

Macaulay, Ambrose. *Dr. Russell of Maynooth.* London: Darton, Longman, and Todd, 1983.

Martin, Brian. *John Henry Newman: His Life and Work.* New York: Oxford University Press, 1982.

McClelland, Vincent. *English Roman Catholics and Higher Education, 1830–1903.* Oxford: The Clarendon Press, 1973.

McElrath, Damien. *Richard Simpson, 1820–1876. A Study in XIX Century English Liberal Catholicism.* Louvain: Publications Universitaires, 1972.

————. *The Syllabus of Pius IX: Some Reactions in England.* Louvain: Publications Universitaires, 1964.

Miller, Edward Jeremy. *John Henry Newman on the Idea of Church.* Shepherdstown, W.Va.: Patmos Press, 1987.

Misner, Paul. *Papacy and Development: Newman and the Primacy of the Pope.* Leiden: E. J. Brill, 1976.

Moody, John. *John Henry Newman.* New York: Sheed and Ward, 1945.

Morley, John. *The Life of William Ewart Gladstone.* 3 vols. London: Macmillan and Co., Ltd., 1903.

Murray, Placid. *Newman the Oratorian.* Leominster, Herefordshire: Fowler Wright Books Ltd, 1980.

Norman, E. R. *Anti-Catholicism in Victorian England. Historical Problems: Studies and Documents.* Edited by G. R. Elton. Vol. 1. New York: Barnes & Noble, Inc., 1968.

_____. *The English Catholic Church in the Nineteenth Church.* Oxford: The Clarendon Press, 1984.

O'Brien, David J. *Isaac Hecker: An American Catholic.* New York and Mahwah, N.J.: Paulist Press, 1992.

O'Gara, Margaret. *Triumph in Defeat: Infallibility, Vatican I, and the French Minority Bishops.* Washington: The Catholic University of America Press, 1988.

Portier, William L. *Isaac Hecker and the First Vatican Council.* Lewiston/Queenstown: The Edwin Mellen Press, 1985.

Purcell, Edmund Sheridan. *Life of Cardinal Manning: Archbishop of Westminster.* 2 vols. New York and London: The Macmillan Company, 1896.

Purcell, Edmund Sheridan, and Edwin Phillipps De Lisle. *The Life and Letters of Ambrose Phillipps De Lisle.* 2 vols. London: Macmillan and Co., Ltd., 1900.

Schiefen, Richard J. *Nicholas Wiseman and the Transformation of English Catholicism.* Shepherdstown: Patmos Press, 1984.

Snead-Cox, J. G. *The Life of Cardinal Vaughan.* London: Burns and Oates, 1910.

Strange, Roderick. "Newman on Infallibility in 1870 and 1970." *Ampleforth Journal* 80 (Spring 1975).

Swisshelm, G. "Newman and the Vatican Definition of Papal Infallibility." *St. Meinrad Essays* 12 (1960).

Trevor, Meriol. *Newman: The Pillar of the Cloud.* London: Macmillan and Co., Ltd., 1962.

_____. *Newman: Light in Winter.* London: Macmillan and Co. Ltd., 1962.

Ward, Wilfrid. *Ten Personal Studies.* London: Longmans, Green, and Co., 1908.

_____. *The Life of John Henry Cardinal Newman.* 2 vols. London: Longmans, Green, and Co., 1912.

_____. *William George Ward and the Catholic Revival.* London and New York: Macmillan and Co., 1893.

Weaver, Mary Jo., ed. *Newman and the Modernists.* Lanham, Md.: The College Theology Society and University Press of America, Inc., 1985.

White, Norman. *Hopkins: A Literary Biography.* Oxford: The Clarendon Press, 1992.

Yearley, Lee H. *The Ideas of Newman: Christianity and Human Religiosity.* University Park and London: The Pennsylvania State University Press, 1978.

Index